Cybercrime and Information Technology

Cybercrime and Information Technology

Theory and Practice: The Computer Network Infrastructure and Computer Security, Cybersecurity Laws, Internet of Things (IoT), and Mobile Devices

Alex Alexandrou

CRC Press
Taylor & Francis Group
Boca Raton London New York

CRC Press is an imprint of the
Taylor & Francis Group, an **informa** business

First edition published 2022
by CRC Press
6000 Broken Sound Parkway NW, Suite 300, Boca Raton, FL 33487-2742

and by CRC Press
2 Park Square, Milton Park, Abingdon, Oxon, OX14 4RN

CRC Press is an imprint of Taylor & Francis Group, LLC

Library of Congress Cataloging-in-Publication Data

Names: Alexandrou, Alex (Professor of information technology security), author.
Title: Cybercrime and Internet technology : theory and practice--the computer network infostructure and computer security, cybersecurity laws, internet of things (IoT), and mobile devices / Alex Alexandrou.
Identifiers: LCCN 2021007948 (print) | LCCN 2021007949 (ebook) | ISBN 9780367251574 (hardback) | ISBN 9781032053851 (paperback) | ISBN 9780429318726 (ebook)
Subjects: LCSH: Computer crimes. | Computer security. | Computer security--Law and legislation. | Computer networks--Security measures.
Classification: LCC HV6773 .A425 2022 (print) | LCC HV6773 (ebook) | DDC 364.16/8--dc23
LC record available at https://lccn.loc.gov/2021007948
LC ebook record available at https://lccn.loc.gov/2021007949

ISBN: 978-0-367-25157-4 (hbk)
ISBN: 978-1-032-05385-1 (pbk)
ISBN: 978-0-429-31872-6 (ebk)

DOI: 10.1201/9781003020080

Typeset in Minion
by Deanta Global Publishing Services, Chennai, India
Access the Support Material: www.crcpress.com/9780367251574

To my parents Achilleas and Maria Alexandrou, who taught me about humility, to have a good work ethic and a willingness to help others.

To my grandmother, Eleni who taught me to be an independent person and NEVER Give UP!

Contents

Preface

My motivation for writing this book stems from my struggle to find a textbook that strengthens student understanding of the fundamentals of computer and network security and includes the study of cybercrime.

Therefore, the primary goal of this book is to provide a strong foundation of cybercrime knowledge along with the fundamental concepts of networking, computer security, Internet of Things (IoTs), and mobile devices.

With this knowledge base, students can also learn to design and implement mitigation strategies and can then follow the processes of developing security policies.

The textbook is appropriate for courses in the Computer Forensics and Criminal Justice curriculum and is relevant to those studying Security Administration, Public Administrations, Police Studies, Business Administration, Computer Science, and Information Systems.

The book is organized into eight chapters.

- **Chapter 1** – This first chapter describes information processing, bytes and bits, Binary, Hexadecimal ASCII, EBCDIC, and UNICODE codes, Boolean algebra, logic gates, color depth, color models and resolution, compression, and a brief history of computing technology.
- **Chapter 2** – This chapter studies the evolution and phases of cybercrime including: motives that make cybercrime alluring, different categories of

cybercrime, the costs and the role of cryptocurrency, online child sexual abuse and exploitation, the connections among cybercrime, machine learning and artificial intelligence, and explains state-sponsored and cyber warfare.

- **Chapter 3** – This chapter provides an overview of the legal system in the United States and the main barriers to prosecuting cybercriminals.
- **Chapter 4** – The chapter describes cyberlaw standards, and regulations affecting cybercrime including anti-hacking laws, data security laws in critical infrastructure, the National Institute of Standards and Technology (NIST) cybersecurity framework, the public and private sector partnerships laws, and surveillance and privacy laws.
- **Chapter 5** – This chapter explores computer networking, its history and evolution, and explains the essential computer network components and terminology, clarifies the different types of networking, and the different theoretical network models such as Open Systems Interconnection (OSI) and Transmission Control Protocol/Internet Protocol (TPC/IP).
- **Chapter 6** – This chapter provides an overview of computer security technology, including its history and evolution, terminology, different types of cyberattacks, computer security prevention mechanisms, and encryption methodology.
- **Chapter 7** – This chapter introduces the Internet of Things (IoTs), applications, and security vulnerabilities.
- **Chapter 8** – The final chapter explains the historical significance of mobile phone technology, cellular networks, and the main components of network architecture, along with security threats and vulnerabilities.

Acknowledgment

First and foremost, I express my heartfelt appreciation to the Taylor and Francis group for the development and production of this book, especially to Mr. Mark Listewnik, for his support, guidance, and patience. Special thanks to John and Patricia Pommells for their support and encouragement. I also owe an enormous debt of gratitude to the reviewers for their thoughtful comments and efforts, including Julia Vonferber, PhD; Muath Obaidat, PhD; Nina Russakoff, JD; and Sylvia Russakoff, MA, MBA.

Finally, I am eternally grateful to Ms. Sylvia Russakoff; without her advice, wisdom, and knowledge, this book would not have been possible.

Author's Bio

Alex Alexandrou is an Assistant Professor in the Department of Security, Fire, and Emergency Management at John Jay College of Criminal Justice. He received his bachelor's degree from Youngstown State University, his master's degree from Brooklyn College of the City University of New York, and his doctorate degree in computing studies from Pace University. Dr. Alexandrou has worked extensively in both business and academic environments. He has 18 years of experience in Health Information Technology and Operations leadership, including software integration, biometric and access control systems, deploying virtualization by transitioned use of physical servers into virtualization technology, and realigning IT architecture with cloud-based networks and security platforms/technologies. Dr. Alexandrou has taught courses in Cybersecurity, Health Information Technology, and Telemedicine at both undergraduate and graduate levels since 2015. He is a firm believer in *Hard work, determination and never giving up on what you really want to do.*

Dr. Alexandrou has conducted research studies on mobile device security in healthcare, Deep Fake videos, Cybercrime, and Biometric authentication. His current research interests include system security and privacy for healthcare applications, mobile forensics investigation, and mobile device vulnerabilities and threats.

Chapter 1

Understanding Essential Computer Concepts

Objectives

After completing this chapter, the student will be able to:

- Understand information processing in computing devices
- Explain the difference between a Bit and a Byte
- Understand Binary, Hexadecimal ASCII, EBCDIC, and UNICODE codes
- Understand Boolean algebra, logic gates, and truth tables
- Explain color depth, color models, and screen resolution
- Understand lossy and lossless compression
- Understand the basics of quantum computing
- Recognize computer terminology
- Understand the history of computers and the technology surrounding them

1.1 Understanding Computation

Conventional Computer Systems

Technological innovation is a combination of the brain's computing power and the desire to mimic human intelligence. The progression of technology is the result of the human desire to solve problems and improve the quality of life.

DOI: 10.4324/9780429318726-1

Electronic devices are technological advancements that correlate with our efforts to solve problems.

The computer is an electronic device that accepts input, processes data by modifying or manipulating it, stores the data for further reference, and produces output, all according to a series of instructions or commands. This group of processes is the von Neumann architecture, or von Neumann concept, published in 1945 by John von Neumann, which describes a proposed architecture for a computer. The concept depicts a stored-program computer with instruction and program data stored in the same memory.[1] "The design consists of a central control, the central arithmetic and logic unit, memory, and input and output."[2] This concept was so powerful and valuable that our computers have always followed this model.

All conventional computing devices still operate through these four basic functions: receiving input, processing data, storing data, and producing output.

First, the user inputs information, using an input device like a touchpad, keyboard, mouse, trackpad, microphone, or video camera. The data is converted into binary data, identified as either 0s or 1s. The central processing unit (CPU), the "brain" of the computer, with the help of the memory, analyzes how to display each character.

Next, the CPU manipulates the binary data and stores it in memory for further reference. The CPU processes the binary data and creates output, viewed on a screen, speaker, or printer. To view the image on a monitor, the CPU works in conjunction with a software application, or program that sends instructions to the computer's graphics card. The graphics card, which controls the visual display, decides how to arrange the screen to create the image. All this happens through a series of instructions or commands that the computer follows. Complex tasks, such as editing high definition video, or 3D modeling and rendering, require more processing power and memory. Lastly, the processed data is stored on the hard drive (HD). Figure 1.1 summarizes information processing in a computing device.

The term computer was initially mathematical. "The word *computer* is a combination of the Latin word *putare,* which means to 'think or train,' and *com,* which means 'together.' The Oxford English Dictionary dates the first use of the word to 1579, linking it with "arithmetical or mathematical

---

[1] Von Neumann, John. "First Draft of a Report on the EDVAC." *IEEE Annals of the History of Computing* 15, no. 4 (1993): 27–75.

[2] Campbell-Kelly, Martin. *Computer, student economy edition: A history of the information machine.* Routledge, 2018.

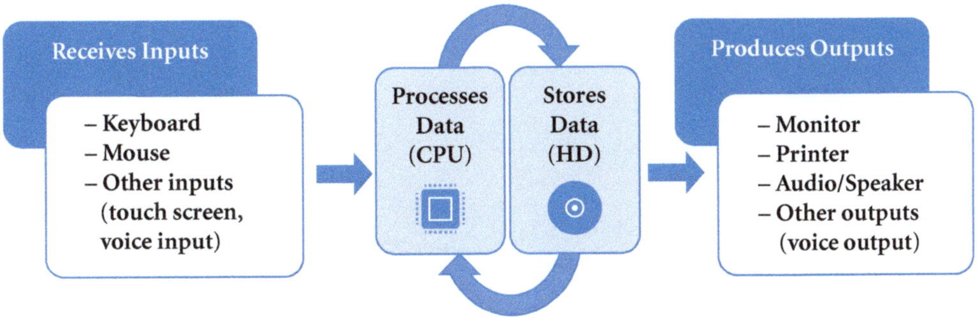

FIGURE 1.1 Information processing in a computing device.

reckoning."[3] Before the advent of machine computers, a computer was a person – a clerical worker who wrote entries, calculated numbers, and kept proper accounts. "The electronic computer can be said to combine the roles of human computer and the human clerk"[4] (Figure 1.2).

It is worth noting that the field of mathematical logic has had a major impact on the development of computer science. One instance of this is in the area of program verification. "Since a computer program is simply a formal description of calculation, it can be verified in the same way that a mathematical theorem can be verified using logic."[5]

The Greek philosopher Aristotle provided a foundation for *mathematical logic* that enabled later ideas to become reality. Aristotle viewed logic as a tool for philosophers and scientists alike.[6] To better understand computing devices, we need to appreciate its evolution, along with the philosophies, theories, and ideas that emerged from mathematical logic.

The American space program of the 1960s, along with the research and development that went into its missions, helped to accelerate the development of the computing industry, causing a dramatic shift in electronics and computing systems (Figures 1.3 and 1.4).

1.2 Input

The user interface (UI) is the way in which the user interacts with the machine (computer). The basic human–computer interaction consists of physical inputs such as keyboards, mouse, voice commands, tabs in screen (with commands run inside), to convert physical actions and conditions to binary data (Figure 1.5).

[3] Garfinkel, Simson L., and Rachel H. Grunspan. *The computer book: From the abacus to artificial intelligence, 250 milestones in the history of computer science*, 2018, Nueva York: Sterling, 2018.

[4] *Id.* at 2.

[5] Ben-Ari, Mordechai. *Mathematical logic for computer science*. Springer Science & Business Media, 2012.

[6] Simpson, Stephen G. "Logic and mathematics." *The examined life: Readings from western philosophy from Plato to Kant*, edited by S. Rosen, pp. 577–605, Random House, 2000.

FIGURE 1.2 **Computers at work – calculating test data. Ames Research Center, c1958. Photograph from National Aeronautics and Space Administration (NASA).**

FIGURE 1.3 **Electronic Machine Computing Branch, IBM 704 Date Processor, c1958. Photograph from National Aeronautics and Space Administration (NASA).**

Understanding Binary Data

Human languages use characters or symbols, letters and images to signify meaning. These characters are unintelligible to the wires and circuits within the computer. The computer does not act as we do; instead, it stores values as electrical charges. More specifically, when electricity flows through a wire, the electrical signal can be represented as either 1 or 0, True or False, Yes or No, or On or Off. Figure 1.6 demonstrates the binary representation of an image.

FIGURE 1.4 **Dr. Werner von Braun (seated) examining a Saturn computer in the Astrionics Laboratory at the Marshall Space Flight Center, c1966. Photograph from National Aeronautics and Space Administration (NASA).**

FIGURE 1.5 **A research to improve the human–computer interface, c1966. MAGIC (Machine for Automatic Graphics Interface to a Computer) Photograph from NIST Digital Archives.**

The 0 or 1 is referred to as a *bit* (short for binary digit), and is the smallest unit of information. The more electrical connections the computer uses, the more bits are flowing through its system.

While a bit can represent only a 0 or a 1, a *byte*, a collection of exactly 8 bits, represents a unique character. Table 1.1 and Figure 1.7 demonstrate the possible patterns or states of 0s and 1s that can be made from 1, 2, 3 and 4 bits.

B5 AD 6F A9 F7 EE BD D2 75 DD 48 73 20 59 19 01 69 0B 1D 00 FA F9
96 4F EA 78 23 FE 23 9F 7E EB DD 44 9D 84 50 19 48 8D 66 94 9F 18
08 0E A1 A4 EA 2B 19 BD 97 FA FD 0F D3 DF BA F7 48 D9 69 C3 AC 92
55 CB AA 10 EB F4 2A 1B 57 25 54 1F AD AF FE 36 FE 9E FD D7 BA 04
B7 64 E2 B2 AE 51 10 1F B3 78 D1 3F DD 81 C7 D0 95 3C 0B 13 C8 07
F1 7B FD 7D FB AF 74 12 E4 E3 60 1C B0 D4 C8 18 48 51 82 09 24 53
76 03 9F C1 BB 31 3F ED FD FB AF 74 14 64 95 35 D5 4A 6F E9 94 D8
C8 DF 56 73 EA D0 7E BC DB 57 F4 02 C0 7B F7 5E E9 EB 19 34 35 18
E8 62 A9 5D 5A C3 42 15 79 94 80 0B 0B 12 2C 18 5C 7D 6D FF 00 11
EF DD 7B AE 54 AC B0 30 85 88 14 E4 48 DA 35 E8 D3 28 20 B8 95 7F
37 16 E4 F1 FD 3D FB AF 74 F0 69 D6 FE 48 55 44 52 97 69 80 22 CC
4F F9 C2 55 B8 E4 58 00 3F D7 1E FD D7 BA C9 45 59 34 2F 35 1C 95
1E 26 D1 33 53 08 B5 34 75 74 AB 19 1A 4F 92 C5 64 53 60 CA 3F AD
C5 81 3E FD D7 BA 3E DB 3E A2 3A FC 46 0E A0 C8 23 63 8B A0 97 52
DB 4C 6D 1C 00 28 0A 7D 56 E4 DB F3 7F AF BF 75 EE 84 3A 9A 45 FB
6B A9 00 BC 8B 29 8F 4F EB 97 F0 F2 FF 00 BC 12 D6 FE 9F 9F 7E EB
DD 07 B9 B8 A2 59 1A 79 0A C8 82 35 21 64 BB 6A 50 FF 00 B8 3D 24
DD 75 7D 47 E4 F1 EF DD 7B A0 33 7A D5 B5 45 16 52 9C AC 34 D4 F3
D3 54 42 ED 16 95 A8 8A 9E 58 99 0C 71 80 09 05 8D 88 BF 36 F7 EE
BD D6 BB 9F 31 FA B2 8B 78 E3 77 B6 D3 9B 19 4C 30 DB CF 6F EE 1D
AD 99 6A F6 F2 52 E5 29 37 0D 13 D3 2D 14 94 AC 39 75 AB F1 4F 1B
B5 95 64 54 BD 83 1F 7E EB DD 69 57 98 A7 97 17 3D 66 1F 72 57 55
63 6B B0 95 79 1C 2E 4E 87 1D 4E B4 9E 1C 8E 26 A5 E8 6B 61 A8 8A
52 4C 6E 93 44 D1 91 6B 29 FC 91 63 EF DD 7B A4 EC 79 BC 5A A2 45
47 33 C8 EF 2B A4 D4 F1 D2 56 2F 83 F0 03 56 86 F5 22 35 80 2B F4
E7 FA 7B F7 5E E9 59 8A 38 AA F8 25 95 B3 55 4F 2A C2 A4 21 DB 75
91 01 2A 9B 2C 47 24 67 65 1C EA B2 E9 B9 1E AB FD 7D FB AF 74 F3
1D 14 49 4D E5 A5 AE 95 1E 39 52 68 96 78 69 2B A9 63 89 D4 F9 55
E0 7D 67 53 7D 40 62 48 FF 00 0B 7B F7 5E EA 68 AF C4 56 54 53 08
25 9A A6 68 E4 54 11 CC E2 28 5E AD D4 44 35 46 C4 46 96 04 AE A3
7E 0F 3E FD D7 BA 6B CB 53 33 4D 51 4E D0 AC 6B 10 6F B7 78 64 12
85 A8 B9 06 29 2A 53 9B 01 70 AF 6B 01 F4 F7 EE BD D4 8C 44 4F 32
AA FD CB CF 57 24 89 11 A6 8C 1F 3C A0 8D 22 28 48 B9 2D F5 5F 4F
36 F7 EE BD D3 C4 99 1C 35 03 C7 05 4E 32 92 6F 1F 89 8C E5 25 FB
A8 F5 BF 26 69 8D D8 16 B1 B9 07 90 38 B7 BF 75 EE 9B 2A B7 06 25
E4 92 5A 48 E5 58 5E 36 24 C8 EF 51 1D 54 51 C9 E4 11 89 09 D5 C5
AF 72 7F C4 DF E9 EF DD 7B A8 F4 D5 58 EA C8 2A 2A E1 F3 D3 A8 A8
45 32 33 79 A2 8E 46 BF 8A 4D 3A 4A 06 7B F1 71 F4 FA 58 FB F7 5E
EB 15 47 F1 33 4C 4D 45 4C 53 AC 2E D2 C5 AC B5 9A 6D 76 12 78 E5
20 EB 2B 6B B0 E0 0E 07 1C 7B F7 5E E9 B6 82 5A D7 99 A2 A8 AC A6
58 A7 8F 54 E2 59 55 5F 59 70 B6 42 01 B5 EC 14 0F C7 E3 DF BA F7
4A 1A 68 0D 9D 64 95 C1 13 32 C4 F1 05 32 AA EA 0B 22 B1 00 30 50

FIGURE 1.6 **The Binary representation of an image.**

TABLE 1.1 Bits and Their Possible Patterns

Bits	Possible Patterns
1 bit (2 possible values)	0 or 1
2 bits (4 values)	00 01 10 11
3 bits (8 values)	000 001 010 011 100 101 110 111

To be able to represent more than 1 and 0, True/False, Yes/No, or On/Off, we collect 8 bits to form 1 byte. With 1 byte we can represent and store the numbers between 0 and 255 (2^8). Therefore, a single byte can represent up to **256** different values.

By arranging bits into bytes, any number up to 255 can be represented using only 0s and 1s. Overall, each additional bit doubles the number of possible patterns (Table 1.2).

In our everyday lives, we use a base-10 numeric system with numbers from 0 to 9 (ten digits), whether we are dealing with money, weight, time, or volume. The prefix "dec-" means ten (deka) from Ancient Greek "δέκα" in the metric system. For example, the *dec*athlon event is equal to 10 meters, and a *dec*agon is a 10-sided polygon. It is quite likely we have been using the base-10 system for thousands of years because humans have 10 fingers or digits, so that counting to 10 felt natural.

As noted earlier, a *binary number* is based on the power of 2 (2^n). Why do almost all computers use the binary system? Computers use the binary number

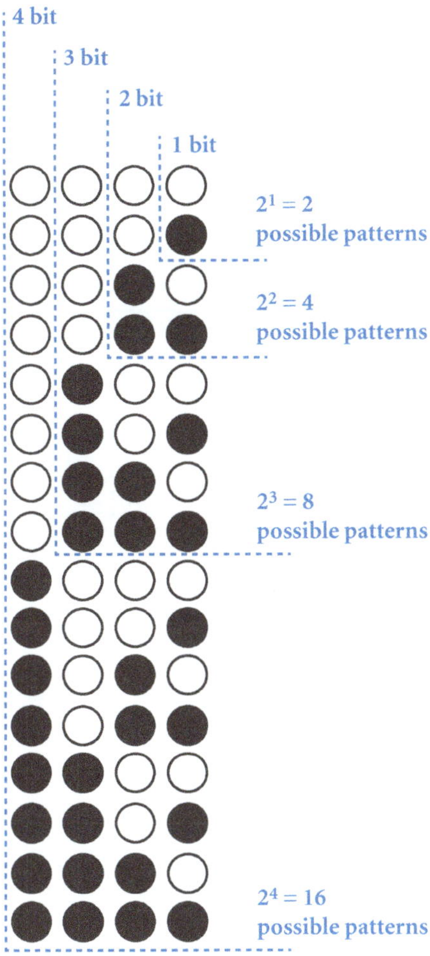

FIGURE 1.7 **Bits possible patterns.**

TABLE 1.2 **Bits and the Number of Patterns with Exponents**

Bits	Patterns	Exponents
1 bit	2	2^1
2 bits	4	2^2
3 bits	8	2^3
4 bits	16	2^4
5 bits	32	2^5
6 bits	64	2^6
7 bits	128	2^7
8 bits (one byte)	256	2^8

system as an alternative to the decimal system because it simplifies program design and makes it easier for the programmer to tell the computer what to do.

The computer understands electrical signals. We convey information through microscopic wires inside the computer. Each wire carries its own electrical signal. There are only two states possible for an electrical signal, charged and not charged. If a wire is carrying an electrical signal (charged), it corresponds to 1. It is in a "signal" state. If the wire is not carrying an electrical signal, it is not in signal state, and corresponds to 0. A bit is always either On (1) or Off (0), and the signal states change according to the instructions the computer is following. In the binary system, groups of 1s and 0s may represent any number. A single wire represents only one bit; many wires represent additional bits. Although a wire can carry variable amounts of electricity, it must interpret its content as either 0 or 1.

When *transistors* were invented, they could control the flow of electricity, acting like digital switches. The transistors inside the computer are so small that we would need an electron microscope to see them. Depending on the transistor and its threshold voltage, the transistor turns on when enough electricity flows through, and turns off when not. For example, if the threshold voltage of a transistor is 5V, any voltage of 3.5V or higher will turn the transistor on. Any voltage lower than 3.5V will turn the transistor off. In practice, when we plug a mouse into a Universal Serial Bus (USB) computer port, a transistor will notice the voltage required by the mouse and translate the state of the mouse to On, telling the computer that an external USB device is plugged into the port.

When we type a letter, number, or symbol on the keyboard, the computer converts each character to binary code instantaneously, simultaneously displaying the character on the monitor.

Computers process large amounts of data measured in MIPS (Millions of Instructions per Second). A single byte (8 bits) represents a single character. For example, the letter A is saved as 01000001, and the number 7 is saved as 0111. The number 77 is saved as 01001101 (see Figure 1.8 and Table 1.10).

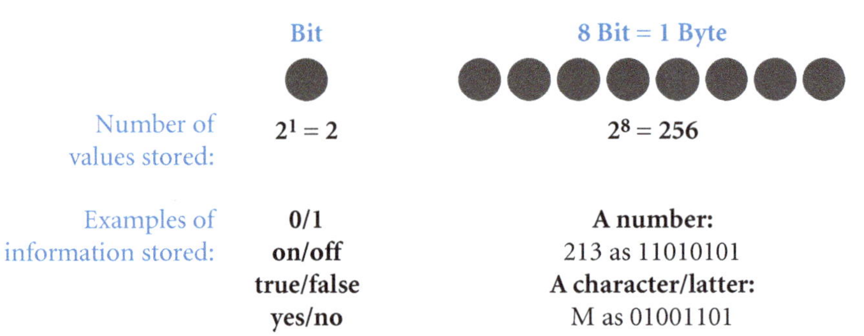

FIGURE 1.8 Demonstrates the difference between a Bit and a Byte.

TABLE 1.3 Decimal vs Binary System

Decimal System The decimal system uses 10 digits from 0 to 9	Binary System The binary system uses only two digits, 0 & 1
The decimal system uses the powers of 10 for calculation (10^0 =1, 10^1=10, 10^2=100, 10^3=1000, 10^4=10000……).	The Binary system uses the powers of 2 (2^0=1, 2^1=2, 2^2=4, 2^3=8, 2^4=16……).

The binary system is the main language used by computers because it is simple and reliable. Furthermore, it is efficient because it requires a minimum number of electric circuits, and is of low-cost, uses little energy, and occupies minimum space.

Computers calculate conversion to binary code much faster than a human could, but it is useful to know how to do conversion by hand (see Table 1.3 Decimal vs Binary Systems and Table 1.4 Computer Data Conversion).

Conversion from Binary to Decimal

We would like to convert Binary 1001 to a decimal number. In Rows 1 and 2 of table 1.5, we see the powers of two and their numerical equivalents written from right to left.

To convert a binary number to decimal, the key is to deconstruct the number as the sum of powers of two.

To find the decimal number represented by the binary code 1001, look at the table and calculate each column. Any 0 in binary will remain 0 in decimal, since the signal is Off. Reading from right to left: 1=1 (2^0), 0=0 (2^1), 0=0 (2^2), 1=1 (2^3). Adding the numbers together yields 9. Therefore, the binary code 1001 is equal to the number 9.

In the next line, we convert 10011011 to its decimal value. Again, the 0s do not change, from right to left; the 1s are equal to 1,2,8,16,128. The sum of these numbers is 155. Therefore, the binary code 10011001 is equal to the number 155 (Table 1.5).

Conversion from Decimal to Binary

Now, let us convert in the other way – the decimal 23 to Binary. What is the largest power of two that is less than the number we are converting? The column represented by 32 (2^5) is larger than 23, therefore we will begin with 16 (2^4). When we omit the 0, the numbers left are 16 + 4 + 2 + 1=23. Therefore, the binary number 10111 is the digit 23. Another example shows that the binary number 111 is the digit 7 (4 + 2 + 1 = 7) (see Table 1.6).

TABLE 1.4 Computer Data Conversion

Units *(byte prefixes)*	Actual number of bytes *(decimal form)*	Base-2 *(Number of bytes)*	Approximate Size in bytes *(decimal form)*	Base-10 *(decimal)*
Kilobyte (KB)	1,024	2^{10}	One-thousand bytes	10^{3}
Megabyte (MB)	1,048,576	2^{20}	One-million bytes	10^{6}
Gigabyte (GB)	1,073,742.824	2^{30}	One-billion bytes	10^{9}
Terabyte (TB)	1,099,511,627,776	2^{40}	One trillion bytes	10^{12}
Petabyte (PB)	1,125,899,906,842,624	2^{50}	One-quadrillion bytes	10^{15}
Exabyte (EB)	1,152,921,504,606,846,976	2^{60}	One-quintillion bytes	10^{18}
Zettabyte (ZB)	1,180,591,620,717,411,303,424	2^{70}	One-sextillion bytes	10^{21}
Yottabyte (YB)	1,208,925,819,614,629,174,706,176	2^{80}	One-septillion bytes	10^{24}

TABLE 1.5 Conversion from Binary to Decimal

2^{10}	2^9	2^8	2^7	2^6	2^5	2^4	2^3	2^2	2^1	2^0	Binary
1024	512	256	128	64	32	16	8	4	2	1	Decimal = 9
							1	0	0	1	Binary Decimal
							8	+0	+0	+1	=155
			1	0	0	1	1	0	1	1	
			128	+0	+0	+16	+8	+0	+2	+1	

Right to Left

TABLE 1.6 Conversion from Decimal to Binary

2^{10}	2^9	2^8	2^7	2^6	2^5	2^4	2^3	2^2	2^1	2^0	Decimals # 23
1024	512	256	128	64	32	16	8	4	2	1	Binary
							16	+0	+4	+2	Decimal # 7 Binary
							1	0	1	1	
									4	+2	
									1	1	

Right to Left

Hexadecimal

Another common number system used in computer science is Hexadecimal or Hex, also called Base 16, because it consists of 16 characters. Hexadecimal is derived from hexa, meaning six, like the six-sided hexagon, and "decimal'"from the number 10. The hexadecimal system uses only 10 digits (0–9), and 6 letters A, B, C, D, E, and F. The system utilizes letters instead of other symbols because it is easier to type them on a keyboard. Hexadecimal calculation is different from binary. Each hexadecimal character is equivalent to 4 bits or half a byte (for example, 1110), and is called a Nibble, or Nybble.

The hexadecimal system is efficient in computer programming, because only a single hexadecimal character represents 4 bits. Table 1.7 displays decimals and hex values from 1 to 31.

For example, the single hexadecimal character E can represent the group of four bits 1110, called a Nybble. A group of eight bits, 1110 1100, called a byte, represents two hexadecimal characters EC. When we use hexadecimal characters in a code, we add **0x** to the beginning of the value, for example **0xEC.** When programmers write codes, they try to represent values as efficiently as possible. For example, the hexadecimal letter A, which represents the number 10, is more manageable than the binary number 1010, which also represents 10. In another example, the decimal number 252 is 1111 1100 in binary code, but in hex it is just FC. Developers of web

TABLE 1.7 Decimals and Hex values

Decimals	Hex	Decimals	Hex
0	0	16	10
1	1	17	11
2	2	18	12
3	3	19	13
4	4	20	14
5	5	21	15
6	6	22	16
7	7	23	17
8	8	24	18
9	9	25	19
10	A	26	1A
11	B	27	1B
12	C	28	1C
13	D	29	1D
14	E	30	1E
15	F	31	1F

pages use Hex to represent the specific colors within Hyper Text Markup Language (HTML) the standard markup language for Web pages within Cascading Style Sheets (CSS).

Cascading Style Sheets are a set of rules that determine how a webpage should look like, telling the browser what colors the developer wants and how to display them. This technology, alongside HTML and JavaScript, is the foundation of the World Wide Web (WWW).

The primary use of hexadecimal code is a human-friendly representation of binary-coded values. The hexadecimal color system is the standard system for all web browsers. Each hexadecimal digit is a number between 0 and 255 in decimal numbers, but it is much easier to read as 2 hexadecimal digits from 00 to FF.

When choosing colors, the developer knows that the base colors Red, Green, and Blue (RGB), when mixed together, can reproduce a wide range of colors on a computer screen. On an 8-bit color screen, 8 bits can represent each color (or $2^8 = 256$). This means there are 256 possible values for each color, 00–255 which can be represented in a double-digit hexadecimal code from 00 to FF, to shorten the HTML code length.

The purest white color in hexadecimal code displays red, green, and blue at the highest possible color brightness of the RGB model and is written in hex as #FFFFFF. In decimals, it would be nine digits, 255,255,255. Hex code makes it possible for 256 numbers to be represented by only two different characters, for example FF is represented by #255. In RGB the hex value of black is written as #000000, because all three colors, Red, Green, and Blue, have zero value. Yellow in RGB hex is written as #FFFF00 and is composed of 100% red or #255, 100% green or #255 value, and 0% or 0 value of Blue. Pure Red in RGB hex is written as #FF0000 and is composed of 100% Red or #255 value, 0% Green, and 0% Blue.

Converting from Hexadecimal to Binary

We learn to count from small numbers to very large ones. In contrast, the hexadecimal system has only 16 *characters* in its set of numbers. In hex we count **0, 1, 2, 3, 4, 5, 6, 7, 8, 9, A, B, C, D, E, F** – and that is it! When we need a value in excess of the letter **F (decimal 15),** we go through the sequence again, but this time always beginning with 1, then with 2, and so on. Therefore, **hex 11** is equal to **decimal 17** and **hex 21** is equal to **decimal 33**. This is displayed in Table 1.8, showing the first 255 hexadecimal numbers.

To convert a hex number to a binary number, once a hex number is larger than a *nybble* (4 bits or half a byte) the left digit is valued more. Look at each *nybble* independently (see Table 1.9).

Conversion from Binary to Hexadecimal

To convert from binary to hexadecimal, follow the reverse of the above examples. The first example **1101** is very simple. The answer is D (13=D) in the hexadecimal system or $\mathbf{D_{16}}$. The second example is little complicated

TABLE 1.8 The first 255 in hexadecimal numbers

Hexadecimal numbers from 0 to 255
0 1 2 3 4 5 6 7 8 9 A B C D E F 10 11 12 13 14 15 16 17 18 19 1A 1B 1C 1D 1E 1F 20 21 22 23
24 25 26 27 28 29 2A 2B 2C 2D 2E 2F 30 31 32 33 34 35 36 37 38 39 3A 3B 3C 3D 3E 3F 40
41 42 43 44 45 46 47 48 49 4A 4B 4C 4D 4E 4F 50 51 52 53 54 55 56 57 58 59 5A 5B 5C 5D
5E 5F 60 61 62 63 64 65 66 67 68 69 6A 6B 6C 6D 6E 6F 70 71 72 73 74 75 76 77 78 79 7A 7B
7C 7D 7E 7F 80 81 82 83 84 85 86 87 88 89 8A 8B 8C 8D 8E 8F 90 91 92 93 94 95 96 97 98 99
9A 9B 9C 9D 9E 9F A0 A1 A2 A3 A4 A5 A6 A7 A8 A9 AA AB AC AD AE AF B0 B1 B2 B3
B4 B5 B6 B7 B8 B9 BA BB BC BD BE BF C0 C1 C2 C3 C4 C5 C6 C7 C8 C9 CA CB CC CD
CE CF D0 D1 D2 D3 D4 D5 D6 D7 D8 D9 DA DB DC DD DE DF E0 E1 E2 E3 E4 E5 E6 E7
E8 E9 EA EB EC ED EE EF F0 F1 F2 F3 F4 F5 F6 F7 F8 F9 FA FB FC FD FE FF

TABLE 1.9 Translate Hex to binary

Hex	Conversion of Each Part	Binary Result
7F	7= 0111 and F=1111	Therefore, Hex 7F=0111 1111 Binary
D4B	D=1101, 4=0100 and b=1011	Therefore, Hex D4B=1101 0100 1011 Binary
FF301B	f=1111, f=1111, 3=0011, 0=0000, 1=0001 and B=1011	Therefore, Hex FF301B =1111 1111 0011 0000 0001 1011 Binary

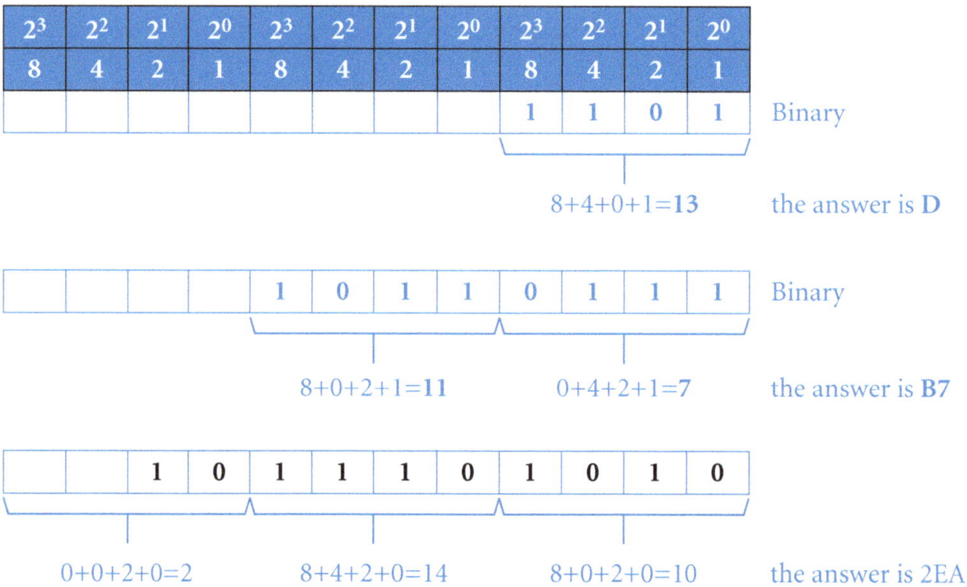

FIGURE 1.9 **Conversion from binary to hexadecimal.**

10110111. Each *nybble* is 4 bits or half a byte. The answer is **B7** (11 is B and 7) in the hexadecimal system or $\mathbf{B7}_{16.}$ In the third example, the binary number is 1011101010 and the answer is **2EA** (2+14 which is E + 10 which is A) in the hexadecimal system or $\mathbf{2EA}_{16}$ (Figure 1.9).

ASCII, EBCDIC and UNICODE

ASCII is an acronym for American Standard Code for Information Interchange. This standard, established in the 1960s and rarely used today, was created to serve as a common language among computers using the English alphabet. The original ASCII code represents 128 characters as standard numeric values, lower and uppercase letters, symbols, numbers, punctuation marks, and control characters. Each character is assigned a number between 0 and 127, and contains 7-bit codes, meaning that there are 128 different characters within seven bits, including seven digits set to 0 or a 1, True or False, Yes or No, On or Off. Besides the printable characters, ASCII code also contains non-printable characters that control how text is processed.[7/8]

Another encoding system is the Extended Binary Coded Decimal Interchange Code (EBCDIC), developed in the late 1950s and early 1960s, and used by International Business Machines (IBM).[9] Since EBCDIC and ASCII have limitations in terms of number of characters, a UNICODE was created jointly by the Unicode Consortium and by The International Organization for Standardization (ISO). The Unicode provides an exclusive number for every character, including emojis, regardless of the platform, program, or language.[10]

Table 1.10 displays the first 25 (0–25) decimals and characters in binary values and ASCII code.

1.3 Processing

Boolean Algebra, Logic Gates, and Truth Tables

As described above, we send bits through the computer using wires that represent 1s and 0s. The computer uses logic gates to enable these 1s and 0s to execute more complicated operations.

A logic gate is a device based on Boolean function that implements logical operations in any digital system. The miniature electronic circuits within the computer are the most basic building blocks, using one or more inputs to produce a single output (1 or 0), based on logical functions. Simply put, logic gates control the flow of electric current through a circuit. Certain circuits may have only a few logic gates, while others, like those found within a microprocessor, may have millions of logic gates. When the computer uses millions of logic gates, it is possible to perform highly complex operations.

Logic gates are the foundation for computers and other modern digital electronics. They are used in microprocessors and microcontrollers, and are embedded in system applications like mobile devices and IoT devices that integrate hardware circuitry and software programming techniques.

To understand logic gates, we need to understand the work of George Boole, the inventor of Boolean algebra. His mathematics are fundamental to computer science. George Boole was an English mathematician of the mid-1800s who developed logical statements that went beyond Aristotle's mathematical logic. Boole wrote *The mathematical analysis of logic* in 1847.[11]

---

[7] Maini, Anil K. *Digital electronics: principles, devices and applications*. John Wiley & Sons, 2007.

[8] Danet, Brenda, and Susan C. Herring. "Introduction: The multilingual internet." *Journal of Computer-Mediated Communication* 9, no. 1 (2003): JCMC9110.

[9] *Id*. at 7.

[10] Unicode standard. https://home.unicode.org/basic-info/overview/

[11] Boole, George. *The mathematical analysis of logic*. Philosophical Library, 1847.

TABLE 1.10 Decimal numbers 0–25 and the alphabet in binary values and ASCII code

Decimals	Binary	Alphabet uppercase	ASCII code	Binary	Alphabet lowercase	ASCII code	Binary
0	0000 0000	A	065	0100 0001	A	097	0110 0001
1	0000 0001	B	066	0100 0010	B	098	0110 0010
2	0000 0010	C	067	0100 0011	C	099	0110 0011
3	0000 0011	D	068	0100 0100	D	100	0110 0100
4	0000 0100	E	069	0100 0101	E	101	0110 0101
5	0000 0101	F	070	0100 0110	F	102	0110 0110
6	0000 0110	G	071	0100 0111	G	103	0110 0111
7	0000 0111	H	072	0100 1000	H	104	0110 1000
8	0000 1000	I	073	0100 1001	I	105	0110 1001
9	0000 1001	J	074	0100 1010	J	106	0110 1010
10	0000 1010	K	075	0100 1011	K	107	0110 1011
11	0000 1011	L	076	0100 1100	L	108	0110 1100
12	0000 1100	M	077	0100 1101	M	109	0110 1101
13	0000 1101	N	078	0100 1110	N	110	0110 1110
14	0000 1110	O	079	0100 1111	O	111	0110 1111
15	0000 1111	P	080	0101 0000	P	112	0111 0000
16	0001 0000	Q	081	0101 0001	Q	113	0111 0001
17	0001 0001	R	082	0101 0010	R	114	0111 0010
18	0001 0010	S	083	0101 0011	S	115	0111 0011
19	0001 0011	T	084	0101 0100	T	116	0111 0100
20	0001 0100	U	085	0101 0101	U	117	0111 0101
21	0001 0101	V	086	0101 0110	V	118	0111 0110
22	0001 0110	W	087	0101 0111	W	119	0111 0111
23	0001 0111	X	088	0101 1000	X	120	0111 1000
24	0001 1000	Y	089	0101 1001	Y	121	0111 1001
25	0001 1001	Z	090	0101 1010	Z	122	0111 1010

In Boolean algebra, the values of variables are expressed only as true or false, while in ordinary algebra the values of variables involve numbers, variables, and operations. Furthermore, the Boolean operation takes a specific input and produces a specific output, based on a set of rules. Logic gates implement basic logical functions and are the vital building blocks of digital integrated circuits.

The three basic logic gates are NOT, AND, and OR. Other gates include XOR, NAND, NOR, and XNOR. All gates are represented by symbols and truth tables. Truth tables help us understand how circuits work. The following are the three basic logic gates with their symbols and truth tables.

- A NOT-gate is the simplest logic gate, also known as an inverter. The NOT-gate has only one input and one output. The output is the reverse of the input, so if the input is 0, the output must be 1, and vice versa. The gate flips True to False, and False to True.

  The following illustration shows the symbol and truth table of a NOT-gate. The letter A represents the Input and the letter O represents the output. The term True is equal to 1 in binary code. This logic gate means that if the input is False the statement is True; if the input is True the statement is False (see Figure 1.10 and Table 1.11).
- The AND-gate consists of two inputs, A and B, and one output, O. If both inputs are turned On (True or 1), the output will turn On (True or 1). If none of the input or only one of the two inputs is turned On (True or 1), the output will be Off (False or 0). The following is the symbol and truth table of an **AND-gate** (see Figure 1.11 and Table 1.12).

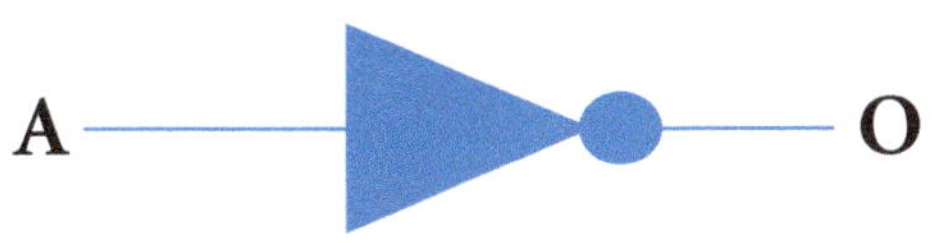

FIGURE 1.10 **NOT-Gate.**

TABLE 1.11 NOT-gate truth tables

Input (A)	Output (O)	Input (A)	Output (O)
True	False	1	0
False	True	0	1

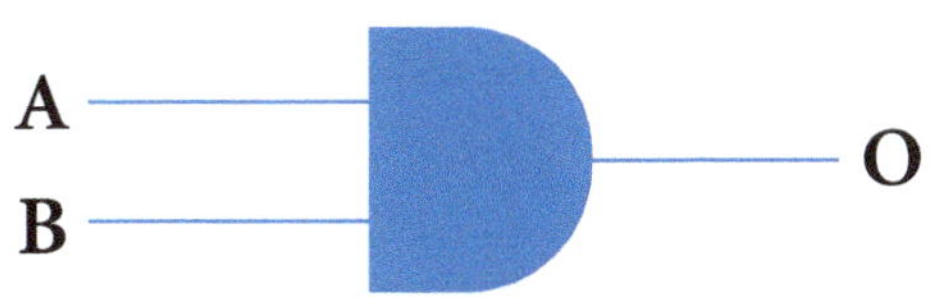

FIGURE 1.11 **AND-Gate.**

TABLE 1.12 AND-gate truth tables

Input (A)	Input (B)	Output (O)	Input (A)	Input (B)	Output (O)
False	False	False	0	0	0
False	True	False	0	1	0
True	False	False	1	0	0
True	True	True	1	1	1

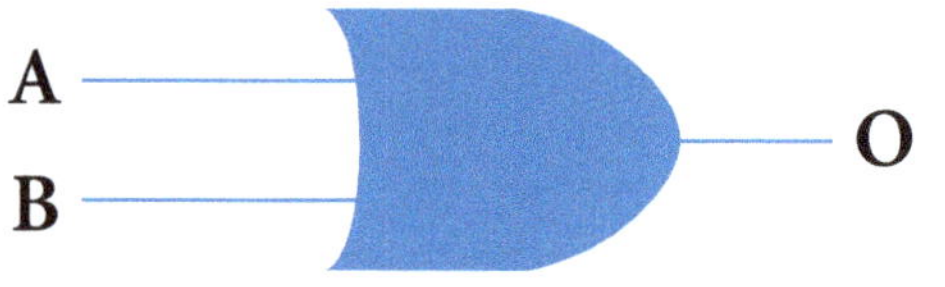

FIGURE 1.12 **OR-Gate.**

TABLE 1.13 OR-Gate truth tables

Input (A)	Input (B)	Output (O)	Input (A)	Input (B)	Output (O)
False	False	False	0	0	0
False	True	True	0	1	1
True	False	True	1	0	1
True	True	True	1	1	1

- The OR-gate consists of two inputs, A and B, and one output (O). If at least one input is turned On (True or 1), the output will be 1. If both inputs are Off (False or 0), the output will be Off (False or 0). The only time that an OR-gate outputs a 0 (False) is if both inputs are 0. The output is True if either input A or input B is True (see Figure 1.12 and Table 1.13).

Developers use other gates, called derived logic gates, made from the combination of two or more of the three basic logic gates. Combining logic gates results in a complicated logical function.[12] Connecting thousands or millions of logic gates makes it possible to perform highly complex operations, and these operations are the core components of digital integrated circuits, including computer memory and microprocessors. Microprocessors and most other digital technology are made of transistors, which may contain more than 100 million logic gates.[13 /14]

[12] Mahmoodi, Hamid, Saihal Mukhopadhyay, and Kaushik Roy. "High performance and low power domino logic using independent gate control in double-gate SOI MOSFETs." In *2004 IEEE International SOI Conference (IEEE Cat. No. 04CH37573)*, pp. 67–68. IEEE, 2004.

[13] Chau, Robert, Brian Doyle, Mark Doczy, Suman Datta, Scott Hareland, Ben Jin, Jack Kavalieros, and Matthew Metz. "Silicon nano-transistors and breaking the 10 nm physical gate length barrier." In *61st Device Research Conference. Conference Digest (Cat. No. 03TH8663)*, pp. 123–126. IEEE, 2003.

[14] Baker, R. Jacob. *CMOS: circuit design, layout, and simulation*. Wiley-IEEE press, 2019.

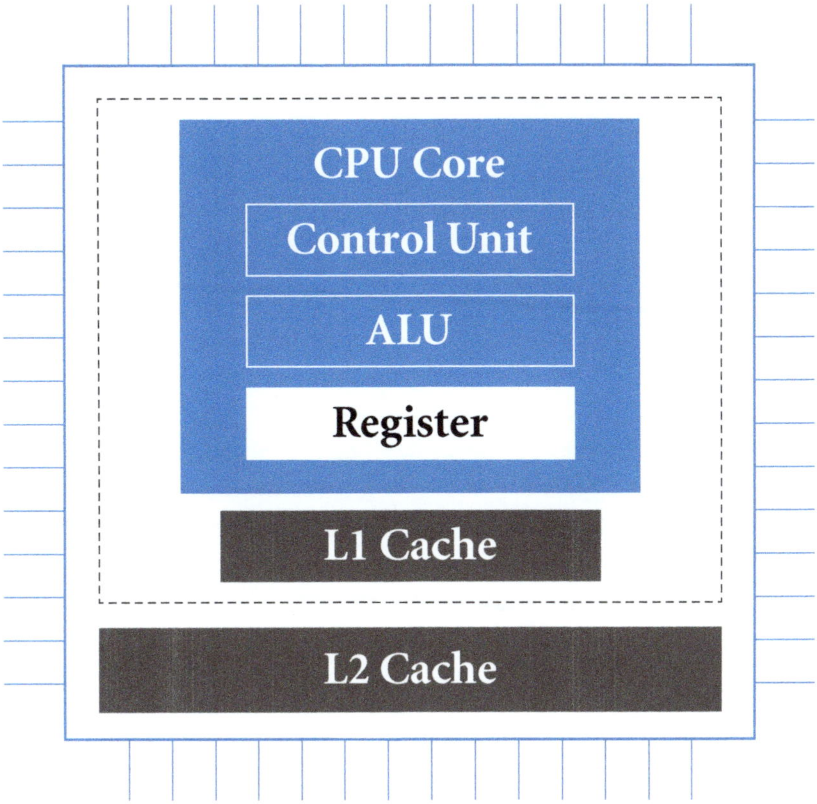

FIGURE 1.13 A typical CPU architecture.

When the gate is On, current flows through the transistor. When the gate is Off, current cannot flow. In the same way, the output of a gate may be connected to the inputs of one or several other gates, resulting in outputs that are even more complicated. Most logic gates are made from metal oxide semiconductor field effect transistors (MOSFET), or metal oxide silicon transistors (MOS).[15/16] In addition to logic gates, the Arithmetic Logic Unit (ALU) performs arithmetic and logic operations on binary numbers. They can be found at the heart of every computing system like the CPU. See Figure 1.13.

Processor Types (32-bit Processors vs 64-bit Processors)

In computing architecture, the two main categories of processors are 32-bit (also known as x86) and 64-bit (also known as x64). The number indicates how the hardware and software, such as the central processing unit (CPU), the operating system (OS), and the software, process data. For example, the 32-bit processor can process 4 bytes ($4 \times 8=32$ bits) for each CPU cycle,

[15] Motoyoshi, Makoto. "Through-silicon via (TSV)." *Proceedings of the IEEE* 97, no. 1 (2009): 43–48.
[16] Bousse, L., J. Shott, and J. D. Meindl. "A process for the combined fabrication of ion sensors and CMOS circuits." *IEEE Electron Device Letters* 9, no. 1 (1988): 44–46.

roughly 4.3 gigabytes of RAM in total. The 64-bit processor can process 8 bytes ($8 \times 8 = 64$ bits) per CPU cycle. Thus, the 64-bit processor can handle twice the amount of data compared to the 32-bit processor.

More specifically, the processor type represents how much data the CPU can load from the main memory (RAM) at a time. The 64-bit processor can calculate data faster, regardless of the processor's clock speed (cycles per second).

- A 32-bit processor (2^{32}) can access a limited amount of RAM. For example, using MS Windows, the processor can address 4,294,967,296 bytes of RAM or physical memory (4 GB of RAM or less). Computers built in the 1990s and early 2000s were built and designed specifically for 32-bit processors.
- 64-bit processors (2^{64}), can theoretically access 8,446,744,073,709,551,616 bytes of RAM or physical memory (any amount of physical memory greater than 4 GB of RAM). The operating systems of these processors must support the 64-bit processors. The number of calculations per second a 64-bit processor can achieve influences the speed of the computer and how fast a request for processing data can be completed. With a 64-bit processor, data in memory is accessed faster and programs load much faster into memory. Furthermore, the central processor clock speed determines how quickly the CPU can retrieve and interpret instructions. The CPU speed is measured, in numeric value such as million instructions per second (MIPS), or billion instructions per second (GIPS). CPU instruction rates are measured in Hz (megahertz or gigahertz). This measurement can be useful when evaluating processors made with similar architecture and a general idea of a computer's speed (Figure 1.13).

1.4 Storage

Data storage is a process for archiving data in a variety of forms. Examples include:

- Hard Drives (HD), a spinning disk with magnetic coatings and read/write heads in the form of magnetic patterns and Solid-State Drive (SSD) using flash memory. Old storage media, such as floppy disks and tapes also store data magnetically.
- Removable media, such as Data storage devices, USB flash drives, CompactFlash cards (CF), Secure Digital cards (SD), and Memory Sticks.
- Electro Optical devices such as Blu-ray, Compact Discs (CD), and Digital Versatile Discs (DVD). These devices use laser light or electromagnetic waves along with a reflective material incorporated into optical discs to read or write binary information.

- Another form of storage is the option for remote data storage, such as the Cloud storage model, in which computers store digital data in multiple servers and sometimes in multiple locations around the world.

Different types of data storage perform different functions in a computing environment. Computer memory/storage is classified into two categories:

Volatile Memory This type of memory loses its data if the power is turned off, for example Random-access memory (RAM).

Non-Volatile Memory This is a type of memory that holds and saves data even when the power is turned off, for example read-only memory (ROM), software that is rarely changed throughout the life of the system, like Complementary metal–oxide–semiconductor (CMOS) memory that holds the startup program (BIOS) of the computer.

Additionally, in computer architecture, it is important to understand *memory hierarchy.* The term defines the level of computer storage (how the computer handles data) by response time. The *memory hierarchy* consists of

Primary Storage

CPU Registers: (very fast computer processor memory used to execute programs and operations efficiently).

Cache Memory: the fastest system memory that provides data storage of programs and instructions for fast access during operation of the CPU.

Secondary Storage

Main Memory or Random Access Memory (RAM):

Fast memory used to temporarily hold programs and data, allowing information to be stored and retrieved while the computer is on.

Virtual Memory: is extra memory that simulates RAM if more is needed. Virtual memory enables a system to run more than one large application at the same time without running out of memory (RAM) by temporarily transferring data from random access memory (RAM) to disk storage.

Hard Drives: Magnetic Disks/SSD

Optical Devices: CDs, DVDs and Blu-ray

Figures 1.14 and 1.15 display the memory hierarchy and schematic overview of computer architecture.

Compression

Even though computers can store large amounts of data, size still matters. When a file is small, it can be stored, handled, and sent more easily, without taking up much space. Therefore, compression algorithms reduce file

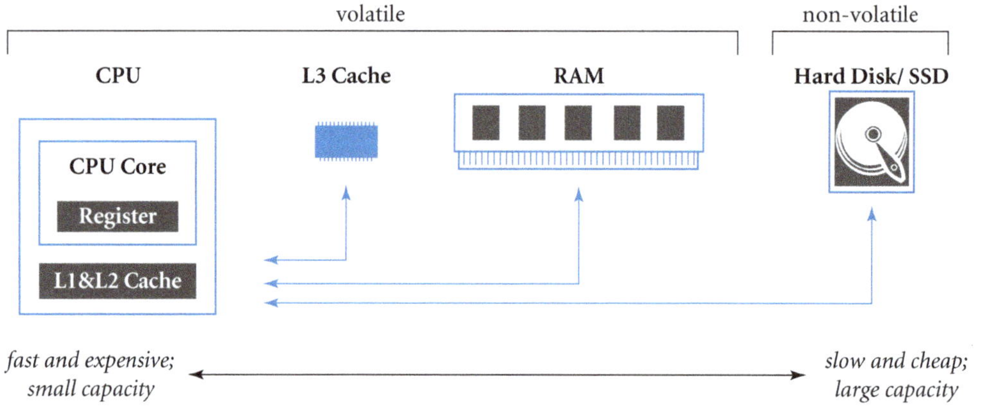

FIGURE 1.14 **Memory hierarchy.**

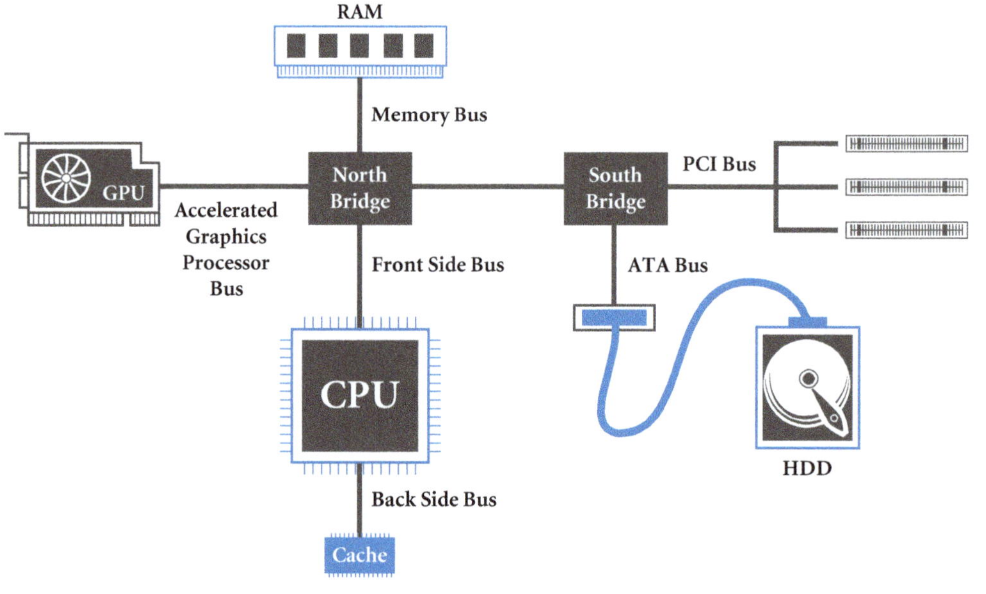

FIGURE 1.15 **Schematic overview of computer architecture.**

size while preserving the data. A compressed file takes up less space and can be sent and received faster (Figure 1.16). The file compression algorithm locates recurrent sequences and replaces them with shorter representations. Essentially, there are two different kinds of compression, lossy and lossless.

Lossy Compression

Lossy compression is an algorithm that reduces file size by discarding bits of information that are less important. The process lowers the number of bits in the file, resulting in significantly smaller file size. However, it also affects file quality, and once lost, data cannot be restored. A compressed lossy file has less data than the original file. Lossy compression is most frequently used

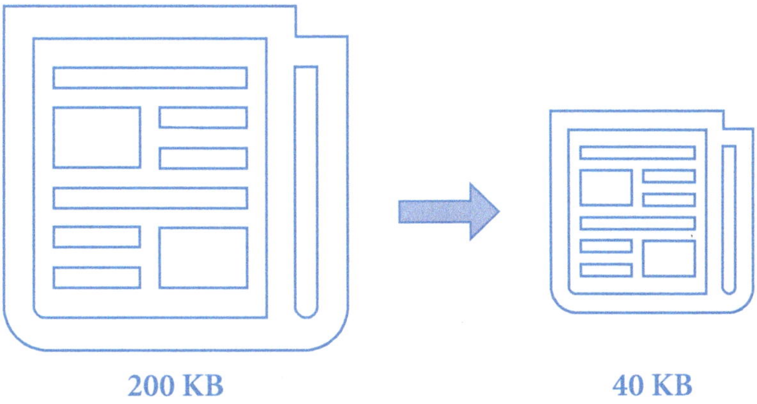

FIGURE 1.16 **Compression.**

for files uploaded to the internet, such as audio, video (streaming media), and images. The advantage to lossy compression is that it keeps the file size small, while preserving relatively high-quality multimedia content.

During lossy compression, images and sounds that repeat are removed. After repeated compression and decompression, the file will progressively lose quality, called generation loss. In audio, for instance the algorithm discards frequencies that the human ear is not likely to detect, and also discards sounds of lower volume that the listener cannot hear, while reducing the size of the audio file and maintaining as much audio quality as possible. Figure 1.17 demonstrates Lossless and Lossy compression.

Computer programs that encode or decode video for viewing are called *codecs*. If you are trying to watch a video, and your computer does not have the right codec, it may prompt you to download it. Some examples of common image and video formats include image compression formats such as JPEG, PNG, video coding standards like MPEG and H.264/AVC, WMA, RealVideo, DivX and audio compression formats like MP3, AAC, and RealAudio.

Lossless Compression

Lossless compression algorithms can reconstruct the original data from the compressed data without any quality loss.[17] The file data is removed temporarily so that the file can be sent. Lossless compression is used for medical images, text documents, spreadsheets, software applications, and images for digital preservation. A common format used to do this is the *.zip* format. Lossless compression algorithms are necessary when the reconstruction must be identical to the original. Some lossless audio compression methods

[17] Kodituwakku, S. R., and U. S. Amarasinghe. "Comparison of lossless data compression algorithms for text data." *Indian Journal of Computer Science and Engineering* 1, no. 4 (2010): 416–425.

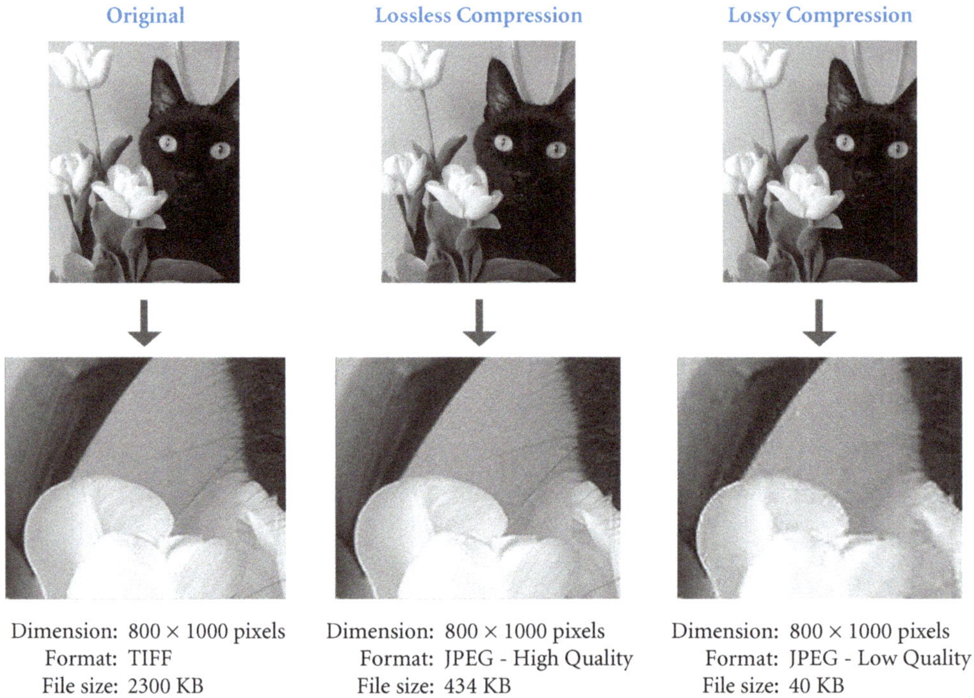

FIGURE 1.17 Compare Lossy and Lossless compression.

are Free Lossless Audio Codec (FLAC), Apple Lossless Audio Code (ALAC), WMA Lossless (Windows Media Lossless). For images, popular formats are TIFF (Tagged Image File Format), which can provide either lossless or lossy compression, (JPEG-LS), both lossless and near-lossless compression. Video examples include Container, associated with file formats such as QuickTime, AVI, and MPEG, and Codecs associated with compression standards (encoding and decoding or compression or decompression of digital files). Examples of these codec include H.264, H.265 compression technology, MPEG-4, DivX, and AOMedia Video 1 (AV1).

1.5 Output

Pixels

All digital photos, videos, and graphics are made of tiny squares called Pixels. A pixel, pel, or picture element, is the smallest unit of a digital image or graphic.[18] The most efficient way to store an image is in black and white, using a gray scale of varying intensity. For instance, 2 bits per pixel will provide us with $2^2=4$ shades of intensity from 0 white to level 3 black, 3 bits

[18] Pavlidis, Theodosios. *Algorithms for graphics and image processing.* Springer Science & Business Media, 2012.

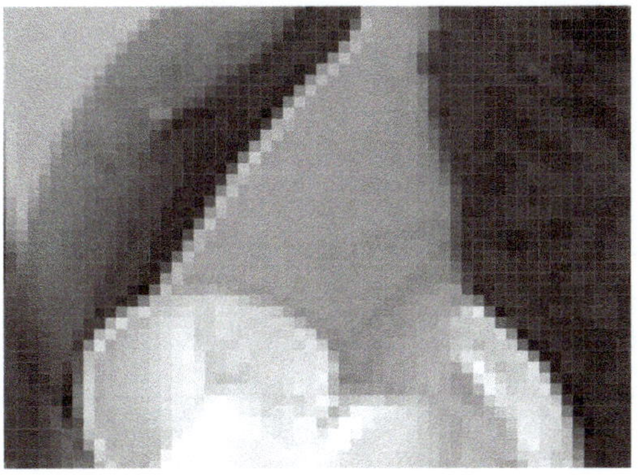

FIGURE 1.18 **Grayscale representation of pixel raster.**

per pixel will provide us with $2^3=8$ shades of intensity from 0 white to level 7 black, and 8 bits per pixel will provide us with $2^8=256$ distinct shades of gray (Figure 1.18).

However, most images today are not black and white, but are in color. Each individual pixel has an individual pixel value. This value is a single number that describes how bright that pixel is, and what color it should be. Each pixel value consists of three numeric color components, Red, Green, and Blue (RGB), that represent its color. Each red, green, and blue setting defines the intensity of the color as an integer between 0 and 255. Each individual pixel that represents a color image in a computer screen has a pixel value. This value describes how bright the pixel is. We use an integer between 0 and 255 because each pixel can be represented by 8 bits or 1 byte.

When we use the value 0, this means there is no contribution from the specific color. At the opposite end of the range, the value of 255 means the greatest or most saturated contribution of this color. Bear in mind that with 1 byte we can efficiently represent up to 255 different colors. For example, Pink is produced by combining three RGB values: Red (255), Green (105), and Blue (180). The color Aqua is Red (0), Green (255), and Blue (255). This model is used efficiently and just as importantly because it is the closest representation to the way the human eye perceives color.[19] Table 1.14 demonstrates the colors in RGB, binary value, and Hex.

Color Depth

The number of "bits" described in reference to an image is the amount of tonal variation in the image, the variation of lightness or darkness of a color. For example, there are numerous tones of a red color available, but they must be described differently to appear correct. All computers support 16-bit color, 24-bit, and 32-bit color.

[19] Koenderink, Jan J. *Color for the sciences*. MIT Press, 2010.

TABLE 1.14 Displays the colors in RGB, binary value and Hex

Color	Decimal RGB	Binary RGB	Hex RGB
Black	(0, 0, 0)	00000000 00000000 00000000	00 00 00
Blue	(0, 0, 255)	00000000 00000000 11111111	00 00 FF
Cyan	(0, 255, 255)	00000000 11111111 11111111	00 FF FF
Gray	(128, 128, 128)	10000000 10000000 10000000	80 80 80
Green	(0, 255, 0)	00000000 11111111 00000000	00 FF 00
Magenta	(255, 0, 255)	11111111 00000000 11111111	FF 00 FF
Red	(255, 0, 0)	11111111 00000000 00000000	FF 00 00
White	(255, 255, 255)	11111111 11111111 11111111	FF FF FF
Yellow	(255, 255, 0)	11001000 10110100 01111000	C8 B4 78

- In the base powers of two numeral systems 8 bits or 1 byte contains one of 256 numeric values ranging from 0 to 255 because (2^8) = 256 colors. In other words, the maximum number of colors the graphical function of the computer can display is 256 per channel, specifically 256 shades of green, 256 shades of blue, and 256 shades of red. At 8 bits per channel, an 8-bit RGB image would have total of 24 bits per pixel (8 for red, 8 for green, and 8 for blue).
- A 16-bit RGB color (or high color) image uses two bytes (8 bits +8 bits) or 256 × 256 = 65,536 tonal values for each color. At 16 bits per channel, the image would have a total of 48 bits per pixel (16 for red, 16 for green, and 16 for blue).
- A 24-bit RGB color (or true color) image uses 3 bytes (8 bits +8 bits + 8 bits) or 256 ×256 ×256 = 16,777,216 million possible combination of color that can be represented.
- A 32-bit RGB color supports 16,777,216 colors like the 24-bit. However, the 32-bit has an alpha channel (an additional byte or 8 bits), therefore it can create more realistic gradients, shadows, and transparencies. A 32-bit color (2^{32}) supports 256 ×256 ×256 ×256 = 4,294,967,296 color combinations.
- A 48-bit RGB color supports (2^{48}) or 281,474,976,710,656 trillion colors). Each RGB channel uses 16 bits per pixel, containing up to 65,536 tone levels, supporting 281,474,976,710,656 trillion colors.

The RGB data value shows how much red, green, and blue intensity levels are combined within an image's pixels. This greater number of bits per pixel provides higher color depth, resulting in more visually appealing features. Then again, with a higher color depth more system resources are required. Table 1.15 below shows the bit depth and the number of colors available.

TABLE 1.15 **Displays bit depth and the number of colors available**

Bit Depth	Number of Colors Available	
8-Bit	256 tonal values for each color (RGB)	(2^8)
16-Bit	65,536 tonal values for each color (RGB)	(2^{16})
24-Bit	16,777,216 tonal values for each color (RGB)	(2^{24})
32-Bit	16,777,216 million possible combination of color + Transparency tonal values for each color (RGB)	(2^{32})
48-Bit	281,474,976,710,656 trillion tonal values for each color (RGB)	(2^{48})

Color Models

There are numerous ways to represent colors with numbers. The most well-known color model is RGB. This model is an additive color model, meaning that it combines red, green, and blue light to create the colors we see on computer devices, and on television screens.[20] The RGB model is best for on-screen applications, or for the display of images in electronic systems. The RGB model is based on the Trichromacy (three-color) theory that three types of receptors in the human retina transmit and receive color information.[21,22] Figure 1.19 shows examples of bit colors.

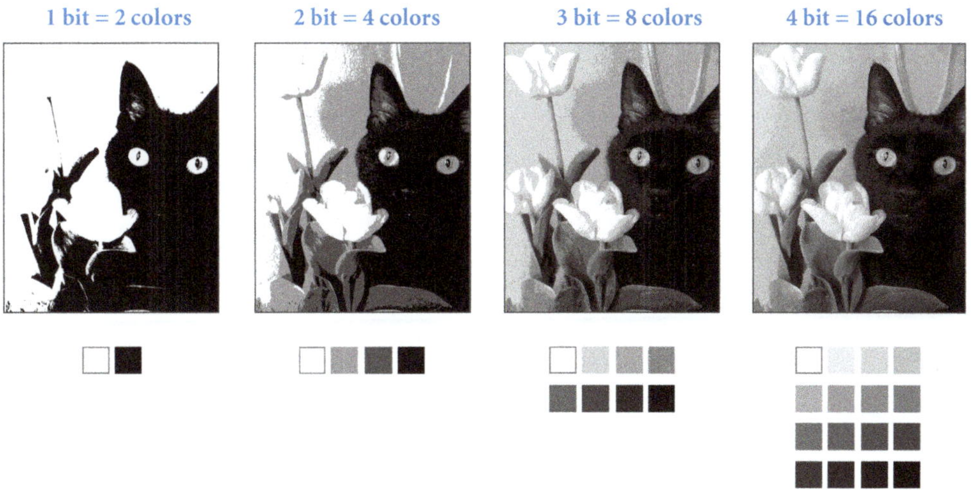

FIGURE 1.19 **Example of bit colors.**

[20] Hirsch, Robert. *Exploring color photography: From film to pixels.* Routledge, 2014.

[21] Horiguchi, Hiroshi, Jonathan Winawer, Robert F. Dougherty, and Brian A. Wandell. "Human trichromacy revisited." *Proceedings of the National Academy of Sciences* 110, no. 3 (2013): E260–E269.

[22] Bowmaker, J. K. "Trichromatic colour vision: why only three receptor channels?" *Trends in Neurosciences* 6 (1983): 41–43.

Another important color model is the CMYK (Cyan, Magenta, Yellow, Black), which is a subtractive color model. A subtractive model reduces the light that is reflected, and is used for printing color images. When printers print colors on paper, they work with reflected light, which determines what colors we see. We see objects when they are illuminated by white light, either sunlight or artificial light. We see a white car, because it reflects all the visible wavelengths of light, and we see a black car because it absorbs all the visible wavelengths of light. We see a red color as we see a red apple, because the object absorbs some of the light but reflects the red.

To be able to do this, computers can use the opposing subtractive primaries of RGB, which are cyan, magenta, and yellow. "Cyan is directly opposed to red; magenta is the opposite of green; and yellow is the opposite of blue."[23] CMYK gives a much wider range of colors compared to the RGB model. Additionally, a color black or K (key color) is added to create deep dark colors, like true black.[24] Computer screens use the RGB model, and the CMYK model is used in printers.

Screen Resolution

The quality of the graphics card and the display monitor dictate the quantity, size, and color of the pixel display resolution. Computer-based images contain a matrix of thousands or millions of pixels. The screen generates the image you see by altering the colors of these tiny square pixels. The screen resolution depends upon how many pixels the screen can display horizontally and vertically. Computer screens of different sizes can still have the same screen resolution. A computer screen with a higher resolution (more pixels), will display an image more sharply. For example, a computer display resolution of 3,840 × 2,160, means that we see 3,840 pixels horizontally and 2,160 vertical pixels vertically (written as width × height). This resolution is commonly known as 4K Ultra HD, and refers to horizontal resolutions of around 4,000 pixels, which is exactly twice as many pixel rows and columns as a High Definition Television 1080p (1920 ×1080 pixels). However, the higher resolution also means that icons and text will look smaller.

In addition to screen resolution, brightness, color representation, and refresh rates are also very important. The refresh rate, or vertical refresh rate, is the number of times per second, measured in Hertz or Hz, that the monitor updates the screen with new information. Higher numbers are equivalent to better and less choppy images.

[23] Mouw, T. "Additive vs. subtractive color models," Pantone. Last modified April 2018. https://www.xrite.com/blog/additive-subtractive-color-models

[24] Verikas, Antanas, Jens Lundström, Marija Bacauskiene, and Adas Gelzinis. "Advances in computational intelligence-based print quality assessment and control in offset colour printing." *Expert Systems with Applications* 38, no. 10 (2011): 13441–13447.

1.6 Beyond Conventional Computing

Quantum Computing Is Poised to Change Everything

In 1981, Richard Feynman introduced the idea of a computer that can harness the power of quantum mechanics.[25] His idea, quantum computing, essentially means the building of better and faster computer systems that play an important role in increasing computation intelligence.

Earlier in this chapter we discussed how conventional computation works. While in conventional computing data is captured in bits, in quantum computing we use *Qubits*. The term stands for Quantum Bit and is the smallest unit of quantum information.

In conventional computing, two bits can have four patterns (00, 01, 10, 11). In quantum computing, two qubits can have the same four patterns, but the qubits can represent and use all four at the same time. When we add more bits to a conventional computer, the computer still works with one state at a time. When we add qubits, because so many more computations happen simultaneously, the power of the quantum computer is exponentially greater.

In physics, we call this phenomenon *superposition*, and it describes the ability of a quantum system to be in several states at the same time. In other words, the state can exist in a superposition of 0s and 1s. A byte can be not merely a 0 or a 1, but a superposition of both states. If one qubit can be in a superposition of two states, then two qubits can be in a superposition of four states and three qubits of eight states.

For example, we say that a coin can have two positions, heads (0) or tails (1). In conventional computation, only one of those positions is possible. However, in quantum computation it would be as if the coin could be in both positions at once.

Another example involves using a computer program to crack a password. The conventional computer program will try each individual combination or potential password sequentially until it finds the correct answer. The quantum computer will configure this problem differently. The qubits will be in superposition of all the possible states or all possible password configurations, and by using interference, will amplify some answers and cancel others, finding the correct password much more quickly.

A third example involves using mapping software like Google Maps to go from point A to point B. Normal map computation looks at all the possible paths between A and B, one at a time, to determine the fastest route. A quantum computer will try every possible path between two points simultaneously and will determine the best route in a fraction of the time of a conventional computer.

[25] Feynman, Richard P. *Feynman lectures on computation*. CRC Press, 2018.

A larger number of qubits means that the number of states grows exponentially, creating millions of possibilities, and making possible solutions that are far beyond those of conventional computers. This has practical implications in scientific experiments and simulations, and as part of the development of new drugs and materials.

Even when fully developed, quantum computers will never completely replace conventional computers. However, this new type of computer will solve problems that would take a conventional computer thousands of years to solve. Quantum computers will never stream video from Netflix, nor will they play videos on the Web. Both conventional and quantum computing will coexist, serving different purposes.

The conventional computer may attempt to solve a difficult equation or a problem, calculating in bits and bytes. However, if the problem is too difficult, it may fail. The quantum computer can explore these exponential possibilities much more easily, since its strengths are almost limitless.

If we have "n" qubits, you can simultaneously represent (2^n) states. Three qubits (2^3) = 8 states at the same time; 4 qubits (2^4) = 16; and 64 qubits (2^{64}) = 18,446,744,073,709,600,000 probabilities. The conventional computer can represent this huge number (2^{64}) of states, but with only one state at a time. To cycle through all these combinations would take a conventional computer around 400 years, but the quantum computer will explore these much faster, as Google's quantum research has demonstrated.[26]

Quantum computers could boost the expansion of new advances in science, treatments, and medications, increase the speed of machine learning and artificial intelligence, and help in the discovery of better building materials for more efficient and safer structures.

However, we are not ready to abandon the conventional computer. Quantum computing is still in the experimental stage and will coexist with conventional computers in the foreseeable future.

1.7 A Brief History of Computing Devices

The following is a brief history, highlighting the most significant events in computing history from its beginning to the present.

The history of computers began with the invention of a calculating tool called the *abacus* (Figure 1.20). This first mechanical calculating device worked by manually sliding counters on rods. The exact origin of the abacus is still unknown. While some researchers credit the Babylonians around

[26] Boixo, Sergio, Sergei V. Isakov, Vadim N. Smelyanskiy, Ryan Babbush, Nan Ding, Zhang Jiang, Michael J. Bremner, John M. Martinis, and Hartmut Neven. "Characterizing quantum supremacy in near-term devices." *Nature Physics* 14, no. 6 (2018): 595.

FIGURE 1.20 Ancient abacus calculation device. Courtesy of Shutterstock.

2400 BC,[27] other cultures and civilizations in China, Egypt, Greece, India, and Mesopotamia also played an essential part in its development and evolution.[28]

In 1901, scientists found an important discovery in a shipwreck on the island of Antikythera, in Greece (Figure 1.21). Invented around the second century BC, the Antikythera Mechanism is known as the world's first mechanical computer. This analogue computer was built by the ancient Greeks, who used it to predict the time and color of lunar and solar eclipses with impressive accuracy.[29] It was invented to "predict the future," by taking astronomical theories and

FIGURE 1.21 Antikythera Mechanism. Courtesy of Shutterstock.

[27] Teresi, Dick. *Lost discoveries: The ancient roots of modern science—from the Babylonians to the Maya.* Simon and Schuster, 2002.

[28] Smith, David E. *History of mathematics.* Vol. 1. Courier Corporation, 1958.

[29] Seiradakis, J. H., and M. G. Edmunds. "Our current knowledge of the Antikythera Mechanism." *Nature Astronomy* 2, no. 1 (2018): 35.

FIGURE 1.22 **Mechanical bird. Courtesy of Shutterstock**

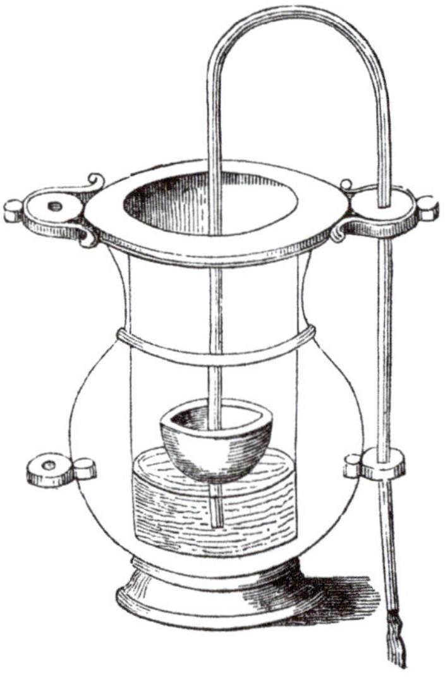

FIGURE 1.23 **Siphon float and constant flow of Heron of Alexandria. Courtesy of Shutterstock.**

mechanizing them to see what outputs could be calculated. This was the first time that humans created a mechanical computer device.

During the 4th century BC (428–347), the Greek mathematician *Archytas of Tarentum* designed a mechanical bird called *The Pigeon*, which moved by steam[30] (Figure 1.22). Another ancient innovator was Heron of Alexandria, a fascinating engineer and physicist who lived around AD 10–85. He conceived many innovations, including mechanical, robot-like machines for temples, theaters, and military weapons, including the first steam turbine and a vending machine that served up holy water[31] (Figure 1.23).

[30] Yates, David R., Christophe Vaessen, and Morgan Roupret. "From Leonardo to da Vinci: the history of robot-assisted surgery in urology." *BJU International* 108, no. 11 (2011): 1708–1713.

[31] Papadopoulos, Evangelos. "Heron of Alexandria (c. 10–85 AD)." In *Distinguished figures in mechanism and machine science*, pp. 217–245. Springer, Dordrecht, 2007.

Early modern examples of mechanical computers include the calculators credited to mathematician and physicist, Blaise Pascal and mathematician Gottfried Wilhelm (von) Leibniz in the 17th century.[32]

In 1822, Charles Babbage announced the invention of his calculating machine to the Royal Astronomical Society, in a paper titled "Note on the application of machinery to the computation of astronomical and mathematical tables." Babbage's calculating machine, or *difference engine*, used the decimal number system and was operated by cranking a handle[33] (Figure 1.24). The successor of the difference engine was the *Analytical Engine,* a general purpose, mechanical computer. Babbage continued working on his Analytical Engine, and his son completed it after Babbage's death in 1871. The Analytical Engine is considered the first modern mechanical computer. In 1904, English physicist John Ambrose Fleming invented and patented the thermionic valve or vacuum tube. He based the device on the Edison

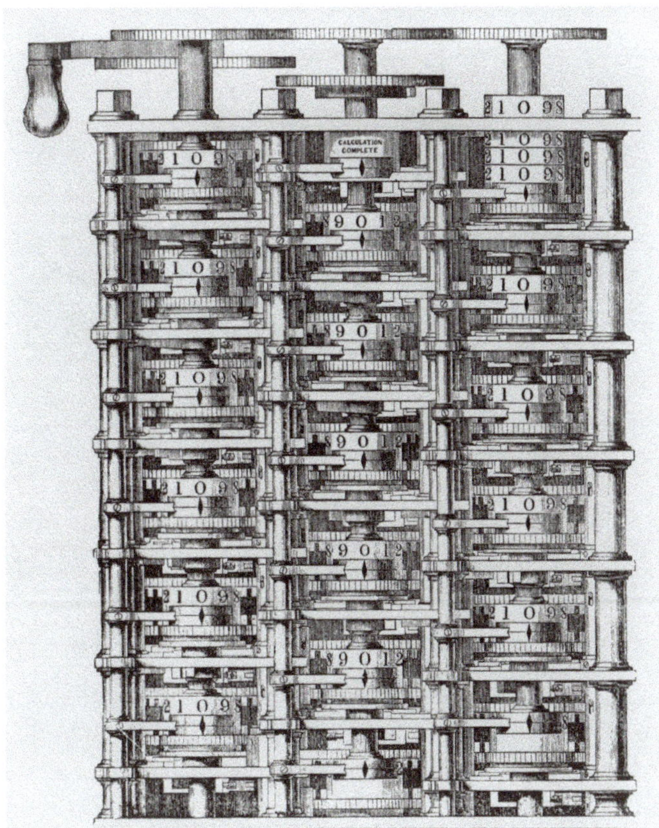

FIGURES 1.24 Small part of Babbage's mechanical calculating engine. Courtesy of Shutterstock.

[32] Ratcliff, Jessica R. "Samuel Morland and his calculating machines c. 1666: the early career of a courtier–inventor in Restoration London." *The British Journal for the History of Science* 40, no. 2 (2007): 159–179.

[33] Randell, Brian, ed. *The origins of digital computers: Selected papers*. Springer, 2013.

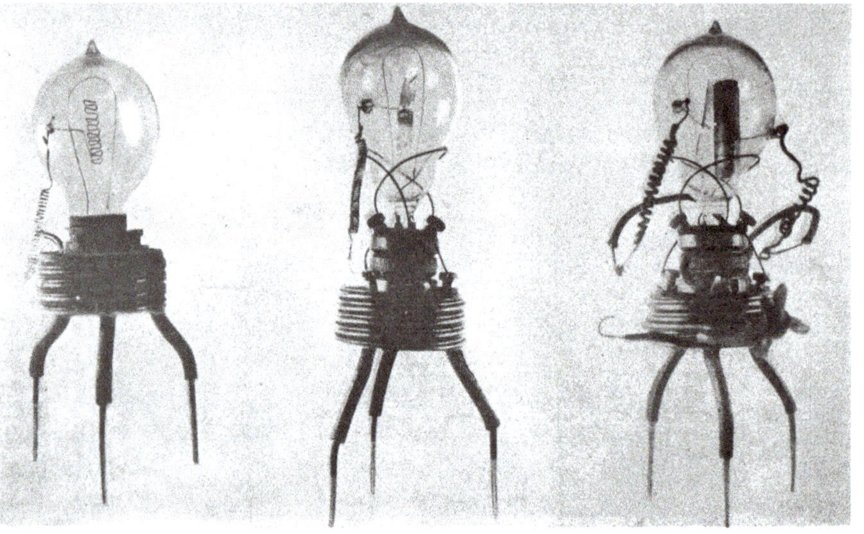

FIGURES 1.25 The thermionic valve.

FIGURE 1.26 Atanasoff-Berry Computer at Durham Center, Iowa State University.

effect describing the behavior of electrodes in a vacuum, and was found in Marconi's wireless systems.[34] The invention and later improvement of the vacuum tube began one of the biggest revolutions in history (Figure 1.25).

After Charles Babbage's Analytical Engine, one of the most important innovations in computing came from John Atanasoff of Iowa State University (Figure 1.26). In 1939, along with Clifford Berry, Atanasoff built

[34] Guarnieri, Massimo. "The age of vacuum tubes: Early devices and the rise of radio communications [historical]." *IEEE Industrial Electronics Magazine* 6, no. 1 (2012): 41–43.

the Atanasoff-Berry Computer (ABC), the first electronic, digital, general-purpose device that used vacuum tubes.[35]

> The ABC was the first linear algebra computer, and its 1940 performance is very close to what Moore's law predicts (the law is described later in this chapter). World War II prevented its innovations from being published and credited to Atanasoff and Berry.[36]

Another innovation, the Z3 Computer, was built in Germany. Designed by *Konrad Zuse* in 1941, this binary machine was the first programmable, controlled, fully automatic digital computer and could store 64 floating-point numbers in binary memory. The original Z3 was destroyed during World War II[37] (Figure 1.27).

Between 1939 and 1945, the British Colossus vacuum tube computing machine was one of the most important tools used against Germany during World War II. Analysts used this computer to break German war codes at England's Bletchley Park. This machine was the first fully functioning electronic digital computer.

In 1946, the American Electronic Numerical Integrator and Computer (ENIAC) first used high-speed vacuum tubes and operated faster than any previous machine (Figure 1.28). Mauchly and Eckert built ENIAC at the

FIGURE 1.27 A replica of the very first electronic computer (Z3) being built by Konrad Zuse. Courtesy of Shutterstock.

[35] Burks, Arthur W. "The invention of the universal electronic computer—how the Electronic Computer Revolution began." *Future Generation Computer Systems* 18, no. 7 (2002): 871–892.

[36] Rojas, Raúl, and Ulf Hashagen, eds. *The first computers: History and architectures.* MIT Press, 2002.

[37] Rojas, Raúl. "Konrad Zuse's legacy: the architecture of the Z1 and Z3." *IEEE Annals of the History of Computing* 19, no. 2 (1997): 5–16.

FIGURES 1.28 The ENIAC computer. Courtesy of the Library of Congress.

University of Pennsylvania's Moore School of Electrical Engineering.[38] The computer weighed more than 30 tons, contained 19,000 vacuum tubes and 6000 switches, and could add 5,000 numbers in a single second, a significant achievement at the time.[39] Although the vacuum tube was a great innovation, its high power consumption, high cost, large size, and reliability, led to the replacement of glass by transistors. Dr. John Bardeen, Dr. Walter Brattain, and Dr. William Shockley at Bell Labs in Murray Hill, New Jersey invented the transistor in 1947.[40] The transistor is considered an amplifier or switch (ON/OFF) of a current flow. In 1965, Drs. Bardeen, Brattain, and Shockley received the Nobel Prize in Physics for their research on semiconductors, and the discovery of the transistor effect. Figure 1.29 displays the historical timeline of computer technology.

In the 1950s and 1960s, Remington Rand Inc. introduced the Eckert-Mauchly Computer Corporation's ERA 1101, or UNIVAC 1101, to the United States. This was the first computer commercially available, and the first customer was the U.S. government (Figure 1.30). The ERA's magnetic drums used magnetic tapes and could hold up to two million bits, or 65,000 30-bit words. Its access time ranged from 8 to 64 milliseconds.[41,42] The commercial version was called the UNIVAC 1103.

[38] Ceruzzi, Paul E. *A history of modern computing*. MIT Press, 2003.

[39] Neukom, Hans. "The second life of ENIAC." *IEEE Annals of the History of Computing* 28, no. 2 (2006): 4–16.

[40] Brinkman, William F., Douglas E. Haggan, and William W. Troutman. "A history of the invention of the transistor and where it will lead us." *IEEE Journal of Solid-State Circuits* 32, no. 12 (1997): 1858–1865.

[41] *Id.* at 38.

[42] Tomash, Erwin, and Arnold A. Cohen. "The birth of an ERA: Engineering Associates, Inc. 1946–1955." *Annals of the History of Computing* 1, no. 2 (1979): 83–97.

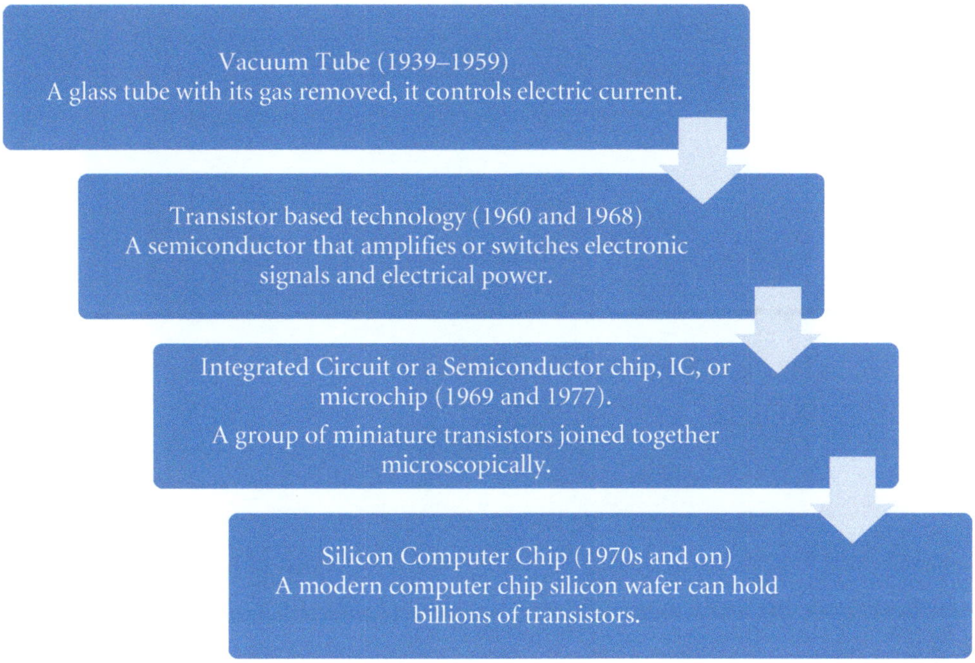

FIGURE 1.29 The historical timeline of the beginnings of modern computer technology.

FIGURE 1.30 ERA 1103 UNIVAC 2 Calculating Machine. Photograph from National Aeronautics and Space Administration (NASA).

In 1958, Jack St. Clair Kilby, an electrical engineer from Texas Instruments, manufactured the first integrated circuit or semiconductor chip, IC, also called a microchip.

The microchip is a group of miniature transistors joined in microscopic form during the manufacturing process. A modern computer chip, or

FIGURE 1.31 **The IBM 7090 Data Processing System at Data Processing and Data Reduction at the NASA Ames Research Center, c1963. Photograph from National Aeronautics and Space Administration (NASA).**

silicon wafer, can hold billions of transistors.[43] These integrated circuits transformed computing and electronics during the 1960s and 1970s.

For his invention, Jack St. Clair Kilby was awarded the Nobel Prize in Physics in the year 2000.[44] Without Kilby's chip we would not have today's TVs, mobile phones, tablets, digital watches, missiles, satellites, navigation systems, and almost all the electronics we use every day.

In 1964, International Business Machines (IBM) introduced the IBM System/360. It was intended for business and science uses. IBM offered the 360 in a family of six models, small to large, that all used the same programs, thereby saving the customers money. By 1971, IBM's net earnings exceeded 1 billion US dollars. The company became a leader in computer production and was unable to keep up with demand[45] (Figure 1.31).

In 1965, Gordon E. Moore, hypothesized that the number of components on an integrated circuit would double every two years for the next 10 years. This hypothesis became Moore's Law, predicting that as computation would increase in power, its cost would decrease exponentially. Moore's Law is the barometer for the electronics industry, and a catalyst for innovation. Moore is the co-founder of the Intel Corporation.[46]

As of 1969, in addition to continued developments in machinery, the ARPANET (Advanced Research Projects Agency network) emerged as the

---

[43] Ayers, John E. *Digital integrated circuits: Analysis and design*. CRC Press, 2018.

[44] Kilby, Jack St Clair. "Turning potential into realities: The invention of the integrated circuit (Nobel lecture)." *ChemPhysChem* 2, no. 8–9 (2001): 482–489.

[45] *Id.* at 36.

[46] Schaller, Robert R. "Moore's law: Past, present and future." *IEEE Spectrum* 34, no. 6 (1997): 52–59.

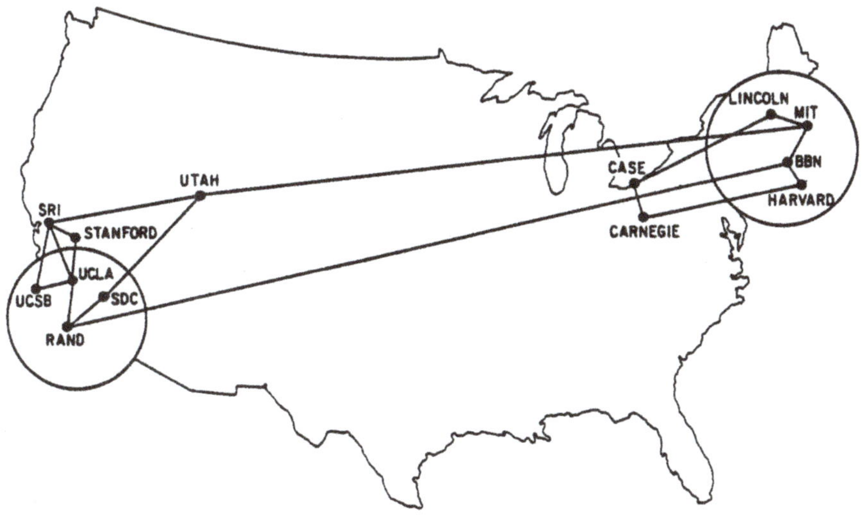

FIGURE 1.32 **A map of the ARPANET in December 1970. Courtesy of DARPA.**

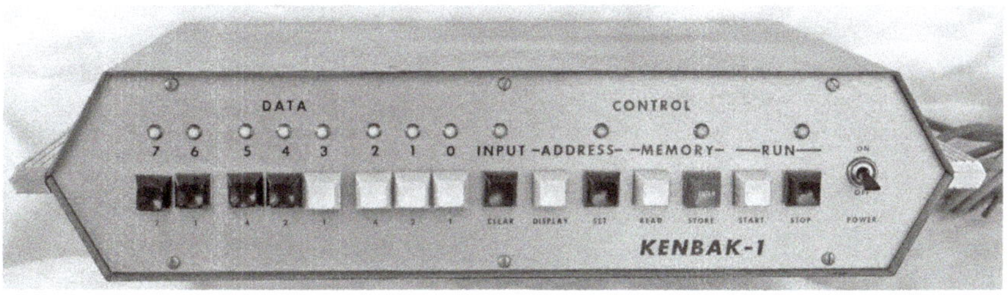

FIGURE 1.33 **Kenbak-1. Photo courtesy of Mr. John Blankenbaker**

precursor of the Internet. The ARPANET began as a military computer network, using early packet-switching technology. It was the first network to implement the Transmission Control Protocol and Internet Protocol TCP/IP suite for more effective transmission over this early Internet (Figure 1.32).

The first personal computer was Kenbak-1. It sold for $750 in *Scientific American* magazine in 1971. The Kenbak-1 did not sell well, but it did increase public awareness of home-based computers[47] (Figure 1.33).

In 1972, Ray Tomlinson invented the e-mail system we know today. While working as an ARPANET contractor, Tomlinson selected the @ symbol *to* structure the address of a single user and its host (name-of-the-user@name-of-the-computer).[48]

In 1976, Steve Jobs and Steve Wozniak founded the Apple Computer Company. In 1977, the Apple II revolutionized personal computers and created a device we easily recognize today. The Apple II was the first successful mass-produced

[47] Bosworth, Seymour, and Michel E. Kabay, eds. *Computer security handbook*. John Wiley & Sons, 2002.

[48] Brown, Bruce C. *The complete guide to e-mail marketing: how to create successful, spam-free campaigns to reach your target audience and increase sales*. Vol. 978, no. 1-60045. Atlantic Publishing Company, 2007.

FIGURE 1.34 The Apple II computer. Courtesy of Shutterstock.

microcomputer aimed at the general public. It had a plastic case and had the ability to display color graphics. It featured expandable RAM, 4K or 8K, the BASIC programming language, and included two game paddles, color graphics, and a demo cassette for $1,298 USD, $5,603 in today's dollars (Figure 1.34).

In 1981, IBM introduced the IBM Personal Computer, or IBM PC. It used the 8088 Intel microprocessor, and its operating system was PC-DOS, licensed from Microsoft. The IBM PC was so successful that "By 1984, IBM replaced Apple as the number one supplier of microcomputers. Apple had 26% of the PC business. IBM's share had grown to 41%."[49] This success represents the beginning of the mass desktop computer market (Figure 1.35).

In the same year, Adam Osborne created the Osborne 1, the first commercially available portable computer, weighing 24.5 pounds and costing $1,795[50](Figure 1.36).

In 1984, Apple introduced the Macintosh, which included a Graphical User Interface (GUI) and a much faster processor, the Motorola 68000 chip. The Macintosh included a monitor, keyboard, mouse, and a floppy drive that took 400 kB 3.5″ inch disks. The price for the Macintosh was $2,495[51] (Figure 1.37).

In 1991, Tim Berners Lee, a scientist at the CERN laboratory in Switzerland invented the World Wide Web (WWW).[52] The WWW used application

[49] Chesbrough, Henry W., and David J. Teece. "Organizing for innovation." *The Strategic Management of Intellectual Capital* (2009): 27.

[50] Diem, Richard A., and Michael J. Berson, eds. *Technology in retrospect: Social studies in the information age, 19842009.* IAP, 2010.

[51] Linzmayer, Owen W. *Apple confidential 2.0: The definitive history of the world's most colorful company.* No Starch Press, 2004.

[52] Mowery, David C., and Timothy Simcoe. "Is the Internet a US invention?—an economic and technological history of computer networking." *Research Policy* 31, no. 8–9 (2002): 1369–1387.

FIGURE 1.35 **The IBM PC. Courtesy of Shutterstock.**

FIGURE 1.36 **The Osborne 1.**

software called a browser to retrieve, read, and display Internet sites from countries around the world written in Hypertext Markup Language (HTML). It was a browser called Mosaic that launched the WWW.

Bill Gates and Microsoft Corp released Windows 3.1 in 1992.[53] The Windows 3.1 Operating System made IBM PCs more user-friendly, integrating a new graphic user interface (GUI) that replaced the old Windows command line from MS-DOS. This GUI was the Macintosh OS. Windows 3.1 eventually progressed to Windows 95, and then Windows 98, ME, NT,

[53] Bank, David. *Breaking windows: how Bill Gates fumbled the future of Microsoft*. Simon & Schuster, 2001.

FIGURE 1.37 **The Macintosh. Courtesy of Shutterstock.**

2000, XP, Vista, Windows 7, 8, and 10. The Mac uses many additional operating systems, including Apple's OS, Linux OS, Chrome, Ubuntu, UNIX, and Symbian, among others.

In 1995, the US Federal Networking Council (FNC) passed a resolution to define the Internet, in consultation with members of the internet and intellectual property rights communities.

> Internet refers to the global information system that (a) is logically linked together by a globally unique address space, based on the Internet Protocol (IP) or its subsequent extensions/follow-ons; (b) is able to support communications using the Transmission Control Protocol/Internet Protocol (TCP/IP) suite or its subsequent extensions/follow-ons, and/or other IP-compatible protocols; and (c) provides, uses or makes accessible, either publicly or privately, high level services layered on the communications and related infrastructure described herein.[54]

By 1995, Internet service providers (ISPs), such as AOL, MCI, Sprint, and UUNET, began offering their services to large numbers of customers.[55] Along with the arrival of the Internet, in 1996, Personal Digital Assistants (PDA), like the PalmPilot 1000 became available to the consumer.[56] These devices provided calendar information, played games and music, did numeric calculations, and

---

[54] Adelsberger, Heimo H., Betty Collis, and Jan Martin Pawlowski, eds. *Handbook on information technologies for education and training.* Springer Science & Business Media, 2013.

[55] Campbell-Kelly, Martin, and Daniel D. Garcia-Swartz. "The history of the internet: The missing narratives." *Journal of Information Technology* 28, no. 1 (2013): 18–33.

[56] Baumgart, Daniel C. "Personal digital assistants in health care: Experienced clinicians in the palm of your hand?" *The Lancet* 366, no. 9492 (2005): 1210–1222.

downloaded information from the Internet. The combination of PDA and the mobile phone created the first multi-purpose mobile computing device.

Since the beginning of the new millennium, the global positioning system (GPS) has been available to civilians. Previously available only to the military, GPS[57] has become an essential technology for cellular telephones, global navigation, and other wireless media. It is difficult to imagine the world without GPS-enabled smartphones. In addition to GPS, a hi-speed Universal Serial Bus (USB) 2.0 device was released in 2000.[58] The USB standardizes the connection of computer peripherals, such as keyboards, pointing devices, printers, and disk drives. Furthermore, it has replaced serial and parallel ports, and has provided easy-to-use communication and electrical power to a plethora of devices in plug & play mode.

In the early 2000s, the dotcom or internet bubble burst after the U.S. technology stock market over-invested in internet-based companies.[59]

At the same time, social media platforms started attracting attention and gaining momentum. In 2003, MySpace and LinkedIn were launched, Facebook appeared in 2004, and YouTube in 2005.[60] Social media has changed our way of living and how we communicate. It has had a profound influence on the concept of privacy as our lives have become progressively more public. At the same time, the use of social media to manipulate public opinion has become a dangerous threat to public life around the world.

In 2004, Google was the first major web company to go public.[61] At that time, there was not a single internet search company trading on the U.S. Stock Exchange. Google launched Gmail in 2004,[62] Google Maps in 2005,[63] and Google Chrome in 2008.[64] Google Maps, along with AJAX (Asynchronous JavaScript and XML), a key component of Web 2.0, the second generation of the web, brought more ease of use and more interaction to end users, and has made navigation systems essential to our daily lives.[65]

---

[57] McNeff, Jules G. "The global positioning system." *IEEE Transactions on Microwave theory and techniques* 50, no. 3 (2002): 645–652.

[58] Axelson, Jan. *USB complete: The developer's guide*. Lakeview research LLC, 2015.

[59] Buenstorf, Guido, and Dirk Fornahl. "B2C—bubble to cluster: The dot-com boom, spin-off entrepreneurship, and regional agglomeration." *Journal of Evolutionary Economics* 19, no. 3 (2009): 349–378.

[60] Edosomwan, Simeon, Sitalaskshmi Kalangot Prakasan, Doriane Kouame, Jonelle Watson, and Tom Seymour. "The history of social media and its impact on business." *Journal of Applied Management and Entrepreneurship* 16, no. 3 (2011): 79–91.

[61] Vise, David. "The google story." *Strategic Direction* 23, no. 10 (2007).

[62] "Google Company: Our history in depth." Last modified April 2019. https://web.archive.org/web/20160406123606/ http://www.google.co.uk/about/company/history/#2005

[63] Miller, Christopher C. "A beast in the field: The Google Maps mashup as GIS/2." *Cartographica: The International Journal for Geographic Information and Geovisualization* 41, no. 3 (2006): 187–199.

[64] *Id.* at 62.

[65] O'reilly, Tim. "What is Web 2.0: Design patterns and business models for the next generation of software." *Communications & Strategies* 1 (2007): 17.

FIGURE 1.38 **The iPhone c2007. Courtesy of Shutterstock.**

In 2006, the commercialization of Cloud computing began when Amazon introduced its Web Service.[66] Apple introduced the iPhone in 2007,[67] and changed the computing, television, movie, gaming, photography, healthcare, and music industries, releasing the first version of iTunes in early 2001[68]. (Figure 1.38) In 2008, Google introduced the Android[69] mobile operating system, inspired by Apple's iOS. With the introduction of Google Android smartwatches in 2014[70] and the Apple iWatch in 2015,[71] we were able to appreciate and experience the miniaturization of mobile technology. Additionally, we have seen how quickly mobile computing technology has spread around the world. According to the Pew Research Center, out of a total world population of 7.7 billion people, more than 5 billion now own mobile devices.[72]

As technology becomes smaller, faster, and cheaper, people want to take their mobile devices with them. The Internet has infiltrated all technologies today, resulting in the growth of the Internet of Things (IoT). Today, we can connect

---

[66] Qian, Ling, Zhiguo Luo, Yujian Du, and Leitao Guo. "Cloud computing: An overview." In *IEEE International Conference on Cloud Computing*, pp. 626–631. Springer, Berlin, Heidelberg, 2009.

[67] Goggin, Gerard. "Adapting the mobile phone: The iPhone and its consumption." *Continuum* 23, no. 2 (2009): 231–244.

[68] Tilson, David, Carsten Sørensen, and Kalle Lyytinen. "Platform complexity: Lessons from the music industry." In *2013 46th Hawaii International Conference on System Sciences*, pp. 4625–4634. IEEE, 2013.

[69] *Id.* at 67.

[70] Mishra, Sanjay M. *Wearable android: android wear and google fit app development*. John Wiley & Sons, 2015.

[71] Turban, Efraim, Judy Whiteside, David King, and Jon Outland. "Mobile commerce and the internet of things." In *Introduction to Electronic Commerce and Social Commerce*, pp. 167–199. Springer, Cham, 2017.

[72] Taylor, Kyle, and Laura Silver, "Smartphone ownership is growing rapidly around the world, but not always equally." Pew Research Center, Washington, D.C., February 5, 2019. https://www.pewresearch.org/global/2019/02/05/smartphone-ownership-is-growing-rapidly-around-the-world-but-not-always-equally/

almost every device we purchase to the internet and to other devices. Smart locks, Bluetooth trackers, smart home devices, machine-learning devices like Amazon Echo, Apple Homepod, and Google Home can all now connect to the internet and be networked to other devices. These devices can and do distribute information anywhere in the world, despite security and privacy concerns.

In 2012, Cisco Systems introduced Fog computing,[73] which entails extending the cloud-computing model to the enterprise network. Instead of sending data from IoT devices to the cloud continually, the fog-computing paradigm gives organizations more options. Some data require priority, like healthcare IoTs, including cancer treatment, glucose, and insulin pen monitoring. The fog-computing paradigm helps reduce latency and worry, and enables increasing growth of IoT devices. Now, the fast-growing number of connected devices can be processed more efficiently.[74]

In computer evolution, we have witnessed major advances in Artificial Intelligence (AI), Machine Learning (ML), and Robotic process automation. The field of Artificial Intelligence was founded in the 1950s, and the term "AI" was created by John McCarthy in 1956 at the Dartmouth Conference.[75,76]

According to John McCarthy, AI "is the science and engineering of making intelligent machines."[77] Artificial intelligence (AI) is the formation of intelligence established by machines/computers, capable of learning or mimicking human or animal intellect. To be able to simulate human behavior, AI must continuously improve its performance, using its knowledge and experience, and adjusting its behavior according to prior performance and new inputs. In contrast, the human brain learns, adapts, and solves problems independently, without always requiring new information. AI is not yet at that point; AI technology is still taking baby steps when it comes to reasoning and human/animal interaction.

Currently, what we have is termed Machine learning (ML), a division of AI. ML is a computer algorithm that teaches computers to learn by performing data analysis, identifying patterns, and making decisions based on what it has learned. The goal of ML is to understand the formation of data, and to organize that data into models so it may be comprehended and used by humans.

Some examples of first-generation AI or ML technology are Apple's Siri, Amazon's Alexa, IBM Watson, Amazon Go, Music and Media streaming services such as Spotify, Netflix, and YouTube, Social Media feeds, Smart Home

---

[73] Mahmud, Redowan, Ramamohanarao Kotagiri, and Rajkumar Buyya. "Fog computing: A taxonomy, survey and future directions." In *Internet of everything*, pp. 103–130. Springer, Singapore, 2018.

[74] Dastjerdi, Amir Vahid, and Rajkumar Buyya. "Fog computing: Helping the Internet of Things realize its potential." *Computer* 49, no. 8 (2016): 112–116.

[75] Nilsson, Nils J., and Nils Johan Nilsson. *Artificial intelligence: a new synthesis*. Morgan Kaufmann, 1998.

[76] McCarthy, John, Marvin L. Minsky, Nathaniel Rochester, and Claude E. Shannon. "A proposal for the dartmouth summer research project on artificial intelligence, August 31, 1955." *AI Magazine* 27, no. 4 (2006): 12–12.

[77] McCarthy John. "What is artificial intelligence?" Last revised November 12, 2007. http://jmc.stanford.edu/articles/whatisai.html.

devices, and Google and Apple Maps. These applications use ML technology to classify queries and requests using spoken human language, and then to respond with answers from a database. ML utilizes neural network algorithms to model the data to provide the user with a sense that the computer actually understands the query – hence the belief in AI is established and strengthened.

In 2015, Google released an open source machine learning or deep learning tool called TensorFlow.[78] TensorFlow was developed by the Google Brain Team (machine intelligence and deep neural networks research), and it is based on the first-generation machine learning tool called DistBelief.[79] TensorFlow is the second-generation tool, and focuses on deep learning. It can understand the context of the messages it receives, and to predict the replies that will be sent. This tool also can decode spoken search queries and can recognize faces in a photo.

One example of how TensorFlow is used is in the detection of diabetic retinopathy. It utilizes a database of images provided and sorted by ophthalmologists. TensorFlow compares the images in its database with a patient's image and can predict whether the patient's diabetes has damaged the retina. Other examples include voice and sound recognition, voice search, sentiment analysis in customer relationship dialogues, text-based applications like Google Translate, image recognition, and video detection.

Using machine learning, computers can employ a command line interface and move into Neural Networks. "An artificial neural network (ANN) is an interconnected group of artificial neurons simulating the thinking process. One can consider an ANN as a 'magical' black box trained to achieve expected intelligent processes, alongside the input and output information stream."[80] The human brain is composed of more than 100 billion neurons, and it transmits electrochemical signals like wires in a computer.[81]Neural Networks learn from data and try to simulate human perception.

To understand this, imagine taking a train for the first time and watching the train make every stop. The next time you take the train to the same destination, you might take the express train and go directly or close to the destination without making the local stops. Like the human brain, the Neural Network requires data to learn. The more data, the more precise the results will become. Gradually the algorithm becomes more efficient and makes connections that are more direct with fewer mistakes. To train Neural Networks, we need to transfer information to the dataset for the

---

[78] Abadi, Martín, Ashish Agarwal, Paul Barham, Eugene Brevdo, Zhifeng Chen, Craig Citro, Greg S. Corrado, et al. "Tensorflow: Large-scale machine learning on heterogeneous distributed systems." *arXiv preprint arXiv:1603.04467* (2016).

[79] Abadi, Martín, Paul Barham, Jianmin Chen, Zhifeng Chen, Andy Davis, Jeffrey Dean, Matthieu Devin, et al. "Tensorflow: A system for large-scale machine learning." In *12th {USENIX} Symposium on Operating Systems Design and Implementation ({OSDI} 16)*, pp. 265–283, 2016.

[80] Wu, Stephen Gang, Forrest Sheng Bao, Eric You Xu, Yu-Xuan Wang, Yi-Fan Chang, and Qiao-Liang Xiang. "A leaf recognition algorithm for plant classification using probabilistic neural network." In *2007 IEEE international symposium on signal processing and information technology*, pp. 11–16. IEEE, 2007.

[81] Stiles, J., and T.L. Jernigan, 2010. The basics of brain development. *Neuropsychology Review*, *20*(4), pp. 327–348.

algorithm to learn the correlation between labels and raw data. This process is called supervised learning. After the algorithm understands the raw data, it decides which label to assign to new data based on the pattern. Following are some examples in our everyday life:

- Face identification and facial expression recognition (happiness, sadness, and anger from face images)
- Gesture recognition system
- Recognition and understanding of images and scenes
- Spam Classification (classifying text as spam or fraudulent)
- Voice-identification systems (detect voices, transcribe speech to text, voice cloning, mimicking the voices of friends, enemies, and celebrities

When it comes to common sense, reasoning, and human/animal interaction/behavior, AI is still in its infancy. Nonetheless, every piece of software can claim some level of AI technology based on a predefined algorithm that responds to a desired input by a programmer, and/or automatically adjusts to a user's behavior.

Many believe that Artificial Intelligence is misused and mischaracterized in our data-driven society. As we see in movies like "The Terminator," HBO's series "Westworld," and books and prophecies by the Singularity evangelist Ray Kurzweil ("The Singularity is Near"[82] and "Ethics and emerging technologies"[83]) one can conclude that computers utilizing processes like AI will become exponentially smarter than human beings, and will eventually take over the world. According to Ray Kurzweil, exponential progress in computing power will lead to the hypothesis called "technological singularity," at which point computers will attain human-level intelligence.

Others strongly disagree, saying that we are not even close to the hypothesis described in Singularity, and will not ever get closer, since we do not fully understand the structure of the brain and how it responds to everyday changes.[84,85] Once, we considered computers to be high-end machines for scientists and skillful professionals. Today, they are for everyone, becoming smaller, lighter, more intuitive, easier to use, and displaying some level of intelligence.

Is the human mind able to build a cognitive computer simulating human behavior or reasoning? No one knows the answer – and no one knows how computers will evolve in the future.

Table 1.16 summarizes major technological advancements in computing since 2000, and Table 1.17 lists some of the most important definitions in computer science.

---

[82] Kurzweil, Ray. *The singularity is near: When humans transcend biology.* Penguin, 2005.

[83] Kurzweil, Ray. "The singularity is near." In *Ethics and emerging technologies*, pp. 393–406. Palgrave Macmillan, London, 2014.

[84] Modis, Theodore. "The singularity myth." *Technological Forecasting & Social Change* 73, no. 2 (2006): 104–112.

[85] Allen, P., & M. Greaves. "The singularity isn't near." *MIT Technology Review.* Last revised October 12, 2011. https://www.technologyreview.com/s/425733/paul-allen-the-singularity-isnt-near/.

TABLE 1.16 Technological advances in computing since 2000

	Major Technological Advancements in Computing Since 2000
2000	USB Flash drives introduced; Global Positioning System (GPS) goes mainstream.
2001	Mac OS X and Microsoft XP operating systems released; iTunes released.
2002	Supercomputer Earth Simulator is a massive, vector-based system that costs nearly 60 billion yen (roughly $600 million at the time).
2003	Blu-ray released; The Computer Science and Artificial Intelligence Laboratory (CSAIL) at MIT is formed by the merger of the Laboratory for Computer Science and the Artificial Intelligence Laboratory; MySpace founded; PowerMac G5 tower computer released
2004	Google is the first major Web company to float a publicly traded stock; "Web 2.0" brings back Interactivity.
2005	Lenovo acquires IBM's PC business; YouTube channel founded.
2006	"The Cloud": Computer utilities return; WikiLeaks established; Hulu founded; Twitter & Amazon introduce the Web Service (cloud computing); FAA issued commercial drone permit.
2007	Dropbox founded; First 1 TB (terabyte) hard disk drive (HDD); Apple's iPhone introduced; Amazon Kindle released
2008	"Satoshi Nakamoto," likely a pseudonym, publishes Bitcoin. MacBook Air is released; Android's OS introduced;
2009	Vendors announce cloud-based network-attached storage solutions for online backup; Roadrunner, IBM's supercomputer, is completed; Nakamoto 'mines' the first Bitcoins in January 2009, and a year later, a user orders two pizzas with them. Bitcoins' value explodes in November 2013 before a gradual devaluation.
2010	Angry Birds becomes top-selling mobile game; China's Tianhe supercomputers are operational; IBM's Watson and Brad Rutter appear on Jeopardy! Apple iPad is released
2011	Arab Spring protests spread by social media; The Nest's Learning Thermostat is an early product made for the emerging "Internet of Things"; Siri is introduced as a built-in feature with the Apple iPhone 4S smartphone; Passing of Steve Jobs.
2012	Facebook acquires Instagram; Raspberry Pi, a credit-card-size single board computer, is released as a tool to promote science education
2013	Amazon announces that the company is considering using drones.; Former CIA employee and NSA contractor Edward Snowden copies hundreds of thousands of classified documents; Microsoft Office 365 is unveiled; Microsoft introduces Xbox One; Sony releases PlayStation 4
2014	Apple Pay mobile payment system is introduced; HTML 5 replaces HTML 4
2015	Apple Watch is released
2016	In March, 2016, Amazon introduces the first version of the Amazon Echo Dot; Microsoft announces agreement to acquire LinkedIn for $26.2 billion.

(*Continued*)

TABLE 1.16 (CONTINUED) Technological advances in computing since 2000

	Major Technological Advancements in Computing Since 2000
2017	Open AI became the first AI to defeat the world's best DotA 2 player Danil "Dendi" Ishutin in a 1v1 game. The AI learned to play the game by playing against itself in less than a month with little coaching from humans.
2018	Google introduced the Google Pay service for all Android and iOS devices on January 8, 2018.; Stephen Hawking passed away; Microsoft began rolling out the Windows 10 Fall Creators Update on Oct. 17, 2017; Paul Allen passed away
2019	Huawei banned from doing business with U.S. companies due to the trade war with China.
2020	Machine Learning and AI, Robotic process automation, Blockchain technology, Virtual Reality (VR) & Internet of Things (IoT).

1.8 Conclusion

The invention of the computer represents the desire of humans to explore, explain, and manipulate the environment. From finger counting to Aristotle's mathematical logic, to Boolean algebra, logic gates, machine learning, and AI, the human brain continues to innovate.

Typical programming relies on simple statements (if A, then B). Nothing that goes into a computer is processed as entered, but as a code. A computer can do a billion things in a second but is still unable to imitate the complexity of intelligent human behavior. For the present, a computer is still just a machine without intellect.

As AI and Machine Learning progress, computing technology will continue to change our lives. The computer is one of the most powerful human innovations in history, and our lives are linked inseparably to its technologies. It is possible that some time in the future machine intelligence will "simply outlast" human intelligence. Maybe! However, for the moment we enthusiastically and cautiously enjoy the ride of technological advancements, which can be both positive and negative.

TABLE 1.17 Glossary of Common Terms in Computer Science

Name	Computer Definitions
AI	Artificial Intelligence
Application (App)	A software program designed to execute a sequence of instructions used to accomplish a certain task, or an operation in a computing device.
ASCII	American Standard Code for Information Interchange. A character-encoding standard for electronic communication
Bluetooth	A short-range wireless standard for exchanging data between computing devices using Ultra High Frequency (UHF) radio signals. Uses less power, easy to use, and costs less to implement than Wi-Fi technology
Binary	A system based on powers of the two numeral system (2^n), which uses only two numbers: 0 and 1.
Bit (binary digit)	The smallest unit of digital information in computing.
Bytes	A larger unit of digital information. A byte is a collection of 8 bits.
BIOS	Abbreviation for Basic Input Output System. It performs the booting process (starts up the computer).
CMOS	Complementary Metal Oxide Semiconductor is a technology for building integrated circuits, including microprocessors.
CPU	Central Processing Unit, or main processor of the computer. Also identified as the computer's Chip.
Multi-Core CPU	A CPU with two or more separate processing units. The parts of the processor that do parallel processing or multitasking tasks at a given time.
Firmware	A small piece of software that supports a specific piece of hardware. Examples include BIOS, keyboards, hard drive, or graphic card, etc.
GUI	Graphical User Interface. The screen(s) that enable users to interact with a computing device using menus, icons, and graphics.
Integrated Circuit	A group of miniature transistors joined microscopically.
Interface	The methods which describe the exchange of information between two or more separate components of a computer system or between a user and a computer.
ML	Machine Learning, a division of AI. ML is a computer algorithm that teaches computers to learn by performing data analysis, identifying patterns, and making decisions based on what has been learned.
Motherboard	A circuit board that comprises the principal components of a computer.
Non-Volatile	Retains stored information even when not powered. Examples include flash memory, hard drives, magnetic tape and optical discs.

(*Continued*)

TABLE 1.17 (CONTINUED) Glossary of Common Terms in Computer Science

Name	Computer Definitions
Nybble (Nibble)	4 bits or half a byte.
OS	Operating System. The main system software that interfaces and controls software and hardware on any computing device. Examples include Windows and Linux.
Power Supply	Hardware that converts alternating current (AC) to low-voltage direct current (DC) for the internal components of the computer. It also regulates voltage to limit overheating.
Quantum Computing	Quantum computing makes direct use of quantum mechanics to distribute better processing power and more intelligence in computation.
RAM	Random Access Memory. Temporarily stores data while the CPU is performing other tasks. With more RAM on the computer, the CPU can read less data from the external or secondary memory, allowing the computer to work with more information.
Software	A generic term for a computer program in a computer or other device.
Transistor	The transistor is an amplifier or a switch (On/Off) that controls an electrical current flow.
Utility	A utility is a piece of software in the computer that analyzes, configures, monitors, and maintains it. Usually comes installed with the OS.
Volatile Memory	Requires power to maintain the stored information. Example: RAM
Wi-Fi or Wireless Fidelity	A technology that utilizes radio waves to send and receive data to provide wireless local area networking (WLAN). This wireless technology is based on the IEEE 802.11 group of standards.

1.9 Key Words

Abacus
Artificial Intelligence (AI)
Application (App)
Binary Data
Bit
Bluetooth
Boolean Algebra
Byte
Central Processing Unit (CPU)
Color Depth
Computer
Decimals
Graphics Card
Hard Drive
Hexadecimals
Integrated Circuit
Internet of Things (IoT)
Logic Gates
Lossless compression
Lossy Compression
Machine Learning (ML)
Mathematical Logic
Pixels
Processor
Quantum Computing
Screen Resolution
Storage
Transistor
Vacuum Tube.

Chapter 2

Cybercrime in a Data-Driven and Techno-Centric Society

Objectives

After completing this chapter, the student will be able to:

- Understand the evolution and phases of cybercrime.
- Recognize cybercrime weapons.
- Explain the motives that make cybercrime attractive.
- Recognize the categories of cybercrime.
- Understand the cybercriminal.
- Discuss the Internet of Things (IoT) and cybercrime.
- Recognize the connections among Cybercrime, Machine Learning and Artificial Intelligence (AI).
- Understand the costs of cybercrime and the role of cryptocurrency.
- Understand online Child Sexual Abuse and Exploitation (CSAE).
- Explain state-sponsored and cyber warfare.

2.1 Cybercrime and the Cybercriminal

It is hard to imagine our world without the Internet. Television and radio may shorten the distances between us or let us imagine the world from afar, but the Internet has changed our planet into a virtual global village with no boundaries.

DOI: 10.4324/9780429318726-2

New technologies and the Internet have transformed the way we communicate, how we access information, how we form opinions, and how we find and enjoy entertainment. It has changed the shopping experience and has altered the face of crime. While there are drawbacks to the techno-centric world of the 21st century, the Internet is generally seen as a powerful space that we would never choose to give up.

As the Internet and computing technologies continue to evolve, criminals have found ways to use these technologies to commit unlawful acts, giving rise to massive cybercriminal activity. Cybercrime, a relatively new type of crime, is committed using a computing device and the Internet. While in the 20th-century oil was our most valuable commodity, today, the most precious commodity is data,[1] and cybercriminals are masters at finding and using our data while abusing our right to privacy. Cybercrimes encompass a broad category of offenses. One attraction to cybercrime is that it is so easy to be anonymous in cyberspace. The borderless nature of the Internet, and its lack of territorial jurisdiction enable the cybercriminal to pursue personal gain and rarely get caught.

As Figure 2.1 illustrates the most common motivations for cybercrime are:

- **Financial gain:** skimming bankcard numbers and PINs, payment system fraud (PayPal, Bitcoin), identity theft, and use of tools like malware, ransomware, and phishing
- **Espionage or spying:** accessing information/data from political entities, the military, government, industries, manufacturers, and corporations
- **Ideology:** hacktivism, disagreement over politics or values, cyberterrorism, cyber warfare, or the desire to evoke fear
- **Harassment, revenge, and fun:** seeking of revenge, fun, fame, thrill-seeking, recognition, or to control, manipulate, bully, or stalk.

Today, financial cybercrime is the biggest threat to companies and organizations. Cybercriminals may seek access to valuable data to sell them on the Dark Web. These data are personal, financial, and medical, as well as purchase-based consumer and social media data. The cybercriminal utilizes anonymous communication devices, such as The Onion Router (Tor) and OpenBazaar, an open source e-commerce protocol that uses cryptocurrency to hide illegal transactions.

However, not all cybercriminals seek financial gain. An Internet activist, or hacktivist, is a person who uses unauthorized data for political and subversive goals. Hacktivism began as a protest on the internet to effect change. A hacktivist needs to rebel and to spread an ideology. Some of the most infamous examples of hacktivism are the groups Anonymous, Lulz Security

---

[1] *The Economist*. The world's most valuable resource is no longer oil, but data (2017). Retrieved from https://www.economist.com/news/leaders/21721656-data-economy-demands-new-approach-antitrust-rules-worlds-most-valuable-resource

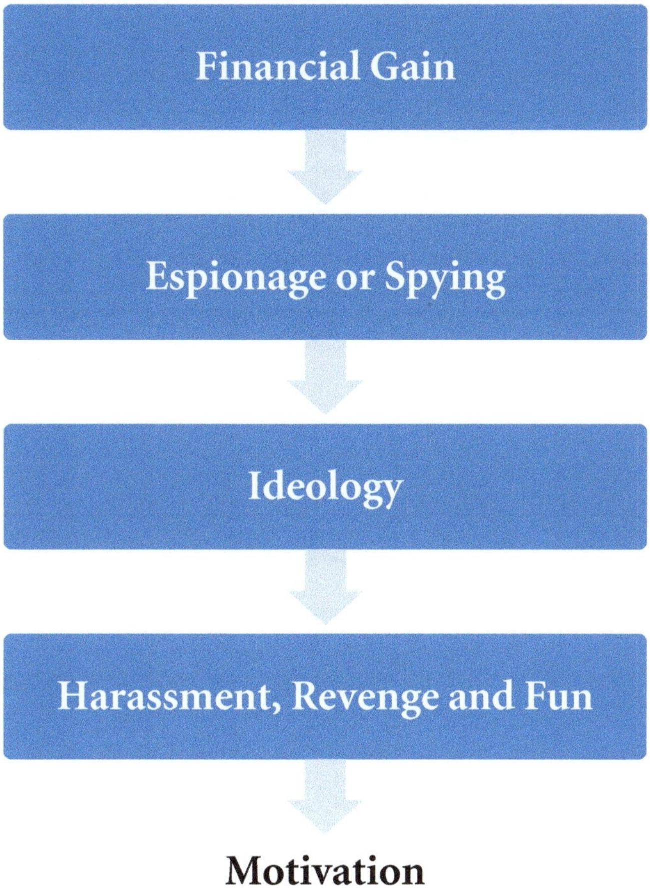

FIGURE 2.1 **Motives for Cybercrime.**

(LulzSec), Ghost Security Group (GhostSec) and WikiLeaks. The ultimate purpose of hacktivism is to spread a political or social message and cause a social change. In addition, the hacker becomes part of a community providing each member with emotional, political, or religious support, and a shared desire for power. Table 2.1 summarizes cybercrime weapons:

2.2 The Origin and Definition of Cybercrime – It's the Data, Always the Data

During the 1992 presidential campaign, James Carville, a campaign strategist of Bill Clinton, said repeatedly "It's the economy, stupid." He intended to remind the staff to keep focused on the issues.[2] Today, what matters more

[2] Bennett, Anthony J. "1992: 'It's the Economy, Stupid!'." *In the race for the White House from Reagan to Clinton*, pp. 123–159. Palgrave Macmillan, New York, 2013.

TABLE 2.1 A Summary of Cybercrime Weapons

Crime-as-a-Service (CaaS): An on-demand marketplace where one can purchase cybercrime services and attack tools like exploit kits, ransomware, worms, and phishing tools. Found on the Dark Web
Cyberterrorism: The use of the Internet as a tool to promote propaganda, cause fear, provide training, and disseminate advice on making bombs, promoting radicalization and planning attacks. Cyberterrorists use hacking tools to target critical social media infrastructure, with the intent of provoking fear, weakening government and diminishing social cohesion.
Cyberwarfare: A nation-state-sponsored cyber-attack on another nation-state to harm, alter, destroy, or steal information, or to conduct espionage and sabotage a computer network. Examples include distribution of malware that destroys files, and social media attacks that distribute false information and manipulate people to change their opinions and loyalties.
Cyberbullying or Cyber Harassment: A form of intimidation or mistreatment of an individual, targeting the victim online and sometimes extorting money.
Denial of service (DoS): An attack that occurs when a hacker makes computer resources inaccessible to its users by flooding the network with information, causing it to crash. DoS uses only a single computer to carry out the attack.
Distributed denial-of-service (DDoS): These more complex attacks occur when a hacker exploits security vulnerability to take control of multiple computers and turns them into botnets (zombie computers), and then uses the botnets to attack other computers or networks. DDoS attacks frequently extend worldwide.
Fraud and financial crime: A form of theft involving funds or property. A cybercriminal pretends to be a lawful merchant and advertises nonexistent goods and services, collecting money or property. Crimes include online purchase scams, auction fraud, mortgage fraud, sales fraud, embezzlement, Ponzi and pyramid schemes, credit and debit card fraud, money laundering and health care fraud.
Hacker: An individual accessing a computer device or computer system without the user's knowledge and authorization.
Hacktivist: An individual hacker driven by an ideology or politically inspired reason.
Identity theft: A broad range of crimes, including theft of personal or medical information, accessing a victim's bank accounts, credit cards, tax refunds, or impersonating another individual when apprehended for a crime. Personal data may be stolen and then sold to marketing firms worldwide. These data purchases can cost the marketing firms far less than traditional marketing research.
Malware: The term Malware is short for 'malicious software', and consists of computer viruses, worms, Trojan horses, ransomware, spyware, and all other types of destructive software or code. These impair or infiltrate a device or system without the user's knowledge to execute specific damage.
Phishing: Phishing is a deceitful attempt to gather personal information such as usernames, passwords, and credit card information by using deceptive e-mails masked as legitimate.
Ransomware: Use of malicious software to extort victims by locking and encrypting their data unless the victim pays a ransom in cryptocurrency. Even after payment the data may not be restored.
Spam: Any unwelcome electronic message sent in bulk. Spam may be an advertising campaign or a malicious worm or virus with a primary mission to infect.
Worm: A type of malware that duplicates itself and spreads from computer to computer using removable media, e-mail attachments, or by downloading infected files from the Internet.

than anything else is the data – what it says, what it can be made to say, and how it can help you decide what to do.

Today, data, information, hacking tools, and simple instructions for using them are available to anyone interested in cybercrime, with or without prior computer training. Cybercriminals make significant amounts of money by selling or trading data. These data, whether personal, medical, or financial, are the currency of a thriving underworld industry.

The data does not always have to be real. In the 2016 and 2020 U.S. presidential elections, falsified information was used as a tool of influence, in cyber attacks against the country's critical infrastructure. [3,4]

In the law, cybercrime is not distinct from other crimes.[5,6] When a hacker penetrates a security system to steal information, the hacker commits theft. The hacker is like any other thief, the only difference being the tools or methods used. Therefore, conventional and cybercriminals both break the law and are punished in similar ways. Cybercrimes were committed long before the Internet existed; as soon as computing technology became widely available individuals began to think about how they could take advantage of these new opportunities and cybercrime was born. Figure 2.2 displays a chronological timeline of major Cybercrime incidents.

Users can browse the Dark Web anonymously, buying and selling illegal goods in the form of data. Once purchased, the data can be sorted into categories, for purchase or for exploitation.

As these crimes transform and evolve, replacing older and clumsier tactics with new and more agile cyber tools and behaviors, our understanding of cybercrime is constantly expanding.

The cybercriminal's weapon is not a gun or knife, but instead is a computing device that links to a network. He or she accesses the Internet and directly commits theft or vandalism. The current expansion of cybercrime coincides with the development of more advanced artificial intelligence (AI) and machine learning algorithms. We have defined cybercrime as a computer-based criminal act utilizing a computing device and a network. This act transcends national and international borders and raises jurisdictional issues that one nation alone cannot address.

---

[3] Trautman, Lawrence J. "Is cyberattack the next pearl harbor." *NCJL & Tech.* 18 (2016): 233.

[4] Robert S. Mueller, "Report on the Investigation into Russian Interference in the 2016 Presidential Election," The United States Department of Justice, March 2019. Retrieved from https://www.justice.gov/sco

[5] Kirwan, Gráinne, ed. *The psychology of cyber crime: Concepts and principles.* Igi Global, 2011.

[6] Seger, Alexander. "Cybercrime and economic crime." *Financial Crimes: A Threat to Global Security* (2012): 119–146.

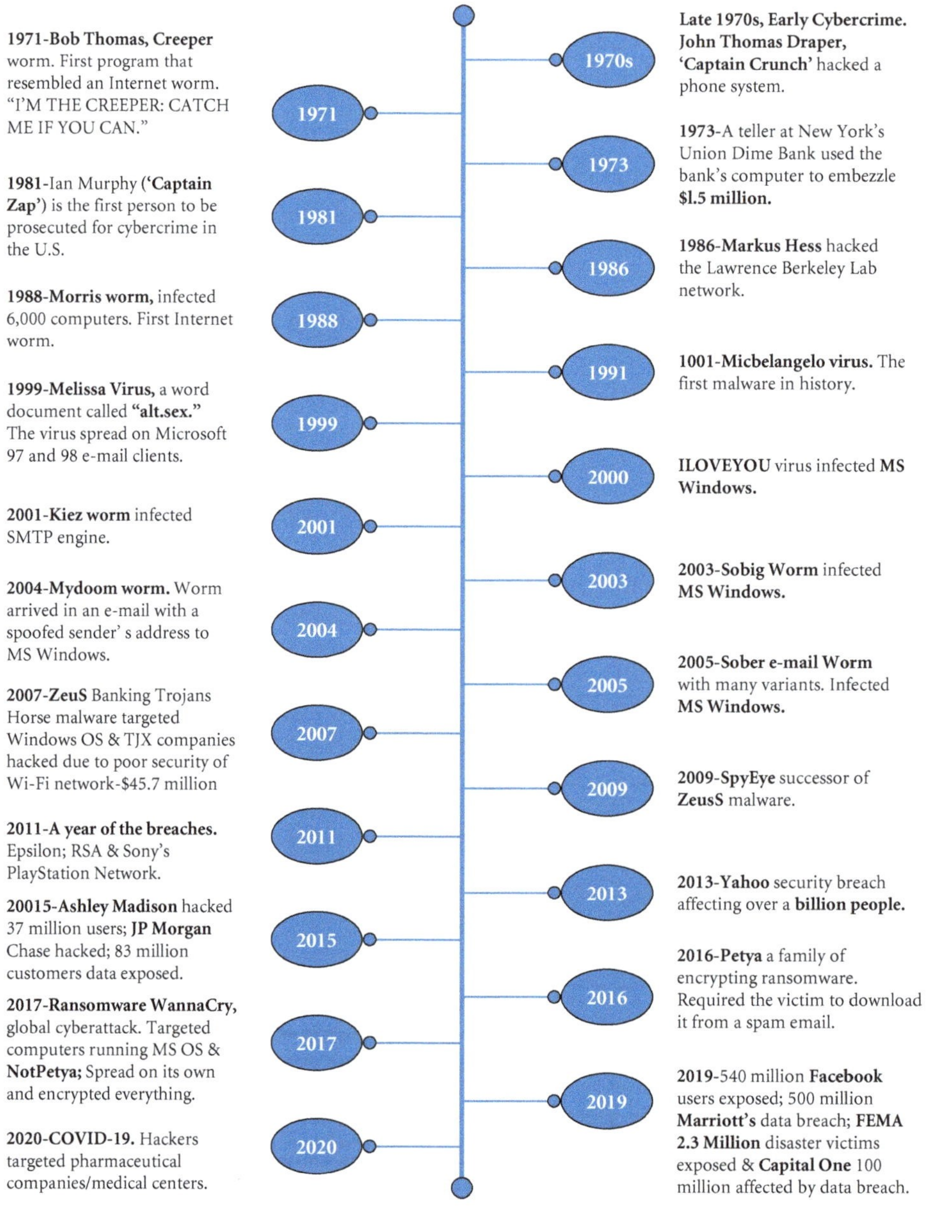

FIGURE 2.2 Timeline of major Cybercrime incidents.

2.3 Brief Summary of the Phases and Evolution of Cybercrime

Most Internet technologies are connected, using servers that cross political and cultural boundaries. These technologies provide a vast array of services and resources that are merely a click away. Valuable benefits, such as cheap storage using cloud computing, fast connectivity to businesses using e-commerce, and access to governments can be reached on a global scale in seconds. These technologies provide a rich environment for activities such as hacking, theft of information, installation of malware, and interference with network integrity and availability.

As we examine the history of cybercrime, we see four phases. However, the beginning of a new phase does not signal the end of the previous one; it is merely an addition to the repertory of cybercrimes. Today (2020), we can look back and observe all four phases.

The first phase began during the 1970s and 1980s. In this phase, we see an exploratory or experimental effort to control situations from a distance, using computer technology.

The second phase begins in the latter part of the 1980s. We see the formation of hacking groups, and the creation of a few highly effective viruses and worms aimed at crippling large systems.

The third phase originated in the early 2000s. Here we see the widespread adoption of Internet technology and use of social media, leading to crimes that are mostly financial.

The fourth phase commenced in 2011, a particularly challenging year for the Security industry. In this phase, we see massive breaches into organizations such as the Sony PlayStation Network and Nasdaq.[7] Its most distinct characteristic is the state-sponsored attack, and pervasive assaults on democracy by foreign powers. Figure 2.3 demonstrates the Phases of cybercrime.

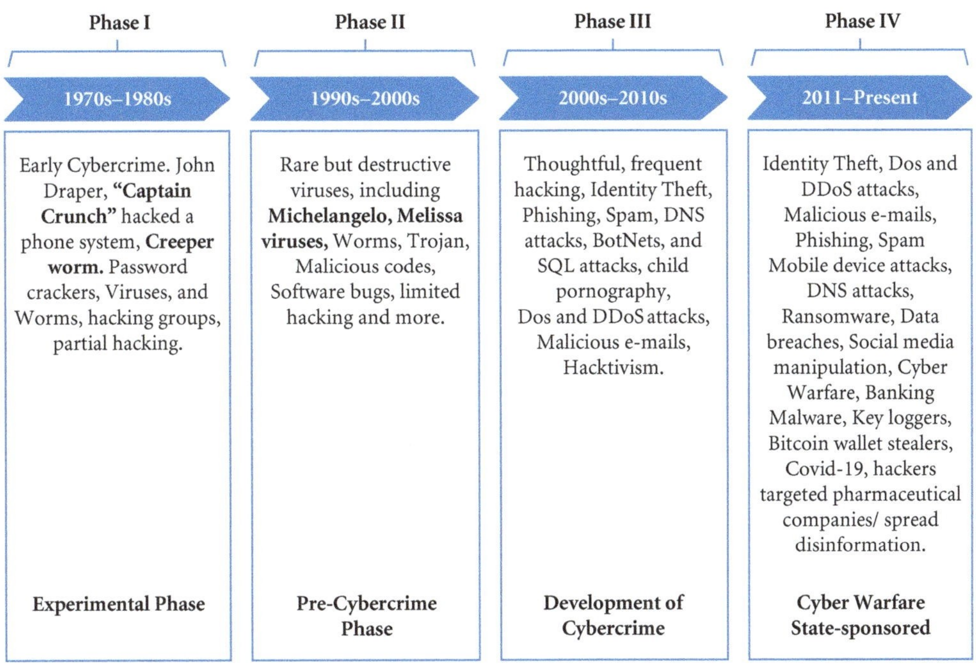

FIGURE 2.3 Phases of Cybercrime.

[7] Bonner, Lance. "Cyber risk: How the 2011 Sony data breach and the need for cyber risk insurance policies should direct the federal response to rising data breaches." *Washington University Journal of Law & Policy Introduction* 40 (2012): 257.

Cybercrime continues to evolve along with the Internet, now including Wi-Fi, cryptocurrency, leading to the crime of Cryptojacking, social media, and the Internet of Things (IoT).

Now, let us understand these phases in more detail.

Phase I

Phase I dates from the late 70s, with the first computer worm, the "Creeper." Between the 1970s and 1980s we saw the expansion of the ARPANET (Advanced Research Projects Agency Network), an early network initially funded by the US Department of Defense, and its metamorphosis into the fledgling Internet.

Phase I can be summarized as *You can build it, but I can break it.* It features direct attacks against systems, with the goal of bringing them down or causing damage. In this phase budding criminals are becoming almost gleefully aware of their ability to cause damage within this new environment. Some tools of this period include malicious code, Trojans (a type of malware disguised as a legitimate piece of software), advanced worms, and viruses that replicate and crash systems or damage files.

When the Creeper worm appeared on the ARPANET,[8] infected systems would display the message: "I'M THE CREEPER: CATCH ME IF YOU CAN."[9] This act was the first illegal attempt to alter a software program to transmit a specific message, but it was merely a boast, and could not damage or change any data.

One of the most important innovations of this time was the development and use of e-mail. Earlier, emails were designed to deliver messages and files directly to printers. One of the first email systems, created by Tom Van Vleck and Noel Morris in 1965 at The Massachusetts Institute of Technology, was called the Compatible Time-Sharing System (CTSS).

Ray Tomlinson is credited with inventing the e-mail system as we know it today. While working with ARPANET, Tomlinson chose the symbol @ to designate a particular user and its host, and to differentiate between one computer and another: name-of-the-user@name-of-the-computer.[10] Today, experts believe that global e-mail use will grow to over 4.1 billion users by the end of 2021.[11]

---

[8] Lukasik, Stephen. "Why the ARPANET was built." *IEEE Annals of the History of Computing* 33, no. 3 (2010): 4–21.

[9] Chen, Thomas M., and Jean-Marc Robert. "The evolution of viruses and worms." *Statistical Methods in Computer Security* 1 (2004).

[10] Brown, Bruce C. *The complete guide to e-mail marketing: How to create successful, spam-free campaigns to reach your target audience and increase sales.* Vol. 978, no. 1-60045. Atlantic Publishing Company, 2007.

[11] Shuaib, Maryam, Olawale Surajudeen Adebayo, Oluwafemi Osho, Ismaila Idris, John K. Alhassan, and Nadim Rana. "Whale optimization algorithm-based email spam feature selection method using rotation forest algorithm for classification." *SN Applied Sciences* 1, no. 5 (2019): 390.

Once computers became part of our daily lives, more incidents began to follow. In 1971, at General Motor's Oshawa (Canada) factory, thieves hacked into the system and created false purchase requisitions; they then placed purchase orders and invoices in the accounting system to make matters appear legitimate. In 1973, a teller at New York's Union Dime Bank used the bank's computer to embezzle $1.5 million.[12]

The term *Hacking* originated in the 1960s at MIT. It was originally a positive term and described the use of a modification to a product or procedure to correct a problem. Students learned to modify computer code to control a program in new ways, demonstrating that they were worthy of calling themselves Hackers. The term was used for amusement and recognition, not for illegal activity.

Phase I is also characterized by a new character – a curious, brilliant, and solitary individual in search of thrill and adventure, seeking to show off his abilities (*I'm better than you, I can hack anything*). In the 1980s, hackers joined hacking groups such as the Chaos Computer Club, Legions of Doom, and NuPrometheus League.[13] When IBM introduced the Personal Computer (PC) in 1982, businesses were already using computers to improve productivity, and the new PCs began to appear in homes around the country.

The romantic veneration of computers is perfectly displayed in the 1983 movie *War Games*, in which a young hacker finds his way into a U.S. military supercomputer and comes close to starting a 'global thermonuclear war'. The movie was released during the time when people believed computers were magic and hackers were geniuses, and while a classic representation of this period, it remains popular to this day.

In 1984, U.S. Congress passed the first hacking-related legislation; the Computer Fraud and Abuse Act (CFAA). It was enacted as an amendment to existing computer fraud law (18 U.S.C. § 1030). However, the first person to face prosecution for cybercrime in the United states was Ian Murphy ("Captain Zap") in 1981. Murphy hacked into AT&T's computers and changed their internal clocks to charge less during peak times. He received 1,000 hours of community service and 2.5 years of probation.[14/15]

In 1986, in an attack chronicled by author and investigator Cliff Stoll in "The Cuckoo's Egg", German hacker Markus Hess hacked into the Lawrence Berkeley Laboratory computer network[16]obtaining wide access to military information; then selling much it to the KGB, part of the Russian government.

---

[12] Carroll, John M. *Computer security*. Butterworth-Heinemann, 2014.

[13] Corera, Gordon. *Cyberspies: The secret history of surveillance, hacking, and digital espionage*. Pegasus Books, 2016.

[14] Brenner, Susan W. "History of computer crime." In *The history of information security*, pp. 705–721. Elsevier Science BV, 2007.

[15] Kizza, Joseph Migga. *Computer network security and cyber ethics*. McFarland, 2014.

[16] Futter, Andrew. *Hacking the bomb: Cyber threats and nuclear weapons*. Georgetown University Press, 2018.

The laboratory, a U.S. national laboratory near Berkeley, California, conducts research for the US Department of Energy (DOE).

In 1988, Robert Morris, a Cornell University student, embedded his *Morris worm* in the University's UNIX system. A worm is a standalone malware program that works by multiplying itself and spreading from one computer to another. The *Morris worm* multiplied itself thousands of times, moving from computer to computer across a huge network of computers from many universities, and eventually brought the system to a crashing halt. This worm destroyed more than 6,000 computers and resulted in $98 million in damages. Although still a student, Robert Morris was prosecuted and convicted of violating 18 U.S. Code § 1030 (fraud and related activity in connection with computers). The *Morris worm* is known as the first Internet worm.

Phase II

Phase II dates from the beginning of the 1990s to the year 2000. With the advancement of web browsers in the 1990s, it became easier to send viruses through Internet connections. These viruses caused the computers to run slowly or allowed annoying pop-up ads to appear.

In 1991 the *Michelangelo virus* appeared.[17] It was like nothing that had been seen before and has been called the first public malware in history. *Michelangelo* is a boot sector virus, infecting storage devices such as floppy disks, or the master boot section of the operating system, where the booting up process of the hard drive begins.

The next important virus, the *Melissa Virus*,[18] appeared in 1999, when David L. Smith hacked an America Online (AOL) account and posted an infected Word document called **alt.sex** on an Internet newsgroup. Since the file was a Microsoft Word document, people assumed it was harmless. As a result, the *Melissa Virus* spread among millions of Microsoft 97 and 98 e-mail clients. The virus required several large companies to shut down their e-mail systems and is estimated to have cost $80 million worth of damages.[19] David L. Smith was sentenced to 20 months in prison and fined $5,000 for introducing the virus.

---

[17] Gragido, Will, Daniel Molina, John Pirc, and Nick Selby. *Blackhatonomics: An inside look at the economics of cybercrime.* Newnes, 2012.

[18] Zou, Cliff C., Don Towsley, and Weibo Gong. "Email virus propagation modeling and analysis." *Department of Electrical and Computer Engineering, University of Massachusetts, Amherst, Technical Report: TR-CSE-03-04* (2003).

[19] Hovav, Anat, and John D'Arcy. "The impact of virus attack announcements on the market value of firms." *Information Systems Security* 13, no. 3 (2004): 32–40.

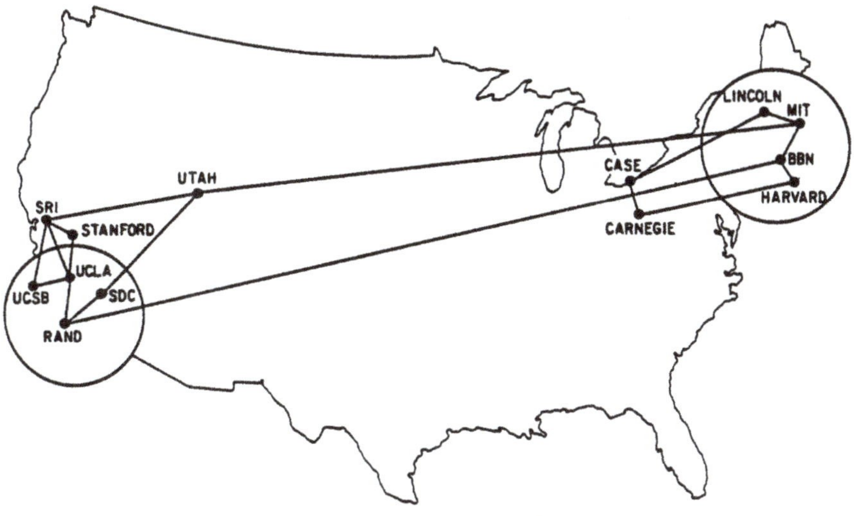

FIGURE 2.4 A map of the ARPANET in December 1970. Courtesy of DARPA.

Phase III

Phase III arose in the early 2000s, after the ARPANET and the National Science Foundation's NSFNet were transformed into a larger network, becoming the Internet (Figure 2.4). After establishing the Internet as their main channel of communication and illegal e-commerce, cybercriminals began targeting big data. During this phase, cybercrime became a for-profit enterprise. We define this phase by the proliferation of monetary crimes, including identity and credit card theft, phishing, Domain Name System (DNS) attacks, botnets, and use of ransomware and spyware. Cybercriminals evaded justice worldwide by using secure software and proxy servers to conceal their locations and communications, thus remaining anonymous. When social media was born and users flooded it with their personal information, theft of personal data became the crime of the new millennium, with cybercriminals accessing bank accounts, setting up fraudulent credit cards, and engaging in other forms of financial fraud.[20]

The number and types of online attacks grew exponentially. Large denial-of-service (DDoS) attacks occurred, including attacks at Amazon, AOL, CNN, eBay, Yahoo, and numerous others. The *ILOVEYOU* virus[21] spread across the Internet by e-mail in 2000, with the subject line reading "ILOVEYOU" and an attachment, 'LOVE-LETTER-FOR-YOU.txt.vbs'. If the receiver opened the attachment, a script written in *Visual Basic* script was executed; the virus was launched, and the computer was infected.

[20] Hoar, Sean B. "Identity theft: The crime of the new millennium." *Oregon School of Law* 80 (2001): 1423.
[21] Knight, Peter. "ILOVEYOU: Viruses, paranoia, and the environment of risk." *The Sociological Review* 48, no. 2_suppl (2000): 17–30.

In 2001, the *Klez* worm infected its host with a symbiotic virus, Elkern .cav, through an e-mail.[22] The worm used its own Simple Mail Transfer Protocol (SMTP) engine to spoof the *From*: field. The worm replicated and mailed itself to every person in the victim's address book, infecting everyone it reached.

In response to the attacks of September 11, 2001, Congress enacted the 2001 USA PATRIOT Act,[23] Uniting and Strengthening America by Providing Appropriate Tools Required to Intercept and Obstruct Terrorism. The Act brought changes to U.S. laws affecting intelligence, communication, and privacy, including the Electronic Communications Privacy Act (EPCA), which modifies Title III of the Omnibus Crime Control and Safe Streets Act (the Wiretap Act), the Foreign Intelligence Surveillance Act of 1978 (FISA); and the Communications Act of 1934.

The changes in the USA PATRIOT Act appeared logical and necessary, given the circumstances. The law relaxes restrictions on how much personal information about citizens and non-citizens the government can acquire. Additionally, it authorizes the federal government to improve surveillance procedures, provides for increased monitoring of financial transactions, extends permission for wiretapping, and gives government the power to request electronic communications, as well as the ability to relax search warrant requirements for suspected terrorists. This law remains a subject of contention, as it was intended to deal with a temporary state of emergency, and yet remains in effect twenty years later.

During this time, websites like MySpace and LinkedIn gained fame. YouTube first appeared in 2005, devising new ways for people to communicate and share videos. In 2006, Facebook and Twitter became available to users across the world. This period was characterized by the miniaturization of technology, and the rapid spread of mobile devices (smartphones and tablets).

In 2003, the *Sobig* worm was introduced, infecting millions of Internet and Windows PC users by e-mail.[24] When executed, *Sobig*, would copy itself to the Windows folder as Winmgm32.exe. The file extension .exe means that the file is an "Executable" file, a file containing a program that can be run, used in operating systems such as Windows, MS-DOS, OpenVMS, or ReactOS. The program runs when a user opens the file. Executable files do not require any other program to run. Thus, *Sobig* was not only a computer

---

[22] Kienzle, Darrell M., and Matthew C. Elder. "Recent worms: a survey and trends." In *Proceedings of the 2003 ACM workshop on Rapid malcode*, pp. 1–10. ACM, 2003.

[23] USA PATRIOT Act of 2001, Pub. L. No. 107–56. Retrieved from https://www.congress.gov/107/plaws/publ56/PLAW-107publ56.pdf

[24] Chen, Thomas M., and J-M. Robert. "Worm epidemics in high-speed networks." *Computer* 37, no. 6 (2004): 48–53.

worm, but also a *Trojan horse*, doing damage after being allowed to enter the computer's operating system.

Trojan horse malware obtained its name from Homer's novel, The Iliad. When the Greeks tried to conquer the city of Troy, they had difficulty getting into the fortified city. The Greeks deceived the Trojans by giving them a giant wooden horse and pretending to sail away after the Trojans dragged the wooden horse into their city. During the night, Greek soldiers hidden inside the horse crawled out and opened the gates for the rest of the Greek army, after which they captured the city. Similarly, a Trojan horse is a type of malware (malicious software) that masquerades as genuine but contains a hidden destructive element.

When you receive an email and click an innocent looking attachment, you may unknowingly install a program that will infect files throughout your computer or network. That attachment is called a Trojan horse. Mostly, the Trojan horse stays hidden until a specific action is taken, such as accessing an online banking website or paying a bill online. At that point, the Trojan activates a malicious code and carries out its instructions, stealing passwords or transferring money. The Trojan horse may be scripted to delete itself after completing the task.

Mydoom, one of the most damaging viruses or worms, appeared in 2004.[25] It arrived in an e-mail with a spoofed (fake) sender's address. When *Mydoom* executed, it would duplicate itself to the Windows system folder as Taskmon.exe. A legitimate file with this name is found in the Windows folder. It also created the file Shimgapi.dll, which was similarly placed in the system folder. *Mydoom* is a backdoor Trojan, or secret file. It opened and used the Transmission Control Protocol (TCP), and thus exploited the Internet Explorer browser.

Another devastating worm was the *Sober* email worm and its variants. The *Sober* worm is a family of computer worms. They are generally independent programs, and do not need human interaction to replicate across networks. The worm may arrive in an email, fake webpage, fake pop-up ad, or fake advertisement, and will contain subject lines such as, sex, love, and even computer virus warnings. "Upon execution, *Sober* copies itself to one of several files in the Windows system folder, as an .exe file, with a name that is constructed from the following strings: sys, host, dir, explorer, win, run, log, 32, disc, crypt, data, diag, spool,service,smss32."[26]

Three notable technological advancements became so widespread in this period that they changed how people interact with each other. These technologies are the Apple iPhone, first introduced in 2007, and the Android Operating System (OS), introduced in 2008. The third development is Cloud

[25] *Id.* at 24.

[26] "Sophos W32/Sober-I." Last modified January 2005. Retrieved from https://www.sophos.com/en-us/threat-center/threat-analyses/viruses-and-spyware/W32~Sober-I/detailed-analysis.aspx

Computing, although John McCarthy first introduced a much more basic version of this technology in the 1960s.[27]

In 2006, Amazon introduced its Web Service AWS, and other cloud-computing providers, such as Google, IBM and Microsoft followed. Cloud Computing is the distribution of computing services such as database, storage, applications, and analytics, over the Internet. Cloud computing provides business and individuals around the world flexibility, savings in cost, time, and resources, enabling less reliance on traditional data centers and support teams. However, a great concern with cloud computing has been the issue of security and data privacy. Depending on the cloud computing model used, data may no longer belong completely to a business or individual. The cloud service provider stores the user's data on its own servers and has full access to the data, confidential or not. Additionally, physical storage of the data often spans multiple servers in different countries, making it easier for cyber criminals to manipulate the connection to the cloud or attack the data centers.

An example in April 2019 involved the Facebook data bridge that was posted publicly on Amazon cloud servers. Five hundred and forty million records of Facebook user data were publicly exposed. According to UpGuard,[28] a Mexico-based media company called Cultura Colectiva was responsible for the leak. It exposed 146 gigabytes of Facebook user data, including account names, IDs, and other details. It is unclear exactly how many individual users had data exposed.

Named after Zeus, the Greek king of the gods, the *Zeus* virus, was identified in 2007. Like other Trojan malware, it targets Microsoft Windows, and cybercriminals use it to steal online financial transactions. *Zeus* creates a botnet, and gathers massive amounts of information including passwords, configuration files, and online credentials. Botnets or "bots" are internet-based computing devices that have been infected with malware and programmed remotely for fraudulent purposes.

Additionally, the *Zeus* virus corrupts computers, while it communicates with and controls servers. *Zeus* infected over 3.6 million computers in the United States.[29] Between 2009 and 2011, a *Zeus* successor, *SpyEye*, remotely infected and controlled computers, stealing personal and financial information. The two hackers who spread *SpyEye*, Russian national Aleksandr Andreevich Panin and Algerian national Hamza "B × 1" Bendelladj, were prosecuted and received a combined term of 24 years in prison. Both are

---

[27] Chen, Yanpei, Vern Paxson, and Randy H. Katz. "What's new about cloud computing security." *University of California, Berkeley Report No. UCB/EECS-2010-5*, January 20, no. 2010 (2010): 2010–15.

[28] "Losing face: Two more cases of third-party facebook app data exposure." *UpGuard*. Last modified April 3, 2019. Retrieved from https://www.upguard.com/breaches/facebook-user-data-leak

[29] Binsalleeh, Hamad, Thomas Ormerod, Amine Boukhtouta, Prosenjit Sinha, Amr Youssef, Mourad Debbabi, and Lingyu Wang. "On the analysis of the zeus botnet crimeware toolkit." In *2010 Eighth International Conference on Privacy, Security and Trust*, pp. 31–38. IEEE, 2010.

responsible for the development, marketing, and customization of the malware according to the specific needs of each cybercriminal.[30] This is an example of the Crime-as-a-Service (CaaS) model. Since 2008, a self-updating worm called *Conficker* has been aggressively spreading across the Internet. Chinese hackers offered to sell this worm for the equivalent of $37.80.[31]

In 2009, the Health Information Technology for Economic and Clinical Health Act (HITECH), steered healthcare providers in the United States toward an expansion of secure Electronic Medical Records (EMR). Once personal medical information was online, cybercriminals began targeting these healthcare records. They realized that while data stolen from financial institutions becomes useless once the breach is uncovered and passwords are changed, medical histories cannot change and last for a lifetime.

In 2010, the *Stuxnet* worm appeared. *Stuxnet* was a Cyber-warfare tool created by U.S. and Israeli governments to disrupt Iran's nuclear program.[32] This sophisticated computer worm targeted Supervisory Control and Data Acquisition, (SCADA) systems. These military systems are responsible for gathering and analyzing real-time data. The *Stuxnet* worm is believed to be responsible for causing considerable damage to Iran's nuclear program.

Phase IV

Phase IV begins after 2011 and extends into the present. This phase comprises state-sponsored cyberattacks, espionage, breaches to government privacy and confidentiality, and the manipulation of public opinion through persuasion over social media platforms. Additionally, in this phase we see the rise of fake news, and the death of personal privacy. We now live in the age of surveillance, eerily like George Orwell's descriptions in his novel, 1984.

The year 2011 was a year of sizable data breaches. Epsilon Data Management, whose clients include Eddie Bauer, Ethan Allen, and TD Ameritrade, lost enormous amounts of data. Also hit were Sony's PlayStation Network and Qriocity services, drawing the public's attention to data security, privacy, and the role of governments in preventing such attacks.[33] Additionally, in 2011, RSA's two-factor SecurID, used by U.S. government agencies and contractors, was attacked and sensitive information was stolen. The stolen data enabled attacks against third-party companies, such as Lockheed Martin

---

[30] "Two major international hackers who developed the 'SpyEye' malware get over 24 years combined in federal prison." *United States Department of Justice*. Last modified April 20, 2016. Retrieved from https://www.justice.gov/usao-ndga/pr/two-major-international-hackers-who-developed-spyeye-malware-get-over-24-years-combined

[31] Porras, Phillip, Hassen Saidi, and Vinod Yegneswaran. "An analysis of conficker's logic and rendezvous points." *Computer Science Laboratory, SRI International, Tech. Rep* (2009): 36.

[32] Kenney, Michael. "Cyber-terrorism in a post-stuxnet world." *Orbis* 59, no. 1 (2015): 111–128.

[33] *Id.* at 7.

and other U.S. defense contractors. Later investigation revealed that hackers from the Chinese army orchestrated the cyberattack.[34/35]

In 2013–14, Yahoo experienced the largest security breach in its history, affecting over a billion users.[36] Yahoo never disclosed the timeline of the event nor the exact number of users compromised.

Another famous example of a state-sponsored attack occurred against Sony Pictures Entertainment (SPE) in 2014. The company detected extensive network intrusions, followed by demands that it refrain from releasing its new action comedy film, 'The Interview'. The film was a satire about Americans sent to North Korea to assassinate its president, Kim Jung Un. Sony claimed that the film was not a political attack but was intended only as entertainment. Sony employees were threatened with physical harm unless they signed a document denouncing the film. Sony did not accede to the demands and released the film as planned. It was later verified that the government of North Korea was responsible for the attack and demands that followed.[37]

In 2015, a hacking group called "The Impact Team" hacked into Ashley Madison's database and stole personal information from 37 million users. Ashley Madison is a website dedicated to extramarital affairs.[38] After the data breach, cybercriminals leaked subscribers' personal information to the public, resulting in humiliation, embarrassment, and extortion.

Additionally, cybersecurity attacks continued to affect the healthcare industry. Health insurer Anthem Inc. and Primera Blue Cross suffered massive data breaches. Cyber thieves stole approximately 91 million patient records, including social security numbers, medical data, and financial information.[39]

In 2016, as the U.S. presidential election approached, the country experienced a wave of political cybercrime, characterized by manipulation of social media as well as theft or purchase of personal profiles. In this case, cybercriminals from other countries chose targets to influence based on their political orientation, levels of education, opinions, and other factors that made them persuadable and vulnerable. This type of hacking campaign manipulates social media data and attacks voters without their

---

[34] Virvilis, Nikos, Oscar Serrano, and Luc Dandurand. "Big data analytics for sophisticated attack detection." *Isaca Journal* 3 (2014): 22–25.

[35] Sanger, David E., David Barboza, and Nicole Perlroth. "Chinese army unit is seen as tied to hacking against US." *New York Times*, February 18, 2013.

[36] Steinmetz, Kevin F., and Matt R. Nobles, eds. *Technocrime and criminological theory*. Routledge, 2017.

[37] Haggard, Stephan, and Jon R. Lindsay. "North Korea and the Sony hack: Exporting instability through cyberspace" (2015).

[38] Edwards, Benjamin, Steven Hofmeyr, and Stephanie Forrest. "Hype and heavy tails: A closer look at data breaches." *Journal of Cybersecurity* 2, no. 1 (2016): 3–14.

[39] Khan, Shahidul Islam, and Abu Sayed Md Latiful Hoque. "Digital health data: A comprehensive review of privacy and security risks and some recommendations." *Computer Science Journal of Moldova* 24, no. 2 (2016).

consent, using social media bots, creating propaganda, and promoting fake news. Since the majority of American adults (62%) get their news on social media, a large number of those who see these stories accept them and believe they are true.[40] The propaganda they see presents an alternative reality to the victims, and they also accept the traditional media as purveyors of 'fake news'. The intelligence community reported these intrusions as coming from Russia, but this has not yet been universally accepted.

Democratic presidential candidate Hillary Clinton and other Democrats were attacked with ads and persuasive Facebook material containing false information, with the goal of changing votes and creating voting blocs in vulnerable states, ultimately leading to social unrest and unexpected election results, namely the election of Donald Trump, and finally to the possibility of a changed balance of national and international power.

We have seen these hacking campaigns not only in the U.S. election of 2016,[41] but in European elections and referenda as well.[42] In addition, we have seen Russian hackers target critical infrastructure, like electrical grids in Europe and the United States.[43]

New evidence discovered in 2018 showed that a British political consulting firm, Cambridge Analytica, and other companies harvested personal information in order to alter the outcome and influence voter behavior in both the U.S. presidential election and the U.K.'s Brexit referendum of 2016.[44,45,46,47] More specifically, Cambridge Analytica purchased data from Facebook without user knowledge or consent. The company developed a tool based on research by Kosinski, Stillwell, and Graepel, using data from Facebook Likes to predict personal attributes such as political views, sexual

---

[40] Allcott, Hunt, and Matthew Gentzkow. "Social media and fake news in the 2016 election." *Journal of Economic Perspectives* 31, no. 2 (2017): 211–36.

[41] Persily, Nathaniel. "The 2016 US election: Can democracy survive the internet?." *Journal of Democracy* 28, no. 2 (2017): 63–76.

[42] Sunstein, Cass R. *# Republic: Divided democracy in the age of social media*. Princeton University Press, 2018.

[43] Kshetri, Nir, and Jeffrey Voas. "Hacking power grids: a current problem." *Computer* 50, no. 12 (2017): 91–95.

[44] *Id.* at 41.

[45] Rosenberg, Matthew, Nicholas Confessore, and Carole Cadwalladr. "How Trump consultants exploited the Facebook data of millions." *The New York Times*, March 17, 2018. Retrieved from https://www.nytimes.com/2018/03/17/us/politics/cambridge-analytica-trump-campaign.html

[46] Cadwalladr, Carole, and Emma Graham-Harrison. "Revealed: 50 million Facebook profiles harvested for Cambridge Analytica in major data breach." *The Guardian* and *The Observer*, March 17, 2018. https://www.theguardian.com/news/2018/mar/17/cambridge-analytica-facebook-influence-us-election

[47] Schotz, Mai. "Cambridge analytica took 50M Facebook users' data—and both companies owe answers." *Wired*, March 17, 2018. Retrieved from https://www.wired.com/story/cambridge-analytica-50m-facebook-users-data/

orientation, religious ethnicity, personality, intellect and age.[48,49] They analyzed the data and successfully targeted individuals with selected ads in order to influence their behavior and political beliefs.

An example of this behavior manipulation occurred in the small Welsh town of Ebbw Vale. According to National Public Radio, the town voted overwhelmingly in favor of Brexit. Using news feeds from Facebook, which later disappeared, and advertisements from Google and YouTube, people were persuaded to believe that immigrant and refugee populations had overwhelmed the city, even though the town actually has one of the lowest rates of immigration in the country. Although the European Union had invested heavily in the town, people came to believe it had done nothing for them. The advertisements and fake news provoked specific human emotions and consequent behavior among people.[50]

The use of psychographic techniques to manipulate behavior emerged as one of the results of corporate greed from Facebook, Twitter, and even Google. Psychographic analysis puts an emphasis on consumer lifestyle. It is used to understand the cognitive processes that affect spending habits, hobbies, opinions, attitudes, interests, and lifestyles, who we buy from, and why we choose to purchase things.

In 2018, the UK's protection watchdog fined Facebook £500,000 for the role it played in the Cambridge Analytica scandal. Later in 2019, after an investigation of Facebook showed it gave Cambridge Analytica access to 87 million Facebook users' personal data without their knowledge, the U.S Federal Trade Commission (FTC) fined Google $5 billion. The FTC found that Facebook violated rules against deceptive practices by revealing phone numbers collected during the two-factor (2FA) authentication used for advertising.[51 /52]

Cambridge Analytica gained additional information by using mobile apps to collect data, and by tracking location and contact/address lists. One

[48] Kosinski, Michal, David Stillwell, and Thore Graepel. "Private traits and attributes are predictable from digital records of human behavior." *Proceedings of the National Academy of Sciences* 110, no. 15 (2013): 5802–5805.

[49] Cadwalladr, Carole, and E. Graham-Harrison. "The Cambridge analytica files." *The Guardian* 21 (2018): 6–7.

[50] Raz, Guy. "Carole Cadwalladr: How did social media manipulate our votes and our elections?" *npr News*, July 12, 2019. Retrieved from https://www.npr.org/templates/transcript/transcript.php?storyId=740771021

[51] "$5b privacy fine against Facebook seen as 'chump change'" *Naked Security*, July 19, 2019. Retrieved from https://nakedsecurity.sophos.com/2019/07/16/5b-privacy-fine-against-facebook-seen-as-chump-change/

[52] "Facebook to pay record $5bn to settle privacy concerns." *BBC News*, July 24, 2019. Retrieved from https://www.bbc.com/news/business-49099364

app used was called "Cruz Crew" and was used by the campaign for the re-election of U.S. Senator Ted Cruz of Texas.[53,54]

In addition, during Phase IV we continue to experience older forms of cybercrime, including banking malware, bitcoin wallet theft, mobile device hacks, and extortion through ransomware.

With both new and old threats, in Phase IV we see cybercrime grow beyond hacking and identity theft to a more sophisticated and better-organized global threat. Cybercrime now resembles a silent worldwide war. It knows no boundaries and concerns every nation on the planet.

The dissemination of fake news, a critical part of election interference, has been a great source of revenue for social media. This use of disinformation can be stopped only through government supervision, education, and continuous monitoring. As of now, we can only conclude that the word 'truth' has lost its meaning. Instead we have "alternative truth or facts."

We first loved Google and Facebook because they were "free"; we now understand that social media is far from free. We must now think of ourselves as not only users, but also as sources of revenue, with our private information a commodity that can be bought and sold. Social media may have been designed to bring us together, but it now divides us.

Between 2016 and 2017, an encrypting ransomware program called *Petya* and its newer version, *NotPetya*, appeared. Both were intended to encrypt and lock the hard drive of infected computers. File access could be restored only by paying a ransom. The malware usually arrived on the victim's computer attached to an email. *Petya* could run only if it succeeded in tricking the victim to download its file from a spam email. It targeted the Windows Operating System (OS), infecting the master boot record, encrypting the hard drive's file system and preventing the computer from booting up. Frequently, cybercriminals demand that the victim make payment to regain access through Bitcoin.[55]

In 2016 we experienced the *Mirai* strain of malware. This type of malware turns IoT devices running on Linux into remotely controlled "bots".[56]

In 2017, ransomware called *WannaCry* exploited a weakness in Windows computers worldwide. Like *Mirai*, the ransomware was able to encrypt a computer's files and then lock out users, making it impossible for them to access their own information. At that point, ransom payments in

---

[53] Detrow, Scott. "Cruz's Crew: you play the game, but it's the cruz campaign that scores." *Npr News*, November 9, 2015. Retrieved from https://www.npr.org/2015/11/09/455225893/cruzs-crew-you-play-the-game-but-its-the-cruz-campaign-that-scores

[54] *Id.* at 41.

[55] Fayi, Sharifah Yaqoub A. "What Petya/NotPetya ransomware is and what its remidiations are." In *Information Technology—New Generations*, pp. 93–100. Springer, Cham, 2018.

[56] Kambourakis, Georgios, Constantinos Kolias, and Angelos Stavrou. "The mirai botnet and the iot zombie armies." In *MILCOM 2017-2017 IEEE Military Communications Conference (MILCOM)*, pp. 267–272. IEEE, 2017.

Bitcoin cryptocurrency were required to permit users to access their own information.

WannaCry infiltrated the United Kingdom's National Health Service (NHS) computers, bringing down the entire medical records system. Medical personnel could not register patients, access medical records, or prescribe medication, delaying crucial procedures, and creating chaos for millions of patients and personnel.[57] "There are two components to the malware. One uses the 'EternalBlue' exploit against a vulnerability of Windows' Server Message Block (SMB), and the other is a WannaCry ransomware encryption component." [58]

The EternalBlue exploit is a code that takes advantage of a software vulnerability, in this case MS Windows OS. It was allegedly stolen from the National Security Agency (NSA) in 2016 and was leaked by a hacker group called the Shadow Brokers. It was then was used in *WannaCry* ransomware.[59]

WannaCry and *NotPetya* did not target individuals, but instead attacked critical infrastructures of the largest systems, banks, state agencies, and ministries. These attacks did not come from lone criminals, but instead were designed by intelligence or cyberwarfare agencies.[60] A major cyber-security breach occurred in September 2017 in the data analytics company Equifax, located in the U.S. Cybercriminals accessed approximately 145.5 million pieces of personal data, including names, dates of birth, driver license numbers, and social security numbers.[61] This comprised all the information needed to commit the perfect cybercrime. None of the data had been circulated. In 2020, the U.S. government has charged members of the Chinese military with a hack.[62]

In 2018, the European Union implemented legislation to combat cybercrime. The General Data Protection Regulation (GDPR) replaced the Data Protection Directive 95/46/EC,[63] and gives individuals better control over their personal data. In the United States, California's governor, Jerry Brown,

---

[57] Clarke, Rachel, and Taryn Youngstein. "Cyberattack on Britain's National Health Service—a wake-up call for modern medicine." *The New England Journal of Medicine* 377, no. 5 (2017): 409–11.

[58] Chen, Qian, and Robert A. Bridges. "Automated behavioral analysis of malware: A case study of wannacry ransomware." In *2017 16th IEEE International Conference on Machine Learning and Applications (ICMLA)*, pp. 454–460. IEEE, 2017.

[59] Bowden, Mark. "The worm that nearly ate the Internet." *The New York Times*, June 9, 2019. Retrieved from https://www.nytimes.com/2019/06/29/opinion/sunday/conficker-worm-ukraine.html

[60] Farral, Travis. "Nation-state attacks: Practical defences against advanced adversaries." *Network Security* 2017, no. 9 (2017): 5–7.

[61] Kenny, Caitlin. "The Equifax data breach and the resulting legal recourse." *Brooklyn Journal of Corporate, Financial & Commercial Law* 13 (2018): 215.

[62] The U.S. Department of Justice, "Criminal indictment." Retrieved from https://www.justice.gov/opa/press-release/file/1246891/download

[63] "European Commission-Data Protection Directive 95/46/ec." Last modified June 28, 2018. Retrieved from https://eur-lex.europa.eu/LexUriServ/LexUriServ.do?uri=CELEX%3A31995L0046%3Aen%3AHTML

signed into law the California Consumer Privacy Act (CCPA),[64] which improves privacy rights and consumer protection for California residents.

In 2018, Marriott International announced that hackers had breached its Starwood reservation system and had stolen the information of 500 million of its customers worldwide.[65]

In 2019, Facebook, the subject of numerous cybersecurity concerns in the past, suffered another breach. Because unsecured Facebook personal databases were insufficiently protected by a cybersecurity firm called Upguard, more than 540 million records from Facebook users were exposed publicly on Amazon's cloud computing service.

In 2019, the US Federal Emergency Management Agency (FEMA) announced in a management alert that the confidential personal information of 2.3 million disaster victims of the 2017 California wildfires and hurricanes Harvey, Irma, and Maria had been exposed.[66]

In 2019, we saw growth in Artificial Intelligence (AI) and Machine Learning (ML) algorithms that have revolutionized the creation of believable audios and videos called 'deepfakes.' This technology provides the ability to trade one person's face for another in a video clip or image. Deepfake videos can make anyone do or say anything, and they are not easy to detect. The impact of this powerful technology can range from harmless parody to bullying and extortion of victims, and have enabled the creation of X-rated videos used in political attacks in major election campaigns. It becomes increasingly difficult to spot these fakes and persuade others that they are not credible. Thus, the power of Artificial Intelligence provides another weapon to the cybercriminal.

2.4 Cybercrime Categories

The Three Cybercrime Categories

Cybercrime may be organized into three categories: cybercrime against government, cybercrime committed against individuals, and cybercrime against property or a corporation. Each category has different goals and requires different methods to achieve these goals.

[64]"California Legislation Information-Assembly Bill No. 375, CHAPTER 55." Last modified November 23, 1995. Retrieved from https://leginfo.legislature.ca.gov/faces/billTextClient.xhtml?bill_id=201720180AB375

[65]Hammouchi, Hicham, Othmane Cherqi, Ghita Mezzour, Mounir Ghogho, and Mohammed El Koutbi. "Digging deeper into data breaches: An exploratory data analysis of hacking breaches over time." *Procedia Computer Science* 151 (2019): 1004–1009.

[66]"Management alert – FEMA did not safeguard disaster survivors' sensitive personally identifiable information." Office of Inspector General Department of Homeland Security. Last modified March 15, 2019. Retrieved from https://www.oig.dhs.gov/sites/default/files/assets/2019-03/OIG-19-32-Mar19.pdf; https://www.oig.dhs.gov/reports/2019/management-alert-fema-did-not-safeguard-disaster-survivors-sensitive-personally-identifiable-information-redacted/oig-19-32-mar19

- **Cybercrime against government:** Cybercrime against a government is an attack against a state or nation's sovereignty and is an attempt to limit its power. This act of terrorism is also called cyberwarfare.

  - Cybercrime against a government includes hacking into government, military, or defense contractors' websites, attacks against critical infrastructure, distribution of malware, denial-of-service (DoS and DDoS) attacks, and ransomware attacks. Additionally, it includes manipulation of social media platforms and the distribution of propaganda to influence people into the adoption of certain beliefs and attitudes.
  - Examples include Russian manipulation of social media platforms in the United States and Europe (U.S. presidential election of 2016,[67] and referenda Brexit),[68] as well as Chinese manipulation of news meant to undermine the Hong Kong protests.
  - State-sponsored intellectual property theft and cyber-enabled espionage evading U.S. laws. The use of copyrights, patents, or trade secrets, and trademarks without permission.
  - Examples include Chinese hackers acting on behalf of China's Ministry of State Security (MSS) to target aviation companies in Europe and U.S. aerospace companies, banking and finance, telecommunications, consumer electronics, medical equipment, and government agencies.[69] In 2018, the U.S. Justice Department announced criminal indictments of Chinese nationals in the Southern District of New York.[70]
- **Cybercrime against corporations or against property:** This type of cybercrime is characterized by unauthorized computer intrusion into the private information of any corporation or any property.

  - This includes unauthorized transfer, theft, or possession of data, use of a computer or network without permission, computer or network vandalism, and attacks using malicious software such as spyware, ransomware, malware, and key logger software.

---

[67] *Id.* at 41.

[68] Sunstein, Cass R. *# Republic: Divided democracy in the age of social media*. Princeton University Press, 2018.

[69] Inkster, Nigel. *China's Cyber Power*. Routledge, 2018.

[70] "US Justice Department announced criminal indictments in Southern District of New York." Last modified December 2018. Retrieved from https://www.documentcloud.org/documents/5638932-Chinese-economic-espionage-indictment.html#document/p1

- **Cybercrime committed against a person:** This category involves a computer-related crime that targets an individual.
  - This includes the use of malware, ransomware, hacking, spamming, phishing, identity theft, and online scams. It also includes extortion, cyberbullying, cyberstalking, cyber harassment through distribution of hateful or illegal information on the internet or social media, online libel or slander, sexting, and distribution of child pornography and other pornographic material (Figure 2.5).

Cybercriminals favor the most efficient methods, and those requiring the least effort. To understand this, let us look at the Crime-as-a-Service (CaaS) model. This criminal marketplace is located on the Dark Web, offering cybercriminals on-demand services such as password cracking, cloud cracking, distributed denial-of-service, and malware.[71] Both *SpyEye* and *Zeus malware* were available as on-demand services for anyone who could afford them, and cybercriminals Andreevich Panin and Hamza "Bx1" Bendelladj were able to customize the malware according to their own customers' needs.

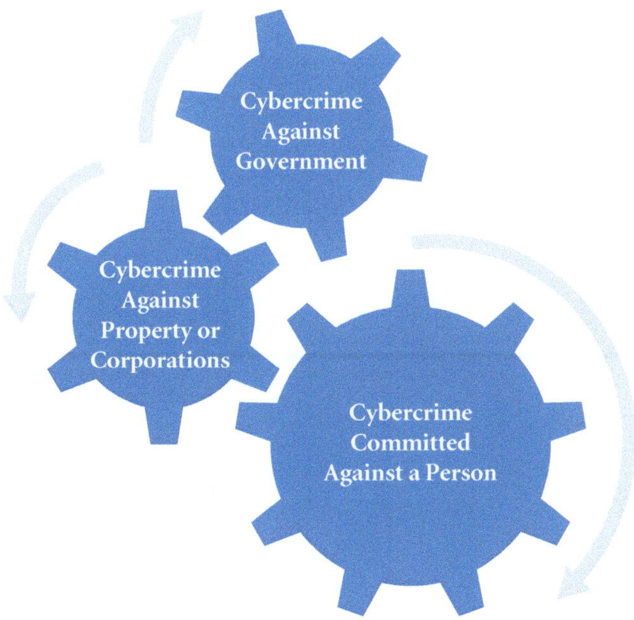

FIGURE 2.5 Cybercrime categories.

[71] Manky, Derek. "Cybercrime as a service: A very modern business." *Computer Fraud & Security* 2013, no. 6 (2013): 9–13.

CaaS provides services and products for anyone, including the non tech-savvy, to buy and use. A 2018 Internet Organized Crime Threat Assessment by Europol reports that cybercriminals and state sponsored actors all use the CaaS model.[72] The report also emphasizes that it is becoming increasingly difficult for law enforcement to distinguish among high-level cybercrime, state sponsored actors, and cybercrime amateurs who use tools they bought on the dark web.

The increasing presence of worldwide high-speed Internet makes people more likely to experience cybercrime as victims. The attackers may be from an organized crime group, a corporation engaged in espionage, participants in hacktivism, cyber warfare or cyberterrorism, or criminals looking for financial gain. While conventional crime is a social and economic occurrence, cybercrime is a business, and seeks financial success and quick profit. Thus, cybercrime encompasses economic enticements and methodically selected targets. Cybercriminals generate substantial revenues by selling, obstructing access, or holding data to ransom through the dark web. It fills needs, evolves, and adapts. You may be a victim of cybercrime without ever being aware that your data is being sold to a third party to meet that entity's goals.

Cybercrime is an inevitable consequence of our data-centric society. Proliferation of cybercrime is associated with the rapid expansion of the Internet, growth of broadband networks, and awareness of the ways in which our unprotected data may be used.

2.5 The Future of Cybercrime

The Making of the Cybercriminal

Like many of us, cybercriminals often belong to online forums, which facilitate peer-to-peer communication and the buying and selling of hacking tools and services. These activities take place in the Deep Web and the Dark Web.

The Surface Web (Visible Web or Indexed Web), which we know and use every day, does not contain all the content available online. Familiar Search engines like Google and Bing, can only retrieve content in the Surface Web.

Access to the Surface Web requires a direct query, or keywords. But it is exceedingly difficult to find information on the Deep Web since most of its contents are not indexed and will not be recognized by search engines.

The Deep Web is larger than the Surface Web, and is growing exponentially.[73,74] All emails, social media profiles, subscriptions, and all

[72] "Internet Organized Crime Threat Assessment by Europol (IOCTA 2018)." Last modified 2018. Retrieved from https://www.europol.europa.eu/internet-organised-crime-threat-assessment-2018

[73] Weimann, Gabriel. "Going dark: Terrorism on the dark web." *Studies in Conflict & Terrorism* 39, no. 3 (2016): 195–206.

[74] Bergman, Michael K. "White paper: The deep web: surfacing hidden value." *Journal of Electronic Publishing* 7, no. 1 (2001).

information for applications and PDF forms go to the Deep Web. In other words, the Deep Web holds all information that is not easily obtained or is invisible to the Surface Web.

The Dark Web is a portion of the Deep Web and contains content and sites that are purposely concealed and encrypted. It contains illegal activities such as child pornography, sensitive information, money laundering, copyright infringement, identity theft, illegal sales of weapons and other kinds of illegal sales. The Dark Web is accessed only by using specialized software like The Onion Router (TOR) or the Invisible Internet Project (I2P). The user must use encrypting software that masks his IP address, and makes him hard to identify. The most publicized site related to Dark Web is the Silk Road, an online black-market drug store selling everything from weed to heroin[75] (Figure 2.6).

Essentially, the Dark Web is an illicit marketplace providing services to terrorists, contract killers, human organ black market sellers, and other criminals. It flourishes because of its borderless nature. Its anonymity and speed serve illegal lucrative businesses around the world.

Small businesses are especially vulnerable to the Dark Web, since it provides data they cannot afford to buy; the full-scale Information Technology (IT) teams and secure networks of larger organizations are out of reach for them. These small businesses are also susceptible to the threat of

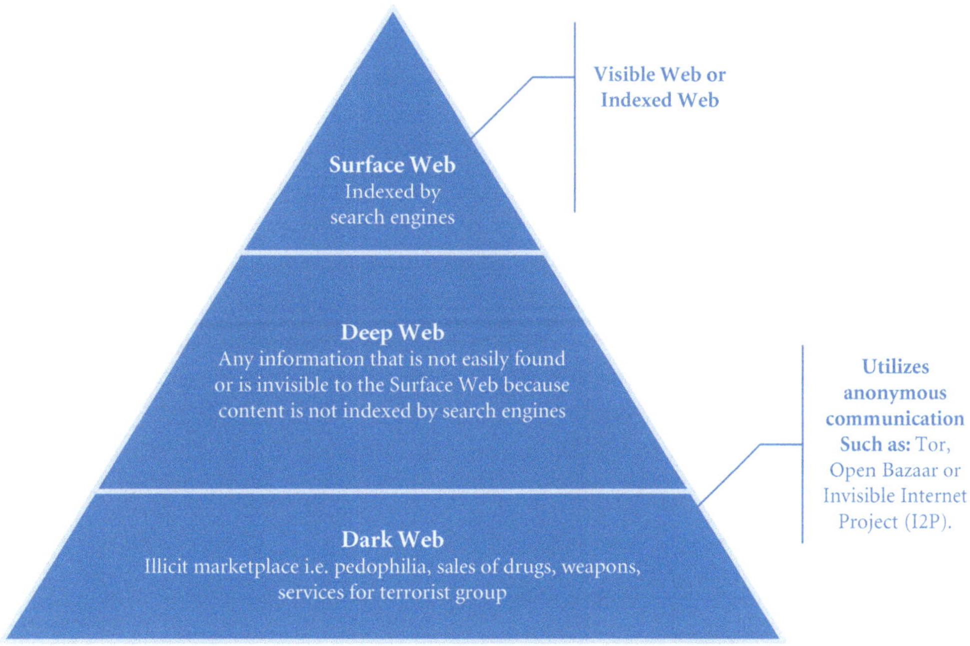

FIGURE 2.6 The Surface Web, Deep Web, and Dark Web.

[75] Bradbury, Danny. "Unveiling the dark web." *Network Security* 2014, no. 4 (2014): 14–17.

Ransomware.[76] Any business depends on its data to survive and flourish; the threat of losing this data makes it vulnerable to criminals using Ransomware. Larger businesses are more likely to refuse to negotiate with criminals, but the smaller targets feel they have no choice.

In general, cybercriminals prefer to hack smaller targets with smaller financial payouts rather than attack large enterprises. They use both simple and cutting-edge technologies to carry out their attacks and constantly seek new methods and techniques.

Cybercrime and the Internet of Things (IoT)

The IoT encompasses millions of computer-based devices that transmit data over the internet autonomously. These include smart home devices and automation products like smart thermostats, smart bulbs, smart TVs, and wearable sensors like heart rate and respiratory rate monitors. Due to technological advances, cheap data storage, and fast internet connections, the Internet of Things (IoT) is everywhere.

Protecting the devices comprising the IoT is a security nightmare. In 2018, The FBI warned that cyber criminals are now targeting IoT devices, looking to exploit their vulnerability and use them as a pathway to other attacks.[77]

The *Mirai* malware attack in 2016 targeted IoT devices, demonstrating the risks these devices faced.[78] IoT risk is expected to grow, consistently outperforming the security meant to protect them, especially with the introduction of fifth-generation cellular wireless (5G).

5G is the next generation of mobile broadband that will ultimately replace current 4G LTE connections. 5G has been developed with three major improvements: superior speed, lesser latency (the time it takes for data to go back and forth, and the ability to connect more IoT devices at once.[79] The growing number of devices will give rise to large cyber attacks, and we must remember that every device connected to the internet is always under threat of assault.

IoT devices make our lives better, more comfortable, and healthier, utilizing real-time monitoring, medical assistance, tracking and alerts. Consequently, cybercriminals will have access to more and more personal and medical information. Many IoT devices have being manufactured using unsecured communications protocols and open source codes, allowing anyone to use or modify a code or a program. Additionally, manufacturers often use and share code from

---

[76] Brewer, Ross. "Ransomware attacks: Detection, prevention and cure." *Network Security* 2016, no. 9 (2016): 5–9.

[77] "The Federal Bureau of Investigation—cyber actors use internet of things devices as proxies for anonymity and pursuit of malicious cyber activities" Last modified August 2, 2018. Retrieved from https://www.ic3.gov/media/2018/180802.aspx

[78] Lindqvist, Ulf, and Peter G. Neumann. "The future of the Internet of Things." *Communications of the ACM* 60, no. 2 (2017): 26–30.

[79] Al-Falahy, Naser, and Omar Y. Alani. "Technologies for 5G networks: Challenges and opportunities." *IT Professional* 19, no. 1 (2017): 12–20.

a single source across devices and multiple brands. As a result, many IoT devices have hard coded backdoor passwords built into them, meaning that anyone can type in the default password and gain access. In some cases, the password can be found on the internet (YouTube) or hacking forums.

Cybercriminals perform these attacks remotely and anonymously. Thus, the ability to impose ransomware thousands of miles away to owners of countless IoT devices is possible. Cybercriminals are constantly looking for ways to gain control of them via password cracking and exploiting additional vulnerabilities.

Cybercrime: Machine Learning and Artificial Intelligence

However, despite the threats already discussed, Machine Learning (ML) and Artificial Intelligence (AI) may be beneficial in the fight against cyberattacks. ML, a subdivision of AI, enables a computer to learn from experience and behave with a semblance of human-like intellect. This goal is still largely in the future. ML can improve cyber security by spotting abnormal activity patterns in an attack much faster than a human. Using deception as an automated response, AI can send decoys that deceive cyber-attackers, while still adapting to new situations, learning from them, and preventing future attacks. AI technologies can help analysts cope with the potential threats coming from IoT and other new technologies.

Nevertheless, Newton's third law reminds us that for every action, there is an equal and opposite reaction.[80] The more we apply machine intelligence to defend ourselves from cyberattacks, the more cybercriminals will learn to understand this technology, avoid detection and succeed in their attacks. Some examples: weaponized drones ("killer robots"), used to attack people, networks, and the adoption of machine learning algorithms to improve malware and ransomware.

Furthermore, AI can help cybercriminals analyze large volumes of data, create personalized emails or messages, and target specific people for propaganda and psychological warfare.

Google's TensorFlow[81] software enables criminals to deceive us as we view online videos. This software makes sophisticated video manipulation available to everyone. As machine learning improves, users will find it easier to edit and manipulate video and audio. Deepfake technology, created using TensorFlow, uses Google's image search feature to locate and then almost flawlessly replace faces in videos. The program does not need human supervision after the initial machine learning process; its algorithm works automatically to improve the process. Anyone can switch the faces in pornographic videos so that they feature celebrities, politicians, friends,

[80] Hellingman, Cornellis. "Newton's third law revisited." *Physics Education* 27, no. 2 (1992): 112.

[81] "An end-to-end open source machine learning platform." Google. Last modified May 2018. Retrieved from https://www.tensorflow.org/

and enemies. Individuals use the results for revenge porn, bullying, video evidence, political sabotage, propaganda, fake news video, and blackmail. The machine-learning algorithm may be used to blackmail those who now 'star' in these videos, and the videos can produce fake news, consisting of methodical disinformation and propaganda that distorts actual news and facts by replacing them with false images and information.

Machine Learning and Artificial Intelligence can be beneficial, but are also a major threat.

Online Child Sexual Abuse and Exploitation (CSAE)

Besides financial rewards, cybercriminals are enticed by cyberbullying, pedophilia, and sexual exploitation, and goals that are political and ideological. The internet has exponentially increased the production, distribution, and possession of child pornography images and child sexual abuse material (CSAM). The United States has addressed online child pornography with the Child Pornography Prevention Act of 1996 (CPPA)[82] and the PROTECT Act of 2003.[83] Furthermore, the Council of Europe (COE)[84] criminalized online activities related to child pornography and classified such behaviors as cybercrimes in its Convention on Cybercrime.

Many consider child sexual abuse and exploitation to be the most shocking aspect of cybercrime. Although this type of abuse occurred prior to the internet, its existence enables new methods and means of exploitation. The growing number of children who can access the internet and social media allows cybercriminals to connect with them as well as with adults.

Technologies like encryption enable offenders to hide their identity and avoid law enforcement. Faster internet speeds, lack of physical boundaries, cloud services around the world, and data encryption make detection exceedingly difficult. Since young social media users link self-esteem to 'likes' and 'dislikes' the promise of thousands of followers if they carry out offenders' requests is a powerful incentive. This allows criminals to use persuasion, temptation, or coercive methods to control the behavior of minors. According to the Internet Organized Crime Threat Assessment by Europol (IOCTA 2018),[85] Child Sexual Abuse and Exploitation (CSAE) will see continuous exponential growth on the internet, and for extreme material on the Dark Web.

Another form of CSAE is live streaming. This tool does not require storage of pornographic material and presents a limited forensic trail. Additionally,

---

[82] Child Pornography Prevention Act of 1996. Retrieved from https://www.congress.gov/bill/104th-congress/house-bill/4123

[83] Prosecutorial Remedies and Other Tools to End the Exploitation of Children Today Act of 2003 (PROTECT Act). Retrieved from https://www.congress.gov/bill/108th-congress/senate-bill/151/titles

[84] Council of Europe Convention on the Protection of Children against Sexual Exploitation and Sexual Abuse-CETS No.201. Last modified October 25, 2007. Retrieved from https://www.coe.int/en/web/conventions/full-list/-/conventions/treaty/201

[85] *Id.* at 72.

forensic investigations are very tricky when they involve crossing international borders and jurisdictions.

Cost of Cybercrime

According to *The Economist*, now that over 50% of the world population has access to the internet, the second half of the internet revolution has begun. "Most new users are in the emerging world; some 726 million people came online in the past three years alone. China is still growing fast. But much of the rise is coming from poorer places, notably India and Africa."[86] Online business and e-commerce around the world continue to boom in our digital world.

What is the financial cost of cybercrime? In 2014, cybercrime cost almost $500 billion; by 2018, the cost rose to $600 billion.[87] What about the nonfinancial costs to human suffering and freedom? Impossible to calculate.

A 2018 RAND Corporation report estimates that global cybercrime "has direct gross domestic product (GDP) costs of $275 billion to $6.6 trillion, and total GDP costs (direct plus systemic) of $799 billion to $22.5 trillion, representing 1.1 to 32.4 percent of GDP."[88] Worldwide, cybercrime is one of the largest and costliest types of crimes.

The Role of Cryptocurrency in Cybercrime

Cryptocurrency is an electronic monetary system or digital currency that uses cryptographic technology, permitting instantaneous and borderless transactions. The best-known cryptocurrency is Bitcoin, but there are many others. Financial institutions and governments have no jurisdiction or control over digital currency. Cryptocurrency uses public and private cryptography keys for privacy, security, and anonymity. Cryptocurrency crimes cannot be predicted or punished properly due to user anonymity and lack of oversight by government and financial regulators.

Cryptocurrency crimes include theft of money from financial exchanges, software that tracks secret keys for transactions, called electronic wallets, suspicious services and cryptocurrency Ponzi schemes. In addition, hackers can take over personal computers and other devices, or can infect a computer with crypto mining malware to stealthily mine cryptocurrencies.[89] Furthermore, cybercriminals use decentralized exchanges (DEX) to

---

[86] "The second half of humanity is joining the internet." *The Economist*. Last modified June 8, 2019. Retrieved from https://www.economist.com/leaders/2019/06/08/the-second-half-of-humanity-is-joining-the-internet

[87] Lewis, James. *McAfee report—Economic Impact of Cybercrime—No Slowing Down*. Last modified February, 2018. Retrieved from https://www.mcafee.com/enterprise/en-us/solutions/lp/economics-cybercrime.html

[88] Dreyer Paul, Jones Therese, Klima Kelly, Oberholtzer Jenny, Strong Aaron, Welburn William Jonathan, Winkelman Zev. *Estimating the global cost of cyber risk calculator*. RAND Corporation, 2018. Last modified January 15, 2018. Retrieved from https://www.rand.org/pubs/tools/TL281.html

[89] *Id.* at 72.

launder currency with peer-to-peer trading of cryptocurrencies without a third-party service to hold the customer's funds.[90]

Cybercriminals have been buying and selling cryptocurrencies anonymously at peer-to-peer markets like Dream Market, The Wall Street Market and AlphaBay. Cryptocurrency laundering occurs when an offender uses electronic money, video game currency and digital payment systems to convert illegally obtained funds to clean funds. These currencies have become the preferred tools criminals use for money laundering for the following reasons:

- **Anonymity, security and privacy:** (no real name required for transactions; criminals can remain unknown)
- **Lack of universal regulations:** (regulation of cryptocurrency varies around the world; little or no oversight by government regulators)
- **No financial institutions or government control:** (not governed by any central authority and not monitored)
- **Tax evasion**
- **Transportation:** (no detection across international borders, no monitoring from banking institutions)
- **Speed:** (quick processing of cryptocurrency into cash)

The growing criminal use of cryptocurrency is creating problems for the global financial system and governments (Figure 2.7). Criminals hide their money trails and confuse law enforcement agencies by converting stolen income into video game currency or virtual goods. Virtual goods include gaming merchandise like weapons for a specific game, clothing, or other items that a player needs. The criminals then transform these items into cryptocurrencies or property purchases like Bitcoin Real Estate. Some of the most popular video games for cryptocurrency laundering are Minecraft, FIFA, Final Fantasy, Star Wars Online, and Warcraft. Virtual goods can be purchased at online games sites, cell phone apps, and games on social media. According to the Cipher Trace Cryptocurrency Anti-Money Laundering Report, crime in the cryptocurrency sector in 2018 reached $1.7 billion USD. In the first quarter of 2019, theft of cryptocurrencies from exchanges and infrastructure frauds came to more than $356 million USD.[91] In addition, the New York State Attorney General's Office revealed that the cryptocurrency exchange "Bitfinex," which also controls the "tether" virtual currency, has engaged in a cover-up to hide the apparent loss of $850 million USD.[92]

[90] Ponsford, Matthew P. "A comparative analysis of Bitcoin and other decentralised virtual currencies: Legal regulation in the people's republic of China, Canada, and the United States." *Hong Kong Journal of Legal Studies* 9 (2015): 29.

[91] CipherTrace. "Cryptocurrency anti-Money laundering report, 2019." Last modified April 2019. Retrieved from https://ciphertrace.com/wp-content/uploads/2019/05/ciphertrace-q1-2019-cryptocurrency-anti-money-laundering-report.pdf

[92] Lelitia James, NY Attorney General. "Attorney General James announces court order against 'crypto' currency company under investigation for fraud." Last modified April 25, 2019. Retrieved from https://ag.ny.gov/press-release/attorney-general-james-announces-court-order-against-crypto-currency-company-under

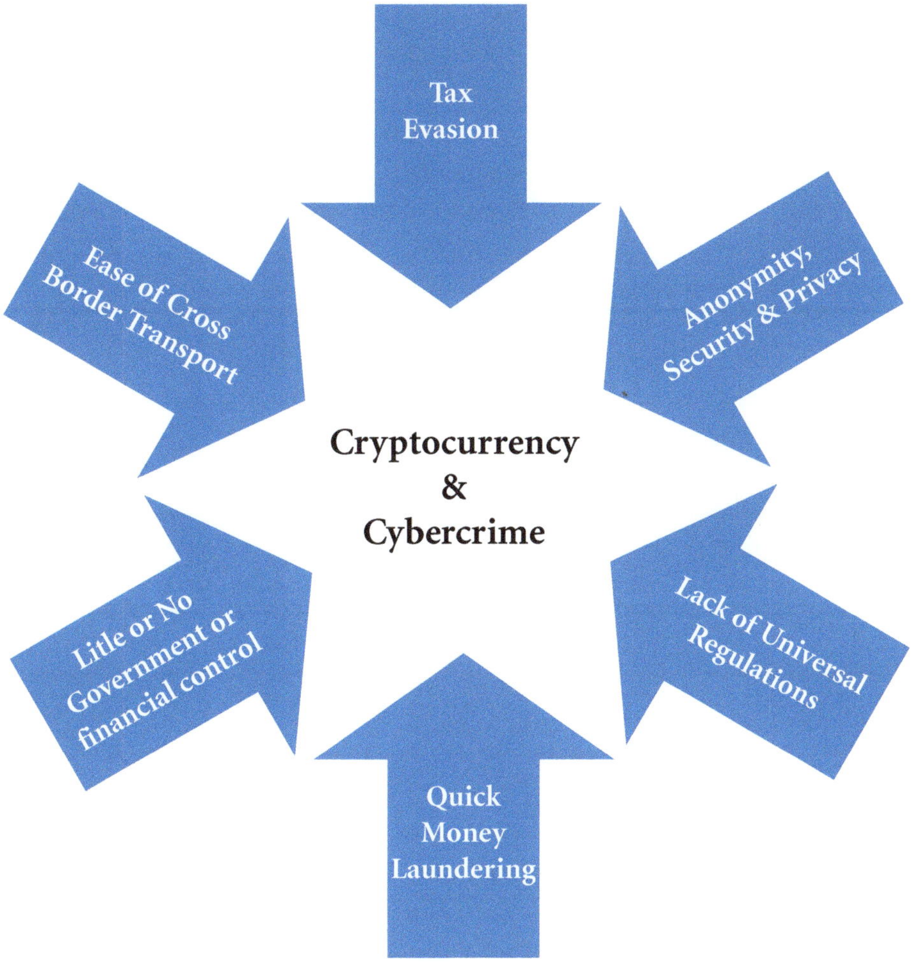

FIGURE 2.7 Cybercrime and Money Laundering.

State-Sponsored Cyberwarfare and Industrial Espionage

The present phase of cybercrime (Phase IV) is characterized by state-sponsored cyber warfare, particularly attacks on Western nations.[93]

State-sponsored hackers target countries and their citizens by using ransomware, data theft, critical infrastructure attacks (electricity, gas, and water supply systems) and social media manipulation with trolls, bots, and fake news.

This cyber warfare is an operation with specific objectives, undertaken by one nation attacking another. Special military units are dedicated to cyber warfare, such as the Chinese "PLA Unit 61398" or Russia's "Information Countermeasures" or IPb (informatsionnoye protivoborstvo). In addition, intelligence agencies around the world pay hackers to keep the breach secret. As a result, cyberwarfare actors receive funding, technical support, and

[93] Lawson, Sean, and Michael K. Middleton. "Cyber Pearl Harbor: Analogy, fear, and the framing of cyber security threats in the United States, 1991–2016." *First Monday* 24, no. 3 (2019).

equipment from a country's intelligence or military agencies to execute the attack. The operation consists of psychological warfare, containing propaganda messages and espionage.

Cyberwarfare continues to be an effective weapon in political conflicts around the world. The 2015 attack on Ukraine's power grid,[94] Russia's attacks on the 2016 U.S. presidential election,[95] and the 2017 ransomware on UK health system are powerful examples.[96]

The usual suspects in cyber attacks on Western countries are China, Iran, North Korea, and Russia. We know that Russia interfered with the American presidential election in 2016, and that North Korea and China have both been accused of cyber espionage.[97] However, on the other side of the political spectrum, *Stuxnet*, the malicious computer worm developed by American/Israeli intelligence agencies, targeted the development of the Iranian nuclear warfare systems.[98]

2.6 Conclusion

Cybercrime is persistent and will not stop any time soon. Motivations for cybercrime include:

- **Cybercrime as a business:** Financial motives are appealing and are frequently easy to achieve. The increased number of unsuspected new users, the growth of Cybercrime-as-a-Service and the vast amount of data give cybercriminals access to power and wealth.
- **Hard to prosecute cybercriminals:** Jurisdiction is the biggest barrier in the prosecution of cybercriminals. When the cybercriminal committing a crime is located outside of the jurisdiction, the likelihood of being apprehended is low.
- **Politically motivated:** Hacktivists can carry out cyber attacks and hate crimes, spreading propaganda, making political statements and protests, destruction, and retaliatory actions.
- **Script kiddies[99] or amateurs:** Individuals who use tools and instructions that are easily found online. Assumed to be juveniles who lack the ability to write complex programs or exploits, their main objectives are to impress their friends, curiosity, enjoyment of a challenge, or trying to enter a professional hacking group.

---

[94] Kostyuk, Nadiya, and Yuri M. Zhukov. "Invisible digital front: Can cyber attacks shape battlefield events?." *Journal of Conflict Resolution* 63, no. 2 (2019): 317–347.

[95] *Id.* at 93.

[96] *Id.* at 60.

[97] Hjortdal, Magnus. "China's use of cyber warfare: Espionage meets strategic deterrence." *Journal of Strategic Security* 4, no. 2 (2011): 1–24.

[98] Farwell, James P., and Rafal Rohozinski. "Stuxnet and the future of cyber war." *Survival* 53, no. 1 (2011): 23–40.

[99] Shachaf, Pnina, and Noriko Hara. "Beyond vandalism: Wikipedia trolls." *Journal of Information Science* 36, no. 3 (2010): 357–370.

- **Cyberwarfare and industrial espionage:** Goals include sabotage, controlling critical infrastructure, developing biases, influencing behavior, and creating political unrest.

Today, we are all experiencing the most dangerous type of cybercrime, with corporations and social media platforms selling our private information, and foreign powers manipulating data to influence public perception. Data, targeted emails, and Facebook posts containing lies, can manipulate recipients maliciously, and can only be described as weapons. Unfortunately, most people do not recognize or understand this threat. Most people can be manipulated and made to believe just about anything. Western democracies have been disrupted by lies, manipulation, and corporate greed.

As cybercrime has increased it has gone far beyond identity theft or a worm in a computer. It has evolved and is now a pandemic that threatens our way of life.

2.7 Key Words

Cybercrime:
- evolution, motivations and phases,
- categories,
- Hacking,

Cybercrime weapons:
- Crime-as-a-Service (CaaS)
- State-Sponsored Cyberwarfare and Industrial Espionage
- Cyberbullying or Cyber Harassment
- Denial of service (DoS)
- Fraud and financial crime
- Identity theft
- Malware
- Phishing
- Ransomware
- Spam

Viruses
Worms
Internet of Things (IoT)
Cybercrime
Machine Learning and Artificial Intelligence
Online Child Sexual Abuse and Exploitation
Cost of Cybercrime
Role of Cryptocurrency in Cybercrime
Cybercrime and Money Laundering
Surface Web
Deep Web & Dark Web
Deepfake, Fake news

Chapter 3

Understanding the U.S. Legal System

Objectives

After completing this chapter, the student will be able to:

- Understand the main barriers to prosecuting cybercriminals.
- Understand the legal system in the United States.
- Distinguish among types of laws.

3.1 Introduction

Gathering information for a criminal case is a laborious and rarely accurate process. As people produce more and more searchable data, our understanding of how and why crimes are committed has changed.

Smartphones can log our daily routines, and by giving them permission to track our every move they can pinpoint our exact location. Apps record our psychographic information (personality, values, attitudes, interests, and lifestyles), and other apps use this information to reveal our preferences and political views. As more Internet of Things (IoT) devices and their apps become networked, information about the people who own them will grow significantly. To track a criminal's movements, conversations, and behavior, we can by-pass a smartphone's encryption and security and access its metadata.

DOI: 10.4324/9780429318726-3

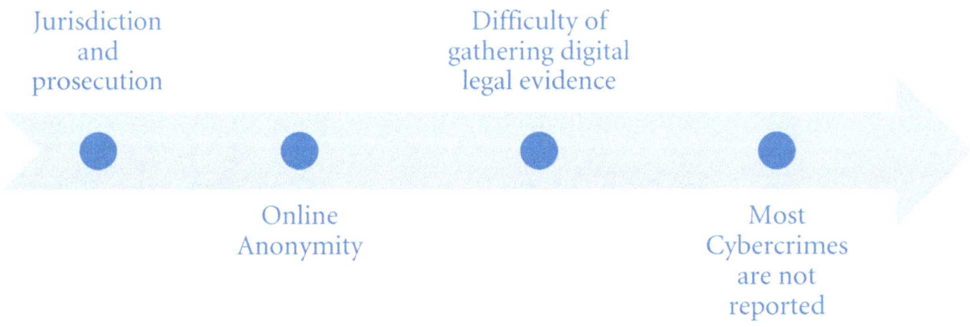

FIGURE 3.1 Barriers to prosecuting cybercriminals.

In response, privacy laws are changing around the world, since previous laws were written during the coin-operated public telephone era. Crime scene investigation in the past was about fingerprints; today it is about our digital footprints. Smartphones, cloud computing, jurisdiction, and IoT devices are making things ever more complex.

The four main barriers to prosecuting cybercriminals are: *Jurisdiction over prosecution*, *Anonymity*, *Difficulty of gathering digital legal evidence*, and *the fact that most cybercrimes are not reported* (Figure 3.1).

I. Jurisdiction and Extradition

Jurisdiction over cybercrime and prosecution of the cybercriminal is incredibly challenging, involving multiple countries and regions around the world, and the difficulty of providing the court with authority to exercise jurisdiction over these matters.

Law enforcement bureaus around the world have dedicated special divisions to combating cybercrime. But where does the crime occur – in the country where the cybercriminal operates, or in the country where the victim resides? Unfortunately, it is difficult if not impossible to successfully prosecute cybercriminals when they reside outside of the country and are therefore outside the legal jurisdiction of a court.

Can the accused criminal be brought to the country where the victim lives? Extradition is a process that occurs when a state or nation sends an accused or convicted individual to another jurisdiction for prosecution.[1] Even when the United States can identify and locate a cybercriminal and collect all the necessary evidence, many countries will never honor warrants of extradition because the United States does not have extradition treaties

1 Sadoff, David A. *Bringing international fugitives to justice: Extradition and its alternatives*. Cambridge University Press, 2016.

with them. Countries like China, Iran, North Korea, and Russia actively target the U.S. government, its allies, and businesses, by launching cyber-attacks against critical infrastructure, conducting espionage, and influencing individuals' opinions and behaviors.[2]

In addition, laws differ from state to state and nation to nation. A criminal act that violates a law in one place may not be illegal in another. Law enforcement agencies can only enforce the law within their jurisdiction. The police department in New York has no authority to arrest someone in Florida, and the Federal Bureau of Investigation can't arrest someone in France, with infrequent exceptions.

Similarly, the laws of extradition vary from nation to nation. According to international law, a nation has no responsibility to turn over a criminal to the requesting body or nation unless both nations have signed a treaty. In some cases, nations grant extradition without a treaty; in other cases, even with a treaty, extradition is a time-consuming process, often taking years.[3,4] At this time, cybercriminals from China, North Korea, Iran, and Russia will not be extradited to the United States for arrest and trial.

II. Online Anonymity

Online anonymity is a complex topic. Some argue that anonymity is a sign of free speech and expression, and is a right belonging to every citizen, according to the First Amendment of the U.S. Constitution. Second, some believe that no website should ever be permitted to track their online behavior, citing the right to anonymity and privacy.

To protect themselves, many people, both criminals and law-abiding citizens, use Virtual Private Networks (VPNs). These allow the user to create a secure connection to another network over the Internet, thereby reducing their digital footprint and providing a greater degree of anonymity. However, there are financial costs associated with VPNs, and some will sacrifice their anonymity and privacy for convenience and less expense.

Finally, anonymity is precious to cybercriminals, allowing their illegal efforts to thrive.[5] When law enforcement makes efforts to track online

---

[2] Coats, Daniel R. "Worldwide Threat Assessment." *Testimony, Washington, DC*, May 23 (2017): 428610-1.

[3] Kofele-Kale, Ndiva. *The international law of responsibility for economic crimes: Holding state officials individually liable for acts of fraudulent enrichment*. Routledge, 2016

[4] Miquelon-Weismann, Miriam F. "The convention on cybercrime: a harmonized implementation of international penal law: what prospects for procedural due process?." In *Computer Crime*, pp. 171–204. Routledge, 2017.

[5] Jardine, Eric. "The Dark Web dilemma: Tor, anonymity and online policing." *Global Commission on Internet Governance Paper Series* 21 (2015).

identity or to access encrypted or locked computing devices, not only are privacy issues raised, but the agency may also feel political backlash. In summation, cybercriminals exploit the privileges of a free and open society.

III. Digital Evidence

Digital evidence is volatile and fragile. Improper handling of this evidence can taint or misplace it. Inexperienced forensic investigators may further exacerbate these difficulties. Digital evidence is more complex than physical evidence because it is not easy to touch, see, or photograph, and any improper handling can make the evidence inadmissible in court. Keeping the integrity of digital evidence and maintaining its chain of custody (the chronological documentation of ownership) is always critical.

The forensic investigator must obtain possession of the evidence with a proper warrant. In some cases, the owner of a computer must voluntarily provide access to the data; in other cases, a proper subpoena must be in place. In child pornography, it can be very difficult to prove which individual downloaded the illegal material. Likewise, as hacking attacks have become more common, a defendant can claim that someone else installed illegal material on their computer without their permission or knowledge. Another difficulty may be the reliability of the evidence, and whether the tools and processes used by the forensic investigator meet the standards for admissible evidence. It is not unheard of for innocent persons to be convicted because of false digital evidence.

Computer forensics investigation is still in its infancy and requires broad universal scientific standards and tools. The enormous amount of data saved in every computing device, along with what may have been stored in the cloud, presents significant challenges. For example, if the cloud that hosts certain data has servers in several different countries, more than one country may have concurrent jurisdiction over the data.

IV. Most Cybercrimes Are not Reported

Most cybercrimes against individuals are not reported because of *humiliation*, and the perception that *law enforcement won't be able to help*, especially if the cybercriminal is in a different country. Unfortunately, law enforcement agencies around the globe are rarely sure how many cybercrimes have been committed, particularly when they don't have the weapons to pursue the cybercriminals and stop the crime.

Corporations also report cybercrime infrequently, unless required by law to report a cybercrime involving personal or medical information under the Health Insurance Portability and Accountability Act of 1996 (HIPAA) in the United States, or the Personal Information Protection and Electronic Documents Act (PIPEDA) in Canada. Companies in the EU are under the General Data Protection Regulation (EU) 2016/679 (GDPR), are ahead of most of the world in these matters, and are legally obliged to notify the Information Commissioner's Office (ICO) of any personal data breach.

If not obligated, companies will usually not report a cybercrime, preferring to handle it internally. Why? The answer involves the time and expense involved, and the probability of further disruption of business, but also the damage to the reputation and perceived vulnerability of the company. When companies are attacked and ransom is demanded, the perception is that a criminal investigation is unlikely to help recover money or data, or to prevent future incidents. In many cases companies choose to pay the ransom. Of course, paying a ransom does not guarantee that data will be returned, or a promised decryption key will be delivered. And, since the cybercriminals now possess the stolen data, they may turn and sell them after payment has been made.

3.2 A Brief Overview of the Legal System in the United States

According to Aristotle's *Politics (350 B.C.E.)* man, when perfected, is the best of animals, but, when separated from law and justice, he is the worst of all.[6] The figure below shows the main sources of law in the United States (Figure 3.2).

In the United States the main categories of law are *Constitutional, Statutory and Agency Regulations, Judicial Decisions or Case law,* and *Administrative law.*

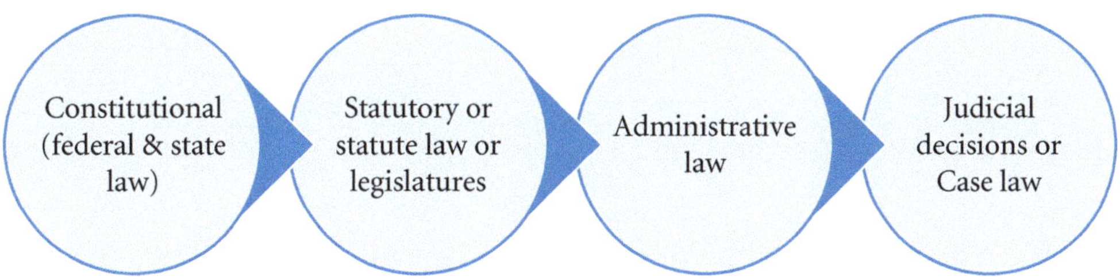

FIGURE 3.2 A basic guide to the main sources of law in the United States.

[6] Jowett, Benjamin. *Politics by Aristotle (Written 350 B.C.E).* Indo-European Publishing, 2012.

I. The Constitution

The U.S. Constitution,[7] ratified in 1789, is the highest law of the land. It is unique because it is a self-limiting document. The Tenth Amendment specifically limits the federal government's powers to those enlisted in the Constitution and reserves the rest to the States and/or the people themselves. To this extent, state laws are even more important in some arenas. Since one of those areas is law enforcement, it's not clear which is "higher" law – the federal or the state constitution for some of these cybercrime cases. An example would be a cyberbullying case between two children who live in the same state and have a local network provider. Federal issues of First Amendment speech are implicated, but so are state- and even local-level laws regarding harassment and stalking.

In addition to the Constitution, each of the 50 states has its own constitution. The U.S. Constitution specifies the powers and duties of the government and guarantees specific rights to the people. It is considered a living document, since it can evolve and be amended over time.

The Constitution is separated into three sections; Preamble, Articles I through VII, and 27 Amendments. The first section, the Preamble, describes the intent and purpose of the Constitution(Figure 3.3).

> We the People of the United States, in Order to form a more perfect Union, establish Justice, insure domestic Tranquility, provide for the common defense, promote the general Welfare, and secure the Blessings of Liberty to ourselves and our Posterity, do ordain and establish this Constitution for the United States of America.[8]

The second section consists of seven Articles. They determine how the government is organized and how the Constitution may be revised. The final section lists the 27 Amendments to the Constitution. The first 10 amendments are known collectively as the Bill of Rights. It is the federal courts that interpret and evaluate the constitutionality of both federal and state laws.

> This Constitution, and the Laws of the United States which shall be made in Pursuance thereof; and all Treaties made, or which shall be made, under the

FIGURE 3.3 The Constitution of the United States (1791). Photograph from the National Archives and Records Administration (NARA).

[7] "United States Senate," Constitution of the United States, https://www.senate.gov/civics/constitution_item/constitution.htm

[8] U.S. Constitution, pmbl.

FIGURE 3.4 **The U.S. Const. Art. VI, Clause 2. Photograph from the National Archives and Records Administration (NARA).**

Authority of the United States, shall be the supreme Law of the Land; and the Judges in every State shall be bound thereby, any Thing in the Constitution or Laws of any State to the Contrary notwithstanding.[9] (Figure 3.4).

II. Statutory or Statute Law

Statutory or Statute Law consists of laws ratified by a legislative body. Because the Supremacy clause in Article VI of the constitution mandates that federal law is the highest form of law in the judicial system, a statute from any state cannot supersede federal law. When a bill is passed by the Congress and signed by the President, it becomes a Public Law (Pub.L.). When there is a conflict between state and federal laws, judges are required to follow federal law.

Most laws passed by Congress are public laws. The first full version of public and private laws, also known as *slip laws*, consists of the entire bill as it was passed by both legislative houses and signed by the President.

Public laws influence issues that affect the general population or society. Because identical versions of public laws must pass each legislative chamber and be signed by the President, the process of negotiation between the Senate and the House of Representatives can lead to public laws that address disparate subject matters.

Private laws, on the other hand, influence the rights and responsibilities of specifically identified individuals, families, businesses, or small groups. For example, if the government wants to grant citizenship to an individual who would be ineligible based on applicable immigration law, that measure would be passed as a private law. See, e.g., Private Law 112-1 (Dec. 28, 2012).[10]

When a Public law is enacted, the legislature assigns it a specific number. This number includes the session of Congress in which it was passed. For example, Pub. L. 116-7 is the seventh law enacted during the 116th Congress. They are collected and codified in the Office of the Law Revision Counsel of the United States House of Representatives (OLRC).[11] OLRC is responsible for placing – and

[9] U.S. Const. Art. VI, Clause 2.

[10] Private Law 112-1—An act for the relief of Sopuruchi Chukwueke. Retrieved from https://www.congress.gov/112/plaws/pvtl1/PLAW-112pvtl1.pdf

[11] "Office of the Law Revision Counsel of the United States House of Representatives," United States Code, last modified August 23, 2019, http://uscode.house.gov.

sometimes breaking up – Public Laws so that they can be incorporated into the sections of the federal laws that address the appropriate subject matter(s).

The U.S. Code contains the federal laws of the United States arranged into *54 broad titles*, according to subject matter.[12] Each title of the Code is subdivided into subtitles, chapters, subchapters, parts, subparts, and sections. Sections are frequently subdivided into subsections, paragraphs, subparagraphs, clauses, subclauses, and items. The closely-related U.S. Code Annotated (U.S.C.) includes statutory descriptions that provide more information, displayed as statutory notes, such as references to related provisions in the Constitution, federal court rulings, and Presidential documents, such as Executive orders, and proclamations.[13]

For example, **18 U.S. Code § 1030 (a)(3)** may be understood as follows:

- Title **18 of the U.S. Code** is the principal criminal code of the federal government for crime and criminal procedures.
- In Title 18, Chapter 47 covers Fraud and false statements (18 USC Ch. 47: FRAUD AND FALSE STATEMENTS),[14]
- § **1030** is the section covering Fraud and related activity in connection with computers. This refers to the Computer Fraud and Abuse Act (CFAA), which outlaws conduct that victimizes computer systems.
- Paragraph (a)(3) condemns unauthorized intrusion ("hacking") into federal government computers.

The section sign § is a typographical symbol that refers to a reference in a particular section of a document in the legal code. It is also called the *double S* or the *sectional symbol or sign*. In Latin this is known as *signum sectionis*, meaning section symbol(Figure 3.5).

When Congress passes laws, it can codify standards or delegate the codification of standards, indicating which federal agencies implement, manage, and evaluate statutorily-authorized programs. The U.S. Code system (U.S.C.), described above, is a codification system for federal laws, while the Code of Federal Regulations (C.F.R.) codifies permanent rules issued by the departments and agencies of the federal government. The CFR is also split by subject matter. It contains *50 titles* that represent wide-ranging areas and subjects of federal regulation.[15]

---

[12] *Id.* at 11.

[13] "Office of the Law Revision Counsel of the United States House of Representatives," Detailed Guide to the United States Code Content and Features United States Code, last modified August 23, 2019, https://uscode.house.gov/detailed_guide.xhtml

[14] "Office of the Law Revision Counsel of the United States House of Representatives, Title 18/Part I/Chapter 47—Fraud and False Statements, United States Code, last modified August 23, 2019, https://uscode.house.gov/view.xhtml?path=/prelim@title18/part1/chapter47&edition=prelim

[15] Electronic Code of Federal Regulations. Retrieved from https://www.ecfr.gov/cgi-bin/ECFR?page=browse

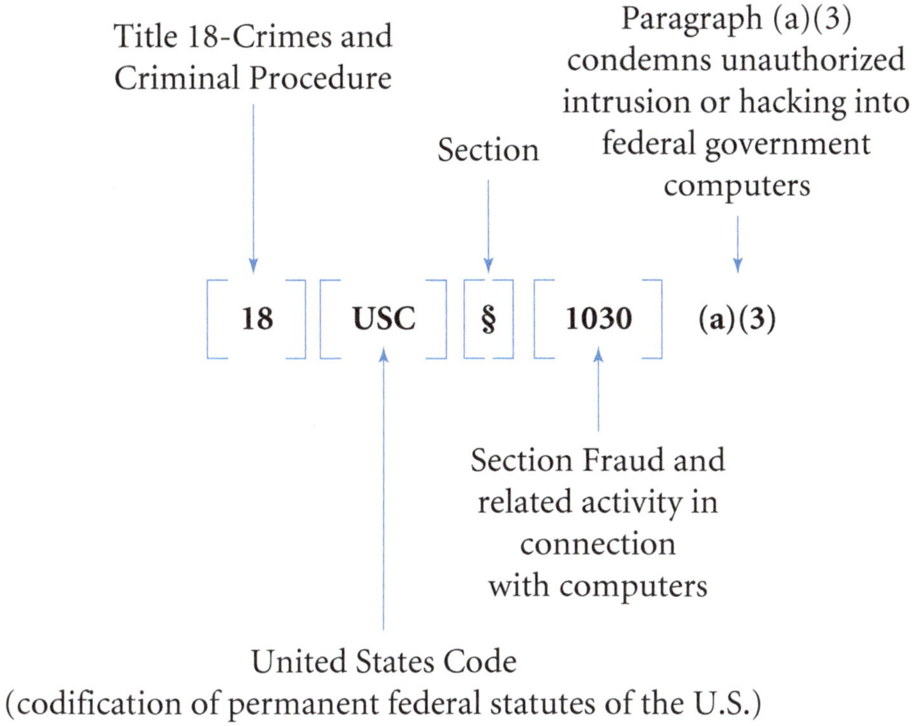

FIGURE 3.5 **Understanding a Statute Citation.**

III. Administrative Laws (Agency Regulations) and Ordinance Law

Administrative laws are also known as Agency Regulations. Ordinance Laws are considered local. Administrative Regulations are crafted by administrative agencies of federal and state governments. Administrative law is supposed to be enacted by "experts" in a certain field rather than elected representatives. Federal administrative agencies ratify, enforce, and sometimes even judge these violations. For example, the Food and Drug Administration (FDA), an agency within the U.S. Department of Health and Human Services (HHS), is authorized to pursue both civil and criminal actions, during which they can seize and regulate foods, human and veterinary drugs, vaccines, medical devices intended for human use, radiation-emitting electronic products, cosmetics, dietary supplements, and tobacco products. The FDA does not regulate meat, poultry, and egg products, which are regulated by the U.S. Department of Agriculture (USDA). The USDA can authorize both civil and criminal remedies for violations. Administrative agencies interpret laws and apply their own guidelines and standards to enforce them.

An *Ordinance* is a law passed by the governing body of a municipality like a city or county. These governing bodies include city and county councils, boards of supervisors, and county commissions. Ordinances govern matters that do not conflict with state or federal laws. Some examples of ordinance law are safety, and city zoning and building regulations, which regulate construction and repair of damaged buildings.

Finally, chief executives (the President and the Governors) can issue executive orders that have the effect of law.

IV. Judicial Decisions or Precedents or Case Law

This type of law originates from English *Common Law*, where precedents and authority are set by previous court rulings. Case law is created when judges follow the judicial decisions made by court rulings in a prior case. Case law is used by lower courts and judges to identify which law applies to a dispute, to establish criminal procedure, or to create a criminal defense for a crime. In 49 states, laws are largely derived from English Common Law, but in Louisiana, laws are based on the French Civil Code.

In the United States, laws are ratified, explained, and enforced by the federal, state, and local levels of government. The hierarchy of the laws of the United States is:

- U.S. Constitution
- Laws enacted by U.S Congress
- Agency regulations by federal agencies
- State Constitutions
- Laws ratified by a State Legislation
- Rules and regulations by State Agencies
- Ordinances (city or county)
- Rules and regulations by Local or City agencies.

3.2.1 The Courts System

The Judicial system is classified by a hierarchical structure at both state and federal levels. federal and state governments, along with U.S. territories, have separate court systems. For the most part, each has *District* courts, *Appeals* courts, and *Supreme* courts, in addition to various courts at local levels, for example traffic court.

Federal jurisdiction consists of U.S. District Courts and U.S. Courts of Appeals or Circuit Courts, which are the first level of appeal, and finally the U.S. Supreme Court, the final level of appeal. Although Article III of the U.S. Constitution requires the establishment of District Courts, these were established pursuant to the Judiciary Act of 1789. U.S. District Courts handle civil and criminal trials within the federal court system. These 94 district or trial courts are organized in 12 regional circuits.

The U.S Appeals Court consists of 13 appellate courts. These courts oversee civil and criminal cases inside clear geographic or subject areas. Federal Courts function differently than State courts.

Federal courts hear only cases authorized by the U.S. Constitution or federal statutes. The federal government can prosecute criminal offenses only in federal courts, and the States must bring criminal prosecutions only in State courts. In addition, according to the Fifth Amendment to the U.S. Constitution, the legal term *Double Jeopardy* means that a defendant cannot be prosecuted twice for the same or similar charges.

> No person shall be held to answer for a capital, or otherwise infamous crime, unless on a presentment or indictment of a Grand Jury, except in cases arising in the land or naval forces, or in the Militia, when in actual service in time of War or public danger; nor shall any person be subject for the same offence to be twice put in jeopardy of life or limb; nor shall be compelled in any criminal case to be a witness against himself, nor be deprived of life, liberty, or property, without due process of law; nor shall private property be taken for public use, without just compensation. (U.S. Const. amend. V (1791); see Figure 3.6).

Nonetheless, Double Jeopardy is not reciprocal between federal and state governments. The federal government can bring its own prosecution if the defendant violated both state and federal laws; if a state brings charges and does not win a conviction, the federal government may file charges against the defendant if the act is also illegal under federal law. Furthermore, double jeopardy applies only to criminal cases, not civil cases. In the Supreme Court case *Gamble v. United States*, 139 S. Ct. 1960; 204 L. Ed. 2d 322, 587 U. S. ____ (2019), the court held that under the Dual-Sovereignty Doctrine, both state and federal courts may prosecute an individual without violating Double Jeopardy. Thus, a state may prosecute a defendant under state law even though the federal government has prosecuted the defendant for the same conduct under federal law. Justice Alito wrote in the majority opinion that "Under this 'dual-sovereignty' doctrine, a State may prosecute a defendant under State law even if the Federal Government has prosecuted him for the same conduct under a Federal statute. Or, the reverse may happen, as it did here."[16]

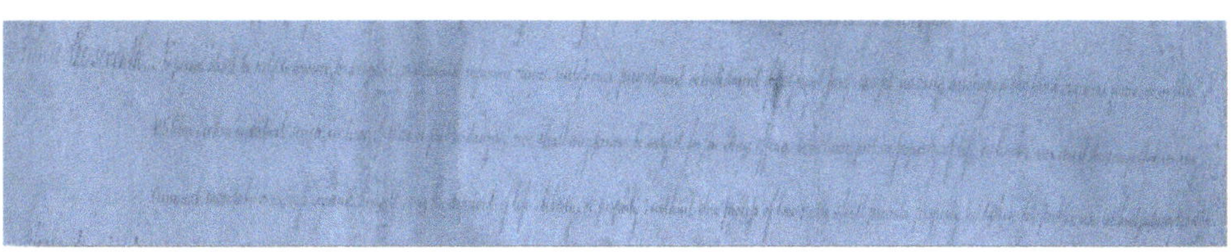

FIGURE 3.6 The U.S. Const. amend. V (1791). Photograph from the National Archives and Records Administration (NARA).

[16] "Supreme Court of the United Stated," *Gamble v. United States*, https://www.supremecourt.gov/search.aspx?Search=Gamble+v.+United+States&type=Site https://www.supremecourt.gov/opinions/18pdf/17-646_new2_1an2.pdf

The Supreme Court has the discretion to choose the cases it will hear, and not all cases are heard. When most of the justices vote to hear a case, this is called *granting certiorari*, often condensed to *cert*.

The Supreme Court hears appeals from the U.S. Courts of Appeals or Circuit Courts, as well as U.S. military courts and State Supreme Courts on decisions involving the U.S. Constitution or federal laws and regulations. Because the U.S. Supreme Court is the highest court in the federal court system, once the Supreme Court hands down a decision it is final. The Supreme Court's decision is considered a binding precedent on all lower courts.

Supreme Court justices and justices of the lower federal courts are appointed by the President and must be confirmed by the U.S. Senate. They usually hold their positions for life. According to U.S. Const. art. III, § 1, "The Judges, both of the supreme and inferior Courts, shall hold their Offices during good Behaviour." Figure 3.7 displays the three-part structure of the federal court system.

For most states, the judicial system consists of State Trial courts, State Appellate courts, and State Supreme courts. Cases begin in the Trial courts, and the plaintiff and defendant present evidence to prove the facts in a case. A jury of citizens sworn to listen to the facts and make decisions, brings in the verdict.

The trial courts and federal district courts are the only courts that use the Jury system. Although there are codified rules governing the admissibility of evidence, District court judges, can determine what evidence may be used. These courts follow constitutional and legal precedents set by higher courts like Appeals and Supreme courts.

If a defendant considers the verdict unfair, the case may be appealed, and it is sent to the appropriate Appellate court, usually called the Appeals court.

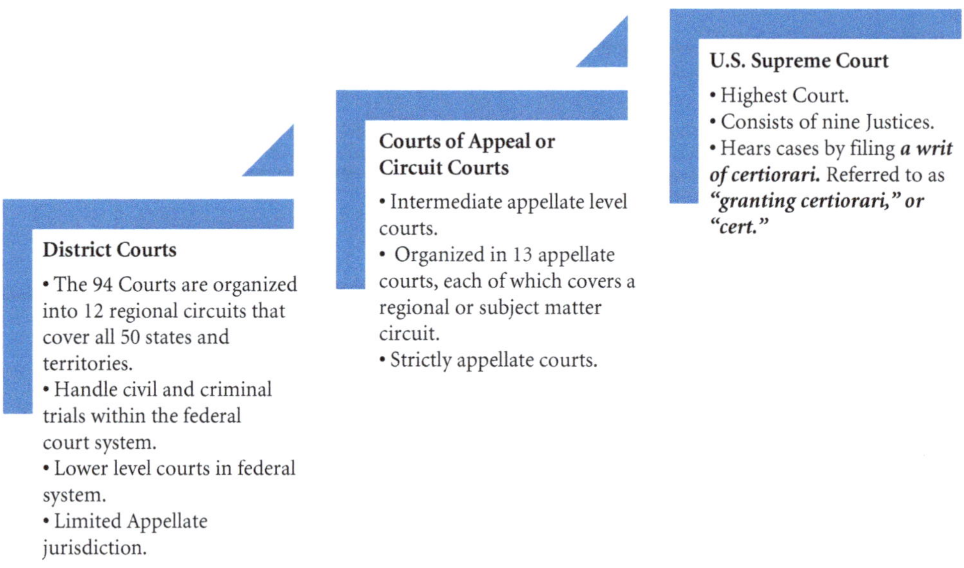

FIGURE 3.7 The three-part structure of the federal court system.

This court hears and reviews legal cases that have already been heard in a lower court. In Appellate court, the lawyers argue before a judge or a panel of judges, focusing on legal and policy principles.

Each State in the United States plus the District of Columbia has at least one Supreme Court. Oklahoma and Texas each have two Supreme Courts, one for civil and one for criminal appeals. While the State Supreme Courts hear appeals on legal issues from lower state courts, the U.S. federal courts may overrule a state Supreme Court decision if it is a ruling on a question of federal law.

3.3 Types of Laws

Major areas of the law include Bankruptcy, Business or Corporate, Civil Rights, Cyber, Entertainment, Environmental Law, Family, Health, Intellectual Property, International, Labor or Employment Law, Maritime, Real Estate, and Tax Law.

The three types of law that concern cybercriminals are Administrative, Civil, and Criminal laws. These laws are administered during legal proceedings.

A legal proceeding is a procedure or legal action in a court of law or arbitration panel instituted in order to enforce the law. In a proceeding, the participants present evidence based on an argument that supports their claims on how to interpret the law.

3.3.1 Administrative Law

Earlier in the chapter we defined Administrative law as powers, or regulations created and enforced by administrative agencies of federal, state, and local levels of government. Administrative law is also comprised of less binding guidance that is supposed to help industry participants understand and implement the governing regulations.

The U.S. Constitution refers to the three branches of government as: Legislative, Executive, and Judicial according to "U.S. Const. art. I", "U.S. Const. art. II", and "U.S. Const. art. III". Administrative agencies are not referred to in the U.S. Constitution, but unofficially, have been called the fourth branch of government. They are officially part of the Executive branch, which is why their department heads are appointed by the President.

Executive Orders are enforceable to the extent they act within an administrative sphere. Other important groups referred to in this manner include the press, advocacy groups, and institutions that are perceived to have influence in the three branches of government. While the free press is called the fourth estate, it is incorrect to call it the fourth branch of government – instead it is an outside entity designed to limit the power of government.

Federal agencies are responsible for protecting the public and ensuring compliance with civil rights, privacy, security, and safety. For example, the Clean Air Act of 1963, 42 U.S.C. § 7401, is administered by Environmental Protection Agency (EPA). The agency has the power to enforce, inspect, investigate complaints, hold hearings, and issue penalties for violations without prior judicial process. This is called non-judicial enforcement. These actions are enforced in coordination with state and local governments.

Certain agencies are authorized to pursue legal action for violations of rules, regulations, or statutes. For example, the Securities and Exchange Commission (SEC) and Drug Enforcement Administration (DEA), which is part of the Justice Department (DOJ), both have the authority to begin civil or criminal litigation against a person or business. The table below lists some of the federal agencies in the United States (Table 3.1).

3.3.2 Civil Law

Civil law covers disagreements between two or more private individuals, an organization, a company, or two private parties (*person vs person*). In a civil trial, the party making a claim of wrongdoing is called the *plaintiff*. The accused party is called the *defendant*, and the process of settling or resolving a dispute is called *litigation*. In both civil and criminal trials, an individual may be sued for the same act. An example is found in the notorious O.J. Simpson case, which involved a criminal trial for murder and a civil trial for wrongful death.

A *tort* is a Civil wrong, meaning an injury that causes a plaintiff to suffer loss or harm and permits a lawsuit seeking monetary compensation. The goal of a *tort suit* (civil lawsuit) is to compensate the plaintiff for any injuries.

> Wrong; injury; the opposite of right, So called, according to Lord Coke, because it is wrested, or crooked, being contrary to that which is right and straight.[17]

3.3.3 Criminal Law

Criminal law deals with individuals who commit criminal wrongs, violating one or more of society's laws. These laws keep the public safe and deter criminal conduct. In criminal cases, it is the government or the state, not another person, that brings charges against a person or persons. In a criminal case, the state is represented by a *prosecutor* or *district attorney*, and the *defendant* by a

[17] Black, Henry Campbell, Bryan A. Garner, Becky R. McDaniel, David W. Schultz, and West Publishing Company. *Black's Law Dictionary*. Vol. 196. St. Paul, MN: West Group, 1999.

TABLE 3.1 Major Federal Agencies in the United States

Major Federal Agencies	
Agriculture Department	Interior Department
Arms Control	International Development Agency
Central Intelligence Agency (CIA)	International Trade Commission (USITC)
Civil Rights Commission	Justice Department (DOJ)
Commerce Department	Labor Department
Commodity Futures Trading	National Aeronautics and Space Administration (NASA)
Consumer Products Safety	National Archives
Census Bureau	National Foundation of Arts & Humanities (NEH)
Defense Department	National Labor Relations Board (NLRB)
Defense Nuclear Safety Board	National Science Foundation (NSF)
Education Department	National Transportation Safety Board (NTSB)
Energy Department	Nuclear Regulatory Commission (NRC)
Environmental Protection Agency (EPA)	Occupational Safety & Health (OSH)
Equal Employment Opportunity	Office of Government Ethics (OGE)
Federal Communications Commission (FCC)	Office of Personnel Management (OPM)
Federal Election Commission (FEC)	Peace Corps
Federal Emergency Management Agency (FEMA)	Postal Service (USPS)
Federal Labor Relations (FLRA)	Securities and Exchange (SEC)
Federal Maritime Commission (FMC)	Small Business Administration
Federal Mine Safety	Social Security Administration
Federal Trade Commission (FTC)	State Department
Food and Drug Administration (FDA)	Trade & Development Agency (USTDA)
Health & Human Services (HHS)	Transportation Department
Homeland Security	Treasury Department
Housing and Urban Development (HUD)	Veteran's Affairs (VA)

criminal defense lawyer. A victim of a crime may file a complaint and report a crime to the police, but only the government or the state can bring criminal charges. Criminal offenses are divided into two categories based on the severity of the offense: *felonies*, severe crimes such as murder, rape, burglary, kidnapping, and arson, and *misdemeanors*, less severe crimes punishable by a fine and/or imprisonment. Figure 3.8 illustrates the U.S. legal process, including international laws and treaties. Table 3.2 provides brief definitions for legal terms used in this chapter.

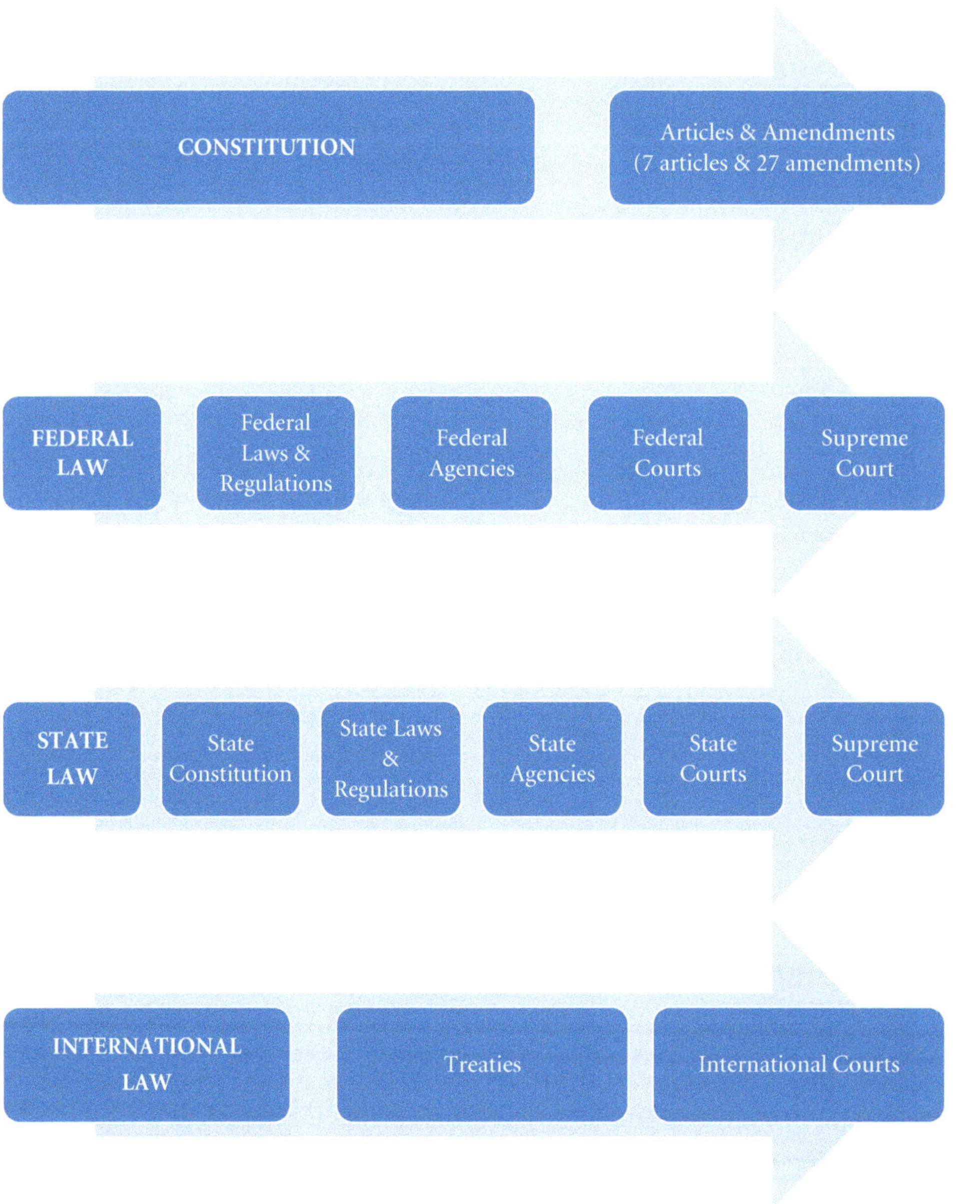

FIGURE 3.8 **The legal process in the United States including international laws and treaties.**

3.4 Conclusion

Cybercrime is continually on the rise, and governments around the world have enacted cybersecurity-related legislation to safeguard privacy, enhance security, and protect the rights of citizens. Before we can understand the complexity of this legislation, we must have a basic understanding of the organization and workings of the U.S. Judicial System. Learning the basics

TABLE 3.2 Glossary of the Legal Terms

Glossary	
Admissible	Evidence that may be considered in civil and criminal cases.
Affidavit	A sworn statement (written or printed) prepared under oath.
Burdens of Proof civil cases	The burden of proof in a civil case is "preponderance of the evidence," meaning the plaintiff must prove the case with most – at least 51% – of the evidence.
Burdens of Proof criminal cases	The burden of proof for a prosecutor to successfully prove a criminal case is "beyond a reasonable doubt." The defendant is by law assumed innocent until the prosecution proves his or her guilt. If the prosecution fails to prove guilt, the defendant goes free.
Class action lawsuit or class suit	Lawsuit to address the injuries of a group of people instead of an individual.
Common Law	Originating from the English Common Law, in accordance with custom and legal precedents and authority set by previous court ruling.
Circumstantial evidence	Circumstantial evidence is evidence gleaned not from direct observation but by inference. For example, finding one's fingerprints at the scene of a crime is circumstantial evidence that one was present.
Digital or Electronic evidence	Digital information that may be used as evidence in a lawsuit or trial, such as e-mails, pictures, videos, browser history, files stored on a computer hard drive, file fragments or data items stored in memory, and information transmitted over a network, like data found in cloud storage.
Probable cause	Probable cause is enough evidence for the government to arrest a suspect or press charges.
Subpoena	A written summons to make an individual to testify, often before a court or in other proceedings. If an individual does not comply, he or she may be held in civil or criminal contempt.
Search Warrant	A legal document issued by a judge or magistrate allowing law enforcement or other officials to enter and search a location. The Fourth Amendment of the U.S. Constitution restricts the government against unreasonable searches and seizures without a warrant.
Testimony	Testimony is information provided under oath in a hearing or other official procedure.
Writ Certiorari or Cert	When a party is not satisfied with a decision by a lower court, the party requests that the U.S. Supreme Court hear the case by petition for *Writ of Certiorari.*

of law can help us identify which legislation is pertinent to a particular cybercrime.

Citizens and businesses can be more proactive about protecting their rights and their data if they understand how laws are structured and know how to take action against cybercrime.

3.5 Key Words

Administrative law
Agency Regulations
Anonymity
Burdens of Proof
Case law
Circumstantial evidence
Civil law
Common Law
Courts system
Criminal law Extradition
Defendant
Digital evidence
Double Jeopardy
Felony
Jurisdiction
Legal system (Supreme, Courts of Appeal or Circuit Courts, District Courts)
Misdemeanor
Ordinance
Plaintiff
Probable cause
Prosecutor
Search Warrant
Subpoena
Tort
U.S. Constitution

Chapter 4

Laws, Standards, and Regulations Affecting Cybercrime

Objectives

After completing this chapter, the student will be able to:

- Define cyber law.
- Understand anti-hacking laws.
- Understand data security laws in critical infrastructure, financial institutions, and healthcare.
- Understand the National Institute of Standards and Technology (NIST) Cybersecurity Framework.
- Understand public and private sector partnerships laws.
- Understand surveillance laws and privacy law.

4.1 Introduction

Cyber law, also called information technology law, or Internet law, pertains to laws involving technology related to the Internet and includes computers and networks. Cyber law is a newer area of the legal system. It pulls from many areas of traditional law and provides legal protection for individuals using the Internet.

This type of law is wide reaching, encompassing cyberbullying and cyberstalking, access to the Internet, intellectual property infringement, consumer

DOI: 10.4324/9780429318726-4

protection, financial crimes, freedom of expression, online privacy, jurisdiction, and First and Fourth Amendment rights.

Cybersecurity is one of the fastest-growing challenges across the globe and is becoming increasingly important. Furthermore, cybersecurity has enormous implications for government security, economic prosperity, and public safety. Cyber laws have been enacted by every nation. In the United States, the federal government and individual states are improving cybersecurity through legislation, better security measures and security practices, increasing fines for computer crimes, and addressing the most serious cyber risks to critical infrastructure.

4.1.1 Current Legislative Framework in the United States

Like other countries, the United States does not have a single piece of national legislation but instead has many statutes and regulations enacted by federal agencies, called Federal Regulations (CFR), that address various aspects of cybersecurity.

Additionally, the U.S. Constitution provides privacy protection through the First Amendment, which ensures the freedoms of Religion, Speech, Press, Assembly, and Petition—"U.S. Const. Amend. I (1791)"—and the Fourth Amendment, with its provisions against Search and Seizure—"U.S. Const. Amend. IV (1791)."

It is impossible within the scope of this chapter to outline all federal, state, and local laws related to cyberspace. Accordingly, this chapter will outline the most important cyberlaws and highlight the importance of federal agencies in creating them.

Furthermore, some laws in this chapter may overlap with others, and some laws will address different issues that arise from the same events. In some cases, we will return to laws we have discussed before when they address different aspects of cybercrime.

The chapter is organized into six major categories. Each outlines the most important legislation in that category, as well as the agencies responsible for enforcing the laws and for issuing criminal charges or penalties. Case studies will clarify how these laws make us safer.

I. **Anti-hacking (unauthorized computer access) laws**
   - Computer Fraud and Abuse Act (CFAA) (18 U.S.C. § 1030)
   - The Economic Espionage Act of 1996 (EEA) (18 U.S.C. § 1831 et seq.)
   - The Digital Millennium Copyright Act (DMCA)

II. **Data security laws and regulations in private sector entities**
   - National Institute of Standards and Technology (NIST); Cybersecurity Framework for private sector organizations

- Laws Dealing with Healthcare: The Health Insurance Portability and Accountability Act (HIPAA), and Health Information Technology for Economic and Clinical Health Act (HITECH)
- Federal Trade Commission (FTC) and Section 5
- Laws Affecting Financial Institutions (The Gramm–Leach–Bliley Act of 1999 (GLBA), Red Flags Rule)
- Laws Affecting Utilities (The Federal Energy Regulatory Commission (FERC), and Nuclear Regulatory Commission (NRC))

III. **Cybersecurity in public and private sector entities partnerships**
- Cybersecurity Information Sharing Act of 2015 (CISA), designed to increase the sharing of cybersecurity threats between the federal and private sector entities to protect privacy and civil liberties
- The Cybersecurity and Infrastructure Security Agency (CISA), The National Cybersecurity and Critical Infrastructure Protection Act of 2014 (NCPA), and the Cybersecurity Enhancement Act of 2014 (CEA)

IV. **Cybersecurity requirements for federal government contractors**
- Federal Information Security Modernization Act of 2014 (FISMA)
- NIST Information Security Controls for Government Agencies and Contractors

V. **Most important Internet surveillance laws in the United States**
- The Fourth Amendment
- USA PATRIOT Act and Freedom Act
- Electronic Communication Privacy Act (ECPA) of 1986
- Communication Assistant for Law Enforcement Act of 1994 (CALEA)
- All Writs Act

VI. **Key privacy laws in the United States**
- Privacy Act of 1974
- Controlling the Assault of Non-Solicited Pornography and Marketing Act of 2003 (CAN-SPAM Act). Unsolicited commercial e-mails “spam,” false or misleading header information, misleading subject lines, and commercial email that can be identified as an advertisement
- 18 U.S.C. § 1037. Fraud and Related Activity in Connection with Electronic Mail
- 18 U.S.C. § 1029. Fraud and Related Activity in Connection with Access Devices
- 18 U.S.C. § 1028. Fraud and Related Activity in Connection with Identification Documents, Authentication Features, and Information

- Children's Online Privacy Protection Act of 1998 (COPPA)
- Video Privacy Protection Act (VPPA) of 1988
- Why the United States began taking privacy seriously (California's Privacy Law and Illinois Biometric Information Privacy Act)

State and local governments have enacted laws to protect their citizens from concerns over surveillance and the right to privacy when using mobile devices and the Internet of Things (IoTs).[1]

It is important to note how differently nations and states view privacy and surveillance. For example, when the USA PATRIOT Act: Preserving Life and Liberty[2] was enacted after the attacks of 9/11, it demonstrated how vulnerable our country felt. The Act made it much easier for the government to monitor individuals and obtain their private information. It included provisions for monitoring financial transactions and established a DNA identification bank of terrorists and other offenders, dramatically increasing the power of the Central Intelligence Agency (CIA) and the Federal Bureau of Investigation (FBI).

Internationally, one of the most important laws on privacy and data protection is the European Union's General Data Protection Regulation (GDPR).[3] The GDPR sets guidelines for the collection and processing of personal information, requiring businesses to protect personal data, and ensures privacy for all EU citizens.

In contrast, Australia passed a controversial law that has been viewed as a repression of freedom. The Telecommunications and Other Legislation Amendment Act of 2018[4] is designed to require technology companies to grant authorities, including police and security agencies, access to encrypted messages.

Some nations recognize their responsibility to protect data and will introduce or modify cyber laws to protect individuals' personal information. Other nations have quite a different approach, pushing back against encryption protocols that could protect their citizens against terrorist threats and crime. It is important to understand that security relies on this cryptography to keep information secure. People depend on secure communication for shopping online, managing their bank accounts, or using technology for personal or business communications.

---

1 Greenwald, Glenn. *No place to hide: Edward Snowden, the NSA, and the US surveillance state.* Macmillan, 2014.

2 USA Patriot Act, The United States Department of Justice. U.S. Government Publishing Office. Retrieved from https://www.govinfo.gov/content/pkg/PLAW-107publ56/pdf/PLAW-107publ56.pdf

3 European Union Law, *Official Journal of the European Union*, Regulation (EU) 2016/679 of the European Parliament and of the Council of 27 April 2016, General Data Protection Regulation. Retrieved from https://eur-lex.europa.eu/eli/reg/2016/679/oj

4 Australian Government, Federal Register of Legislation. https://www.legislation.gov.au/Details/C2018A00148

It is worth noting that state governments like California have enacted their own privacy laws to protect consumers and give them more control over their data. One of the first of its kind, the California Consumer Privacy Act (CCPA)[5] creates new provisions regulating how businesses deal with the personal information of California residents. The new legislation provides the right to know and access their information, and the right to delete or opt out when participation is no longer wanted, to California consumers under the age of 16.

Cybersecurity laws and regulations are designed to protect individuals' privacy rights and systems and information from cyberattacks. The following are the six categories of U.S. law associated with cyberspace in either federal or private sectors. Additionally, at the end of the chapter, Tables 4.5 and 4.6 summarize the most important federal laws concerning cybercrime in the United States.

4.2 Anti-Hacking Laws

Anti-hacking laws enable the government to bring criminal charges against individuals who hack computer systems without consent or lawful authorization. Criminal sentences can result in a prison sentence of 1 year for accessing a computer and obtaining information, up to 10 years for obtaining national security information, and/or a fine (see Table 4.1). Even though penalties are mostly for criminal offenses, they may also include causes of action for civil suits in addition to criminal prosecution. Most computer hacking charges are prosecuted under the Computer Fraud and Abuse Act (18 U.S.C. § 1030).[6,7,8]

4.2.1 The Federal Computer Fraud and Abuse Act

In the United States, the Computer Fraud and Abuse Act is the principal federal anti-hacking statute that prohibits unauthorized access to computers and networks. The Act provides both criminal and civil penalties. In the

5 The California Consumer Privacy Act of 2018 (CCPA), California Legislative information. Retrieved from https://leginfo.legislature.ca.gov/faces/billTextClient.xhtml?bill_id=201720180AB375https://leginfo.legislature.ca.gov/faces/billCompareClient.xhtml?bill_id=201720180AB375

6 18 U.S.C. 1030—Fraud and related activity in connection with computers. U.S. Government Publishing Office. Retrieved from https://www.govinfo.gov/app/details/USCODE-2010-title18/USCODE-2010-title18-partI-chap47-sec1030/summary

7 "Office of the Law Revision Counsel of the United States House of Representatives, Title 18/Part I/Chapter 47—Fraud and false statements, United States Code, last modified August 23, 2019, https://uscode.house.gov/view.xhtml?path=/prelim@title18/part1/chapter47&edition=prelim

8 U.S. Congress, Computer Fraud and Abuse Act of 1986, https://www.congress.gov/bill/99th-congress/house-bill/4562

TABLE 4.1 Summary of CFAA Convictions

CFAA Section	Offense	Sentence (First Conviction)	Maximum Sentence (For Second Conviction)
(a)(1)	Obtaining National Security Information	10 years	20 years
(a)(2)	Accessing a Computer and Obtaining Information	1 or 5 years	10 years
(a)(3)	Trespassing in a Government Computer	1 year	10 years
(a)(4)	Accessing a Computer to Defraud and Obtain Value	5 years	10 years
(a)(5)(A)	Intentionally Damaging by Knowing Transmission	1 or 10 years	20 years
(a)(5)(B)	Recklessly Damaging by Intentional Access	1 or 5 years	20 years
(a)(5)(C)	Negligently Causing Damage and Loss by Intentional Access	1 year	10 years
(a)(6)	Trafficking in Passwords	1 year	10 years
(a)(7)	Extortion Involving Computers	5 years	10 years

Adapted from Prosecuting Computer Crimes, published by the Department of Justice.
Source: Prosecuting Computer Crimes. Department of Justice. Retrieved from https://www.justice.gov/sites/default/files/criminal-ccips/legacy/2015/01/14/ccmanual.pdf

early 1980s, the release of the movie *WarGames* brought panic and concern to the public about computer-related crimes.[9] The movie is about a young hacker who finds a way to control a U.S. military supercomputer with the potential to start a "global thermonuclear war." Law enforcement, facing the dawn of the computer security age, understood the lack of laws available to fight computer crimes like those portrayed in the movie. As a result, Congress included provisions that addressed the unauthorized access and use of computers and computer networks in the Comprehensive Crime Control Act of 1984.[10]

This was the first anti-hacking law put in place to address computer crime.

The CFAA was originally intended to address federal computer-related offenses and to protect government computer systems and financial

[9] Skibell, Reid. "Cybercrime & (and) Misdemeanors: A Reevaluation of the Computer Fraud and Abuse Act." *Berkeley Tech. LJ* 18 (2003): 909.

[10] U.S. Congress, Comprehensive Crime Control Act of 1984, https://www.congress.gov/bill/98th-congress/senate-bill/1762

institutions. The Act expanded with amendments in 1988, 1989, 1990, 1994, 1996, and 2001; it was expanded again by the USA PATRIOT Act 2002 and expanded once more in 2008 to include nearly any computer in the United States. The CFAA makes it a felony to deliberately access a computer without authorization. The CFAA's prosecutions were all criminal; however, this was expanded in the 1994 amendment to include civil lawsuits as well, punishing unauthorized computer access, spreading spam, destroying computer data, password trafficking, seizure of property, and impounding the stolen information and equipment used in the attack.

In addition, the Act makes it an offense to access financial records or credit histories stored in a financial institution or to intrude into a governmental computer system. Furthermore, the Act limits federal jurisdiction to cases with a compelling federal interest, "where computers of the federal government or certain financial institutions are involved or where the crime itself is interstate in nature."[11,12]

The Act is amended as 18 U.S.C. § 1030 and was first enacted by Congress in 1986 to combat computer crime. The Act is located at Title 18, Crimes and Criminal Procedure § 1030, Fraud and Related Activity in Connection with Computers of the United States Code (unannotated).

The following is a brief summary of the seven paragraphs of subsection 1030(a).

- **Hacking and cyber espionage**: The Federal Bureau of Investigation shall have primary authority to investigate offenses for any cases involving espionage, foreign counterintelligence, information protected against unauthorized disclosure for reasons of national defense or foreign relations, or restricted data, as defined in section 11y of the Atomic Energy Act of 1954 (42 U.S.C. 2014(y)), (a)(1). See Appendix A.
- **Hacking to acquire information**: Hacking by means of such conduct as to having obtained information to certain governmental or financial records of a financial institution, credit, or information from any protected computer, (a)(2).
- **Hacking in federal government's computer**: Hacking in a governmental computer (nonpublic computer of a department or agency of the United States), (a)(3).
- **Hacking to commit computer fraud**: Knowingly and with intent to committing fraud and obtain anything of value, unless the object of the fraud and the thing obtained consists only of the use of the

[11] Jarrett, H. M., and M. W. Bailie. *Prosecution of computer. Office of Legal Education Executive Office for United States Attorneys*. Retrieved from https://www.justice.gov/sites/default/files/criminal-ccips/legacy/2015/01/14/ccmanual.pdf

[12] Doyle, C. *Cybercrime: A sketch of 18 USC 1030 and related Federal criminal laws*. Congressional Research Service, 2014. Retrieved from https://fas.org/sgp/crs/misc/RS20830.pdf

computer, and the value of such use is not more than $5,000 in any 1-year period, (a)(4).

- **Hacking to commit damage and loss**: Damage and loss of a governmental computer or knowingly causing the transmission of a program, code, or command, and as a result of such conduct, intentionally causing damage without authorization to a protected computer (for example, worm, computer virus, Trojan horse, time bomb, a denial-of-service attack, and other forms of cyberattack, cybercrime, or cyberterrorism), (a)(5).
- **Password trafficking**: Password trafficking for a governmental computer or affecting interstate or foreign commerce. Knowingly and with intent to defraud trafficking in computer passwords or through which a computer may be accessed, (a)(6).
- **Hacking and threads**: Threatening with intent to extort from any person any money or other thing of value, transmitting in interstate or foreign commerce any communication containing any demand or request for money or other things of value in relation to damage to a protected computer, where such damage was caused to facilitate the extortion, (a)(7).

4.2.1.1 Key Terms and Major Cases to Understand CFAA

4.2.1.1.1 Terms

- First, the term "Without Authorization" in 18 U.S.C. §§ 1030(a)(3), (a)(5)(B), and (a)(5)(C) means an individual who does not have authorization to access a computer system. This term is differentiated from the crime "Exceed Authorized Access," described below. An example is the case of the *United States v. Ivanov.*[13] A Russian hacker accessed a victim company's computer system (a Connecticut corporation called Online Information Bureau, Inc.) without authorization and obtained key passwords to control OIB's network. Another case is the *United States v. Valle.*[14] In this case a New York police officer (Gilberto Valle) had an Internet sex fetish. Among the charges against him was a CFAA violation wherein he was charged with improperly accessing a government computer and obtaining information, in violation of section 1030(a)(2)(B).
- Second, the term "Exceed Authorized Access" in 18 U.S.C. §§ 1030(a)(1), (a)(2), and (a)(4). This term means "to access a computer with authorization and to use such access to obtain or alter information in the computer that the accessor is not entitled so to obtain or alter."[15]

[13] *United States v. Ivanov*, 175 F. Supp. 2d 367 (D. Conn. 2001).
[14] *United States v. Valle*, 807 F.3d 508 (2d Cir. 2015).
[15] 18 U.S.C. §1030(e)(6).

On the other hand, numerous civil cases have taken place where the defendants lost their authorization to access computer systems when they breached a duty of loyalty and good faith (*accessing the computer for an improper purpose*). Examples include the *United States v. Nosal*[16] and *International Airport Centers, LLC v. Citrin*.[17]

4.2.1.1.2 Significant Cases

1. When the law went into effect in 1986, the first person convicted was Robert Morris in the case the *United States v. Morris*.[18] Morris was a Cornell student who unleashed the world's first Internet worm in 1988, called the "Morris worm." The objective of the worm was to highlight the vulnerabilities of a computer network by exploiting its security defects. In addition, the worm was difficult to detect and read and would be difficult to "kill." Morris was found guilty, following a jury trial, of violating the new law 18 U.S.C. § 1030(a)(5)(C), Hacking to commit damage and loss. The defendant was sentenced to 3 years' probation, 400 hours of community service, a fine of $10,050, and the costs of his supervision.
2. The *United States v. Nosal*[19] was a U.S. Court of Appeals case for the Ninth Circuit. The defendant, David Nosal, was a former employee of Korn/Ferry International (KFI). After leaving the company, David Nosal convinced former colleagues to use their login credentials to provide him with confidential information to help him start a competing business. As a result, the government indicted David Nosal on 20 counts, including conspiracy, violations of the Computer Fraud and Abuse Act, mail fraud, and trade secret theft, more specifically with violations of 18 U.S.C.S. § 1030(a)(4), for

> (4) knowingly and with intent to defraud, accessing a protected computer without authorization, or exceeding authorized access, and by means of such conduct furthering the intended fraud and obtaining anything of value, unless the object of the fraud and the thing obtained consists only of the use of the computer and the value of such use is not more than $5,000 in any 1-year period.[20]

David Nosal filed a motion to dismiss, arguing that the CFAA is used to prosecute hackers, not individuals who accessed a computer with authorization and then afterward misused that

[16] *United States v. Nosal*, 676 F.3d 854 (9th Cir. 2012).
[17] *International Airport Centers, LLC v. Citrin*, 440 F.3d 418, 420 (7th Cir. 2006).
[18] *United States v. Morris*, 928 F.2d 504, 505 (2d Cir. 1991).
[19] *United States v. Nosal*, 676 F.3d 854 (9th Cir.2012) (en banc).
[20] 18 U.S.C. 1030—Fraud and related activity in connection with computers. U.S. Government Publishing Office https://www.govinfo.gov/content/pkg/USCODE-2010-title18/html/USCODE-2010-title18-partI-chap47-sec1030.htm

information. Furthermore, he argued that his co-conspirators had permission to access KFI's computers and could not have acted "without authorization"; nor could they have "exceeded authorized access."[21] The district court agreed with the defendant and dismissed some of the CFAA charges. The government appealed to the Ninth Circuit Court of Appeals, claiming that accessing a workplace computer in violation of a corporate policy is not a CFAA violation. As a result, the court concluded that employees who violate the computer use policies of their employers have not "exceeded their authorization" for the purposes of prosecution under the Act.

3. In *Int'l Airport Ctrs., LLC v. Citrin*, the defendant Jacob Citrin was employed by the plaintiffs. He decided to quit the company and go into business for himself, in breach of his employment contract. Before returning the company's computer, he erased all files by loading a program, designed to write over the files and prevent their recovery. The court concluded that Citrin violated 1030(a)(5)(B) and ruled that he had breached his duty of loyalty to the company and had exceeded authorized access. Later, the district court dismissed the plaintiff's suit for failure to state a claim.
4. In the *United States v. Drew*[22] the defendant Lori Drew set up a fictitious profile, pretending to be a 16-year-old juvenile named Josh Evans on the MySpace website. The defendant posted a photograph of a boy without the boy's knowledge or permission for the purpose of communicating with a 13-year-old girl named Megan Meier. Drew then started flirting with Megan using the pseudonym Josh Evans. After some period, he informed Megan Meier that he was moving away and no longer liked her and that the world would be a better place without her in it. After Megan Meier had killed herself, Drew deleted the account. The jury found the defendant guilty of accessing a computer involved in interstate or foreign communication without authorization or in excess of authorization to obtain information in violation of Title 18, U.S. Code, section 1030(a)(2)(C) and (c)(2)(A), a misdemeanor.
5. Another interesting case is the *United States v. John*.[23] The defendant, Eva Lavon John, was a Citigroup employee who used her credentials to provide customer information to her half-brother, who used the information to commit fraud. She was convicted

[21] *United States v. Nosal*, 676 F.3d 854 (9th Cir.2012) (en banc), Retrieved from http://cdn.ca9.uscourts.gov/datastore/opinions/2011/04/28/10-10038.pdf
[22] *United States v. Drew*, 259 F.R.D. 449, 461 (C.D.Cal. 2009).
[23] *United States v. John*, 597 F.3d 263 (5th Cir. 2010).

of numerous counts, including exceeding authorized access to a protected computer in violation of 18 U.S.C. §§ 1030(a)(2)(A) and (C). The defendant appealed and argued that she had not exceeded authorized access because she was authorized to access customer information as a Citigroup employee. The U.S Court of Appeals for the Fifth Circuit rejected the argument. The court concluded that authorized access to a computer and information may exceed its purposes. The court wrote "To give but one example, an employer may 'authorize' employees to utilize computers for any lawful purpose but not for unlawful purposes and only in furtherance of the employer's business."[24]

6. In the case *United States v. Rodriguez*,[25] the defendant, Roberto Rodriguez, worked as a TeleService representative for the Social Security Administration (SSA). SSA policy forbids any employee from gaining information from a database without a business reason. The defendant violated the policy by accessing the social security records of 17 individuals without business reasons. Rodriguez argued that he did not violate section 1030(a)(2)(B) because he accessed only databases that he was authorized to use as a representative. The court concluded that the employee "exceeded authorized access" under the CFAA when he obtained information for a non-business purpose, in violation of the SSA's policies, and returned a guilty verdict on all 17 counts.

These cases describe the wide range of readings by the courts of 18 U.S.C. 1030 in the understanding of "Without Authorization" and "Exceeded Authorized Access." The courts are divided as to whether an individual can be found guilty of violating the CFAA simply by misusing the information to which the individual had proper access. Eventually, the U.S. Supreme Court will have to resolve the issue, as the federal courts continue to apply different definitions.

The CFAA has been used in the United States as the primary hacking law. In addition to criminal proceedings, the law allows hacking victims to bring civil lawsuits against perpetrators in certain conditions. Furthermore, many states have additional computer crime laws, and most address unauthorized access or computer hacking. The CFAA has been criticized for harsh punishment in minor offenses, unclear description of punishments, and neither deterring foreign criminals nor effectively protecting the United States against emerging cybercrime.

[24] *Id.* at 23.

[25] *United States v. Rodriguez*, 628 F.3d 1258 (11th Cir. 2010).

4.2.1.2 Limitations of the CFAA

The CFAA Act fails to describe which offenses to prohibit, specifically regarding the terms "without authorization," "exceeding authorized access," and "unauthorized damage to a computer." The courts should not be debating over whether a matter was authorized or not. Also, compensation should be restricted to real damage to data or to the methodology of accessing the computer system. Harmless or senseless examples of employees deleting emails or backing up databases when data redundancy is available should not be considered. Criminalizing acts like editing a document or shutting down a computer system without permission should not be prosecuted. The civil cases under CFAA are potentially serious crimes. The Act has become a convenient way to impose intellectual property litigation penalties by bringing a claim of theft of trade secrets. Corporations can take legal action against former employees for deleting, copying, or transferring files before or after they have left their jobs. Nevertheless, the Department of Justice has never criminally prosecuted companies for espionage, violation, or data theft. Additionally, defendants face harsh sentences of up to 20 years, depending on what part of the CFAA they violate, at times for offenses with few real damages or merits. Table 4.1 demonstrates the CFAA's convictions.

One example was an outrageous indictment for computer fraud, in the case of the *United States of America v. Aaron Swartz*.[26] Aaron Swartz was a computer programmer and a research fellow at Harvard University. He helped develop the RSS web feed, a computer file format that allows users to access updates to websites and the popular site Reddit. As he was working at Harvard University, he connected to the Massachusetts Institute of Technology (MIT) network and without authorization downloaded thousands of academic articles from a not-for-profit digital library called JSTOR. Any MIT student could access MIT's computer network and JSTOR; however, JSTOR had limited the number of articles that could be downloaded at one time. "He was neither a malicious hacker nor a vandalistic 'script kiddie,' but rather a well-known programmer and political activist."[27] He was first indicted in 2011,[28] but federal prosecutors filed a superseding indictment in 2012,[29] adding nine more felony counts. Swartz committed suicide

[26] U.S. Attorney's Office District of Massachusetts. "Alleged hacker charged with stealing over four million documents from MIT network" (July 19, 2011). Press release. Retrieved from http://www.justice.gov/usao/ma/news/2011/July/SwartzAaronPR.html

[27] Peters, Justin. *The idealist: Aaron Swartz and the rise of free culture on the Internet*. Simon and Schuster, 2016.

[28] *Id.* at 27.

[29] *Superseding indictment, U.S. v. Aaron Swartz*. Crim. No. 1:11-cr-10260-NMG (D. Mass. 2012).

in 2013 before his case was concluded. His family accused the government of obsessive prosecution for a nonviolent crime.[30]

Table 4.1 displays the penalties of the CFAA Act.

For a complete text of the CFAA and the additional amendments see Appendix A.

4.2.2 Computer Hacking Laws from Individual States

So far, in the federal courts, most individuals accused of hacking are charged under the CFAA. In addition, all 50 states have their own computer crime laws, and most address unauthorized access to computer-based information systems or computer intrusion.

It is important to acknowledge the significance of state law. State hacking laws differ widely. Certain states prohibit unauthorized access, computer trespass, and the use of viruses and malware by addressing specific cybercrimes like Denial-of-Service (DoS), Phishing, Ransomware, and Spyware. Florida categorizes DoS as a felony in the first degree,[31] and other states, including California, criminalize Ransomware.[32] In addition, California penalizes computer-related crime with Penal Code 502[33] and Penal Code section 530.5.[34] The National Conference of State Legislatures (NCSL) provides a comprehensive list and complete texts of each state's anti-hacking laws.[35]

4.2.3 The Economic Espionage Act of 1996 (EEA)

The EEA Act,[36,37] 18 U.S.C. § 1831, criminalizes two forms of trade secret theft and was the first federal statute to do so. The two forms are *economic*

[30] Broadhurst, Roderic, Peter Grabosky, Mamoun Alazab, Brigitte Bouhours, and Steve Chon. "An analysis of the nature of groups engaged in cybercrime. An analysis of the nature of groups engaged in cyber crime." *International Journal of Cyber Criminology* 8, no. 1 (2014): 1–20.

[31] Official Internet site of the Florida Legislature. Florida Statutes Title XLVI. Crimes § 815.01. Retrieved from http://www.leg.state.fl.us/Statutes/index.cfm?App_mode=Display_Statute&URL=0800-0899/0815/Sections/0815.06.html

[32] California Legislative Information. Penal Code PC §523(b). Retrieved from https://leginfo.legislature.ca.gov/faces/codes_displaySection.xhtml?lawCode=PEN&sectionNum=523.

[33] California Legislative Information. Penal Code PC §502. Retrieved from https://leginfo.legislature.ca.gov/faces/codes_displaySection.xhtml?sectionNum=502.&lawCode=PEN

[34] California Legislative Information. Penal Code PC §530.5. Retrieved from https://leginfo.legislature.ca.gov/faces/codes_displaySection.xhtml?lawCode=PEN&sectionNum=530.5

[35] The National Conference of State Legislatures (NCSL). Laws Addressing Hacking, Unauthorized Access, Computer Trespass, Viruses, Malware. Retrieved from http://www.ncsl.org/research/telecommunications-and-information-technology/computer-hacking-and-unauthorized-access-laws.aspx#Hacking

[36] The United States Department of Justice. 18 U.S.C. §1831 (economic espionage) and 18 U.S.C. §1832 (theft of trade secrets). Retrieved from https://www.justice.gov/jm/criminal-resource-manual-1122-introduction-economic-espionage-act

[37] Economic Espionage Act of 1996. Retrieved from https://www.congress.gov/104/plaws/publ294/PLAW-104publ294.htm

espionage (18 U.S.C. § 1831), which benefits a foreign entity, and *theft of trade secrets* (18 U.S.C. § 1832), known as theft for pecuniary gain.

Theft of trade secrets extends from electronic storage to actual theft. Additionally, section 1836[38] allows victims to sue for civil damages and attorneys' fees. The Act was primarily aimed at former spies, currently jobless, who could steal American companies' trade secrets and sell them to foreign entities. The Act requires the government to prove beyond a reasonable doubt that the defendant stole, plotted, or attempted to steal information or data that was proprietary, had no claim to it, and was a trade secret.

The Economic Espionage Act was passed in 1996 and provided punishment for foreign and corporate espionage. It was amended in 2016. The Act now allows companies to bring civil litigation for trade secrets theft;[39] increases criminal penalties to $5 million or three times the trade secret's value, whichever is greater;[40] and provides protection to whistleblowers who make confidential disclosures to a government official.[41]

4.2.3.1 Important Cases

1. Notable cases include *U.S. v. Liew*. Walter Liew[42] was the first person convicted under the EEA and was sentenced to 15 years in prison and ordered to pay a penalty of $27.8 million gained in illegal profits and $511,667.82 in restitution.[43] The defendant and his company, USA Performance Technology, were convicted of numerous other offenses, including the disclosure of trade secrets to a third party. The trade secrets related to DuPont's technology for manufacturing titanium dioxide (TiO_2).[44]

DuPont had identified titanium dioxide (TiO_2) as a "trade secret," and according to the Act

> (A) the owner thereof has taken reasonable measures to keep such information secret; and (B) the information derives independent economic value, actual or potential, from not being generally known to, and not being readily

38 18 U.S.C. §1836.

39 18 U.S.C. § 1836.

40 18 U.S.C. § 1832(b).

41 18 U.S.C. § 1833.

42 *U.S. v. Liew CR 11-00573-1*, 4 JSW (N.D. Cal. Jun. 9, 2014). Retrieved from http://cdn.ca9.uscourts.gov/datastore/opinions/2017/05/05/14-10367.pdf

43 U.S. Attorney's Office, The Federal Bureau of Investigation. Retrieved from https://www.fbi.gov/contact-us/field-offices/sanfrancisco/news/press-releases/walter-liew-sentenced-to-15-years-in-prison-for-economic-espionage

44 *Id.* at 42.

ascertainable through proper means by another person who can obtain economic value from the disclosure or use of the information.[45]

2. The case of *United States of America v. Wang Dong, Sun Kailiang, Wen Xinyu, Huang Zhenyu, Gu Chunhui*[46] signifies the first time charges were brought against known Chinese military hackers. They were indicted on 31 counts of computer hacking and cyberespionage, including theft of trade secrets, over 9 years between 2006 and 2014 by a federal grand jury in Pennsylvania. Since the incident occurred in the United States, the court's decision is unlikely to be implemented in China.

4.2.4 The Digital Millennium Copyright Act

The DMCA emphasizes anti-circumvention laws and aims to prevent copyright infringement by punishing unauthorized users who evade or hack into copyrighted technology or software. The word "circumvention" means lack of authorization or hacking into access controls or technological protection measures (TPM), like a burglar attempting to pick a locked door.

On October 28, 1998, President Clinton signed into law the Digital Millennium Copyright Act.[47] This law implemented two 1996 treaties of the World Intellectual Property Organization (WIPO): first, the WIPO Copyright Treaty, and, second, the WIPO Performances and Phonograms Treaty. The Act also reinforced the law's protection of intellectual property rights on the Internet, including unauthorized access to copyrighted work.[48] In other words the DMCA modernized U.S. law to meet the requirements of international copyright treaties and addressed copyrighted material in the digital age. The law has five titles:[49]

[45] Office of the Law Revision Counsel of the United States House of Representatives. United States Code, Retrieved from https://uscode.house.gov/view.xhtml?req=granuleid:USC-prelim-title18-section1839&num=0&edition=prelim

[46] The United States Department of Justice. Retrieved from https://www.justice.gov/opa/pr/us-charges-five-chinese-military-hackers-cyber-espionage-against-us-corporations-and-labor

[47] Pub. L. No. 105-304, 112 Stat. 2860 (Oct. 28, 1998).

[48] U.S. Government Publishing Office. Title 17—Copyrights Chapter 5—Copyright Infringement and Remedies Sec. 506—Criminal offenses. U.S. Government Publishing Office. U.S. Government Publishing Office. Retrieved from https://www.govinfo.gov/content/pkg/USCODE-2010-title17/html/USCODE-2010-title17-chap5-sec506.htm

[49] The Digital Millennium Copyright Act of 1998. U.S. Government Publishing Office. Retrieved from https://www.govinfo.gov/content/pkg/CRPT-105srpt190/html/CRPT-105srpt190.htm

- **Title I**: "WIPO Copyright and Performances and Phonograms Treaties Implementation Act of 1998." This title implements the WIPO Copyright Treaty.
- **Title II**: "Online Copyright Infringement Liability Limitation Act." This title creates a so-called *safe harbor* regarding the liability of online service providers (OSPs) for copyright infringement.
- **Title III**: "Computer Maintenance Competition Assurance Act." This title creates an exemption for making temporary, limited copies of a computer program for purposes of maintenance or repair.
- **Title IV**: "Covers six miscellaneous provisions." These provisions relate to the functions of the Copyright Office. It clarifies the duties of the Copyright Office, ephemeral copy for broadcasters, provisions to facilitate distance education, provisions to assist libraries with keeping and making recordings, "webcasting" of sound recordings on the Internet, and provisions of collective bargaining agreements for the transfer of movie rights.
- **Title V**: "Vessel Hull Design Protection Act." Protection for vessel hulls design.

Among the sections, Title II, known as the Online Copyright Infringement Liability Limitation Act, is codified as Section 512, Title 17, of the United States Code (17 U.S.C. § 512). The law protects online service providers and websites from liability for copyright infringements in certain cases. More specifically, the law contains safe-harbor provisions for service providers. The safe harbor protects them from copyright infringements, until the copyright owner establishes notice for the prompt removal of content (notice and takedown). The DMCA offers safe harbor only to OSP; individuals or subscribers may still be held liable. Lack of knowledge of the law will not exempt the user from legal consequences. Furthermore, the OSP is obligated to provide all users access to information for dealing with copyright infringement notifications and to inform users concerning violations of copyright or other intellectual property laws.

Section 107 of the Copyright Act (17 U.S.C. § 107) offers the right to use copyrighted content or work without the permission of the owner in certain conditions. This is called Fair Use. The legally permissible purposes for which the copyrighted content can be used include: News Reporting, Commentary, Research, Criticism, Scholarship, and Teaching. According to § 107,

> In determining whether the use made of a work in any particular case is a fair use the factors to be considered shall include: the purpose and character of the use, including whether such use is of a commercial nature or is for nonprofit educational purposes; the nature of the copyrighted work; the amount and substantiality of the portion used in relation to the copyrighted

work as a whole; and the effect of the use upon the potential market for or value of the copyrighted work.[50]

The purpose of Fair Use is to promote commentary, discussion, creativity, criticism, innovation, research, scholarship, and teaching.

Cybersecurity legislation involves section 1201 of the DMCA. This section was created to accomplish the aims of the WIPO Copyright Treaty and criminalizes those who "circumvent technological measures used to prevent unauthorized access to copyrighted works, including copyrighted books, movies, video games, and computer software."[51] Section § 1201 aims to protect copyrighted works from those circumventing access control measures. The following are three primary provisions:

- § 1201(a)(1) "No person shall circumvent a technological measure that effectively controls access to a work protected under this title." This section forbids technological measures to encrypt a work, or to avoid, evade, remove, deactivate, or impair, without the authority of the copyright owner. For instance, it forbids avoiding access controls by decrypting encrypted Blu-ray/DVD disks and playing them on an unauthorized device or evading password access to music streaming services. Other examples include password cracking or evading authentication codes in video game systems to prevent playing pirated games.
- § 1201(a)(2) "No person shall manufacture, import, offer to the public, provide, or otherwise traffic in any technology, product, service, device, or component that was designed to evade a lawful control."[52]
- § 1201(b)(1) "No person shall manufacture, import, offer to the public, provide, or otherwise traffic in any technology, product, service, device, component, or part thereof, that—".[53] This section forbids manufacture or trafficking in devices or services, i.e., software and other TPM that can be employed to circumvent protected access. These measures are called Access Controls or Copy Controls. They protect against unlawful use of a copyrighted work once gained access to legally (Figure 4.1).

[50] Office of the Law Revision Counsel of the United States House of Representatives. United States Code. Retrieved from https://uscode.house.gov/view.xhtml?req=granuleid:USC-prelim-title17-section107&num=0&edition=prelim

[51] 17 U.S.C. § 1201.

[52] U.S. Congress. H. Rept. No. 105-551-WIPO Copyright Treaties Implementation and On-Line Copyright Infringement Liability Limitation. Retrieved from https://www.congress.gov/congressional-report/105th-congress/house-report/551/1

[53] 17 U.S.C. § 1201 (b) (1).

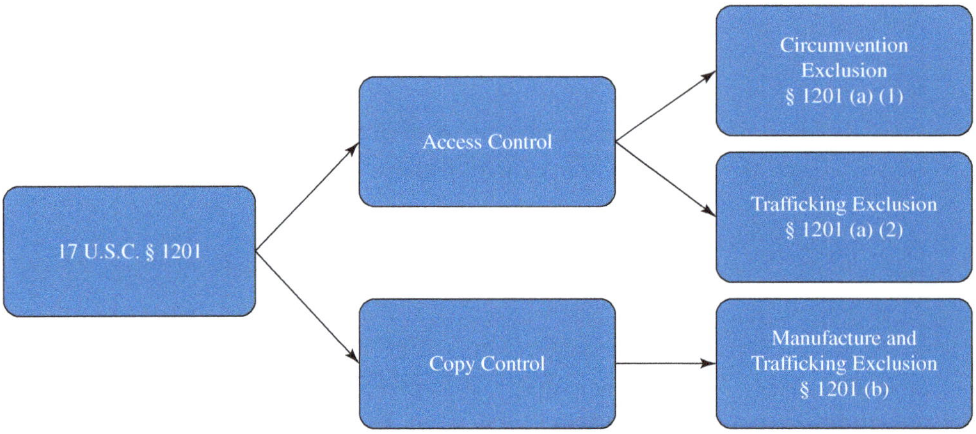

FIGURE 4.1 The 17 U.S.C. § 1201 statutory structure.

4.2.4.1 Penalties for 17 U.S.C. § 1201

A civil suit in a federal court can be brought by an individual injured by a violation of sections 1201 or 1202.

Section § 1201 refers to

(a) False Copyright Management Information.—No person shall knowingly and with the intent to induce, enable, facilitate, or conceal infringement—
  (1) provide copyright management information that is false, or
  (2) distribute or import for distribution copyright management information that is false.
(b) Removal or Alteration of Copyright Management Information.—No person shall, without the authority of the copyright owner or the law—
  (1) intentionally remove or alter any copyright management information,
  (2) distribute or import for distribution copyright management information, knowing that the copyright management information has been removed or altered without authority of the copyright owner or the law, or
  (3) distribute, import for distribution, or publicly perform works, copies of works, or phonorecords, knowing that copyright management information has been removed or altered without authority of the copyright owner or the law.[54]

Section 1203[55] allows the court to grant equitable and monetary remedies as well as statutory damages. The court in its discretion may reduce or remit the damages

[54] 17 U.S.C. § 1202.
United States Code. 17 U.S.C. § 1202—Integrity of copyright management information. U.S. Government Publishing Office. U.S. Government Publishing Office. Retrieved from https://www.govinfo.gov/app/details/USCODE-2016-title17/USCODE-2016-title17-chap12-sec1202

[55] 17 U.S.C. § 1203—Civil remedies.

in cases of innocent or unintentional violation. Criminal violation under section 1204[56] punishments ranges not more than $500,000 fine or imprisonment for not more than 5 years for the first offense, and not more than $1,000,000 fine or imprisonment for not more than 10 years for subsequent offenses.

(a) In General.—Any person who violates section 1201 or 1202 willfully and for purposes of commercial advantage or private financial gain—
  (1) shall be fined not more than $500,000 or imprisoned for not more than 5 years, or both, for the first offense; and
  (2) shall be fined not more than $1,000,000 or imprisoned for not more than 10 years, or both, for any subsequent offense.

(b) Limitation for Nonprofit Library, Archives, or Educational Institution.—Subsection (a) shall not apply to a nonprofit library, archives, or educational institution.

(c) Statute of Limitations.—No criminal proceeding shall be brought under this section unless such proceeding is commenced within 5 years after the cause of action arose.[57]

4.2.4.2 Important Cases

1. In the case of *Friedman v. Live Nation Merchandise*,[58] a photographer, Glen Friedman, took photographs of the hip-hop group Run DMC. He published the photographs in a book and granted Sony Music a license to reproduce and alter some of the photographs. Live Nation Merchandise, Inc., a music merchandising company, used some of the pictures in a wall calendar and three T-shirts. When Glen Friedman discovered that his pictures were used by Live Nation, he filed a complaint alleging copyright infringement and removal of copyright management information (CMI). The district court decided that the plaintiff had not provided enough evidence to establish that the defendant knew it was using his photographs without permission, removing the CMI. Finally, the court determined that the plaintiff was limited to one award per work infringed by the defendant. The court acknowledged the likelihood of multiple legal damages, but in cases of mass marketing, the plaintiff must seek separate legal damages against each retailer and then pursue damages against the wholesaler.

[56] 17 U.S.C. § 1204.

[57] United States Code. 17 U.S.C. § 1204—Criminal offenses and penalties. U.S. Government Publishing Office. Retrieved from https://www.govinfo.gov/app/details/USCODE-1998-title17/USCODE-1998-title17-chap12-sec1204

[58] *Friedman v. Live Nation Merch., Inc.*, No. 14-55302 (9th Cir. Aug.18, 2016). United States Court of Appeals for the Ninth Circuit. Retrieved from https://cdn.ca9.uscourts.gov/datastore/opinions/2016/08/18/14-55302.pdf

Because there was sufficient evidence in the record to allow a reasonable jury to conclude that Live Nation willfully infringed Friedman's copyrights and knowingly removed CMI from the images it used, we reverse the district court's grant of summary judgment to Live Nation on those issues. We affirm the district court's ruling as to statutory damages.[59]

2. Another interesting case is *Craigslist, Inc. v. Naturemarket*[60] in which the plaintiff Craigslist sued the defendant Naturemarket because the defendant sold software that allowed its customers to automatically post multiple ads, spam, and email messages to Craigslist. Craigslist used CAPTCHA software and telephone verification to avoid the defendant's automatic postings. Craigslist claimed that the defendant copied part of Craigslist's website to facilitate automated access and to circumvent the CAPTCHA software. Because of the protected measure CAPTCHA used by Craigslist to safeguard its copyright rights, the court concluded that the defendant violated § 1201(b)(1). The court granted plaintiff Craigslist the amount of $1,712.07 and $65,038.20 for attorneys' fees.[61]
3. *MDY Industries, Inc. LLC v. Blizzard Entertainment*[62] is about a worldwide multiplayer online role-playing game known as World of Warcraft (WoW), created by the defendant Blizzard Entertainment. The plaintiff, MDY Industries, created a software bot, a web robot named Glider, that lets users play WoW unattended, instead of as the defendant intended. MDY Industries had created Glider for its own purposes in directing how users played the game. At the district court level, the plaintiff MDY Industries had been found liable under section 1201(a)(2) for selling software (trafficking in technology) that contributed to the breach of Blizzard's software bot.[63] The district judge decided against MDY Industries and its founder Michael Donnelly, levying a penalty of $6.5 million for violating DMCA. After an appeal by MDY Industries, the court decision against MDY for related copyright infringement was reversed.

---

[59] *Id.* at 58.
[60] *Craigslist, Inc. v. Naturemarket, Inc.*, 694 F. Supp. 2d 1039, 1048–49 (N.D. Cal. 2010).
[61] *Craigslist, Inc. v. Naturemarket, Inc.* Case Retrieved from Google scholar https://scholar.google.com/scholar_case?case=14733453541646660370&q=Craigslist,+Inc.+v.+Naturemarket,+Inc.,&hl=en&as_sdt=6,33&as_vis=1
[62] *MDY Industries, Inc. LLC v. Blizzard Entertainment*, 629 F.3d 928 (9th Cir. 2010).
[63] District of Arizona, azd-2:2006-cv-02555. *MDY Industries, LLC v. Blizzard Entertainment, Inc. et al.* No. CV-06-2555-PHX-DGC. Retrieved from https://www.docketbird.com/court-documents/MDY-Industries-LLC-v-Blizzard-Entertainment-Inc-et-al/ORDER-re-bench-trial-Signed-by-Judge-David-G-Campbell-on-1-28-2009/azd-2:2006-cv-02555-00108

> We conclude that for a licensee's violation of a contract to constitute copyright infringement, there must be a nexus between the condition and the licensor's exclusive rights of copyright. Here, WoW players do not commit copyright infringement by using Glider in violation of its Terms of Use. MDY is thus not liable for secondary copyright infringement, which requires the existence of direct copyright infringement.[64]

In conclusion, the court upheld the judgment that MDY Industries violated the provisions of the DMCA against section 1201(a)(2) that prohibits the circumvention of technological measures but not for related copyright infringement. This case shows the importance of contract drafting in a business relationship.

For a complete text of section 1201, see Appendix B.

4.3 Data Security Laws and Regulations in the Private Sector Entities

This section emphasizes the importance of partnerships between public and private sectors in terms of data security and privacy through the cooperation of federal agencies and departments working collaboratively with the private sector (Figure 4.2).

FIGURE 4.2 The importance and intersection between public and private sector partnerships.

The private sector consists of organizations that generate profits for their stakeholders and are not controlled by the government. In a public–private partnership, a government agency and private sector company may collaborate to deliver services or business ventures to the public. Since government agencies regularly collect and store citizens' personal information, the government must agree to protect the privacy of its citizens when dealing with the private sector. As a result, the federal government, along with many states, has passed data security laws and regulations that apply to private entities involved in government

[64] United States Court of Appeals for the Ninth Circuit. *MDY Industries, Inc. LLC v. Blizzard Entertainment*, 629 F.3d 928 (9th Cir. 2010). Retrieved from http://cdn.ca9.uscourts.gov/datastore/opinions/2011/02/17/09-15932.pdf

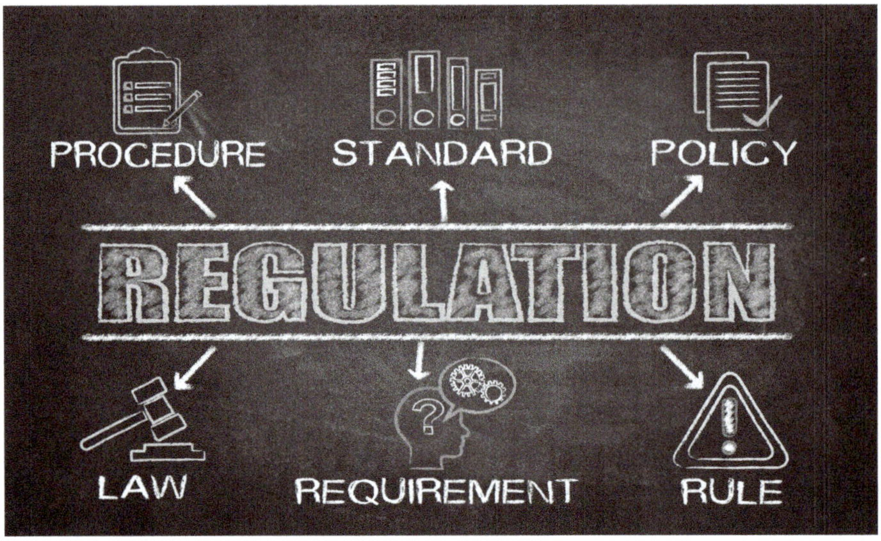

FIGURE 4.3 **Regulations. Courtesy of Shutterstock.**

business (Figure 4.3). *Failure to comply can lead to criminal and civil investigations, huge fines and penalties, sanctions, and class-action lawsuits.*

4.3.1 The National Institute of Standards and Technology Cybersecurity Framework

The National Institute of Standards and Technology is an agency of the U.S. Department of Commerce. It was founded in 1901 to set official standards for weights and measures and to serve as the national physical laboratory for the United States. From 1901 to 1988 it was known as the National Bureau of Standards (NBS) and the National Metrological Institute (NMI). In 1988, its name was changed to the National Institute of Standards and Technology (Figure 4.4).[65] NIST is a non-regulatory federal agency of the U.S. Department of Commerce. Its "mission is to develop and promote measurement, standards and technology to enhance productivity, facilitate trade, and improve the quality of life."[66] NIST research areas consist of Advanced Communications, Advanced Manufacturing, Cyber-Physical Systems, Disaster Resilience, Forensic Science, Healthcare, and IT and Cybersecurity.

[65] NIST Timeline. Retrieved from https://www.nist.gov/timeline#event-774241
[66] NIST. Retrieved from https://www.nist.gov/

The NIST Framework for Improving Critical Infrastructure Cybersecurity or the Cybersecurity Framework offers a voluntary policy framework of computer security for the private sector in the United States. While the use of the framework has been voluntary for the private sector, it has been mandated for all U.S. federal agencies by Presidents Obama and Donald Trump by executive order.[67,68,69] The framework has been translated into many languages and has been utilized by other governments like Japan and Israel. The framework *improves, prevents, detects, and responds* to cyberattacks.[70] Figure 4.5 demonstrates the evolution of the framework.

National Institute of Standards and Technology
U.S. Department of Commerce

FIGURE 4.4 NIST logo.

In 2014, after an executive order, NIST released version 1.0 of the Framework for Improving Critical Infrastructure Cybersecurity. Congress approved the role of NIST's Framework in the Cybersecurity Enhancement Act of 2014[71] by continuing the development of the framework. The first update, version 1.1, was released in April 2018. The updated version contains

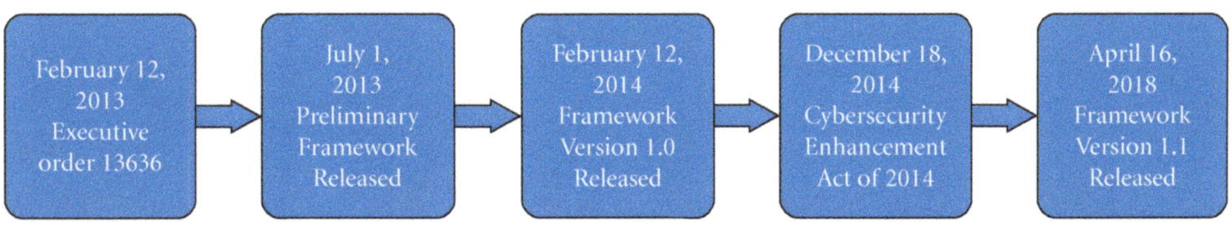

FIGURE 4.5 Evolution of the Cybersecurity Framework. Adopted from NIST.

Source: The National Institute of Standards and Technology (NIST), History and Creation of the Framework. Retrieved from https://www.nist.gov/cyberframework/online-learning/history-and-creation-framework; Barrett, Matthew P. "Framework for improving critical infrastructure cybersecurity." National Institute of Standards and Technology, Gaithersburg, MD, USA, Tech. Rep (2018).

[67] Presidential Executive Order on Improving Critical Infrastructure (February 12, 2013) https://obamawhitehouse.archives.gov/the-press-office/2013/02/12/executive-order-improving-critical-infrastructure-cybersecurity

[68] Presidential Executive Order on Strengthening the Cybersecurity of Federal Networks and Critical Infrastructure. (May 11, 2017). Retrieved from https://www.whitehouse.gov/presidential-actions/presidential-executive-order-strengthening-cybersecurity-federal-networks-critical-infrastructure/

[69] Presidential Executive Order on America's Cybersecurity Workforce (May 2, 2019). Retrieved from https://www.whitehouse.gov/presidential-actions/executive-order-americas-cybersecurity-workforce/

[70] *Id.* at 66.

[71] U.S. Congress Cybersecurity Enhancement Act of 2014. Retrieved from https://www.congress.gov/bill/113th-congress/senate-bill/1353/text

three main components: *Five Functions or Core*, *Implementation Tiers*, and *Profiles*.

I. The **Core** comprises three parts: Functions, Categories, and Subcategories. The five functions, also shown in Table 4.2, are:
- Identify—Develop the organizational understanding to manage cybersecurity risk to systems, assets, data, and capabilities.
- Protect—Develop and implement the appropriate safeguards to ensure delivery of critical infrastructure services.
- Detect—Develop and implement the appropriate activities to identify the occurrence of a cybersecurity event.
- Respond—Develop and implement the appropriate activities to take action regarding a detected cybersecurity event.
- Recover—Develop and implement the appropriate activities to maintain plans for resilience and to restore any capabilities or services that were impaired due to a cybersecurity event.[72]

II. The **Implementation Tiers** describe how an organization assesses, evaluates, and manages the cybersecurity risk as defined in the framework. The four tiers show progress from Partial (Tier 1) to Risk Informed (Tier 2) Repeatable (Tier 3), and finally Adaptive (Tier 4).

III. In the **Profiles** an organization may conduct a self-assessment and identify and improve cybersecurity outcomes based on business needs.

4.3.2 Laws Dealing with Healthcare

4.3.2.1 The Health Insurance Portability and Accountability Act (HIPAA)

HIPAA is a federal law that requires the formation of national standards to protect patients' privacy, confidentiality, and security of health information (Figure 4.6). Specifically, the law protects patients' medical information from disclosure without the patient's knowledge and permission. The law (Pub. L. 104–191)[73] was enacted by the U.S. Congress and signed by President Bill Clinton in 1996. It has also been known as the Edward Kennedy and Nancy

[72] Framework for Improving Critical Infrastructure Cybersecurity. Version 1.1 National Institute of Standards and Technology. April 16, 2018. Retrieved from https://nvlpubs.nist.gov/nistpubs/CSWP/NIST.CSWP.04162018.pdf

[73] U.S. Government Publishing Office. Retrieved from https://www.govinfo.gov/content/pkg/PLAW-104publ191/pdf/PLAW-104publ191.pdf

TABLE 4.2 The Core

Function	Category
Identify What are we protecting?	Asset Management
	Business Environment
	Governance
	Risk Assessment
	Risk Management Strategy
	Supply Chain Risk Management
Protect What protections are available?	Identity Management, Authentication, and Access Control
	Awareness and Training
	Data Security
	Information Protection Processes and Procedures
	Maintenance
	Protective Technology
Detect What methods and techniques identify an incident?	Anomalies and Events
	Security Continuous Monitoring
	Detection Processes
Respond What methods and techniques can manage the impacts of an incident?	Response Planning
	Communications
	Analysis
	Mitigation
	Improvements
Recover How can we restore and recover from an incident?	Recovery Planning
	Improvements
	Communications

Adapted from Cybersecurity Framework Version 1.1
Note: Id at 72.

FIGURE 4.6 HIPAA logo.

Kassebaum Act after two of its leading sponsors.[74] According to HIPAA, the Department of Health and Human Services (HHS) is required to develop regulations protecting privacy and security. These regulations are known as the *HIPAA Privacy Rule*[75] and the *HIPAA Security Rule*.[76] In HHS, the Office for Civil Rights (OCR) is responsible for enforcing the rules with voluntary compliance and civil money penalties.

The *Privacy Rule* protects "individually identifiable health information"[77] in both paper and electronic form, by creating national regulations. Additionally, the law enables the patient to examine/see and receive copies of their health information records upon request.

The *Security Rule* concentrates on the technical safeguards—"technology and the policy and procedures for its use that protect electronic protected health information and control access to it"[78]—for the health information by protecting electronic health information created, received, used, or maintained by a covered entity. The Security Rule identifies two main entities, "covered entities" and their "business associates." A *covered entity* is one of the following:

I. **Health care provider**: doctors, clinics, psychologists, dentists, nursing home pharmacists.
II. **A health plan**: health insurance companies, health maintenance organization (HMO), company health plans, government-sponsored programs like Medicare and Medicaid, and veterans' health care programs.
III. **A health care clearinghouse**: "public or private entity, including a billing service, repricing company, or community health information system, which processes non-standard data or transactions received from one entity into standard transactions or data elements, or vice versa."[79]

The "covered entities" are defined in the HIPAA rules as "(a) Except as otherwise provided, the standards, requirements, and implementation specifications adopted under this subchapter apply to the following entities: (1) a health plan, (2) a health care clearinghouse, (3) a health care provider who transmits any health information in electronic form in connection with a transaction covered by this subchapter. (b) Where provided, the standards,

[74] U.S. Congress. H.R.3103—Health Insurance Portability and Accountability Act of 1996104th Congress (1995–1996). Retrieved from https://www.congress.gov/bill/104th-congress/house-bill/3103/text
[75] U.S. Department of Health and Human Services. OCR privacy Brief, Summary of HIPAA Privacy Rules. Retrieved from https://www.hhs.gov/sites/default/files/privacysummary.pdf
[76] Pub. L. 104-191.
[77] *Id.* at 76.
[78] 45 C.F.R. § 164.304.
[79] Health and Human Services. Health Information Privacy Cover. Covered Entities and Business Associates. Retrieved from https://www.hhs.gov/hipaa/for-professionals/covered-entities/index.html

requirements, and implementation specifications adopted under this subchapter apply to a business associate."[80]

"Business Associates" are individuals or organizations who come in contact with or may disclose Protected Health Information (PHI). Examples include accountants, billing company services, cloud storage, email services, healthcare app developers, legal services, IT contractors, and web hosting services. In addition, HIPAA requires a contract or a "Business Associate Agreement" with companies or individuals to safeguard the PHI it receives or creates on behalf of the *covered entity.*

"Business Associates" are defined as (i) a health information organization, e-prescribing gateway, or other "person that provides data transmission services with respect to protected health information to a covered entity and that requires access on a routine basis to such protected health information. (ii) A person that offers a personal health record to one or more individuals on behalf of a covered entity. (iii) A subcontractor that creates, receives, maintains, or transmits protected health information on behalf of the business associate."[81]

4.3.2.2 Penalties for Violating HIPAA Rule

Violations under HIPAA are very costly. The penalties are based on the level of negligence and can be both civil and criminal. Also, penalties may be imposed on a person or covered entity. For example, under section 13410(D) of the HITECH Act, when a covered entity or person did not know of a violation, "and by exercising reasonable diligence would not have known,"[82] a fine of $100 to $50,000 for every violation, up to a maximum of $1.5 million for identical provisions during a calendar year, may be imposed.

For HIPAA Act sections: § 164.308 Administrative safeguards, § 164.310 Physical safeguards, § 164.312 Technical safeguards, and § 164.314 Organizational requirements see Appendix C.

4.3.3 Health Information Technology for Economic and Clinical Health Act

The HITECH Act[83] was signed into law by President Barack Obama on February 17, 2009, and is a part of the American Recovery and Reinvestment

[80] 45 CFR § 160.103.
[81] *Id.* at 80.
[82] The American Recovery and Reinvestment Act of 2009. TITLE XIII—The Health Information Technology for Economic and Clinical Health (HITECH) Act. SEC. 13410. Improved Enforcement. U.S. Government Publishing Office. Retrieved from https://www.govinfo.gov/content/pkg/PLAW-111publ5/pdf/PLAW-111publ5.pdf
[83] *Id.*at 82.

Act of 2009 (ARRA) (Pub. L. 111–5),[84] under Title XIII. The law was established to advance and expand the adoption of Electronic Health Records (EHRs) with its concept of "Meaningful Use." This means the adoption and use of a certified EHR technology, for example e-prescribing, in a manner that improves the quality of health care. The Act strengthens the civil and criminal enforcement of HIPAA regulations with section 13410(D) regarding privacy and security concerns associated with electronic transmission of EHR.

For HITECH Act, § 13410 Improved Enforcement, see Appendix D.

4.3.4 Protecting Consumers' Privacy Rights with FTC's Section 5: Federal Trade Commission Act

The Federal Trade Commission is a U.S. federal agency responsible for protecting consumers from unfair business practices and for improving competition across the economy (Figure 4.7). The FTC Act of 1914 founded the Commission and was signed into law by President Woodrow Wilson.[85] In the area of data security, its primary legal authority comes from FTC, section 5,[86] where "unfair or deceptive Acts or practices in or affecting commerce … are … declared unlawful."[87] The law does not reference data security, but the FTC claims authority for the safety of the Web, also defining as unlawful "unfair or deceptive acts or practices including those involving foreign commerce that (i) cause or are likely to cause reasonably foreseeable injury within the United States; or (ii) involve material conduct occurring within the United States."[88]

FIGURE 4.7 Federal Trade Commission logo.

The FTC has extensive authority to enforce a variety of laws covering privacy and data security. These include the Truth in Lending Act (TILA),[89] which protects against unfair credit card practices and specifies that

[84] Public Law 111—5—American Recovery and Reinvestment Act of 2009. U.S. Government Publishing Office. Retrieved from https://www.govinfo.gov/app/details/PLAW-111publ5

[85] Hoofnagle, Chris Jay. Federal Trade Commission privacy law and policy. Cambridge University Press, 2016.

[86] 15 U.S.C. § 45.

[87] 15 U.S.C. Sec. 45(a)(1).

[88] 15 U.S.C. Sec. 45(a)(4)(A).

[89] 15 U.S.C. §§ 1601-1667f. Retrieved from https://uscode.house.gov/view.xhtml?req=granuleid%3AUSC-prelim-title15-chapter41-subchapter1&edition=prelim

information regarding finance charges must be disclosed; the CAN-SPAM Act,[90] which protects consumers from spam emails and establishes rules for commercial email and messages, addressing penalties for violations of the Act; and the Children's Online Privacy Protection Act (COPPA),[91] which institutes requirements on websites or online services focused on children under 13 years old. COPPA also gives parents control over the collection or use of the child's information. The Equal Credit Opportunity Act (ECOA)[92] prohibits credit discrimination, while the Fair Credit Reporting Act (FCRA)[93] regulates the collection of consumers' credit information and access to credit reports. The Fair Debt Collection Practices Act[94] protects consumers from debt collectors who use abusive, unfair, or deceptive practices. Finally, the Telemarketing and Consumer Fraud and Abuse Prevention Act[95] protects consumers from telemarketing deception and abuse, for example unsolicited phone calls that are deemed an invasion of privacy.

4.3.4.1 Important FTC Cases

The FTC has charged offenders who have violated section 5 of the FTC Act. Additionally, it imposes other federal laws regarding consumers' privacy and security.

1. *Google LLC and YouTube, LLC* (Civil Action Number:1:19-cv-02642). In 2019, the FTC and the New York Attorney General's office claimed that Google and YouTube collected personal information from children under 13 years without parental consent. Specifically, YouTube's video sharing service violated the law by using cookies to track children's personal information without parental consent. As a result, Google and its subsidiary YouTube agreed to pay a $170 million civil penalty to settle the allegations.
2. In another case, CVS Pharmacy (FTC File No. 072 3119) (C-2459), one of the largest pharmacies in the United States, was charged with failing to take appropriate security measures to protect sensitive financial and medical information for its customers and employees.

---

[90] 15 U.S.C. 103—Controlling the Assault of Non-Solicited Pornography and Marketing. U.S. Government Publishing Office. Retrieved from https://www.govinfo.gov/content/pkg/USCODE-2011-title15/html/USCODE-2011-title15-chap103.htm

[91] 15 U.S.C. §§ 6501–6505 Children's Online Privacy Protection. Retrieved from https://uscode.house.gov/view.xhtml?req=granuleid%3AUSC-prelim-title15-section6501&edition=prelim

[92] 15 U.S.C. §§ 1691–1691f. Retrieved from https://www.govinfo.gov/content/pkg/USCODE-2011-title15/html/USCODE-2011-title15-chap41-subchapIV-sec1691.htm and https://www.govinfo.gov/content/pkg/USCODE-2011-title15/html/USCODE-2011-title15-chap41-subchapIV-sec1691f.htm

[93] 15 U.S.C. § 1681. U.S. Government Publishing Office. Retrieved from https://www.govinfo.gov/content/pkg/USCODE-2018-title15/html/USCODE-2018-title15-chap41-subchapIII-sec1681.htm

[94] 15 U.S.C. §§ 1692–1692p Debt Collection Practices. U.S. Government Publishing Office. Retrieved from https://www.govinfo.gov/content/pkg/USCODE-2011-title15/html/USCODE-2011-title15-chap41-subchapV.htm

[95] 15 U.S.C. §§ 6101–6108 U.S. Government Publishing Office. Retrieved from https://www.govinfo.gov/content/pkg/USCODE-2011-title15/html/USCODE-2011-title15-chap87-sec6101.htm

> CVS pharmacies around the country threw confidential information into the garbage, including pill bottles with patient information, orders with social security numbers, credit card numbers, and driver's license numbers. HHS opened its own investigation into CVS's disposal of health information protected by HIPAA. As a result, the company agreed to pay $2.25 million to settle the matter with HHS.

Most cases settle with FTC without the expense and publicity of a trial. One example is the $5 billion penalty imposed on Facebook for violating consumers' privacy, the largest privacy or data security penalty imposed worldwide.

> "Despite repeated promises to its billions of users worldwide that they could control how their personal information is shared, Facebook undermined consumers' choices," said FTC Chairman Joe Simons. "The magnitude of the $5 billion penalty and sweeping conduct relief are unprecedented in the history of the FTC. The relief is designed not only to punish future violations but, more importantly, to change Facebook's entire privacy culture to decrease the likelihood of continued violations. The Commission takes consumer privacy seriously and will enforce FTC orders to the fullest extent of the law."[96]

The FTC has extraordinary powers; Congress has given it unparalleled investigative and prosecutory power. It can investigate any business practice in the name of consumer protection.

For FTC's § 5 see Appendix E.

4.3.5 Laws Affecting Financial Institutions

4.3.5.1 The Gramm-Leach-Bliley Act of 1999 (GLBA)

FINANCIAL INSTITUTION

The growth of mobile technology and the digital transformation of financial institutions have produced major concerns about privacy and misuse of data. Each financial institution retains information about its customers: names, addresses, email addresses, motor vehicle license numbers, passport numbers, financial data, and social security numbers. Penalties for not protecting this data carry hefty consequences including loss of coverage from the Federal Deposit Insurance Corporation (FDIC), resulting at the end of the financial firm's business.

The Gramm–Leach–Bliley Act[97] is also known as the Gramm–Leach–Bliley Financial Services Modernization Act. Its main function is to protect

---

[96] The Federal Trade Commission. FTC Imposes $5 Billion Penalty and Sweeping New Privacy Restrictions on Facebook. Retrieved from https://www.ftc.gov/news-events/press-releases/2019/07/ftc-imposes-5-billion-penalty-sweeping-new-privacy-restrictions

[97] Public Law 106–102—Nov. 12, 1999. The Gramm-Leach-Bliley Act. Retrieved from https://www.govinfo.gov/content/pkg/PLAW-106publ102/pdf/PLAW-106publ102.pdf

the consumer's financial privacy by regulating the handling of personal information obtained by financial institutions. The term "financial institutions" has a broad definition and includes banks, insurance companies, securities firms, investment banks, investment companies, brokerage firms, non-bank mortgage lenders, automotive dealers, and tax return preparers. The law requires these institutions to explain their information sharing practices and how they safeguard the sensitive data of their customers.

The most significant section of the GLBA is the Safeguards Rule, stating that any financial institution must protect the consumer information they collect. In addition to having measures in place to keep customer information secure, Gramm–Leach–Bliley requires federal regulating agencies to adopt administrative, technical, and physical safeguards for the instructions that they regulate.

> TITLE V—PRIVACY Subtitle A—Disclosure of Nonpublic Personal Information
>
> 15 USC 6801. SEC. 501. PROTECTION OF NONPUBLIC PERSONAL INFORMATION.
>
> (a) PRIVACY OBLIGATION POLICY. It is the policy of the Congress that each financial institution has an affirmative and continuing obligation to respect the privacy of its customers and to protect the security and confidentiality of those customers' nonpublic personal information.
>
> (b) FINANCIAL INSTITUTIONS SAFEGUARDS. In furtherance of the policy in subsection (a), each agency or authority described in section 505(a) shall establish appropriate standards for the financial institutions subject to their jurisdiction relating to administrative, technical, and physical safeguards
>
> (1) to insure the security and confidentiality of customer records and information;
>
> (2) to protect against any anticipated threats or hazards to the security or integrity of such records; and
>
> (3) to protect against unauthorized access to or use of such records or information which could result in substantial harm or inconvenience to any customer.[98]

The law refers to the term "non-public personal information" in § 6809(4) and defines it as personally identifiable information of a financial nature provided by a consumer to a financial institution, resulting from a transaction or service performed for the consumer, or otherwise obtained by a financial institution.

[98] 15 U.S.C. § 6801(a)(b).

(4) NONPUBLIC PERSONAL INFORMATION. (A) The term "nonpublic personal information" means personally identifiable financial information

(i) provided by a consumer to a financial institution;
(ii) resulting from any transaction with the consumer or any service performed for the consumer; or
(iii) otherwise obtained by the financial institution."[99]

Some examples of "nonpublic personal information" include: contact information, consumer account number and application information, consumer report information gained by the financial institution such as employee's credit worthiness, credit standing, credit capacity, social security number, and Internet cookie information.

Under the Safeguards Rule, the financial institutions must develop, implement, and maintain a comprehensive information security plan to protect the confidentiality of the client's data. Furthermore, the financial institution must assign an employee to ensure the security and confidentiality of consumer information, "to protect against any anticipated threats or hazards to the security or integrity of such records."[100] In addition, the security program must include employee training on information security; information system risk management; how to properly dispose of customer information; identifying and managing system failures; and detecting, responding, and maintaining procedures for a security breach. On December 4, 2015, Congress passed a new section of the law, section 503(f), requiring financial institutions to provide their customers with initial and annual privacy notices concerning the institution's privacy policies.[101]

4.3.5.1.1 Enforcement and Penalties for Violating the GLBA

The *Securities and Exchange Commission (SEC)* is an independent U.S. Federal Agency in charge of protecting investors; maintaining fair, orderly, and efficient markets; and facilitating capital formation (Figure 4.8). The SEC adopted Regulation S-P § 248.30, covering procedures to safeguard customer records and information and the disposal of consumer report information, in accordance with the GLBA Safeguard Rules requirements.[102] The SEC enforces federal laws regulating the securities industry: securities markets,

---

[99] 15 U.S.C. § 6809(4).
[100] *Id.* at 98.
[101] 12 C.F.R. § 1016.9 Retrieved from https://www.govinfo.gov/content/pkg/CFR-2014-title12-vol8/pdf/CFR-2014-title12-vol8-sec1016-9.pdf and https://www.federalregister.gov/documents/2018/08/17/2018-17572/amendment-to-the-annual-privacy-notice-requirement-under-the-gramm-leach-bliley-act-regulation-p
[102] 17 C.F.R. §248.30.

stock exchanges, stock markets, mutual funds, and the electronic securities markets in the United States.

In addition to the SEC, the FTC aggressively enforces the Safeguard Rules. The agency monitors Title V, subtitle A, of GLBA,[103] ensuring that financial institutions protect consumers' financial privacy and most importantly their personal financial data.

FIGURE 4.8 The Securities and Exchange Commission (SEC) logo.

> SEC. 505. ENFORCEMENT. (a) IN GENERAL.—This subtitle and the regulations prescribed thereunder shall be enforced by the Federal functional regulators, the State insurance authorities, and the Federal Trade Commission with respect to financial institutions and other persons subject to their jurisdiction under applicable law.[104]

The enforcement and penalties for violations include monetary damages, forfeiture, and imprisonment. In some cases, these could exceed $1 million and the likelihood of losing FDIC insurance, resulting at the end of the financial firm's business.

4.3.5.2 Red Flags Rule

The Fair and Accurate Credit Transactions Act (FACT)[105] was enacted by Congress in 2003 and signed by President George W. Bush as the Fair Credit Reporting Act.[106] The Act protects consumers' information in their credit reports and regulates the collection, distribution, and use of consumer information, including credit information. In particular, the "Red Flags Rule" part of the Act was created to protect consumers against identity theft. The Red Flags Rule requires banking regulators to develop regulations requiring financial institutions to avert, detect, and respond to identity theft patterns.[107] Furthermore, the act makes financial institutions become more preemptive with consumers' privacy and prevention of identity theft. Finally, it allows every consumer to access their credit report yearly at no cost.

For part 681—Identity Theft Rules see Appendix F.

---

[103] 15 U.S.C. § 6801 et seq.

[104] 15 U.S.C. § 6805.

[105] U.S. Congress. H.R.2622—Fair and Accurate Credit Transactions Act of 2003, Public Law No: 108–159 (12/04/2003). Retrieved from https://www.congress.gov/bill/108th-congress/house-bill/2622/text

[106] 15 U.S.C. § 1681.

[107] 15 U.S.C. § 1681m.

4.3.6 Laws Affecting Utilities

4.3.6.1 The Federal Energy Regulatory Commission

Under the Energy Policy Act of 2005[108] Congress authorized the Federal Energy Regulatory Commission to regulate and oversee the national electric utilities (Figure 4.9). The FERG is a federal[109] independent agency[110] that regulates interstate electric utilities, natural gas, and oil.

FIGURE 4.9 The Federal Energy Regulatory Commission (FERC) logo.

One of the biggest threats to electric utilities and power companies is the growing danger of cyberattacks and their effect on the operations and security of the U.S. Electric Power Grid. The electric grid depends on the Industrial Control System (ICS). The grid's ICS network sensors monitor important components. A common ICS network system is the Supervisory Control and Data Acquisition (SCADA), which collects information from remote stations.[111,112] Since SCADA is connected to the Internet, it is vulnerable to cyberattacks. One cyberattack occurred in the Ukrainian Power Grid in 2015 when hackers attacked the distribution utility substations and turned off power to over 225,000 customers. Similar attacks by Russian hackers occurred in Kiev in 2016, sabotaging infrastructure by shutting down substations which controlled 200 megawatts of capacity.[113]

Besides direct cyberattacks by hackers, other threats exist from infected IoT devices connected to the same network as an electric grid. Hackers can take control of a great number of infected IoT devices and launch denial-of-service or other cyberattacks on an electric grid. Additionally, hackers can spread malware, using IoTs to damage these systems on the network, causing interruptions of electrical system operation or manipulation of information. These kinds of attacks could potentially transpire in U.S. electric grids as well. As a result, in 2017, the president issued Executive Order (EO) 13800 on "Strengthening the Cybersecurity of Federal Networks and

---

[108] Pub.L.109-58; EPACT05-Energy Policy Act of 2005. U.S. Government Publishing Office. Retrieved from https://www.govinfo.gov/content/pkg/PLAW-109publ58/html/PLAW-109publ58.htm

[109] 42 USC 7172.

[110] 42 USC 7171(a).

[111] Congressional Research Service, Electric Grid Cybersecurity (R45312). Updated September 4, 2018. Retrieved from https://crsreports.congress.gov

[112] Cruz, Tiago, Luis Rosa, Jorge Proença, Leandros Maglaras, Matthieu Aubigny, Leonid Lev, Jianmin Jiang, and Paulo Simoes. "A cybersecurity detection framework for supervisory control and data acquisition systems." *IEEE Transactions on Industrial Informatics* 12, no. 6 (2016): 2236–2246.

[113] Whitehead, David E., Kevin Owens, Dennis Gammel, and Jess Smith. "Ukraine cyber-induced power outage: Analysis and practical mitigation strategies." In *2017 70th Annual Conference for Protective Relay Engineers (CPRE)*, pp. 1–8. IEEE, 2017.

Critical Infrastructure."[114] The executive order is meant to avoid the dangers of cyberattack to critical infrastructure and calls for an assessment of the danger, development of the ability to manage and mitigate consequences, and sharing of cyber threat information with the public and private sectors.

The Federal Energy Regulatory Commission has adopted cybersecurity framework standards for critical infrastructu\re protection (CIP).[115] These standards were designed by the North American Electric Reliability Corporation (NERC), a not-for-profit corporation, and are intended to improve the security of our power systems. These cyber and physical security standards are mandatory, and utility companies may be subject to a fine of up to $1 million per violation per day if the standards are not followed. Table 4.3 shows some of NERC's critical infrastructure protection standards.[116]

TABLE 4.3 Several North American Electric Reliability Corporation (NERC) Critical Infrastructure Protection Standards

Standards	Title	Description
CIP-001	Sabotage Reporting	Report sabotage to the appropriate governmental agencies
CIP-002	Critical Cyber Asset Identification	Identify and protect Bulk Electric System (BES) against compromise
CIP-003	Security Management Controls	Use consistent security management controls to protect BES Cyber Systems against compromise
CIP-004	Cyber Security Personnel and Training	Require personnel risk assessment training and security awareness in BES Cyber Systems
CIP-006	Physical Security of BES Cyber Systems	Stipulate a security plan to protect BES Cyber Systems against compromise
CIP-007	Cyber Security System Security Management	Select technical, operational, and procedural requirements to support BES Cyber Systems against compromise
CIP-009	Cyber Security Recovery Plans for BES Cyber Systems	Specify recovery plan requirements for the continued stability, operability, and reliability of the BES
CIP-010	Cyber Security Configuration Change Management and Vulnerability Assessments	Develop changes to prevent and detect unauthorized changes to BES Cyber Systems.

114 Presidential Executive Order on Strengthening the Cybersecurity of Federal Networks and Critical Infrastructure. Retrieved from https://www.whitehouse.gov/presidential-actions/presidential-executive-order-strengthening-cybersecurity-federal-networks-critical-infrastructure/

115 North American Electric Reliability Corporation (NERC), CIP Standards. Retrieved from https://www.nerc.com/pa/Stand/Pages/CIPStandards.aspx

116 *Id.* at 115.

4.3.6.2 Nuclear Regulatory Commission

The *Nuclear Regulatory Commission* is an independent agency regulating and licensing the nuclear power plants in the United States (Figure 4.10). More specifically, the Code of Federal Regulations, 10 C.F.R. § 73.54 protects digital computer and communication systems and networks from cyberattack.[117,118] In addition, it requires protecting the networks from attempts to modify, destroy, or compromise the integrity of data or software.[119] The NRC also stipulates that nuclear power plants will implement a cybersecurity plan and provide an incident response and recovery plan.[120]

FIGURE 4.10 The Nuclear Regulatory Commission (NRC) logo.

4.4 Public and Private Sector Entities Partnerships in Cyberspace

A public and private collaboration is necessary to address some of the biggest challenges in cybersecurity. As escalating cyberattacks continue to affect governments and private entities, the federal government can act as a central repository and distributor of cyberintelligence and guidelines. The federal government must provide cybersecurity tools to safeguard both public and private information. Organizations outside the federal government should play a leading role in public–private partnerships to train employees, improve technology, identify and rectify vulnerabilities, and exchange information.

For a complete 6 U.S.C. § 1501—Domestic Security Chapter 6—Cybersecurity Subchapter I—Cybersecurity Information Sharing Sec. 1501—Definitions see Appendix G.

---

117 10 C.F.R. §73.54—Protection of digital computer and communication systems and networks. U.S. Government Publishing Office. Retrieved from https://www.govinfo.gov/content/pkg/CFR-2012-title10-vol2/pdf/CFR-2012-title10-vol2-sec73-54.pdf

118 10 C.F.R.§ 73.54(a)(1).

119 10 C.F.R.§ 73.54(a)(2).

120 10 C.F.R.§ 73.54(e).

4.4.1 Cybersecurity Information Sharing Act of 2015 (CISA)

On December 18, 2015, President Obama signed the Consolidated Appropriations Act[121] into law (not to be confused with the CISA agency that President Donald Trump created). The Act is found at Division N, Title I of the Cybersecurity Information Sharing Act of 2015 (CISA). It was created to increase the *sharing of cybersecurity threat information* for *cybersecurity purposes* between the public and private sector entities while protecting privacy and civil liberties. CISA defines the term "cybersecurity purpose" as "the purpose of protecting an information system or information that is stored on, processed by, or transiting an information system from a cybersecurity threat or security vulnerability."[122] The law authorizes private entities to monitor and share their information with the federal government on a voluntary basis. Private entities can declare information shared as proprietary and confidential, and shared information will not be subject to state or local freedom of information requests.[123] Under the law, the Department of Homeland Security will collect and assess all cyber threat information coming from private entities. DHS is also responsible for protecting critical infrastructure from physical and cyber threats, along with the National Cybersecurity and Communications Integration Center (NCCIS) and the United States Computer Emergency Readiness Team (US-CERT). The primary advantage of this *cyber threat indicator* is it provides a safe opportunity to share information with the federal government to defend its networks from cyber threats and vulnerabilities identified by other entities.

> The term "cyber threat indicator" means information that is necessary to describe or identify—
>
> (A) malicious reconnaissance, including anomalous patterns of communications that appear to be transmitted for the purpose of gathering technical information related to a cybersecurity threat or security vulnerability;
> (B) a method of defeating a security control or exploitation of a security vulnerability;
> (C) a security vulnerability, including anomalous activity that appears to indicate the existence of a security vulnerability;
> (D) a method of causing a user with legitimate access to an information system or information that is stored on, processed by, or transiting an information system to unwittingly enable the defeat of a security control or exploitation of a security vulnerability;

[121] Pub. L. 114-113 Consolidated Appropriations Act 2016. U.S. Government Publishing Office. Retrieved from https://www.govinfo.gov/content/pkg/PLAW-114publ113/html/PLAW-114publ113.htm
[122] Cybersecurity Information Sharing Act of 2015, § 102.
[123] *Id.*at 122.

(E) malicious cyber command and control;
(F) the actual or potential harm caused by an incident, including a description of the information exfiltrated because of a particular cybersecurity threat.
(G) any other attribute of a cybersecurity threat, if disclosure of such attribute is not otherwise prohibited by law; or
(H) any combination thereof.[124]

4.4.2 The Cybersecurity and Infrastructure Security Agency

A new Act was signed into law on November 16, 2018, by President Donald Trump. Named the Cybersecurity and Infrastructure Security Agency (Figure 4.11), it became the nation's risk advisor.[125,126] Even though its name mirrors that of the Cybersecurity Information Sharing Act of 2015, this new agency is quite different. It is an operational component of DHS and is responsible for protecting the critical infrastructure from physical and cyber threats. The CISA is expected to have a positive effect in cybersecurity and in the 16 identified sectors of critical infrastructure which include Chemical, Commercial Facilities, Communications, Critical Manufacturing, Dams, Defense Industry, Emergency Services, Energy Infrastructure; Financial; Food and Agriculture; Government Facilities; Healthcare and Public Health; Information Technology; Nuclear Reactor Materials and Waste; Transportation; and Wastewater Systems.[127] In addition, the agency will coordinate with private and public sectors and will bring its technical assistance and assessments to infrastructure owners and operators.

FIGURE 4.11 The Cybersecurity and Infrastructure Security Agency (CISA) logo.

---

[124] *Id.*at 122.

[125] Cybersecurity and Infrastructure Security Agency (CISA). Retrieved from https://www.cisa.gov/

[126] U.S. Congress, Cybersecurity and Infrastructure Security Agency Act of 2018. Retrieved from https://www.congress.gov/bill/115th-congress/house-bill/3359/text

[127] CISA, Critical Infrastructure Sectors. Retrieved from https://www.cisa.gov/critical-infrastructure-sectors

4.4.3 The National Cybersecurity and Critical Infrastructure Protection Act of 2014 (NCPA)

The National Cybersecurity and Critical Infrastructure Protection Act of 2014[128] amended the Homeland Security Act of 2002 (HSA). The act requires DHS to conduct cybersecurity activities; critical infrastructure protection; and the sharing of information among federal entities, state and local governments, private entities, and critical infrastructure relevant to cyber threat information. The act emphasizes promoting information sharing between the government and the private sector through DHS. Two of the most important titles concerning cybersecurity are:[129]

- **Title I**—Securing the Nation against Cyber Attack
  - designates the 16 critical infrastructure sectors.
  - creates the National Cybersecurity and Communications Integration Center (NCCIC) as a federal civilian information sharing organization.
  - promotes ongoing multidirectional sharing of information.
  - reports cyber incidents, threats, and vulnerabilities impacting federal civilian information systems and critical infrastructure systems.
- **Title II**—Public–Private Collaboration on Cybersecurity.
  - directs NIST to develop a voluntary cybersecurity framework.
  - forbids NIST from requiring the use of specific solutions, products, services, or manufacturing or design techniques.

4.4.4 Cybersecurity Enhancement Act of 2014 (CEA)

The Cybersecurity Enhancement Act of 2014 (CEA)[130] provides voluntary public–private partnerships to improve cybersecurity and supports cybersecurity research and development, education, and awareness. This act focuses on empowering NIST to enable the development of a voluntary cybersecurity framework for critical infrastructure organizations that could be adopted in the private sector and that would strengthen cyber protocols in the event of regulatory oversight. The NIST is not granted any regulatory authority. Below is a short description of all titles of this Act.[131]

- **Title I**: Public–Private Collaboration on Cybersecurity (Sec. 101)

---

[128] U.S. Congress, National Cybersecurity and Critical Infrastructure Protection Act of 2014. Retrieved from https://www.congress.gov/bill/113th-congress/house-bill/3696

[129] *Id.* at 128.

[130] *Id.* at 71.

[131] *Id.* at 71.

- strengthens, facilitates, and supports the development of the cybersecurity framework for critical infrastructure organizations by NIST.
- **Title II**: Cybersecurity Research and Development (Sec. 201)
  - directs the National Science Foundation (NSF) to support cybersecurity research; allows research and development grants for secure fundamental protocols, software engineering, monitoring, detection, mitigation, and rapid recovery methods; and secure wireless networks, mobile devices, and cloud infrastructure.
- **Title III**: Education and Workforce Development (Sec. 301)
  - The NSF should continue the federal cyber scholarship for cybersecurity programs in the public sector workforce.
- **Title IV**: Cybersecurity Awareness and Preparedness (Sec. 401)
  - distributes technical standards and identify best practices by individuals, businesses, and educational institutions
- **Title V**: Advancement of Cybersecurity Technical Standards (Sec. 502)
  - NIST to coordinate federal agencies in the development of international technical standards related to information system security.

4.5 Cybersecurity Requirements for Federal Government Contractors

The U.S. federal government has been a frequent target of cybersecurity attacks. Fortunately, Congress has recognized the importance of information security inside the federal government and has enacted laws to ensure information security controls and to regulate how contractors handle personal data. In addition, federal agencies have strengthened cybersecurity regulations and standards, especially after the massive leak caused by National Security Agency's contractor Edward Snowden.[132] As a result, the federal government has new security standards and regulations that depend on what kind of information is being handled, stored, and processed. Following are the most important legislations and standards for federal government and contractors.

[132] *Id.* at 1.

4.5.1 Federal Information Security Modernization Act of 2014

On December 17, 2002, President George W. Bush signed into law the **E-Government Act.**[133] It promotes electronic government services, including the Internet and other information technologies, and makes it easier for citizens and businesses to interact with the federal government. The law also acknowledges the importance of information security in the federal government. More significantly, Title III: Information Security Sec. 301 is the **Federal Information Security Management Act of 2002 (FISMA)**[134] that requires the federal government to develop a framework for the government to improve, evaluate, and strengthen its information security controls. The act also strengthened the role of NIST and established an office of the electronic government within the Office of Management and Budget (OMB).

In 2014, the Federal Information Security Management Act of 2002 (FISMA) was replaced by the Federal Information Security Modernization Act of 2014 (FISMA) or FISMA 2014.[135] The new law provides changes and updates to federal cybersecurity practices, providing a better response to evolving cybersecurity threats. It also safeguards the efficiency of information security controls that support federal information systems. The entire federal government, including agencies, contractors, subcontractors, and any entity that interchanges data with federal government systems, must ensure compliance with FISMA. The FBI is responsible for investigating cyberattacks against public and private targets by criminals.[136] Following is a brief overview of the law in strengthening networks, systems, and data of the federal government.

- The law defines "national security system" as any information system or telecommunications system used or operated by an agency or by a contractor of an agency or other organization on behalf of an agency (44 U.S.C. § 3552).
- The law requires federal agencies to have information security and privacy policies and guidelines (44 U.S.C. § 3553).
- The OMB monitors agency implementation of the information security policies and guidelines (§ 3553).

---

[133] Pub. L. 107-347 E-Government Act of 2002. U.S. Government Publishing Office. Retrieved from https ://www.govinfo.gov/content/pkg/CRPT-107hrpt787/html/CRPT-107hrpt787-pt1.htm

[134] Tittle III: Information Security Sec. 301.Federal Information Security Management Act of 2002 (FISMA). U.S. Government Publishing Office. Retrieved from https://www.govinfo.gov/content/pkg/PLAW-107publ347/pdf/PLAW-107publ347.pdf

[135] U.S Congress, Federal Information Security Modernization Act of 2014 (FISMA). Retrieved from https://www.congress.gov/113/plaws/publ283/PLAW-113publ283.pdf or U.S. Government Publishing Office. Retrieved from https://www.govinfo.gov/content/pkg/CRPT-113srpt256/html/CRPT-113srpt256.htm

[136] The Federal Bureau of Investigation. What We Investigate. Retrieved from https://www.fbi.gov/investigate

- The director of OMB is required to notify Congress of major security incidents within 7 days (44 U.S.C. § 3554, § 3558).
- The OMB is responsible for assembling meetings with senior agency officials to help ensure the implementation of information security policies and practices and for collaborating to develop cybersecurity policies and cybersecurity programs and to coordinate government response to cyberattacks (44 U.S.C. § 3553).
- The law establishes a Federal Chief Information Security Officer for OMB and the Cyber and National Security Unit (44 U.S.C. § 3553).
- Under FISMA, DHS takes the lead in federal cybersecurity and coordinates federal government-wide cybersecurity efforts (44 U.S.C. § 3556).
- NIST is responsible for creating standards for information systems, in coordination with OMB and other federal agencies (44 U.S.C. § 3553).
- The head of each federal agency provides information on security protections and implementation of information security policies and practices for national security systems (44 U.S.C. § 3554).
- The director of the OMB shall ensure that data breach notification policies and guidelines are updated periodically (44 U.S.C. § 3558).

4.5.2 NIST Information Security Controls for Government Agencies and Contractors

As the federal government depends heavily upon contractors for products and services, these contractors are particularly susceptible to cyberattacks. As a result, FISMA 2014 assigned NIST to provide standards and guidance to aid agencies and contractors in meeting legal requirements.[137] These standards are mandatory. However, not all organizations handle the same level of information. Prior to adopting a standard, each organization must determine the security category or potential impact on organizations or individuals of their information systems as provided by the FIPS Publication 199, Standards for Security Categorization of Federal Information and Information Systems.[138] FIPS stands for Federal Information Processing Standards, and its most significant publications are FIPS Publication 200, Minimum Security Requirements for Federal Information and Information Systems,[139] and NIST Special Publication

[137] NIST, Computer Security Resource Center. Publication search. Retrieved from https://csrc.nist.gov/publications/fips

[138] NIST, FIPS Publication 199, Standards for Security Categorization of Federal Information and Information Systems. Retrieved from https://nvlpubs.nist.gov/nistpubs/FIPS/NIST.FIPS.199.pdf

[139] NIST, Computer Security Resource Center. Publication search FIPS series. Retrieved from https://csrc.nist.gov/publications/fips

800-53.[140] Both publications ensure that proper security controls and security requirements are implemented by federal information systems and information.

4.6 Most Important Internet Surveillance Laws in the United States

The arrival of the Internet, the exponential growth in the number of mobile devices along with the advent of the Internet of Things, and biometric technologies, all mean that the job of protecting personal privacy has changed. The Fourth Amendment provides protection from unreasonable searches and seizures and has been used to defend wiretaps and other forms of surveillance. Following are the laws that limit the surveillance of government and private entities in the United States.

4.6.1 All Writs Act

The All Writs Act[141] was part of the Judiciary Act of 1789, which established the Judicial Courts of the United States. The Act allows federal judges to issue "writs" or formal orders, considered orders from the courts. The All Writs Act has limitations and should be used solely in situations where there is no other law or regulation and should not be used to circumvent or evade current laws. The All Writs Act states:

(a) The Supreme Court and all courts established by Act of Congress may issue all writs necessary or appropriate in aid of their respective jurisdictions and agreeable to the usages and principles of law.
(b) An alternative writ or rule nisi may be issued by a justice or judge of a court which has jurisdiction (§ 1651(a)(b)).

4.6.1.1 Significant Case

Nevertheless, in 1977, in the case of the *United States v. New York Telephone Co.*[142] the Supreme Court ruled that the FBI may obtain a court order forcing telephone companies to install pen registers. A pen register, or dialed number recorder (DNR), is an electronic device that records all numbers called from a particular telephone line. The All

[140] NIST, Computer Security Resource Center. Publication search SP 800 series. Retrieved from https://csrc.nist.gov/publications/sp800
[141] 28 U.S.C. § 1651.
[142] *United States v. New York Telephone Co.*, 434 U.S. 159 (1977).

Writs Act gave the court the power to order this assistance from the telephone company.

In other cases, the federal government had used the All Writs Act to access encrypted cell phones like Apple's iPhone. In a Brooklyn drug case, federal law enforcement requested Apple's help in unlocking an iPhone. A federal judge ruled that Apple had complied with 70 All Writs Act orders without objection, but in this case the All Writs Act did not require Apple to assist law enforcement in unlocking the iPhone.[143]

> the relief the government seeks is unavailable because Congress has considered legislation that would achieve the same result but has not adopted it. In addition, applicable case law requires me to consider three factors in deciding whether to issue an order under the [All Writs Act]: the closeness of Apple's relationship to the underlying criminal conduct and government investigation; the burden the requested order would impose on Apple; and the necessity of imposing such a burden on Apple. As explained below, after reviewing the facts in the record and the parties' arguments, I conclude that none of those factors justifies imposing on Apple the obligation to assist the government's investigation against its will. I therefore deny the motion. … Ultimately, the question to be answered in this matter, and in others like it across the country, is not whether the government should be able to force Apple to help it unlock a specific device; it is instead whether the All Writs Act resolves that issue and many others like it yet to come. For the reasons set forth above, I conclude that it does not. (James Orenstein, U.S. Magistrate Judge, February 29, 2016)[144]

4.6.2 Fourth Amendment

The Fourth Amendment to the Constitution is the basis for the individual's right to privacy (Figure 4.12). But, as technology advances, upholding the right to privacy has become a challenge for the legal system in the United States. When there is an imperative government interest, individual privacy rights are diminished. Then again, because the Fourth Amendment is an important constitutional right, this area is ripe for litigation. The Amendment prevents the government from exercising its authority against unreasonable search and seizure of the property of U.S. citizens. Under the Fourth Amendment, *a warrant is required to be issued by a judge based on probable cause*. The Amendment states that:

---

[143] United States District Courteastern District of New York, No. 15-MC-1902 (JO) (E. D. N. Y. Feb. 29, 2016). Retrieved from https://img.nyed.uscourts.gov/files/opinions/Order%2015mc1902.pdf

[144] *Id.* at 143.

FIGURE 4.12 **The Bill of Rights. The first 10 amendments to the Constitution, including the Fourth Amendment, comprise the Bill of Rights. Courtesy of The National Archives.**

> The right of the people to be secure in their persons, houses, papers, and effects, against unreasonable searches and seizures, shall not be violated, and no Warrants shall issue, but upon probable cause, supported by Oath or affirmation, and particularly describing the place to be searched, and the persons or things to be seized.[145]

This following is a brief overview of the Fourth Amendment.

4.6.2.1 Search and Seizure

The Fourth Amendment limits search and seizure by the government and protects people's right to privacy from unreasonable intrusions without a warrant issued by a judge, with only a few exceptions. It is important to recognize that the Fourth Amendment limits only governmental entities and not the private sector under the Fourteenth Amendment's *State Action*

[145] U.S. Const. Amend. IV.

Doctrine that differentiates between governmental entities and private sector independence. [146]

4.6.2.2 Exceptions to the Search Warrant Rule

Exceptions to the Fourth Amendment require urgent circumstances:

- **Exigent circumstances**: In case of an emergency like a life-and-death situation, law enforcement personnel can enter a premise without a warrant. In the Supreme Court case of *Missouri v. McNeely*, the court decided "A variety of circumstances may give rise to an exigency sufficient to justify a warrantless search, including law enforcement's need to provide emergency assistance."[147]
- **Search and seizure incidental to a lawful arrest**: When a police officer observes an individual committing a crime, the officer may search without a warrant. In the Supreme Court case of *Riley v. California*[148] the court decided that police require a search warrant to search cell phones.
- A *consent* is required for law enforcement to search without a warrant. A parent can provide consent for a search of a child's bedroom when no rent is paid by the child, but not a landlord, or a hotel manager. The Supreme Court case of *Illinois v. Rodriguez*[149] states that an individual can consent to a search at the time of entry.
- *In plain view* occurs when a police officer observes illegal evidence in plain view, for example when a police officer sees contraband in a car during a traffic stop. In *Horton v. California*, "the Fourth Amendment does not prohibit the warrantless seizure of evidence in plain view, even though the discovery of the evidence was inadvertent."[150]
- Another exception to the warrant is the *caretaker function*. If a box has been given to the police, the police have the right to open it without a search warrant.
- *Impounded vehicles* may be searched without a search warrant as well. The Supreme Court case of *South Dakota v. Opperman* states that "when vehicles are impounded, police routinely follow

---

[146] U.S. Const. Amend. XIV, sec. 1.

[147] *Missouri v. McNeely*, 569 U.S. 141 (2013). Retrieved from https://www.supremecourt.gov/opinions/12pdf/11-1425_cb8e.pdf

[148] *Riley v. California*, 573 U.S. 373 (2014). Retrieved from https://www.supremecourt.gov/opinions/13pdf/13-132_8l9c.pdf

[149] *Illinois v. Rodriguez* 497 U.S. 177 (1990). Retrieved from https://cdn.loc.gov/service/ll/usrep/usrep497/usrep497177/usrep497177.pdf

[150] *Horton v. California*, 496 U.S. 128 (1990). Retrieved from https://cdn.loc.gov/service/ll/usrep/usrep496/usrep496128/usrep496128.pdf

caretaking procedures by securing and inventorying the cars' contents." [151]

- The *border search exception* is a doctrine that permits the government, specifically U.S. Customs and Border Protection and DHS to conduct warrantless searches at international borders. See also the cases *United States v. Villamonte-Marquez*[152] and *United States v. Ramsey.*[153] In addition to the exception doctrine, warrantless border searches are authorized by the following statutes: 8 U.S.C. § 1225(d)(1) (2014); 8 U.S.C. § 1357(c) (2014); 19 U.S.C. § 482 (2014); 19 U.S.C. § 1467 (2014); 19 U.S.C. § 1496 (2014); 19 U.S.C. § 1499 (2014), and 19 U.S.C. § 1582 (2014).

4.6.2.3 Electronic Surveillance: Private vs Public

4.6.2.3.1 Noteworthy Cases

1. In the case of the *United States V. Richardson,*[154] the defendant, Richardson, had an email account with America Online (AOL), an Internet service provider. AOL used an image detection system and discovered child pornographic images, which were reported to the government.[155] As a result, the defendant was charged based on those findings. The defendant claimed that the search was unconstitutional because it was conducted without a warrant and therefore violated the Fourth Amendment. The Fourth Circuit Court rejected the defendant's claims and decided that AOL was not a governmental agency.

AOL's actions did not equate to governmental conduct triggering constitutional protection. The Fourth Amendment does not protect against searches, no matter how unreasonable, conducted "by private individuals acting in a private capacity."[156]

2. In the area of electronic surveillance (wiretaps), the landmark case of *Katz v. United States*[157] has both historical and legal significance against unreasonable searches and seizures. The defendant, Charles Katz, was a gambler and used a phone booth, placing bets to engage in interstate gambling. This was illegal under federal law. The FBI set up a wiretap on the public phone booth without a search war-

---

[151] *Dakota v. Opperman*, 428 U.S. 364 (1976). Retrieved fromhttps://cdn.loc.gov/service/ll/usrep/usrep428/usrep428364/usrep428364.pdf

[152] *United States v. Villamonte-Marquez*, 462 U.S. 579, 585 (1983).

[153] *United States v. Richardson*, 607 F. 3d 357 (4th Cir. 2010).

[154] *United States V. Richardson*, 607 F. 3d 357 (4th Cir. 2010).

[155] 42 U.S.C. § 13032(b)(1)—Reporting of child pornography by electronic communication service.

[156] *Id.* at 154.

[157] *Katz v. United States*, 389 U.S. 347 (1967). Retrieved from https://cdn.loc.gov/service/ll/usrep/usrep389/usrep389347/usrep389347.pdf

FIGURE 4.13 **The Phone Booth. Courtesy of Shutterstock.**

rant (Figure 4.13). As a result, Katz was arrested and charged for his illegal interstate wagers. The defendant argued that the FBI did not use a warrant, and the surveillance of the phone booth was therefore unconstitutional. The government argued that the phone booth was made partly of glass; therefore the defendant was visible to the outside world. Initially, Katz was convicted by a lower court based on the recordings and appealed to the U.S. Supreme Court, which reversed the defendant's conviction and said that the FBI had violated the Fourth Amendment.

> The petitioner has strenuously argued that the booth was a "constitutionally protected area." The Government has maintained with equal vigor that it was not. But this effort to decide whether a given "area," viewed in the abstract, is "constitutionally protected" deflects attention from the problem presented by this case. For the Fourth Amendment protects people, not places. What a person knowingly exposes to the public, even in his own home or office, is not a subject of Fourth Amendment protection.[158]

Since we now rarely see a phone booth, another landmark case concerning cell phone location information, in relation to the Fourth Amendment, was decided by the U.S. Supreme Court.

3. In the case of *Carpenter v. United States,*[159] the Supreme Court ruled that cell phone location data is protected by the Fourth Amendment, and law enforcement agencies and the police require warrants to obtain data from ISPs.

   Accordingly, when the Government tracks the location of a cell phone it achieves near perfect surveillance, as if it had attached an ankle monitor to the phone's user. Moreover, the retrospective

---

[158] *Id.* at 157.

[159] *Carpenter v. United States,* No. 16-402, 585 U.S. ____ (2018). Retrieved from https://www.supremecourt.gov/opinions/17pdf/16-402_h315.pdf

quality of the data here gives police access to a category of information otherwise unknowable. The Government will be able to use subpoenas to acquire records in the overwhelming majority of these investigations. We hold only that a warrant is required in the rare case where the suspect has a legitimate privacy interest in records held by a third party.[160]

4.6.2.4 Exclusionary Rule and the Good Faith Exception

The exclusionary rule prohibits law enforcement from using evidence obtained illegally in violation of the Fourth Amendment. An exception to this rule is the "good faith exception." When a police officer is acting lawfully and it is later found that the officer made a mistake in conducting a search, the evidence is admissible.[161]

4.6.2.5 The USA PATRIOT Act and the Fourth Amendment

After the September 11, 2001, attacks and the enactment of the USA PATRIOT Act of 2001,[162] the law gave the government unprecedented power to gather intelligence. The legislation was changed to the Freedom Act in 2015, with new constraints on government surveillance.

With the first version of the PATRIOT Act, law enforcement agencies could conduct covert surveillance on U.S citizens and obtain evidence of crime without proving probable cause under § 213, Title II—Enhanced Surveillance. The law gave leeway to "authorities for delaying notice of execution of a warrant."[163] The delaying notice was also known as the "sneak and peak" warrant. In addition, the legislation allowed the National Security Agency (NSA) under § 215 to collect bulk telephone metadata. This section was challenged in the case of *American Civil Liberties Union v. James Clapper*,[164] in which the Southern District of New York decided that § 215 does not authorize the bulk collection of telephone metadata.

In 2015, after the USA PATRIOT Act expired, a new version was enacted, the Uniting and Strengthening America by Fulfilling Rights and Ensuring Effective Discipline over Monitoring Act of 2015 or the USA Freedom Act.[165] The 2015 law contained some limitations that prohibited bulk collec-

---

160 *Id.* at 159.

161 *Mapp v. Ohio*, 367 U.S. 643 (1961).

162 U.S. Congress, House, Uniting and Strengthening America by Providing Appropriate Tools Required to Intercept and Obstruct Terrorism (USA PATRIOT ACT) Act of 2001, HR 3162, 107th. Retrieved from https://www.congress.gov/bill/107th-congress/house-bill/3162/text

163 *Id.* at 162.

164 *American Civil Liberties Union v. James Clapper*, 959 F.Supp. 2d 724, No. 13-3994 (S.D. New York, Dec. 28, 2013).

165 U.S. Congress, House, Uniting and Strengthening America by Fulfilling Rights and Ensuring Effective Discipline Over Monitoring Act of 2015 (USA Freedom Act of 2015), H. Rept. 114-109. Retrieved from https://www.congress.gov/114/plaws/publ23/PLAW-114publ23.pdf

tion of data in "broad geographic regions, including the United States" and provided for the adoption of "minimization procedures" and safeguarding of data collection.

4.6.3 Electronic Communication Privacy Act of 1986

In addition to the Fourth Amendment, the Electronic Communication Privacy Act[166] protects private electronic communications, including emails and telephone conversations, along with electronic data storage places, from being intercepted by the federal government over the wire. The Act is essential for cybersecurity since it restricts the ability of both the government and the private sector to monitor networks. More specifically, it protects personal communications, such as wire, oral, or electronic communication, from being intercepted by another private individual and bars wiretapping and electronic eavesdropping. The Wiretap Act prohibits any person from deliberately intercepting or attempting to intercept a wire, oral, or electronic communication using any "electronic or mechanical or other device" (§ 2510 (3)).

> Interception and disclosure of wire, oral, or electronic communications prohibited. Manufacture, distribution, possession, and advertising of wire, oral, or electronic communication intercepting devices prohibited. (§ 2511)[167]

While the ECPA had revised and updated the original Federal Wiretap Act of 1968, the core of the law has not changed. The ECPA has been amended by the Communications Assistance to Law Enforcement Act (CALEA),[168] the USA PATRIOT Act, and the FISA Amendments Act of 2008.[169] The following is a brief overview of the ECPA:

- 18 U.S. Code CHAPTER 119—WIRE AND ELECTRONIC COMMUNICATIONS INTERCEPTION AND INTERCEPTION OF ORAL COMMUNICATIONS (also called Wiretap Act) (18 U.S.C. §§ 2510-23)
  - Except as otherwise specifically provided in this chapter any person who

[166] Electronic Communications Privacy Act of 1986 (ECPA), 18 U.S.C. §§ 2510-2523. Retrieved from https://uscode.house.gov/view.xhtml?path=/prelim@title18/part1/chapter119&edition=prelim

[167] *Id.* at 166.

[168] U.S. Congress, H.R. 4922—Communications Assistance for Law Enforcement Act 103rd Congress (1993–1994). Retrieved from https://www.congress.gov/bill/103rd-congress/house-bill/4922/text

[169] U.S. Congress, H.R. 6304—FISA Amendments Act of 2008 110th Congress. Retrieved from https://www.congress.gov/bill/110th-congress/house-bill/6304/text

    (a) intentionally intercepts, endeavors to intercept, or procures any other person to intercept or endeavor to intercept, any wire, oral, or electronic communication;
    (b) intentionally uses, endeavors to use, or procures any other person to use or endeavor to use any electronic, mechanical, or other device to intercept any oral communication when—
        - (i) such device is affixed to, or otherwise transmits a signal through, a wire, cable, or other like connection used in wire communication; or
        - (ii) such device transmits communications by radio or interferes with the transmission of such communication" (§ 2510 (1)(a)(b).
  - Prohibits interception and disclosure of wire, oral, or electronic communications (§ 2511).
  - Prohibits the use of illegally obtained communications as evidence (§ 2515).
  - Provides access for Federal and State government to obtain authorized wiretapping (§§ 2516-2518).
  - A warrant needed for interception of communications for up to 30 days by demonstrating probable cause for individual "committing, has committed, or is about to commit a particular offense" (listed at § 2516 and § 2518).
- 18 U.S. Code CHAPTER 121—STORED WIRE AND ELECTRONIC COMMUNICATIONS AND TRANSACTIONAL RECORDS ACCESS (also called Stored Communications Act (SCA) (§§ 2701-13).[170]
  - The SCA criminalizes "intentional accesses without authorization of a facility through which an electronic communication service is provided; or

    intentionally exceeding an authorization to access that facility" § 2701(a)(1)(2).
  - Protects the privacy for data files stored by Internet Service Provider (ISP), and telephone companies, such as subscriber name, billing and records information, and IP addresses or "any person or entity the contents of any communication" (§ 2702).
  - The SCA protects "electronic communication services" and "remote computing services" (§ 2702). The term "electronic communication service" means any service which provides to users thereof the ability to send or receive wire or electronic

[170] U.S. Codes, 18 USC Ch. 121: Stored wire and electronic communications and transactional records access. Retrieved from https://uscode.house.gov/view.xhtml?path=/prelim@title18/part1/chapter121&edition=prelim

communications" (§ 2510) and the term "remote computing service" means the provision to the public of computer storage or processing services by means of an electronic communications system" (§ 2711 (2)).
    - ISPs are not allowed to share content data such as spoken words of a conversation, actual text of the message, and e-mails. Content data are defined as "contents" when used with respect to any wire, oral, or electronic communication, includes any information concerning the substance, purport, or meaning of that communication" (§ 2510).
    - An exception is when ISP permitted to share non-content information, such as telephone numbers, email addresses used, websites visited, logs of account usage, mail header information minus the subject line, and lists of outgoing email addresses (§ 2702 (c)(6)).
- 18 U.S. Code CHAPTER 206—PEN REGISTERS AND TRAP AND TRACE DEVICES (§§ 3121-3127) (also called pen register).[171]
    - The pen register prohibits government entities/law enforcement, to install trap and trace devices without obtaining a warrant. "No person may install or use a pen register or a trap and trace device without first obtaining a court order under section 3123" (§ 3121(a)).

4.6.4 Communication Assistant for Law Enforcement Act of 1994 (CALEA)

The Communication Assistant for Law Enforcement Act[172] gives law enforcement agencies permission to conduct electronic surveillance under lawful warrants and court orders. Congress enacted the law in 1994, requiring telecommunications companies and manufacturers to assist law enforcement in surveillance, and to comply with legal requests for information. Those covered include communications services using wireless services, routing, Internet-based telecommunications in applications, circuit mode equipment, packet mode equipment, broadband Internet access providers, and Voice over Internet Protocols (VoIP) like Skype. The federal agency that is responsible for enforcing CALEA is the Federal Communications Commission (FCC). While the USA PATRIOT Act extended provisions provided by CALEA to assist law enforcement with improved technology to

[171] 18 USC Ch. 206: Pen registers and trap and trace devices. Retrieved from https://uscode.house.gov/view.xhtml?path=/prelim@title18/part2/chapter206&edition=prelim

[172] 47 U.S.C §§1001-10.

fight terrorism, the provisions of CALEA allow law enforcement to conduct electronic surveillance, while protecting the individual's privacy during the investigation. Additionally, CALEA restricts the government's authority over carriers or manufacturers of any equipment or software configuration. This applies to mobile devices which are included in the category of encrypted devices. Sections 1002(b)(1) and 1002(b)(3) of CALEA:

"(1) Design of features and systems configurations. This subchapter does not authorize any law enforcement agency or office
  (A) to require any specific design of equipment, facilities, services, features, or system configurations to be adopted by any provider of a wire or electronic communication service, any manufacturer of telecommunications equipment, or any provider of telecommunications support services.
  (B) to prohibit the adoption of any equipment, facility, service, or feature by any provider of a wire or electronic communication service, any manufacturer of telecommunications equipment, or any provider of telecommunications support services." § 1002(b)(1)

(2) Encryption. A telecommunications carrier shall not be responsible for decrypting, or ensuring the government's ability to decrypt, any communication encrypted by a subscriber or customer, unless the encryption was provided by the carrier and the carrier possesses the information necessary to decrypt the communication. § 1002(b)(3)[173]

4.7 Key Privacy Laws in the United States

The exponential growth and use of new technologies such as tracking by global positioning system (GPS), the use of social media over the Internet, and the use of biometric authentication, all make privacy less important. Are discount coupons that collect behavioral information and online habits and information about what we do online worth our privacy? Cyberspace and the progression of technology have not killed privacy but have altered how it is being managed and handled. It certainly requires more effort to protect our privacy than ever before. The following is the key legislation that safeguards our privacy (Figure 4.14).

FIGURE 4.14 Privacy Laws. Courtesy of Shutterstock.

[173] 47 U.S.C. 1002—Assistance capability requirements. Retrieved from https://www.govinfo.gov/content/pkg/USCODE-2018-title47/pdf/USCODE-2018-title47-chap9-subchapI-sec1002.pdf

4.7.1 Privacy Act of 1974

The Privacy Act of 1974[174,175] established control over the collection, maintenance, use, and dissemination of personal information by the federal government. In addition, the legislation allows a U.S. citizen or permanent resident alien the right to access information related to themselves, to copy and to correct any record held by the federal government, amending the record if it is incomplete. Included in the Act is the right to sue the federal government if it violates the law, for example if it provides unauthorized access to personal information. The Act was amended by the Computer Matching and Privacy Protection Act of 1988,[176] adding new provisions, including protection of personal information when using computers, and providing the opportunity to receive a notice and to disprove information if not true. Finally, the law established a Data Integrity Board to oversee these activities. The Computer Matching and Privacy Protection Act of 1988 is codified as part of the Privacy Act of 1974. In addition, Congress enacted the Computer Matching and Privacy Protection Amendments of 1990[177] that clarified the "due process" provisions guaranteeing the respect of all legal rights at subsection (p).

4.7.2 Controlling the Assault of Non-Solicited Pornography and Marketing Act of 2003 (CAN-SPAM Act)

The CAN-SPAM Act[178] was signed into law by President George W. Bush on December 16, 2003, and created standards for sending unsolicited commercial emails. The law was the result of the growing amount of junk email "spam" in mailboxes. The law prohibits false or misleading header information and misleading subject lines and declares that commercial email be identified as an advertisement. In addition, the recipients of such email must be able to opt out if they choose. In addition, the law requires the FTC to enforce its provisions, requires labelling of sexually explicit commercial email, and establishes criteria for determining the purpose of such emails. The following are some of the main requirements of the legislation.

- Prohibition of false or misleading transmission information (§ 7704 (a)(1))

---

174 5 U.S.C. § 552a.

175 The Privacy Act of 1974, Pub. L. No. 93-579, 88 Stat. 1896. Retrieved from https://www.govinfo.gov/content/pkg/USCODE-2018-title5/pdf/USCODE-2018-title5-partI-chap5-subchapII-sec552a.pdf

176 The Computer Matching and Privacy Protection Act of 1988, Pub. L. No. 100-503. Retrieved from https://www.govinfo.gov/content/pkg/STATUTE-102/pdf/STATUTE-102-Pg2507.pdf#page=7

177 Pub. L. No. 101-508, Subtitle C—Miscellaneous SEC. 7201, Computer Matching of Federal Benefits Information and Privacy Protection. Retrieved from https://www.govinfo.gov/content/pkg/STATUTE-104/pdf/STATUTE-104-Pg1388.pdf

178 15 U.S.C §§ 7701-7713. Retrieved from https://uscode.house.gov/view.xhtml?req=granuleid%3AUSC-prelim-title15-chapter103&edition=prelim

- Prohibition of deceptive subject headings (§ 7704 (a)(2))
- Inclusion of identifier, opt-out, and physical address in commercial electronic mail (§ 7704 (a)(5))
- In this subsection, the term "sexually oriented material" means any material that depicts sexually explicit conduct as that term is defined in section 2256 of title 18—unless the depiction constitutes a small and insignificant part of the whole, the remainder of which is not primarily devoted to sexual matters (§ 7704 (d)(4))
- Exclusive enforcement by FTC ((§ 7705 (c))

4.7.3 18 U.S.C. § 1037 Fraud and Related Activity in Connection with Electronic Mail

SEC. 4. PROHIBITION AGAINST PREDATORY AND ABUSIVE COMMERCIAL E-MAIL of the CAN-SPAM Act, § 1037[179] applies to anybody involved in interstate or foreign commerce who can access a safeguarded computer without authorization. The CAN-SPAM Act extends 18 U.S.C. § 1030 to prosecute hackers who use email for deceitful purposes and prohibits sending sexually explicit emails without a label. The law prohibits the transmission of emails with the aim to deceive or misinform receivers. It is also unlawful to falsify or use misleading header information in multiple commercial emails or to incorrectly represent oneself as a registrant or legitimate successor.

(a) In General.—Whoever, in or affecting interstate or foreign commerce, knowingly—
  (1) accesses a protected computer without authorization, and intentionally initiates the transmission of multiple commercial electronic mail messages from or through such computer,
  (2) uses a protected computer to relay or retransmit multiple commercial electronic mail messages, with the intent to deceive or mislead recipients, or any Internet access service, as to the origin of such messages,
  (3) materially falsifies header information in multiple commercial electronic mail messages and intentionally initiates the transmission of such messages,
  (4) registers, using information that materially falsifies the identity of the actual registrant, for five or more electronic mail accounts or online user accounts or two or more domain names, and intentionally initiates the transmission of multiple commercial

[179] 18 U.S. Code § 1037. Retrieved from https://www.govinfo.gov/content/pkg/USCODE-2011-title18/html/USCODE-2011-title18-partI-chap47-sec1037.htm

electronic mail messages from any combination of such accounts or domain names, or

(5) falsely represents oneself to be the registrant or the legitimate successor in interest to the registrant of 5 or more Internet Protocol addresses, and intentionally initiates the transmission of multiple commercial electronic mail messages from such addresses, or conspires to do so, shall be punished as provided in subsection (b). (§ 1037)

According to § 1037(b)(1)(2), offenders will be punished with a fine and/or jail sentence for not fewer than 3 and up to 5 years. As mentioned earlier, in § 1037, the law prohibits sending sexually explicit emails without a warning label. The law is codified at 15 U.S.C. § 7704(d)[180] and is punishable by a fine, imprisonment for not more than 5 years, or both.

For a complete U.S.C. § 1037 see Appendix H.

4.7.4 18 U.S.C. § 1029 Fraud and Related Activity in Connection with Access Devices

Unauthorized access to a network where data resides compromises the privacy of individuals; such cases commonly involve violations of identity theft statutes. Our credit card information is widely available, and it is quite easy for criminals to commit credit card fraud. Part of the Violent Crime Control and Law Enforcement Act of 1994,[181] subsection (a)(7) of 18 U.S.C. § 1029, criminalizes knowingly, and with intent to defraud, conduct affecting interstate or foreign commerce. Penalties include a fine and/or jail sentence for not more than 10 and up to 15 years. The following are some of the key requirements of the law.

(a) Whoever—

(1) knowingly and with intent to defraud produces, uses, or traffics in one or more counterfeit access devices;

(2) knowingly and with intent to defraud traffics in or uses one or more unauthorized access devices during any one-year period, and by such conduct obtains anything of value aggregating $1,000 or more during that period;

(3) knowingly and with intent to defraud possesses fifteen or more devices which are counterfeit or unauthorized access devices;

(4) knowingly, and with intent to defraud, produces, traffics in, has

[180] 15 U.S.C. 7704—Other protections for users of commercial electronic mail. Retrieved from https://www.govinfo.gov/content/pkg/USCODE-2011-title15/pdf/USCODE-2011-title15-chap103-sec7704.pdf

[181] Violent Crime Control and Law Enforcement Act of 1994, Pub. L. No. 103-322, § 250007, 108 Stat. 1796. Retrieved from https://www.govinfo.gov/content/pkg/STATUTE-108/pdf/STATUTE-108-Pg1796.pdf.

control or custody of, or possesses device-making equipment;

(5) knowingly and with intent to defraud effects transactions, with 1 or more access devices issued to another person or persons, to receive payment or any other thing of value during any one-year period the aggregate value of which is equal to or greater than $1,000;

(6) without the authorization of the issuer of the access device, knowingly and with intent to defraud solicits a person for the purpose of—

(A) offering an access device; or

(B) selling information regarding or an application to obtain an access device;

(7) knowingly and with intent to defraud uses, produces, traffics in, has control or custody of, or possesses a telecommunications instrument that has been modified or altered to obtain unauthorized use of telecommunications services;

(8) knowingly and with intent to defraud uses, produces, traffics in, has control or custody of, or possesses a scanning receiver;

(9) knowingly uses, produces, traffics in, has control or custody of, or possesses hardware or software, knowing it has been configured to insert or modify telecommunication identifying information associated with or contained in a telecommunications instrument so that such instrument may be used to obtain telecommunications service without authorization; or

(10) without the authorization of the credit card system member or its agent, knowingly and with intent to defraud causes or arranges for another person to present to the member or its agent, for payment, 1 or more evidences or records of transactions made by an access device;

Shall, if the offense affects interstate or foreign commerce, be punished as provided in subsection (c) of this section. (§ 1029)

4.7.5 18 U.S. Code § 1028 Fraud and Related Activity in Connection with Identification Documents, Authentication Features, and Information

Numerous federal laws apply to identity theft, including section 1028(a)(7), enacted as part of the Identity Theft and Assumption Deterrence Act of 1998,[182] and amended in 2004 by the Identity Theft Penalty Enhancement Act,[183] to include penalties for aggravated identity theft.

[182] U.S Congress H.R. 3601—Identity Theft and Assumption Deterrence Act of 1998. Retrieved from https://www.congress.gov/bill/105th-congress/house-bill/3601/text

[183] U.S. Congress H.R. 858—Identity Theft Penalty Enhancement Act.

Title 18, United States Code, section 1028 criminalizes identity theft involving fraudulent identification documents or the unlawful use of identification information. The law made identity theft a federal crime and can impose punishments of up to 15 years imprisonment and a maximum fine of $250,000. The law allows for the identity theft victim to seek restitution if there is a conviction. In addition, the law establishes the FTC[184] as the central federal agency to act as a "clearinghouse" to serve as the federal government's central repository for identity theft complaints and to provide victim assistance and consumer education. According to section 1028(a)(7)

> Whoever, in a circumstance described in subsection (c) of this section—
> (7) knowingly transfers, possesses, or uses, without lawful authority, a means of identification of another person with the intent to commit, to aid or abet, or in connection with any unlawful activity that constitutes a violation of Federal law, or that constitutes a felony under any applicable State or local law; or
> (8) knowingly traffics in false or actual authentication features for use in false identification documents, document-making implements, or means of identification;
> a. Shall be punished as provided in subsection (b) of this section.

4.7.6 Children's Online Privacy Protection Act of 1998

The Children's Online Privacy Protection Act of 1998[185] prevents online operators of websites or online services from collecting the personal information of children under 13 years of age. The term "child" means an individual under the age of 13 (§ 6501). Under COPPA, the FTC has the authority to issue regulations[186] and enforce COPPA law.

More specifically, the law applies to any online services and operators of commercial websites including mobile apps, Internet-connected toys, or any devices that collect, use, or disclose personal information from minors under 13 years old. According to the FTC, personal information is listed in Table 4.4.[187]

Additionally, the law applies to operators of general audience websites or online services that have "actual knowledge of collecting, using, or disclosing personal information from children" (§ 312.4). Any online services and websites covered under COPPA law must provide notice and "verifiable

[184] Federal Trade Commission, Identity Theft and Assumption Deterrence Act. Retrieved from https://www.ftc.gov/node/119459

[185] 15 U.S.C. §§ 6501–06.

[186] 16 C.F.R. § 312.

[187] 16 C.F.R. § 312.2.

TABLE 4.4 Personal Information

Personal information means individually identifiable information
(1) A first and last name
(2) A home or other physical address including street name and name of a city or town
(3) Online contact information as defined in this section
(4) A screen or username where it functions in the same manner as online contact information, as defined in this section
(5) A telephone number
(6) A Social Security number
(7) A persistent identifier that can be used to recognize a user over time and across different Web sites or online services. Such persistent identifier includes, but is not limited to, a customer number held in a cookie, an Internet Protocol (IP) address, a processor or device serial number, or unique device identifier
(8) A photograph, video, or audio file where such file contains a child's image or voice
(9) Geolocation information sufficient to identify street name and name of a city or town
(10) Information concerning the child or the parents of that child that the operator collects online from the child and combines with an identifier described in this definition

Adopted from 16 C.F. R. § 312.2

parental consent" before collecting, using, or disclosing personal information from children.

> (a) General principles of notice. It shall be the obligation of the operator to provide notice and obtain verifiable parental consent prior to collecting, using, or disclosing personal information from children. Such notice must be clearly and understandably written, complete, and must contain no unrelated, confusing, or contradictory materials. (§ 312.4 Notice)

The online services and websites "must make reasonable efforts to obtain verifiable parental consent," and "reasonably calculated, in light of available technology, to ensure that the person providing consent is the child's parent."[188] Some examples include the following from section 312.b (b):

- Providing a consent form to be signed by the parent and returned to the operator by postal mail, facsimile, or electronic scan;
- Requiring a parent, in connection with a monetary transaction, to use a credit card, debit card, or other online payment system that provides notification of each discrete transaction to the primary account holder;

[188] 16 C.F.R. § 312.5.

- Having a parent call a toll-free telephone number staffed by trained personnel;
- Having a parent connect to trained personnel via video-conference;
- Verifying a parent's identity by checking a form of government-issued identification against databases of such information, where the parent's identification is deleted by the operator after such verification is complete. (§ 312.b (b))

It is worth noting that under § 312.10 "Data retention and deletion requirements," the FTC has designated the "Safe Harbor Certification program" that the industry may request approval of self-regulatory guidelines. The program ensures best practices for the collection, use, and disclosure of personal information from minors as consistent with COPPA law.

> In general. Industry groups or other persons may apply to the Commission for approval of self-regulatory program guidelines ("safe harbor programs"). The application shall be filed with the Commission's Office of the Secretary. The Commission will publish in the Federal Register a document seeking public comment on the application. The Commission shall issue a written determination within 180 days of the filing of the application. (§ 312.11 Safe harbor programs)

4.7.7 Video Privacy Protection Act (VPPA) of 1988

The Video Privacy Protection Act of 1988[189] was enacted by the U.S. Congress in 1988,[190] and it was passed because of the exposure of Supreme Court nominee Robert Bork's video rental record, published in newspapers and intended to embarrass him. The law is one of the strongest protections of consumer privacy against websites and apps that deliver online video data collection. Furthermore, the law prevents the exposure of personally identifiable rental records and also broadly defines who the law is aimed at as "any person engaged in the business of or affecting interstate or foreign commerce, of rental, sale, or delivery of prerecorded video cassette tapes or similar audio visual materials."

> (4) the term "video tape service provider" means any person engaged in the business, in or affecting interstate or foreign commerce, of rental, sale, or delivery of prerecorded video cassette tapes or similar audiovisual materials, or any person or other entity to whom a disclosure is made under

189 18 U.S.C § 2710.

190 Pub. L. 100–618. Video Privacy Protection Act of 1988. Retrieved from https://www.govinfo.gov/content/pkg/STATUTE-102/pdf/STATUTE-102-Pg3195.pdf#page=3

subparagraph (D) or (E) of subsection (b)(2), but only with respect to the information contained in the disclosure. (§ 2710(4)

As a result, the law includes not only "video rental stores or video tape service providers" but any video streaming from the web. The following are the most significant provisions of the law:

- Unlawful on the disclosure of personally identifiable rental information without written consent.
- Law enforcement requires a valid warrant or court order.
- If any personal, identifiable information concerning any consumer is disclosed, the provider shall be liable.
- Civil remedies, not less than $2500.
- When an account is terminated the "video rental stores or video tape service provider" should destroy rental records in no longer than 1 year.
- The states are free to enact broader protections for individuals' records. The Act does not preempt state law (§ 2710).

4.7.8 When the United States Began Taking Privacy Seriously

As we have pointed out, the United States does not have a single form of national legislation but instead has numerous enacted statutes and regulations addressing various aspects of cybersecurity. States sometimes take initiative from the federal government and implement new privacy laws to protect residents' rights. As a result, two states enacted specially important legislation protecting the individual's privacy. The first is the California Consumer Privacy Act of 2018 (CCPA),[191] and the second is the Illinois Biometric Information Privacy Act.[192]

California's CCPA was enacted in 2018 and is the most significant consumer data protection law in the United States. The law offers residents of California the right to know what data companies collect about them and gives them the right to request that the business delete their personal information. Examples of personal information include *name, alias, postal address, unique identifier, Internet protocol address (IP), email address, social security number, driver's license number, passport number,* and *characteristics such as race, gender, disability,* and others protected by federal and state antidiscrimination laws. In addition to the personal information the law protects commercial information, such as *records of property, products or services provided, obtained, or considered, or other purchasing or consumer*

[191] *Id.* at 5.

[192] 740 ILCS 14/10.

histories or tendencies; biometric data; Internet or other electronic network activity information, including browsing history, search history, and information regarding a consumer's interaction with a website, application, or advertisement.

In synopsis, the law provides the following rights, the right to know, right to access, right to deletion, right of opt-out, right to equal service and price, and right to opt-in for consumers under the age of 16.

The second state law that has had a profound impact concerning privacy is the Illinois Biometric Information Privacy Act (BIPA).[193] The law regulates the privacy and protection of biometric information that is collected by businesses, such as fingerprints, retina scans, and facial images. "Biometric identifier" means "a retina or iris scan, fingerprint, voiceprint, or scan of hand or face geometry."[194] The legislation requires businesses to collect written consent from individuals before acquiring their biometric data. "Written release" means informed written consent or, in the context of employment, a release executed by an employee as a condition of employment."[195] In addition, businesses must develop a written policy, made available to the public.

Tables 4.5 and 4.6 summarize the most significant Federal laws concerning Cybercrime in the United States.

4.8 Conclusion

Cybercrime is a major concern for the U.S government and the private sector. The growth of computing devices and e-commerce affects everyone. Data breaches have become commonplace. The U.S. cyber and privacy rights laws are perhaps the oldest and most effective in the world. Nevertheless, they need to be modernized and equal in effectiveness to California's CCPA and the Illinois Biometric Information Privacy Act. A mixture of federal, state, and local legislation, along with responsible individual and best practices, is the best solution to preventing cyberattacks.

[193] Illinois General Assembly, Illinois Biometric Information Privacy Act. Retrieved from http://www.ilga.gov/legislation/ilcs/ilcs3.asp?ActID=3004&ChapterID=57

[194] 740 ILCS 14/10.

[195] *Id.* at 194.

TABLE 4.5 A Brief Summary of Major Unlawful Contact Concerning Cybercrime

Unlawful Violations	Federal Legislation
Accessing a Computer without Authorization	18 U.S.C. § 1030
A Denial-of-Service (DoS) Attack	18 U.S.C. § 1030, 18 U.S.C. § 1362
Child Pornography	18 U.S.C. §§ 2251, 2252, 18 U.S.C. § 2423, 18 U.S.C. § 1466
Children's Online Privacy Protection	15 U.S.C. §§ 6501-06, 16 C.F. R. § 312
Credit Card Fraud	18 U.S.C. § 1030, 18 U.S.C. § 1029, 15 U.S.C. § 1644, 18 U.S.C. § 1343
Cyberstalking	18 U.S.C. § 2261
Disclosure of Private Information	18 U.S.C. § 2511
Electronic Harassment	47 U.S.C. § 223
Electronic Threats	18 U.S.C. § 875, 18 U.S.C. § 1951, 47 U.S.C. § 223
Espionage	18 U.S.C. § 1030, 18 U.S.C. § 793, 18 U.S.C. § 798
Extortion	18 U.S.C. § 1030, 18 U.S.C. § 875, 18 U.S.C. § 1951
Internet Fraud	18 U.S.C. § 1030, 18 U.S.C. § 1028, 18 U.S.C. § 1343, 18 U.S.C. §§ 1956, 1957, 18 U.S.C. § 1001, 15 U.S.C. § 45, 15 U.S.C. § 52, 15 U.S.C. § 6821
Interception of Electronic Communications	18 U.S.C. § 2511, 18 U.S.C. § 2701, 18 U.S.C. § 1030
Interfering with Government Communication Systems	18 U.S.C. § 1030, 18 U.S.C. § 1362
Password Fraud	18 U.S.C. § 1030, 18 U.S.C. § 1029, 18 U.S.C. § 1343
Intellectual Property Theft/Piracy	17 U.S.C. §§ 1201-1205, 18 U.S.C. § 545, 18 U.S.C. §§ 1831, 1832, 18 U.S.C. § 2318, 17 U.S.C. § 506, 18 U.S.C. § 2319, 18 U.S.C. § 2320, 47 U.S.C. § 553, 18 U.S.C. § 1343
Substitution/Redirection of a Website	18 U.S.C. § 1030
Spam	18 U.S.C. § 1037
Spoofing Email Address	18 U.S.C. § 1037
Transmission of Program, Information, Code, or Command	18 U.S.C. § 1030
Trade Secrets/Economic Espionage	18 U.S.C. § 1831, 18 U.S.C. § 1832, 18 U.S.C. § 1905, 18 U.S.C. §§ 2314, 2315
Use Misleading Domain Name	18 U.S.C. § 225
Video Privacy Protection from the Web	18 U.S.C § 2710

TABLE 4.6 Federal Legislation with Titles

Federal Legislation with Titles	
18 U.S.C. § 1030—The Computer Fraud and Abuse Act (CFAA)	**8 U.S.C. 1957**—Engaging in monetary transactions in property derived from specified unlawful activity
18 U.S.C. § 1362—Communication lines, stations, or systems	**18 U.S.C. § 1001**—Statements or entries generally
18 U.S.C. § 2251—Sexual exploitation of children, **§ 2252**—Certain activities relating to material involving the sexual exploitation of minors	**15 U.S.C. § 45**—Unfair methods of competition unlawful; prevention by Commission
18 U.S.C § 2710—Wrongful disclosure of video tape rental or sale records	**15 U.S.C. § 52**—Dissemination of false advertisements
18 U.S.C. § 2423—Transportation of minors	**15 U.S.C. § 6821**—Privacy protection for customer information of financial institutions
18 U.S.C. § 1466—Engaging in the business of selling or transferring obscene matter	**18 U.S.C. § 2511**—Interception and disclosure of wire, oral, or electronic communications prohibited
15 U.S.C. § 6501–§ 6506—Children's Online Privacy Protection Rule (COPPA)	**18 U.S.C. § 2701**—Unlawful access to stored communications, **§ 1201**—Savings clause
16 C.F. R. § 312—Children's Online Privacy Protection Rule Safe Harbor Proposed Self-Regulatory Guidelines	**17 U.S.C. § 1205**—Circumvention of copyright protection systems
18 U.S.C. § 1029—Fraud and related activity in connection with access devices	**18 U.S.C. § 545**—Smuggling goods into the United States
15 U.S.C. § 1644—Fraudulent use of credit cards; penalties	**18 U.S.C. § 1831**—Economic espionage
18 U.S.C. § 1343—Fraud by wire, radio, or television	**18 U.S.C. 1832**—Theft of trade secrets
18 U.S.C. § 2261—Interstate domestic violence	**18 U.S.C. § 2318**—Trafficking in counterfeit labels, illicit labels, or counterfeit documentation or packaging
18 U.S.C. § 2315—Sale or receipt of stolen goods, securities, moneys, or fraudulent state tax stamps	**17 U.S.C. § 506**—Criminal offenses (if the infringement was committed)
47 U.S.C. § 223—Obscene or harassing telephone calls in the District of Columbia or in interstate or foreign communications	**18 U.S.C. § 2319**—Criminal infringement of a copyright
18 U.S.C. § 875—Interstate communications	**18 U.S.C. § 2320**—Trafficking in counterfeit goods or services

(*Continued*)

TABLE 4.6 (CONTINUED) Federal Legislation with Titles

Federal Legislation with Titles	
18 U.S.C. § 1951—Interference with commerce by threats or violence	**47 U.S.C. § 553**—Unauthorized reception of cable service
18 U.S.C. § 793—Gathering, transmitting, or losing defense information	**18 U.S.C. § 1037**—Fraud and related activity in connection with electronic mail
18 U.S.C. § 798—Disclosure of classified information	**18 U.S.C. § 1905**—Disclosure of confidential information generally
18 U.S.C. § 1028—Fraud and related activity in connection with identification documents, authentication features, and information	**18 U.S.C. § 2314**—Transportation of stolen goods, securities, moneys, fraudulent state tax stamps, or articles used in counterfeiting
18 U.S.C. § 1956—Laundering of monetary instruments	**18 U.S.C. § 225**—Continuing financial crimes enterprise

4.9 Key Words

Anti-Hacking Laws
Authorized Access
Business Associate Agreement
Business Associates
Commission
Consumer Fraud
Consent
Copyright
Covered Entities
Cybersecurity Framework
Cyber Laws
Electric Utilities
Economic Espionage
Exceed Authorized Access
Exigent Circumstances
Fair Use
Federal Government
Financial Institutions
Healthcare
Infringement Liability
Intellectual Property
Meaningful Use
Online Privacy
Password Trafficking
Public
Private Sector
Plain View
Protection
Red Flags Rule
Telemarketing
Safe Harbor
Search and Seizure
Warrant

Chapter 5

The Networking Environment

Objectives

After completing this chapter, the student will be able to:

- Understand computer networking, its history, and evolution
- Identify the advantages and disadvantages of computer networking
- Understand essential computer network components and terminology
- Understand different types of networking
- Understand the Open Systems Interconnection (OSI) and Transmission Control Protocol/Internet Protocol (TPC/IP) Models

Matthew types www.linkedin.com *into the address bar of his browser and searches for "Jobs in Computer Security." The browser looks for a Domain Name System (DNS) record to find the IP address of* www.linkedin.com. *Instantly, he receives a response, and the site appears.*

But what happens behind the scenes?

- Domain Name System (DNS) Search
- Network communication using Transmission Control Protocol (TCP)
  - Browser sends a Hypertext Transfer Protocol Secure (HTTPS) request
  - Server sends back HTTPS response

DOI: 10.4324/9780429318726-5

    - Server acknowledges and sends back the requested Hypertext Markup Language (HTML) file
- Browser renders HTML
- Browser sends additional requests (GET request) for additional components
- Matthew receives requested information

First, the browser checks for a Domain Name System (DNS) record to find the corresponding IP address of www.linkedin.com. Every Web page on the Internet has a unique IP address assigned to it. While the Uniform Resource Locator (URL) is a reference to a specific website, the DNS is the "phonebook" of the Internet and contains a list of every URL and its IP addresses. To find www.linkedin.com, the browser checks four caches, the Browser cache, Computer Operating System (OS) cache, Router cache, and Internet service provider (ISP) DNS cache. A cache can be hardware or software. It stores data so that future requests for that data can be found more quickly.

If the IP address is not found, the DNS server starts a new DNS query to find the IP address of www.linkedin.com. As soon as the browser locates the right IP address, it tells the server that has found the IP address for www.linkedin.com and wants to transfer the information.

How does it do that? There are several types of network protocols, but the TCP is the most common protocol used to establish and maintain network communication. The browser sends a Hypertext Transfer Protocol (HTTP) request. HTTP is a protocol that runs on top of TCP. TCP transfers data packets between Matthew's computer, the client, and the server. This connection is known as a three-way handshake: 1-SYN or a request from the server is sent to synchronize devices; 2-SYN/ACK or the client (Matthew) hears the request; and 3-ACK or the request is acknowledged. This establishes the connection between the network and the devices. After the TCP/IP connection is established, the data can be delivered to Matthew's computer.

The browser receives a HTML file that needs to be understood and displayed. First, it renders the HTML, and then it checks the HTML tags and sends out a GET method request for additional components on the Web page, like an image or a graph. Now Matthew can see the result of "Jobs in Computer Security" appearing on his browser.

All these events take place while Matthew blinks. In this chapter you will learn to understand each of these steps and appreciate the network devices and processes that make them possible.

The term "computer network" refers to two or more interconnected computing devices or machines that can communicate with each other. The fundamental goal of *computer networking* is simple—to securely share information and resources. It is the execution that is not simple at all.

5.1 Introduction to Computer Networking

Over the centuries, some human inventions have provided transformative changes in our lives. Inventions such as the wheel, compass, concrete, steel, gunpowder, and nails have extended the boundaries of civilization and human knowledge and have moved innovation forward.

The end of the 18th century brought the age of the steam engine,[1] powered by coal. In the late 19th century, commerce changed again due to the discovery of oil and innovations in manufacturing, such as Henry Ford's assembly line and the work of Frederick Winslow Taylor, the father of scientific management.[2]

The 20th century brought us automation, information gathering and processing, the Internet, and mobile phones.[3] In the 21st century the word "connected" now describes the significant advancements in technology that has changed our world once again.

The Internet is an enormous global network of networks that can connect every computing device to its vast resources and to every other computer on the planet. In the 1960s, the Advanced Research Projects Agency (ARPA), part of the Department of Defense, funded a proposed network project called the Advanced Research Projects Agency Network (ARPANET), through the Association for Computing Machinery (ACM).

In 1969, the experimental ARPANET was constructed (Figure 5.1). Only universities with ties to the Department of Defense were considered for this project. The new network connected the Universities of California Los Angeles (UCLA) and California at Santa Barbara (UCSB), the Stanford Research Institute (SRI), and the University of Utah (UTAH) through the Internet Message Processor (IMP)[4] (Figure 5.2). The four universities formed a network and communicated using software called the Network Control Program (NCP), which later came to be known as a protocol or a host-to-host protocol[5] (Figure 5.3). In 1981, the National Science Foundation (NSF) sponsored the creation of CSNET. This network was created for universities that were not qualified to use the ARPANET because they did not have ties to the Defense Advanced Research Projects Agency (DARPA).

However, it is worth noting that Bolt Beranek and Newman (BBN) Inc. was awarded the contract to build the ARPANET. Consequently, BBN

[1] Deane, Phyllis M., and Phyllis M. Deane. *The first industrial revolution*. Cambridge University Press, 1979.

[2] Kanigel, Robert. "The one best way: Frederick Winslow Taylor and the enigma of efficiency." *MIT Press Books* 1 (2005).

[3] Morrar, Rabeh, Husam Arman, and Saeed Mousa. "The fourth industrial revolution (Industry 4.0): A social innovation perspective." *Technology Innovation Management Review* 7, no. 11 (2017): 12–20.

[4] Forouzan, Behrouz A. *TCP/IP protocol suite*. McGraw-Hill, Inc., 2002.

[5] Hauben, Michael. "History of ARPANET." *Site de l'Instituto Superior de Engenharia do Porto* 17 (2007).

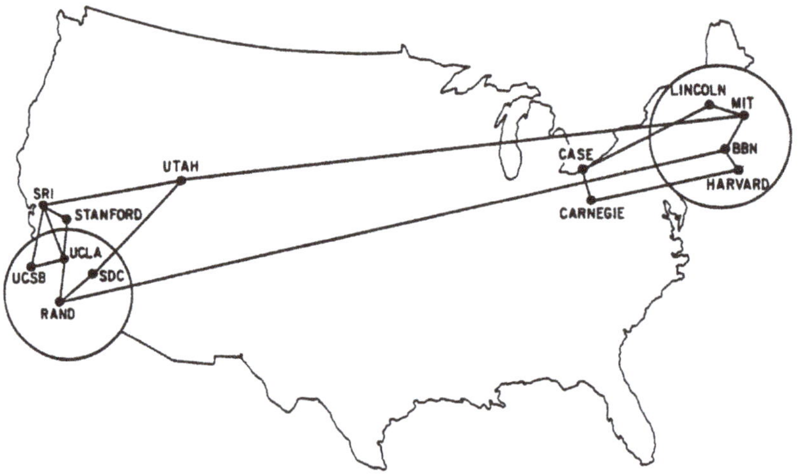

FIGURE 5.1 **A map of the ARPANET in December 1970. Courtesy of DARPA.**

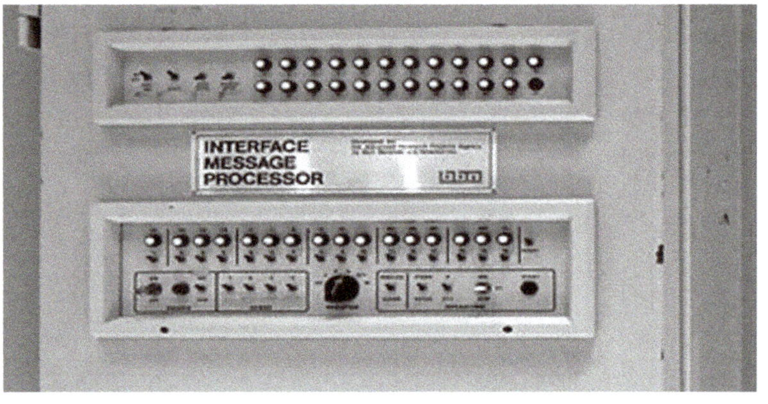

FIGURE 5.2 **The first routers, known as Interface Message Processors or IMPs. Courtesy of DARPA.**

created Telenet Communications Corp. to commercialize the packet switching technology. Telenet received a Federal Communications Commission (FCC) license in 1974. In 1975, Telenet launched the first commercial packet switching with network service that cost $0.60 per kilo packet with no distance restrictions and $0.90–2.40 per hour for computer terminals dialing into the local Telenet node. The company expanded its network globally and played a vital role in generating the standard for commercial packet networks.[6]

Most institutions with computer science programs were part of CSNET. In 1983, TCP/IP became the official protocol for ARPANET. The term "protocol" will be explained shortly.

[6] Mathison, Stuart L., Lawrence G. Roberts, and Philip M. Walker. "The history of telenet and the commercialization of packet switching in the US." *IEEE Communications Magazine* 50, no. 5 (2012): 28–45.

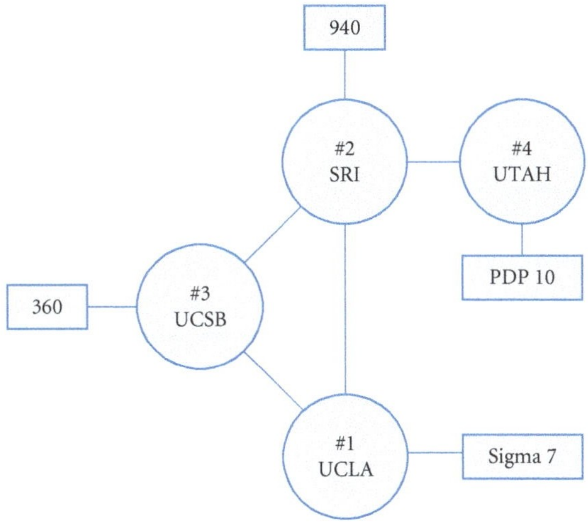

FIGURE 5.3 The first rough conceptual design of ARPANET in 1969 with four nodes. Adopted from DARPA.

In 1983, the ARPANET split into two separate networks, the MILNET for military installations and the ARPANET for civilian use (mainly dedicated to research). In 1986, the National Science Foundation (NSF) sponsored the development of the National Science Foundation Network (NSFNET), which promoted advanced research in networking.[7]

In 1989, while working for the European Organization for Nuclear Research (CERN), Tim Berners-Lee invented the World Wide Web (WWW). The idea was the creation of a service that merged HTML, URL, and HTTP so that all computers could understand each other in an easy-to-use global information system.[8]

In 1990, the ARPANET was replaced by NSFNET. In 1995, the network became largely commercial and grew exponentially.[9] However, it was the ARPANET, not the NSFNET, that was the predecessor to our Internet. Today we take for granted this global network infrastructure called the Internet.

5.1.1 Protocols

A protocol is a digital language and set of specifications and procedures followed throughout the network so that computers in different locations can share information and resources, making the network viable. Networks can connect many different types of computers and share resources that reside

---

[7] *Id.* at 4.

[8] Where the Web was born, European Organization for Nuclear Research (CERN). Retrieved from https://home.cern/science/computing/birth-web/short-history-web

[9] National Science Foundation. A Brief History of NSF and the Internet. Retrieved from https://www.nsf.gov/news/news_summ.jsp?cntn_id=103050

on widely different types of servers. Without a viable protocol, no network can function.

During the early years of the ARPANET the Network Working Group (NWG) was formed to monitor and oversee the network's technical aspects. The NWG was instrumental in the development of the ARPANET and set the stage for the development of the Network Control Protocol (NCP) and later the Transmission Control Protocol/Internet Protocol (TCP/IP), the most widely used communications protocol to this day. In 1970, the NWG, under the supervision of Steve Crocker, completed the host-to-host protocol called the NCP. Between 1970 and 1972 the NCP was implemented on the ARPANET, enabling network users to develop applications. Besides Crocker, Vinton G. Cerf, one of the co-founders of TCP/IP, had been involved in NCP design and development.[10]

In1974, Vinton G. Cerf and Robert E. Kahn published a paper called "A Protocol for Packet Network Intercommunication Researchers," which recognized the significance of network intercommunication involving different types of computers, flow control, end-to-end error checking, and topologies.[11,12] Thus, they designed the TCP/IP protocol along with the basic architecture used to transmit data over the Internet. Their contribution is of immense significance to the digital revolution that followed. Dr. Cerf is commonly known as the "Father of the Internet."

Later in the 1970s, the government decided to split TCP into two protocols. In 1981, UC Berkeley, working under a contract with DARPA, expanded TCP/IP to include error correction, segmentation, and reassembly. As a result, in 1981, the government eliminated the NCP and adopted TCP/IP as the official protocol for the ARPANET.[13] In 1983, the ARPANET replaced NCP with TCP/IP and allowed the ARPANET to split into MILNET for military and the ARPANET for research communications.[14] Figure 5.4 demonstrates key events in the development of the Internet.

5.1.2 The World Wide Web and the Internet

The Internet and the World Wide Web (WWW) are not the same. The Internet is a global network of networks that are structured to connect each

[10] Leiner, Barry M., Vinton G. Cerf, David D. Clark, Robert E. Kahn, Leonard Kleinrock, Daniel C. Lynch, Jon Postel, Lawrence G. Roberts, and Stephen S. Wolff. "The past and future history of the Internet." *Communications of the ACM* 40, no. 2 (1997): 102–108.

[11] Cerf, V., and R. Icahn. "A protocol for packet network intercommunication." *IEEE Transactions on Communications* 22, no. 5 (May 1974): 637–648. doi: 10.1109/TCOM.1974.1092259.

[12] Cerf, Vinton G., and Robert E. Icahn. "A protocol for packet network intercommunication." *ACM SIGCOMM Computer Communication Review* 35, no. 2 (2005): 71–82.

[13] *Id.* at 4.

[14] *Id.* at 10.

1995
- The US Federal Networking Council (FNC) passed a resolution to define the Internet.

1989
- Tim Berners Lee, a scientist at the CERN laboratory in Switzerland, invented the World Wide Web (WWW), or the Web.

1986
- The National Science Foundation (NSF) sponsored the development of the National Science Foundation Network (NSFNET), which promoted advanced research in networking.

1983
- The ARPANET split into two separate networks, the MILNET for military installations and the ARPANET for civilian use (mainly dedicated to research).

1983
- TCP/IP becames the official protocol for ARPANET.

1975
- Telenet launched the first commercial packet switching with network service.

1974
- Drs.Vinton Cerf and Robert Kahn invented the TCP/IP protocol. The software code is used to transmit data over the Internet.

1972
- Ray Tomlinson invented the e-mail system we know today by selecting the @ symbol to structure the address of a single user and its host (name-of-the @name-of-the-computer).

1970
- The Network Working Group (NWG) under the supervision of Steve Crocker completed the firts host-to-host protocol, called the Network Control Protocol (NCP).

1969
- Advanced Research Projects Agency Network (ARPANET) began with the Advanced Research Projects Agency (ARPA) by the Department of Defense and through the Association for Computing Machinery (ACM).

FIGURE 5.4 A timeline of key network and computer events.

FIGURE 5.5 **Ethernet cables. Courtesy of Shutterstock.**

other, whereas the Web is a service that runs on top of this infrastructure. Imagine our lives today without it!

In the past, the computer center was a room in the basement of a company from which all computer operations were run. With the introduction of networking and the ability to connect to resources and businesses around the world, the old room became outdated and was replaced by enterprise-wide data centers in various locations, with servers connected to the network. Now, these enterprise data centers have been overtaken by cloud computing, virtualization, mobile devices, and the Internet of Things (IoTs), all using edge computing paradigms and fog standards that bring their applications closer to the user. These are discussed more fully in Chapter 7.

The connection into a network by any device occurs either *wired* or *wirelessly*. In a wired connection, we physically connect a computer into a router using Ethernet cables (Figure 5.5). In a wireless connection the computer is connected to the network via a radio signal. The Institute of Electrical and Electronics Engineers (IEEE) has defined the standard for wireless communications with Wi-Fi-enabled devices as IEEE 802.11, and for Ethernet wired standard connections as IEEE 802.3.

5.1.3 Advantages and Disadvantages

Some of the advantages of *computer networking* are the following:

- **Central data storage**: data is shared between computing devices/users, and users can access data remotely.
- **Cost benefits of shared resources**: when multiple users share resources, such as printers, scanners, copiers, and applications, the

business saves money. In addition, by storing data in one centralized database and by sharing peripherals and Internet access, redundancy is reduced, and efficiency is increased.

- **Centralized protection and monitoring**
- **Ability to access information at a very fast speed**
- **Network backup reliability**: ensures that data is backed up onto multiple servers.
- **Security**: through authentication that validates the identity of an authorized user, thereby preventing theft or unauthorized accessing of data.

In addition to these advantages, networks have disadvantages as well. Some are:

- **Cost** of network management and maintenance, including expensive hardware and applications, uninterruptible power supply (UPS), fire suppression equipment, air conditioning, stable temperature maintenance, humidity control, air filtration for dust and other airborne particles, and the training of personnel to run the data center.
- **Virus and malware**: Infections can quickly spread on a network system, and repair is time consuming and may interrupt the flow of business.

5.1.4 Essential Computer Network Components and Terminology

A computer network requires different components, which must work together properly. These components are the building blocks of the network and provide the resources to perform its tasks. In addition, the network provides methods and techniques to prevent and monitor unauthorized access, called data breaches.

The most basic form of networking is *peer-to-peer (P2P)*. The P2P network is created when two or more computing devices share resources like storage devices, files, and printers without using a server. All computing devices can function as both a client and server (Figure 5.6).

FIGURE 5.6 A peer-to-peer (P2P) network.

What is a server? The term refers to a piece of hardware or software used to provide resources for other computers or devices, called "clients."

In networking, a "node" refers to any addressable device, redistribution point, connection point, or communication endpoint that is connected to a network. A node can create, process, recognize, receive, transmit, or store data and requires a unique address for identification to be part of a network. Examples of nodes include computers, network bridges, IoT devices, modems, printers, routers, and switches.[15] A "client" is a computing device that can utilize and share network resources. A computing device on a TCP/IP network that handles network and node requests for applications and offers resources and services is called a "host." An example is a server that provides clients with network connectivity and access to information stored in databases. A host is also a physical network node. Figures 5.7 and 5.8 demonstrate the client server process.

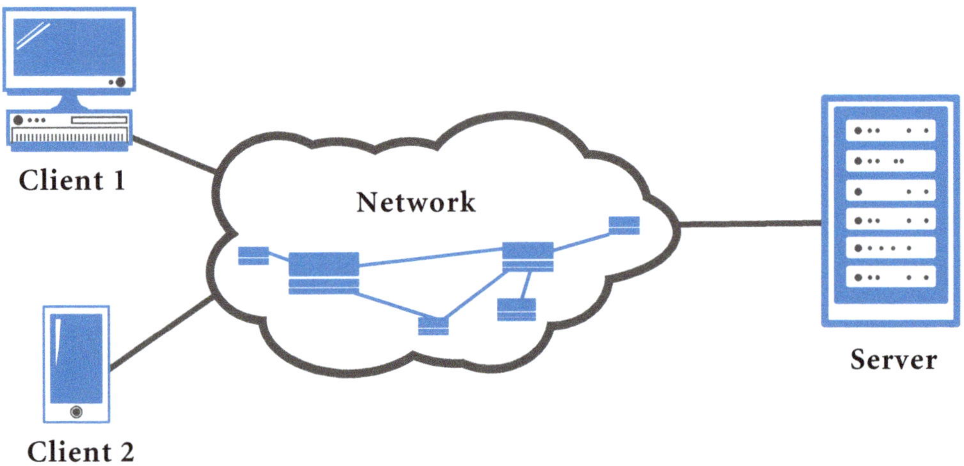

FIGURE 5.7 A network with two clients and a server.

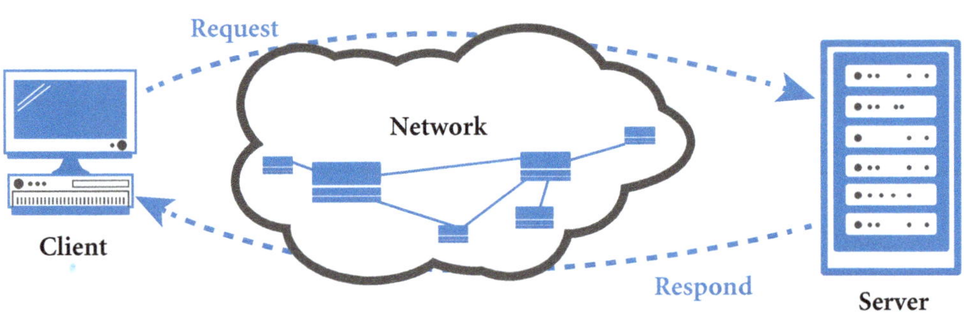

FIGURE 5.8 The client-server communication.

[15] The Internet Engineering Task Force (IETF). Retrieved from https://tools.ietf.org/html/rfc2460#section-2

In a corporate setting, a network will include a client computer for every employee connected to a server. The client sends and receives requests. A server provides resources to the client such as access to the Internet and to connections like printers, files, programs, and external processing power. Communication occurs when the client sends a message to the server over the network and then waits for a reply. When the server receives the request, it will process it and send back a reply.

The purpose of networking is back-and-forth communication. A network allows computing devices to exchange packets of data safely and securely. To be able to comprehend complex network interactions, we need to understand in detail all the devices that comprise it. All *network devices*, also called *network hardware*, are physical devices that can communicate and interact over the network. *Network software* refers to the application program that runs the network, helping administrators deploy, manage, and/or monitor it. *Network architecture* signifies the way network devices and services are configured and structured. Below are the most important key networking terms, devices, and concepts.

Access Point (AP) or *Wireless Access Point (WAP)* is a networking device that contains a radio transmitter and a receiver signal, enabling other computing devices to connect to the network and communicate with each other (Figure 5.9). An access point can connect routers, switches, and hubs via Ethernet cables or Wi-Fi signals. It can provide a solution to a networking problem, for example, when we want to enable Wi-Fi access to a specific area and we are not within range of the router. The solution is to install an access point and run an Ethernet cable from it to the server. This small, wired connection allows the wireless network to broadcast in a designated

FIGURE 5.9 **A ceiling access point Wi-Fi. Courtesy of Shutterstock.**

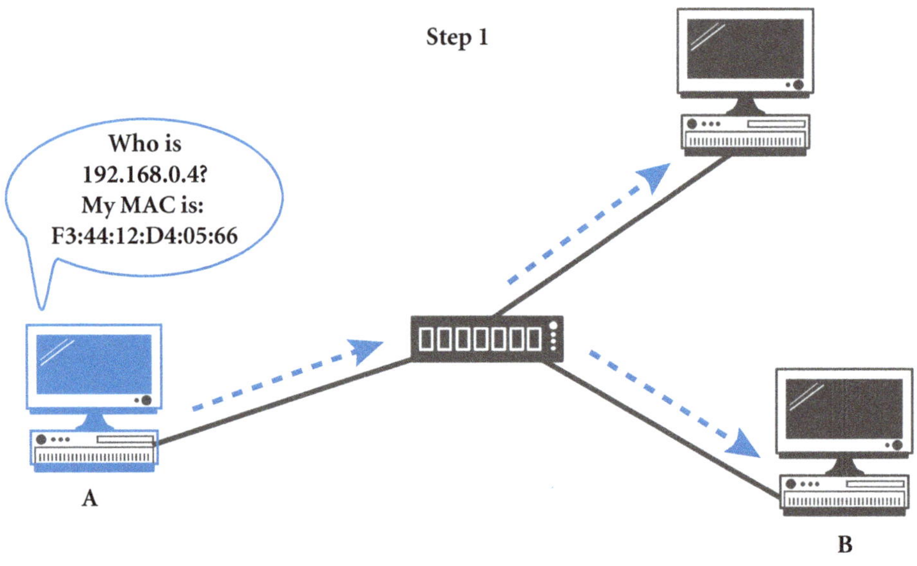

FIGURE 5.10 Address Resolution Protocol (ARP)—Step 1 translates IP addresses to MAC addresses.

area. Access Points operate at Layer 2–Data Link of the OSI model. We will discuss the OSI model later in this chapter.

Address Resolution Protocol (ARP) is a network protocol that finds the Media Access Control (MAC) address of a device from an IP address. Figures 5.10 to 5.12 describe the ARP process.

A *bridge* is a network device that connects two or more networks or segments. The bridge is responsible for regulating incoming traffic by inspecting it and deciding whether to forward it or to filter it (block it), thereby reducing unnecessary traffic. A bridge can also store MAC addresses.

Data packets are units of data sent over a TCP/IP network, with the goal of transmitting data efficiently and reliably. When we send something over the Internet, the data is divided into small pieces (using the specific size in bytes) to ensure each part is transmitted successfully and to accommodate various bandwidths. By breaking the data into parts, the data packets can evade network congestion caused by simultaneous transfers and can be rerouted via less congested paths. When an email leaves a computing device, the network splits it into data packets. When the packets reach their destination, they are reconstructed and put into the sequence as a single file. Think about it as mailing a jigsaw puzzle. It doesn't matter which route each mosaic piece is mailed to, as long as all mosaic pieces arrive at the destination and the recipient can combine the shapes into a picture. The reverse happens when we receive an email or a Webpage. We will discuss data packets further in relation to the OSI model.

A packet contains both delivery information and the actual data of the sender. The precise synthesis of a packet differs between protocols, but a typical packet contains three sections, the *header*, the *payload*, and the *trailer* or

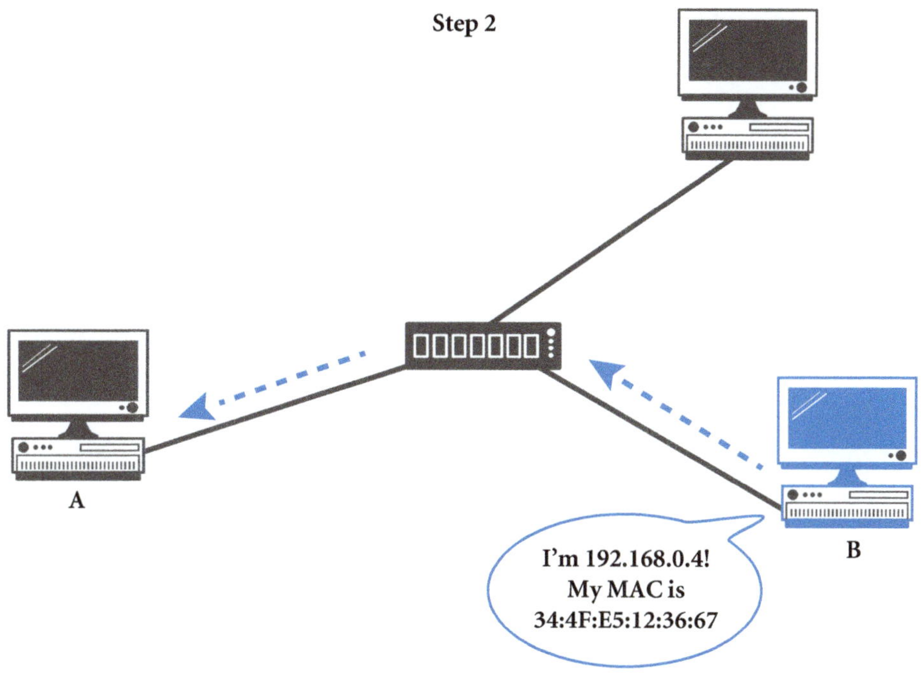

FIGURE 5.11 Address Resolution Protocol (ARP)—Step 2.

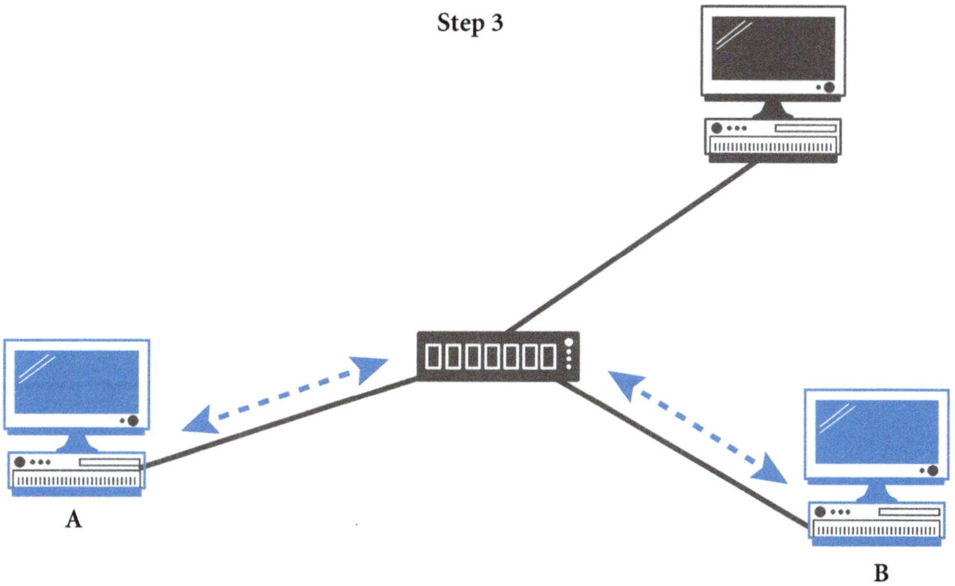

FIGURE 5.12 Address Resolution Protocol (ARP)—Step 3 translates MAC addresses to IP addresses.

footer. For example, in Internet Protocol version 6 (IPv6), the first section of each data packet is the *IPv6 header*. IPv6 will be described later in the chapter. The main components of an IPv6 header are the following.[16]

Version indicates the version of the IP. The header size is 4 bits.

Traffic class designates the class or priority settings of IPv6 packet. Its size is 8 bits.

- **Flow label**: specifies that packets belong to a specific sequence. Examples include real-time data such as voice and video. The size is 20 bits.
- **Payload length**: defines the length of the IPv6 payload in octets. An octet is a unit measuring digital information and consists of 8 bits. The size is 16 bits.
- **Next header**: indicates the type of the first extension header or the Protocol Data Unit (PDU). This could be TCP, User Datagram Protocol (UDP), or others. The size is 8 bits.
- **Hop limit**: designates the maximum number of links that the IPv6 packet can travel before the packet is released. The size is 8 bits.
- **Source address**: the originating IPv6 host address. The size is 128 bits.
- **Destination of IPv6 address**: stores the destination host. The size is 128 bits.

The *payload* delivers the actual data to its destination, and the *trailer* encompasses information about the destination of the packet.

Dynamic Host Configuration Protocol (DHCP) is the client or server that is responsible for assigning dynamic IP addresses to client computers and other related configuration information.

Domain Name System (DNS) is a directory of the IP addresses of the entire Internet. The DNS translates domain names, which people can remember, or maps host names into IP addresses. In other words, the DNS allows people to use words in place of an IP address when searching. For example, when we type www.CISCO.com into a browser, the browser asks the DNS to find the IP address. The DNS will return the IP address for CISCO's domain name (72.163.4.185), and the browser will connect to the IP address. The user can find an IP address or a website by typing C:\> nslookup at the command prompt in Windows or at a terminal in Linux. Another way to find an IP address is with ARIN WHOIS IP Address Database Search[17] (Table 5.1).

In addition to translating domain names into IP addresses, the DNS has anti-spam defenses, including routing security like the Resource Public Key Infrastructure (RPKI) that safeguards the Internet's routing infrastructure

---

[16] CISCO SYSTEMS. IPv6 Extension Headers Review and Considerations. https://www.cisco.com/en/US/technologies/tk648/tk872/technologies_white_paper0900aecd8054d37d.html

[17] ARIN WHOIS IP Address Database Search. Retrieved from http://itools.com/tool/arin-whois-domain-search

TABLE 5.1 Example of DNS Names and Corresponding IP Addresses

Name: **Address:**	microsoft.com 131.107.0.89
Name: **Addresses:**	CISCO.com 2001:420:1101:1::185 72.163.4.185

and firewalls.[18] Also, the DNS can contain an open standard called the Sender Policy Framework (SPF),[19] an email authentication method that is used to prevent spam messages sent on behalf of the user's domain. This standard helps identify the mail servers that are authorized by the domain owner to send email. SPF defines the correct IP addresses the user can send emails from. More specifically, SPF looks at the domain of the return-path value (in the email's headers) for a proper SPF value.

Another standard created for the same purpose as SPF is the Domain Keys Identified Mail (DKIM).[20] It also prevents cybercriminals from identifying the user as an email sender. DKIM can be added to the DNS server and provides validation for the domain name identity of the email sender through cryptographic authentication. Yes, it's really me! sending this message!

Cybercriminals use phishing attacks, to create fake but real-looking websites, tricking users into clicking links in the sites and then giving out personal information. These fake domains impersonate legitimate websites but have entirely different IP addresses.

The DNS is essential because it protects users and businesses from phishing attacks. Therefore, the communication between the user's computer and the DNS system is vital to direct the correct IP address assigned to a domain name. Usually the Internet Service Provider (ISP) automatically assigns its own default DNS server, but this can change the system's DNS settings to other free and secure services such as Google Public DNS,[21] OpenDNS,[22] and Quad9 Internet Security & Privacy DNS.[23]

Gateway or *Protocol Converters* are network devices (nodes) that can be employed as software, hardware, or a combination of both to connect two dissimilar networks. The gateway is an entry or exit point between networks. The gateway takes data from one network, interprets it, and transfers it to another network. Gateways are usually complex, and since they are found at the edges of a network, they are integrated into routers, firewalls, servers, or

[18] Klein, Amit, Haya Shulman, and Michael Waidner. "Internet-wide study of dns cache injections." In *IEEE INFOCOM 2017—IEEE Conference on Computer Communications*, pp. 1-9. IEEE, 2017.

[19] Sender Policy Framework (SPF). Retrieved from http://www.open-spf.org/Project_Overview/

[20] DomainKeys Identified Mail (DKIM). Retrieved from http://www.dkim.org/)

[21] Google Public DNS. Retrieved from https://developers.google.com/speed/public-dns/docs/using

[22] DNS services for your home or small business. Retrieved from https://www.opendns.com/home-internet-security/

[23] Quad9 Internet Security & Privacy DNS. Retrieved from https://www.quad9.net/

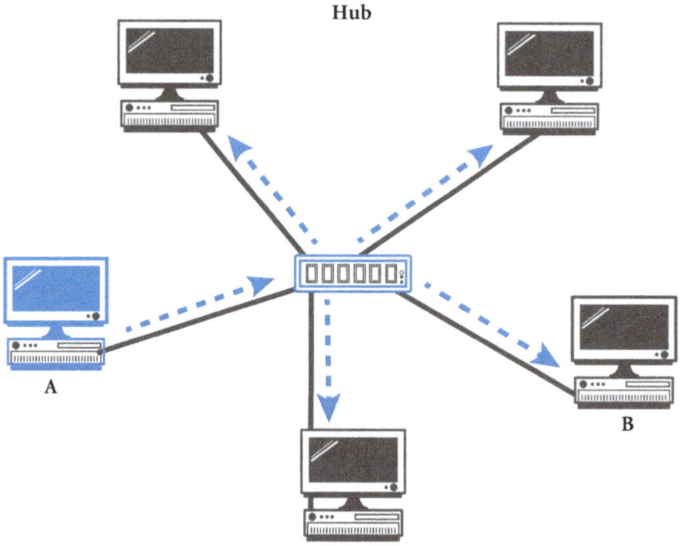

FIGURE 5.13 A hub broadcasts data to all connected hosts.

other devices that enable traffic to flow in and out of the network. Without gateways we would not be able to communicate with devices, nodes, or networks outside of our own network.

A *hub* connects computing devices and serves as a connection point within a private network or Local Area Network (LAN) by broadcasting packets of data to other connected computing devices (Figure 5.13). Because the data packets will stay within the local network, the hub does not perform filtering or routing. The drawback of using multiple hubs in a private network is that there may be a *collision* when two or more devices send data at the same time. Another weakness is that when the available bandwidth is split among connected devices, the speed will slow. Hubs operate at Layer 1—Physical layer of the OSI model. Bandwidth is defined as the maximum rate of data transmitted across a network path per unit of time and measured in bits per second.

Internet Protocol address (IP address) is a unique identifier assigned to every single computing device on a TCP/IP network. The IP address has two primary functions: it identifies the host's or network interface identification and location addressing. When a computing device sends data to another device, the data headers contain information about the sending device's IP address along with the destination device's IP address. The IP address is like a physical home address for the computer that determines where the mail should be delivered. In 1982, when TCP/IP became the official protocol for ARPANET, IP addresses first emerged. As mentioned earlier, the first version of modern TCP was written in 1973 by Cerf and Kahn.

The first and second Internet Protocols, IPvland IPv2, were never defined; IPv3 and IPv5 were experimental. Internet Protocol 4, IPv4, was the first version that was used publicly and carried a theoretical limit of 4.3 billion (2^{32})

addresses. So far, IPv4 is the most popular version ever deployed. But, as the Internet grew exponentially, IPv4 ran out of IP addresses, especially after the emergence of mobile and IoT devices. As a result, in 1998, the Internet Engineering Task Force (IETF) created IPv6 to solve this problem.[24] In the 1980s, when IPv4 was first implemented, no one could have foreseen that in 20 years we would have more than four billion devices connected to the Internet.

The organization that is responsible for allocating and maintaining global IP addresses is the Internet Assigned Numbers Authority (IANA).[25] IANA has been a division of the Internet Corporation for Assigned Names and Numbers (ICANN) since 1998 and is responsible for maintaining the Central Internet Address pools and the DNS root zone. ICANN does not control content or access to the Internet but coordinates how IP addresses are supplied to avoid repetition or clashes, along with the growth and evolution of the Internet.[26] In addition, IANA assigns IP address blocks to five international Regional Internet Registries (RIR). Globally, these five regions create smaller address blocks available to the respective Local Internet Registries (LIR) and the National Internet Registries (NIR) (Figure 5.14). Then, they are distributed to the Internet Service Providers (ISPs). The ISPs assign IP addresses to the users. At present, IANA is issuing two types of IP addresses, IP version 4 (IPv4) and IP version 6 (IPv6). Table 5.2 lists the regional internet registries (RIR).[27]

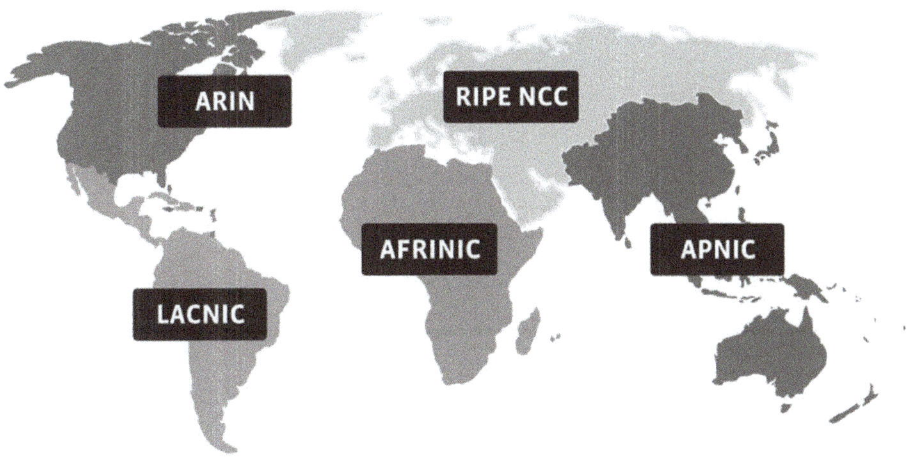

FIGURE 5.14 Map of Regional Internet Registry (RIR RIR). The map was adapted from IANA.

[24] The Internet Engineering Task Force. IPv6 is an Internet Standard. Retrieved from https://ietf.org/blog/ipv6-internet-standard/ and https://www.ietf.org/rfc/rfc2460.txt

[25] Internet Assigned Numbers Authority (IANA). Retrieved by https://www.iana.org/about

[26] Internet Corporation for Assigned Names and Numbers (ICANN). What Does ICANN Do? Retrieved from https://www.icann.org/ and https://www.icann.org/resources/pages/what-2012-02-25-en

[27] Internet Assigned Numbers Authority (IANA). Number Resources. Retrieved from https://www.iana.org/numbers

TABLE 5.2 The Regional Internet Registries (RIR)

Registry	Area
AFRINIC	Africa Region
APNIC	Asia/Pacific Region
ARIN	Canada, USA, and some Caribbean Islands
LACNIC	Latin America and some Caribbean Islands
RIPE NCC	Europe, the Middle East, and Central Asia

The table was adapted from IANA.

- **IPv4**, first deployed in 1983, uses a 32-bit address and can handle 4,294,967,296 (2^{32}) unique addresses. It is still the most widely used IP version.[28] Because IPv4 is currently running out of addresses, ISPs are switching to IPv6. At the present time, IPv4 coexists harmoniously with the newer IPv6, which will eventually replace it, at which point IPv4 will become a legacy protocol.
- **IPv6** uses a 128-bit address, theoretically delivering 2^{128} unique addresses. It offers about 340 trillion trillion trillion combinations, called undecillion, or sextillion or dodekillion and is equal to 10^{36}. As opposed to IPv4, which is written in dotted decimal notation, IPv6 is written using hexadecimal notation. An example of an IP address provided by IPv6 for the Microsoft Corporation in Redmond, Washington, United States is 2a01:111: f400:5254::2.

5.1.5 Basic Anatomy of IPv6

IPv6 splits the address into two 64-bit segments, and consists of eight sets of 16-bit hexadecimal values or blocks, separated by colons (:).

For example, if we convert hex 2001 to binary the result is 0010 0000 0000 0001, and if we convert hex 1234 to binary the result is 0001 0010 0011 0100. For more information on hex and binary, see Chapter 1. The figure below demonstrates the IPv6 structure in hexadecimal. The left four values or blocks indicate the network ID, which is administratively assigned. The right four values or blocks indicate the host or interface ID and are configured manually or automatically (e.g. DHCPv6 or randomly generated numbers). If you think of each value or block as an address, the street is on the network side, left, and the house number is on the right. Figure 5.15 represents one of many different configurations of IPv6 address.

More specifically, the network ID side is split into two smaller parts, the 48-bit *routing prefix* and the 16-bit *Subnet ID* (see figure). The *routing prefix* contains the global network addresses and is assigned by ARIN or the ISP.

[28] *Id.* at 27.

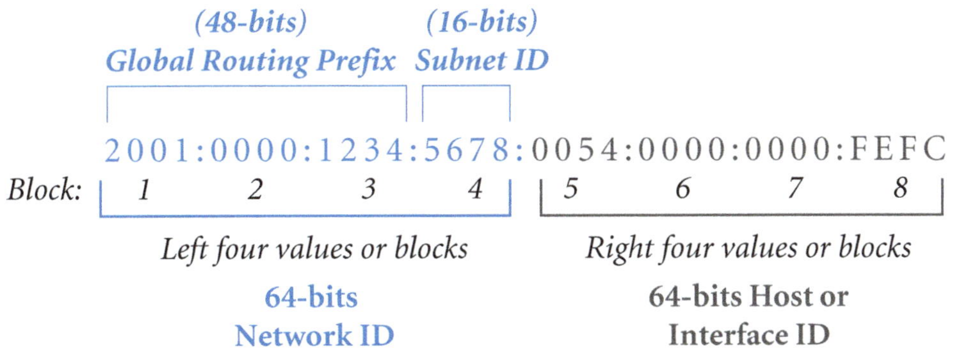

FIGURE 5.15 **IPv6 structure.**

This part is used for routing over the internet. The second part, the *subnet*, is created by the customer on an internal network and is controlled by the network administrator. A *subnet* or *a subnetwork* is a segment of a larger network structure, or a network inside a network. *Subnetting* is been used by administrators to make networks more efficient by allowing traffic to travel shorter distances. The final part, the *Interface ID*, is the unique identifier for a host or a node connected to the network. [29]

The first two blocks of IPv6 show which block the IP came from. The numbers above the block number indicate ARIN's specific IPv6 allocation block.[30] The third block shows the region or site location. The fourth block is the *subnet*, which can be customized or controlled by the local network administrator. The last four blocks (5–8) consist of an auto-configured 64-bit unique identifier for the hosts or nodes.[31]

Since the IPv6 specification is exceptionally long, the protocol allows us to shorten the address by omitting leading zeros. For example, in block 5, the hex 0054 can become 54.

If we have consecutive zeros in contiguous blocks, as in blocks 6&7, we can omit them and substitute a double colon (**: :**). Then, the IPv6 looks like this: **2001:0:1234:5678:54::FEFC.**

In the IP world, there are two types of IP addresses: *static and dynamic*. The *static IP* does not change until the device is retired. This type of IP is assigned by the Internet Service Provider (ISP) or by a network administrator.

- A *static IP* address is assigned to important external computing devices, a server (web server, email server, printer shared within the network) or websites that need to use the IP address so other devices

[29] The American Registry for Internet Numbers (ARIN). Retrieved from https://www.arin.net/resources/guide/ipv6/first_request/

[30] IP Address Blocks ARIN Issues From. Retrieved from https://www.arin.net/reference/research/statistics/ip_blocks/

[31] The American Registry for Internet Numbers (ARIN). Number Resource Policy Manual. Retrieved from https://www.arin.net/participate/policy/nrpm/#6-5-3-1-subsequent-allocations-for-transition

can connect to it quickly. Another example is a Virtual Private Network (VPN). Because Virtual Private Networks (VPN) trust specific IPs, the static IP address provides an easier way to locate the device, more easily set it up, and get better support through the DNS server. This makes it easier to work remotely using VPN and provides better reliability when communicating using Voice over Internet Protocol (VoIP) and video conferencing. However, along with these advantages, the most significant disadvantage of the *static IP* is lessened security. Cybercriminals like hackers know the location of each server on the Internet and the static IP makes it easier to attack since it cannot be disguised. Another disadvantage is that ISPs usually charge more for *static IP* addresses.

- The *dynamic IP* is subject to change and is assigned by Dynamic Host Configuration Protocol (DHCP) servers. Some of its advantages include better security. It is harder for hackers to find the location and target networked equipment they are looking for, since the address may have changed. Also, the *dynamic IP* is easier to set up with automatic configuration by the DHCP server. The DHCP automatically assigns computing devices with unlimited IP addresses and is constantly reusing them. The use of *dynamic IP* addresses is less expensive than static IPs. For example, in homes or offices, the ISP's DHCP server could assign a *dynamic IP* address to a router or other computing devices. When they are disconnected, that IP address may then be assigned to another device. To prevent a conflict when two devices try to use the same *dynamic IP* address, the network or the router automatically removes the old IP and assigns another one. Examples of dynamic address apps include Hulu, DirecTV, and SlingTV.

By default, an ISP or cable company will assign a *dynamic* IP address, unless the user requests a *static* IP. Also, within a network, computing devices are assigned *dynamic* IPs by default. To switch an IP address, the user will need to go to the router's interface, locate the device, and then change the IP address manually. Typically, a network administrator or the ISP can assign a *static* IP. Additionally, an IP can be classified as either a *public* or a *private* IP address. A *public* IP address can be either *static or dynamic* and is accessible to everyone on the Internet. It is unique for each device and is provided by ISPs as soon as the computing device is connected to the Internet gateway.

When the ISP assigns an IP address to a gateway, the gateway permits multiple devices to access the Internet through a single *public IP* address through a process called Network Address Translation (NAT). The NAT limits the number of *public IPs* that an organization must use by translating a *public IP* to *private IP* for security and cost-effective purposes. From a security perspective, NAT enhances security by hiding the internal network from the outside world. NAT is a process in which one or multiple *private IPs* are translated (mapped) into one or multiple *public or global* IP addresses and vice versa. NAT was introduced due to the need for more IPv4 addresses and the vast amount of IT devices.

A *private IP* address is used locally only, for example in a LAN, and is never routed outside of the network. The Internet Assigned Numbers Authority (IANA) reserves IP address ranges for use on private networks.

IPv6 also includes a *type* and a *scope* for interfacing. The three major *types* are *Unicast*, *Multicast*, and *Anycast*.[32,33]

- *Unicast addresses* locate a single interface or a node on a network. Once a packet goes to a *unicast* address, the traffic goes from one sender to one receiver or to a specified destination.
- *Multicast addresses* locate a set of interfaces or nodes in the network. As soon as a packet goes to a multicast address, the traffic is transported to all interfaces or nodes in the group or within the same physical medium.
- *Anycast* addresses locate a set of interfaces or nodes on different physical media. Once the packet goes to an anycast address, it is transported to the closest member of the group or nearest interface or node in the group but not to all interfaces.

An IPv6 address has a specific *scop*e that classifies the topological area for an interface (see Figure 5.16). These scopes are the *global unicast addresses*

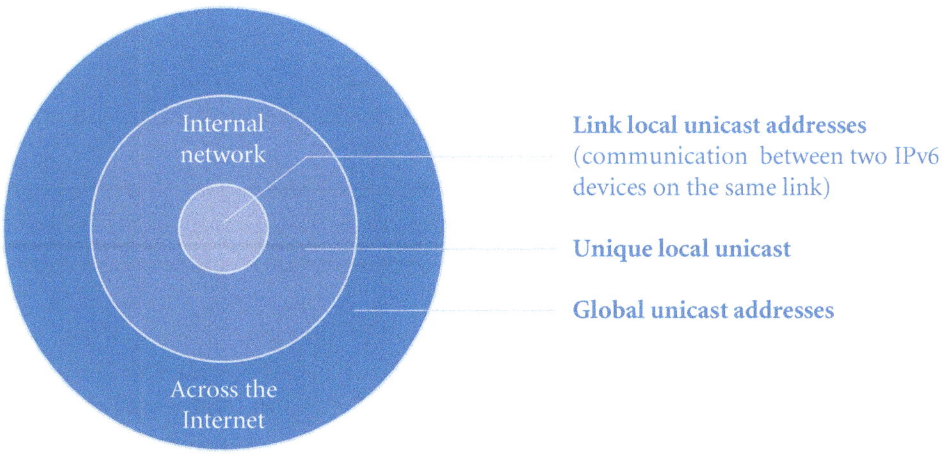

FIGURE 5.16 The scope of IPv6 address.

[32] CISCO Systems, IPv6 Deployment Guide for Cisco Collaboration Systems Release. Retrieved from https://www.cisco.com/c/en/us/td/docs/voice_ip_comm/uc_system/IPv6/vtgs_b_ipv6-deployment-guide-for-cisco/vtgs_b_ipv6-deployment-guide-for-cisco_chapter_01.html

[33] JUNIPER, IPv6 Address Types. Retrieved from https://www.juniper.net/documentation/en_US/junos/topics/concept/subscriber-management-dual-stack-ipv6-address-types.html

and are universally routable across the Internet, with the Prefix always set to binary 001. *Unique local unicast addresses* are for local communication and are routable only inside an internal network and are not routed on the Internet. An example of a unique local unicast address might be an inter-site VPN, a virtual private network across existing Internet connections. The prefix is always set to hex FD or binary 1111 110. Finally, *link local unicast addresses* are used for communication among two IPv6 devices on the same link and are not routed on the Internet, meaning packets cannot move outside the link or to joined networks. This address always starts with hex FE80 or binary 1111 1110 1000 0000.[34]

Protocols are a set of specifications and procedures used by systems to communicate with each other. Important protocols are the TCP and HTTPS.

A *port* is a number used to identify a communication endpoint on a network. More specifically, it is a programming docking point to which information flows. Table 5.3. demonstrates the most common protocols used on the internet with their *port* numbers.[35]

Protocol Data Unit (PDU) is a term describing the names for data packets as they travel in different layers of the OSI model (Figure 5.17). When a *PDU* arrives at the *Transport Layer*, it is called a *TCP segment* or a *UDP datagram* (most applications use the TCP protocol); when the unit travels into the *Network Layer* it is called a *packet*, and when it moves into the *Data Link Layer* it is called a *frame*. We will discuss segments, packets, and frames along with the OSI model later in this chapter.

Media Access Control Address or *Physical Address* is a unique, 48-bit, identification number allocated to every computing device's Network Interface Card (NIC) by the manufacturer. The MAC address does not change; it is hard coded into the NIC or stored in Read Only Memory (ROM). The uniqueness of MAC addresses is registered by the IEEE, which assigns blocks of MAC addresses for a fee to manufacturers. Nonetheless, the address can be configured using manufacturer-supplied software.[36] The MAC address is used to connect the device to the network and to filter the process on wireless networks. For example, since the IP address is *dynamic* and changes, the MAC address can be used to identify the device. From a security point of view, a weakness is that the MAC address can be used to track a computing device on a Wi-Fi network. One way to do this is called MAC spoofing, a method used by hackers to manipulate and change a factory-assigned MAC address and then attempt to conceal his/her identity or to bypass the MAC address control list by pretend-

[34] ORACLE, System Administration Guide: IP Services. Retrieved from https://docs.oracle.com/cd/E23823_01/html/816-4554/ipv6-overview-10.html

[35] IANA. Assigned Internet Protocol Numbers. Retrieved from https://www.iana.org/assignments/protocol-numbers/protocol-numbers.xml

[36] Martin, Jeremy, Travis Mayberry, Collin Donahue, Lucas Foppe, Lamont Brown, Chadwick Riggins, Erik C. Rye, and Dane Brown. "A study of MAC address randomization in mobile devices and when it fails." *Proceedings on Privacy Enhancing Technologies* 2017, no. 4 (2017): 365–383.

TABLE 5.3 Common Protocols Used on the Internet with Their Port Numbers

Port #	Protocol Name	Purpose
67 & 68	DHCP—Dynamic Host Configuration Protocol	Automatically assigns dynamic configuration of IP addresses to clients (client/server protocol).
53	DNS—Domain Name System	A standard protocol that translates host names into IP addresses. This naming scheme governs how computers exchange data on the Internet.
20 & 21	FTP—File Transfer Protocol	A network protocol used for the transfer of files between a client and a server on a network.
80	HTTP—Hyper Text Transfer Protocol	An application protocol for displaying and distributing Web pages. Its main goal is to send data between the web browser and a website.
443	HTTPS—Hyper Text Transfer Protocol Secure	An encrypted version of HTTP protocol with SSL/TLS used in communication. The main goal is to increase the security of data transfer. This secure protocol ensures: *authenticity*—being on the real website, *confidentiality*—the connection is encrypted, *integrity*—ensures that data has not been tampered or modified between the client (visitor) and the server (website).
1	ICMP—Internet Control Message Protocol	This protocol is for error testing, reporting, and querying for connectivity issues.
119	NNTP—Network News Transfer Protocol	An application protocol for distributing, inquiring, retrieving, posting, and transferring newsgroup articles (USENET) from both client/server and server/server.
110	POP3—Post Office Protocol version 3	Protocol for retrieving email from a server.
22	SFTP—Secure File Transfer Protocol	Secure file transfer.
25	SMTP—Simple Mail Transfer Protocol	Email is sent using this protocol.
22	SSH—Secure Shell	A protocol for secure remote access to a remote computer or a server. A secure (encrypted) method for file transferring. Is intended to execute commands like login remotely.
443	SSL—Secure Socket Layer	Like the TLC, creates an encrypted HTTPS connection between two computers over the Internet. Intended for data transmission.
23	Telnet	This client-server protocol for remote access or login via text-based inputs and outputs (command-line utility). This is an insecure connection.
443	TLC—Transport Layer Security protocol	An encryption protocol that provides confidentiality and integrity between two computers over the Internet.

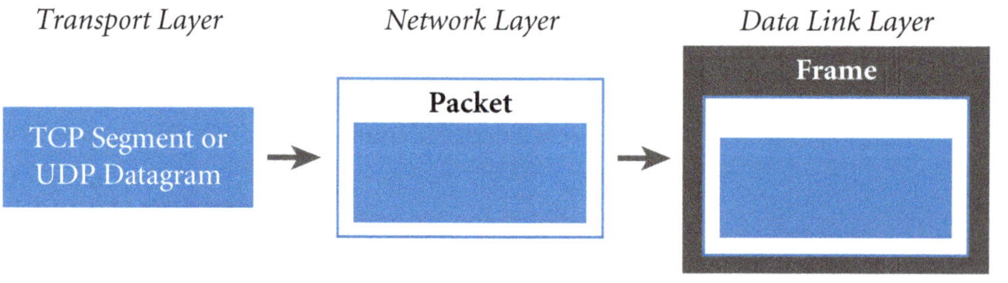

FIGURE 5.17 The Protocol Data Unit (PDU) at the different layers of the OSI model.

ing to be an authorized user. Additionally, the hacker can deny services on a wireless network, inject packets, send frames to all the wireless users using a broadcast address, and manipulate any packet field.[37] Companies like Android, Linux, iOS, and Windows have implemented *MAC address randomization*, which allows mobile devices to rotate across random hardware addresses.[38,39] An interesting point is that MAC spoofing attacks happen via the Address Resolution Protocol (ARP). An ARP allows an IP node to verify the hardware MAC addresses. More specifically, the ARP maps a network to find out the MAC address of a device from an IP address.

MAC addresses consist of 12-digit hexadecimal numbers, 48 bits or 6 bytes. The first 3 bytes (24 bits or 2^{24}) represent the Organizationally Unique Identifier (OUI) or manufacturer's code assigned by the IEEE. The following 3 bytes (24 bits or 2^{24}) identify the NIC from its manufacturer.[40] For example, NIC identifiers for manufacturers such as CISCO Systems are assigned 00-00-0C or 00-40-96. APPLE Computers are assigned 08-00-07, and 08-00-09 is used for the Hewlett-Packard Company. Figure 5.18 demonstrates the MAC address structure.

Network Address Translation (NAT) allows network devices like routers to connect private IP networks to the Internet by replacing the private IP with a public IP address. The NAT acts as a "receptionist or a dispatcher" between the Internet (public IPs) and local network (private IPs). With this method, only a single IP address is needed to connect an entire group of local computing devices to the Internet.[41]

---

[37] Alotaibi, Bandar, and Khaled Elleithy. "A new mac address spoofing detection technique based on random forests." *Sensors* 16, no. 3 (2016): 281.

[38] Vanhoef, Mathy, Célestin Matte, Mathieu Cunche, Leonardo S. Cardoso, and Frank Piessens. "Why MAC address randomization is not enough: An analysis of Wi-Fi network discovery mechanisms." In *Proceedings of the 11th ACM on Asia Conference on Computer and Communications Security*, pp. 413–424. 2016.

[39] Martin, Jeremy, Travis Mayberry, Collin Donahue, Lucas Foppe, Lamont Brown, Chadwick Riggins, Erik C. Rye, and Dane Brown. "A study of MAC address randomization in mobile devices and when it fails." *Proceedings on Privacy Enhancing Technologies* 2017, no. 4 (2017): 365–383.

[40] *Id.* at 39.

[41] CISCO Systems. Network Address Translation (NAT). Retrieved from https://www.cisco.com/c/en/us/support/docs/ip/network-address-translation-nat/26704-nat-faq-00.html

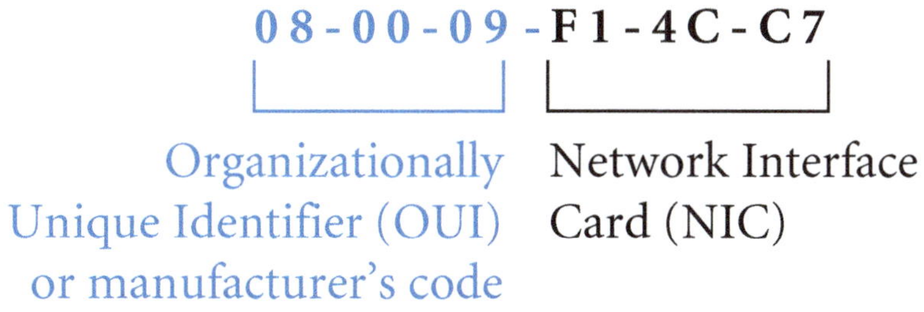

FIGURE 5.18 **The MAC address structure.**

The *Network Interface Card*, also known as *Network Interface Controller* or *Network Adapter*, is a piece of computer hardware that permits a computing device to connect to a network via wired or wireless connections. A NIC card's address is the MAC address of the device.

5.1.6 Using Network Utilities

Network Utilities are software tools that analyze, diagnose, and configure many aspects of computer networking and begin working on solutions. Some of the most common open source utilities include:

- **Angry IP Scanner**: a cross-platform network scanner.[42]
- **CISCO Packet Tracer**: network simulation, used to test network environments before implementation. It may work across different platforms.
- **iPerf3**: network problem solving, performance measurement, and tuning (Microsoft Windows, MacOS, Linux).[43]
- **Netstat** or **Network statistics**: delivers basic statistics on network activities on most operating systems.[44]
- **Nmap**: network scanner and monitor for unauthorized devices and open ports (supports cross-platform).[45]
- **PuTTY**: used to access and configure network devices (Microsoft Windows, MacOS, Linux).[46]
- **Wireshark**: collects and interprets network traffic (supported cross-platform).[47]

Additionally, some of the key network utilities included with the common operating systems (OS) are the following:

- **arp**

[42] Angry IP Scanner. Retrieved from https://angryip.org/
[43] iPerf3. Retrieved from https://iperf.fr/
[44] Netstat. Retrieved from https://netstatagent.com/download/
[45] Nmap. Retrieved from https://nmap.org/
[46] PuTTY. Retrieved from https://www.puttygen.com/download-putty
[47] Wireshark. Retrieved from https://www.wireshark.org/

- The *arp* utility command is used to display and modify the Address Resolution Protocol (ARP) cache and to list the IP and MAC addresses for any devices. The command *arp-a* displays the MAC addresses.

  To use this command, in Windows, go to Search, and type **cmd** to get the command prompt screen; then type the command **arp**.

  In Unix or Linux, go to the *Terminal app* and type **arp**.
- **ipconfig**
- The *internet protocol configuration* is a utility that is used to display information on TCP/IP configuration and information on how to set or display the IP address and netmask of a network interface. Once we type **ipconfig** in the command prompt screen, the operating system will return a signal containing IPv4 and IPv6 addresses, subnets, and default gateways which are connections to the Internet. This command can also verify if the computer has the right IP configuration.

  To use *ipconfig*, in Windows, go to Search, and type **cmd** to get the command prompt screen; then type the command. Entering **ipconfig/all** command will get the full TCP/IP configuration; **ipconfig/flushdns** empties the DNS cache with name resolution issues. As mentioned earlier, the DNS server converts domain names into numerical addresses. Depending upon the operating system or browser, the DNS temporarily stores information about previous DNS searches. We use this command to "flush the DNS" in order to hide search behavior/history, uncover security reasons such as manipulation and DNS spoofing, and solve technical problems like incorrect or old IPs and updated IP information. Linux has replaced **ifconfig** with ip. For example, **ip-4 a** is to see IPv4 information and **ip-6** is to see IPv6 information.[48]

  You can also use the **ifconfig** command to see all network-connected devices, including their IP and MAC addresses.
- **ping**
  - This command is used for confirming network connectivity with TCP/IP and local computers. The command also provides reports on any packet loss. You can use *ping* at the Windows **cmd** prompt, and at the *Terminal app* on Unix or Linux.
- **netstat**

  This command displays information about incoming and outgoing activity in the network connection. *Netstat* will display all active TCP/IP connections and can be used with Windows, Terminal app, Unix, or Linux.

---

[48] Replacing ifconfig with ip. Retrieved from https://www.linux.com/training-tutorials/replacing-ifconfig-ip/

- **tracert**
  - This command is like ping, but *tracert* delivers more detail on packet routes that went through to the destination and also measures transit delays, including "hops," switches, routers, and DNS information.

  To use tracert, at the Windows cmd, enter **tracert**; on Unix or Linux use the Terminal app command and enter **traceroute.**

  Repeater is a network device that receives and regenerates the signal over the same network. A repeater does not understand frames or packets or headers and cannot perform intelligent routing but only regenerates and reproduces the signal. The repeater operates at the Layer 1—Physical Layer of the OSI model.

Routers are virtual or physical network devices that function as dispatchers by forwarding data packets between different IP networks. Additionally, a router evaluates data packets and chooses the best routes on which to send them.

Servers are computer hardware or software that accept and respond to requests made by a client over a network. The client creates the request and sends it to the server, the server then returns the requested information to the client. A server runs on a remote computing device, providing services to the clients, and a client is a program that runs on the local computing device that requests services from a server (Figure 5.19).

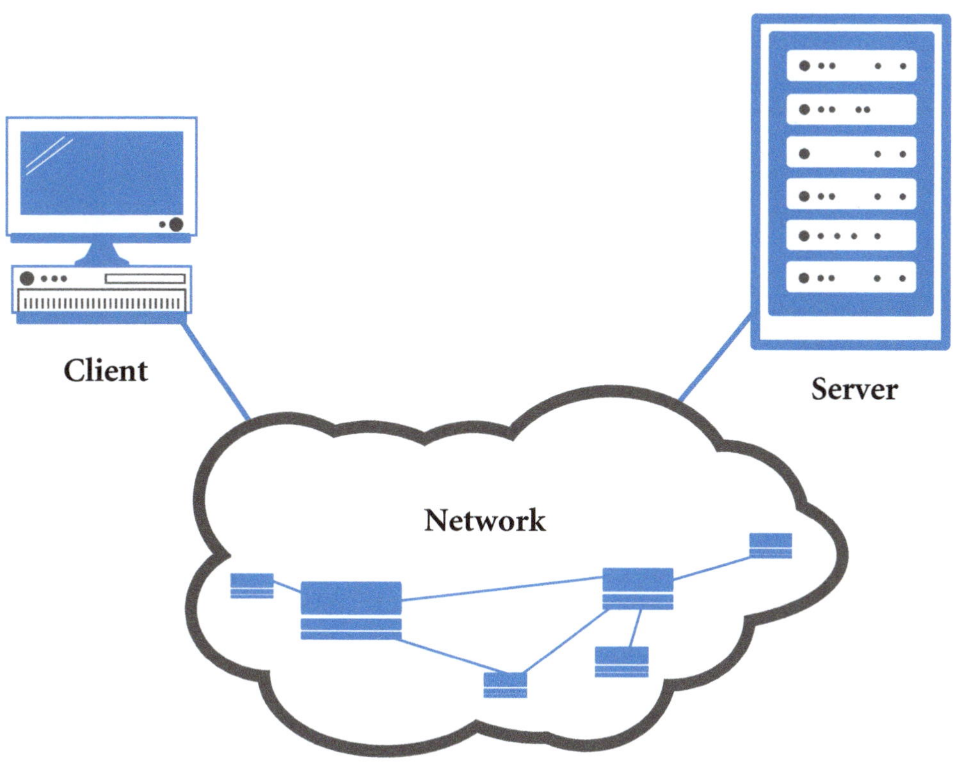

FIGURE 5.19 **The client-server model.**

Standards are sets of rules for components and systems manufacturers that define how to communicate in different settings. For example, Ethernet-based networks are defined by IEEE 802.3 standards, issued by the IEEE, and Bluetooth devices are defined by Bluetooth Low Energy 5.1, which is a wireless technology standard for exchanging data over short distances.

Switches are multiport devices that connect computing devices in a network and act like controllers. Switches vary from *hubs* because they handle data packets differently, by performing error checking and by not forwarding data packets that have errors. Therefore, switches improve efficiency and performance. Additionally, a *switch* is a device in the data link layer or layer two of the seven-layer OSI model (see OSI model) that allows devices on a network to communicate with each other as well as with other networks. Switches operate at Layer 2—Data Link of the OSI model (Figure 5.20).

Virtualization in computing or *VM* is the technology of creating software-based or virtual services like operating systems and servers by distributing capabilities and enabling a single machine to act like multiple simulated devices. *Virtualization* is a cost-saving method. A *hypervisor* is the software that creates and manages virtual machines (Figure 5.21).

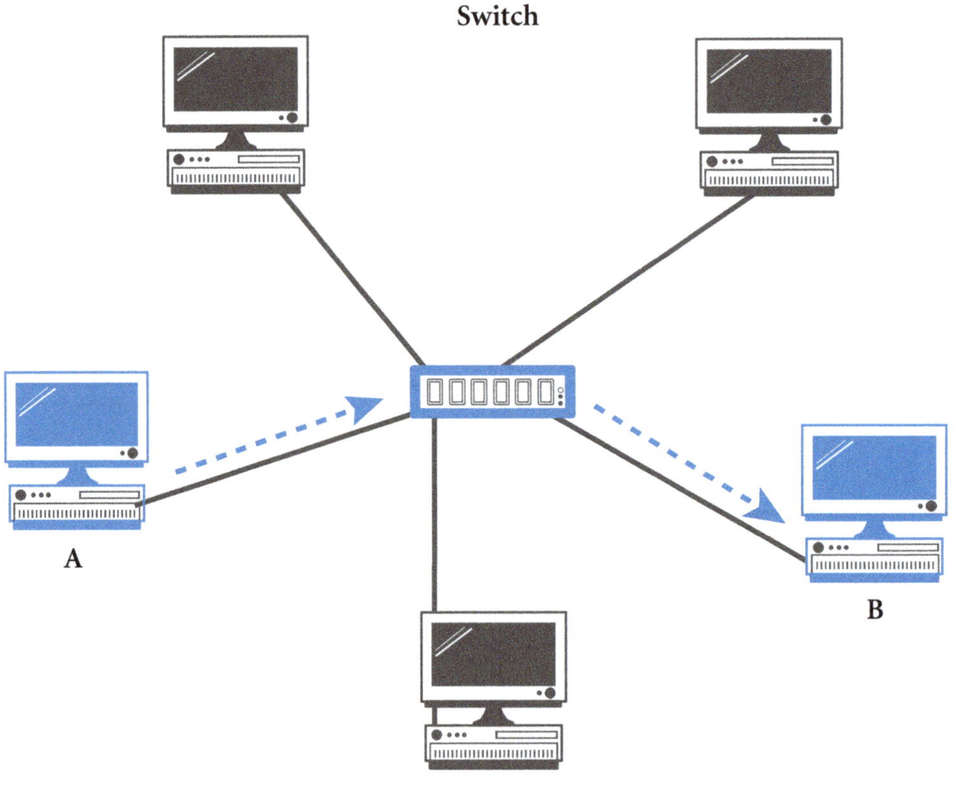

FIGURE 5.20 **The Network Switch.**

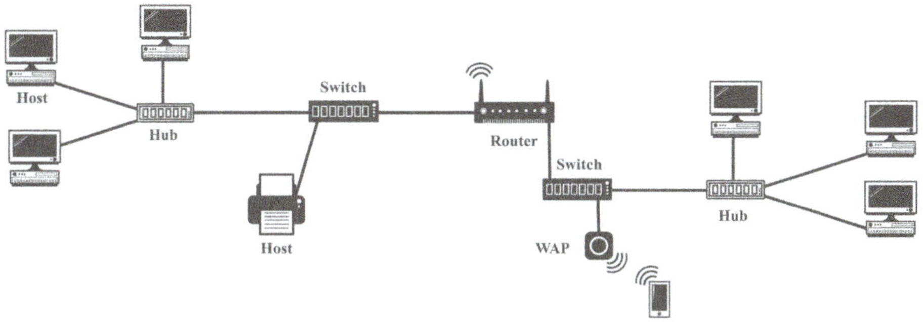

FIGURE 5.21 **A Typical Network.**

5.2 Types of Networks

To be able to meet evolving demands and needs, different types of networks have been designed.

The most common types of networks (Figure 5.21) are the following:

- **CAN (Campus Area Network)**: As the name indicates, this type of network is designed for educational institutions like campuses, colleges, schools, and universities. A CAN network is larger than a LAN and smaller than a Wide Area Network (WAN) (Figure 5.22).
- **PAN (Personal Area Network)**: It is a short-range network that serves one person as the name indicates. For example, using an app on a mobile device like a wrist fitness tracker, heart rate monitor, or pedometer with a Bluetooth device is a PAN. When a person connects any two devices such as a mobile phone and a computing device or shares emails, photos, text messages, and more, this is also done within a Personal Area Network (Figure 5.23).

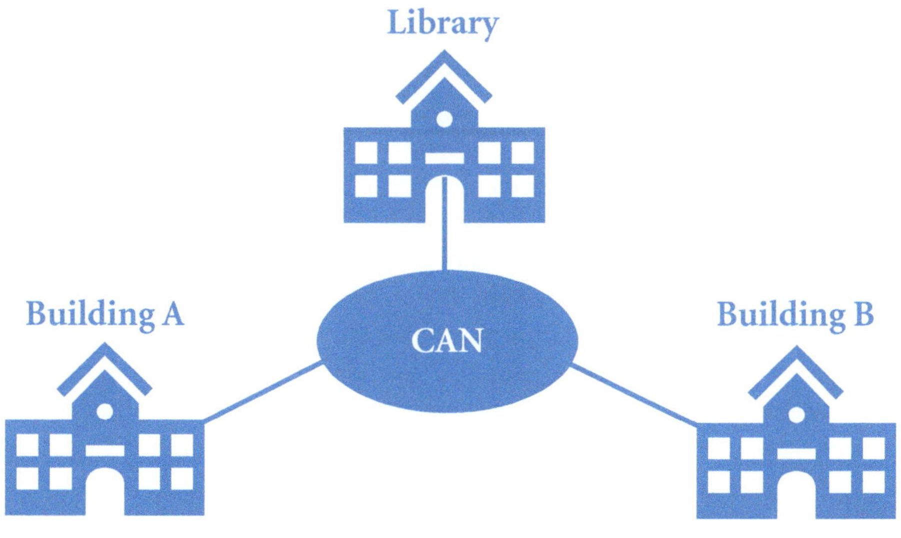

FIGURE 5.22 **A CAN.**

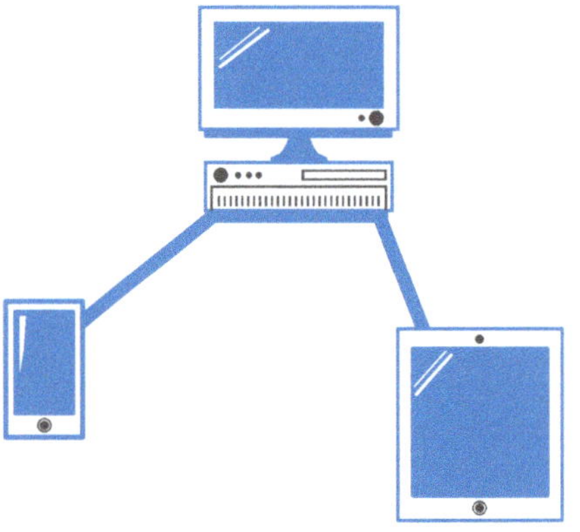

FIGURE 5.23 **A PAN.**

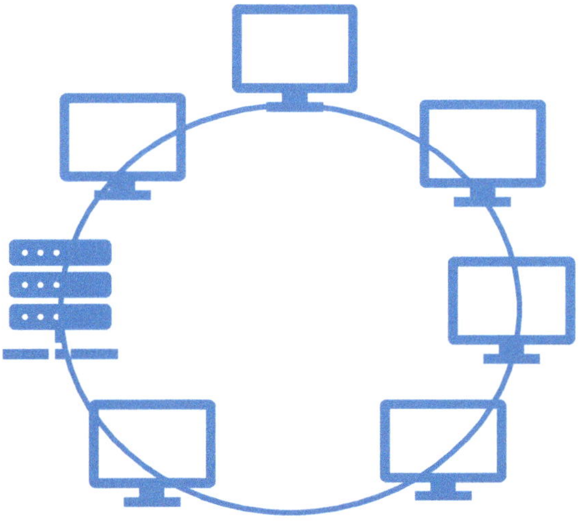

FIGURE 5.24 **A LAN.**

- **LAN**: It is a medium-range network that spans an area inside a single room, building or group of buildings, office, factory, or school, allowing the sharing of data, files, and resources. A LAN might connect all the computers in a school or a building and could contain both wired and wireless devices (Figure 5.24).
- **MAN (Metropolitan Area Network)**: It is a long-range network that provides communications over a larger area than a LAN and a smaller area than a WAN. Examples include citywide networks; governmental bodies typically own and administer MANs (Figure 5.25).
- **WAN (Wide Area Network)**: It is the largest area communications network. It can span a large geographic area and can connect multiple networks in a country, from region to region or throughout the world. The largest WAN is the Internet, connecting millions of networks around the globe. WAN connectivity can be accomplished by leased fiber lines and satellite links.

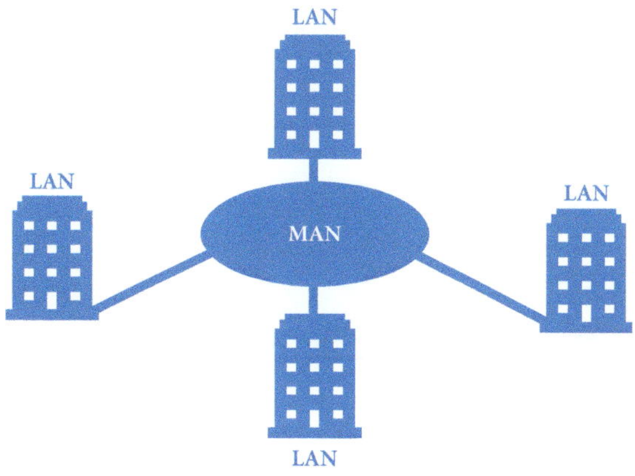

FIGURE 5.25 A MAN.

FIGURE 5.26 A WLAN.

- **WLAN (Wireless Local Area Network)**: It is like a traditional LAN, but instead of Ethernet cable it uses high-frequency radio waves to connect and communicate wirelessly (Figure 5.26).
- **Virtual Local Area Network (VLAN)**: It is a logical instead of physical connection of different nodes in one or more LANs. Additionally, the LANs are configured to communicate as if they are physically connected.[49] For example, LAN nodes can be connected to each other with switches or repeaters and can propagate or broadcast data throughout the network. Usually, when two people try to send data at the same time, a data collision may occur, and the switches or repeaters will continue to propagate on the network. After a collision, the original data must be resent once the collision is repaired. A VLAN, on the other hand,

[49] CISCO Systems, Understanding and Configuring VLANs. Received from https://www.cisco.com/c/en/us/td/docs/switches/lan/catalyst4500/12-2/25ew/configuration/guide/conf/vlans.html

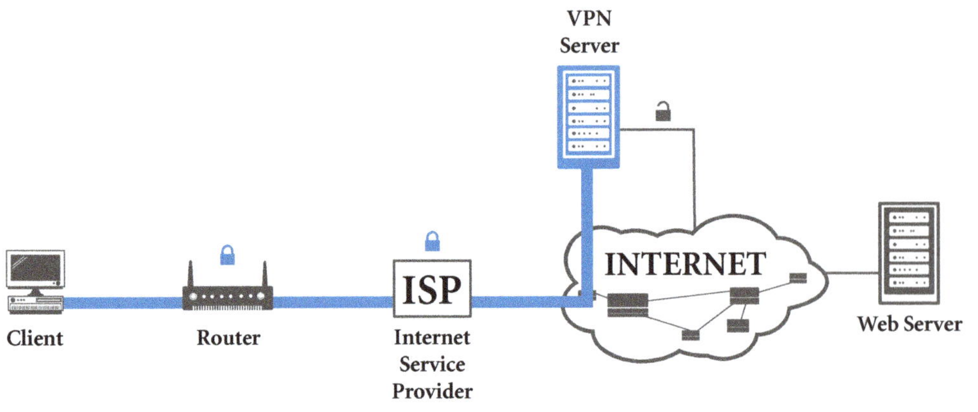

FIGURE 5.27 **A Virtual Private Network.**

allows a network administrator to logically change segments into different broadcast domains. VLANs help to reduce traffic passing through routers by dividing and creating segments without having to disconnect physical nodes or modify existing LANs.

- **VPN (Virtual Private Network)**: It is a point-to-point secure network connection for traffic in transit across the Internet. Significantly, a VPN establishes some privacy by encrypting a personal tunnel and encircling the user's identity. More specifically, it directs the user's traffic through a VPN server and masks the user's IP original address, acting as a middleman. As a result, the mixture of routing to a VPN server, masking of IP address, and the private tunnel encryption makes snooping more difficult for cybercriminals, the government, and ISPs (Figure 5.27).

5.3 Network Topology

Network topology shows the layout of the network and how its nodes and links are structured to forward, receive, send, and store data. Network topology consists of two categories: *physical*, which contains the devices, maintenance, and wires; and *logical*, which describes the way the network transmits and how data flows.

The correct topology improves performance by assigning resources efficiently across the network and helps in finding errors. The following are the most common types of network topology.

- A *bus network topology* or *line topology* is when all network nodes and computing devices are connected to a central continuous cable in a single direction. More specifically, the data moves in one direction and follows the route of the central cable. Bus network topology features a simple layout and is a cost-effective method for smaller

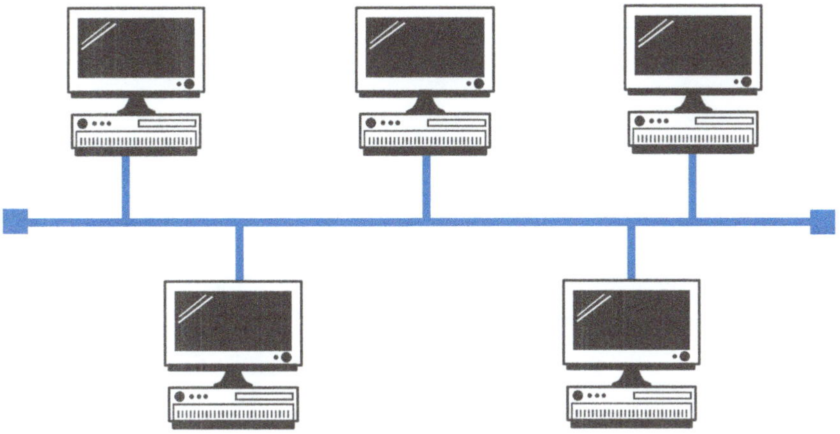

FIGURE 5.28 **A bus network topology connects all network nodes and computing devices to a central continuous cable in a single direction.**

networks. However, this topology may be vulnerable, since the network is based on one central cable, and if the cable fails the entire network will go down (Figure 5.28).

- A ***mesh topology*** is used when network nodes and computing devices have multiple paths or have overlapped connections. There are two types of mesh topology, *full mesh topology*, in which every node is connected to every other node in a network (see Figure 5.29), and *partial mesh topology* (Figure 5.30), where only selected nodes are connected to each other, and others are connected to only one or two devices in the network (see Figure 5.30). Mesh topology provides

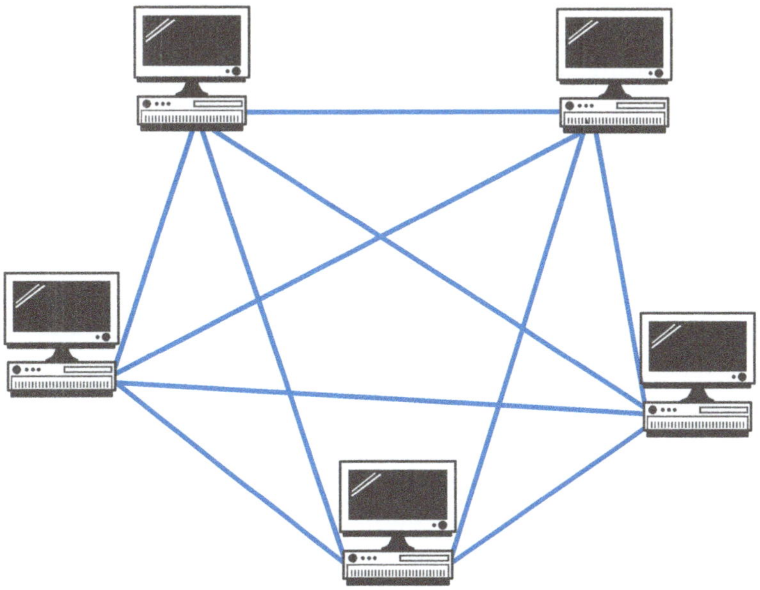

FIGURE 5.29 **A full mesh topology.**

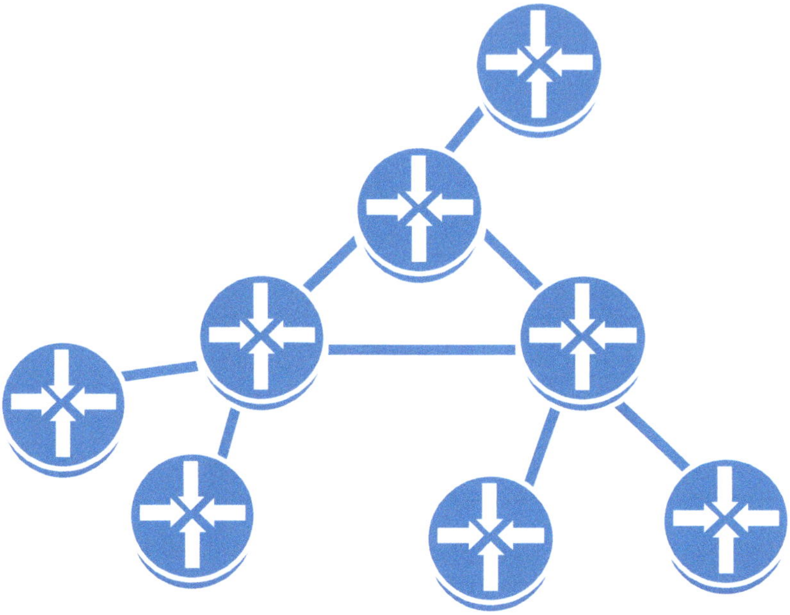

FIGURE 5.30 **In partial mesh topology, only selected nodes are connected to each other.**

reliability and robustness, because it offers redundancy to avoid failure; one link cannot cause a break in the network or in the transmission of data or affect other links. Nonetheless, full mesh topology can be expensive due to the cost of cabling. It is also time consuming and labor intensive to implement. Partial mesh, on the other hand, offers fewer redundancies and is less expensive to implement.

- A *point-to-point topology* is the simplest communication connection between two nodes directly connected to each other. Examples include a connection between two computers (Figure 5.31), a connection between two routers (Figure 5.32), and a connection between two segments (Figure 5.33).
- A *ring topology* is a configuration where all network nodes and computing devices are connected in a ring or circle (Figure 5.34). Data can travel either direction, and each node has only two neighbors. This topology is characterized by efficiency in transmitting data without errors and without collision in the network and is easy to troubleshoot. A possible disadvantage is that when we take the ring network down to reconfigure devices or troubleshoot, the entire network is offline. Another disadvantage in this topology is that computer devices share bandwidth, which means there is more traffic on the network, and more delays.
- A *star network topology* is configured when all network nodes and computing devices are connected to a central switch that manages data transmission (Figure 5.35). Data flows from any node through a

FIGURE 5.31 A point-to-point connection between two computers.

FIGURE 5.32 A point-to-point connection between two routers.

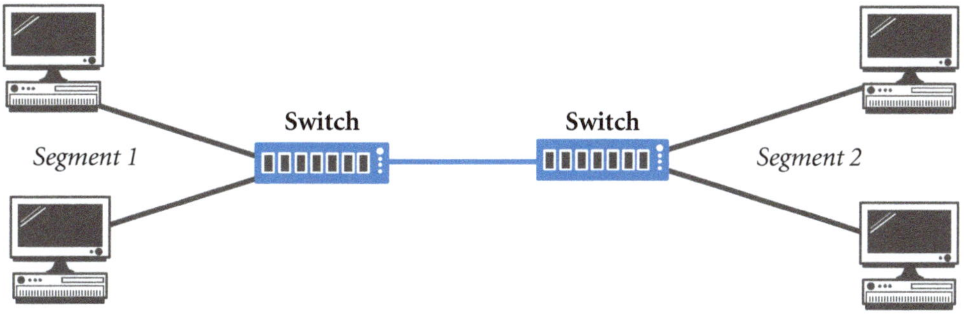

FIGURE 5.33 A point-to-point connection between two networks.

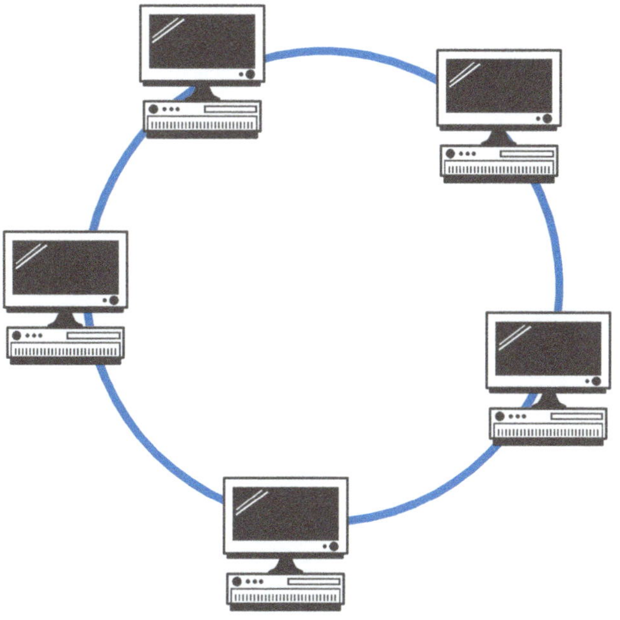

FIGURE 5.34 A ring topology connects computing devices in a ring or a circle configuration.

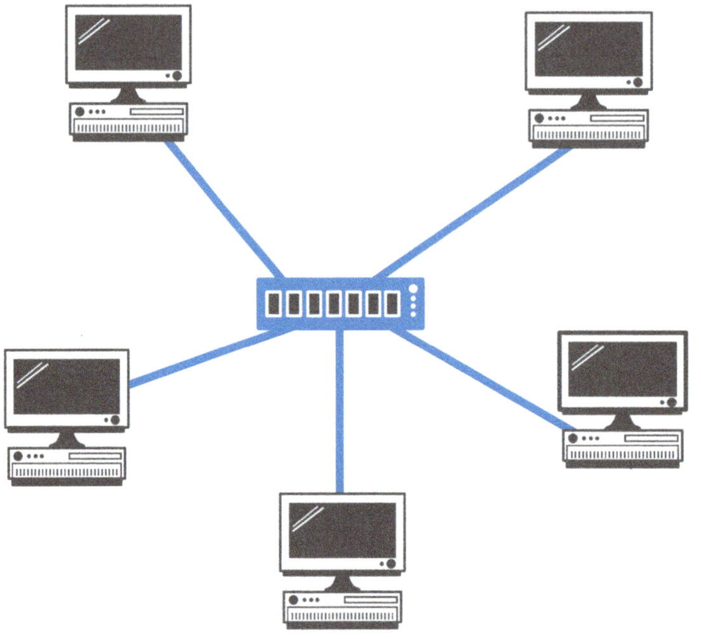

FIGURE 5.35 **A star network topology connecting all network nodes and computing devices with a central switch.**

central hub, which works as a repeater, preventing data loss. The star is the most popular topology, providing higher data transfer speed, easy installation, and management from a single location. A major disadvantage is that when the central switch fails, the entire network cannot function. Also, the cost of installation is higher for the star topology than for other network topologies.

Additional network topologies include the Hybrid and Tree topologies. Since every network topology or configuration is designed for a different purpose, decisions are made by looking at the overall network size, the objectives of the network, and, of course, the budget.

5.4 The Open Systems Interconnection (OSI) Model

The *Open Systems Interconnection (OSI)* is a reference or conceptual model that describes the functions and specified protocols and standards of each conceptual layer, tier, or stratum of a network communication. It was created in 1984, when the International Organization for Standardization (ISO) and the International Telegraph and Telephone Consultative Committee, known in France as the Comité Consultatif International Téléphonique et Télégraphique (CCITT), merged their ideas and procedures to shape the

OSI Reference Model.[50] The OSI model divides the Internet into seven theoretical layers and provides a visual narrative to a particular network system. These "layers" make it easier to understand the tasks of network communication and the order in which they occur.

Besides its educational usages, the OSI helps network administrators troubleshoot a problem within a specific layer, and it helps vendors and manufacturers assist customers in recognizing in which layer their product works. Also, it helps programmers as they develop an application to know where in the model the application will work. The ITU Telecommunication Standardization Sector (ITU-T) provides the OSI standards as recommendations X.200 standards.[51] Each layer has a specific task to fulfill, at the end of which it transfers the data to the next layer.

The OSI model is not meant to be an exact science, but it does define the network framework and should be viewed as a guideline; often it does not match the real world exactly (see Figure 5.37). We will describe the layers starting with the user interface and move down to the physical connections.

- **Layer 7—Application** is the interface between the user and the network. This layer is closest to the end user, allowing access to network services like email, Directory Services, Web browsers, video conferencing applications like Zoom and Skype, file transfer, and more. The hands-on work of the user is done in Layer 7.
- **Layer 6—Presentation** handles the *syntax*, which is the structure, format, or organization of data, and *semantics*, the "meaning" of the data, of the information being transmitted by the network. This layer specifies and handles the presentation of data by translating and changing the native data representations to the transfer syntax. Examples include encryption by transforming the original information to another form or ciphertext, and decryption by transforming the message to its original form or to plain text. This layer also provides data compression to reduce the size of the data and code conversion, including ASCII, Unicode, EBCDIC, TIFF, GIF, PICT, JPEG, MPEG, MIDI, DOCX, HTML, MP3, AVI, and others. The protocols used in this layer are Network Data Representation (NDR) and Lightweight Presentation Protocol (LPP).
- **Layer 5—Session** coordinates the mechanisms that organize and structure communication between application processes. Simply put, when two machines need to talk to each other, a session is established to synchronize which machine has the right to transmit or to re-synchronize in case of an error. The *Session layer* is involved in

[50] Russell, Andrew L. *Open standards and the digital age*. Cambridge University Press, 2014.

[51] The ITU Telecommunication Standardization Sector (ITU-T). Recommendation X.200. Retrieved from https://www.itu.int/rec/T-REC-X.200/en

coordinating, setting up, managing, and ending sessions between applications.

- **Layer 4—Transport** delivers end-to-end reliable communication over the network. More specifically, this layer receives data from the upper layers (5–7), at which point the data is broken into smaller pieces called *segments* and is passed to the Network layer. The *Transport layer* also ensures that the *segments* correctly reach their destination. Examples of protocols used in Layer 4 are the TCP and User Datagram Protocol (UDP). See Figure 5.41.
- **Layer 3—Network** is responsible for transferring and routing *packets* through different routers between sub-networks. In this layer, the *segments* are further processed and form *packets*. A *segment* is inside a *packet* and consists of control information such as the source and destination of an IP address, version of IP used, headers, trailer and data payload (size of the data, defined in octets), and more (Figure 5.36). This layer is responsible for *packet* forwarding, including routing/switching the packets through different routers, and through error and congestion control. For example, if we would like to connect to a server in Germany, the router at this layer will find the most efficient way to reach the server. Examples of protocols used are IP, NAT, and ICMP. Next, the *packets* are forward to the *Data Link layer.*
- **Layer 2—Data Link** coordinates node-to-node data transfers, detects and corrects transmitting errors, forms *packets* into *frames*, and synchronizes the frames. A *frame* is a collection of bits. MAC addresses are part of the frames because frames use MAC addresses, rather than IP addresses.

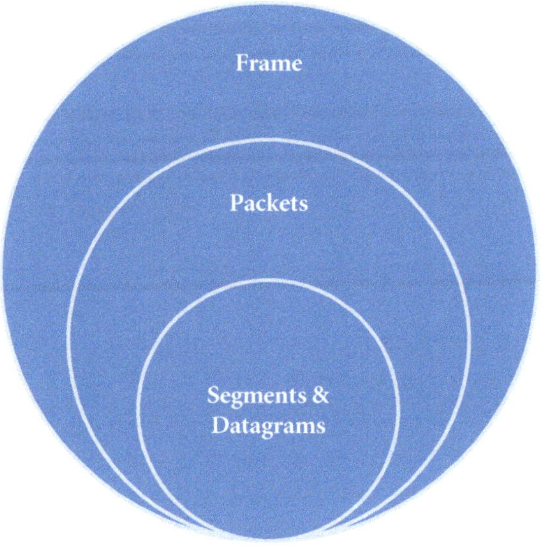

FIGURE 5.36 **Segment, packet and a frame.**

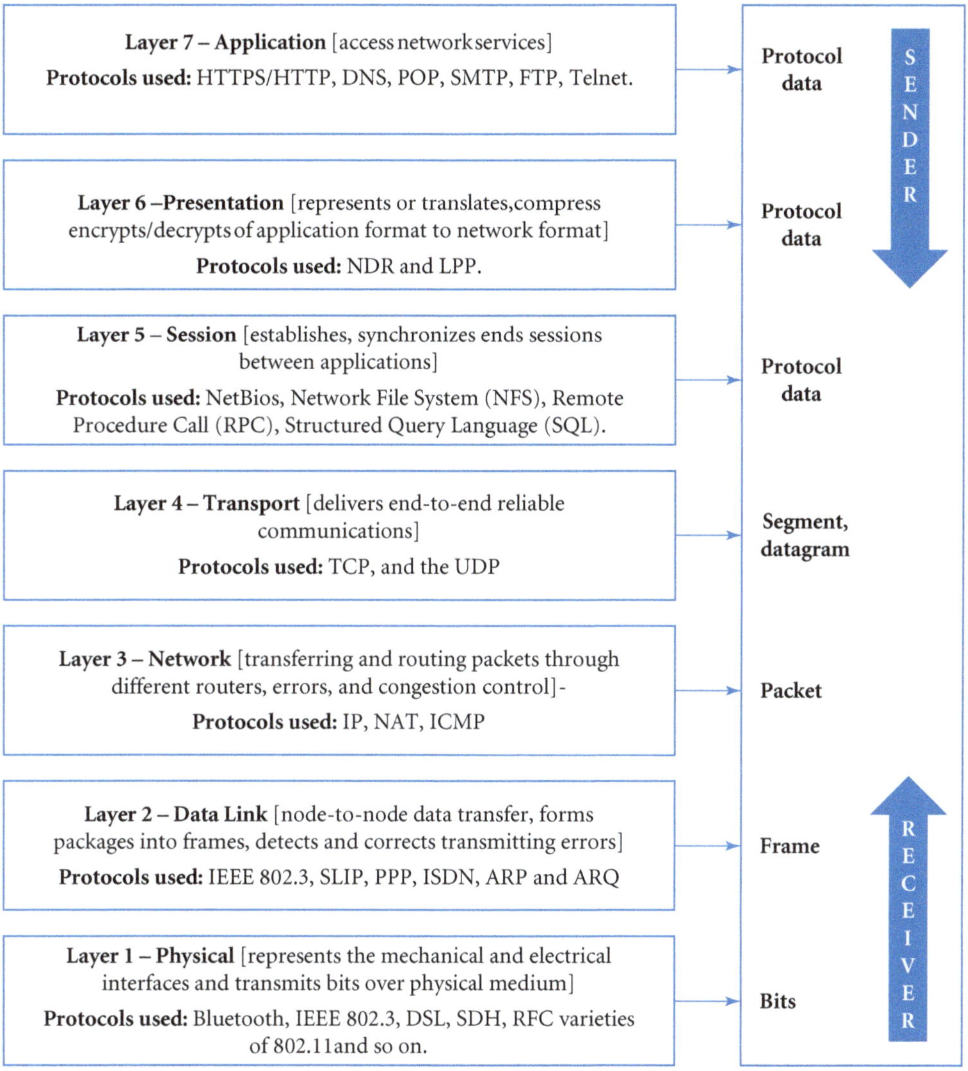

FIGURE 5.37 **The open systems interconnection (OSI) conceptual model.**

The *Data Link layer* accepts packets from the Network layer and adds headers and trailers, making them into frames. Next, the data link layer sends them to the *Physical layer*. In order to fulfill these tasks, the Physical layer is split into two sublayers. The first is the upper sublayer known as the Logical Link Control (LLC) sublayer, which provides data transfer by communicating with the Network layer and is responsible for frame synchronization, flow and error control, and multiplexing (transmission of multiple data simultaneously over a shared link). The lower sublayer, known as the MAC sublayer, is responsible for communicating with the *Physical layer*. The protocols used in this layer are the Serial Line Internet Protocol (SLIP), Point-to-Point Protocol (PPP), Address Resolution Protocol (ARP) Automatic

Repeat ReQuest (ARQ), Asynchronous Transfer Mode (ATM), Integrated Services Digital Network (ISDN), and IEEE 802.3.

Layer 1—Physical represents the mechanical and electrical interfaces, a setup of physical connections between devices such as Ethernet cables, optical fiber or radio signals, NIC cards, procedures, and functions of the network. In addition, the *Physical layer* receives *frames* from the *Data Link layer*, converts them into a signal, and transmits them over local media. The protocols used in this layer are Bluetooth, IEEE 802.3, Digital Subscriber Line (DSL), synchronous digital hierarchy (SDH), Request for Comments (RFCs), and varieties of 802.11.

These seven layers consist of two major groups and have different levels of significance (Figure 5.37). Layers 1–4 (Physical, Data Link, Network, and Transport) are the *lower layers* and perform the processes for data transfer around the network. The primary goal of the *lower layers* is formatting, encoding, and transmission of data, using both hardware and software.

Layers 5–7 (Session, Presentation, and Application) comprise the *upper layers* and signify the application component or application-level data. Their primary goal is to interact with the user interface and run applications to fulfill the user's requests.

5.5 The Internet Protocol Suite (TPC/IP)

The TCP/IP protocol suite is a large family of protocols that are named after TCP and IP. TCP/IP enables the Internet to work by helping computers talk to each other from anywhere on the Internet. Its procedures are consistent and stable, and they are used reliably. The TPC/IP model emerged from the ARPANET.

As mentioned earlier, TCP/IP was invented in 1974 by Drs. Vinton G. Cerf and Robert E. Kahn.[52,53] In 1982, the government adopted TCP/IP as the official protocol for the ARPANET.[54]

The TCP/IP model contains four layers and constitutes a simplified version of the OSI model. The OSI and TCP/IP models are the two most widely used networking models for Internet communications. TCP/IP encompasses multiple processes that are required for sending and receiving data; these processes must be sent using the same interface, the IP layer. The data is then directed to the transport layer and is managed there by either TCP or UDP. As a result, TCP/IP can perform multiplexing by mixing multiple

---

[52] *Id.* at 12.
[53] *Id.* at 12.
[54] *Id.* at 4.

signals into one signal or session or into several applications, using the same IP address to communicate with the network.

Examining the layers, we can see that TCP/IP is essentially a shorter version of the OSI model, consisting of four instead of seven layers. The four layers are:

- **Application Layer** (corresponding to layers 5–7 in OSI): This layer is responsible for the user interface, allowing users to access its services. Examples of these services include the web browser, email client, and file transfer clients. Like the *Application layer* of the OSI model, the following are protocols used by this layer:
  - Dynamic Host Configuration Protocol (DHCP)
  - Domain Name System (DNS)
  - File Transfer Protocol (FTP)
  - Hypertext Transfer Protocol (HTTP)
  - Multipurpose Internet Mail Extensions (MIME)
  - Post Office Protocol (POP)
  - Real-Time Streaming Protocol (RTSP)
  - Secure Hypertext Transfer Protocol (SHTTP)
  - Simple Mail Transfer Protocol (SMTP)
  - Secure Shell Protocol (SSH)
  - Telnet Remote Protocol (Telnet)
  - Trivial File transfer Protocol (TFTP)
  - Transport Layer Security Protocol (TLS)
  - Universe Resource Locator (URL)
- **Host-to-Host Layer** (layer 4 in OSI): This layer corresponds to the *Transport layer* of the OSI model, providing flow control, segmentation, data transmission, reliability, error control, and end-to-end data integrity. This layer uses the following protocols:
  - Transmission Control Protocol
  - User Datagram Protocol (UDP)
  - Datagram Congestion Control Protocol (DCCP)
  - Stream Control Transmission Protocol (SCTP)

The standard protocols used by the *Host-to-Host layer* to provide transfer data and ensure functionality between end systems are the User Datagram Protocol (UDP) and TCP. Both protocols move data between the Application layer and the *Internet layer*. More specifically, the TCP protocol provides a reliable service and connection by ensuring that data packets are resubmitted in case of error.

Unlike TCP, which is a connection-oriented protocol, UDP provides unreliable connectionless services. UDP provides fast transmission and leaves reliability to be controlled by the Application layer. Both TCP and UDP divide data into packets, including the IP addresses of the sender and receiver, along with several configurations, the trailer that indicates the end of the packet and the actual application data. The main difference between the two protocols is how the data packets are transported. Table 5.4 provides a brief summary of key characteristics of each protocol.

5.5.1 TCP

The TCP is a reliable host-to-host, connection-based protocol. Connection-based protocol means that before any data can be transmitted, a reliable connection between hosts must be achieved and acknowledged. Its speed is slower than UDP, but it is more reliable, with fewer errors occurring. All packets sent are traced so no data is lost or corrupted during transit. TCP, unlike UDP, requires the recipient and the sender to communicate and establish a connection, acknowledging that packets have been received. If packets are not acknowledged by the recipient, they are sent again. Consequently, this back-and-forth communication makes TCP slower than UDP. TCP guarantees delivery of data packets to *port* 4321 just as they were sent. As defined earlier, a port is a physical interface or an endpoint that identifies a transaction over a network by the host and the service. See Table 5.3.

Because TCP is connection-oriented, only when the connection has been established and checked can it be verified that a message has been received. If the message has not been received the TCP sends it again. Only when the connection is established can the user's data be sent from either direction. This connection is called a "handshake."

TCP uses a *three-way handshake*. The three parts of the handshake are **SYN** for Synchronize; **SYN-ACK**, for Synchronize Acknowledgment; and **ACL** for Acknowledgment, respectively. Figure 5.38 demonstrates the *handshake* process.

When two hosts want to send information back and forth, they can negotiate the parameters of the connection before requesting the connection be

TABLE 5.4 A Brief Summary of Key Characteristics of TCP and UDP Protocols

TCP	UDP
Reliable protocol	Unreliable datagram protocol
Lower speed	Higher speed
Connection-oriented protocol	Connectionless
Error detection and correction	No error detection and correction
Congestion control	No congestion control
Acknowledge segments	Only via checksum
Segment retransition and flow control	No retransition and flow control

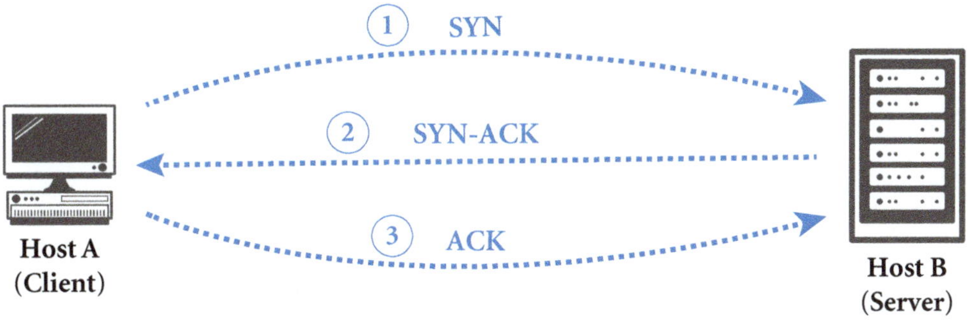

FIGURE 5.38 **TCP uses a three-way handshake.**

set up or before transmitting data. To start a TCP session, the host sends a **SYN** packet to the server. This is a request to synchronize the devices. The server receives the **SYN** and responds with a **SYN-ACK** packet. This means that the SYN request has been received and acknowledged. Finally, the host receives the server's **SYN-ACK** and sends an ACK packet and the TCP socket connection is established. The *three-way handshake* is a process which is used to describe client (host A) and server (host B) communications on a TCP/IP network. This is a standard method for computing devices to communicate regardless of the brand.

The essential function of this protocol is to provide host-to-host or end-to-end communication services between an application program and the IP. Another important role for TCP is to handle and detect errors and request retransmission of out-of-order delivery packets. When the network is congested, IP packets can be misplaced, duplicated, or arrive out of order. The protocol can detect these problems and request retransmission of misplaced packets, or it can sort the out-of-order queue and reduce the congestion. As soon as the protocol reassembles the packet data in the correct order, it transmits the packet to the application program. Additionally, TCP can identify duplicate messages and will reject them. Finally, TCP uses *flow control mechanisms* to slow data transfer and avoid senders sending data too fast for the TCP receiver. All these features make TCP an end-to-end reliable transport protocol.

5.5.2 UDP

The User Datagram Protocol (UDP) is a faster communication protocol than TCP, but it is unreliable. UDP is a transport layer protocol defined by RFC 768.[55] Like TCP, this protocol divides data into datagrams or packets. The term "datagram" is a basic transfer unit associated with a packet-switched network and provides a connectionless communication. Datagrams are

[55] User Datagram Protocol. Retrieved from https://tools.ietf.org/html/rfc768

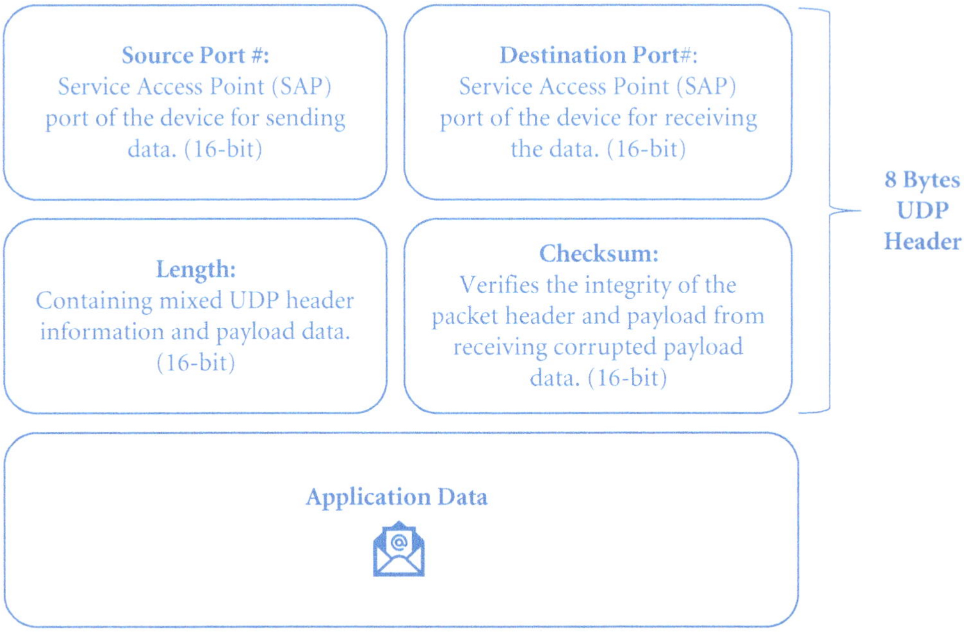

FIGURE 5.39 The User Datagram Protocol (RFC 768).

synonymous with the packets used by UDP. However, a datagram's arrival and its content are not guaranteed by UDP.

Both protocols are built on top of the Internet Protocol (IP), and both send data across the Internet from one IP address to another. TCP allows applications to exchange data with the lowest amount of overhead. UDP, however, instead provides unreliable datagram connectionless services and cares about fast transmission, leaving reliability to be controlled by the Application layer. The word "unreliable" means that the protocol does not have a method for confirming that data packets have reached their destination correctly. Another important distinction between TCP and UDP is that UDP does not provide any communication security. For security protection against eavesdropping, message forgery, and tampering, additional protocols are required.

In summary, UDP does not offer reliable delivery and extra security overhead, offering no acknowledgment that packets have been received. This speeds up connections and reduces latency. With UDP, when one computing device sends packets of data to another, delivery cannot be guaranteed, a kind of "send it and forget it" technique. UDP is faster than TCP because it eliminates functions like error checking and recovery services. UDP chooses speed over integrity, and data received may not exactly match the data sent. UDP is faster and TCP is more reliable. UDP is used for streaming games, live broadcasts, and videos. Figure 5.39 demonstrates the UDP protocol.

- **Internet Layer**: This layer provides the same services as OSI's Network layer. The layer routes packets, or datagrams, from a source to a destination host and defines addressing of the host by identifying on which network the device resides. The IP uses the TCP/IP transmission method. The main task of this layer is to send packets, regardless of the route they use to arrive at the *destination*. The protocols used are:
  - IP-Internet Protocol (IPv4/IPv6)
  - Internet Control Message Protocol (ICMP)
  - Internet Group Management Protocol (IGMP)
  - IPsec (Internet Protocol Security)
- **Network Access or Network Interface** (Layers 1–2): This layer is responsible for physical connections to the network, providing a blend of the OSI model's *Data link* and *Physical layers*. The Network

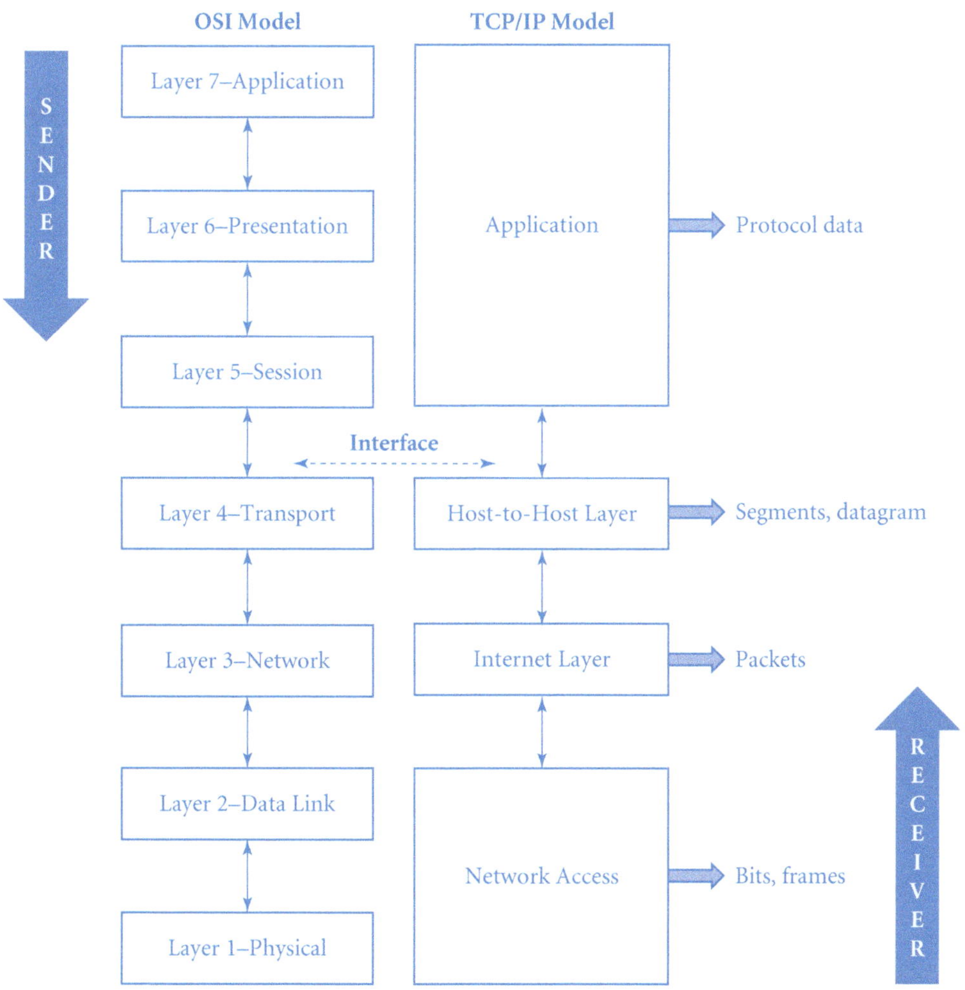

FIGURE 5.40 **The OSI and the TCP/IP models.**

layer includes Ethernet and optical, or wireless, radio wave technology, such as cellular and Wi-Fi standards that work along with the NIC card on a computer device. This allows the computer to access the network infrastructure and send data to other devices. The main responsibility for this layer is to transmit information over the same network between devices. The following protocols are used in this layer.

- Address Resolution Protocol (ARP)
- Reverse Address Resolution Protocol (RARP)
- Serial Line Internet Protocol (SLIP)
- Ethernet (IEEE)
- Point-to-Point Protocol (PPP)

Figure 5.40 demonstrates the OSI and the TCP/IP models.

5.6 How Everything Works Together on the Internet: A Review

- On a network, every single computing device can connect to the network or to another device with a wired or wireless connection. All these devices share data and resources.
- Every computing device has two unique identifiers, the IP address and the MAC Address or Physical Address. The IP address identifies a computing device globally on the Internet, and the MAC address identifies the device on the local network. Therefore, both addresses are needed to transfer a data packet from the source to the destination. Think of it like sending a postal letter to California. The *data packet* is the actual letter. The envelope resembles the *IP header* that contains the information required to *route* data on the Internet and reach the destination. *Routing* is when a networked computer decides how to send the data packets. Like the postal service, the letter goes from a substation to another substation, until it reaches its destination. Inside the envelope is the actual letter which is called the *payload*. The IP address is like the zip code, and the addresses with the recipient's name, street name, street address, and house number are the MAC address.
- When we use a search engine, the computer sends a request for the information to the network and attaches the device's IP address to the request.
- The search engine now knows where to send the request. Hence, it responds—and with ads as well.
- When a computer sends a request and receives an answer, a rule or a protocol manages the communication between all devices that are

involved. The TCP/IP protocol suite is a large family of protocols. It defines the communications standards and procedures between devices and governs how data should route and interconnect in a network or Internet.

- To be able to connect to a computer network, a device must use either a wired or a wireless connection. If a wired Ethernet connection is required, IEEE 802.3 is the signaling standard that is used. The wireless standard that defines wireless communications is IEEE 802.11 and IEEE 802.16.[56] Both wired and wireless standards are developed by the IEEE.
- One of many examples of network types is a surveillance network, with cameras installed throughout a city to monitor congestion and accidents, detect automatic incidents, issue traffic tickets to drivers who run red lights, and monitor closures and crowd flow.
- Another example is a peer-to-peer or device-to-device network that establishes connections between mobile devices and IoTs, using a *mesh network* design to allow communication using extend wireless communication such as Bluetooth or Wi-Fi. Each node communicates with the other, and if one module cannot relay information to another, the network will try a different route. The mesh network is often used to enable communication in areas with poor connectivity, like disaster zones, or when the area is without Internet connection or is in a remote location.
- The *switch* connects computing devices and manages node-to-node communication inside a network, using packet switching, to receive and forward data, ensuring that the packets reach their ultimate destination.
- Protocols define the format of these communications and set out how they are sent and received.
- An *access point* connects the computing devices via a radio transmitter and a receiver signal, without the use of cables.
- The *routers*, virtual or physical, act like dispatchers, forwarding data packets between different IP networks and determining the best route for them to reach their destination. Additionally, *routers* protect information from outside security threats by enabling firewalls and acting like a fence between the Internet and computer devices, blocking any information requests from the Internet.

[56] IEEE GET Program. Retrieved from https://standards.ieee.org/products-services/ieee-get-program.html

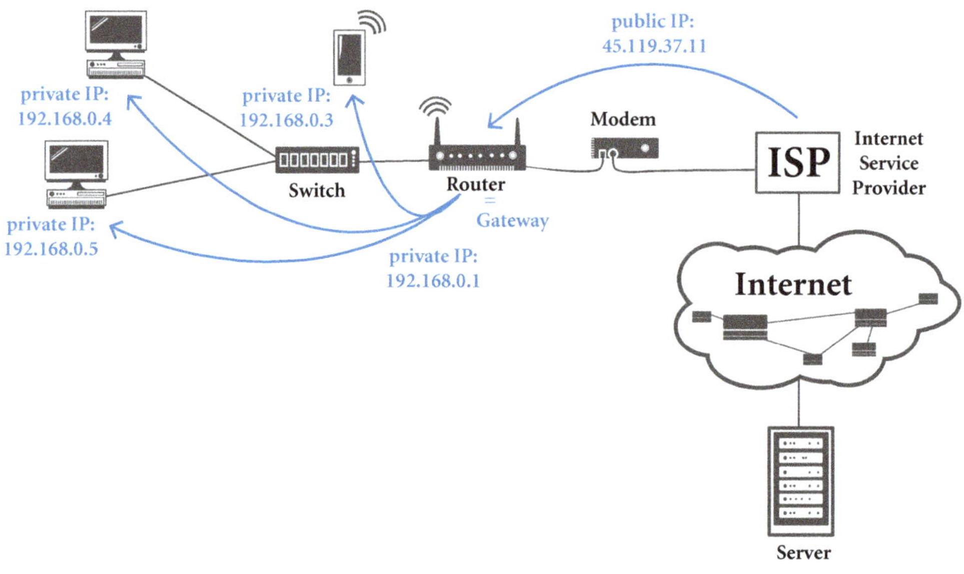

FIGURE 5.41 A typical LAN connected to the Internet.

- The computer architecture describes the functionality, the physical and logical framework, and how devices are organized in a computing network.

Figure 5.41 illustrates a typical LAN Network.

5.7 Conclusion

Network connectivity has been in a constant state of evolution, with improved virtualization of servers and data centers, the adoption of multi-cloud systems, and the improvement of networking through AI and machine learning. Machine learning will continue to improve troubleshooting by collecting relevant data, correlating them, and then being able to identify a network or application problem. Additionally, machine learning will improve network security by creating a real-time database of security threats, behavior, and detection.

A final technology gaining momentum is the Software-Defined Wide Area Network (SD-WAN) that simplifies and centralizes the operation of a WAN. SD-WANs improve performance by virtualizing the WAN with centralized controls and intelligent management software, providing the network with cost-effective solutions to its problems.

In wireless networking, 5G wireless network technology, Wi-Fi 6 and Mesh networking will soon change how we access the Internet. An autonomous, fast, and intelligent network is the next evolutionary revolution in technology yet to come.

5.8 Key Words

Access Point
APRA
ARPANET
Assigned Names and Numbers (ICANN)
Bridge
Campus Area Network (CAN)
Client
Defense Advanced Research Projects Agency (DARPA)
Domain Name System (DNS)
Dynamic IP
Dynamic Host Configuration Protocol (DHCP)
Electrical and Electronics Engineers (IEEE)
Frame
Gateway
Host
Hub
Internet Assigned Numbers Authority (IANA)
Internet
Internet Protocol (IP)
Local Area Network (LAN)
Metropolitan Area Network (MAN)
Media Access Control (MAC) Addresses
MILNET
Network
Network Address Translation (NAT)
Network Architecture
Network Interface Card (NIC)
Network Software
Network Topology
Node
Open Systems Interconnection (OSI)
Personal Area Network (PAN)
Payload
Private or Public IP Address
Protocol
Protocol Data Unit (PDU)
Ports
Repeater
Routers
Segment
Server
Standards
Static IP
Switch
Transmission Control Protocol/ Internet Protocol (TPC/IP)
User Datagram Protocol (UDP)
Transmission Control Protocol (TCP)
Virtualization
Virtual Local Area Network (VLAN)
Virtual Private Network (VPN)
Wide Area Network (WAN)
Wireless Local Area Network (WLAN)
Wired
World Wide Web (WWW)

Chapter 6

Computer Security Technology and Principles

Objectives

After completing this chapter, the student will be able to:

- Understand computer security technology, its history, and evolution
- Understand the CIA Triad Model and NIST's Standards for Security Categorization of Federal Information and Information Systems (FIPS 199)
- Recognize the significance of identification, authentication, and authorization in computer security
- Understand different types of cyberattacks
- Recognize computer security prevention mechanisms
- Understand modern encryption methodology

6.1 Introduction

For every type of cyberattack, there is a defense mechanism. For every defense mechanism, there is a new and unknown cyberattack.

Imagine that you sent a personal email to a close friend. How would you feel if this email were intercepted and the content posted on social media for everyone to see? To prevent this, we use *security* measures that permit access to authorized users and detect and deny access to potential intruders or

DOI: 10.4324/9780429318726-6

cybercriminals. This chapter will provide an overview of computer security technology and principles, including terminology, types of cyberattacks, and basic encryption.

Ancient civilizations invented various clever ways to hide information and messages from adversaries. Two well-known techniques for keeping information confidential are *steganography* and *cryptography*. The first term, *steganography*, means *covered writing* and derives from the Greek word *steganós* (στεγανός), meaning *covered*, and *graphy* (γραφή), *writing*.[1] The second term, *cryptography*, means *hidden writing*, and originates from the Greek words *crypto* (κρυπτός), meaning *hidden*, and *graphy* (γραφή), *writing*.

In *steganography*, information is *concealed* or *hidden from view*, and no means are used to change the structure of the information. In *cryptography*, information is encrypted by encoding or *changing the information structure*.

The Greek historian Herodotus (c.486–425 B.C.),[2] the father of history provided several examples of *steganography* in his book *Histories* (Figure 6.1). The first example concerns an aristocrat, Histaeus, who wanted to

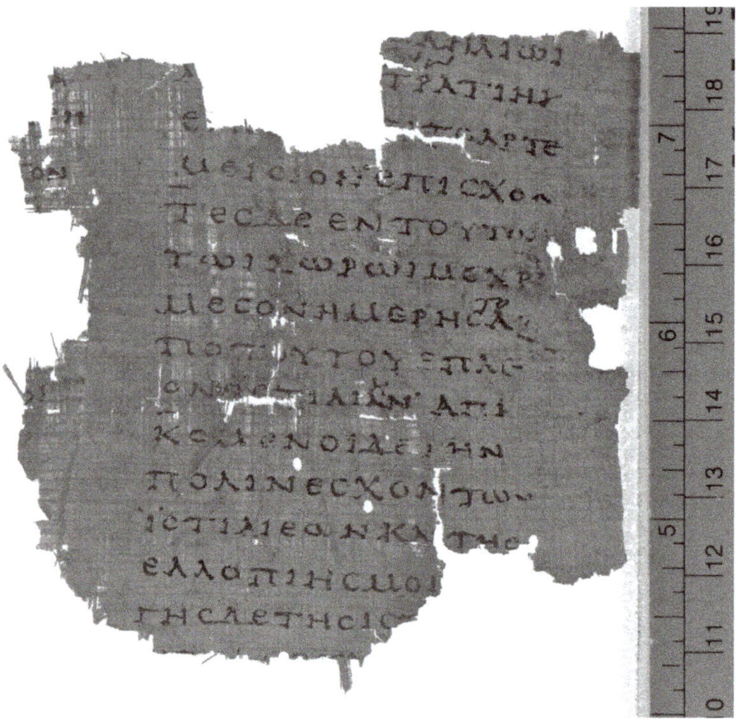

FIGURE 6.1 Fragment from Herodotus Histories Book VIII. Photograph from Papyrus Oxyrhynchus 2099.

[1] Morkel, Tayana, Jan H. P. Eloff, and Martin S. Olivier. "An overview of image steganography." In *ISSA*, vol. 1, no. 2. 2005.

[2] Luce, Torrey James. *The Greek historians*. Psychology Press, 1997.

send a secret message to his son-in-law in Greece, urging revolt against the Persians. Histaeus shaved the head of a trustworthy slave and tattooed the message onto his scalp. After the hair grew back, the slave was sent to deliver the message.[3] Another example from Herodotus concerns Demeratus, who alerted Sparta to an invasion from the Persians by concealing the message under writing tablets using wax. "These were usually two pieces of wood, hinged as a book, with each face covered with wax. One wrote on the wax; the recipient melted the wax and reused the tablet."[4]

Cryptography began thousands of years ago, protecting secrets by applying a code to encrypt and then decrypt a message. A parallel technique, called *cryptanalysis*, was invented to breach or break the adversary's code. According to the book *The Art of War* by the ancient Chinese military strategist Sun Tsu (c. 5th century B.C.), "Knowledge of the enemy's dispositions can only be obtained from other men. Hence the use of spies, of whom there are five classes: (1) Local spies; (2) inward spies; (3) converted spies; (4) doomed spies; (5) surviving spies."[5]

Ancient civilizations invented ingenious ways to encrypt or decrypt secret messages. The algorithm or process of implementing both encryption and decryption is called *cipher* or *cypher*. Some examples include evidence of concealed information found in clay tablets as early as 1500 B.C. in Mesopotamia.[6] Furthermore, the Old Testament contains encrypted text using *Atbash* ciphers, a traditional Hebrew method (c. 600–500 B.C.), accomplished by replacing a letter with another letter that is an equal number of places from the end of the alphabet. For example, the letter "A" would be replaced by the letter "Z" and the letter "B" by the letter "Y."[7] In India, according to the *Kama Sutra*, an ancient text on sexuality written between 400 BCE and 300 CE, lovers would encrypt writing communication between themselves.[8]

Ancient Greeks also used a wooden baton or *scytale* (σκυτάλη) to send cipher messages during military conflicts (Figure 6.2). Spartans used a belt containing a strip of parchment that contained a written message. When the messenger, wearing the belt, arrived at his destination, the receiver decrypted the message, by wrapping the parchment strip around a *scytale* of the same diameter.[9] In addition to the *scytale*, a Greek scolar, Polybius,

---

3 Herodotus. (2003). "The Histories, Book 5." Trans. Aubrey De Selincourt. Rev. John Marincola. London: Penguin Group.

4 Kahn, David. "The history of steganography." In *International Workshop on Information Hiding*, pp. 1–5. Springer, Berlin, Heidelberg, 1996.

5 Tzu, Sun, Sun Tzu, Wu Sun, and Sun Cu Vu. *The art of war*. Vol. 361. Oxford University Press, 1971.

6 Kahn, David. *The Codebreakers: The comprehensive history of secret communication from ancient times to the internet*. Simon and Schuster, 1996.

7 Singh, Simon. *The code book: The science of secrecy from ancient Egypt to quantum cryptography*. Anchor, 2000.

8 *Id*. at 7.

9 *Id*. at 7.

invented the *Polybius Square*. According to the Greek historian Herodotus, in *Polybius' Histories*,[10] the *Polybius Square* was invented by Cleoxenus and Democleitus and was further developed by Polybius. The method divides the alphabet into five rows of squares, each described by coordinates in the grid (Table 6.1). To decrypt the message the recipient must know the letters represented by each set of coordinates. Using this simple example, the word "Love" (letters underlined) converts to 31 34 51 15.

Julius Caesar, on the other hand, used a method called the Caesar cipher or Caesar code, that moved each letter a fixed number of places.[11] Table 6.2 demonstrates the alphabet with three shifted places. For example the word "LOVE" becomes "ILSB" and the word "THE" becomes "QEB" by replacing each letter with the letter three places to the left.

During World War II, the Germans developed and used numerous mechanical and electromechanical machines for encrypting communication. Their best-known cipher machines are the *Enigma* (Figure 6.3), built by the Chiffriermaschinen Aktiengesellschaft (Cipher Machines Corporation), and the *SZ-40/SZ-42*, built by Standard Elektrik Lorenz (Figure 6.4). The British gave these encrypting machines the codename FISH Machines.[12] Modern cryptography

FIGURE 6.2 A scytale. Photograph from Free Software Foundation

TABLE 6.1 Polybius Square

	1	2	3	4	5
1	A	B	C	D	E
2	F	G	H	I/J	K
3	L	M	N	O	P
4	Q	R	S	T	U
5	V	W	X	Y	Z

[10] McGing, Brian C. *Polybius' Histories*. Oxford University Press, 2010.
[11] Id. at 7.
[12] Id. at 6.

TABLE 6.2 The Caesar Cipher with Three Shifted Places

Plain Alphabet												
A	B	C	D	E	F	G	H	I	J	K	L	M
X	Y	Z	A	B	C	D	E	F	G	H	I	J

M	N	O	P	Q	R	S	T	U	V	W	X	Y	Z
J	K	L	M	N	O	P	Q	R	S	T	U	V	W
Caesar Cipher													

FIGURE 6.3 **Enigma machine. Courtesy of Shutterstock**

FIGURE 6.4 **Lorenz-SZ42 machine.**

uses complicated algorithms such as blockchain, public key cryptography, and cryptographic hash functions. They will be discussed later in this chapter.

Different terminologies have been used to describe computer security. All the terms relate to the protection of Internet-connected computing.

The most important subcategories of computer security include:

- *Application security* is a general term for securing applications. It includes security features within applications and measures often used for finding, fixing, and preventing security vulnerabilities against cyberthreats. Examples include email, Directory Services, Web browsers, video conferencing applications like Zoom and Skype, and file transfers.

  Application security concentrates on keeping applications and computing devices secure from SQL injection, DoS attacks, data breaches, and more. For additional information on the OSI model and the application layer, see Chapter 5.
- *Cybersecurity* refers to protection from criminal activity facilitated by the Internet. It also relates to the protection of Internet-connected devices, computer programs, networks, and data from cybercriminals. In other words, cybersecurity protects physical security, which consists of sites, equipment, infrastructure, etc., and logical security, which consists of software safeguards such as user passwords, access, and authentication of Information and Communications Technology (ICT). Additionally, cybersecurity includes neglected and non-intentional incidents that compromise the confidentiality, integrity, and availability of computing systems and data.
- *Network security* involves the use of countermeasures to protect the networking infrastructure, both software and hardware, from intruders.
- *Information security*, or *InfoSec*, refers to safeguarding data in storage, in transit, and while being used.

According to 44 U.S.C. 3542—Definitions[13]

(1) The term "information security" means protecting information and information systems from unauthorized access, use, disclosure, disruption, modification, or destruction to provide—

(A) *Integrity*, which means guarding against improper information modification or destruction, and includes ensuring information

[13] United States Code, 2006 Edition, Supplement 5, Title 44—Public Printing and Documents. 44 U.S.C. 3542—Definitions. Retrieved from https://www.govinfo.gov/app/details/USCODE-2011-title44/USCODE-2011-title44-chap35-subchapIII-sec3542

nonrepudiation and authenticity. Integrity safeguards that data and systems are authentic, neither modified nor corrupted.

(B) *Confidentiality*, which means preserving authorized restrictions on access and disclosure, including means for protecting personal privacy and proprietary information. Confidentiality ensures that only authorized users can access or modify data and systems and includes methods for protecting privacy. A loss of confidentiality occurs when unauthorized access or security breach occurs.

(C) *Availability*, which means ensuring timely and reliable access to and use of information. Availability ensures accessibility and reliability by authorized users.

These three concepts are commonly known as the *CIA Triad Model*, which has been used in information security to direct policies of keeping and protecting confidential and sensitive data. The National Institute of Standards and Technology (NIST)[14] has used this model to define information security and cybersecurity and to help organizations implement information security programs. Figure 6.5 demonstrates the *CIA Triad Model*.

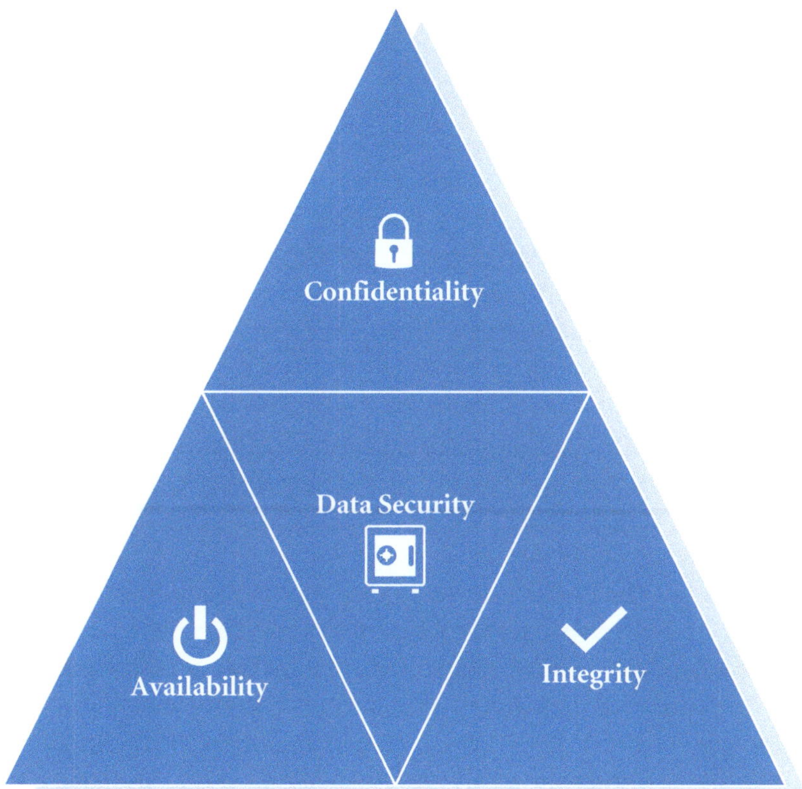

FIGURE 6.5 **The CIA Triad model.**

[14] NIST, Small business information security: The fundamentals. Retrieved from https://csrc.nist.gov/publications/detail/nistir/7621/rev-1/final

Vulnerability in any of these areas of security can vary, and it has been necessary to categorize the levels of threat they pose. Therefore, the NIST's Standards for Security Categorization of Federal Information and Information Systems (FIPS 199) has defined the levels of potential impact for Confidentiality, Integrity, and Availability as Low, Moderate, and High.

The potential impact is **LOW** if—

- The loss of confidentiality, integrity, or availability could be expected to have a **limilted** adverse effect on organizational operations, organizational assets, or individuals.

  A limited adverse effect means that, for example, the loss of confidentiality, integrity, or availability might: (i) cause a degradation in mission capability to an extent and duration that the organization is able to perform its primary functions, but the effectiveness of the functions is noticeably reduced; (ii) result in minor damage to organizational assets; (iii) result in minor financial loss; or (iv) result in minor harm to individuals.

The potential impact is **MODERATE** if—

- The loss of confidentiality, integrity, or availability could be expected to have a **serious** adverse effect on organizational operations, organizational assets, or individuals.

  A serious adverse effect means that, for example, the loss of confidentiality, integrity, or availability might: (i) cause a significant degradation in mission capability to an extent and duration that the organization is able to perform its primary functions, but the effectiveness of the functions is significantly reduced; (ii) result in significant damage to organizational assets; (iii) result in significant financial loss; or (iv) result in significant harm to individuals that does not involve loss of life or serious life threatening injuries.

The potential impact is **HIGH** if—

- The loss of confidentiality, integrity, or availability could be expected to have a severe or catastrophic adverse effect on organizational operations, organizational assets, or individuals.

  A **severe or catastrophic** adverse effect means that, for example, the loss of confidentiality, integrity, or availability might: (i) cause a severe degradation in or loss of mission capability to an extent and duration that the organization is not able to perform one or more of its primary functions; (ii) result in major damage to organizational assets; (iii) result in major financial loss; or (iv) result in severe or catastrophic

> harm to individuals involving loss of life or serious life threatening injuries. [15]

Table 6.3 demonstrates the levels of potential impact according to FIPS 199.

The FIPS 199 levels of impact also include an additional component under integrity called *authenticity*, which means "guarding against improper information modification or destruction and includes ensuring information non-repudiation and authenticity."[16] In other words, verify that users are who they say they are and data received are from a trusted source. In addition, NIST has developed the Cybersecurity Framework[17] that provides a structure for evaluating and improving cybersecurity risk and helps tackle cybersecurity threats and vulnerabilities. The framework is a security management tool that helps an organization to *Identify*, *Protect*, *Detect*, *Prevent*, *Respond*, and *Recover* from a cyberattack. For a more detailed description of NIST Cybersecurity Framework, see Chapter 4.

In this chapter we will use *Computer Security* as an umbrella term. We define *Computer Security* as the methodology intended to protect computing

TABLE 6.3 Levels of Potential Impact According to FIPS 199 (Adapted from FIPS 199)

	Low	Moderate	High
Impact on operations, assets, and individuals.	Limited	Serious	Catastrophic
Impact of the loss of confidentiality, integrity, or availability.	Temporary disruption or reduction of services; small financial loss; minor damage to assets; minor harm to individuals.	Significant service disruption while performing the primary function; significant financial loss; significant damage to assets; significant harm to individuals other than physical injuries or loss of life.	Significant service disruption compromising primary function; major financial loss; major damage to assets; severe harm or injury to individuals, including or loss of life.

[15] The National Institute of Standards and Technology, Federal Information Processing Standards (FIPS) Publication 199, Standards for Security Categorization of Federal Information and Information Systems. Retrieved from https://www.nist.gov/privacy-framework/fips-199

[16] *Id.* at 15.

[17] The National Institute of Standards and Technology, Cybersecurity Framework. Retrieved from https://www.nist.gov/cyberframework

systems and networks, including hardware, software, and data from unauthorized intruders.

6.2 Understanding Security Terminology

The world of computer security is constantly changing. Attacks occur daily and continue to evolve. Computer security consists of sets of protocols and best practices showing organizations and individuals how to prevent and monitor unauthorized access. To understand these practices, we will need to understand basic security terminology first. Following are some of the most important terms associated with computer security:

Access control—is a system that permits, restricts, and monitors requests for access to a wide range of hardware and software, including access to computer systems and network resources, information processing services, and entry or exit points to facilities.

Antivirus software or antivirus protection—is a program that prevents, detects, monitors, and removes malicious software from a computing system, device, or network.

Behavioral analytics—in enterprise security, behavioral analytics software senses abnormal network behavior such as patterns of unusual data transfer. Behavior analytics software detects intrusions that elude firewalls and antivirus software.

Biometrics—are unique physical or behavioral characteristics that either identify (*who are you?*) or verify (*prove that it is you … are you who you claim to be?*) the user. Physical or physiological characteristics can consist of DNA, facial patterns, fingerprints, hand geometry, a person's vein patterns, and iris pattern recognition. Behavioral characteristics can include handwriting patterns, voice recognition, typing or keystroke patterns, and signature analysis.

Cloud security—is the safeguarding of cloud-based computing systems, including applications, cloud access, data, and infrastructures, using controls, policies, and systems. The goal of cloud security is to reduce threats and protect users when they are accessing data and applications in the cloud.

Crime-as-a-Service (CaaS)—an on-demand marketplace found on the Dark Web, where one can purchase cybercrime services and attack tools like exploit kits, ransomware, worms, and phishing tools.

Software-as-a-Service (SaaS)—describes the current method of licensing popular software. Instead of purchasing and installing the software from disks, the software is now cloud-based, and we license and download our copies. Examples include Microsoft Office 365, Google Apps, Dropbox, Cisco WebEx, GoToMeeting, and Adobe Photoshop, InDesign, and Acrobat.

Cyberwarfare—a nation-state-sponsored cyberattack on another nation-state to harm, alter, destroy, or steal information; to disseminate lies and misinformation; or to conduct espionage and sabotage a computer network. Examples include the distribution of malware that destroys files and social media attacks that distribute false information, manipulating people rather than technology. Another example is the Advanced Persistent Threat (APT) that hacked the U.S. government agencies in late 2020 using a supply chain of SolarWinds Orion products. The hack was classified by the Cybersecurity and Infrastructure Security Agency (CISA) as AA20-352A.[18]

Data Breach—access to a computer system or network resulting in the disclosure of information. It may transpire *intentionally* or *unintentionally.* When the breach follows hackers gaining unauthorized access, it is *intentional*; when caused by an employee's negligence, such as accidental loss of computing devices, stolen or unattended sensitive documents, the breach is *unintentional.*

Exploit—refers to a program or a code written to attack or take advantage of a vulnerability and break into a computer system or a network.

Hacker—is an individual accessing a computer device or a computer system without the user's knowledge and authorization. Not all hackers are bad. In assessing the hacker, the essential factor is whether a law, for example the Computer Fraud and Abuse Act (18 U.S.C. §1030), is being broken. Hackers are classified into the following types:

- *Black-hat hackers* are cybercriminals who break into or gain unauthorized access to a computer system with malicious intentions. The primary motivations are financial gain, cyber espionage, and competition between hackers.
- *White-hat hackers* or *ethical hackers* are the "good guys of hacking," who utilize the same techniques as black-hat hackers but access systems with permission to identify security vulnerabilities and exploits. Companies hire white-hat hackers to perform penetration testing and find security vulnerabilities before cybercriminals do, performing security audits and checking for security gaps. Professional certifications are offered for ethical

[18] The Cybersecurity and Infrastructure Security Agency (CISA), Advanced Persistent Threat Compromise of Government Agencies, Critical Infrastructure, and Private Sector Organizations. Retrieved from https://us-cert.cisa.gov/ncas/alerts/aa20-352a

FIGURE 6.6 **Black-hat, gray-hat, and white-hat hackers. Courtesy of Shutterstock**

hacking. See Appendix I for information on hacking and other certifications.

- *Gray-hat hackers* are somewhere between black and white hat and do not have criminal motives. They will identify security vulnerabilities and exploits in computing systems without permission from the owner. After the defect is found the gray-hat hacker will inform the owner of the system and demand a small fee to repair the vulnerability, mentioning that otherwise the hack might be published. The motive is mostly personal enjoyment (Figure 6.6).
- *Script kiddies* or *amateurs* are individuals who use tools and follow instructions that are easily found online. Assumed to be juveniles who lack the ability to write complex programs or exploits, their main objectives are to impress friends, curiosity, enjoyment of a challenge, or an attempt to enter a professional hacking group.
- *Hacktivists* are individual hackers driven by an ideology or are politically inspired.

Intrusion Detection System (IDS)—is a hardware or a software application installed on the network that detects, logs, and screens for malicious attacks and intrusions based on security policies or rule violations on the network. The IDS identifies possible incidents, compares anomalies to normal activities, and recognizes deviations.

Intrusion Prevention System (IPS)—is a hardware or a software application that detects and blocks intrusions on the network by examining network traffic flows and attempts to prevent any exploit from reaching its destination. More specifically, the IPS is designed to block threats, analyze, and stop data packets from being delivered based on a predefined set of security rules and policies.

Protocols—are a digital language and set of specifications used by systems to communicate with each another. Important protocols are the Transmission Control Protocol (TCP) and Hypertext Transfer

Protocol Secure (HTTPS). Each protocol uses precise rules and has an exact purpose on a specific port (see Chapter 5). Some of the most common security protocols include:

- Secure Sockets Layer (SSL) and Transport Layer Security (TLS), protocols for encrypting and securing communications over a network. The SSL has been replaced by the TLC but is still commonly used.
- The Secure Shell (SSH) protocol provides secure remote login from one computer to another via an unsecured network (SSH client connecting to the SSH server).
- The Hypertext Transfer Protocol Secure (HTTPS) sends data between a Web browser and a website. HTTPS is encrypted using TLS in order to increase the security of data transfer.
- The Pretty Good Privacy (PGP) is an encryption protocol that allows a receiver to authenticate the identity of a sender who has sent the message and verifies that it was not altered in transit. The PGP uses a combination of symmetric and asymmetric encryption and has been used in encrypting and decrypting texts, emails, files, and other messages.

Security Audit—is an impartial assessment and examination of an organization's information security systems. The Security Audit should include the following:

- Review of regulations, operational procedures, and practices.
- Assessment of infrastructure such as security architecture, evaluation of internal and external vulnerabilities, and assessment of security configuration.
- Audit of specific applications such as penetration testing and source code reviews.
- Assessment of physical security, including the protection of facilities, personnel, equipment, property, alarms and access controls, and surveillance cameras that display sensitive areas such as data centers.

Security Threat—refers to a possibility or an action that can compromise computing systems.

Spam—any unwelcome electronic messages sent in bulk. Spam may be an advertising campaign or a malicious worm or virus with a primary mission to infect.\

Virtual Private Network (VPN)—is a point-to-point secure network connection for traffic across the Internet. Significantly, a VPN is built on top of existing physical networks and establishes some privacy by encrypting a personal secure tunnel, which encircles the user's identity. As a result, the combination of routing traffic to a VPN server, masking of IP address, and the private tunnel encryption makes intrusion and interference more difficult for cybercriminals, the government, and ISPs.

Why Is a VPN Necessary?—When we open a Web page on the Internet, data flows from our modem to our Internet Service Provider (ISP), and then across the Internet until it finds its destination Web server. The server replies with data that comes back via the same route. All these data require IP addresses. As a result, every network *logs* our IP address and the address that has been requested. The Web server then connects and collects data about us and about our destination. These sites are often not secure, and hackers can easily steal data. In addition, some countries allow ISPs to sell or to provide consumer data to their governments.

How Does a VPN Work?—The VPN enables a computer user to create an encrypted private connection over public networks (Internet) and disguises the actual IP address and location. The IP address communicating with the Web server will no longer display the user's IP address but instead will display the IP address of the VPN service. The VPN server assigns a new IP address and transmits data through encrypted tunnels.

The VPN application first encrypts data and then sends it to the VPN server via a secure connection. Next, the VPN server decrypts the data and sends it over the Internet, waiting for a reply. The VPN is like a bridge or a middleman between a user's computing device, like a cellphone, tablet or home network, and the Internet. Each message is encrypted before being sent and then decrypted by the VPN server when it is received. The VPN creates a safe and encrypted connection over a less secure Internet. Some of the most common VPN protocols are IPsec—Internet Protocol Security, IKEv2—Internet Key Exchange version 2, Secure Socket Tunneling Protocol (SSTP), SSL/TLS—Transport Security Layer (TLS) and its predecessor secure socket layer, and L2TP/IPSec—Layer 2 Tunnel Protocol. Figure 6.7 demonstrates a typical VPN connection.

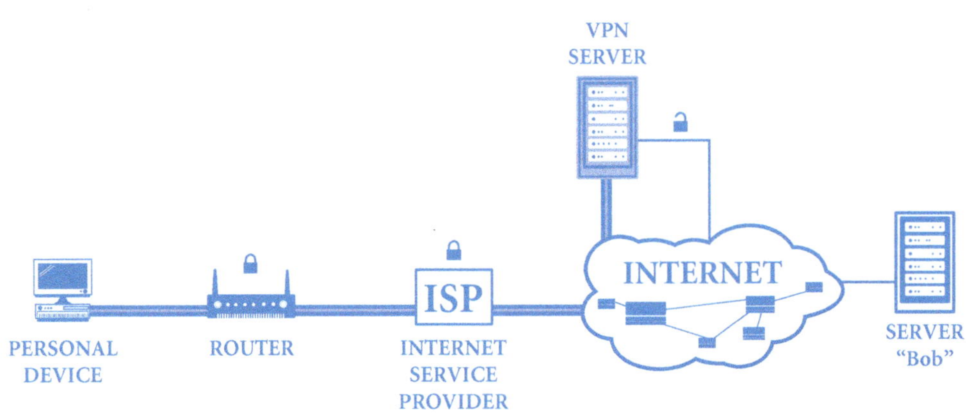

FIGURE 6.7 A typical VPN connection.

Vulnerability—refers to a security flaw or weakness in a computing system or software that can be exploited by hackers. They may attempt to gain unauthorized access by forcing computing systems to act in unintended ways, run the hacker's codes, install malware, and destroy, modify, or steal sensitive data.

6.3 Types of Cyberattacks

The interconnected world makes our lives easier but also makes us vulnerable to cybersecurity attacks. These attacks infect our computing systems with malicious code, modify data, and threaten our civil liberties by exposing our personal information. Starting in the 1970s with John Draper's hack of a phone system, cybercriminals have continued to become more sophisticated and rarely get caught (see Chapter 2).

Cybercrime today is a large-scale sophisticated enterprise that adjusts the business model to meet customer's demands. In some cases, cybercriminals or hackers for hire are connected to governments or other large organizations, penetrating computer systems or networks around the world. An example is the APT attack associated with nation-state criminal organizations.

In computer security, cyberattacks are classified as *Active* and *Passive*.[19] When cybercriminals modify system resources, data, or affect the operation, the attack is classified as *Active*. When cybercriminals do not modify system resources but instead use the information by monitoring or copying, the attack is classified as *Passive*.

Example of *Active* attacks include exploits, DoS, DDoS, malware, phishing, and brute-force attacks like password cracking, viruses, and worms. *Passive* attacks consist of system surveillance like keystroke loggers that record every keystroke, malware that can eavesdrop on emails, and other communications like voice recordings and metadata analysis.

Attacks may occur from inside an organization's network or from an outside source like a hacker. Figure 6.8 shows active and passive attacks.

A *cyberattack* is an intentional exploitation and malicious action that targets computing systems, networks, and personal computing devices. Cybercriminals use a broad range of techniques to cause maximum disruption and increase their profit.

The *attack vector* in cybersecurity refers to methods used to gain unauthorized access or to penetrate the targeted computing system.

A database that provides references and descriptions of officially known security vulnerabilities and exposures is called the Common Vulnerabilities and Exposures (CVE).[20] The CVE standardizes and classifies security vul-

[19] Stallings, William, and Lawrie Brown. *Computer security: principles and practice*, fourth edition. Pearson Education, 2017.

[20] Common Vulnerabilities and Exposures (CVE). Retrieved from https://cve.mitre.org/

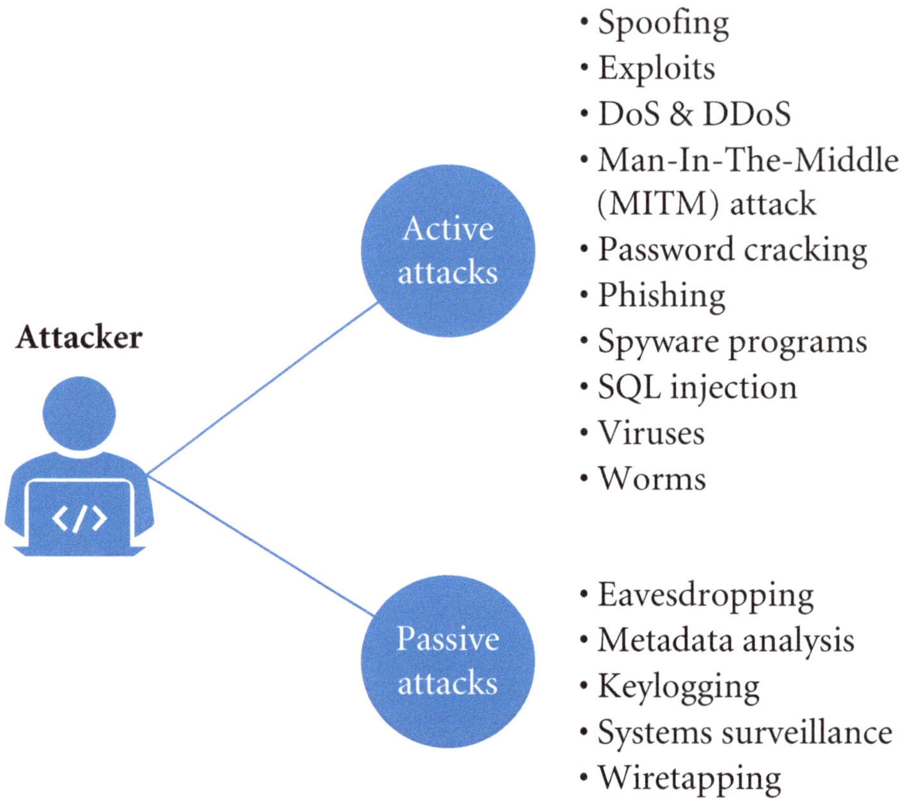

FIGURE 6.8 Active and passive attacks.

nerabilities for public use. This database system was launched in 1992 and is sponsored by the U.S. Department of Homeland Security (DHS) and the Cybersecurity Infrastructure Security Agency (CISA), which operates as DHS's Federally Funded Research and Development Center. The MITRE Corporation is a not-for-profit organization that manages and maintains the CVE list and website.[21] An example of a recent vulnerability described in the CVE is the Android version of Chrome named CVE-2020-16010 and refers to an exploit that cybercriminals are abusing and which needs to be patched.

The main reasons that cybercriminals or hackers access unauthorized computing systems are *Cyberwarfare*, *Disgruntled employees*, *Revenge*, *Nuisance*, *Espionage*, *Financial gain*, *Fun*, *Hacking enthusiasts*, *Intellectual challenge*, *Hacktivism*, *Malicious competition among businesses*, *Slow network performance (DoS attacks)*, and *ransom*.

Figure 6.9 demonstrates the various motivations of a cyberattack.

What are these attacks like? Following are some of the most common types of cyberattacks.

[21] CVE, frequently asked questions. Retrieved from https://cve.mitre.org/about/faqs.html

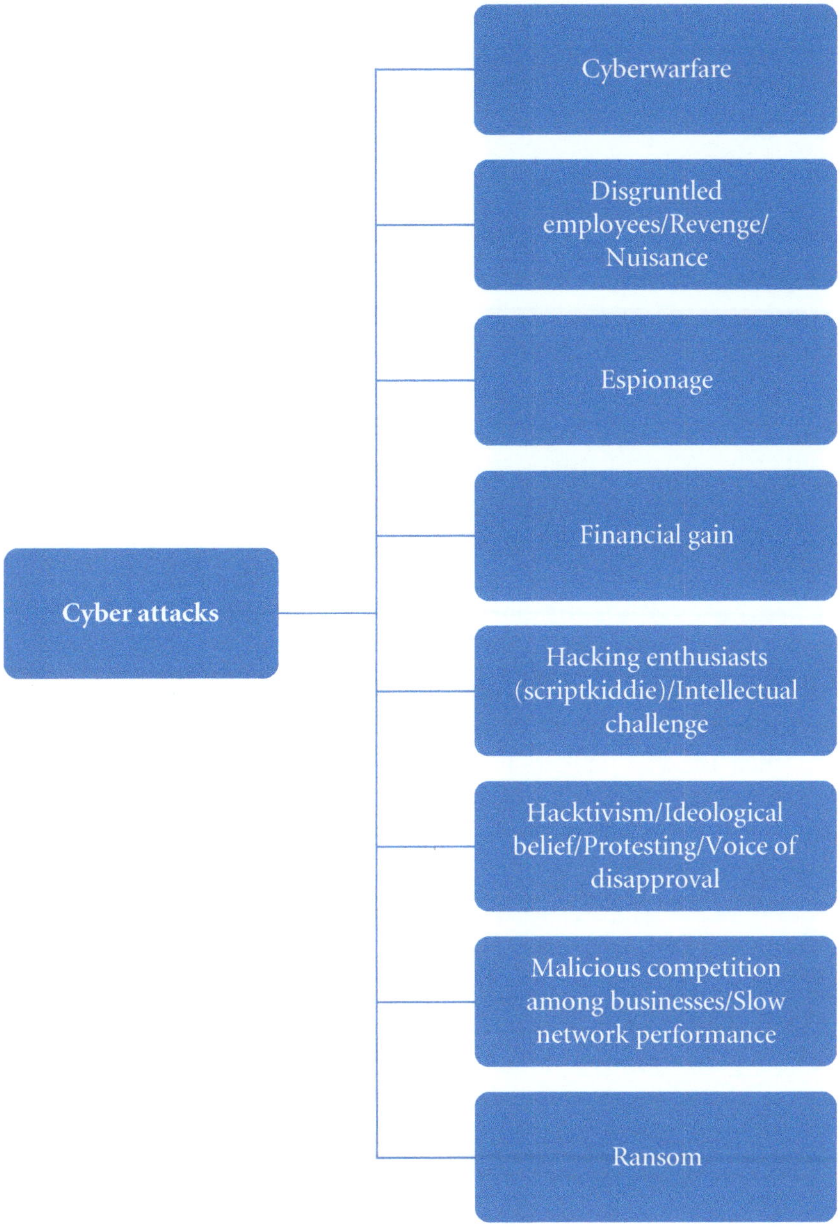

FIGURE 6.9 Various motivations of cyberattacks.

6.3.1 Adware

Adware, or advertising-supported software, is considered undesirable software, intended to force the user to view or click on an advertisement on the screen. Adware is a *Potentially Unwanted Program (PUP)*, meaning that it is a minor threat and is below the classification of malware. This unwanted software is often placed within a Web browser to generate revenue for its developer or in a user interface as a third-party sponsor that urges the user to install it. Adware exists in all computing device platforms and is usually safe, legitimate, and not malicious. However, cybercriminals could take advantage of the adware developers and might use it as a gateway for malware infection.[22]

6.3.2 Denial-of-Service Attacks

Denial of service (DoS) is an attack that occurs when a hacker makes computer resources inaccessible to its users. There are a variety of ways to begin the attack when the aim is to overload the network. The two common methods of DoS attacks are flooding network services by using up resources and crashing network services. One way to execute a DoS attack is to develop a small virus whose only purpose is to launch a flood of messages against the target. Additionally, an attacker can compromise the availability of a system by creating an error or buffer overflow (e.g. ping of death). Any attack against the availability of a service is categorized as a denial-of-service attack.

DoS uses only a single computing device to carry out the attack. Figure 6.10 demonstrates a DoS attack.

Denial-of-service attacks come in various forms and can be classified as *Application Layer Attacks* (measured in requests per second), *Protocol Attacks* (measured in packets per second), and *Volumetric or Volume-based Attacks* (measured in bits per second).[23]

Figure 6.11 explains the three types of denial-of-service attacks with examples for each category.

Denial-of-service attacks do not need a specific program like malware to run but instead take advantage of the security vulnerabilities of the network's communication applications.

The goal of a DoS attack is not to infiltrate computing systems, servers, or networks to gain confidential information but to cut users off from a resource

FIGURE 6.10 A DoS attack.

[22] Gao, Jun, Li Li, Pingfan Kong, Tegawendé F. Bissyandé, and Jacques Klein. "Should you consider adware as malware in your study?" In *2019 IEEE 26th International Conference on Software Analysis, Evolution and Reengineering (SANER)*, pp. 604–608. IEEE, 2019.

[23] Gupta, B. B., and Omkar P. Badve. "Taxonomy of DoS and DDoS attacks and desirable defense mechanism in a cloud computing environment." *Neural Computing and Applications* 28, no. 12 (2017): 3655–3682.

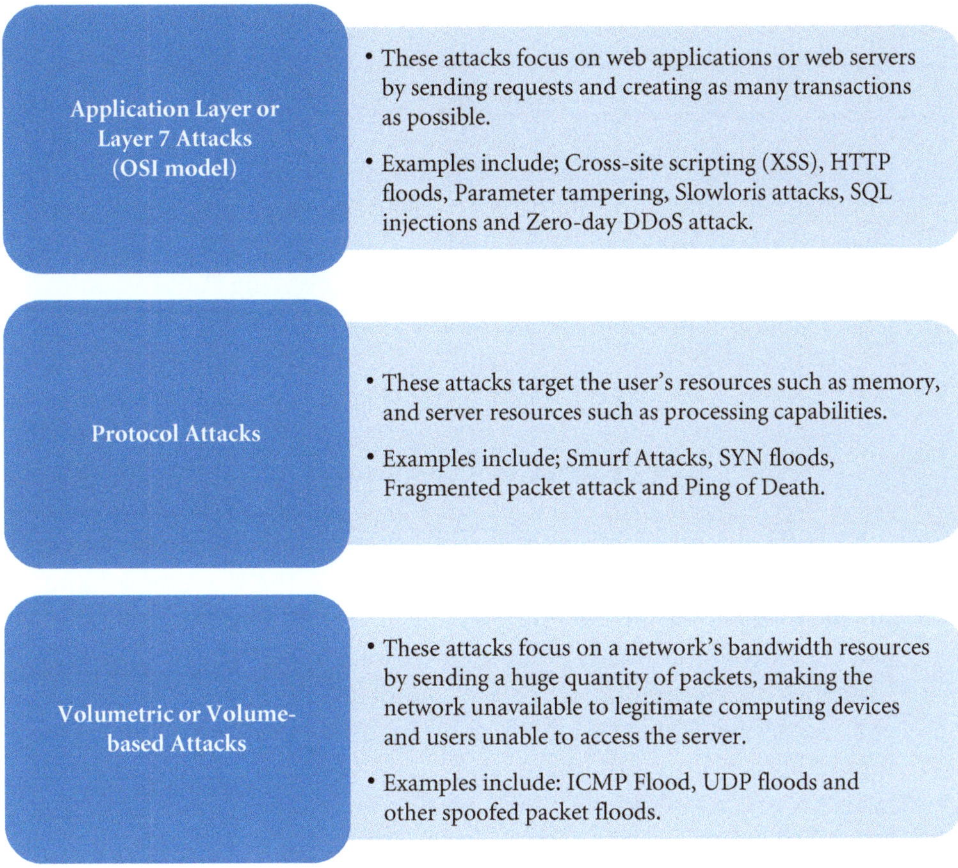

FIGURE 6.11 **Types of denial-of-service attacks.**

by overwhelming them with requests. Since every computer device has an operational limit, the cybercriminal sends numerous requests to the target server, overloading it with traffic it cannot handle. The computing system eventually makes the service unavailable to legitimate users. Following are some common DoS attacks:

- An *Internet Control Message Protocol (ICMP)* or *ping flood* attack. This type of attack happens when a hacker sends ICMP echo requests or pings with the purpose of flooding a computing system.[24] The ping flood is the most basic technique used for a DoS attack. The overwhelming number of requests from incoming messages (echo request) and outgoing responses (echo-reply) consumes a good deal of the bandwidth of a system.

[24] Khalaf, Bashar Ahmed, S. A. Mostafa, Aida Mustapha, Azizan Ismaila, M. A. Mahmoud, Mohammed Ahmed Jubaira, and M. H. Hassan. "A simulation study of syn flood attack in cloud computing environment." *REVISTA AUS* 26, no. 1 (2019): 1–19.

At first, the computer system slows down, and then it forces a disconnection through a timeout. As a result, when the target is flooded with more pings than it can process and respond to efficiently, denial of service transpires. Reconfiguring the ICMP perimeter firewall to block pings can prevent this type of attack.

When we click on something on a website, our computer sends a query to the website's server saying "Hi." This is a GET request. The website's server responds with a short message saying "OK," meaning that the request has succeeded. Next, the Hypertext Transfer Protocol (HTTP) is established. The second HTTP request loads the webpage and communication is established, as stated in the Location field.

In a DoS attack, the hacker sends not just one "Hi" but thousands. The website's server cannot handle so many requests and either crashes or slows down.

- A *SYN flood* happens when the attacker exploits weaknesses in the TCP connection sequence, by not supporting the three-way handshake. Every connection establishing using TCP requires a three-way handshake, and this is the foundation for every connection. In a normal connection the three-way handshake occurs between a client and server. First the client sends an SYN packet and the server replies with acknowledgment, such as SYN-ACK. The server sends back an acknowledgment ACK packet followed by the data. The handshake is completed (see Figure 6.12).

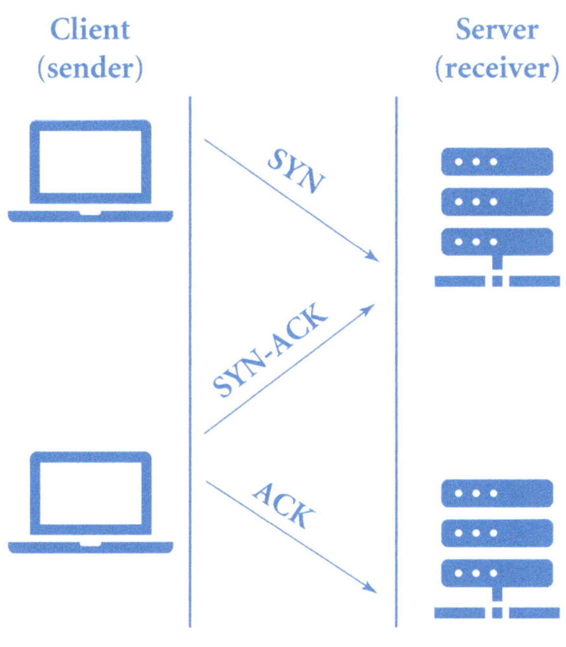

FIGURE 6.12 **The three-way handshake.**

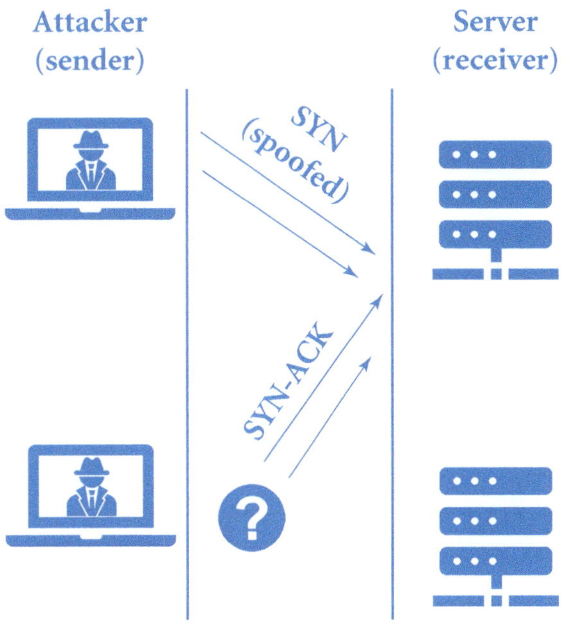

FIGURE 6.13 **The SYN flood attack. The three-way handshake is not completed.**

The attacker, on the other hand, sends a synchronized (SYN) packet to begin the handshake. The server responds with the acknowledgment (SYN-ACK), but the attacker does not reply with an acknowledgment ACK packet. As a result, the three-way handshake is not completed and leaves the connected port of the server inaccessible for further requests (see Figure 6.13). The attacker will continue sending more and more requests to prevent anyone else from connecting to the server or network. Defense against SYN flood includes a Software-Defined Networking (SDN) paradigm,[25] SYN cookies, SYN cache, SYN proxy, Firewalls, IDS,[26] or by managing the three-way handshake process in the cloud, until the TCP connection sequence is completed.

- A *Smurf attack* is a denial-of-service attack that exploits weaknesses of the Internet Protocol (IP) and ICMP by using a source code called "smurf." A hacker uses this source code to broadcast numerous ICMP packets, by making requests with a spoofed IP address.

  The hacker first creates a spoofed (fake) network packet that has its source address set to the real IP address of the server that he wants to target. Next, the hacker sends an ICMP echo request (ping) to an IP broadcast address of the router, asking a network device or a node

---

[25] Sahoo, Kshira Sagar, Sanjaya Kumar Panda, Sampa Sahoo, Bibhudatta Sahoo, and Ratnakar Dash. "Toward secure software-defined networks against distributed denial of service attack." *The Journal of Supercomputing* 75, no. 8 (2019): 4829–4874.

[26] Kumar, Prashant, Meenakshi Tripathi, Ajay Nehra, Mauro Conti, and Chhagan Lal. "Safety: Early detection and mitigation of tcp syn flood utilizing entropy in sdn." *IEEE Transactions on Network and Service Management* 15, no. 4 (2018): 1545–1559.

to send a reply. Each device responds to the spoofed address with pinged reply packets, resulting in flooding of the targeted IP address and the setting up of an infinite loop since the target and the receiver are the same. Thus, the targeted network is flooded with a large volume of pings from the attacker.[27] Every IP address in the network that was attacked is left hanging due to responding to an invalid message request, and there is soon a complete Denial of Service. Disabling the IP broadcasting address in network routers and firewalls, configuring hosts, and routers so they do not respond to ICMP echo requests and guarding against Trojan horses can prevent Smurf attacks.[28]

- *Buffer overflow* occurs when a hacker modifies a computer's memory or overflows the buffer's limit, overwriting memory locations to control program execution and inserting malicious code into the memory of a program.[29]

  The hacker's goal is to insert malicious code in a memory location that the system will execute. The buffer is a *temporary storage area*, like RAM, in which data is held in a computing device. To mitigate a buffer overflow attack, an Address Space Layout Randomization (ASLR) has been used as a successful defense.[30]
- The *Ping of Death*: This attack is like a *Smurf* attack. It occurs when a hacker manipulates an IP protocol by sending large packets with the maximum value allowed in the IP header to a target. When the targeted computing device tries to reassemble these large packets, the packets overload the network resources, causing the buffer to overflow, slowing the network, or crashing the operating system. This causes a denial of service for legitimate packets.[31] One way to mitigate against this attack is to create a memory buffer with sufficient space to handle packets that exceed the expected size.

Distributed denial-of-service (DDoS) attacks are more advanced. They occur when multiple computing systems coordinate a synchronized attack. A hacker exploits security vulnerability to take control of multiple computers and turns them into botnets or bots (zombie computers). The hacker then uses the bots to attack other computers or networks. The botnets can be made up of a single handful of bots or thousands of them, located around the world. These infected computers are managed through a command-and-control

---

[27] *Id.* at 25.

[28] Easttom, Chuck. *Network defense and countermeasures: Principles and practices.* New Jersey: Pearson Prentice Hall, 2006.

[29] Nicula, Ștefan, and Răzvan Daniel Zota. "Exploiting stack-based buffer overflow using modern day techniques." *Procedia Computer Science* 160 (2019): 9–14.

[30] Seo, Jaebaek, Byoungyoung Lee, Seong Min Kim, Ming-Wei Shih, Insik Shin, Dongsu Han, and Taesoo Kim. "SGX-shield: Enabling address space layout randomization for SGX programs." In *NDSS*. 2017.

[31] *Id.* at 23.

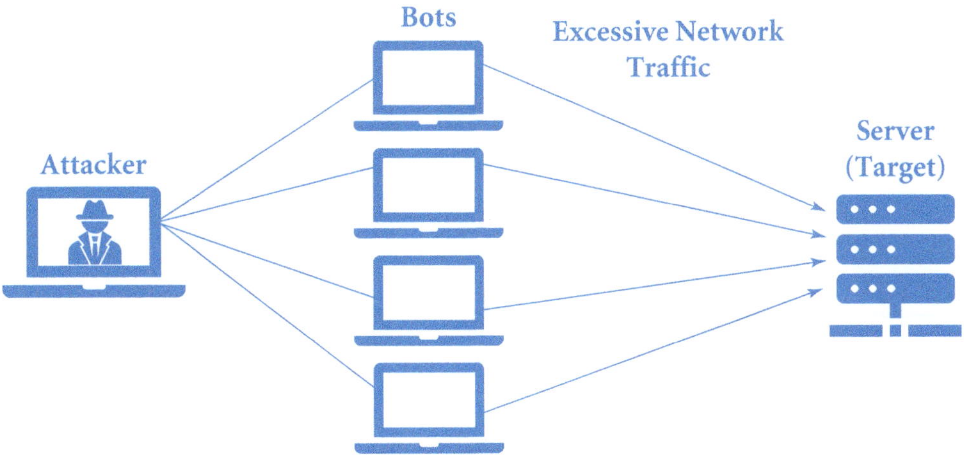

FIGURE 6.14 A DDoS attack.

server. DDoS attacks provide an opportunity for hackers to gain access to numerous compromised computing devices. Figure 6.14 demonstrates a typical DDoS attack.

In addition to the above DoS attacks that can be utilized by a DDoS as well, the most common DDoS attacks are:

- The *User Datagram Protocol (UDP) Flood* is like the *ping flood.* The attacker floods the targeted network with UDP packets. Since the UDP protocol is connectionless it does not require any link to be established between the source and destination before data transfer occurs. The goal of this kind of attack is to flood random ports on a remote host with data. Because there is no established connection, the target computer is unable to find an application-sending data and tells the sender that the destination is unreachable. This process consumes host resources, which can ultimately result in denial of services. To defend against UDP floods, firewalls that block malicious UDP packets along with the use of IP routing technology have been used to prevent an attacker from overwhelming a computing system.[32,33]
- A *Slowloris attack* occurs when an attacker overwhelms a targeted server by sending numerous HTTP requests until the server cannot make any more connections. The attacker is using a legitimate HTTP request. As a result, the server is forced to keep existing connections open indefinitely. To keep the connections open and alive, the attacker periodically sends partial requests (HTTP headers) to

[32] Gillman, David, Yin Lin, Bruce Maggs, and Ramesh K. Sitaraman. "Protecting websites from attack with secure delivery networks." *Computer* 48, no. 4 (2015): 26–34.

[33] Wong, FuiFui, and Cheng Xiang Tan. "A survey of trends in massive DDoS attacks and cloud-based mitigations." *International Journal of Network Security & Its Applications* 6, no. 3 (2014): 57.

the server saying, "Hey server I'm still here." Therefore, these unfinished requests exhaust bandwidth and affect the server's ability to respond to additional traffic requests.[34] A *Slowloris* attack can be mitigated by fingerprint traffic application behavior[35] and by limiting the number of connections and duration for each IP address.[36] Figure 6.15 demonstrates a normal HTTP connection between the sender and the server. Figure 6.16 displays an unfinished *Slowloris* attack.

- *Zero-Day DDoS attacks* or *0-day* is used as a blanket term to refer to all unknown new DDoS attacks that exploit vulnerabilities that have not yet been discovered. Since these types of attacks are not understood, they are exceptionally destructive since the targets have

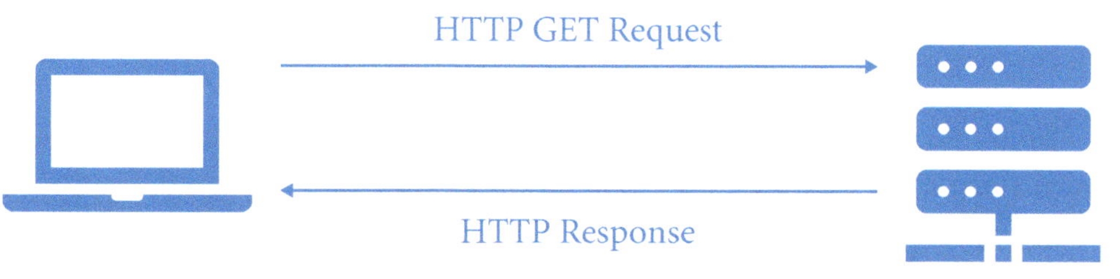

FIGURE 6.15 A normal HTTP request.

FIGURE 6.16 A Slowloris attack with unfinished simultaneous HTTP request.

[34] Cambiaso, Enrico, Gianluca Papaleo, Giovanni Chiola, and Maurizio Aiello. "Slow DoS attacks: Definition and categorisation." *International Journal of Trust Management in Computing and Communications* 1, no. 3–4 (2013): 300–319.

[35] Ahmed, Muhammad Ejaz, Saeed Ullah, and Hyoungshick Kim. "Statistical application fingerprinting for DDoS attack mitigation." *IEEE Transactions on Information Forensics and Security* 14, no. 6 (2018): 1471–1484.

[36] Hirakawa, Tetsuya, Kanayo Ogura, Bhed Bahadur Bista, and Toyoo Takata. "A defense method against distributed slow http dos attack." In *2016 19th International Conference on Network-Based Information Systems (NBiS)*, pp. 152–158. IEEE, 2016.

no defense. In other words, a new attack can be called a vector's zero-days.[37]

6.3.2.1 Notable DDoS Attacks

- The 2020 Amazon Web Services massive DDoS attack. The attack lasted 3 days and peaked at 2.3 terabytes per second.[38]
- The 2018 DDoS attack on GitHub, a platform for hosting software development. GitHub got hit by1.35 Tb per second traffic at once.[39]
- In 2016, the Mirai strain of malware infected the Internet of Things (IoT) running on Linux, turning the devices into remotely controlled bots that created DDoS attacks.[40,41]
- In 2013, *spamhaus.org*, an anti-spam organization, suffered a DDoS attack with an estimated size of more than 300 Gb per second of attack traffic.[42]

6.3.2.2 DoS Attacking Tools

Some of the most common and free DoS attack tools are the following:

- *DoSHTTP*, an easy-to-use and powerful DoS tool that generates HTTP flooding
- *High Orbit Ion Cannon (HOIC)*, intended to attack more than one URL at the same time using HTTP (Hypertext Transfer Protocol)
- *HTTP Unbearable Load King (HULK)*, a DoS attack tool that generates a unique demand for every request to the Web server
- *Layer 7 DDoS Simulator (DDOSIM)*, a DoS attacking tool that mimics several zombie hosts with full TCP connections
- *Low Orbit Ion Cannon (LOIC)*, an open-source network stress testing and DoS attack application
- *R-U-Dead-Yet*, an HTTP POST DoS attack tool
- *Tor's Hammer*, an attacking tool for slow-rate attacks using HTTP POST requests
- *XOIC*, a DoS attack application for any server with an IP address

[37] Sun, Xiaoyan, Jun Dai, Peng Liu, Anoop Singhal, and John Yen. "Using Bayesian networks for probabilistic identification of zero-day attack paths." *IEEE Transactions on Information Forensics and Security* 13, no. 10 (2018): 2506–2521.

[38] AWS Shield Threat Landscape Report—Q1 2020. Retrieved from https://aws-shield-tlr.s3.amazonaws.com/2020-Q1_AWS_Shield_TLR.pdf

[39] Hameed, Sufian, and Usman Ali. "HADEC: hadoop-based live DDoS detection framework." *EURASIP Journal on Information Security* 2018, no. 1 (2018): 1–19.

[40] Kambourakis, Georgios, Constantinos Kolias, and Angelos Stavrou. "The mirai botnet and the iot zombie armies." In *MILCOM 2017-2017 IEEE Military Communications Conference (MILCOM)*, pp. 267–272. IEEE, 2017.

[41] Lindqvist, Ulf, and Peter G. Neumann. "The future of the Internet of Things." *Communications of the ACM* 60, no. 2 (2017): 26–30.

[42] Wong, FuiFui, and Cheng Xiang Tan. "A survey of trends in massive DDoS attacks and cloud-based mitigations." *International Journal of Network Security & Its Applications* 6, no. 3 (2014): 57.

6.3.3 Malware

Malware is short for "malicious software" and consists of computer viruses, worms, Trojan horses, ransomware, spyware, and other types of destructive software or code. Malware impairs or infiltrates a computing device or system to execute specific damage, without the user's knowledge. Java Scripts are commonly used for placing malware on a victim's computing device.[43] JavaScript is a programming language used in website coding for browser appearance and functionality, and it can be also added to Portable Document Format (PDF) files to create user interface actions that apply to the entire PDF document.

- *Virus* is a type of malicious code or a program that replicates and spreads from one computer to another after initial execution. A computer virus requires a *host program* and *user action*. Typically, a virus is attached to a computer program, file, or document. For example, a malicious macro infection can be attached to a Word or PDF file. For this code to infect a computing device, the user must run the infected program, and then the executing code can pass the virus to the device.
- A *Trojan horse* is named after the famous wooden horse that tricked the Trojans and allowed the ancient Greeks to conquer the city of Troy. Trojan horses are scripts or computer programs camouflaged as legitimate software. Instead, they are delivery vehicles for a variety of threats. For example, when a user innocently downloads a utility, game, or movie from a website considered safe and runs it or opens an attachment containing the infected file, the following may occur:
- A backdoor may open, providing hackers with unauthorized remote access.
- An exploit occurs that takes advantage of a weakness of the software or hardware.
- Harmful software is installed, or files are deleted.

  Some examples of Trojans are the *Zeus* or *Zbot Trojan* malware that hacked the U.S. Department of Transportation;[44] the *Wirenet* password-stealing Trojan that was able to steal data from Linux, Mac, and Windows[45] environments; and mobile banking Trojans that steal user login credentials and credit card details.[46]

---

[43] Fass, Aurore, Michael Backes, and Ben Stock. "Hidenoseek: Camouflaging malicious javascript in benign asts." In *Proceedings of the 2019 ACM SIGSAC Conference on Computer and Communications Security*, pp. 1899–1913. 2019.

[44] Mane, Yogita Deepak. "Detect and deactivate P2P Zeus bot." In 2017 8th International Conference on Computing, Communication and Networking Technologies (ICCCNT), pp. 1–7. IEEE, 2017.

[45] Komatwar, Rupali, and Manesh Kokare. "A survey on malware detection and classification." *Journal of Applied Security Research* (2020): 1–31.

[46] Kiwia, Dennis, Ali Dehghantanha, Kim-Kwang Raymond Choo, and Jim Slaughter. "A cyber kill chain based taxonomy of banking Trojans for evolutionary computational intelligence." *Journal of Computational Science* 27 (2018): 394–409.

- A *ransomware* attack occurs when a hacker uses malicious software, usually malware or phishing spam, to extort victims by locking and encrypting their data until the victim pays a ransom in cryptocurrency. Even after payment the data may not be made available.

  A ransomware report alert was issued by the CISA, the FBI, and the HHS (U.S. Department of Health and Human Services).[47] This ransomware alert (AA20-302A) targeted the Healthcare and Public health sector.

  Ransomware frequently indicates the end of a lengthy cyberattack chain or cyber kill chain. The attacker has usually spent many days or weeks laying the groundwork for ransomware in the victim's network.

  When using ransomware, the attacker first encrypts the victim's files so they are unusable and then blackmails the victim to pay for the decryption key. When ransomware occurs in a corporation, the attackers threaten to reveal sensitive data to shareholders, the media, and competitors unless payment is made. Some of the signs a computing system may have been infected by ransomware attacks include:

  - Unusual malware warning reports
  - Infrequent warning reports from hacking tools such as network scanners
  - Unusual phishing attacks

  To defend against ransomware attacks, the following preventive measures should be considered:

  - Perform frequent updates and patches to the operating systems and applications
  - Educate users about phishing attacks in circulation and use an anti-phishing testing system and spam filters
  - Use a strong password and the system should require two-factor or multi-factor authentication
  - Disable all remote services such as Remote Desktop Protocol (RDP)
  - Backup data regularly and keep the backup copy *offline*, in a *cold backup*, where the database is offline, or *off-site*, and where the data is processed externally
  - Disable the autoplay function and file sharing
  - Monitor the network for suspicious network behavior
  - Download only from trusted sites and think twice before clicking
  - File a report with the FBI[48]

---

[47] CISA Ransomware Report Alert, Ransomware Activity Targeting the Healthcare and Public Health Sector (AA20-302A). Retrieved from https://us-cert.cisa.gov/ncas/alerts/aa20-302a

[48] FBI Internet Crime Complaint Center. Retrieved from https://www.ic3.gov/

- *Spyware* is a type of malicious software that invades a computing device to gather information. It does not self-replicate, evades detection, and runs undetected in the background of a computing device. More specifically, it records passwords, login credentials, and credit card information, forwarding the information and providing access to its spyware author.
- A *Worm* is an executable malicious program capable of replicating and distributing itself. In contrast to a virus, a worm does not require user activity to be activated. Usually, worms transmit malware like ransomware.

6.3.4 Phishing

Phishing is a deceitful attempt to gather personal information such as usernames, passwords, and credit card information by using deceptive emails masked as legitimate. For example, a user may receive an email from a financial institution, asking for "missing" information. The email looks genuine, and all the user needs to do is click and answer the questions. But, when the user clicks on the link, the hacker installs malware which spreads to the user's network within seconds. Then several different types of attacks may occur:

- *Deceptive Phishing* is one of the most widely used phishing scams. The goal is to mislead the user into revealing personal confidential information by imitating a legitimate source. The phishing email usually gives the impression of urgency—that the user needs to act fast. Following are two phishing email examples.
    - *I have tried to email this account many times but have received no response. If you receive this email,*
      Contact me as soon as possible for more details.
      Sincerely,
      Benjamin Ezeife
      Your account is on hold
    - *Hi Dear, we're having some trouble with your current billing information. We'll try again. But in the meantime, you may want to update your payment.*
    - UPDATE ACCOUNT NOW
    - *Need help? We are here if you need it. Visit the Help Center or contact us now. Your friends at Netflix*
- *Spear Phishing* is when an attacker targets specific individuals or groups within an organization or business. The attacker usually needs to gather information on the target to compile a convincing phishing email. Often intended to steal data, an attacker may also

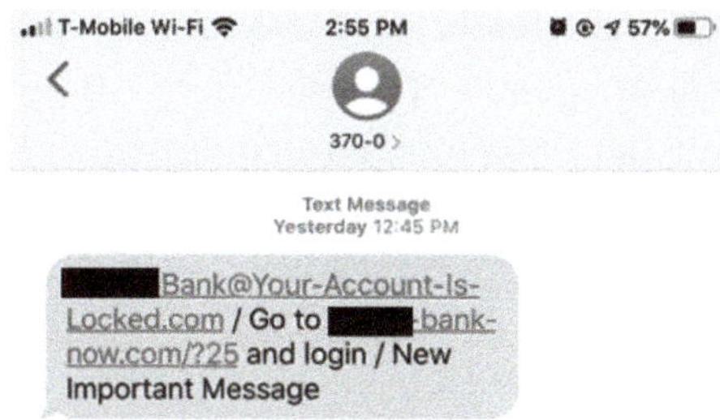

FIGURE 6.17 Example of smishing technique.

intend to install malware on a targeted individual's computer. This technique targets individuals by email, social media, instant messaging (IM), and more. Frequently, a spear phishing technique contains an email and attachment. Social media sites are ideal hunting grounds for phishing attacks.

- *Vishing* is a voice phishing technique that uses verbal scams to deceive users into sharing confidential information. It flourishes when a cybercriminal has some information about the victim and uses this knowledge to create a sense of urgency to get the user to perform some type of action.
- *Smishing* is a mixture of texting and phishing that uses text messages instead of emails. The *smishing* technique lures users into sharing private information or clicking a malicious link and activating a code (Figure 6.17).
- *Pharming* is a combination of two words "phishing" and "farming." The hacker directs an Internet user to a fake website instead of a legitimate one. The hacker may install malware on a user's computer that changes the computer's host file in order to direct traffic to a malicious website instead. Another way to "pharm" is when a hacker may "poison" the DNS server, causing numerous users to visit the fake website. This method exploits Internet browsing. Since a Domain Name System (DNS) server converts domain names like www.google.com into IP addresses, the *pharming* method targets the DNS server and replaces the IP address with a malicious one. When a user visits a website with the replaced IP address, a DNS cache forms, and the user will be sent to the malicious site on each visit. Both the DNS cache and the DNS server can be corrupted by the pharming technique. To protect against pharming, users should avoid suspicious websites and use only secure Web connections with Hypertext Transfer Protocol Secure (HTTPS) in the web address. In addition, they must utilize a password manager that stores the official website's direct link, employ strong passwords, enable two-factor

authentication on websites, use a VPN, remember to install updates on a regular basis, and use a trusted ISP.

- *Social engineering* happens when a cybercriminal tricks victims into revealing confidential information, such as usernames and passwords. For example, a cybercriminal could pose as an IT support technician and then trick the victim into providing login credentials.

6.3.5 Spoofing

Spoofing refers to a deceptive method that tricks the user by hiding a malicious origin as a legitimate source. Examples of some of the common spoofing attacks include:

- *Address Resolution Protocol (ARP) spoofing* or *ARP poisoning* is a man-in-the-middle (MITM) attack. A hacker infiltrates a Local Area Network (LAN) by intercepting communication between network devices. The hacker changes the Media Access Control (MAC) address on the device and thereafter attacks the LAN by modifying the target with a falsified ARP request using a spoofing tool, like *Arpspoof* or *Driftnet*. The hacker can then view all the information passing between the devices and can collect all the traffic via port monitoring. To be able to achieve this type of spoofing attack, the hacker must have access to the network.
- *DNS spoofing or DNS cache poisoning* occurs when cybercriminals alter the DNS record of URLs and then redirect online traffic to a falsified website by changing its IP address. Then, they harvest personal information or infect the computer with malware. The DNS is the "phonebook" of the Internet and contains a list of URLs and their IP addresses. Once hacked, a tremendous volume of traffic can be misdirected.
- *Email spoofing* occurs when a cybercriminal creates and sends email messages from a forged sender's email address and makes the recipient believe that the email was sent from a legitimate source. Email spoofing is the most widely used method to execute phishing attacks.[49] The spoofed emails occasionally contain attachments, which, when opened, install malware.
- *IP spoofing* occurs when hackers modify an IP packet by falsifying its source address. This attack is often used to set up DDoS attacks. The IP spoofing attack has become less common since ISPs have started performing egress filtering and packet filtering to detect and

[49] Iyer, R. Padmavathi, Pradeep K. Atrey, Gaurav Varshney, and Manoj Misra. "Email spoofing detection using volatile memory forensics." In *2017 IEEE Conference on Communications and Network Security (CNS)*, pp. 619–625. IEEE, 2017.

discard spoofed IP packets. Now, it is quite difficult to spoof an IP address outside of a LAN connection. Nevertheless, in cloud computing, hackers use IP spoofing techniques to launch DDoS attacks and masquerade the source's identity.[50,51]

- *MAC spoofing* changes the factory-assigned MAC, the physical address of a computing device's network interface controller (NIC), also known as a network interface card. If a hacker can exploit backdoor vulnerabilities in the device's drivers and modify the MAC address, he is seen as an authorized user. Then, the hacker presents himself at the default gateway and copies all the data without being detected. With these data, the hacker has detailed knowledge about the applications in use and destination host IP addresses. Additionally, the hacker can deny services on a wireless network, inject packets, send frames to all the wireless users using a broadcast address, and manipulate any packet field.[52]
- *Website spoofing* occurs when a cybercriminal creates a fake replica of a real website like that of a bank or a university, and when a user logs into the fraudulent website, the hacker obtains the user's credentials. Nevertheless, this type of spoofing first requires a phishing email that baits the user into clicking on a malicious link.

6.3.6 Structured Query Language (SQL) Injection or (SQLI)

Structured Query Language, or SQL, is a programming language used with databases to query the database for specific information. An SQL query is basically a request for data. Examples include data retrieval, updates, and data removal. To query a database, a Web page is usually designed that accepts a specific type of identification, like username and password. When a user enters the information, it is checked for authentication. If correct, the user is granted entry. If not, access to the database is denied.

SQL injection is a type of cyberattack where hackers "inject" malicious SQL code to manipulate the database and gain access to information illicitly. In other words, the hacker exploits software vulnerability by adding malicious SQL code to Web applications. Since most Web pages have no way of refusing authenticated requests, once authenticated, the hacker can enter

[50] Agrawal, Neha, and Shashikala Tapaswi. "A lightweight approach to detect the low/high rate IP spoofed cloud DDoS attacks." In *2017 IEEE 7th International Symposium on Cloud and Service Computing (SC2)*, pp. 118–123. IEEE, 2017.

[51] Vlajic, Natalija, Mashruf Chowdhury, and Marin Litoiu. "IP Spoofing in and out of the public cloud: From policy to practice." *Computers* 8, no. 4 (2019): 81.

[52] Alotaibi, Bandar, and Khaled Elleithy. "A new mac address spoofing detection technique based on random forests." *Sensors* 16, no. 3 (2016): 281.

a malicious code in the SQL code that changes the query. As a result, the hacker breaks into the database and steals, alters, or destroys data.

6.3.7 Wi-Fi Hacking

A Wi-Fi connection offers a seamless wireless connection to the Internet. As a result, hackers target Wi-Fi connections and attempt to exploit their vulnerabilities, particularly targeting Wi-Fi in home networks. Once the hacker gains access to the network, he will either target the network itself or go after its connected devices. The hacker will usually focus on the link with the vulnerabilities that are easiest to exploit. Most wireless networks are vulnerable since there is no physical connection to deal with. Established wireless security protocols are frequently exploited to gain unauthorized access to Wi-Fi networks. For example, the security protocol Wired Equivalent Privacy (WEP), introduced in 1999, is the least secure, and the Wi-Fi Protected Access (WPA) protocol also has security vulnerabilities.[53] The Wi-Fi Protected Access II (WPA2)[54] and Wi-Fi Protected Access 3 (WPA3) display vulnerabilities that attackers can exploit as well[55] but are currently the most secure choices.

Some of the most common Wi-Fi attacks are the following:

- *Cracking attacks* occur when a hacker uses different password-cracking techniques to break into a Wi-Fi network and gain access. Some of these include:
  - *Brute-force attacks*, meaning the hacker uses every possible combination of letters in a series of password-cracking attempts, struggling by trial and error to "force" its way until the correct password is found. For example, the simplest cipher is the Caesar cipher that can easily be cracked using a brute-force attack. Since the Caesar cipher has only 26 possible keys, by using brute force we can easily try all 26 possible key combinations.
  - *Dictionary attacks* are like *brute-force attacks* but use passwords from a list containing words from the dictionary that many people like to use for their password. The hacker may try words like "password," "attack," or "profanity" or credentials stolen from a third-party resource with information about the target's name, birthday month, etc.

[53] Nikolov, Linko G. "Wireless network vulnerabilities estimation." *Security & Future* 2, no. 2 (2018): 80–82.

[54] Vanhoef, Mathy, and Frank Piessens. "Key reinstallation attacks: Forcing nonce reuse in WPA2." In *Proceedings of the 2017 ACM SIGSAC Conference on Computer and Communications Security*, pp. 1313–1328. 2017.

[55] Kohlios, Christopher P., and Thaier Hayajneh. "A comprehensive attack flow model and security analysis for wi-fi and wpa3." *Electronics* 7, no. 11 (2018): 284.

  - *Phishing*, as discussed earlier, is a dishonest attempt to gather personal information, including usernames and passwords.
  - *Rainbow table* is a password-cracking technique that uses the rainbow hash table. This table is used in cryptography to encrypt and store important values like passwords using pre-computed hash values for every possible combination of characters. The passwords in almost all online services and computer systems are stored as hashes. We will discuss the hash value further in the chapter.
- *Jamming Wi-Fi signals* occurs when a hacker blocks a signal, using an illegal jamming device, for the purpose of creating noise and denying users access to a wireless point. According to the Federal Communications Commission (FCC), jamming critical communications like 911 and other emergency calls poses serious risks to public safety.

  "It is unlawful to advertise, sell, distribute, import, or otherwise market jamming devices to consumers in the United States."[56] The applicable laws for jamming are the Communications Act of 1934, FCC Rules, and the U.S. Criminal Code, enforced by the Department of Justice or the Department of Homeland Security.[57]
- A *Wi-Fi de-authentication attack* occurs when a hacker targets a communication when it is traveling between the Wi-Fi Access Point and the device. This is actually a type of denial-of-service (DoS) attack. The goal is to send fake de-authentication packets to wireless users to capture their handshake and other data. These packets may spoof the user's IP address.[58,59]
- *Wi-Fi protected setup (WPS) attack*. The WPS standard uses a Personal Identification Number, which is an 8-digit pin, or a push button to connect to the router. This standard was created by Cisco and was designed to simplify connectivity between a wireless device and a router.[60] During the attack, the hacker may use a tool called a *Reaver* to intercept the PIN and steal the Wi-Fi Protected Access 2 password. This vulnerability is in the code of the Wi-Fi Protected

---

[56] Federal Communications Commission (FCC), Jammer Enforcement. Retrieved from https://www.fcc.gov/general/jammer-enforcement

[57] *Id.* at 56.

[58] Noman, Haitham Ameen, Shahidan M. Abdullah, and Haydar Imad Mohammed. "An automated approach to detect deauthentication and disassociation dos attacks on wireless 802.11 networks." *International Journal of Computer Science Issues (IJCSI)* 12, no. 4 (2015): 107.

[59] Villain, J., V. Deniau, A. Fleury, E. P. Simon, C. Gransart, and R. Kousri. "EM monitoring and classification of IEMI and protocol-based attacks on IEEE 802.11 n communication networks." *IEEE Transactions on Electromagnetic Compatibility* 61, no. 6 (2019): 1771–1781.

[60] CISCO Systems, Wi-Fi Protected Setup (WPS) Enrollment Configuration on the WAP121 and WAP321 Access Points. https://www.cisco.com/c/en/us/support/docs/smb/wireless/cisco-small-business-300-series-wireless-access-points/smb2485-wi-fi-protected-setup-wps-enrollment-configuration-on-the-wa.html

Setup and not in the WPA or WPA2 Wi-Fi security protocols and allows the hacker to crack the protocol.[61,62]

WPA consists of a family of Wi-Fi security certifications or security technologies developed by the Wi-Fi Alliance to secure wireless computer networks.[63] Some of the hacker's tools used to crack Wi-Fi passwords are *aircrack-ng*, *airmon-ng*, *airodump-ng*, and *aireplay-ng*.[64]

- *Public Wi-Fi security issues.* Free Wi-Fi can be found in public places such as airports, coffee shops, malls, restaurants, and hotels. Most Wi-Fi hotspots are convenient but are often not secure. The hotspots are becoming more widespread because people want to use their devices 24/7, but the risks are considerable.

Some of the risks of using these free hot spots include:

- *Man-in-the-Middle (MITM) attacks*, a type of cyber eavesdropping that occurs when data sent from point A to point B is intercepted by an attacker. The attacker then interjects himself into the communication process and accesses the victim's computing system to monitor the online activity. Sometimes, the hacker can intercept login credentials and steal credit card information, alter the contents of the messages, or mimic the user. Every time we connect to a public Wi-Fi hotspot, we should assume that everything is being watched.
- *Unsecured Wi-Fi connections* can be used by hackers to distribute malware. If the user allows file sharing when using an unsecure Wi-Fi connection, the hacker can easily plant malware on the victim's computer.
- In some cases, a hacker may create a rogue hotspot and name it with a well-known store or location, hope to trick users into signing on with their devices.

How can users remain safe?

Some preventive measures when using a public Wi-Fi connection are:

- Set up a VPN, which can provide protection against man-in-the-middle attacks.
- Use a strong password along with two-factor authentication (2FA), requiring an additional step to log into an account, like a passcode text to a mobile phone or a physical key inserted into a computer.

---

[61] Čisar, P., and S. Maravić Čisar. "Ethical hacking of wireless networks in kali linux environment." *Annals of the Faculty of Engineering Hunedoara* 16, no. 3 (2018): 181–186.

[62] Nikolov, Linko G. "Wireless network vulnerabilities estimation." *Security & Future* 2, no. 2 (2018): 80–82.

[63] Wi-Fi Alliance introduces Wi-Fi Certified WPA3 security. Retrieved from https://www.wi-fi.org/news-events/newsroom/wi-fi-alliance-introduces-wi-fi-certified-wpa3-security

[64] *Id.* at 61.

- Disable the auto-connect functionality for Wi-Fi.
- Visit the safest websites using Hypertext Transfer Protocol Secure (HTTPS).
- Beware of phishing scams when using a public Wi-Fi connection.

Figure 6.18 demonstrates the evolution of the most significant cyberattacks from the early 2000s until the present. From early 2000 to 2004 we've seen

FIGURE 6.18 The evolution of the most important attacks.

mainly worms; from 2005 to 2012 we've seen the rise of modern malware, and from 2013 to the present we've experienced ransomware and APT attacks associated with nation-state criminal organizations. These nation-state actors target government and commercial networks containing sensitive data, such as research for COVID-19 vaccines, and critical infrastructure.

6.4 Prevention Mechanisms

6.4.1 If You Connect It, Protect It

A *firewall* is a piece of hardware, sometimes a standalone system or part of a router, or software application, or a combination of both, that screens incoming and outcoming traffic to or from a network, according to a defined set of rules.

Along with firewalls, other systems such as *IDS* and *IPS* are part of the network security environment.

- The firewall is the first line of defense, like a fence between a trusted internal network, called the subnet, and the unsafe Internet. The firewall makes sure only specific types of traffic are allowed into and out of a network.
- The IDS system detects the attack, identifies it using a database of attack types, registers the attack, and sends an alert to an IT administrator if it is malicious.
- The IPS inspects traffic flowing in the network, looking for anything suspicious, and prevents or blocks a connection that is suspect, provides alerts, and cleans up malicious network traffic to keep it from getting to the rest of the network. Like the IDS, the IPS resides between the firewall and the rest of the network.

> The best example of the difference between security gates in IDS and IPS is that an IDS security gate works like a patrol car within the borders of its neighborhood, monitoring activities and looking for abnormal situations. An IPS security gate operates like a security guard at the gate, allowing and denying access based on credentials and a predefined rule set, or policy. No matter how strong the security at the gate is, the patrols continue to operate in a system that provides its own checks.[65]

The separation between a computing device on an internal network and the Internet, or the outside world, is referred to as the *Demilitarized Zone (DMZ)* or *perimeter network*. This area sits between the internal network and external network. The Internet cannot establish connections directly to

[65] Ashoor, Asmaa Shaker, and Sharad Gore. "Difference between intrusion detection system (IDS) and intrusion prevention system (IPS)." In *International Conference on Network Security and Applications*, pp. 497–501. Springer, 2011.

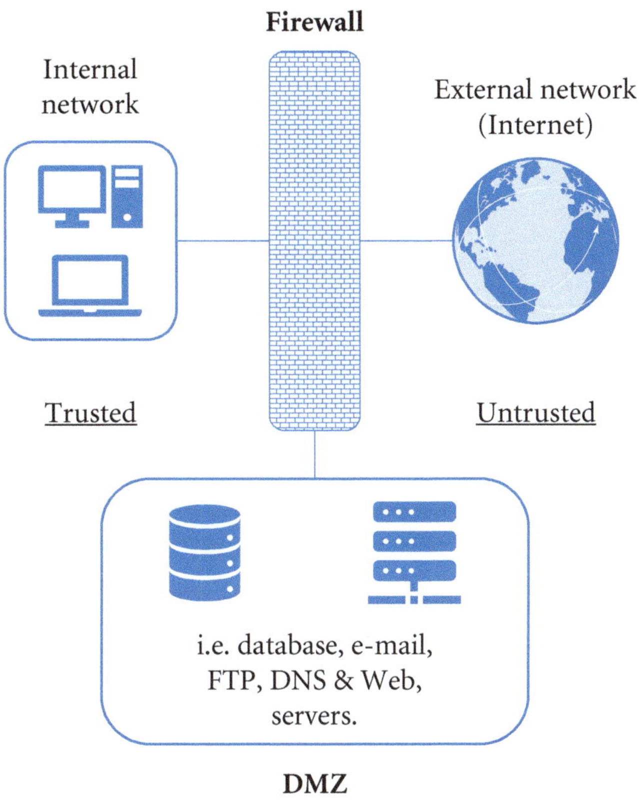

FIGURE 6.19 **The single firewall model.**

the internal network, but it can establish connections with the DMZ. If you think of network security as an onion, the DMZ is the peel, or the first layer of the onion.

There are several ways to implement a DMZ in a network. One way is to use the *single firewall model* (Figure 6.19), which requires three network interfaces (devices) or a three-legged firewall. In this case the DMZ will be positioned inside of this firewall. The first network interface, considered Untrusted, is connected to the external public Internet connection. The second interface, considered trusted, is connected to the internal network or LAN. The third interface is connected directly to the DMZ. Normally, inside the DMZ you will find the email server, File Transfer Protocol (FTP) server, DNS server, Web server, domain controller, database servers, and HTTPS traffic.

The *dual firewall model* utilizes two separate firewalls. One faces the Internet, called the *front-end firewall*, and the other faces the trusted internal network, or subnet, and is called the *back-end firewall*. The *front-end firewall* is configured to allow only traffic destined for the DMZ. The *back-end firewall* is responsible for regulating network traffic on the trusted internal network or traffic from the DMZ to the internal network.

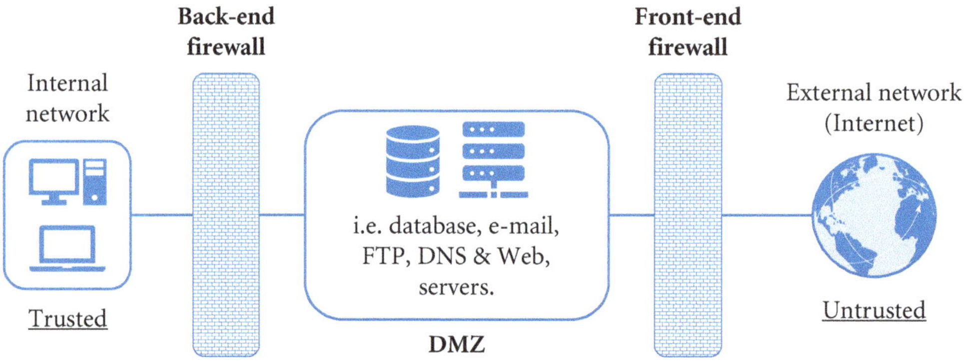

FIGURE 6.20 The dual firewall model.

Cloud computing has changed the role of the DMZ by allowing secure access between the local or on-premises network and cloud-based networks through the use of a VPN service to connect the networks. Most companies use cloud service providers and deploy SaaS applications. DMZs are an important part of network security restricting remote access and guard against unauthorized access to internal servers. Figure 6.20 demonstrates the dual firewall model.

How does the firewall perform its job of monitoring services and blocking malicious or unwanted traffic? What does it block?

A firewall does the following:

- On the device interface, the firewall filters source and destination ports, including OSI model, Layer 2 traffic.
- Regarding packet headers, the firewall filters traffic on the source and destination IP addresses, including OSI model, Layer 3 routed interface IPv4 and IPv6 interfaces. It provides different levels of protection based on parameters within the packet header information, including protocols such as TCP, UDP, and ICMP.
- The firewall rejects or accepts network traffic packet by packet, with or without notification, to the sender.
- The firewall records packet information.
- The firewall enforces security policies such as the setting of alarms, filtering rules and modifying packets, and detects, blocks, and rejects malicious requests when hackers scan public IP addresses for open ports.

On most operating systems the server includes a built-in firewall along with its wireless routers. For example, a firewall is built into Mac OS. It is found under System Preferences, Security & Privacy, Firewall. A firewall is included on Linux and on the Windows OS, where it is called Windows Defender. Additional firewall solutions for personal use are available from security companies such as Bitdefender, Kaspersky, Norton, and McAfee, and from

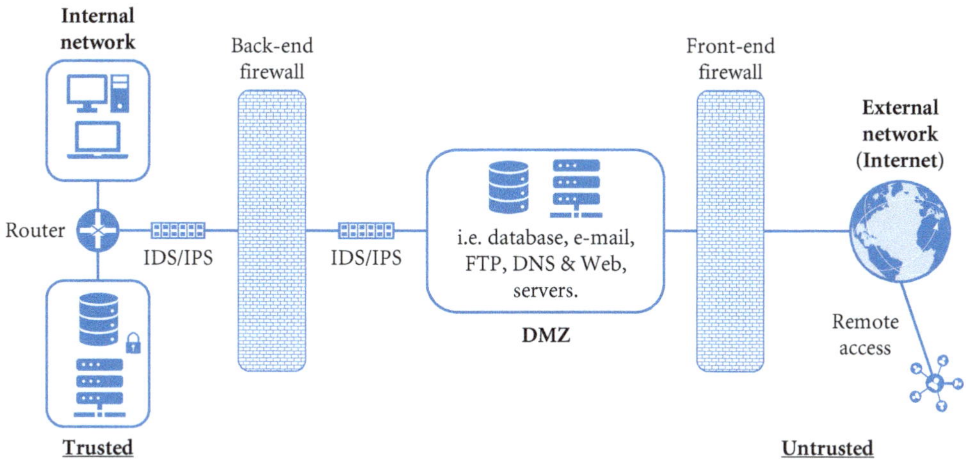

FIGURE 6.21 A typical firewall setup on a network.

ISPs. On an enterprise-level, network firewalls must be able to secure more complex networks such as cloud environments, data center deployments, and remote sites. Some of the leading companies providing enterprise-level firewalls are Barracuda Networks, Check Point, Cisco systems, Juniper, Palo Alto Networks, and SonicWall. Figure 6.21 displays a typical firewall setup on a network.

6.4.2 Types of Firewalls

Firewalls use predetermined rules to analyze incoming traffic at entry points known as ports. Ports are communication endpoints that determine how external devices exchange information and communicate on a network. Some predetermine rules include how to handle trusted IP addresses, protocols, port numbers, and destination IP addresses. Additionally, there are other firewall types based on the method of operation and varying levels of security. Some of the most common firewall types include the following:

- *Packet-filtering firewalls* are the most basic type, inspecting inbound packets arriving from the network router. Only packets that match the firewall's criteria are allowed in. Packet filtering operates at the network layer (OSI model, Layer 3), and the firewall inspects the port number, protocol, source, destination, and IP address. Packet firewalls can be either *stateless* or *stateful*. *Stateless* firewalls employ older firewall technology and analyze individual packets based on static information like source and destination. This method is not preferred by security professionals because it does not address vulnerabilities such as those leading to DDoS attacks. *Stateful* firewalls, on the other hand, are more secure and are a significant improvement, because they continuously monitor the network and the active connections. They can recognize the context of incoming traffic and data packets and can detect whether the packet is a part of an abnormal stream as in a DoS attack. Additionally, the *stateful* firewall, by default, permits connections or access from a trusted network to external servers and denies connections from outside to inside servers. However, overall, the packet-filtering firewall is not considered very secure. Its disadvantages are that it only offers basic protection, and it neither examines the packet nor compares it to the previous packet. Furthermore, it does not support user authentication of connections and is therefore vulnerable.

- *Proxy firewalls*, or *application-level firewalls*, or *gateway firewalls*, inspect the application and the server-side of the application. They monitor traffic at the application layer, using protocols like DNS, FTP, HTTP, and HTTPS, where traffic moves from one network to another and where the application connects. This type of firewall spots malicious traffic at layers 3, 4, 5, and 7 of the OSI model. A proxy firewall provides detailed log reports and analysis, filters application data, authenticates individuals, not devices, and prevents buffer overflow attempts, DoS attacks, unauthorized access, and spoofing attacks.
- A *Network Address Translation (NAT) firewall* allows network devices like routers to connect private IP networks to the Internet by replacing the private IP with a public IP address. The NAT acts as "receptionist or a dispatcher" between the public Internet and local network by remapping an IP address space into another one. The NAT firewall was developed to improve network security by filtering all incoming traffic, identifying threats and malicious actions, and blocking them. The firewall operates on a router to protect the local network's devices as they connect with outside traffic on the Internet. First, the firewall allows Internet traffic to pass into the local network upon request by a device. Every incoming packet must have been requested by a device. Second, when a device is connected to the Internet, the router assigns it an external public IP address. When a device is connected to the router in the local network, the device is given a private IP address and the firewall does not allow the device to directly communicate with the Internet. Every device sends a request to a Web server by sending data packets. The packets include the sender and receiver's IP addresses, port numbers, and what kind of information is requested. The NAT changes the data packet's public IP to private IP to hide or masquerade the IP addresses of any devices from outside the local network behind a single global address.
- The *next-generation firewall (NGFW)* is one of the most popular firewalls. It provides advanced inspection threat beyond what is

offered by traditional *stateful* firewall detection, featuring excellent application awareness and control, and the ability to block malware, prevent intrusion, recognize cloud-based threat intelligence, and prevent other security applications from entering a network.

- *Virtual firewalls* or *Cloud-based firewalls* or *Firewall-as-a-Service* refer to a virtual appliance located in a private cloud that monitors traffic on physical and virtual networks with cost-efficient solutions. This type of firewall provides the same protection in an off-network connection.
- A *Web application firewall* (WAF) is a type of firewall that blocks, filters, and protects data traveling in and out of Web services by analyzing each HTTP and HTTPS request at the application layer.

6.5 Identification, Authentication, and Authorization

In computer security it is important to comprehend the difference among these three terms, Identification, Authentication, and Authorization

Identification indicates the user's or the thing's identity, for example, a username.

Authentication, from the Greek word "αὐθεντικός" authentikos, meaning "real" or "legitimate," is the method that confirms the user's identity and provides access to a computer system, for example, checking the accuracy of a password. Password authentication is the most common method of confirming a user's identity, but passwords have many weaknesses and are susceptible to phishing attacks and password-cracking techniques. Because complicated passwords are hard to remember, users tend to choose convenience over security, hence the "12345" password. In addition to the password checking method, other common authentications include:

- Multi-factor authentication (MFA), sometimes referred to as two-factor authentication (2FA), which means requiring two or more ways to identify a user. For example, users can receive one-time passwords (OTP), requiring a code that is often received via email, text, or from a mobile app like the Google Authenticator. For additional security, a biometric authentication like a fingerprint, face recognition, IRIS scan, or voice recognition can be used. Another security measure is the use of a hardware-based security key based on the FIDO U2F standard.[66] FIDO is administered by the FIDO Alliance and is a set of protocols intended to support authentication methods including biometrics, Bluetooth technology, Near Field Communication

[66] FIDO Alliance. Retrieved from Alliance https://fidoalliance.org/

(NFC) for mobile devices, and USB security tokens. Some popular security keys are Yubico's YubiKey, CryptoTrust OnlyKey, Thetis FIDO U2F Security Key, and Google Titan Security Keys.

Users can authenticate with the following authentication factors:

- Something the user knows, such as a password, a PIN, or answers to a set of questions.
- Something the user has, such as a smart card or a hardware-based security key.
- Something the user is or does such as biometric characteristics.

- Biometric authentication includes physiological, including fingerprints, face recognition, palm vein scan, iris scan, retinal pattern, and DNA, and behavioral, including voice pitch, typing patterns, and signature.
- Token-based authentication requires a unique generated encrypted code, or token, to verify the user's identity. The token can be sent to a mobile app or a small hardware device. An example of a token is the RSA SecurID token offered in RSA SecurID two-factor authentication.

Authorization happens when a user is provided with certain privileges or permissions to access computer systems or resources such as databases, files, services, computer programs, and applications. Authorization access is based on the level of assigned permissions given to the user, as defined by certain conditions.

An *authentication protocol* is a set of rules that exchanges authentication data between two or more entities, allowing them to operate securely with minimal effort. A simple example of Point-to-Point Protocol (PPP) authentication protocol goes like this:

> *Bob sends Alice his password in a packet. Alice checks Bob's received password against the one saved in her database. If the password is correct, she sends a packet with an acknowledgment of successful authentication; if not, Bob is denied.*

Common authentication protocols include PPP, Extensible Authentication Protocol (EAP), Kerberos, Challenge-handshake authentication protocol (CHAP), Password Authentication Protocol (PAP), Secure Shell protocol (SSH), and Shiva Password Authentication Protocol (SPAP).

6.6 Modern Encryption

As we discussed earlier, cryptographic techniques have been used for thousands of years for secure communication. The need for people to exchange data easily and securely became more important with the introduction of computers. Encryption is one of the most effective ways to protect data by scrambling data into secret codes, called ciphers, as they travel across the Internet.

Complex encryption algorithms have been developed that are hard to break. The summary below describes a general understanding of modern encryption methods that can protect *data at rest*, *data in transit*, and *data in use*. It can also keep data safe from lost and stolen computers. However, encryption can also be used by cybercriminals to encrypt data after a ransomware attack, making it almost impossible to retrieve and use. Encryption can be good or evil, protecting us or used as a weapon against us.

6.6.1 Symmetric Encryption or Secret Key Cryptography (SKC)

Symmetric encryption method, also referred to as symmetric key cryptography, secret key, or shared secret, is a method that uses the same key to both encrypt and then decrypt a message. A simple example of symmetric encryption is the Caesar cipher, described earlier, which shifts each letter a fixed number of places. Another example occurred in 1586 when Blaise de Vigenère used an entire word as the shift key.[67] In symmetric encryption, both parties must have the same secret key or else know the code to decrypt the message.

Since the device uses only one key for both encryption and decryption, symmetric encryption may be vulnerable. Another drawback to symmetric encryption is that all parties must exchange the key (key sharing), to encrypt and decrypt data, and this is not always convenient. To solve this problem, another type of encryption, asymmetric encryption, creates a pair of keys, one public and one secret. The following is a simple example of symmetric encryption.

Bob and Alice need the same secret key for decryption and encryption. Bob and Alice must first exchange the secret key so that they can communicate privately. When Bob and Alice would like to store private information, they always store it in an encrypted form, using their secret key. If the server or cloud is compromised by someone else, no one can read their messages because the data is encrypted.

In other words, a cryptographic algorithm converts data into an unreadable form like *qJ4#j!UFO&Cps3#6@tc#Rb50*. Returning it to its original form by decrypting it requires a key or a password.

[67] Traina, P., M. Gramegna, Alessio Avella, A. Cavanna, D. Carpentras, I. P. Degiovanni, G. Brida, and M. Genovese. "Review on recent groundbreaking experiments on quantum communication with orthogonal states." *Quantum Matter* 2, no. 3 (2013): 153–166.

2^{32} = 4,294,967,296 (4.3 billion).
2^{64} = 18,446,744,073,709,551,616 (18.4 quintillion)
2^{128} = 340,282,366,920,938,463,463,374,607,431,768,211,456 (340 undecillion), 282 decillion, 366 nonillion, 920 octillion, 938 septillion.....).

FIGURE 6.22 The length of the AES encryption.

A symmetric key cipher can be Block Cipher or Stream Cipher. Block Cipher is used to encrypt blocks of data, frequently 64 or 128 bits. For example, the cipher may encrypt a 64-bit block and will return the blocks of cipher text in the same size.[68] This is illustrated in Figure 6.22. A Stream Cipher starts with a secret key, or "seed," and generates a keystream or stream of random or pseudorandom characters that combine the stream with the plain text to produce the ciphertext. The ciphertext typically uses the XOR function, which is a Boolean logic function that compares two input bits and generates one output bit. If the bits are the same, the outcome is 0. If the bits are different, the outcome is 1. In a stream cipher, the "transformation of each block of plaintext message is dependent not only on the current internal state of the cipher, but also on the block's location in the message."[69] In other words, the message is processed bit by bit and is therefore different than the block cipher. The key is a secret known only to the sender and the recipient. It is not sent with the ciphertext. The stream cipher provides high-speed streams of cryptographic algorithms, offering simplicity with low hardware and software complexity, and high cryptographic properties.[70] Some examples of symmetric encryption algorithms include:

- Data Encryption Standard (DES) (uses 56-bit key length)
- Advance Encryption Standards (AES) (uses 128-bit, 192-bit, or 256-bit keys)
- Blowfish (key lengths vary from 32 to 448-bits length)
- RC4 (Rivest Cipher 4) (key can be any length up to 2048 bits)
- RC5 (Rivest Cipher 5) key size up to 2040 bits)
- RC6 (Rivest Cipher 6) (key sizes of 128, 192, and 256 bits up to 2040 bits)
- 3DES (uses key length 56, 112, or 168 bits)

[68] Cruz, Bryan F., Keinaz N. Domingo, Froilan E. De Guzman, Jhinia B. Cotiangco, and Christopher B. Hilario. "Expanded 128-bit data encryption standard." *International Journal of Computer Science and Mobile Computing* 68, no. 8 (2017): 133–142.

[69] Kuznetsov, Olexandr, Mariya Lutsenko, and Dmytro Ivanenko. "Strumok stream cipher: Specification and basic properties." In *2016 Third International Scientific-Practical Conference Problems of Infocommunications Science and Technology (PIC S&T)*, pp. 59–62. IEEE, 2016.

[70] *Id.* at 69.

- IDEA (International Data Encryption Algorithm) (encrypts 64-bit blocks using 128-bit key) and ChaCha20 (Google has replaced RC4 with ChaCha20 stream cipher) algorithms. [71,72]
- Another stream cipher the Salsa20, which is related to ChaCha20, takes a 256-bit key. So far, researchers have not found any vulnerabilities in ChaCha20 algorithm.[73]

The key lengths indicate the number of bits in a solution used by a cryptographic algorithm. We can't cover all the different types of encryption algorithms, but we will look at the most common.

In 1970s, IBM developed its DES, which was the first major symmetric algorithm developed for computers in the United States.[74] The DES's input key is 64 bits long, and the actual key used is 56 bits.[75] This 56-bit key refers to the size of the key used to encrypt data. The 56-bit key can result in over 70 quadrillion possible combinations.

The AES is one of the most widely used symmetric encryption ciphers. It uses 128-bit, 192-bit, or 256-bit keys. Figure 6.22 demonstrates the length of its encryption.

If a computer tries 2^{40} (1,099,511,627,7760) solutions per day, it will take approximately about 848 sextillion years to brute-force the solution to a 128-bit key.

The IDEA was developed in 1991. It works with 64-bit block of data and uses a 128-bit key.[76] The cryptographic algorithm ChaCha20, a stream cipher that generates a one-time secret key, along with Poly1305, the authenticator, has been used in the TLS protocol designed to provide communications security, and with the open Secure Shell (SSH), a cryptographic network protocol used by Google to secure the connection between a client and a server. Figure 6.23 demonstrates symmetric encryption. As described earlier, the TLS/SSL protocols use both asymmetric encryption and symmetric encryption. During the handshake, the client and the server agree on a new

[71] Abdullaziz, Osamah Ibrahiem, Li-Chun Wang, and Yu-Jia Chen. "HiAuth: Hidden authentication for protecting software defined networks." *IEEE Transactions on Network and Service Management* 16, no. 2 (2019): 618–631.

[72] De Santis, Fabrizio, Andreas Schauer, and Georg Sigl. "ChaCha20-Poly1305 authenticated encryption for high-speed embedded IoT applications." In *Design, Automation & Test in Europe Conference & Exhibition (DATE), 2017*, pp. 692–697. IEEE, 2017.

[73] McLaren, Peter, William J. Buchanan, Gordon Russell, and Zhiyuan Tan. "Deriving ChaCha20 key streams from targeted memory analysis." *Journal of Information Security and Applications* 48 (2019): 102372.

[74] Coppersmith, Don. "The Data Encryption Standard (DES) and its strength against attacks." *IBM Journal of Research and Development* 38, no. 3 (1994): 243–250.

[75] Singh, Gurpreet. "A study of encryption algorithms (RSA, DES, 3DES and AES) for information security." *International Journal of Computer Applications* 67, no. 19 (2013).

[76] Abdullah, Dahlan, Robbi Rahim, Andysah Putera Utama Siahaan, Ananda Faridhatul Ulva, Zahratul Fitri, M. Malahayati, and H. Harun. "Super-encryption cryptography with IDEA and WAKE algorithm." *Journal of Physics: Conference Series* 1019, no. 1 (2018): 012039.

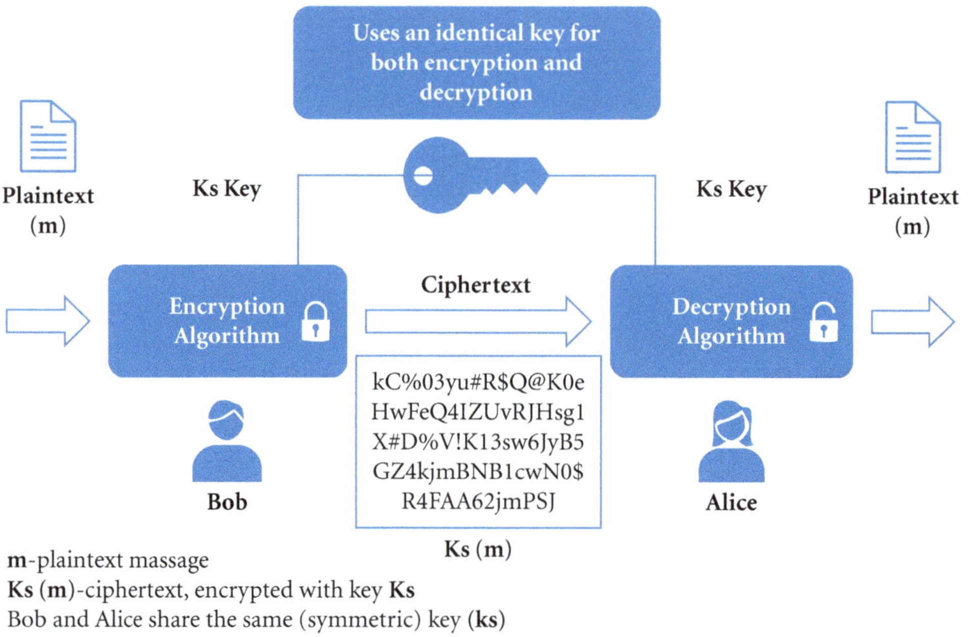

FIGURE 6.23 Symmetric encryption.

key to use for symmetric encryption for that session. Each new communication session will begin with a new and secure TLS handshake.

6.6.2 Asymmetric Encryption or Public Key Cryptography or Asymmetric Cryptography

We have used cipher systems or symmetric encryption for thousands of years. In 1976, a revolutionary paper by Whitfield Diffie and Martin Hellman titled "New Directions in Cryptography" proposed a major change.[77] The two researchers, along with Ralph Merkle, were the first to publish the concepts of public key cryptography, and they received U.S. patent 4200770 for it.[78]

This type of encryption uses two mathematically different but connected cryptographic keys. Instead of a single key as in symmetric encryption, the public key encryption system uses a pair of keys. One key is public, and the other is a private or secret key. The public key may be accessed by anyone, and the private key only by the owner.

The sender encrypts a message using the receiver's public key; however, the receiver can only decrypt this encrypted message with his or her private key. One key will not reveal the other.

---

[77] Diffie, Whitfield, and Martin Hellman. "New directions in cryptography." *IEEE transactions on Information Theory* 22, no. 6 (1976): 644–654.

[78] Hellman, Martin E., Bailey W. Diffie, Ralph C. Merkle. Cryptographic apparatus and method. Retrieved from https://cr.yp.to/patents/us/4200770/text

The keys are linked mathematically so that anything encrypted with key "A" can only be decrypted with key "B."

- A sender can use a recipient's public key to encrypt the message; then, only the recipient can decrypt using his or her private key.
- Or, the message can be encrypted using both the sender's private key and the recipient's public key.
- If the sender encrypts a message with his private key, it can be decrypted by anyone that has the matching public key.
- A recipient with the sender's public key can verify that it was the sender who created the message. This is called a digital signature. In other words, the sender and the recipient only need to exchange public keys, which can be done over open communication lines. Because the public key is available to everyone, other parties can use it to encrypt messages. As a result, every user must generate a pair of public and private keys. The mathematics behind the asymmetric encryption is extraordinarily complex and beyond the scope of this chapter.

The public and private keys are associated with each other via a mathematical relationship. It is not feasible to calculate the private key from the public key because the mathematical relationship cannot work backward. In comparison with symmetric encryption, asymmetric encryption is much slower but offers better security because of the two different keys. Figure 6.24 demonstrates the Asymmetric Encryption or Public Key Cryptography (PKC).

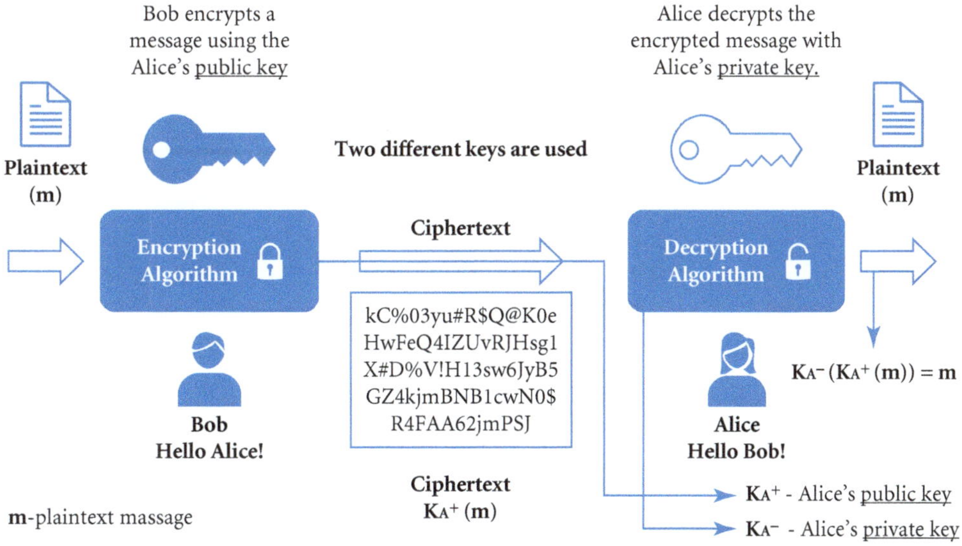

FIGURE 6.24 **The asymmetric encryption or public key cryptography (PKC).**

Bob and Alice have their own separate public keys, which they share with the world, including their friend Eve, and their own private keys which they keep to themselves. Bob encrypts a secret message (a love letter) with Alice's public key. Even though Eve knows that Bob used Alice's public key, she cannot decrypt the message and read the secret love letter. Only Alice, using her private key, can decrypt the message. Eve would need both keys to decrypt the encrypted data. The private key is kept safe on the user's computer. The public key, on the other hand, is exchanged on the Internet (Figure 6.25).

There are different public key encryption schemes that use widely differing mathematical algorithms from the ones used with Symmetric Cryptography. The following are mathematical algorithms used in asymmetric cryptography:

- The Rivest, Shamir, Adleman (RSA) Algorithm
- The Diffie Hellman Algorithm
- The ElGamal Cryptosystem
- The Elliptical Wave Theory Algorithm
- The Digital Signature Algorithm (DSA)
- The Elliptic-Curve cryptography (ECC)

Table 6.4 compares symmetric and asymmetric encryption.

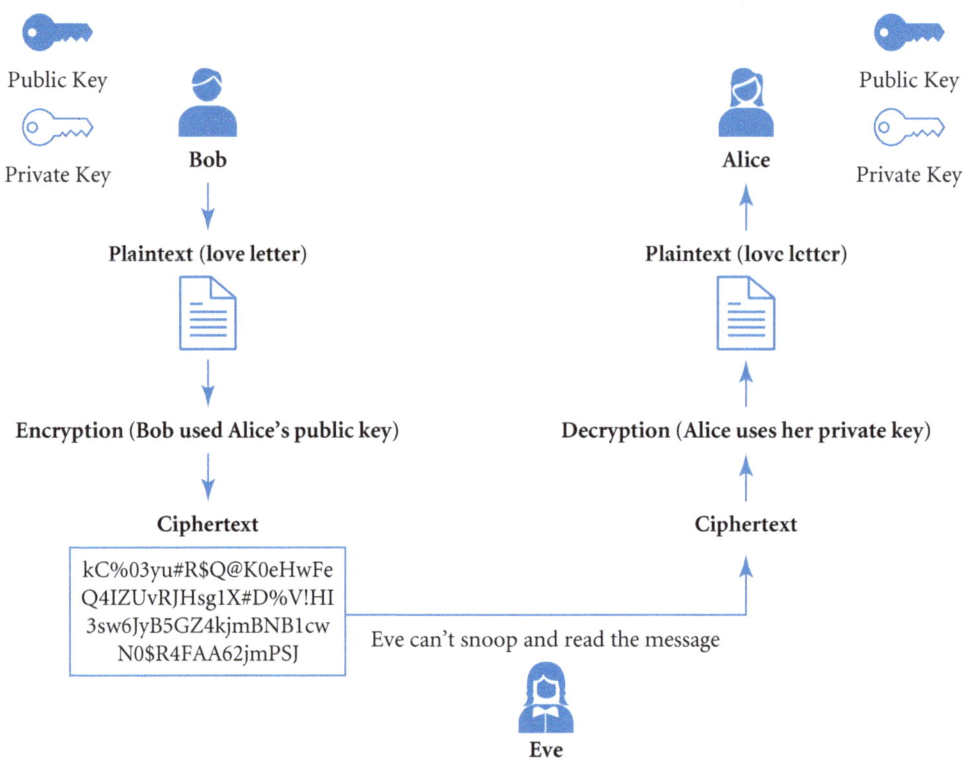

FIGURE 6.25 The asymmetric encryption Bob, Eve, and Alice.

TABLE 6.4 Symmetric vs Asymmetric Encryption

Symmetric Encryption	Asymmetric Encryption
Algorithms example • RC4 • AES • DES • 3DES ChaCha20	Algorithms examples • RSA • Diffie Hellman • ECC • El Gamal DSA
Complexity • Involves one key to encrypt and then decrypt the message. • Uses a simpler encryption method compared to asymmetric encryption because only one key is utilized. • Faster operation compared to asymmetric encryption.	Complexity • Uses two different mathematically connected cryptographic keys, the public key, and the private or secret key. • Sender and receiver do not share the secret key. The public key is known to all. Private key is known only to the receiver. • Uses a complex mathematical process. Slower operation but offers better security because two keys are used.
Usage examples • Banking sector (credit card information). • Data at rest (storage encryption). • SSL/TLS and SSH protocols use both symmetric/asymmetric encryptions and hashing algorithms. Pretty Good Privacy (PGP) uses asymmetric encryption data.	Usage examples • Digital signatures (provides authentication of a source sending a message). • Blockchain uses asymmetric encryption to authenticate the authorized transactions in cryptocurrency. • SSL/TLS, SSH, PGP protocols.

As a result of the strengths and weaknesses of symmetric and asymmetric encryption, they have been employed in different ways. *Typically, symmetric encryption safeguards the message, and asymmetric encryption is used to send the symmetric key securely.*

6.6.3 Digital Certificates and Certificate Authority

At this point we should mention that in cryptography, *public key certificates* are widely distributed by the *Certificate Authority (CA)*. The CA consists of trusted third parties that validate the identities of an entity by issuing *digital certificates* like email addresses, and websites, to individual users. Think of these digital certificates as passports or electronic ID cards that establish the identity of an ID holder. Essentially, the public key certificate certifies ownership of the public key.

To be able to generate a new digital certificate, the applicant or owner needs to generate a *Certificate Signing Request (CSR)*, along with a pair of private and public keys on the computing system where the certificate will be installed. This request provides information about the applicant. Then, the CA verifies the information, and issues, or "signs," the certificate, that now contains a public key and the identity of the applicant. The matching private key is kept secret by the user. In other words, the CA confirms that the public key enclosed in the certificate belongs to the owner of the computing system in the certificate.

In summary, digital certificate technology is based on public key cryptography, where every entity has two keys, public and private, that work only when they are used together and act as keys to a user's encryption scheme. A digital certificate links the public and private key with its owner and allows a user to verify to whom a certificate has been issued. Also, the Certificate Authority makes sure that the owner is not claiming a false identity. The user keeps the private key in a secure location and does not share it, while the public key is sent to every user with whom the user wants to communicate. The most common international framework for digital certificates is defined by the X.509[79] standard. The contents of an X.509 certificate include:

- Issuer's distinguished name
- Subject; contains owner's information
- Public key; contains the actual public key
- Certificate; serial number of the certificate
- Digital signature of the issuer
- Validity period; when issued and date of expiration

Some certificate providers are Comodo, IdenTrust, GeoTrus, Network Solutions, RapidSSL, Symantec, Thawte, DigiCert, GoDaddy, GlobalSign, and Trustwave.

The Certificate Authority can verify a bank's website. Therefore, when we connect to the website, we can be sure that it is the real website and not a fraud. The digital certificate for the bank's website is issued by the same Certificate Authority. A public key from the user's browser encrypts data, such as deposits and withdrawals, and sends them to the bank's website. The private key from the bank's website decrypts the data sent by the browser.

6.6.4 Hash Functions or Hashing Algorithms

The hash algorithm converts data or a message of any length to a fixed length.[80] We call this "hashing the data." The hash will be smaller than the data it represents.

---

[79] ITU Telecommunication Standardization. X.509: Information technology—Open Systems Interconnection—The Directory: Public-key and attribute certificate frameworks. Retrieved from https://www.itu.int/rec/T-REC-X.509

[80] Dang, Quynh. *Recommendation for applications using approved hash algorithms.* U.S. Department of Commerce, National Institute of Standards and Technology, 2008.

The purpose of hash functions is data integrity. A hash algorithm (H) accepts a variable length of data (M) as input and produces a fixed-length output hash value (h). h = H(M). When we change any bit or bits of (M) this results in a change to the hash code.[81]

To be able to find the solution to a hash message, one must guess it by trying a brute-force attack, where the attacker inputs random passwords to see if they match, or by use of a rainbow table of matched hashes.[82] In other words, the hash is an encryption process that converts plain input text to encrypted hash value using a mathematical algorithm. Instead of storing a password in plain text, computers generate and store passwords using hash functions.

Bob creates a hash algorithm into an authentication tag. Alice runs the same computation and checks its result against the tag. If they match, the message is authenticated, if not the packet is discarded.

In a university, each student is assigned a unique number that can be used to retrieve information. That number may be kept safe by hashing it. Hashing is used for the authentication of passwords, digital signatures, which authenticate the identity of the sender and ensure message integrity, Message Authentication Codes (MAC), tags attached to confirm the authenticity of a message, and biometrics. For example, a typical password in a computer might be stored as "0d7006cd055e94cf614587e1d."

The hash function is easy to compute for any given message, but it is impossible to then calculate the original input. In contrast to cryptography, a hash algorithm is a one-way mechanism. It is not reversible.

Figure 6.26 demonstrates a hash function that takes a variable-length input and generates a fixed-length output. Figure 6.27a and b shows the difference between encryption and hashing algorithm.

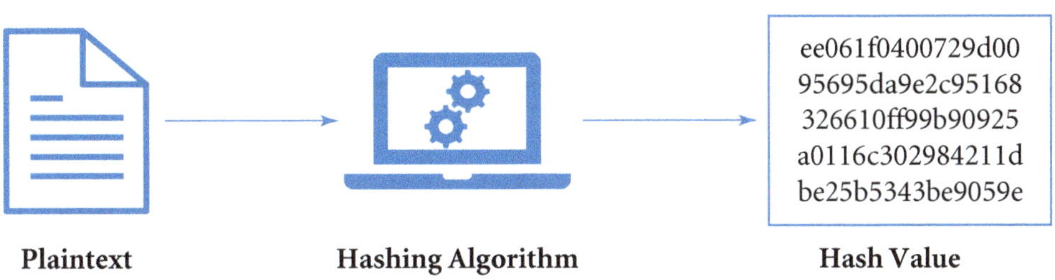

FIGURE 6.26 The hashing algorithm.

[81] Stallings, William, Lawrie Brown, Michael D. Bauer, and Arup Kumar Bhattacharjee. *Computer security: Principles and practice*. Pearson Education, 2012.

[82] Harnik, Danny, Joe Kilian, Moni Naor, Omer Reingold, and Alon Rosen. "On robust combiners for oblivious transfer and other primitives." In *Annual International Conference on the Theory and Applications of Cryptographic Techniques*, pp. 96–113. Springer, 2005.

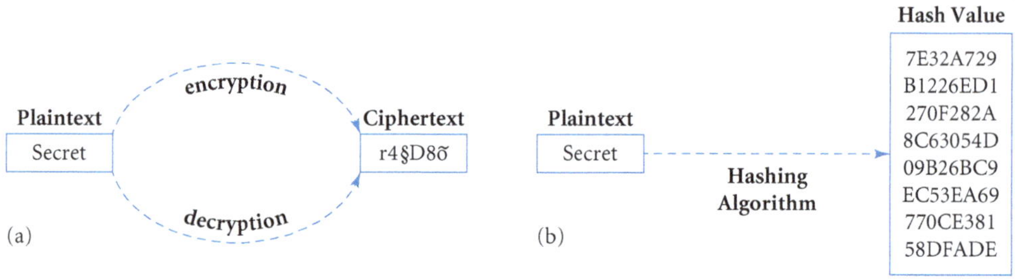

FIGURE 6.27A AND B The difference between encryption and hashing algorithm.

What Does "Salting" a Hashtag Mean?

In hashing, the term "Salt" describes a unique use of random characters added to a one-way function. Salting uses the additional input to safeguard password hashes against dictionary attacks. A new salt is randomly generated for each password and increases the computational power of hashed passwords. In other words, the Salt and the password are concatenated and processed, making a password hash output unique and much less vulnerable to attack. For example, if Bob and Alice use the same password, such as *123456*, both would share the same hash. Consequently, the hacker can predict the password that maps to that hash value by using the dictionary and brute-force attacks. If the password is known, the hacker can access all the accounts that use the hash. With Salt added before the hashing process, the passwords are unique and can better safeguard passwords in storage.

- If we take the most common password, *123456*, by applying the Secure Hash Algorithm (SHA-256),[83] the password will be stored as b59936bb842a7bccc54004091069467d78b85b7372e0f843c2b346c186daa14
- When Salt is added *A1ndQngn2m3* to the password *123456*, and we hash it then, the salted input becomes :*123456A1ndQngn2m3*. As a result, the hash algorithm will be something like this 70c1e0b744121ea8197422639cfee796282696f1b1070165186b1e446abada94

The length of the hash depends on the hashing algorithm. Some common hashing algorithms include:

- *Message Digest Algorithm 5 (MD5)* was introduced in 1992 and creates 128-bit outputs. The MD5 algorithm has been shown to have weaknesses which make it easy to break. Although a hash function is designed to work only in one direction, MD5 is easy to reverse.[84]

---

[83] SHA-256 hash calculator. Retrieved from https://xorbin.com/tools/sha256-hash-calculator

[84] Cilardo, Alessandro, and Nicola Mazzocca. "Exploiting vulnerabilities in cryptographic hash functions based on reconfigurable hardware." *IEEE Transactions on Information Forensics and Security* 8, no. 5 (2013): 810–820.

- *Secure Hash Algorithm (SHA)* family
  - SHA-1 was designed by the National Security Agency (NSA) in 1993 and creates 160-bit hash values.
  - SHA-2 creates hash values with 224-bit, 256-bit, 384-bit, or 512-bits. It was designed by the NSA in 2001 and is recommended for secure hashing.[85,86] The SHA-2 hash algorithm is an essential part of creating a digital signature.
  - SHA-3 is the latest version of SHA family and was developed by the NSA in 2012. It is designed to protect against brute-force attacks.[87]

6.7 Conclusion

As more smart devices connect to the Internet, cybercrime will continue to evolve transnationally. The threats posed by the different forms of cybercrime will increasingly dominate our lives. As we create barriers to their crimes, hackers will continue to become more sophisticated and will always develop new techniques and tools.

Lack of information security, knowledge, and training lead to errors in the mishandling of sensitive data and hacking attacks. Electronic health records (EHRs) and sensitive payment information from credit cards continue to be used for fraud or sold on the Dark Web for profit. Our expectations of privacy continue to suffer.

But then, for any type of cyberattack, there is, hopefully, a defense that we must learn and use.

So far, we humans have been the weakest link in cybersecurity. With IoT and other devices proliferating, the future of cybersecurity relies on a combination of machine learning, artificial intelligence (AI), and savvy people to detect security threats and malicious activities and secure computing devices and networks. Ultimately, understanding and influencing human behavior will help create a better approach to cybersecurity.

---

[85] Guo, Jian, San Ling, Christian Rechberger, and Huaxiong Wang. "Advanced meet-in-the-middle preimage attacks: First results on full Tiger, and improved results on MD4 and SHA-2." In *International Conference on the Theory and Application of Cryptology and Information Security*, pp. 56–75. Springer, 2010.

[86] Glabb, Ryan, Laurent Imbert, Graham Jullien, Arnaud Tisserand, and Nicolas Veyrat-Charvillon. "Multi-mode operator for SHA-2 hash functions." *Journal of Systems Architecture* 53, no. 2–3 (2007): 127–138.

[87] Kelsey, John, Shu-jen Chang, and Ray Perlner. *SHA-3 derived functions: cSHAKE, KMAC, TupleHash, and ParallelHash*. No. NIST Special Publication (SP) 800-185 (Draft). National Institute of Standards and Technology, 2016.

6.8 Key Words

Access Control
Active Attacks
Advanced Encryption Standards (AES)
Adware
Antivirus Software
Application Security
Authorization
Authentication
Asymmetric Encryption
Behavioral Analytics
Biometrics
Caesar cipher
CIA Triad Model
Cloud Security
Crime-as-a-Service (CaaS)
Cryptography
Confidentiality
Cybersecurity
Cyberwarfare
Data Breach
Demilitarized Zone (DMZ)
Denial of service (DoS)
Digital Certificates and Certificate Authority (CA)
Exploit
Firewall
FIPS 199
Hacker
Hash Functions
Integrity
Information Security
Intrusion Detection System (IDS)
Intrusion Prevention System (IPS)
Malware
Network Security
Passive Attacks
Phishing
Protocols
Security Audit
Security Threat
Software-as-a-Service (SaaS)
Spam
Spoofing
SQL Injection
Steganography
Symmetric Encryption
Virtual Private Network (VPN)
Vulnerability
Wi-Fi Hacking

Chapter 7

Internet of Things (IoTs)

Objectives

After completing this chapter, the student will be able to:

- Understand the Internet of Things (IoTs) and the four different lead stages
- Understand real-world applications
- Understand industrial IoT and its relation to manufacturing
- Illustrate IoT architecture
- Explain different types of IoT protocols and standards
- Describe the IoT ecosystem—bandwidth, interoperability, power usage, and range
- Understand the importance of security in IoT devices

The Neuwirth family is returning from a weekend visiting relatives in a neighboring state. As they reach a point about an hour from home, they want to make the house ready for their arrival. Using their phone, they set the thermostat in the downstairs and bedrooms to 70 degrees; turn on the lights in the family room and kitchen; notify their pet sitter that they will be stopping by to pick up Roddy, their golden retriever; and turn on the oven, setting it to 350 degrees so they can pop in a prepared casserole as soon as they arrive.

Sara Taffley, a second grader, has had Type 1 diabetes since the age of 3. She wears an insulin delivery pump to make sure that her glucose level does not go

DOI: 10.4324/9780429318726-7

out of bounds. At 10 o'clock one morning, her mother receives an alert on her smartphone that Sara's glucose has exceeded 200 mg/dl and she has just received 30 units of insulin to bring it down. Sara's pediatrician has received the same alert, as has the nurse's office in her school. Sara's mother leaves work and heads to Sara's school. By the time she arrives, Sara is resting comfortably in the nurse's office, and her doctor has already checked in with the school. Sara's glucose is now 99 mg/dl, a normal reading.

7.1 The Internet of Things—An Introduction

Like the *Industrial Revolution*, which began around 1760[1] and led to the rapid transformation of our society, culture, and economy, the Internet has undoubtedly transformed our lives. Along with the Internet, our ability to transmit and store data has also developed with astonishing speed. As wireless technologies evolve, inexpensive data storage such as cloud computing has enabled the Internet of Things (IoTs) to flourish. IoTs are an important part of today's Internet, just as the steam engine, mass production, railroad, and telegraphy typify the Industrial Revolution.

The phrase "Internet of Things" was coined by Kevin Ashton in 1999.[2] Like most inventions, it began with a new solution to an old problem. Ashton was assigned to help launch a cosmetics line. When he couldn't locate a specific color of lipstick in stock, he came up with the idea of using a new technology called radio-frequency identification (RFID), to tag each tube of lipstick and communicate with a radio receiver to keep track of exactly where it was.[3]

A few years later, a book[4] by Neil Gershenfeld, *When Things Start to Think*, jumpstarted the development and use of IoTs.

Modern computing began after World War II when the aftermath of the war and the space program of the 1960s brought considerable changes to computing technologies. Despite their massive costs, computers were expected to have long-term benefits for governments and big corporations. Their early adoption can be considered the *first stage* of modern computing. The *second stage* followed the introduction of microcomputers and the development of the personal computer (PC) in the early 1980s.

Over time, the cost of computers fell and became affordable for consumers. As computers became smaller and lighter, the transition to laptops and

---

1 Deane, Phyllis M., and Phyllis M. Deane. *The first industrial revolution*. Cambridge University Press, 1979.

2 Ashton, Kevin. "That 'internet of things' thing." *RFID Journal* 22, no. 7 (2009): 97–114.

3 Dudhe, P. V., N. V. Kadam, R. M. Hushangabade, and M. S. Deshmukh. "Internet of Things (IoT): An overview and its applications." In *2017 International Conference on Energy, Communication, Data Analytics and Soft Computing (ICECDS)*, pp. 2650–2653. IEEE, 2017.

4 Gershenfeld, Neil A., and Neil Gershenfeld. *When things start to think*. Macmillan, 2000.

ultimately to mobile devices began. This is considered the *third stage*. The *fourth stage* is the gradual evolution of IoTs and the steady trend toward Internet-connected devices. This stage includes not only the development of IoTs but the computerization of everything in our lives (Figure 7.1).

The recent advances in wireless communications, 5G mobile broadband and the architectural integration of cloud computing, have led to a greater proliferation of IoT devices. Previous researchers have defined IoTs in several ways; there is no concise agreement on a definition.[5,6]

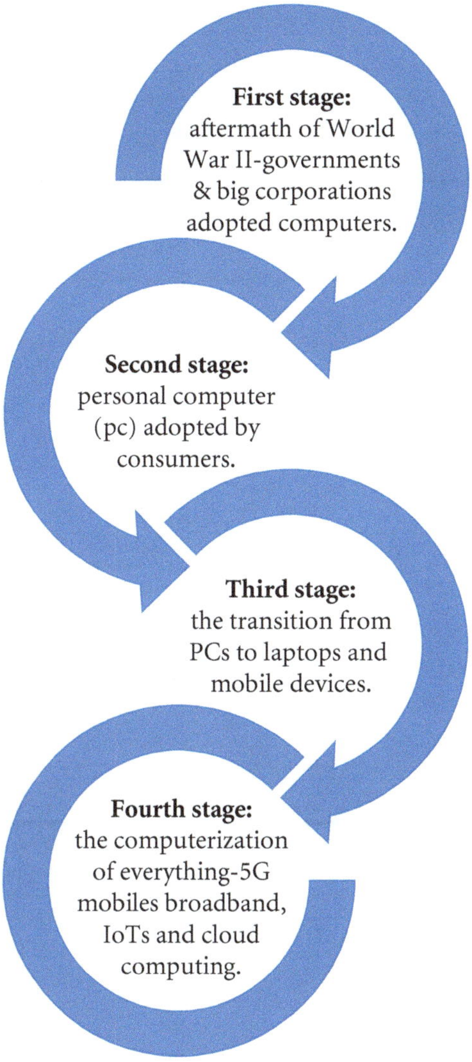

FIGURE 7.1 The four stages of modern computing adoption.

[5] Vermesan, Ovidiu, Peter Friess, Patrick Guillemin, Sergio Gusmeroli, Harald Sundmaeker, Alessandro Bassi, Ignacio Soler Jubert, et al. "Internet of things strategic research roadmap." *Internet of Things—Global Technological and Societal Trends* 1, no. 2011 (2011): 9–52.

[6] Peña-López, Ismael. "ITU Internet report 2005: the internet of things" (2005).

We will define the *Internet of Things* as *intelligent network-connected devices or systems, embedded in the physical environment, to improve the lives of people with minimal or no human intervention.*

IoTs connect the physical world and the digital or virtual world to enhance the quality of life for humans with minimal or no human intervention.

These devices or systems cleverly integrate networking, Information and Communications Technology (ICT), machine learning, edge, fog and cloud computing, and the delivery of products and services. IoTs provide efficiency, enhanced safety, and convenience for humans, completing tasks remotely and with little or no effort. The next generation of mobile networks, 5G, will enable the creation of a new wave of IoTs with higher bandwidth, greater reliability, and very high speed (up to 10 Gbps), which translates to low latency (the time needed for data to travel between two points). As IoTs need to communicate, 5G mobile broadband will offer an enormous amount of new bandwidth connection and will be able to support a vast diversity of devices and services. According to the tech analyst company IDC, the total number of connected IoT devices will be 41.6 billion by 2025 and will generate 79.4 zettabytes (ZB) of data.[7] According to the McKinsey Global Institute, IoTs will potentially have an economic impact of $3.9 trillion to $11.1 trillion a year by 2025.[8]

IoTs connect the physical with the digital world. Any tangible and visible physical object can be converted into an IoT device by connecting the device to the Internet and making it able to store, process, and transmit information. Additionally, the device must be able to communicate with the network independently or be controlled remotely.

Examples of IoT devices include lightbulbs that can be controlled by a phone app, motion sensors, smart thermostats, smart locks, smart light switches, smoke alarms, doorbells, virtual assistants, and speakers like Amazon Echo and Google Home. Furthermore, an IoT can be installed in a child's toy. Medical IoTs and implants monitor and control conditions such as diabetes, hearing loss, and heart rate. IoTs can be embedded in airplanes, collecting and transmitting data about the engine's operation, airframes, and other aspects of operations.

---

[7] International Data Corporation (IDC). "The growth in connected IoT devices is expected to generate 79.4ZB of data in 2025, according to a new IDC forecast." Retrieved from https://www.idc.com/getdoc.jsp?containerId=prUS45213219 (Accessed January 18, 2019).

[8] Manyika, James, Michael Chui, Peter Bisson, Jonathan Woetzel, Richard Dobbs, Jacques Bughin, and Dan Aharon, "Unlocking the potential of the Internet of Things," McKinsey Global Institute, June 2015 report. Retrieved from https://www.mckinsey.com/business-functions/mckinsey-digital/our-insights/the-internet-of-things-the-value-of-digitizing-the-physical-world

However, it is critically important to understand that while IoT devices have numerous benefits, they also pose security concerns, and since they are connected to the Internet they can be hacked and misused.

This chapter outlines IoT applications, architecture, protocols, and standards, as well as bandwidth, interoperability, range, and security.

7.2 A Summary of IoT Applications

The advantages of IoTs, along with the data they produce, have significantly impacted our lives. A physician thousands of miles away can monitor a patient's vital organs, or a city can monitor its trash collection and assess the reliability of its roads and bridges. The possibilities are endless.

Figure 7.2 summarizes IoT applications in our lives.

7.2.1 Automotive Sector

In the automotive industry, sensors collect enormous amounts of data that are processed, conceptualized into a visual format and streamed to the cloud. The data can be accessed from any device via the Internet. These sensory data are vital components of the automotive IoT environment. For

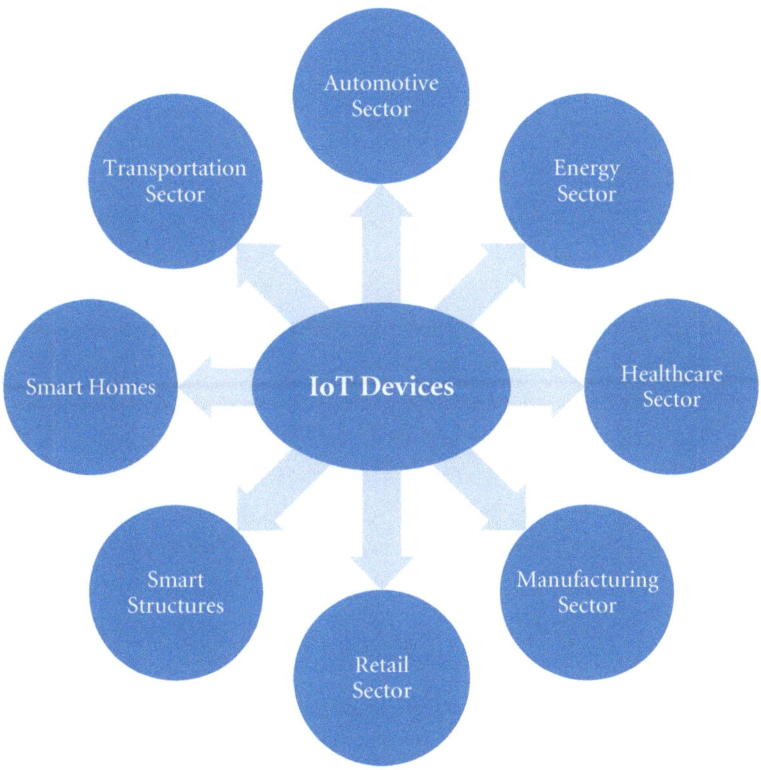

FIGURE 7.2 The range of IoT applications.

example, an automotive fleet operator managing 25 or more vehicles for government or business can easily use these data to monitor parameters like driver behavior, vehicle maintenance, on-board diagnostics, fuel monitoring, and delivery delays. In addition, many vehicles we drive feature Internet connectivity. These connected vehicles can share their Internet access with a range of devices within and outside the vehicle.

The Vehicular ad hoc Network (VANET) helps vehicles communicate with each other and their surrounding environment via wireless connectivity. Communication paths include vehicle-to-vehicle (V2V), vehicle-to-infrastructure (V2I), vehicle-to-sensor on-board (V2S), and vehicle-to-Internet (V2I).[9,10]

These features are evolving rapidly. Many new vehicles come with software platforms that offer mobile devices integration, in-car voice assistants, navigation systems, remote-control parking features, or sensors that allow parents to monitor and control teen drivers.

Eventually, the increase of IoT devices in the automotive industry will lead to the autonomous vehicle, the car that drives itself. Since a range of sensors and algorithms will be needed to ensure the motorist's safety, developing these applications is currently the greatest challenge to the auto industry. We are scratching only the surface of how we interact with our vehicles.

7.2.2 Energy Sector

The energy sector is also undergoing a massive transformation as it becomes more energy efficient. IoT-enabled sensors and devices provide intelligence and detailed data analytics to energy companies and consumers. They track smart energy from generation to transmission and distribution. Smart devices monitor and manage equipment, measure vibration and temperature, monitor wear, and improve maintenance schedules. All these functions are performed remotely, without human intervention, and significantly improve worker safety, reduce costs, and enable virtual troubleshooting before equipment fails.

With the installation of smart meters and smart thermostats consumers become more informed about their energy consumption. A consumer can remotely control a thermostat via a phone app. A smart meter provides accurate energy bills, and other smart devices measure the power consumption of each appliance and device.

Furthermore, IoT devices can transform the energy grid into a smart grid by helping to distribute changes in electricity supply, demand, and

---

[9] Lu, Ning, Nan Cheng, Ning Zhang, Xuemin Shen, and Jon W. Mark. "Connected vehicles: Solutions and challenges." *IEEE Internet of Things Journal* 1, no. 4 (2014): 289–299.

[10] Obaidat, Muath, Matluba Khodjaeva, Jennifer Holst, and Mohamed Ben Zid. "Security and privacy challenges in vehicular ad hoc networks." *Connected vehicles in the Internet of things*, pp. 223–251. Springer, 2020.

distribution. Thanks to IoTs, the energy industry is smarter, more efficient, and more reliable.

7.2.3 Healthcare Sector

In the healthcare sector, IoT devices have been revolutionizing the diagnosis, treatment, and management of patient care. These devices open up a world of possibilities for telemedicine and education paradigms for patients, providing data to help patients and healthcare professionals gain a deeper understanding of the human body. In addition, the devices have been shown to improve outcomes and reduce costs.[11] Remote monitoring can reduce the number of days patients stay in hospitals and empower their engagement and interaction with healthcare providers. One of the most important aspects of IoT devices is the collection and analysis of real-time medical data on a massive scale and over a broad range of issues. These analytics provide additional understanding into symptoms, identify trends, and potentially improve care, save lives, and lower costs related to health care.

Examples of current IoT healthcare devices include automated insulin delivery pumps[12] that monitor a patient's blood glucose levels and regulate the amount of insulin delivered, ingestible sensors that monitor a patient's medication intake, and wearable smart asthma monitors that sense oncoming asthma attacks by monitoring vital signs.

In addition to remote patient monitoring devices, hospital medical equipment is becoming smarter. Examples include defibrillators, electrocardiograms (EKG or ECG), glucose monitoring, smart hospital beds that contain sensors and automatically adjust pressure and can provide patient monitoring, smart thermometers, ultrasound technology, nebulizers, and other monitoring equipment. One example is diabetic management system for children, where a sensor collects data from the child's body (diet, insulin intake, physical activity) and then transmits the data to a Web-centric disease management hub for further instructions or advice from a medical professional.[13] Another example of IoTs in healthcare is a bio-fluid ana-

[11] Alam, Muhammad Mahtab, Hassan Malik, Muhidul Islam Khan, Tamas Pardy, Alar Kuusik, and Yannick Le Moullec. "A survey on the roles of communication technologies in IoT-based personalized healthcare applications." *IEEE Access* 6 (2018): 36611–36631.

[12] Obaidat, M., S. O., J. Holst, A. Al H., J. B, "A Comprehensive and systematic survey on the Internet of things: Security and privacy challenges, security frameworks, enabling technologies, threats, vulnerabilities and countermeasures", *Computers—IoT: Security, Privacy and Best Practices*. Multidisciplinary Digital Publishing Institute (MDPI)-Basel, Switzerland. 2020/5/30. Obaidat, Muath A., Suhaib Obeidat, Jennifer Holst, Abdullah Al Hayajneh, and Joseph Brown. "A Comprehensive and Systematic Survey on the Internet of Things: Security and Privacy Challenges, Security Frameworks, Enabling Technologies, Threats, Vulnerabilities and Countermeasures." *Computers* 9, no. 2 (2020): 44.

[13] Al-Taee, Majid A., Waleed Al-Nuaimy, Zahra J. Muhsin, and Ali Al-Ataby. ""Robot assistant in management of diabetes in children based on the Internet of things." *IEEE Internet of Things Journal* 4, no. 2 (2016): 437–445.

lyzer known as the LoRa/Bluetooth-enabled Electronic Reader. This system uses an app and disposable test "key" that detects urinary tract infections through automated analysis of urine samples. This system enables patients to receive remote monitoring and care outside a medical facility.[14]

While these devices can make our lives better, they are not without challenges. Their enormous bandwidth consumption, along with concerns about data security of sensitive patient information, is concerning.

Nevertheless, we will continue to witness these intelligent devices connecting to the Internet, analyzing data in real time, and extracting meaningful information that will improve healthcare delivery and disease control around the world.

7.2.4 Manufacturing Sector

In the manufacturing sector, IoT devices add intelligence to industrial manufacturing and are poised to transform equipment, processing, and management. Industrial IoT devices, along with 5G mobile broadband, will improve productivity and product quality and will reduce the maintenance of manufacturing technologies through real-time data analytics. This developing trend toward automation, smart factories, real-time data analysis, and network connectivity is called the *Fourth Industrial Revolution or Industry 4.0.*[15,16]

Historically, near the end of the 18th century, the *First Industrial Revolution* was characterized by the steam engine, powered by coal. The *Second Industrial Revolution* began in the late 19th century with the discovery of oil, and early innovations in manufacturing, such as Henry Ford's assembly line for the mass production of automobiles, and the work of Frederick Winslow Taylor, the father of scientific management.[17] The *Third Industrial Revolution* began when manufacturing data moved from analog and mechanical to digital in the 1970s. The changes that Internet computers brought to automation bore a resemblance to the scale of those brought about by steam engine technology.[18]

As we continue to move into the 21st century, interconnected IoT devices have been transforming the traditional manufacturing landscape with

[14] Catherwood, Philip A., David Steele, Mike Little, Stephen Mccomb, and James McLaughlin. "A community-based IoT personalized wireless healthcare solution trial." *IEEE Journal of Translational Engineering in Health and Medicine* 6 (2018): 1–13.

[15] Lu, Yang. "Industry 4.0: A survey on technologies, applications and open research issues." *Journal of Industrial Information Integration* 6 (2017): 1–10.

[16] Wollschlaeger, Martin, Thilo Sauter, and Juergen Jasperneite. "The future of industrial communication: Automation networks in the era of the internet of things and industry 4.0." *IEEE Industrial Electronics Magazine* 11, no. 1 (2017): 17–27.

[17] Kanigel, Robert. "The one best way: Frederick Winslow Taylor and the enigma of efficiency." *MIT Press Books* 1 (2005).

[18] Morrar, Rabeh, Husam Arman, and Saeed Mousa. "The fourth industrial revolution (Industry 4.0): A social innovation perspective." *Technology Innovation Management Review* 7, no. 11 (2017): 12–20.

real-time connectivity, replacing traditional manufacturing processes. Examples include 3D printers, which can print just about anything, smart home devices, autonomous vehicles, logistics management, automation, and robotics machinery.

Industry 4.0 has transformed the world's economic outlook and will continue to innovate and effect change. According to Rifkin (2014) the "zero marginal cost society," along with real-time connectivity, will have a major impact on the current economic system as we know it, and IoT devices are spearheading this endeavor[19] (Figure 7.3).

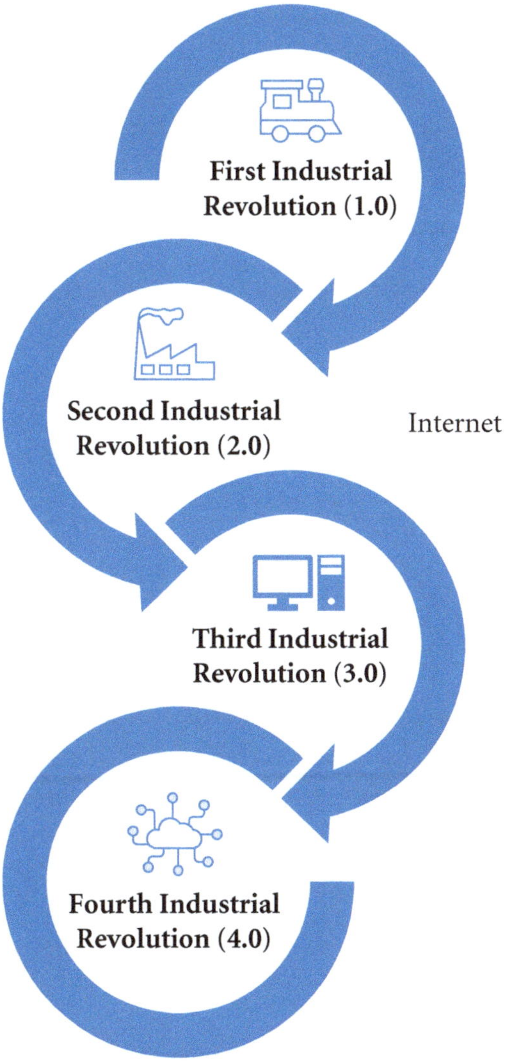

FIGURE 7.3 The four phases of the industrial revolution.

[19] Rifkin, Jeremy. *The zero marginal cost society: The internet of things, the collaborative commons, and the eclipse of capitalism*. St. Martin's Press, 2014.

Thus, industrial IoT devices embedded within cloud-based machine learning capabilities will improve decision making and productivity and will enable the further development of smart products and smart services.

7.2.5 Retail Sector

In the retail sector, IoT devices will help customers make more informed decisions and will help retailers redefine the customer experience. An example of a smart store is *Amazon Go*, in which shopping occurs without the need to stop and check out with a cashier. Other examples include the ability to search for products, compare prices, provide feedback, and receive coupons for a relevant product while customers are still in the store. The smart store uses these technologies to improve the customer experience by understanding their shopping behavior and offering a level of personalized marketing.

Retailers, on the other hand, will be able to grow sales by obtaining and analyzing real-time customer data and identifying each customer's gender, age, education level, eating behavior, habits, and taste preferences. These retailers will be able to identify loyal customers, predict their behavior, and deliver the products and services they desire. They will use heatmap analysis to track customers' actual time spent in specific locations of the store. In addition, stores will monitor inventory levels in real time by using RFID and shelf-sensors to track inventory levels and monitor maintenance equipment before problems arise.[20]

IoT algorithms, not people, will calculate and influence every stage of the customer's shopping experience in the smart store of the future.

7.2.6 Smart Structures (Buildings, Roads, and Bridges Sector)

Any structure that communicates wirelessly, or one that is wired and sends and receives autonomous responses, is considered a smart structure. IoT devices that collect data in smart structures are proliferating.[21] These devices transmit and receive data between systems to provide air conditioning and heating temperature controls. They can switch lights on or off and have security controls like motion detection and can show whether people are

[20] Khodjaeva, Matluba, Muath Obaidat, and Douglas Salane. "Mitigating threats and vulnerabilities of RFID in IoT through outsourcing computations for public key cryptography." In *Security, privacy and trust in the IoT environment*, pp. 39-60. Springer, Cham, 2019.

[21] Zhang, Xiangyu, Rajendra Adhikari, Manisa Pipattanasomporn, Murat Kuzlu, and Saifur Rahman. "Deploying IoT devices to make buildings smart: Performance evaluation and deployment experience." In *2016 IEEE 3rd World Forum on Internet of Things (WF-IoT)*, pp. 530–535. IEEE, 2016.

present or absent. Sensors constantly collect data in real time to inform effective decision making. IoT devices, mobile broadband, and the Internet have transformed the physical world into an immense information system. As technology becomes less expensive, IoT devices have become the solution to many human problems. Today, urban challenges can be addressed by designing a smart city infrastructure. For example, in the U.K., cities like Birmingham, Bristol, Manchester, Milton Keynes, and Peterborough boast smart urban developments, featuring digital infrastructure that demonstrates evolving control of issues, monitoring traffic flow and parking, watching pedestrian crossings, and providing energy savings and intelligent street lighting.[22]

The primary motivation behind these smart building innovations is to reduce costs and improve sustainability and energy efficiency.

In the field of structural design technology, including roads, bridges, and tunnels, IoT devices serve as an early detection system. Sensors monitor structural cracks, vibrations, temperature, and acceleration and, when applied to machine learning models, can predict defects or quality deviations, ultimately saving lives.

7.2.7 Smart Homes

Smart home automation, or the smart home ecosystem, refers to all Internet-connected and integrated devices in our homes, such as appliances, smart light bulbs and switches, smart climate control systems, entertainment systems, and security systems like smart door locks, motion detectors, and security cameras. All these devices can be controlled through one home automation system, offered by tech companies such as Amazon, Apple, Google, and Logitech.

Smart home IoT devices can be remotely monitored anytime and from anywhere using the home network and a voice or remote-control command or by an IoT-enabled application from any computing device. The development of easy-to-use apps along with the success of smartphones and tablets has helped to extend the use of IoT devices throughout the world. If smartphones and tablets are constantly connected to the Internet, then IoT devices may always be controlled and monitored. All current home electronic devices have built-in IoT-enabled technology, and so will those of the future, as this trend is still at the beginning of its journey within *Industry 4.0*.

[22] Caird, Sally P., and Stephen H. Hallett. "Towards evaluation design for smart city development." *Journal of Urban Design* 24, no. 2 (2019): 188–209.

7.2.8 Transportation Sector

One of the basic functions of daily living in both urban and rural environments is transportation. We all try to get from point A to point B faster, safer, and cheaper. The transportation sector consists of many different types of businesses that transport people and goods. Examples include airlines, railroads, marine, freight, public transportation, and the transportation infrastructure. IoT devices provide solutions to their challenges through systems integration and centralized data gathering systems. Hence, this underlying technology creates a smart environment that allows people and business to use data in meaningful ways such as:

- Improved travel with better communication
- Enhanced safety, including sensors to maintain train speeds, the condition of aircraft parts, and roadway safety for trucks and cars
- Environmental effects to reduce energy use, congestion control, including traffic patterns, control of traffic lights, monitoring CO_2 emissions, location and speed control applications on buses and taxis, streetlights that automatically adjust to changing light conditions, pothole location, and communication of accurate weather conditions
- Vehicle-tracking systems, enabling monitoring with GPS tracking and analysis, provision of fleet information, including maintenance, advanced engine diagnostics, the ability to reduce fuel costs and promote better fuel efficiency, and information and security about a vehicle's exact location.
- For maritime applications, IoT devices help by streamlining data operations across a fleet, tracking individual vessels, monitoring equipment and machinery in real time, forecasting maintenance needs, improving planning, reduction of fuel consumption, and safeguarding passengers and crews

Industry 4.0 is emerging in almost every conceivable industry or sector as each industry incorporates IoT devices to keep pace with competitors and future-proof the business. The underlying technology offers major advantages in automation, real-time data collection, and analysis but comes with security risks and challenges. As IoT devices continue to grow, security risks and privacy issues continue to loom.

7.3 IoT Components, Data Processing Architectures, and Protocols

7.3.1 Basic Components and Data Processing

IoT devices consist of a collection of various technologies that work together seamlessly. Basic IoT hardware includes a *sensor*, an *actuator*, a *transceiver*, and a *power supply*.[23] New nanotechnology-enabled sensors convert physical characteristics into electrical signals. IoT devices are embedded with software and essential IoT hardware.

- The sensor captures physical characteristics. It first processes them into electrical signals and then interprets them to provide readable information. An excellent example is the microphone. The microphone converts air vibrations (sound waves) into electrical energy (audio signals).[24] The most commonly used sensors measure acceleration, rotational motion (gyroscope), gas, thermal radiation, light detection, moisture, optical, pressure, proximity, smoke, and temperature. 
- An actuator converts electrical signals into action. An actuator turns an electric signal into a motion, for example turning a furnace on or off. 
- A processor processes and stores data within an application, on a server or in the cloud. 
- A wireless communication transceiver provides communication through wireless links, allowing people to monitor or configure IoT devices and enabling interaction between the owner and the device. 
- A power supply may be either alternating current (AC) or direct current (DC). All IoTs require power. The power supply must be reliable, affordable, efficient, and space-saving. 

The sensors and actuators are the devices that interact with the physical world. A sensor wirelessly collects and transmits data to the control center after processing. In general, the control center decides, based on the software, to send a command to an actuator in response to the data collected. Data processing and storage can be performed on the edge of the network, in the cloud servers or on the device itself. Cloud computing provides centralization of computing resources, including storage, easy access to data and cost savings. Data processing capability is limited by the resources

[23] Sethi, Pallavi, and Smruti R. Sarangi. "Internet of things: architectures, protocols, and applications." *Journal of Electrical and Computer Engineering* 2017 (2017).

[24] Sultana, Ayesha, Md Mehebub Alam, Sujoy Kumar Ghosh, Tapas Ranjan Middya, and Dipankar Mandal. "Energy harvesting and self-powered microphone application on multifunctional inorganic-organic hybrid nanogenerator." *Energy* 166 (2019): 963–971.

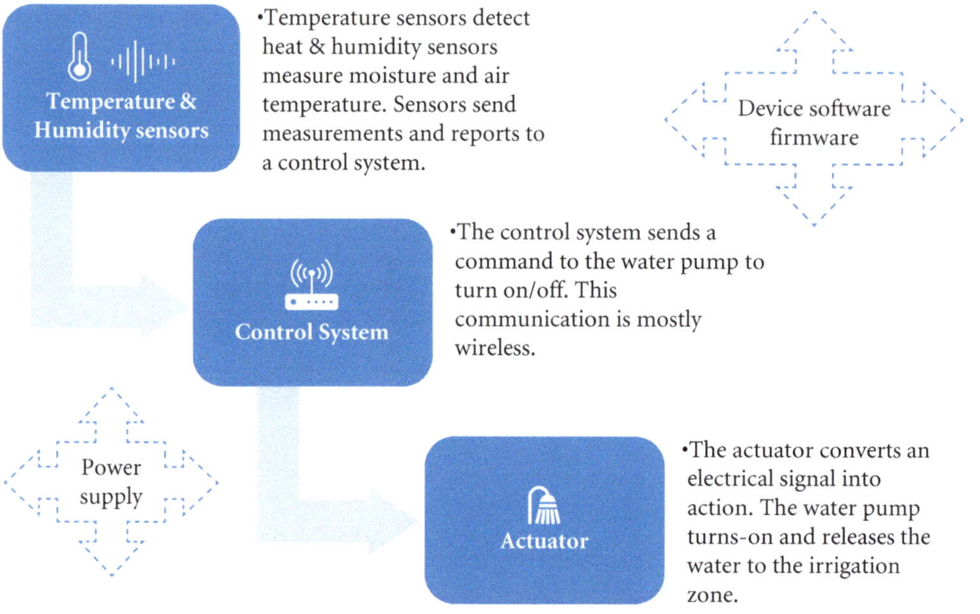

FIGURE 7.4 An example of how an IoT system works.

available, size, energy, power, and computational capability.[25] Figure 7.4 displays a typical IoT system.

7.3.2 Big Data in IoT

The increasing number of IoT devices and the vast amount of data being generated, along with the increasing use of processing power, together create delays and performance issues, especially when the centralized cloud computing model is used.[26,27] To address this, a paradigm called *edge computing* eliminates the centralized cloud servers and brings processing closer to the IoT device or data source. Edge computing makes IoT devices more flexible, by removing the limits of centralized cloud servers, minimizing delays, and theoretically providing more security, since all data are not in the same place.

Data processing happens on the *edge* of the network or nearer to the source of the data. The *edge computing paradigm* allows processing in real

[25] *Id.* at 23.

[26] Yousefpour, Ashkan, Genya Ishigaki, and Jason P. Jue. "Fog computing: Towards minimizing delay in the internet of things." In *2017 IEEE International Conference on Edge Computing (EDGE)*, pp. 17–24. IEEE, 2017.

[27] El-Sayed, Hesham, Sharmi Sankar, Mukesh Prasad, Deepak Puthal, Akshansh Gupta, Manoranjan Mohanty, and Chin-Teng Lin. "Edge of things: The big picture on the integration of edge, IoT and the cloud in a distributed computing environment." *IEEE Access* 6 (2017): 1706–1717.

time at a location closer to the user, resulting in shorter response time and more efficient processing.[28]

> It works on both downstream data on behalf of cloud services and upstream data on behalf of IoT services. An edge device is any computing or networking resource residing between data sources and cloud-based datacenters.[29]

In addition to edge computing, a standard introduced by Cisco, called *fog computing*, defines how edge computing should work.[30] The *fog standard* brings intelligence down to the Local Area Network (LAN) architecture and processes the data in a *fog* node. They are called fog nodes because they can be implemented anywhere within a network connection (classrooms, factory floor, power poles, parks, streets, train tracks, etc.).[31] In other words, a fog node can be any computing device with storage and network connectivity. These devices include controllers, switches, routers, servers, video surveillance cameras, and more.

In contrast, in edge computing, the data processing occurs on internal LAN devices like access points, switches, routers, and other devices near the sensors. "Within the network, IoT data are collected, processed, and stored at the **Fog/edge** node, also referred as the IoT gateway through which the fog interacts with the Cloud."[32] Both fog and edge paradigms complement cloud computing by reducing the amount of data that needs to be sent to the cloud and by generating intelligence close to the IoT device.

In retrospect, edge computing and the fog standard remove the workload from the network and bring it closer to the IoT devices, using machine learning, and a cloud computing backend.

To understand latency better, a security camera system with artificial intelligence (AI)-driven analysis and resolution of 2288 × 1712 over the cloud will create latency when transferring massive amounts of video data back and forth between the cloud servers and the device. However, if the security camera system can perform most of the data processing itself and then send information to the cloud servers for archiving, it

[28] Shi, Weisong, and Schahram Dustdar. "The promise of edge computing." *Computer* 49, no. 5 (2016): 78–81.

[29] *Id.* at 28.

[30] David Linthicum. *Edge computing vs. fog computing: Definitions and enterprise uses.* Retrieved from https://www.cisco.com/c/en/us/solutions/enterprise-networks/edge-computing.html

[31] Iorga, Michaela, Larry Feldman, Robert Barton, Michael J. Martin, Nedim Goren, and Charif Mahmoudi. *Fog computing conceptual model recommendations of the National Institute of Standards and Technology (NIST).* March 2018. Retrieved from https://nvlpubs.nist.gov/nistpubs/SpecialPublications/NIST.SP.500-325.pdf

[32] Pramanik, Pijush Kanti Dutta, Prasenjit Choudhury, S. K. Shandilya, S. A. Chun, S. Shandilya, and E. Weippl. "IoT data processing: the different archetypes and their security & privacy assessments." *Internet of Things (IoT) Security: Fundamentals, Techniques and Applications* (2018): 37–54.

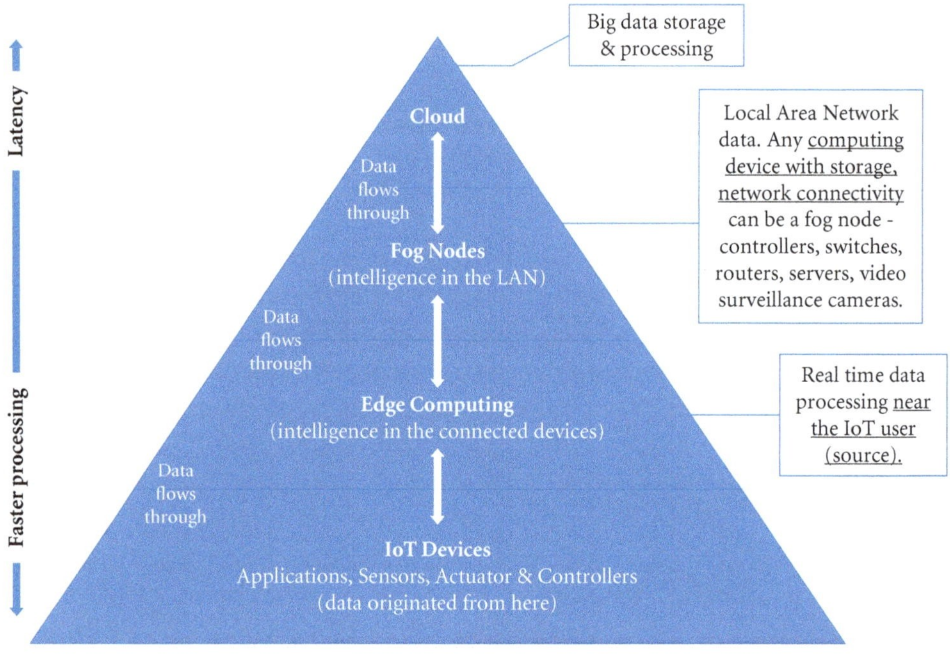

FIGURE 7.5 The edge and fog processing paradigms.

takes less time, reducing latency and lowering the cost of data transfer. In addition, outage reduction and sporadic connectivity work better with edge computing paradigms since this paradigm does not rely only on cloud servers for processing.

Another example requires us to look at the autonomous vehicles of the future, which will contain numerous sensors and will therefore require massive bandwidth and continuous real-time processing. Edge computing paradigms can analyze data faster from numerous sensors in real time and will be able to make better immediate decisions. The future success of IoTs is about making them smarter, faster, and more secure. Figure 7.5 delineates edge and fog processing paradigms in relation to cloud computing.

7.3.3 Architectures

Although the IoT network comprises many interdependent components, its primary purpose is to provide a complete solution and work flawlessly. All components of an IoT system must be integrated and must follow rules that define the interface between hardware and software. Like any computing device, IoT architecture contains a set of rules or building blocks describing how each part functions, organizes, and integrates with the other parts. There is no standard IoT architecture model. Researchers, however, have proposed different architecture models. The most common are the *three-* and the *five-layer* architecture (see Figure 7.7).[33,34,35,36]

The basic three-layer architecture consists of the following:

- The *perception layer* is the physical layer, where the collection, transfer, and sending of data about the physical environment are accomplished, using sensors, networks-sensors and actuators, tags, near field communication (NFC), and radio-frequency identification.
- In the *network layer*, IoT devices connect to other smart devices and network devices such as gateways, wireless access points, servers, routers, switches, hubs, and repeaters. This layer is responsible for transmitting and processing data from the sensors, using gateway controls (physical devices or software that connects to cloud servers), Wi-Fi, Ethernet, cellular, and wide area networks (Figure 7.6).
- The *application layer* is where the data is delivered to the IoT user. We have seen this described in all the sectors we have discussed.

The three-layer architecture has been expanded to contain three additional layers: the *transport layer*, the *processing layer*, and the *business layer* (see Figure 7.7).

- The *transport layer* resembles the network layer, which is responsible for transmitting the data from the sensors of the perception layer to the processing layer across the network.
- The *processing layer* or *middleware layer* is responsible for aggregating data, data storage (cloud computing and databases), processing data received from the transport layer,[37] and protecting against security attacks.
- The *business layer* functions as the manager of the IoT system. This layer is responsible for operating the applications, user privacy, and managing how data is created, stored, and used.

In addition to three- and five-layer architecture, a real-time business architecture solution is needed to authorize devices to improve the management of IoT devices. The *management component* of the IoT ecosystem is based on IoT device modeling, configuration, controlling data

[33] *Id.* at 23.

[34] Jamali, Jabraeil, Bahareh Bahrami, Arash Heidari, Parisa Allahverdizadeh, and Farhad Norouzi. *Towards the Internet of Things*. Springer International Publishing, 2020.

[35] Mashal, Ibrahim, Osama Alsaryrah, Tein-Yaw Chung, Cheng-Zen Yang, Wen-Hsing Kuo, and Dharma P. Agrawal. "Choices for interaction with things on Internet and underlying issues." *Ad Hoc Networks* 28 (2015): 68–90.

[36] Khan, Rafiullah, Sarmad Ullah Khan, Rifaqat Zaheer, and Shahid Khan. "Future internet: The internet of things architecture, possible applications and key challenges." In *2012 10th International Conference on Frontiers of Information Technology*, pp. 257–260. IEEE, 2012.

[37] Ashraf, Q. M. and M.H. Habaebi. Autonomic schemes for threat mitigation in Internet of Things. *The Journal of Network and Computer Applications* 49 (2015): 112–127. doi: 10.1016/j.jnca.2014.11.011

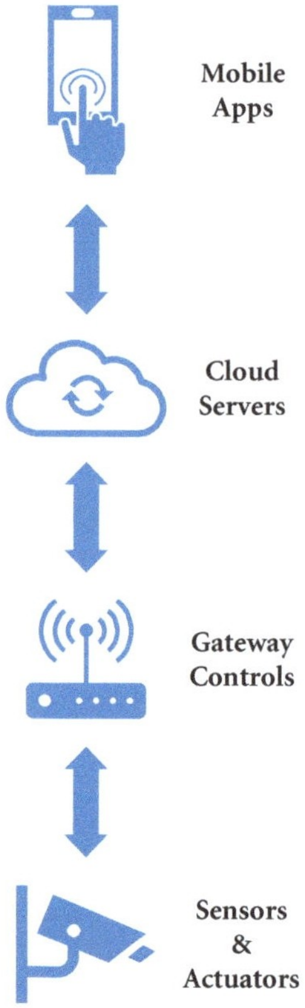

FIGURE 7.6 **The IoT connectivity.**

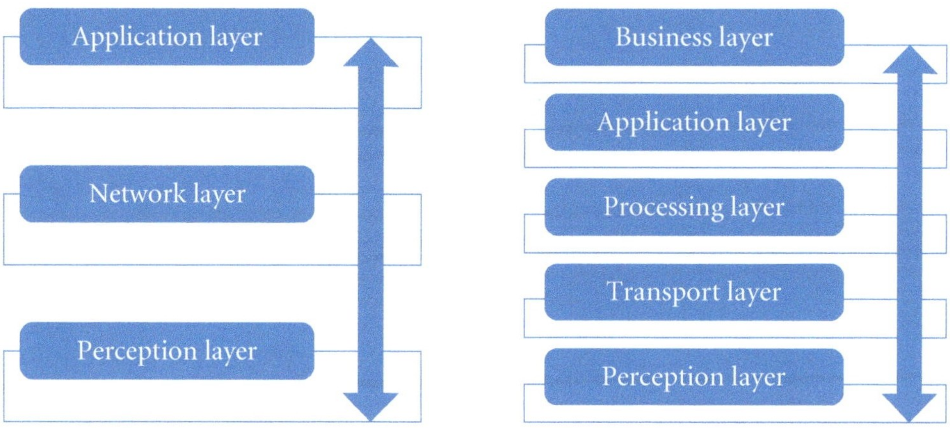

FIGURE 7.7 **The three- and five-layer IoT architectures.**

flow, and security controls. As IoT devices become more powerful, dealing with huge amounts of data along with *edge* and *fog paradigms*, Cisco IoT and Azure IoT suite architecture has developed a pre-integrated reference model called Cisco Edge. It works with the Microsoft Azure IoT Hub solution and includes software, hardware, security, and cloud services for enterprise IoTs.[38] This initiative is an example of how far IoT devices have evolved and how they will continue to use the Internet with increasing levels of sophistication (Figure 7.7).

7.3.4 Protocols and Standards

A *protocol* is a procedure or set of rules used by systems to communicate with one another. Well-known examples include Transmission Control Protocol (TCP) and Hypertext Transfer Protocol Secure (HTTPS).

A *standard*, in this context, is a set of rules followed by systems manufacturers that define how devices communicate in different settings. For example, Ethernet-based networks are defined by IEEE 802.3 standards, issued by the Institute of Electrical and Electronics Engineers (IEEE), and Bluetooth devices are defined by Bluetooth Low Energy 5.1, which is a wireless technology standard for exchanging data over short distances,

> *Protocols and standards define how IoT devices are managed and how data are transmitted via networks.*

Standards and protocols are developed by different regulatory organizations and industrial bodies. Among the best known are the recommendations for IoT device manufacturers by the Internet Engineering Task Force (IETF), the Institute of Electrical and Electronics Engineers, the Organization for the Advancement of Structured Information Standards (OASIS), the International Telecommunication Union (ITU), and the NIST's (National Institute of Standards and Technology) (NISTIR 8259).

While it is not possible to present all protocols and standards, this section will present some of the most frequently used.

To explain how the parts of the IoT interconnect, we will look at the Open Systems Interconnection Model (OSI) and its short version, called the Transmission Control Protocol/Internet Protocol (TCP/IP) model. TCP/IP has been around for a long time. It was developed in the 1970s and adopted as the protocol standard for the ARPANET (predecessor to the Internet) in 1983.

TCP/IP contains four layers and constitutes a simplified version of the OSI model. Both models have been discussed in detail in Chapter 5. The OSI and TCP/IP models are the two most widely used networking models in Internet communications, including for IoT devices.

In general, networking protocols can be understood best when grouped into layers, where each layer describes a different function. See Table 7.1.

---

[38] Bakhshi, Zeinab, Ali Balador, and Jawad Mustafa. "Industrial IoT security threats and concerns by considering Cisco and Microsoft IoT reference models." In *2018 IEEE Wireless Communications and Networking Conference Workshops (WCNCW)*, pp. 173–178. IEEE, 2018.

TABLE 7.1 OSI and TCP/IP Models

OSI Model	TCP/IP Model
(7) Application layer	Application layer
(6) Presentation layer	
(5) Session layer	
(4) Transport layer	Transport layer
(3) Network layer	Internet layer
(2) Data link layer	Network access layer
(1) Physical layer	

Both the OSI and TCP/IP models will help us understand how the parts of the IoT ecosystem work together. In Figure 7.1 we see that the TCP/IP model condenses the seven-layer OSI model into four layers. TCP/IP is actually a simpler version of OSI, and IoT networking protocols map more closely to TCP/IP levels than to OSI levels.[39] The IoT ecosystem is therefore comprised of the following four layers: Network Access & Physical, Internet, Transport, and Application. Each of the four layers uses different protocols, which are described below:

I. **Application layer (layers 5–7 in OSI)**: In this layer the user employs the interface given by the IoT to interact with the IoT device or other application. Protocols used in this layer:
   - **AMQP**: Advanced Message Queuing Protocol is used to pass messages between applications, called Message Exchange and Communication. AMQP is dependable over a distance or over poor networks. AMQP is similar to MQTT, Message Queuing Telemetry Transport, and follows the publish/subscribe (pub/sub) protocol of communication, which is standardized by OASIS.[40] This means that messages are exchanged without specifying the identity of the sender or recipient.[41]
   - **CoAP**: Constrained Application Protocol is a machine-to-machine (M2M) protocol and, like Hypertext Transfer Protocol (HTTP), works between a client and a server with a minimum number of resources, making it perfect for IoT devices. Also,

[39] Irons-Mclean, Rik, Anthony Sabella, Marcelo Yannuzzi, "IoT and Security Standards and Best Practices," January 14, 2019, CISCO. Retrieved from https://www.ciscopress.com/articles/article.asp?p=2923211&seqNum=6

[40] Advancement of Structured Information Standards (OASIS). AMQP v1.0. Retrieved from https://docs.oasis-open.org/amqp/core/v1.0/os/amqp-core-complete-v1.0-os.pdf

[41] Yassein, Muneer Bani, and Mohammed Q. Shatnawi. "Application layer protocols for the Internet of Things: A survey." In *2016 International Conference on Engineering & MIS (ICEMIS)*, pp. 1–4. IEEE, 2016.

CoAP provides simplicity since it runs over the User Datagram Protocol (UDP) but offers less reliability.[42]

- **DDS**: Data Distribution Service is a machine-to-machine (M2M) communication protocol that provides low-latency (faster) data connectivity and reliability. It also follows the pub/sub protocol for real-time and embedded systems. DDS was designed by the Object Management Group (OMG)[43] to support IoT applications and M2M protocols.
- **MQTT**: Message Queuing Telemetry Transport is standardized by OASIS[44] and ISO/IEC 20922.[45] MQTT runs messages between applications, services, and IoT devices. This is like a client-server environment, featuring low bandwidth, low power, and high latency. [46]

II. **Transport layer (layer 4 in OSI)**: This layer enables host-to-host data communication between layers. Examples of transport protocols are TCP and UDP. Both transport protocols work on top of the IP (Internet Protocol) to send bits of data known as packets from an IoT device to different routers.

- **DTLS**: Datagram Transport Layer Security is a communications protocol that provides excellent security. This protocol has been used by CoAP (Constrained Application Protocol) and IPsec (Internet Protocol Security) for authentication, integrity, and encryption between two communication points across the IP network.[47]
- **UDP**: User Datagram Protocol is a faster communication protocol, but it is less reliable. This protocol works similarly to TCP by dividing data into smaller units called datagrams or packets. Both protocols are built on top of the IP, and both send data across the Internet from one IP address to another. UDP, unlike TCP, does not guarantee delivery and has less overhead, offering no acknowledgment that packets have been received. This speeds the connection and reduces latency but reduces reliability. When using this protocol, a computing device sends packets of data to another device without guaranteeing delivery; this is a

---

[42] Naik, Nitin. "Choice of effective messaging protocols for IoT systems: MQTT, CoAP, AMQP and HTTP." In *2017 IEEE International Systems Engineering Symposium (ISSE)*, pp. 1–7. IEEE, 2017.

[43] Object Management Group (OMG), Data Distribution Service (DDS). Retrieved from https://www.omg.org/omg-dds-portal/

[44] Advancement of Structured Information Standards (OASIS), MQTT Version 3.1.1 Plus Errata 01. Retrieved from https://docs.oasis-open.org/mqtt/mqtt/v3.1.1/mqtt-v3.1.1.html

[45] International Organization of Standardization (ISO), ISO/IEC 20922:2016 Information technology—Message Queuing Telemetry Transport (MQTT) v3.1.1. Retrieved from https://www.iso.org/standard/69466.html

[46] *Id.* at 41.

[47] *Id.* at 42.

"send it and forget it" method. UDP is faster than TCP, because it eliminates functions like error checking and recovery services. It chooses speed over integrity, and data received may not exactly match the data sent. UDP is faster and TCP is more reliable. UDP is used for streaming games, live broadcasts, and video.

- **TCP** is a much more reliable host-to-host connection-based protocol. Its speed is slower than UDP, but TCP's greater reliability guarantees fewer errors. The packets sent are traced so no data is lost or corrupted during transit. TCP, unlike UDP, requires the recipient and the sender to communicate and establish a connection, acknowledging that packets have been received. If packets are not acknowledged by the recipient, they are sent again. Consequently, this back-and-forth communication makes TCP slower than UDP.

III. **Internet layer (layer 3 in OSI)**: In this layer routers transport packets of data between the source host and the destination host. The IoT device communicates with the router using logical IP addressing to deliver packets of information between different networks. Following are some of the protocols the routers use:

- **IPv4**: Internet Protocol uses a 32-bit address and can handle 4,294,967,296 (2^{32}) unique addresses. Because IPv4 is currently running out of addresses the protocol is switching to IPv6.
- **Ipv6**: Internet Protocol uses a 128-bit address, theoretically delivering 2^{128} unique addresses.
- **RPL**: Routing Protocol for Low-Power and Lossy Networks is for wireless networks and IoT devices with low power consumption. It is a simple and interoperable networking protocol and is resource-constrained.[48] The protocol is standardized by IETF as RFC 6550.[49]
- **6LoWPAN**: Low Power Wireless Personal Area Networks standard makes it possible for IoT devices to transmit IPv6 packets over wireless networks.[50] The 6LoWPAN is standardized by IETF as RFC 6282.[51] The 6LoWPAN has been used with wireless sensors for smart home automation.

IV. **Network access layer (layers 1-2 in OSI)**: This layer oversees how an IoT device is physically connected to the network through Ethernet

[48] Kim, Hyung-Sin, Jeonggil Ko, David E. Culler, and Jeongyeup Paek. "Challenging the IPv6 routing protocol for low-power and lossy networks (RPL): A survey." *IEEE Communications Surveys & Tutorials* 19, no. 4 (2017): 2502–2525.

[49] Internet Engineering Task Force (IETF), RPL: IPv6 Routing Protocol for Low-Power and Lossy Networks. RFC 6550. Last modified January 21, 2020. Retrieved from https://datatracker.ietf.org/doc/rfc6550/

[50] Qiu, Yue, and Maode Ma. "A mutual authentication and key establishment scheme for m2m communication in 6lowpan networks." *IEEE Transactions on Industrial Informatics* 12, no. 6 (2016): 2074–2085.

[51] Internet Engineering Task Force (IETF), Compression Format for IPv6 Datagrams over IEEE 802.15.4-Based Networks RFC 6282. Last modified September 29, 2016. Retrieved from https://datatracker.ietf.org/doc/rfc6282/

wired cables or wireless radio wave technology, using Wi-Fi standards. In addition to this connection, the IoT device is connected to a Media Access Control (MAC) and its protocols. The MAC address is a unique identification number allocated for every device and is used to connect the device to the network. This address is burnt into every device's hardware by the manufacturer. Some of the protocols in this layer include the following:

- *Bluetooth* is a low-energy, short-range wireless communication protocol that has become a central wireless technology for resource-constrained devices such as battery-operated sensors and actuators in the IoT ecosystem. Bluetooth was originally conceived as a wireless alternative by the Bluetooth Special Interest Group and uses the 2.4 GHz industrial, scientific, and medical (ISM) spectrum band (2,400 to 2,483.5 MHz). It has a range of 100 meters.[52,53]
- *Cellular technology* enables mobile communication and addresses low-power IoT communication. For instance, the Low Power Wide Area Network (LPWAN) uses existing cellular technology for broad utilization of low-power IoT devices like wireless sensors and actuators. Cellular technology includes the fourth-generation cellular wireless (4G LTE) long-term evolution, and the emerging fifth-generation cellular wireless (5G). The LTE-advance (LTE-A) is designed specifically for IoT communication in cellular networks.[54]
- *Dash7* is a wireless communication protocol for wireless sensors, actuators, and messaging applications. The protocol was developed by the DASH7 alliance and is based on ISO/IEC 18000-7.[55] In addition, Dash 7 uses active RFID to support encryption, enabling secure communication in the IoT ecosystem.
- *Ethernet* IEEE 802.3 is an entire family of standards and protocols that defines wired connectivity in Local Area Networks (LAN) and includes standards for wiring, signaling, connectors, protocol rules, and more. More precisely, it defines the physical layer and the MAC address (hardware addresses) of the data link layer for wired Ethernet networks.[56] The Ethernet is standard-

[52] Bluetooth SIG. Bluetooth Core Specification. Retrieved from https://www.bluetooth.com/specifications/bluetooth-core-specification/

[53] Hortelano, Diego, Teresa Olivares, M. Carmen Ruiz, Celia Garrido-Hidalgo, and Vicente López. "From sensor networks to internet of things. Bluetooth low energy, a standard for this evolution." *Sensors* 17, no. 2 (2017): 372.

[54] Elsaadany, Mahmoud, Abdelmohsen Ali, and Walaa Hamouda. "Cellular LTE-A technologies for the future Internet-of-Things: Physical layer features and challenges." *IEEE Communications Surveys & Tutorials* 19, no. 4 (2017): 2544–2572.

[55] The DASH7 Alliance Protocol (D7A). Retrieved from https://dash7-alliance.org/

[56] Law, David, Dan Dove, John D'Ambrosia, Marek Hajduczenia, Mark Laubach, and Steve Carlson. "Evolution of Ethernet standards in the IEEE 802.3 working group." *IEEE Communications Magazine* 51, no. 8 (2013): 88–96.

ized by the IEEE. Some of the standards are 802.3cg, 802.3cm, 802.3cq, and 802.3cn.[57]

- *NFC* is a collection of short-range wireless communication protocols, using electromagnetic fields that enable communication with other devices and wireless transfer of data.[58] Standardization of NFC is provided by the NFC Forum. The NFC Forum certifies NFC units compatible to its specifications (ISO/IEC 14443 A, B, ISO/IEC 18092, ISO/IEC 18093, and JIS-X 6319-4).[59]
- *RFID* is a wireless technology that uses radio-frequency waves to read electronic tags from a distance.[60]
- *Wi-Fi IEEE 802.11* is a wireless networking protocol, based on the IEEE wireless communication standard 802.11. The Wi-Fi alliance is responsible for certifying Wi-Fi products, including some of the newest standards such as 802.11ax Wi-Fi 6, 802.11ac Wi-Fi 5, and 802.11n Wi-Fi 4.[61] Specifically, the IEEE 802.11ah standard (also known as Wi-Fi Halo) has been designed for low-energy consumption, as its sensors and IoT applications use a very low transmit power, providing data rates from 150 kb/s to 347 Mb/s. In addition, the standard supports an outdoor application that uses a transmission range up to 1 km at 150 kb/s.[62]
- *ZigBee* is a low-power, low-data-rate, close proximity (i.e., Personal Area Network) wireless communication protocol based on the IEEE 802.15 standard.[63] The ZigBee Alliance is responsible for maintaining and publishing the ZigBee standard.[64] In addition, ZigBee is a mesh network protocol, self-organized and self-configured, where devices communicate with each other using the best path available. ZigBee has a longer range than Bluetooth.

Figure 7.8 demonstrates the TCP/IP model and examples of IoT protocols and standards. Figure 7.9 shows the data from an IoT flow between a sender

[57] The IEEE 802.3 Working Group. 802.3-2018—IEEE Standard for Ethernet. Retrieved from https://standards.ieee.org/standard/802_3-2018.html

[58] Al-Sarawi, Shadi, Mohammed Anbar, Kamal Alieyan, and Mahmood Alzubaidi. "Internet of Things (IoT) communication protocols." In *2017 8th International Conference on Information Technology (ICIT)*, pp. 685–690. IEEE, 2017.

[59] The NFC Forum, Near Field Communication (NFC) protocols. Retrieved from https://nfc-forum.org/what-is-nfc/about-the-technology/

[60] Nath, Badri, Franklin Reynolds, and Roy Want. "RFID technology and applications." *IEEE Pervasive Computing* 5, no. 1 (2006): 22–24.

[61] Wi-Fi Alliance, Wi-Fi generations. Retrieved from https://www.wi-fi.org/discover-wi-fi

[62] Park, Minyoung. "IEEE 802.11 ah: sub-1-GHz license-exempt operation for the internet of things." *IEEE Communications Magazine* 53, no. 9 (2015): 145–151.

[63] Porkodi, R., and V. Bhuvaneswari. "The internet of things (IoT) applications and communication enabling technology standards: An overview." In *2014 International Conference on Intelligent Computing Applications*, pp. 324–329. IEEE, 2014.

[64] ZigBee Alliance, What is Zigbee? Last modified February 10, 2020. Retrieved from https://zigbeealliance.org/solution/zigbee/

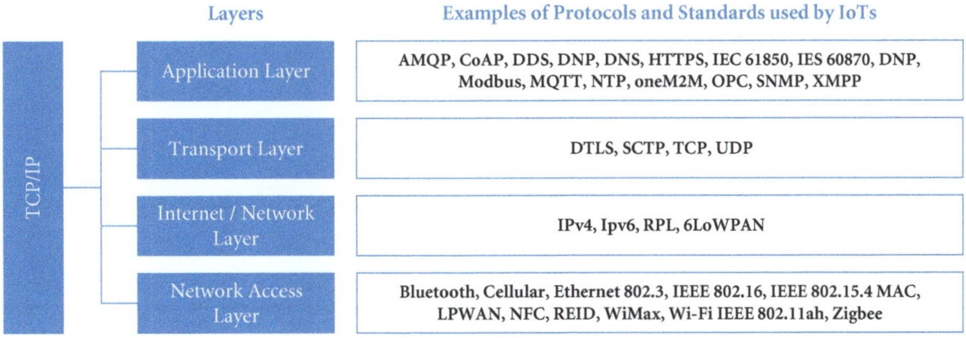

FIGURE 7.8 TCP/IP model, protocols, and standards used by IoTs.

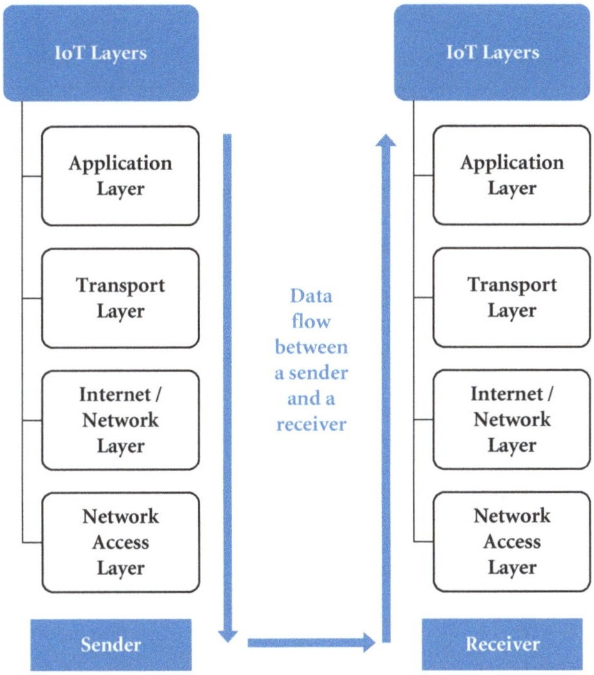

FIGURE 7.9 Data flow between a sender and a receiver.

and a receiver. Both figures provide a good reference point showing how IoTs establish network communication.

7.4 Network Consideration for IoT Devices

In addition to protocols and standards, an IoT ecosystem requires *bandwidth*, *interoperability*, *power usage*, and *range* for successful deployment.

I. **Bandwidth**

Bandwidth defines the maximum rate of data transmitted across a network path per unit of time. "In physical layer communications, the term bandwidth relates to the spectral width of electromagnetic signals or the propagation characteristics of communication systems."[65] Bandwidth is measured in bits per second (bps), kbps (kilobits per second), mbps (megabits per second), gbps (gigabits per second), or tbps (terabits per second). As more and more IoT devices are connecting to the Internet, the growing demand for bandwidth is increasing exponentially. Thus, bandwidth is affected by the number of physical devices deployed, the volume of data each device transmits, and whether data should be processed or transmitted as raw data to the cloud. Technologies such as fog/edge paradigms with smart data preprocessing capabilities and fifth generation mobile network (5G) will reduce latency and enhance network bandwidth, mobility, and security.[66]

II. **Interoperability**

Interoperability refers to the ability of IoT devices to work and interact well with other existing devices, such as equipment and systems utilizing standards and protocols. With the great number of different IoT ecosystems that can be connected, poor interoperability can cause serious issues. The adoption of standards and protocols by manufacturers has been a long-established approach to providing good interoperability.

III. **Power usage**

Every IoT device requires power to process and transmit data. Additionally, most of these devices are small, contain limited battery power, and are "always connected" and transmitting data. "Data rate and payload of protocol affect directly on power consumption. High data rate and long data size of protocol lead to low power consumption."[67]

IV. **Range of networks**

Different types of networks can transfer IoT data from one system to another. Following are the types of networks over which data is usually transmitted by IoT devices. See Figure 7.9 for the different types of network connectivity.

- **PAN (Personal Area Network)** is a short-range network, found, for example, when using an app on a mobile device over a Bluetooth device (wrist fitness trackers, heart rate monitors, and pedometers).

[65] Prasad, Ravi, Constantinos Dovrolis, Margaret Murray, and K. C. Claffy. "Bandwidth estimation: metrics, measurement techniques, and tools." *IEEE Network* 17, no. 6 (2003): 27–35.

[66] Hu, Pengfei, Sahraoui Dhelim, Huansheng Ning, and Tie Qiu. "Survey on fog computing: Architecture, key technologies, applications and open issues." *Journal of Network and Computer Applications* 98 (2017): 27–42.

[67] Mahmoud, Mahmoud S., and Auday AH Mohamad. "A study of efficient power consumption wireless communication techniques/modules for internet of things (IoT) applications." *Advances in Internet of Things* 6 (2016): 19–29.

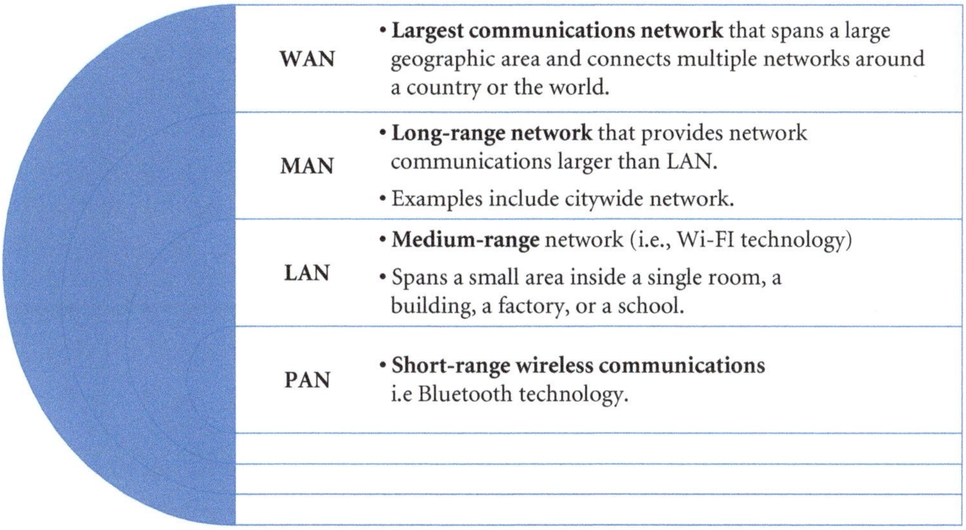

FIGURE 7.10 **The different types of network connectivity for IoTs.**

- **LAN (Local Area Network)** is a medium-range network that spans a small area inside a single room, building or group of buildings, factory, or school. Examples include smart home products such as smart thermostats, surveillance equipment, and IoT devices integrated within an Electronic Health Record (EHR) to monitor a patient's health.
- **MAN (Metropolitan Area Network)** is long-range network that provides communications over a larger area than a LAN. Examples include citywide networks, where IoT sensors can tell the sanitation department when the trash reaches a certain level, or on college campuses, where sensors can collect data about temperature, humidity, and air quality in the classrooms.
- **WAN (Wide Area Network)** is the widest communications network that can span a large geographic area and can connect multiple networks in a country or throughout the world. Multiple sensors within different countries can monitor water quality over the entire water supply. The best-known example of a WAN is the Internet, connecting multiple networks around the globe. Figure 7.10 delineates the different types of networks transferring IoT data from one system to another.

7.5 Security

Since the inception of IoT devices, their security has a great challenge to IoT ecosystems. Security vulnerabilities continue to hound manufacturers and users in every layer of IoT architecture. One of the most infamous IoT security attacks occurred in 2016. An IoT botnet malware called Mirai took advantage of unprotected IoT devices by using default usernames and passwords to log in and infect the IoT devices with malware. It then used the IoTs to issue massive distributed denial-of-service (DDoS) attacks.[68,69]

Because everything can be connected to the Internet in today's digital world, privacy and security are critical. IoT devices provide hackers with new targets and more importantly can become part of a "botnet" army that delivers DDoS attacks. Examples of bad actions caused by the exploitation of IoT weaknesses include taking control of a smart home by unlocking the doors, hacking surveillance cameras, taking control of wearable devices, gathering personal data and tracking the users, hacking medical IoT devices and threatening a patient's safety, or even shutting down a car while it is in motion.

Besides the invasion of our privacy, IoT devices cause additional harm as they interact with our physical world. Cyberattacks caused by IoTs can compromise sensitive data through industrial espionage and eavesdropping, ruin equipment, and even endanger life and property.

The wide variety of IoT applications using different IoT frameworks, the many manufacturers that fail to implement adequate security measures, along with the lack of computing and battery power, makes it very difficult to implement a universal security solution.[70] Some of the major security issues, limitations, and challenges that face IoT devices are the following:

- **Device limitations**: IoT devices generally have short battery lifetimes and limitations in memory and processing power. As a result, they cannot handle all the requirements for advanced cryptography algorithms that would protect them from security threats.[71,72,73]
- **Physical attacks, network attacks, software, and encryption attacks**:
    - Physical attack performed in the proximity of the IoT device (i.e., attacker is close enough to the device to analyze electrical signals such as electromagnetic waves emitted) and can gather sensitive information.[74]

---

[68] Kambourakis, Georgios, Constantinos Kolias, and Angelos Stavrou. "The mirai botnet and the IoT zombie armies." In *MILCOM 2017-2017 IEEE Military Communications Conference (MILCOM)*, pp. 267–272. IEEE, 2017.

[69] Jaramillo, L. E. S. "Malware detection and mitigation techniques: lessons learned from mirai DDOS attack." *Journal of Information Systems Engineering & Management* 3, no. 3 (2018): 19.

[70] Yang, Yuchen, Longfei Wu, Guisheng Yin, Lijie Li, and Hongbin Zhao. "A survey on security and privacy issues in Internet-of-Things." *IEEE Internet of Things Journal* 4, no. 5 (2017): 1250–1258.

[71] *Id.* at 70.

[72] Ammar, Mahmoud, Giovanni Russello, and Bruno Crispo. "Internet of Things: A survey on the security of IoT frameworks." *Journal of Information Security and Applications* 38 (2018): 8–27.

[73] *Id.* at 12.

[74] Andrea, Ioannis, Chrysostomos Chrysostomou, and George Hadjichristofi. "Internet of Things: Security vulnerabilities and challenges." In *2015 IEEE Symposium on Computers and Communication (ISCC)*, pp. 180–187. IEEE, 2015.

- Network attacks occur when an attacker accesses, manipulates, or intercepts an IoT network system remotely and causes damage (a DoS attack, malware, breach, man-in-the-middle attack (MITM), routing information or traffic attack, RFID Spoofing).[75]
- Software attacks, including phishing attacks, malware, virus, worms, Trojan horse, spyware, and adware.[76]
- Encryption attacks: These occur when an attacker tries to break the encryption scheme and obtain the private key to the device. These types of attacks include cryptanalysis attacks, side channel attacks, MITM attacks, sleep deprivation attacks, eavesdropping, and interference.[77,78,79]

- **The lack of security by IoT device manufactures**: Manufacturers are profit driven and rush to produce the latest IoT device, often ignoring the lack of appropriate legislation and other security considerations such as insecure software or firmware. In addition, security software updates have often been largely ignored by device manufacturers. Finally, since IoT devices can be embedded in toys, manufacturers may have violated the Federal Trade Commission's Children's Online Privacy Protection Rule (COPPA).[80]
- **The lack of security awareness by the user**: When it comes to IoT devices, users focus on their advantages and lack the technical knowledge to detect and be aware of security threats.[81] As usual, the human element is the weakest link in IoT security.

Understanding the significance of these security risks, the National Institute of Standards and Technology (NIST) published a set of voluntary rules (NISTIR 8228—Considerations for Managing IoT Cybersecurity and Privacy Risks)[82] aimed at IoT manufacturers and federal agencies to help them comprehend and manage the cybersecurity and privacy risks related

---

[75] *Id.* at 70.

[76] Deogirikar, Jyoti, and Amarsinh Vidhate. "Security attacks in IoT: A survey." In *2017 International Conference on I-SMAC (IoT in Social, Mobile, Analytics and Cloud) (I-SMAC)*, pp. 32–37. IEEE, 2017.

[77] *Id.* at 74.

[78] Zhang, Jing, Dawu Gu, Zheng Guo, and Lei Zhang. "Differential power cryptanalysis attacks against PRESENT implementation." In *2010 3rd International Conference on Advanced Computer Theory and Engineering (ICACTE)*, vol. 6, pp. V6-61. IEEE, 2010.

[79] Lin, Jie, Wei Yu, Nan Zhang, Xinyu Yang, Hanlin Zhang, and Wei Zhao. "A survey on internet of things: Architecture, enabling technologies, security and privacy, and applications." *IEEE Internet of Things Journal* 4, no. 5 (2017): 1125–1142.

[80] Chu, Gordon, Noah Apthorpe, and Nick Feamster. "Security and privacy analyses of Internet of Things children's toys." *IEEE Internet of Things Journal* 6, no. 1 (2018): 978–985.

[81] McDermott, Christopher D., John P. Isaacs, and Andrei V. Petrovski. "Evaluating awareness and perception of botnet activity within consumer internet-of-things (IoT) networks." In *Informatics*, vol. 6, no. 1, p. 8. Multidisciplinary Digital Publishing Institute, 2019.

[82] NISTIR 8228—Considerations for Managing Internet of Things (IoT) Cybersecurity and Privacy Risks. Retrieved from https://nvlpubs.nist.gov/nistpubs/ir/2019/NIST.IR.8228.pdf

to IoT devices. According to the publication, the cybersecurity and privacy risks for IoT devices have three mitigation goals:

- Protect device security
- Protect data security
- Protect individuals' privacy

7.6 Conclusion

IoT devices signify the next giant leap of computing, using the power of the Internet. The combination of IoT and AI is immensely powerful. But IoTs, like other new technologies, need to mature and overcome their security hurdles. The necessity of safeguarding data security and individuals represents a great challenge. We are aware of this challenge and must always remain skeptical and suspicious about anything new that is connected to the Internet. Although firms like Microsoft have developed security applications like Azure Sphere to protect IoT devices, it will take time to earn the knowledge and trust of end users. Like each new technology, IoTs promise enormous benefits and have the potential to bring lasting changes to the world. Time will tell.

7.7 Key Words

Actuators
Automotive Sector
Bandwidth
Cellular Technology
Edge and Fog processing Paradigms
Energy Sector
Fifth-Generation Cellular Wireless (5G)
Fourth-Generation Cellular Wireless (4G LTE)
Healthcare Sector
Industrial Revolution
Industry 4.0
IoT Applications
IoT Architectures
Internet of Things (IoT)
IoT Security
Interoperability
National Institute of Standards and Technology (NIST)
LAN (Local Area Network)
LTE-Advance
MAN (Metropolitan Area Network)
Manufacturing Sector
Open Systems Interconnection Model (OSI)
PAN (Personal Area Network)
Power Usage
Power Supply
Protocols and Standards
Radio-Frequency Identification (RFID)
Range
Retail Sector

Sensor
Smart Home Automation
Smart Structures
Transceiver
Transportation Sector
Transmission Control Protocol/ Internet Protocol (TCP/IP) Model
WAN (Wide Area Network)
Wireless Communication Transceiver

Chapter 8

Mobile Devices

The Smartphone

Objectives

After completing this chapter, the student will be able to:

- Understand the historical significance of mobile phone technology.
- Recognize the device's main components and architecture.
- Understand how cellular networks function.
- Understand the main components, operating systems, applications, and architecture of smartphones.
- Understand tracking of mobile devices.
- Recognize threats to mobile security.

8.1 Introduction

Smartphones and tablets have transformed our lives. The ability to contact just about anyone sits in the palm of your hand; information that took time to find is now available in a single click. Thousands of free apps help us get the best from our technologies without needing great expertise. Typing is no longer needed – launch the speech recognition app when you send a message, and just speak into your phone – thumbs are no longer required!

The term mobile devices refers to all handheld computing devices like e-readers, cellphones, tablets etc., that are portable and support transmission

DOI: 10.4324/9780429318726-8

FIGURE 8.1 **The disappearance of phone booths. Courtesy of Shutterstock.**

of high-quality multimedia data, such as data, voice, and video via wireless transmission and without a physical network connection.

These devices are typically characterized by Wi-Fi and Cellular connectivity, a small rechargeable battery, usually Lithium-ion or Li-ion, a touchscreen interface, a virtual assistant such as Siri or Alexa, and the capacity to download applications or apps.

This chapter will discuss mobile devices, and their functionality, basic components, architecture, cell network structure, and security.

There was a time not long ago, when people who were not at home had to find a phone booth to make a simple phone call (Figure 8.1). The smartphone has forever changed our lives. The indispensable smartphone can do just about everything and has become the *Swiss army knife* for all modern society's needs. It has replaced many things we used to depend on, like alarm clocks, answering machines, calculators, camcorders, cameras, flashlights, GPS devices, landlines, payphones, maps, music players, pagers, watches, address books, and more.

8.2 A Brief History and Significant Milestones of Mobile Phones

The mobile radio has actually been around since the 1800s, when *Heinrich Hertz* proved the possibility of sending and receiving radio waves, based on *James Clerk Maxwell's* electromagnetic theory of light. Additionally, *Guglielmo Marconi* established a radio link between a land base and a boat in 1901.[1]

In the 1970s, mobile phones were used in vehicles and trains but were not handheld devices. In 1973, Motorola introduced the first *portable*

[1] Nassa, Vinay Kumar. "Wireless communications: Past, present and future." *Dronacharya Research Journal* 50, July–Dec., 2011.

FIGURE 8.2 **Motorola's DynaTAC 8000X. Courtesy of Shutterstock.**

radio telephone the Motorola DynaTAC, DYNamic Adaptive Total Area Coverage[2,3] (Figure 8.2). A cellular patent was filed by Dr. Martin Cooper as U.S. Patent 3,906,166.[4] In 1977, the Federal Communications Commission (FCC) approved the installation of the first cellular phone system in Chicago, which went live in 1978. In 1979, the first analog cellular systems were implemented in Tokyo by Nippon Telephone & Telegraph (NTT), and in 1981 one was launched in the Nordic countries (Denmark, Finland, Iceland, Norway, and Sweden) by Nordic Mobile Telephone (NMT). Sweden had 20,000 mobile users by 1981.[5] This was the *first generation (1G) analog automated cellular network* in the world.

In the United States, the first analog automated cellular network was launched in 1983. Called the Advanced Mobile Phone System (AMPS), it was the first-generation mobile standard that decided how mobile devices communicate with the base station, using distinct frequencies for each conversation. This standard was developed by Bell Labs, an AT&T subsidiary.[6] In the same

[2] "Motorola Milestones," last modified September 2018. Retrieved from https://www.motorola.com/us/about/motorola-history-milestones

[3] "Facts about the DynaTAC." Retrieved from https://www.motorola.com/sites/default/files/library/us/about-motorola-history-milestones/pdfs/DynaTAC_facts_73_001.pdf

[4] Cooper, Martin, Richard W. Dronsuth, Albert J. Leitich, Jr Charles N. Lynk, James J. Mikulski, John F. Mitchell, Roy A. Richardson, and John H. Sangster. "Radio telephone system." U.S. Patent 3,906,166, issued September 16, 1975.

[5] Agar, Jon. *Constant touch: A global history of the mobile phone.* Icon Books Ltd, 2013.

[6] *Id.* at 5.

year, the FCC approved Motorola's DynaTAC 8000X, called the *brick*, which was the first commercially available mobile phone. The *brick* mobile phone was 13 inches long and weighed 2.5 pounds, offered 30 minutes of talk time, and cost $3,995, plus a monthly service charge calculated by the minute.[7]

In the 1990s, the *second generation (2G)* of cellular communication emerged with two systems. First was the European Global System for Mobile communication (GSM) that was made mandatory by the European Union, and second was the U.S. developed Code Division Multiple Access (CDMA) standard. The 2G cellular network varied from 1G because it utilized digital transmission. Thus, generation 2G allowed the expansion of capacity and enabled widespread use of cellphones around the globe.

As the demand for faster wireless data transfer grew, 2G was not capable of handling such growth. As a result, the *third generation (3G)* promised a more capable digital cellular network. The 3G communication network appeared in the early 2000s and offered access to multimedia and widespread use of the Internet on cell phones. 3G uses a network of phone towers to transfer signals to and from the cell phone, ensuring a stable and fast connection. Originally, 3G's air data rate was measured between 384 kbit/s coverage and 2 Mbps indoor/microcell coverage. Afterward, the technology progressed into high-speed mobile broadband network coverage, called 3.5G, 3G+ and turbo 3G, delivering faster download speeds, and allowing for data transfer speeds up to 14 Mbps.[8]

In 2007, Apple introduced the iPhone. This was the first mobile phone using a multi-touch interface and signified the beginning of a new era in multimedia.

The two global standards for cellular communication were the GSM and CDMA. Both are 2G communication standards. GSM had captured almost two-fifths of the international market.[9] In Europe, GSM was mandatory, and it spread globally due to its lower-power operation, enabling smaller and lighter devices with greater security and longer battery. In addition, GSM used a mix of Frequency Division Multiple Access (FDMA) and Time Division Multiple Access (TDMA) along with frequency hopping. This means that a frequency is assigned to each user and allows several users to share the same frequency channel by dividing that signal into different time slots.[10,11] In this *time division* system, calls take turns when received. In

7 Annuzzi, Joseph, Lauren Darcey, and Shane Conder. *Introduction to Android application development: Android essentials*. Pearson Education, 2014.

8 Miao, Guowang, Jens Zander, Ki Won Sung, and Slimane Ben Slimane. *Fundamentals of mobile data networks*. Cambridge University Press, 2016.

9 Steinbock, Dan. *The mobile revolution: The making of mobile services worldwide*. Kogan Page Publishers, 2005.

10 Sempere, Javier Gozalvez. "An overview of the GSM system." *IEEE Vehicular Technology Society* (1997): 1–33.

11 *Id.* at 8.

other words, the receiver with assigned time slots obtains the call, with the call pieced together. This process occurs so rapidly that the receiver does not detect the fact that other calls are taking turns sharing the frequency.

To send the call, the voice is first converted from analogue sound waves to data (digital) and transmitted by the cellular network. The subscriber identity module (SIM) card contains the user's mobile information, including the personal number assigned to the mobile user. One of the advantages for GSM users is that the SIM card can be moved to another mobile phone, easily unlocking and transferring the device to another network. However, when using CDMA, the SIM card works only with mobile devices from the company with the same system.

In contrast, CDMA developed in the United States has been categorized as a *code division* system, and is built on a spread-spectrum signaling, resulting in spreading the user's signal within the time-frequency domain. This means that many users can send information instantaneously over a single channel or can share a band of frequencies.[12,13] CDMA offered advantages such as *timing flexibility*, where the signal is not affected by simultaneous transmitted user signals, *quality of transmission*, and *security and privacy*. Since each transmission is assigned a unique code, the conversation is private, and it resists interference.[14] 3G cellular technology made smartphones practical and the 'jack of all trades.'

The arrival of the iPhone in 2007 put the mobile Internet into everyone's hands (Figure 8.3). Its multimedia capabilities and mobile Internet access made 3G a "slow" network. As a result, the *fourth generation (4G)* cellular network, launched in 2010 by Telia Sonera in Finland, promised to support 100 Mbps peak rates and 1 Gbps in low mobility to mobile users.[15,16] In comparison to 3G, 4G provided a faster and more seamless mobile experience, featuring mobile Internet access, a wider range of applications with superior performance and reliability, along with the high quality of videos and images without buffering and pauses. 4G allowed smartphone technology to spread its wings and become more than just a phone.

Different technologies and standards have been used with 4G such as Long-Term Evolution (LTE), Worldwide Interoperability for Microwave Access (WIMAX), Multiple Input Multiple Output (MIMO), Mobile Broadband Wireless Access (MBWA), and Orthogonal Frequency Division

---

[12] Torrieri, Don. *Principles of spread-spectrum communication systems*. Vol. 1. Heidelberg: Springer, 2005.

[13] Stüber, Gordon L., and Gordon L. Stèuber. *Principles of mobile communication*. Vol. 2. Kluwer Academic, 1996.

[14] Pahlavan, Kaveh, and Allen H. Levesque. *Wireless information networks*. Vol. 93. John Wiley & Sons, 2005.

[15] Ezhilarasan, E., and M. Dinakaran. "A review on mobile technologies: 3G, 4G and 5G." In *2017 Second International Conference on Recent Trends and Challenges in Computational Models (ICRTCCM)*, pp. 369–373. IEEE, 2017.

[16] Fagbohun, O. "Comparative studies on 3G, 4G and 5G wireless technology." *IOSR Journal of Electronics and Communication Engineering* 9, no. 3 (2014): 88–94.

FIGURE 8.3 **The first-generation iPhone. Courtesy of Shutterstock.**

Multiplexing (OFDM). Of these, the most significant 4G standard for wireless data transmission is the LTE. The LTE standard was deployed in 2009 and was developed by the 3rd Generation Partnership Project, 3GPP. It established a significant path towards advanced international mobile telephony (IMT Advanced).[17] LTE uses two different radio links to enable better communication, reduced latency, and increased speed from tower to mobile device and back. For the downlink, LTE uses an Orthogonal Frequency Division Multiple Access (OFDMA) ranging from 1.4 to 20 MHz, and for the uplink it uses a Single Carrier Frequency Division Multiple Access (SC-FDMA) for better peak-to-average power ratio than OFDM, allowing less complexity.[18]

4G continues to evolve, using LTE-Advanced and LTE-Advanced Pro, as we move towards *fifth generation (5G)* cellular network technology. 5G mobile networks promise faster speeds than 4G, increased bandwidth, better coverage, less latency, and are expected to offer speeds higher than 1Gbps by using CDMA.[19,20,21] 5G technology will change the way we use smartphones

[17] Astély, David, Erik Dahlman, Anders Furuskär, Ylva Jading, Magnus Lindström, and Stefan Parkvall. "LTE: The evolution of mobile broadband." *IEEE Communications* 47, no. 4 (2009): 44–51.

[18] *Id.* at 17.

[19] Fagbohun, O. "Comparative studies on 3G, 4G and 5G wireless technology." *IOSR Journal of Electronics and Communication Engineering* 9, no. 3 (2014): 88–94.

[20] Al-Falahy, Naser, and Omar Y. Alani. "Technologies for 5G networks: Challenges and opportunities." *IT Professional* 19, no. 1 (2017): 12–20.

[21] Ibrahim, A. N., and M. F. L. Abdullah. "The potential of FBMC over OFDM for the future 5G mobile communication technology." In *AIP Conference Proceedings*, vol. 1883, no. 1, p. 020001. AIP Publishing LLC, 2017.

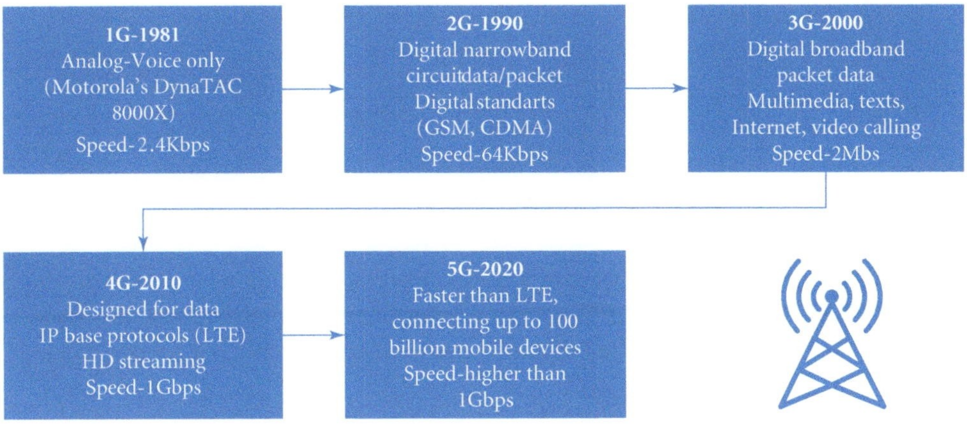

FIGURE 8.4 **The Evolution of Wireless Mobile Systems.**

since will soon be able to connect up to 100 billion mobile devices. Figure 8.4 shows the evolution of consumer mobile technologies.

8.3 Components, Operating Systems (OS), Applications and Architecture

Like any computing device, a mobile phone consists of both hardware and software components. The components work together and form a complex mobile ecosystem. Most of us do not realize the complexity of the engineering processes that take place when we purchase a smartphone or a tablet. Without thinking, we make phone calls, send text messages, access the Internet, look at videos, play music, take multiple pictures, and play games. None of these activities would be possible without the evolution of computer hardware like Global Positioning Systems (GPS), graphic cards, System-on-Chip (SOC), sensors, wireless networking, and many more elements.

Mobile device are small portable computers that offer many of the same possibilities as standard computers but, provide a different user experience in a compact, portable environment.

8.3.1 Main Components

Due to widespread adoption of these devices and their potential security risks and vulnerabilities, it is important to recognize the basic layers of hardware and software they contain and understand how they communicate and function. Additionally, it is important to understand the miniaturization that has gone into the development of mobile technology, such as the camera technology and image sensors, along with the System-on-Chip (SOC), which is an integrated circuit fitted into a single chip. The following are some of the major hardware components of the mobile phone:

- **An antenna**: made of a metallic element, usually copper, that communicates with mobile points using radio frequencies. It is used by the mobile phone for data broadcast, sending its electrical signal via radio waves, in both directions. A typical mobile phone has more than one type of antenna. Examples include the cellular antenna, Wi-Fi and Bluetooth antenna, wireless charging antenna, GPS antenna, and the Near-Field Communication (NFC) antenna.
- **Battery**: the primary source that supplies power to a mobile phone, usually lithium-ion or (Li-ion). Unfortunately, battery technology, has not advanced as fast as other parts of mobile phone technology.
- **Camera**: has evolved and become more sophisticated, with astonishing results. The smartphone camera uses a CMOS image sensor and has a digital zoom feature, which is a software effect that crops the image and mimics the optical zoom. To provide a clear image, the camera must be able to use a great number of pixels; otherwise, the image will be less than satisfactory.
- **Microphone**: converts sound pressure waves from speech into electrical signals. The *Speaker* does the direct opposite, converting electrical signals into sound waves.
- **Mobile phone circuit board or printed circuit board (PCB)**: one of the main components and considered the "brain" of the mobile phone because it manages all parts of the mobile ecosystem. The PCB contains computer chips, flash memory, Read Only Memory (ROM), and more. These circuit boards are constructed of precious metals such as gold, silver, and palladium, which prompt people to recycle their old mobile phones.[22]
- **Smartphone display**: the selling point for every mobile phone since the iPhone of 2007. The display has evolved from a miniature gray screen displaying numbers to a high-resolution touchscreen. The smartphone's display comes in a variety of sizes and resolutions. Where there is a *touchscreen* it will work as both an input and output device. When the finger touches the display, grid wires under the screen produce electrical charges, and the device recognizes the area as a tap (input).

  The two most common types of displays are:
- **Liquid crystal display (LCD) or IPS (in-plane switching) technology**: Its variations display panels shining a bright white backlight behind the screen that passes through polarizing filters and liquid crystals. Depending on the voltage the crystals control the light-like shutters and adjust the angle of polarized light. In front

[22] Kim, Yumi, Hyunhee Seo, and Yul Roh. "Metal recovery from the mobile phone waste by chemical and biological treatments." *Minerals* 8, no. 1 (2018): 8.

of the crystals layer there is a matrix of picture elements or pixels. Each pixel consists of three separate subpixels (Red, Green, and Blue) and produces the picture on the screen.[23] LCDs are cheaper to produce and are reliable, featuring resolution density and peak brightness.[24]

- **Light-emitting diode (LED)**, including Active-Matrix Organic Light-Emitting (AMOLED) and Organic Light Emitting Diode (OLED). Here, the pixels use light-emitting diodes and are self-luminous. That means the display is slimmer and lighter than LCD screens, featuring better energy efficiency, true black state, faster response time, flexible displays, and a wider color range than LCD.[25]
- **Sensors**: devices that detect changes according to certain rules, convert these changes into electrical signals, and interpret them to provide readable information. Examples of mobile device sensors are:
  - **Accelerometer**: senses the orientation of the mobile device and its movements. Measures instantaneous acceleration or deceleration.
  - **Gyroscope**: senses the displacement changes of the device.
  - **Magnetic field sensor**: measures magnetic field for direction concerning mapping and navigation.
  - **Light sensor**: adjust the screen brightness based on the light conditions or by the necessity to preserve battery life.
  - **Proximity sensor**: senses the orientation of nearby objects.
- **System-on-chip (SOC)**: a processing system package or a building block that integrates several computer hardware elements into a single silicon chip such as Camera and Image signal processor, Central Processing Unit (CPU), Flash Storage, Graphics Processing Unit (GPU), Modems (4G LTE, 5G, Wi-Fi, and Bluetooth), mobile Random Access Memory (RAM), video encoder & decoder and more.[26,27] The advantage of SOC integration is efficiency, cost reduction, speed of performance, and space reduction. Besides their use in mobile devices, SOC has been utilized in the Internet of Things

---

[23] Tsai, Pei-Shan, Chia-Kai Liang, Tai-Hsiang Huang, and Homer H. Chen. "Image enhancement for backlight-scaled TFT-LCD displays." *IEEE Transactions on Circuits and Systems for Video Technology* 19, no. 4 (2009): 574–583.

[24] Chen, Hai-Wei, Jiun-Haw Lee, Bo-Yen Lin, Stanley Chen, and Shin-Tson Wu. "Liquid crystal display and organic light-emitting diode display: Present status and future perspectives." *Light: Science & Applications* 7, no. 3 (2018): 17168–17168.

[25] *Id.* at 24.

[26] Hwang, L. James, and Reno L. Sanchez. "Method and system for resource allocation in FPGA-based system-on-chip (SoC)." U.S. Patent 7,058,921, issued June 6, 2006.

[27] Hill, Mark, and Vijay Janapa Reddi. "Gables: A roofline model for mobile SoCs." In *2019 IEEE International Symposium on High Performance Computer Architecture (HPCA)*, pp. 317–330. IEEE, 2019.

(IoT), cars, and laptops. The key manufacturers of SOC processing are Apple, Huawei's HiSilicon, MediaTek, NVIDIA, Qualcomm, and Samsung Semiconductor.

8.3.2 Operating Systems (OS) and Applications (apps)

The mobile operating system is designed to run on mobile devices, including phones, tablets, 2-in-1 computers (tablet + laptop), and other devices. The OS is usually pre-installed and can be initiated by a power button. When the power button is pushed, firmware, the BIOS, begins the boot process. Self-testing begins, followed by debugging and/or modifying, along with additional device initialization codes before the OS loads into the device.

The mobile OS is responsible for its operation, including administration, maintenance, and management of hardware and software resources, including the processor and memory. Also, the OS runs applications and manages cellular and wireless network connectivity, including Bluetooth and Wi-Fi, GPS navigation, and multimedia functions. The most popular mobile Operating Systems are Android OS and Apple's iOS.

- Android OS is the most widely used mobile operating system in the world and is an open source OS. It is based on a modified version of the Linux kernel and was developed by Google.[28] A modified version has been configured for TVs, cars, and smartwatches.
- iPhone OS or iOS is the second most popular operating system and was developed by Apple. The iOS is based on a Unix-like operating system and contains several elements of the Mac OS X operating system. The iOS is only available for Apple devices.[29]

Running above the mobile OS is a series of applications or apps. Initially, the apps were intended to incentivize productivity, like calendar and e-mail apps. As the popularity of mobile devices increased, the demand for apps rapidly expanded into "there's an app for everything and everyone." These application programs or apps are specialized software, that easily enable

[28] Alshahrani, Hani, Harrison Mansourt, Seaver Thorn, Ali Alshehri, Abdulrahman Alzahrani, and Huirong Fu. "DDefender: Android application threat detection using static and dynamic analysis." In *2018 IEEE International Conference on Consumer Electronics (ICCE)*, pp. 1–6. IEEE, 2018.

[29] Novac, Ovidiu Constantin, Mihaela Novac, Cornelia Gordan, Tamas Berczes, and Gyöngyi Bujdosó. "Comparative study of Google Android, Apple iOS and Microsoft Windows phone mobile operating systems." In *2017 14th International Conference on Engineering of Modern Electric Systems (EMES)*, pp. 154–159. IEEE, 2017.

mobile users to perform a specific task. An *Application Program Interface (API)* is a feature of the OS that permits apps to request services and can interact with and acquire data from one another. Examples of APIs that enable shared content between third-party apps are the LinkedIn's API, Facebook's API, Twitter API, Google Maps, and YouTube. A good example is Facebook's API. Facebook's API allows users to sign in, enable social media users, and post content from the Facebook app. It also allows developers to access users' profile identities and get data from Facebook platforms to manage ads and perform other tasks. Users often do not understand the extent of their data that Facebook can use. Facebook's Graph API, a list of specific tags or data about a specific object, was used by Cambridge Analytica to collect Facebook users' personal information, access their social lives, and use them as targets in political campaigns like the 2016 U.S. presidential election, and UK's Brexit referendum campaign.

On a positive note, APIs integrate application components into existing architecture and help businesses to collaborate with customers, harvesting data from old infrastructures with cloud-based apps and sharing the data with them.

To be able to develop an application, developers are using one-stop solution software called *Software Development Kit (SDK)*, a collection of tools, APIs, guidelines, libraries, programs, and other utilities, that help developers create an application for a specific platform. Companies that offer SDK kits include Google, Facebook, and Microsoft.

8.3.3 Platform Architectures

The two most widely deployed mobile operating systems are Google's Android OS and Apple's iOS. Android is the most deployed smartphone OS to the end-user.[30] Both platforms, Android and iOS, run on a Unix-like OS.[31,32]

Android is an open-source OS developed by Google, Open Handset Alliance, and other companies. To be able to use the Android OS, mobile device manufacturers must meet the requirements specified by the Compatibility Definition Document (CDD) and get

[30] Mayrhofer, René, Jeffrey Vander Stoep, Chad Brubaker, and Nick Kralevich. "The Android platform security model." *arXiv preprint* arXiv:1904.05572 (2019).

[31] Dutta, Amitava, Abhinay Puvvala, Rahul Roy, and Priya Seetharaman. "Technology diffusion: Shift happens—The case of iOS and Android handsets." *Technological Forecasting and Social Change* 118 (2017): 28–43.

[32] NOVAC, Ovidiu Constantin, Robert-Gyula MARCZIN, and Mihaela Cornelia NOVAC. "Comparison of hybrid cross-platform mobile applications with native cross-platform applications." *Journal of Computer Science & Control Systems* 9, no. 2 (2016).

permission from Google. The Android OS consists of seven main layers.[33,34] These layers, along with their elements, are integrated to provide an optimal user experience.

- **Linux kernel layer**: at the bottom of the stack and considered the heart of the Android ecosystem, it is responsible for the smooth functioning of the system. This layer interfaces between the device hardware and the upper layer of the Android application software stack. It manages core system services like virtual memory, interfacing to peripheral hardware, networking, and a vast array of device drivers like Bluetooth, camera, display, memory, power management, memory management, and keypad.[35]
- **Hardware abstraction layer (HAL)**: provides an interface for specific hardware components. It consists of multiple modules, for example, the camera or the Bluetooth module.[36] If a framework API would like to access the camera, the Android system loads the module that is needed.
- **Android runtime (ART)**: is the software layer between the Android OS and the applications. It provides an execution environment for running apps written in Kotlin, the programming language for Java Virtual Machine, and other Java language apps. Additionally, ART's predecessor Dalvik should work when running with ART. ART also manages memory and provides a set of core libraries for developers to use when developing apps in the Java language.[37,38]
- **Native C/C++ libraries**: provide standard Java libraries for android apps that support general-purpose tasks like networking and databases. Examples include the SQLite library, which is used to store and share data, the Webkit library, used for browsing the web, the Secure Sockets Layer (SSL) library, which is used for secure communications, and the Audio manager library, which controls the audio subsystem. In addition to these standard libraries, Java-based libraries

[33] Ahvanooey, Milad Taleby, Qianmu Li, Mahdi Rabbani, and Ahmed Raza Rajput. "A survey on smartphones security: software vulnerabilities, malware, and attacks." *arXiv preprint* arXiv:2001.09406 (2020).

[34] Joshi, Jignesh, and Chandresh Parekh. "Android smartphone vulnerabilities: A survey." In *2016 International Conference on Advances in Computing, Communication, & Automation (ICACCA) (Spring)*, pp. 1–5. IEEE, 2016.

[35] *Id.* at 33.

[36] Bhat, Parnika, and Kamlesh Dutta. "A survey on various threats and current state of security in android platform." *ACM Computing Surveys (CSUR)* 52, no. 1 (2019): 1–35.

[37] Li, Bodong, Yuanyuan Zhang, Juanru Li, Wenbo Yang, and Dawu Gu. "AppSpear: automating the hidden-code extraction and reassembling of packed android malware." *Journal of Systems and Software* 140 (2018): 3–16.

[38] *Id.* at 33.

are designed for Android developers.[39] Examples of Android libraries include: *android.database*, used to access data from a content provider, *android.text*, used to render and manipulate text on the device's display, *android.webkit*, which allows web-browsing abilities constructed into an app, *android.opengl*, a cross-platform graphics API, and many more. Most Android apps are written in Java, but other platforms such as C/C++, Python, and Basic are also used.[40] Additionally, the Android developers' documentation page provides reference-object classes and a complete list of packages, including the Android SDK.[41]

- **Java API framework**: provides the building blocks to create Android apps by simplifying the reuse of core, modular system components and services. It also manages the application resources and user interface, including:[42]
  - Activity Manager, which manages the lifecycle of an app and provides common navigation like the back button.
  - Content, which enables apps to access/share/publish data from other apps. For example, contacts app.
  - Notification Manager, which enables apps to display custom alerts.
  - Resource Manager, which provides access to non-code resources like color strings, graphics, and the user interface layout.
  - View System, which builds an app's user interface, including buttons, lists, text boxes, and web browser.
- **System application layer**: provides core apps and third-party apps for email, SMS messaging, calendars, Internet browsing, contacts, and more. The third-party apps can become users' default apps except for the system's Settings app).[43]
- **Hardware and power management**: components built into the system. Every component has a specific interface design for user interaction.

Figure 8.5 demonstrates the major components of the Android platform.

Apple's iOS is based on the NeXTSTEP operating system. NeXTSTEP was created by Steve Jobs' company, NeXT, after he left Apple. When Jobs returned to Apple, NeXTSTEP became the basis of macOS and iOS.

---

[39] Meier, Reto, and Ian Lake. *Professional android*. John Wiley & Sons, 2018.

[40] Wei, Fengguo, Xingwei Lin, Xinming Ou, Ting Chen, and Xiaosong Zhang. "Jn-saf: Precise and efficient ndk/jni-aware inter-language static analysis framework for security vetting of android applications with native code." In *Proceedings of the 2018 ACM SIGSAC Conference on Computer and Communications Security*, pp. 1137–1150. 2018.

[41] Package Index, Android developers. Retrieved from https://developer.android.com/reference/packages

[42] Android Architecture. Retrieved from https://developer.android.com/guide/platform

[43] *Id.* at 42.

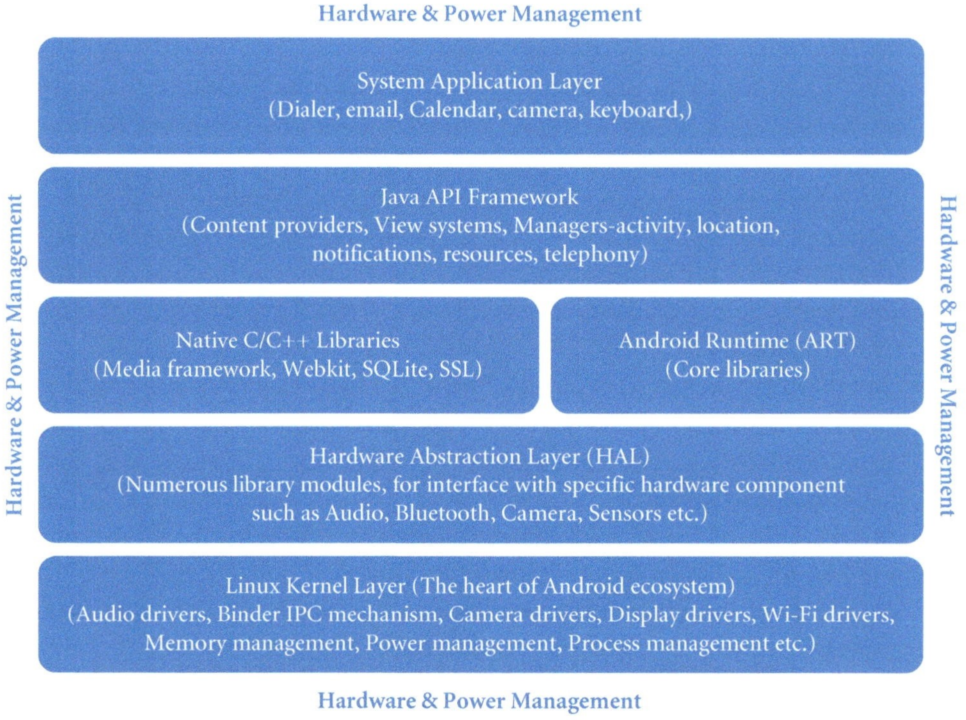

FIGURE 8.5 The Android Platform.

NeXTSTEP was based on Unix and was created using the Carnegie Mellon Mach kernel.[44,45] The Apple iOS architecture is proprietary and consists of the following layers.[46,47] Figure 8.6 displays the iOS architecture.

- **Core OS layer**: Contains lower-level features that most other technologies depend on, like the XNU kernel, which is part of the Darwin OS for use in macOS and iOS operating systems and is the foundation for the entire iOS. The XNU includes the Berkeley Software Distribution (BSD), which provides a portable OS interface and also comprises the file manager, local

[44] Kostakis, Vasilis, and Stelios Stavroulakis. "The parody of the commons." *P2P E INOVAÇÃO* 2, no. 2 (2016): 28–51.
[45] Halvorsen, Ole Henry, and Douglas Clarke. *OS X and iOS kernel programming*. Apress, 2012.
[46] *Id.* at 33.
[47] Pieterse, Heloise, Martin Olivier, and Renier van Heerden. "Evaluation framework for detecting manipulated smartphone data." *SAIEE Africa Research Journal* 110, no. 2 (2019): 67–76.

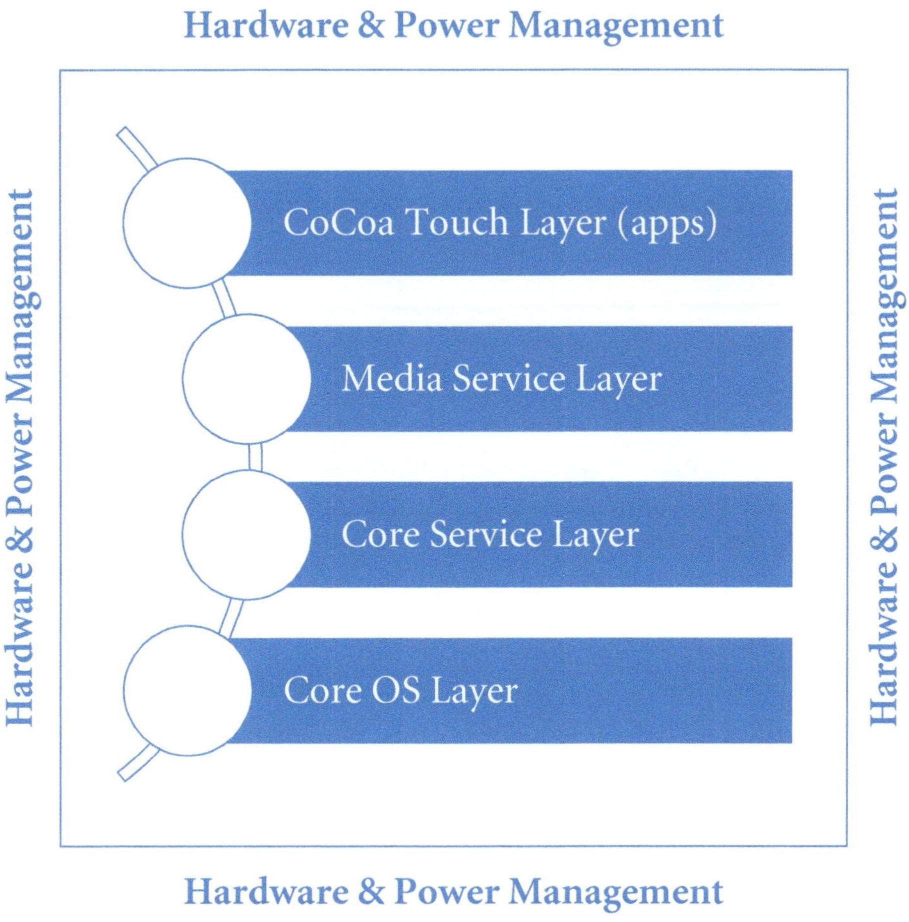

FIGURE 8.6 **The iOS Architecture.**

authentication, security services of the entire system, system utilities, and a Bluetooth framework.[48]

- **Core service layer**: Contains important frameworks such as Address book framework, used with the database, Cloud Kit framework to move data between apps and the iCloud, Core telephony framework to handle telephone lines, Core location to provide location information to apps, and Core motion for accelerometer-based data, Social framework to interface social media accounts, and Health kit to control user's health-related information.[49]
- **Media service layer:** Contains graphics, audio and video, video frameworks such as core graphics framework for vector drawings,

[48] *Id.* at 29.

[49] Junxiang, Gao, and Huang Yu. "Design of mobile learning system for courses of computer science and technology." In *Journal of Physics: Conference Series*, vol. 1237, no. 5, p. 052002. IOP Publishing, 2019.

image 2D rendering, animation, game kit, AV kid, text, and image technology to manage the user interface.

- **Cocoa touch layer**: Contains the user interface of iOS, such as touch-based inputs, notifications, multitasking, cut, copy, paste, Game Kit Framework, MapKit framework, and more.[50]
- **Hardware power management**: Contains components built into the system.

8.4 The Cellular Network

The mobile phone converts audio and data into radio waves and transmits them from the phone's antenna to the nearest cell tower, cellular base station, or cellphone mast. These radio waves are used for cellular communications in a relatively higher frequency because they travel only short distances between the device and the cell towers[51] (Figure 8.7). The radio waves lose strength in the presence of physical objects, electrical equipment, and environmental factors. To overcome these challenges, cell towers enable mobile devices to offer seamless service.

Mobile devices rely on cellular or mobile networks. Cellular technology is based on dividing a geographical area into hexagonal cells. The hexagon is preferred because it covers an entire area without overlapping, and the shape reasonably approximates the circular radiation pattern of an

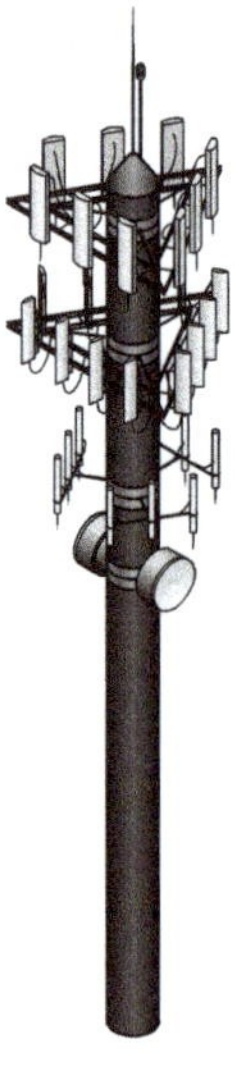

FIGURE 8.7 **A Cell Tower. Courtesy of Shutterstock.**

[50] Mohamed, Ibtisam, and Dhiren Patel. "Android vs iOS security: A comparative study." In *2015 12th International Conference on Information Technology—New Generations*, pp. 725–730. IEEE, 2015.

[51] Gralla, Preston. *How wireless works.* Que, 2002.

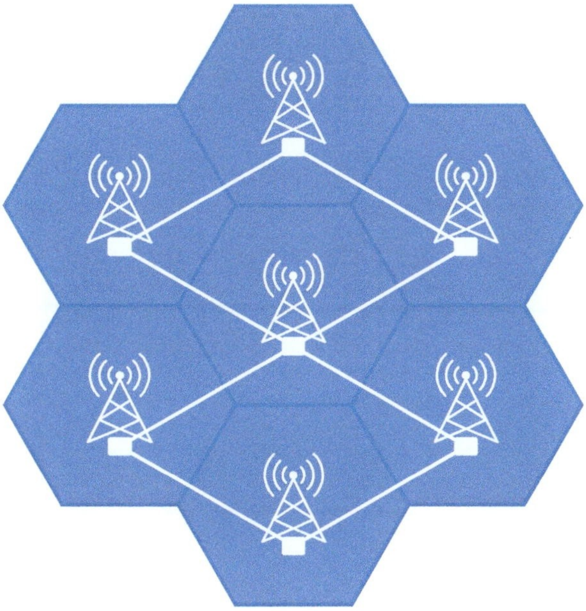

FIGURE 8.8 **The Hexagonal Cellular Network.**

omni-directional cell tower antenna.[52] *Each cell is defined as a geographical element of a cellular network.* Cell towers are interconnected through fiber-optic cables, either underground or underwater to offer national and international connectivity. Thus, wireless does not mean completely wireless (see Figure 8.8).

Cell towers have different traffic densities depending on the number of mobile devices served. For example, during the weekends, cell towers have significantly higher traffic density where people congregate around museums, amusement parks, and shopping centers. Higher traffic occurs near the airports and along highways, compared to rural areas which typically have lower traffic density. Comprehending the traffic density patterns of cellular networks assists with the planning, network capacity, and performance that affect users' satisfaction.[53]

In remote areas, *microwave links* are often used because fiber-optic cables may be impractical or expensive to install. Microwave links are used for point-to-point communication since they have small wavelengths, are cost-effective, easily deployable, and have limited bandwidth compared to fiber optics.[54] Microwave links transmit and receive waves in the microwave

[52] Mozaffari, Mohammad, Ali Taleb Zadeh Kasgari, Walid Saad, Mehdi Bennis, and Mérouane Debbah. "Beyond 5G with UAVs: Foundations of a 3D wireless cellular network." *IEEE Transactions on Wireless Communications* 18, no. 1 (2018): 357–372.

[53] Kim, Heeyoung, Rong Duan, Sungil Kim, Jaehwan Lee, and Guang-Qin Ma. "Spatial cluster detection in mobility networks: A copula approach." *Journal of the Royal Statistical Society: Series C (Applied Statistics)* 68, no. 1 (2019): 99–120.

[54] Rao, R. Srinivasa. *Microwave engineering.* PHI Learning Pvt. Ltd., 2015.

FIGURE 8.9 **Multiple Cellular Antennas (3G, 4G, and 5G). Courtesy of Shutterstock.**

frequency. Microwaves have been used to transmit information in cellular networks, satellite communications, space radio communications and are also used in radar technology. The range of microwave links on the surface of the earth is related to the heights of the antennas, and the curvature of the earth limits the range of communication from 70 to 100 Km.[55]

It is important to point out that with the arrival of 5G cellular systems, traditional cells will be replaced by *Small Cells* that require low power and can be positioned approximately every 250 meters throughout cities. This method will prevent signals from being dropped and provide more effective use of the spectrum[56] (Figure 8.9).

With the exponential growth in demand for *high bandwidth* applications, along with new and old cellular systems being used, more antennas are needed to support more frequencies. The new cellular systems will require greater infrastructure. In the past, cell towers housed 3–4 antennas per tower, now we see dozens of antennas on each tower. With 5G networking, a cell tower can support approximately a hundred ports, so that many more antennas can fit on a single array.[57] The more antennas, the faster that transmission and reception can occur between many more users. In addition to the increase in the number of antennas, optical fiber cables have been used to connect cell towers and antennas. More antennas require more cables up to the towers.

The goal of a cellular network is to communicate seamlessly from one mobile device to another through linked cell towers. Mobile phones have unique key

---

[55] *Id.* at 54.

[56] Nordrum, Amy, and Kristen Clark. "Everything you need to know about 5G." *IEEE Spectrum* 27 (2017).

[57] *Id.* at 56.

identifications to identify the phone's owner and cellular service provider. Following are the most common key identifiers.

- **Electronic serial number (ESN):** is a unique 32-bit binary number embedded by the manufacturer on a mobile phone. The ESN cannot be easily changed by the user; it requires special facilities for alteration.[58] This Mobile Equipment Identifier (MEID)/ESN is commonly used by CDMA and the International Mobile Equipment Identity (IMEI) and is used under the GSM standard to help prevent fraud.[59]
- **Mobile identification number (MIN):** is a 34-bit binary number assigned by the wireless provider within a wireless carrier's network. The binary number consists of MIN1 (24 bits) and MIN2 (10 bits), simply known as MIN. The CDMA standard uses the International Mobile Station Identity (IMSI). The IMSI is usually stored on a Subscriber Identity Module (SIM). In addition, the IMSI includes the Mobile Network Code (MNC) and the Mobile Subscription Identification Number (MSIN).[60]
- **Mobile directory number (MDN):** is the 10-digit cell phone number that we all use. When a number is moved from one wireless service provider to another, the MDN is transferred to a new service provider and another MIN is assigned to identify the new mobile phone on the new carrier. Users can request keeping their MDN, and it is often possible to do so.
- **Mobile equipment identifier (MEID):** is a globally unique number identifying a mobile device in the CDMA. Similarly, the **Mobile Equipment Identifier (IMEI)** in GSM phones with hexadecimal digits is embedded in the device not in the SIM cards.[61]

8.4.1 What Happens When a Mobile Phone Is Turned On?

When we turn on the mobile phone, it listens for a signal and searches for the nearest cell tower approximately every seven seconds.[62] The cellphone tower identifies the mobile phone or mobile device connected to a cellular data network by its Network Identification (NID) and Cellular System Identification number (SID). The combination of SID and NID uniquely identifies the ser-

---

[58] Yacoub, Michel Daoud. *Wireless technology: Protocols, standards, and techniques*. CRC Press, 2017.

[59] Koch, William, Abdelberi Chaabane, Manuel Egele, William Robertson, and Engin Kirda. "Semi-automated discovery of server-based information oversharing vulnerabilities in Android applications." In *Proceedings of the 26th ACM SIGSOFT International Symposium on Software Testing and Analysis*, pp. 147–157. ACM, 2017.

[60] *Id.* at 58.

[61] Bojinov, Hristo, Yan Michalevsky, Gabi Nakibly, and Dan Boneh. "Mobile device identification via sensor fingerprinting." *arXiv preprint* arXiv:1408.1416 (2014).

[62] McLaughlin, Kevin. "The Fourth Amendment and cell phone location tracking: Where are we." *Hastings Communications and Entertainment Law Journal*29 (2006): 421.

vice provider's geographical area. The NID identifies the network within a cellular system, and the SID recognizes the home system, roaming status, and billing information.[63] The mobile device matches the SID to the code programmed by the carrier and recognizes the type of system it is accessing. In the United States, the FCC managed the administration of cellular SIDs until 2003. Since then, cellular SIDs have been transferred to the private sector.[64] Internationally, the International Forum on ANSI-41 Standards Technology (IFAST)[65] has been assigning SID ranges since 1997. Previously, SIDs were allocated by the Telecommunications Industry Association (TIA).[66]

As stated earlier, Radiofrequency (RF) is a type of electromagnetic radiation that has been used to transmit signals containing information in the form of radio waves. The mobile phone uses its antenna to transmit electromagnetic waves, also referred to as Radiofrequency signals, to the nearest cell tower. The cell tower converts the RF signal into light pulses through the Base Transceiver System (BTS) and the Base Station Controller (BSC) and then transmits it over a fiber optic cable into the destination cell tower via the Mobile Telephone Switching Office (MTSO).[67,68] Once the destination cell tower receives the light pulses, it converts them back to RF signals and the reverse process occurs as the mobile device picks up the RF signal and processes it to voice or data.

The Mobile Telephone Switching Office (MTSO), also known as the Mobile Switching Center (MSC),[69] is the heart of a group of cell towers in a specific geographic area and is responsible for controlling the cell towers in that area, coordinating phone calls, managing connections, routing mobile phone calls, maintenance, *handover or handoff management* (the process of keeping the mobile phone connected when it moves from one core network to another), billing, and encryption. Additionally, the MSC maintains a database called Home Location Register (HLR) with all home network subscribers in the area, and an Authentication Centre (AC) that performs authentication tasks for the HLR. All mobile switching centers are interconnected by fiber optic cables. Every center stores the Subscriber Identity Module (SIM) information as well

63 Federal Communications Commission (FCC), Cellular System Identification Number (SID) Administrators. Retrieved from https://www.fcc.gov/wireless/bureau-divisions/mobility-division/cellular-service/cellular-system-identification-number

64 *Id.* at 58.

65 International Forum on ANSI-41 Standards Technology Retrieve, SIDs System Identification Number from http://www.ifast.org/

66 Telecommunications Industry Association (TIA). Retrieved from https://tiaonline.org/

67 Dat, Pham Tien, Atsushi Kanno, and Tetsuya Kawanishi. "Radio-on-radio-over-fiber: efficient fronthauling for small cells and moving cells." *IEEE Wireless Communications* 22, no. 5 (2015): 67–75.

68 Deb, A. B., and N. Kjærgaard. "Radio-over-fiber using an optical antenna based on Rydberg states of atoms." *Applied Physics Letters* 112, no. 21 (2018): 211106.

69 Djordjevic, Ivan B. *Advanced optical and wireless communications systems.* Heidelberg: Springer, 2018.

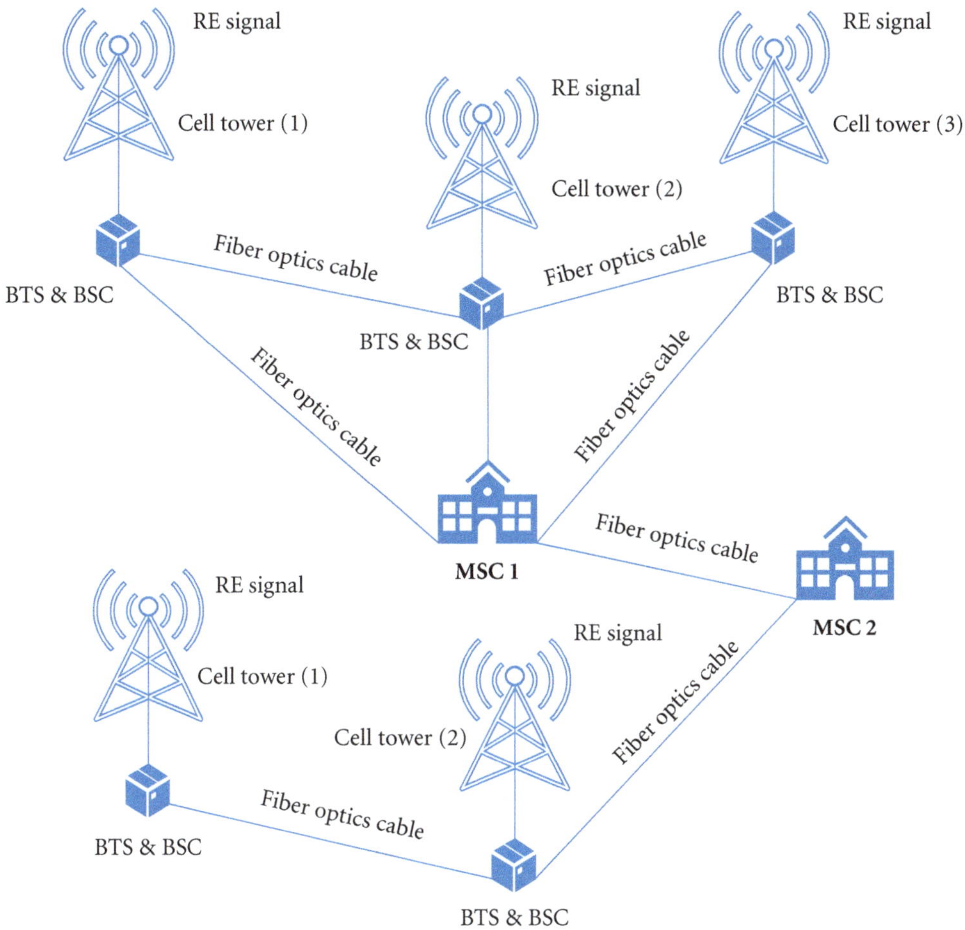

FIGURE 8.10 The Cellular Network.

as its activity status. When the mobile device travels outside the home, the foreign MSC connects with the home MSC and determines the location of the device. If the device is on and is within the range of a cell tower, and is not in airplane mode, the device will be located. The home MSC always knows in which MSC area the device is located. Additionally, the MSC tracks the phone's location in a database and knows which cell area the mobile device is in. Figure 8.10 shows the cellular network.

As was stated earlier, the SIM card is an important component of any mobile phone. This portable memory chip holds subscriber's information that can be read by the mobile device, as well as cellular network information used for authentication and user identification. The most important pieces of information contained in a SIM card are:

- The Integrated Circuit Card ID (ICCID), which consists of 19–20 digits and is a global unique serial number that identifies the SIM card itself and is usually printed on the card,

- The International Mobile Subscriber Identity (IMSI), which identifies the subscriber's cellular network,
- The authentication key (Ki), a 128-bit secret key for authentication assigned by the cellular provider,
- The Local Area Identity (LAI), a unique number that identifies a mobile network,
- Short Message Service Center (SMSC), that manages SMS operations like storing, forwarding, routing, converting, and delivering text messages,
- The SPN Service Provider Name.[70/71]

8.4.2 The Cell Tower or Cellular Base Station

It is important to note the significance of the cell tower, or cellular base station. The transmission of RF signals over fiber optic cables is a technology using intense modulation of a light source with the RF signal.[72] Some of the benefits of RF over fiber technology instead of traditional copper coaxial cables are its high optical bandwidth, enabling a greater number of data transfers from one cell tower to another. This technology allows for higher speed signal processing, greater security against signal interception, no distance limitations, light weight, ease of installation, and low maintenance.[73]

The mobile phone communicates by constantly sending and receiving radio signals to and from an antenna located in the nearest cell tower. When the signal from the mobile phone goes to the cell tower it is called an *uplink*, while the signal coming from a cell tower is called a *downlink*. Each cell tower consists of the following components:

- **The base transceiver system (BTS)**: Consists of radio equipment (transmitter and receiver = transceiver), that handles transmission and reception of the signals. The BTS sends and receives signals by providing radio coverage for a cell or a sector.[74]
- **The base station controller (BSC)**: is a network component that manages and controls several cell towers or base stations from cell-to-cell. In addition, it provides the interface from cell towers

[70] Anwar, Nuril, Imam Riadi, and Ahmad Luthfi. "Forensic SIM card cloning using authentication algorithm." *International Journal of Electronics and Information Engineering* 4, no. 2 (2016): 71–81.

[71] *Id.* at 58.

[72] Caytan, Olivier, Laurens Bogaert, Haolin Li, Joris Van Kerrebrouck, Sam Lemey, Guy Torfs, Johan Bauwelinck et al. "Passive opto-antenna as downlink remote antenna unit for radio frequency over fiber." *Journal of Lightwave Technology* 36, no. 19 (2018): 4445–4459.

[73] Islam, Saveed, Md Ferdous Khan, Md Zakir Hossan, and M. Ashraful Amin. "An Overview of Radio over Fiber (RoF) Technology." In *2019 2nd International Conference on Intelligent Computing, Instrumentation and Control Technologies (ICICICT)*, vol. 1, pp. 749–752. IEEE, 2019.

[74] *Id.* at 58.

to the Mobile Switching Center (MSC) via microwave or fiber optic links.[75]

- **Backup batteries** provide an uninterrupted power supply in the event of an outage.
- **A generator** provides standby power.

8.4.3 Mobile Device Tracking Location: Cell Towers, GPS, and Indoor Localization

There are numerous ways to trace a mobile phone's location, including applications like Android's *Find My Device,* which is built into the smartphone through Google Play or third-party apps like *Prey Anti-Theft*. This app permits the collection of data including pictures from the camera using GPS coordinates and the Media Access Control (MAC) address.

In addition to the Android mobile phone, this app is available to other devices such as laptops, tablets, iOS, Chromebooks, Windows, and Linux. Apple's *Find My iPhone* app comes pre-installed on every iOS device that can use a map to locate the device.

Besides these apps, other methods such as Cell Towers, GPS, and Wi-Fi-based localizations are available if the device is neither turned off nor switched to airplane mode.

First, Cell Tower Triangulation uses multiple cell towers to locate the device. When the mobile device's signal is picked up by three or more cell towers, an overlap is enabled. The cell towers estimate the location of the cell phone based on its distance from the three towers, using angles of radio signals and/or time to find the distance.[76] Some of the main techniques for location of network transmitters are the *Angle of Arrival (AOA)*, *Time Difference of Arrival (TDoA)*, and *Time of Arrival (ToA)*.

- **Angle of arrival (AOA)** estimates the mobile device's location by measuring the arrival angles of radio signals between the device and the cell towers, using basic trigonometry. A minimum of two angles are required. This technique uses the device location at the intersection of lines shaped by the arrival angles of the radio signals (Figure 8.11). This is known as triangulation[77] (Figure 8.12).

---

[75] *Id.* at 58.

[76] Sattarian, Mahbubeh, Javad Rezazadeh, Reza Farahbakhsh, and Alireza Bagheri. "Indoor navigation systems based on data mining techniques in internet of things: A survey." *Wireless Networks* 25, no. 3 (2019): 1385–1402.

[77] Laoudias, Christos, Adriano Moreira, Sunwoo Kim, Sangwoo Lee, Lauri Wirola, and Carlo Fischione. "A survey of enabling technologies for network localization, tracking, and navigation." *IEEE Communications Surveys & Tutorials* 20, no. 4 (2018): 3607–3644.

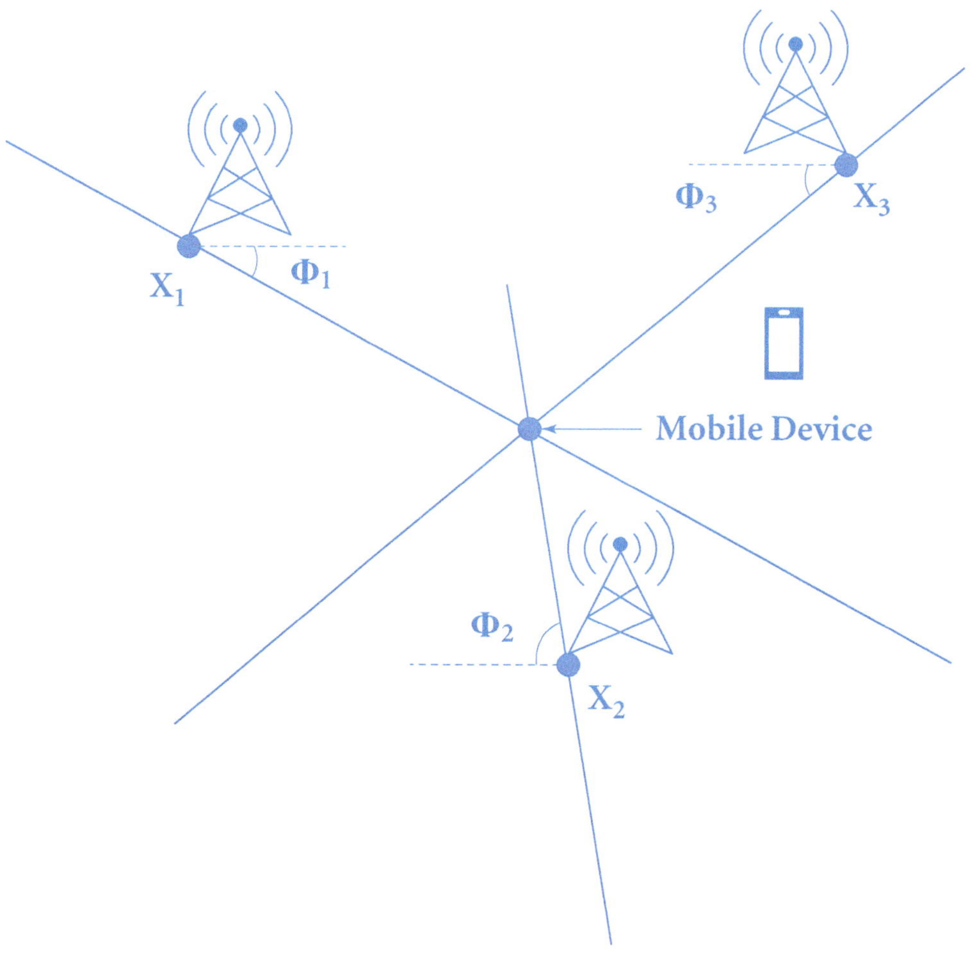

FIGURE 8.11 **Measuring the angles Φ determine the location of a mobile device.**

- **Time of arrival (ToA)** uses an estimation of the distance or distances of the travel time of a signal between a mobile device and several cell towers to determine the position coordinates of the device. This technique uses the transmission time between the device and cell tower directly to find the distance of the device from the tower.[78]
- **Time difference of arrival (TDoA)** Like ToA, this method uses multiple cell towers to locate the mobile device. The TDoA measures the amount of time it takes for the radio signal from cell towers to reach and return to the tower from the cell phone (Figure 8.13). The measurement is defined as a hyperbola, instead of a circle and measures pairs of transmission paths between the device and the cell towers.[79]

---

[78] *Id.* at 77.

[79] Salari, Soheil, Francois Chan, Yiu-Tong Chan, and William Read. "TDOA estimation with compressive sensing measurements and hadamard Matrix." *IEEE Transactions on Aerospace and Electronic Systems* 54, no. 6 (2018): 3137–3142.

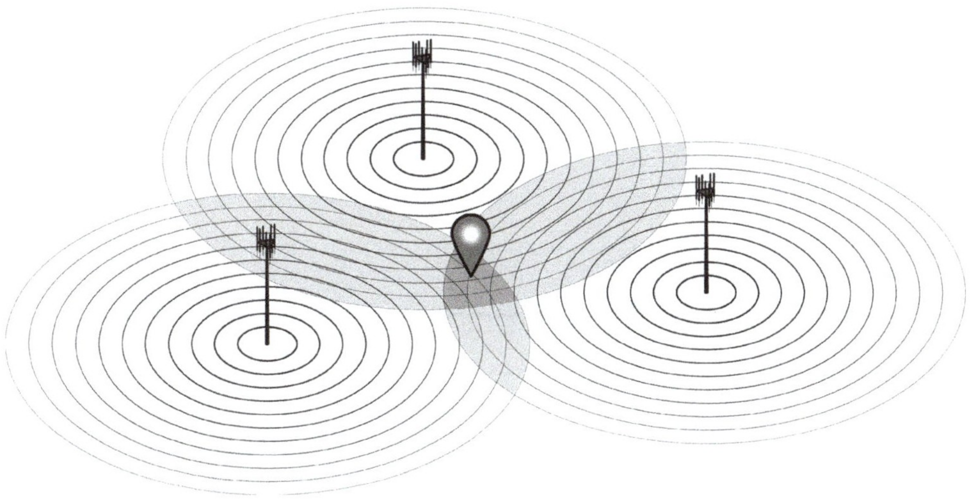

FIGURE 8.12 **Mobile Cell Towers Triangulation. Courtesy of Shutterstock.**

The second method uses the *Global Positioning System (GPS)*, a satellite-based navigation system consisting of 24 satellites orbiting the earth[80,81] (Figure 8.14). All mobile phones have a built-in GPS. The GPS identifies an object based on two mathematical notions. The first notion determines the position of an object from three different satellites. This is called *trilateration*. The second notion is the relationship between distance, rate of travel (speed), and time spent traveling.[82] Use of data from at least three satellites can determine the *latitude, longitude, and altitude* of a mobile device.[83]

In addition to the above methods, indoor techniques may be used to locate devices in an environment when other methods like GPS lack precision. This is called indoor localization and some of the techniques that can be used along with AOA, ToA and TDoA are

- **Bluetooth** and its latest version called Bluetooth Low Energy (BLE), which enables devices like iBeacon to provide proximity detection and indoor localization.[84]

[80] Doshi, Pankti, Pooja Jain, and Abhishek Shakwala. "Location based services and integration of google maps in android." *International Journal of Engineering and Computer Science* 3, no. 3 (2014).

[81] U.S. government information about the Global Positioning System (GPS). Retrieved from https://www.gps.gov/systems/gps/space/

[82] Activity: How to find a position using GPS. Retrieved from https://www.gps.gov/multimedia/tutorials/trilateration/instructions.pdf

[83] Ranacher, Peter, Richard Brunauer, Wolfgang Trutschnig, Stefan Van der Spek, and Siegfried Reich. "Why GPS makes distances bigger than they are." *International Journal of Geographical Information Science* 30, no. 2 (2016): 316–333.

[84] Zafari, Faheem, Athanasios Gkelias, and Kin K. Leung. "A survey of indoor localization systems and technologies." *IEEE Communications Surveys & Tutorials* 21, no. 3 (2019): 2568–2599.

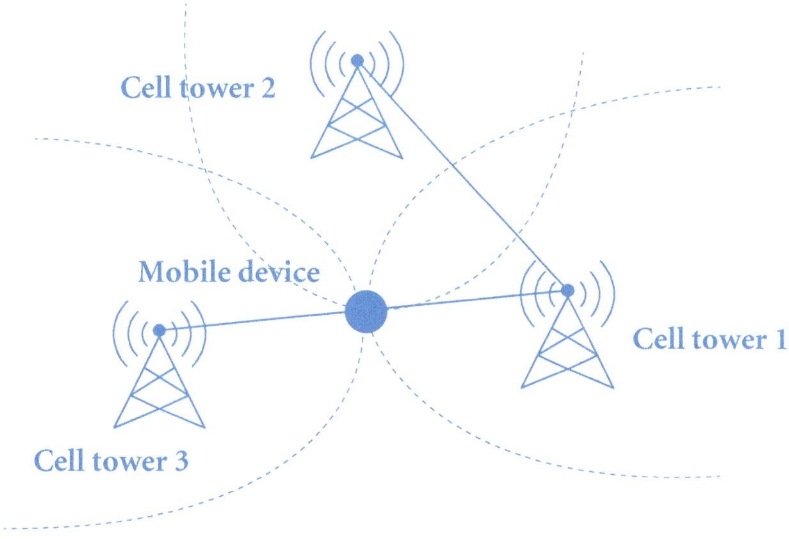

FIGURE 8.13 **The time difference of arrival (TDoA) measurement.**

- **Received signal strength indicator (RSSI)** that can be used to estimate the distance between transmission and reception.[85]
- **Wi-Fi-based localization** finds the position of the Wi-Fi enabled device based on the Wi-Fi hotspots and other wireless access points.[86]

8.5 Security

Because mobile phones have so changed the fabric of our life it is frightening to think how much these devices know about us. For cybercriminals, mobile phones offer a gateway to everything they might want to know about a person, along with paths into their businesses and other organizations. From our phones they can obtain financial information, personal and private data such as e-mails, pictures, messages, personal and business contact lists, and passwords. As a result, security threats are on the rise, especially in corporations.

Safeguarding the security of mobile devices is ever more complex. Almost all employees routinely access corporate data either from a mobile

[85] *Id.* at 84.

[86] Kulshrestha, Tarun, Divya Saxena, Rajdeep Niyogi, Vaskar Raychoudhury, and Manoj Misra. "SmartITS: Smartphone-based identification and tracking using seamless indoor-outdoor localization." *Journal of Network and Computer Applications* 98 (2017): 97–113.

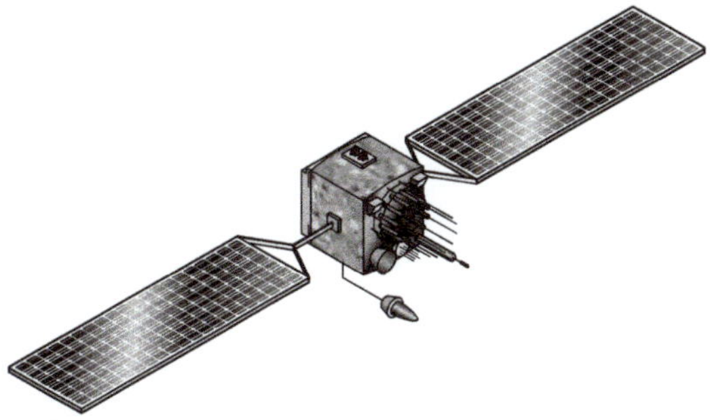

FIGURE 8.14 **A GPS satellite. Courtesy of Shutterstock.**

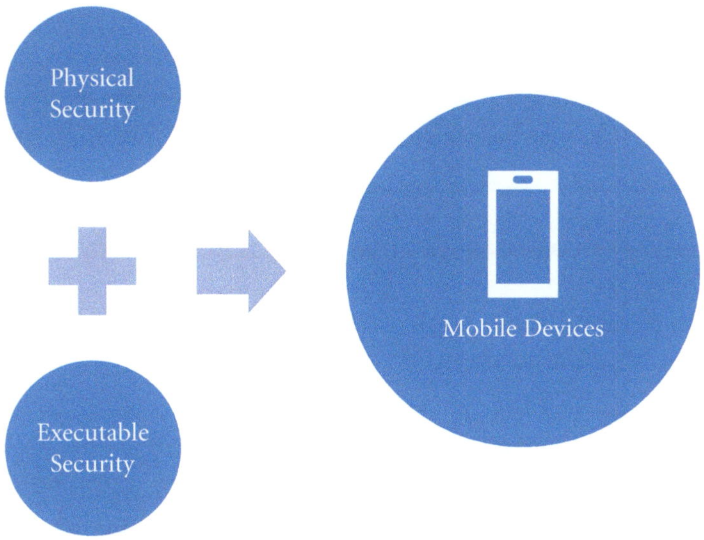

FIGURE 8.15 **Physical and Executable Security.**

device or a personal smartphone. This increases the likelihood of sensitive information getting into the wrong hands. The security risks involved in the use of mobile devices may involve either *physical or executable security* (Figure 8.15).

8.5.1 Physical Security

Physical security, such as theft or loss of the device is one of the greatest threats. Since the devices are easy to carry, they are stolen or lost more frequently than laptop computers. The Cellular Telecommunications and Internet Association (CTIA), which represents the U.S. wireless communications industry, has announced an agreement between major smartphone manufacturers and all of the leading U.S. wireless carriers to enable smartphones with "kill-switch" functionality on phones sold in the United States after July 2015 that can temporarily disable the device. This potentially solves the theft problem, but it is up to the user to enable this "kill-switch" (the human element). As in many so many other security-related issues, the human element is the weakest link.

CTIA has created an online tool that allows anyone to check if a phone has been registered as lost or stolen. All a person needs to perform the check is the IMEI number of the device.[87] This enables the easy sale of stolen phones, with little danger to the thieves that the new owners will check the IMEI number to see if the phone was stolen. In addition, the *Smartphone Theft Prevention Act of 2015* requires smartphone manufacturers and operating system providers to:

I. Delete or render inaccessible all information on the smartphone relating to the account holder
II. Render the smartphone inoperable on the network of any provider of commercial mobile service or commercial mobile data service globally
III. Prevent the smartphone from being reactivated or reprogrammed without a passcode or similar authorization to an unauthorized factory reset
IV. Restore personal information from the smartphone onto a compatible or interoperable device.[88]

Furthermore, the act orders the Federal Communications Commission (FCC) to establish a framework to deter and prevent theft and protect consumers. It prohibits service providers from charging fees for making available such functions as the initial prompt and the ability to opt out. The legislation requires manufacturers such as Google and Apple to include tracking and remote protection software such as Find My iPhone and Find My Device to track the device's last known location and turn on the Activation Lock.

The Global System for Mobile Communications (GSMA) represents the interests of mobile operators worldwide and maintains an International Mobile Equipment Identity Database for mobile devices.[89] This global database comprises the IMEI numbers of millions of devices across the world. Nevertheless, not all countries have signed up with this database; this enables the blacklisting of stolen devices, and therefore the black market of mobile devices thrives. According to GSMA, in the United States alone,

---

[87] CTIA's Stolen Phone Checker. Retrieved from https://stolenphonechecker.org/spc/

[88] Smartphone Theft Prevention Act of 2015. Retrieved from https://www.congress.gov/bill/114th-congress/senate-bill/1076/text

[89] IMEI Database. Retrieved from https://www.gsma.com/aboutus/workinggroups/terminal-steering-group/imei-database

more than 4 million prepaid devices are trafficked annually, at a cost of $900 million USD.[90]

8.5.2 Executable Security

Mobile devices, like other computing devices, are vulnerable to intrusion, intentional intrusion such as hacking, or intrusion through malware that is currently distributed around the Internet. The most common executable security threats (Figure 8.16) are the following:

- **Malicious text messages**

Pegasus was discovered when a political activist received SMS messages that contained malicious links. Instead of clicking on the links, the activist forwarded them to the security labs Citizen Lab and LooKout for examination. If the activist had clicked on the links, his iPhone would have become infected and remotely jailbroken.[91] A group called the NSO Group generated *Pegasus,* which is capable of keylogging, screenshot, and audio capture. *Pegasus* controls unsuspecting users of the malware through SMS messaging and history data extrusion from text messages, including those in applications like WhatsApp, Skype, Facebook, Twitter, and Viber.

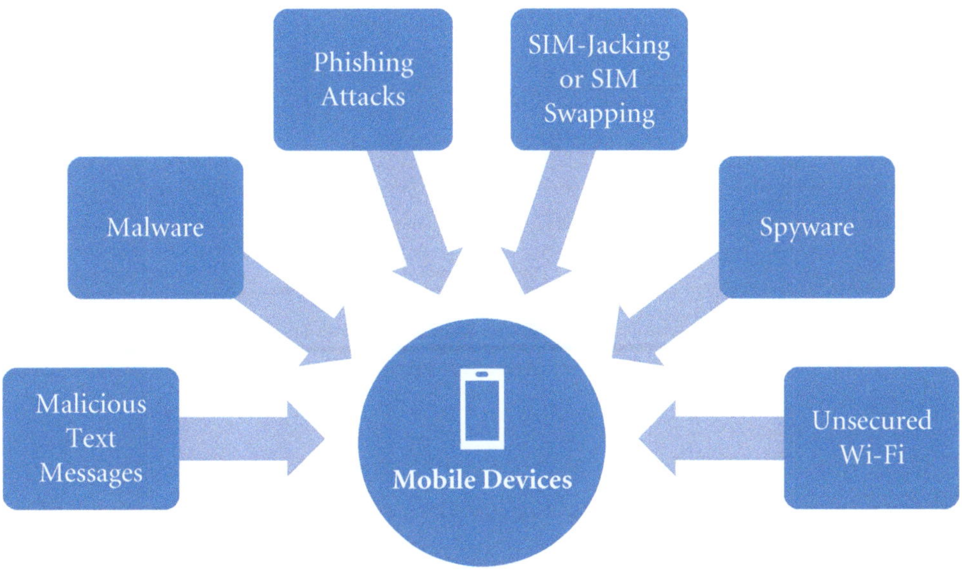

FIGURE 8.16 Some of the Main Executable Security Threats.

[90] Prepaid Device Trafficking. Retrieved from https://www.gsma.com/northamerica/prepaid-device-trafficking/

[91] Marczak, Bill, and John Scott-Railton. "The million dollar dissident: NSO group's iPhone zero-days used against a UAE human rights defender." *Citizen Lab* 24 (2016).

The NSO group, an Israeli surveillance technology company, has developed spyware and other capabilities not intended for the average hacker. According to the company, it provides *authorized governments with technology that helps them combat terror and crime.*[92] The NSO has been targeting human rights activists and journalists in numerous countries.

Two-factor authentication (2FA) codes from SMS adds an additional layer of security that involves not only a username and a password, but also requires an additional layer of authentication, a code that usually comes on an SMS or via e-mail. However, a simple SMS received can still infect a mobile device even if it is protected by 2FA authentication.

In fact, 2FA authentication raises the level of danger associated with infected SMS. For example, Google's 2FA authentication sends a 6-digit code via text message when a user attempts to log in. First, the SMS steals the user's personal information by intercepting SMS messages, then a desktop component phishes the user's computer and tricks the user into installing smartphone malware to prevent 2FA authentication.[93] The interception of SMS can also lead to the theft of a user's credentials, including healthcare information, banking, e-mail, and data that require passwords and payment information.

- **Malware**

The term Malware stands for malicious software. The term is used to describe an intrusive software that impairs a computing device without the user's knowledge. Malware consists of computer viruses, worms, Trojan horses, and spyware. According to a McAfee Mobile Threat Report Q1, 2020, mobile malware has increased the number of attacks on mobile devices, using a wide variety of backdoors that disguise the attacks, making it difficult to identify and remove.[94] Additionally, these malicious codes in numerous configurations remain a concern, mainly, though not exclusively, on the Android platform. Both Apple and Google, scan apps for malicious codes.[95] Malware can search a user's device for specific keywords, running commands and downloads, uploading and infecting devices, and deleting files.

---

[92] Brewster, T. *Forbes*. Everything we know about NSO group: The professional spies who hacked iPhones with a single text. (2016, August 25). Retrieved from https://www.forbes.com/sites/thomasbrewster/2016/08/25/everything-we-know-about-nso-group-the-professional-spies-who-hacked-iphones-with-a-single-text/#547864c33997

[93] Felt, Adrienne Porter, Matthew Finifter, Erika Chin, Steve Hanna, and David Wagner. "A survey of mobile malware in the wild." In *Proceedings of the 1st ACM Workshop on Security and Privacy in Smartphones and Mobile Devices*, pp. 3–14. 2011.

[94] McAfee Mobile Threat Report Q1, 2020. Retrieved from https://www.mcafee.com/content/dam/consumer/en-us/docs/2020-Mobile-Threat-Report.pdf

[95] Sophos 2020 Threat Report. Retrieved from https://www.sophos.com/en-us/medialibrary/pdfs/technical-papers/sophoslabs-uncut-2020-threat-report.pdf

- **Phishing attack**

An additional way to launch malware in a mobile device is through a phishing attack. Phishing refers to attacks that attempt to steal personal or sensitive information, such as usernames, passwords, credit card information, and whatever else is stored on the device's SIM card. Mobile device operating systems and their browsers are not equipped with a security suite that can detect the difference between a fake link and a real link. When an unsuspecting user enters his passwords and credit card information, the phishing attack begins.[96] Phishing attacks can happen on both Android and iOS platforms. All mobile devices support in-application billing, allowing users to purchase products and services without providing credit card information. Such apps often become a target of fraud by malware or phishing attacks. An example is the spear-phishing attack that targets specific employees in order to obtain usable credentials that can be used to break into an organization.[97]

- **SIM-jacking or SIM swapping**

SIM-jacking is when cybercriminals obtain personal information from social media, data breaches or by conning mobile phone users. Then, the hacker uses this information to convince network providers to transfer their numbers to new SIM cards. Once the SIM swap is complete, messages containing codes can be intercepted, and impostors can take over an email, social media, or mobile banking account. The SIM-jacking attacks in the recent past have led to several high-profile thefts of cryptocurrency.[98,99]

- **Spyware**

Spyware is a type of malicious program that gathers personal information from a device, such as its location or text message history, during a designated time. An example is the hidden spyware in a legitimate South Korean transit app that allowed hackers into the developer's Google Play account.[100] Spyware can collect any type of data, including user logins, personal information, web browser history and habits, SMS logs, phone call logs, information from e-mail apps, photos, contact information, saved passwords, audio and video recordings, and data from other apps, especially from apps owned by financial institutions and healthcare institutions.

- **Unsecured Wi-Fi**

One of the major technologies that mobile devices rely on is Wi-Fi technology; we all regularly connect our devices to the nearest Wi-Fi network. Free

[96] *Id.* at 93.
[97] *Id.* at 95.
[98] *Id.* at 95.
[99] FCC-Cell Phone Fraud. Retrieved from https://www.fcc.gov/sites/default/files/cell_phone_fraud.pdf
[100] *Id.* at 94.

or public Wi-Fi nodes, or "hotspots," have been a convenient way for users to enjoy free access to the Internet. Unfortunately, unsecured free access allows hackers to use sniffing apps to intercept and gather data. In addition, mobile devices transmit search requests, looking for nearby networks, and these requests contain the device's unique MAC address. A hacker can then simply display these requests.[101] A privacy technique called MAC Address Randomization protects these devices from being tracked when owners utilize hotspots. This privacy technique changes the number that distinctively identifies the mobile device to a random number. However, research has shown that MAC address randomization alone is not enough to protect the privacy of those using mobile devices.[102],[103] One of the less publicized attacks affecting mobile devices is the Man-in-the-Middle attack. The Man-in-the-Middle attack decrypts and intercepts the traffic between the server and a mobile device app.[104] As a result, traffic between the device and the server is exposed to an attack. This traffic interception can inactivate the validation of digital certificates or fail to authenticate the identity of a server when establishing a connection.

Another way that hackers can fool unsuspecting users is called Network Spoofing, where the attack offers the user what looks like a real Wi-Fi network. Usually set up in a high-traffic public location, the hacker provides access points and might name it, for example, "Free Coffeehouse Wi-Fi Access" to encourage users to connect.

8.6 Conclusion

Mobile devices have come a long way from the brick phone of 40 years ago. They make our lives more efficient, easier, and more enjoyable. They can help us shop, take photos, search the web, identify faces, provide entertainment, replace a credit card, do our banking, and function as a personal assistant. The microprocessor inside today's mobile phone is more powerful than the computer used to send Neil Armstrong to the moon in 1969. Even a modern toaster has more processing power than the Apollo Guidance Computer[105] (Figures 8.17–8.19).

---

[101] Vanhoef, M., Matte, C., Cunche, M., Cardoso, L. S., & Piessens, F. Why MAC address randomization is not enough: An analysis of Wi-Fi network discovery mechanisms. In *Proceedings of the 11th ACM on Asia Conference on Computer and Communications Security* (pp. 413–424). ACM, May 2016.

[102] Martin, Jeremy, Travis Mayberry, Collin Donahue, Lucas Foppe, Lamont Brown, Chadwick Riggins, Erik C. Rye, and Dane Brown. "A study of MAC address randomization in mobile devices and when it fails." *Proceedings on Privacy Enhancing Technologies* 2017, no. 4 (2017): 365–383.

[103] *Id.* at 101.

[104] Shetty, Rushank, George Grispos, and Kim-Kwang Raymond Choo. "Are you dating danger? An interdisciplinary approach to evaluating the (in) security of android dating apps." *IEEE Transactions on Sustainable Computing* (2017).

[105] Chace, Calum. *Artificial intelligence and the two singularities.* CRC Press, 2018.

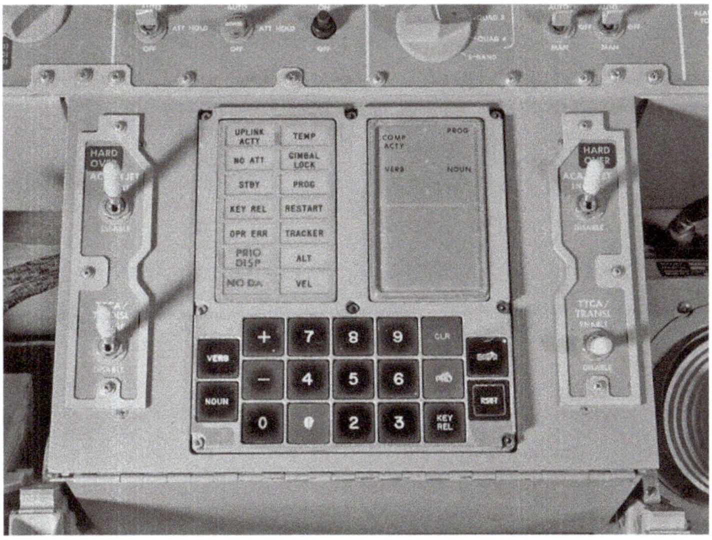

FIGURE 8.17 **The Apollo Guidance and Navigation System. Photograph courtesy Smithsonian Institute.**

FIGURE 8.18 **On July 20, 1969, America's Apollo 11 landed on the moon, c1969. Photograph from National Aeronautics and Space Administration (NASA).**

FIGURE 8.19 **These computers were used during NASA's Project Mercury, 1952–1968. Photograph from National Aeronautics and Space Administration (NASA).**

These small devices will continue to reinvent themselves. They are amazing, but do we rely on and trust them too much?

Nonetheless, mobile phones will become more flexible, will have a longer battery life, and will become more environmentally friendly. They will not begin to lose their central place in our lives until something else replaces them.

8.7 Key Words

Angle of Arrival (AOA)
Android
Antenna
architecture
Apple's iOS
Android Runtime (ART)
Applications (apps)
Application Program Interface (API)
Base Station Controller (BSC)
Base Transceiver system (BTS)
Bluetooth
Cellular
Cellular System Identification number (SID)
Cell Tower Triangulation
Cocoa Touch downlink
Global Positioning System (GPS)
Code Division Multiple Access (CDMA)
Display
Electronic Serial Number (ESN)
Executable security
Fifth Generation (5G)
First Generation (1G)
Fourth Generation (4G)
Global System for Mobile Communication (GSM)
Hexagonal Cellular Network
Hardware Abstraction Layer (HAL)
Hardware
Java API Framework
Long Term Evolution (LTE)
Linux kernel Layer
Malicious Text Messages

Malware
Man-in-the-Middle attack
Media Access Control (MAC)
Media Service Layer
Microphone
Microwave Access (WIMAX)
Microwave links
Mobile Directory Number (MDN)
Mobile Equipment Identifier (MEID)
Mobile devices
Mobile Identification Number (MIN)
Mobile Switching Center (MSC)
Mobile Telephone Switching Office (MTSO)
Native C/C++ Libraries
Network Identification (NID)
Power Management
Printed Circuit Board (PCB)
Operating Systems (OS)
Phishing Attack
Physical Security
Radiofrequency (RF)
Security
Sensors
Second Generation (2G)
SIM Swapping
Smartphone
Spyware
System Application Layer
Software Development Kit (SDK)
Speaker
System-on-Chip (SOC)
Subscriber Identity Module (SIM)
Third Generation (3G)
Time of Arrival (ToA)
Time Difference of Arrival (TDoA)
Unsecured Wi-Fi
Uplink
Wi-Fi Based Localization.

Appendix A
A Complete Text of the Computer Fraud and Abuse Act (CFAA) 18 U.S.C. § 1030.[1]

Fraud and Related Activity in Connection with Computers

a) Whoever—

(1) having knowingly accessed a computer without authorization or exceeding,

(2) and by means of such conduct having obtained information that has been determined by the United States Government pursuant to an Executive order or statute to require protection against unauthorized disclosure for reasons of national defense or foreign relations, or any restricted data, as defined in paragraph y. of section 11 of the Atomic Energy Act of 1954, with reason to believe that such information so obtained could be used to the injury of the United States, or to the advantage of any foreign nation willfully communicates, delivers, transmits, or causes to be communicated, delivered, or transmitted, or attempts to communicate, deliver, transmit or cause to be communicated, delivered, or transmitted the same to any person not entitled to receive it, or willfully retains the same and fails to deliver it to the officer or employee of the United States entitled to receive it;

[1] 18 U.S.C. 1030 - Fraud and related activity in connection with computers, Retrieved from https://www.gov info.gov/content/pkg/USCODE-2010-title18/html/USCODE-2010-title18-partI-chap47-sec1030.htm

DOI: 10.4324/9780429318726-9

(2) intentionally accesses a computer without authorization or exceeds authorized access, and thereby obtains—

(A) information contained in a financial record of a financial institution, or of a card issuer as defined in section 1602(n) of title 15, or contained in a file of a consumer reporting agency on a consumer, as such terms are defined in the Fair Credit Reporting Act (15 U.S.C. 1681 et seq.);

(B) information from any department or agency of the United States; or

(C) information from any protected computer;

(3) intentionally, without authorization to access any nonpublic computer of a department or agency of the United States, accesses such a computer of that department or agency that is exclusively for the use of the Government of the United States or, in the case of a computer not exclusively for such use, is used by or for the Government of the United States and such conduct affects that use by or for the Government of the United States;

(4) knowingly and with intent to defraud, accesses a protected computer without authorization, or exceeds authorized access, and by means of such conduct furthers the intended fraud and obtains anything of value, unless the object of the fraud and the thing obtained consists only of the use of the computer and the value of such use is not more than $5,000 in any 1-year period;

(5)

(A) knowingly causes the transmission of a program, information, code, or command, and as a result of such conduct, intentionally causes damage without authorization, to a protected computer;

(B) intentionally accesses a protected computer without authorization, and as a result of such conduct, recklessly causes damage; or

(C) intentionally accesses a protected computer without authorization, and as a result of such conduct, causes damage and loss.

(6) knowingly and with intent to defraud traffics (as defined in section 1029) in any password or similar information through which a computer may be accessed without authorization, if—

(A) such trafficking affects interstate or foreign commerce; or

(B) such computer is used by or for the Government of the United States;

(7) with intent to extort from any person any money or other thing of value, transmits in interstate or foreign commerce any communication containing any—

(A) threat to cause damage to a protected computer;

(B) threat to obtain information from a protected computer without authorization or in excess of authorization or to impair the confidentiality of information obtained from a protected computer without authorization or by exceeding authorized access; or

(C) demand or request for money or other thing of value in relation to damage to a protected computer, where such damage was caused to facilitate the extortion;

shall be punished as provided in subsection (c) of this section.

b) Whoever conspires to commit or attempts to commit an offense under subsection (a) of this section shall be punished as provided in subsection (c) of this section.

c) The punishment for an offense under subsection (a) or (b) of this section is—

(1)

(A) a fine under this title or imprisonment for not more than ten years, or both, in the case of an offense under subsection (a)(1) of this section which does not occur after a conviction for another offense under this section, or an attempt to commit an offense punishable under this subparagraph; and

(B) a fine under this title or imprisonment for not more than twenty years, or both, in the case of an offense under subsection (a)(1) of this section which occurs after a conviction for another offense under this section, or an attempt to commit an offense punishable under this subparagraph;

(2)

(A) except as provided in subparagraph (B), a fine under this title or imprisonment for not more than one year, or both, in the case of an offense under subsection (a)(2), (a)(3), or (a)(6) of this section which does not occur after a conviction for another offense under this section, or an attempt to commit an offense punishable under this subparagraph;

(B) a fine under this title or imprisonment for not more than 5 years, or both, in the case of an offense under subsection (a)(2), or an attempt to commit an offense punishable under this subparagraph, if—

(i) the offense was committed for purposes of commercial advantage or private financial gain;

(ii) the offense was committed in furtherance of any criminal or tortious act in violation of the Constitution or laws of the United States or of any State; or

(iii) the value of the information obtained exceeds $5,000; and

(C) a fine under this title or imprisonment for not more than ten years, or both, in the case of an offense under subsection (a)(2), (a)(3) or (a)(6) of this section which occurs after a conviction for another offense under this section, or an attempt to commit an offense punishable under this subparagraph;

(3)

(A) a fine under this title or imprisonment for not more than five years, or both, in the case of an offense under subsection (a)(4) or (a)(7) of this section which does not occur after a conviction for another offense under this section, or an attempt to commit an offense punishable under this subparagraph; and

(B) a fine under this title or imprisonment for not more than ten years, or both, in the case of an offense under subsection (a)(4), or (a)(7) of this section which occurs after a conviction for another offense under this section, or an attempt to commit an offense punishable under this subparagraph;

(4)

(A) except as provided in subparagraphs (E) and (F), a fine under this title, imprisonment for not more than 5 years, or both, in the case of—

(i) an offense under subsection (a)(5)(B), which does not occur after a conviction for another offense under this section, if the offense caused (or, in the case of an attempted offense, would, if completed, have caused)—

(I) loss to 1 or more persons during any 1-year period (and, for purposes of an investigation, prosecution, or other proceeding brought by the United States only, loss resulting from a related course of conduct affecting 1 or more other protected computers) aggregating at least $5,000 in value;

(II) the modification or impairment, or potential modification or impairment, of the medical examination, diagnosis, treatment, or care of 1 or more individuals;

(III) physical injury to any person;

(IV) a threat to public health or safety;

(V) damage affecting a computer used by or for an entity of the United States Government in furtherance of the administration of justice, national defense, or national security; or

(VI) damage affecting 10 or more protected computers during any 1-year period; or

(ii) an attempt to commit an offense punishable under this subparagraph;

(B) except as provided in subparagraphs (E) and (F), a fine under this title, imprisonment for not more than 10 years, or both, in the case of—

(i) an offense under subsection (a)(5)(A), which does not occur after a conviction for another offense under this section, if the offense caused (or, in the case of an attempted offense, would, if completed, have caused) a harm provided in subclauses (I) through (VI) of subparagraph (A)(i); or

(ii) an attempt to commit an offense punishable under this subparagraph;

(C) except as provided in subparagraphs (E) and (F), a fine under this title, imprisonment for not more than 20 years, or both, in the case of—

(i) an offense or an attempt to commit an offense under subparagraphs (A) or (B) of subsection (a)(5) that occurs after a conviction for another offense under this section; or

(ii) an attempt to commit an offense punishable under this subparagraph;

(D) a fine under this title, imprisonment for not more than 10 years, or both, in the case of—

(i) an offense or an attempt to commit an offense under subsection (a)(5)(C) that occurs after a conviction for another offense under this section; or

(ii) an attempt to commit an offense punishable under this subparagraph;

(E) if the offender attempts to cause or knowingly or recklessly causes serious bodily injury from conduct in violation of subsection (a)(5)(A), a fine under this title, imprisonment for not more than 20 years, or both;

(F) if the offender attempts to cause or knowingly or recklessly causes death from conduct in violation of subsection (a)(5)(A), a fine under this title, imprisonment for any term of years or for life, or both; or

(G) a fine under this title, imprisonment for not more than 1 year, or both, for—

(i) any other offense under subsection (a)(5); or

(ii) an attempt to commit an offense punishable under this subparagraph.

(1) The United States Secret Service shall, in addition to any other agency having such authority, have the authority to investigate offenses under this section.

(2) The Federal Bureau of Investigation shall have primary authority to investigate offenses under subsection (a)(1) for any cases involving espionage, foreign counterintelligence, information protected against unauthorized disclosure for reasons of national defense or foreign relations, or Restricted Data (as that term is defined in section 11y of the Atomic Energy Act of 1954 (42 U.S.C. 2014(y)), except for offenses affecting the duties of the United States Secret Service pursuant to section 3056(a) of this title.

(3) Such authority shall be exercised in accordance with an agreement which shall be entered into by the Secretary of the Treasury and the Attorney General.

d) As used in this section—

(1) the term "computer" means an electronic, magnetic, optical, electrochemical, or other high speed data processing device performing logical, arithmetic, or storage functions, and includes any data storage facility or communications facility directly related to or operating in conjunction with such device, but such term does not include an automated typewriter or typesetter, a portable hand held calculator, or other similar device;

(2) the term "protected computer" means a computer—

(A) exclusively for the use of a financial institution or the United States Government, or, in the case of a computer not exclusively for such use, used by or for a financial institution or the United States Government and the conduct constituting the offense affects that use by or for the financial institution or the Government; or

(B) which is used in or affecting interstate or foreign commerce or communication, including a computer located outside the United States that is used in a manner that affects interstate or foreign commerce or communication of the United States;

(3) the term "State" includes the District of Columbia, the Commonwealth of Puerto Rico, and any other commonwealth, possession or territory of the United States;

(4) the term "financial institution" means—

(A) an institution, with deposits insured by the Federal Deposit Insurance Corporation;

(B) the Federal Reserve or a member of the Federal Reserve including any Federal Reserve Bank;

(C) a credit union with accounts insured by the National Credit Union Administration;

(D) a member of the Federal home loan bank system and any home loan bank;

(E) any institution of the Farm Credit System under the Farm Credit Act of 1971;

(F) a broker-dealer registered with the Securities and Exchange Commission pursuant to section 15 of the Securities Exchange Act of 1934;

(G) the Securities Investor Protection Corporation;

(H) a branch or agency of a foreign bank (as such terms are defined in paragraphs (1) and (3) of section 1(b) of the International Banking Act of 1978); and

(I) an organization operating under section 25 or section 25(a)[4] of the Federal Reserve Act;

(5) the term "financial record" means information derived from any record held by a financial institution pertaining to a customer's relationship with the financial institution;

(6) the term "exceeds authorized access" means to access a computer with authorization and to use such access to obtain or alter information in the computer that the accesser is not entitled so to obtain or alter;

(7) the term "department of the United States" means the legislative or judicial branch of the Government or one of the executive departments enumerated in section 101 of title 5;

(8) the term "damage" means any impairment to the integrity or availability of data, a program, a system, or information;

(9) the term "government entity" includes the Government of the United States, any State or political subdivision of the United States, any foreign country, and any state, province, municipality, or other political subdivision of a foreign country;

(10) the term "conviction" shall include a conviction under the law of any State for a crime punishable by imprisonment for more than 1 year, an element of which is unauthorized access, or exceeding authorized access, to a computer;

(11) the term "loss" means any reasonable cost to any victim, including the cost of responding to an offense, conducting a damage

assessment, and restoring the data, program, system, or information to its condition prior to the offense, and any revenue lost, cost incurred, or other consequential damages incurred because of interruption of service; and

(12) the term "person" means any individual, firm, corporation, educational institution, financial institution, governmental entity, or legal or other entity.

e) This section does not prohibit any lawfully authorized investigative, protective, or intelligence activity of a law enforcement agency of the United States, a State, or a political subdivision of a State, or of an intelligence agency of the United States.

f) Any person who suffers damage or loss by reason of a violation of this section may maintain a civil action against the violator to obtain compensatory damages and injunctive relief or other equitable relief. A civil action for a violation of this section may be brought only if the conduct involves 1 of the factors set forth in subclauses [5] (I), (II), (III), (IV), or (V) of subsection (c)(4)(A)(i). Damages for a violation involving only conduct described in subsection (c)(4)(A)(i)(I) are limited to economic damages. No action may be brought under this subsection unless such action is begun within 2 years of the date of the act complained of or the date of the discovery of the damage. No action may be brought under this subsection for the negligent design or manufacture of computer hardware, computer software, or firmware.

g) The Attorney General and the Secretary of the Treasury shall report to the Congress annually, during the first 3 years following the date of the enactment of this subsection, concerning investigations and prosecutions under subsection (a)(5).

h)

(1) The court, in imposing sentence on any person convicted of a violation of this section, or convicted of conspiracy to violate this section, shall order, in addition to any other sentence imposed and irrespective of any provision of State law, that such person forfeit to the United States—

(B) such person's interest in any personal property that was used or intended to be used to commit or to facilitate the commission of such violation; and

(C) any property, real or personal, constituting or derived from, any proceeds that such person obtained, directly or indirectly, as a result of such violation.

(2) The criminal forfeiture of property under this subsection, any seizure and disposition thereof, and any judicial proceeding in

relation thereto, shall be governed by the provisions of section 413 of the Comprehensive Drug Abuse Prevention and Control Act of 1970 (21 U.S.C. 853), except subsection (d) of that section.

i) For purposes of subsection (i), the following shall be subject to forfeiture to the United States and no property right shall exist in them:

(1) Any personal property used or intended to be used to commit or to facilitate the commission of any violation of this section, or a conspiracy to violate this section.

(2) Any property, real or personal, which constitutes or is derived from proceeds traceable to any violation of this section, or a conspiracy to violate this section

Amendments

2008—Subsec. (a)(2)(C). Pub. L. 110–326, §203, struck out "if the conduct involved an interstate or foreign communication" after "computer".

Subsec. (a)(5). Pub. L. 110–326, §204(a)(1), redesignated cls. (i) to (iii) of subpar. (A) as subpars. (A) to (C), respectively, substituted "damage and loss." for "damage; and" in subpar. (C), and struck out former subpar. (B) which read as follows:

"(B) by conduct described in clause (i), (ii), or (iii) of subparagraph (A), caused (or, in the case of an attempted offense, would, if completed, have caused)—

"(i) loss to 1 or more persons during any 1-year period (and, for purposes of an investigation, prosecution, or other proceeding brought by the United States only, loss resulting from a related course of conduct affecting 1 or more other protected computers) aggregating at least $5,000 in value;

"(ii) the modification or impairment, or potential modification or impairment, of the medical examination, diagnosis, treatment, or care of 1 or more individuals;

"(iii) physical injury to any person;

"(iv) a threat to public health or safety; or

"(v) damage affecting a computer system used by or for a government entity in furtherance of the administration of justice, national defense, or national security;".

Subsec. (a)(7). Pub. L. 110–326, §205, amended par. (7) generally. Prior to amendment, par. (7) read as follows: "with intent to extort from any person any money or other thing of value, transmits in interstate or foreign commerce any communication containing any threat to cause damage to a protected computer;".

Subsec. (b). Pub. L. 110–326, §206, inserted "conspires to commit or" after "Whoever".

Subsec. (c)(2)(A). Pub. L. 110–326, §204(a)(2)(A), struck out "(a)(5)(A)(iii)," after "(a)(3),".

Subsec. (c)(3)(B). Pub. L. 110–326, §204(a)(2)(B), struck out "(a)(5)(A)(iii)," after "(a)(4),".

Subsec. (c)(4). Pub. L. 110–326, §204(a)(2)(C), amended par. (4) generally. Prior to amendment, par. (4) related to fines and imprisonment for intentionally or recklessly causing damage to a protected computer without authorization.

Subsec. (c)(5). Pub. L. 110–326, §204(a)(2)(D), struck out par. (5) which related to fine or imprisonment for knowingly or recklessly causing or attempting to cause serious bodily injury or death from certain conduct damaging a protected computer.

Subsec. (e)(2)(B). Pub. L. 110–326, §207, inserted "or affecting" after "which is used in".

Subsec. (g). Pub. L. 110–326, §204(a)(3)(B), in the third sentence, substituted "subsection (c)(4)(A)(i)(I)" for "subsection (a)(5)(B)(i)".

Pub. L. 110–326, §204(a)(3)(A), which directed substitution of "in subclauses (I), (II), (III), (IV), or (V) of subsection (c)(4)(A)(i)" for "in clauses (i), (ii), (iii), (iv), or (v) of subsection (a)(5)(B)" in the second sentence, was executed by making the substitution for "in clause (i), (ii), (iii), (iv), or (v) of subsection (a)(5)(B)" to reflect the probable intent of Congress.

Subsecs. (i), (j). Pub. L. 110–326, §208, added subsecs. (i) and (j).

2002—Subsec. (a)(5)(B). Pub. L. 107–273, §4005(a)(3), realigned margins.

Subsec. (c)(2)(B). Pub. L. 107–273, §4002(b)(1), realigned margins.

Subsec. (c)(2)(B)(iii). Pub. L. 107–273, §4002(b)(12)(A), inserted "and" at end.

Subsec. (c)(3)(B). Pub. L. 107–273, §4005(d)(3), inserted comma after "(a)(4)".

Subsec. (c)(4)(A), (C). Pub. L. 107–296, §225(g)(2), inserted "except as provided in paragraph (5)," before "a fine under this title".

Subsec. (c)(5). Pub. L. 107–296, §225(g)(1), (3), (4), added par. (5).

Subsec. (e)(4)(I). Pub. L. 107–273, §4002(b)(12)(B), substituted semicolon for period at end.

2001—Subsec. (a)(5)(A). Pub. L. 107–56, §814(a)(1)–(3), designated existing provisions as cl. (i), redesignated subpars. (B) and (C) as cls. (ii) and (iii), respectively, of subpar. (A), and inserted "and" at end of cl. (iii).

Subsec. (a)(5)(B). Pub. L. 107–56, §814(a)(4), added subpar. (B). Former subpar. (B) redesignated cl. (ii) of subpar. (A).

Subsec. (a)(5)(C). Pub. L. 107–56, §814(a)(2), redesignated subpar. (C) as cl. (iii) of subpar. (A).

Subsec. (a)(7). Pub. L. 107–56, §814(b), struck out ", firm, association, educational institution, financial institution, government entity, or other legal entity," before "any money or other thing of value".

Subsec. (c)(2)(A). Pub. L. 107–56, §814(c)(1)(A), inserted "except as provided in subparagraph (B)," before "a fine", substituted "(a)(5)(A)(iii)" for "(a)(5)(C)", and struck out "and" at end.

Subsec. (c)(2)(B). Pub. L. 107–56, §814(c)(1)(B), inserted "or an attempt to commit an offense punishable under this subparagraph," after "subsection (a)(2)," in introductory provisions.

Subsec. (c)(2)(C). Pub. L. 107–56, §814(c)(1)(C), struck out "and" at end.

Subsec. (c)(3). Pub. L. 107–56, §814(c)(2), struck out ", (a)(5)(A), (a)(5)(B)," after "subsection (a)(4)" in subpars. (A) and (B) and substituted "(a)(5)(A)(iii)" for "(a)(5)(C)" in subpar. (B).

Subsec. (c)(4). Pub. L. 107–56, §814(c)(3), added par. (4).

Subsec. (d). Pub. L. 107–56, §506(a), amended subsec. (d) generally. Prior to amendment, subsec. (d) read as follows: "The United States Secret Service shall, in addition to any other agency having such authority, have the authority to investigate offenses under subsections (a)(2)(A), (a)(2)(B), (a)(3), (a)(4), (a)(5), and (a)(6) of this section. Such authority of the United States Secret Service shall be exercised in accordance with an agreement which shall be entered into by the Secretary of the Treasury and the Attorney General."

Subsec. (e)(2)(B). Pub. L. 107–56, §814(d)(1), inserted ", including a computer located outside the United States that is used in a manner that affects interstate or foreign commerce or communication of the United States" before semicolon.

Subsec. (e)(7). Pub. L. 107–56, §814(d)(2), struck out "and" at end.

Subsec. (e)(8). Pub. L. 107–56, §814(d)(3), added par. (8) and struck out former par. (8) which read as follows: "the term 'damage' means any impairment to the integrity or availability of data, a program, a system, or information, that—

"(A) causes loss aggregating at least $5,000 in value during any 1-year period to one or more individuals;

"(B) modifies or impairs, or potentially modifies or impairs, the medical examination, diagnosis, treatment, or care of one or more individuals;

"(C) causes physical injury to any person; or

"(D) threatens public health or safety; and".

Subsec. (e)(10) to (12). Pub. L. 107–56, §814(d)(4), (5), added pars. (10) to (12).

Subsec. (g). Pub. L. 107–56, §814(e), substituted "A civil action for a violation of this section may be brought only if the conduct involves 1 of the factors set forth in clause (i), (ii), (iii), (iv), or (v) of subsection (a)(5)(B). Damages for a violation involving only conduct described in subsection (a)(5)(B)(i) are limited to economic damages." for "Damages for violations involving damage as defined in subsection (e)(8)(A) are limited to economic damages." and inserted at end "No action may be brought under this subsection for the negligent design or manufacture of computer hardware, computer software, or firmware."

1996—Subsec. (a)(1). Pub. L. 104–294, §201(1)(A), substituted "having knowingly accessed" for "knowingly accesses", "exceeding authorized access" for "exceeds authorized access", "such conduct having obtained information" for "such conduct obtains information", and "could be used to the injury of the United States" for "is to be used to the injury of the United States", struck out "the intent or" before "reason to believe", and inserted before semicolon at end "willfully communicates, delivers, transmits, or causes to be communicated, delivered, or transmitted, or attempts to communicate, deliver, transmit or cause to be communicated, delivered, or transmitted the same to any person not entitled to receive it, or willfully retains the same and fails to deliver it to the officer or employee of the United States entitled to receive it".

Subsec. (a)(2). Pub. L. 104–294, §201(1)(B), inserted dash after "thereby obtains", redesignated remainder of par. (2) as subpar. (A), and added subpars. (B) and (C).

Subsec. (a)(3). Pub. L. 104–294, §201(1)(C), inserted "nonpublic" before "computer of a department or agency", struck out "adversely" after "and such conduct", and substituted "that use by or for the Government of the United States" for "the use of the Government's operation of such computer".

Subsec. (a)(4). Pub. L. 104–294, §201(1)(D), substituted "protected computer" for "Federal interest computer" and inserted "and the value of such use is not more than $5,000 in any 1-year period" before semicolon at end.

Subsec. (a)(5). Pub. L. 104–294, §201(1)(E), inserted par. (5) and struck out former par. (5) which related to fraud in connection with computers in causing transmission of program, information, code, or command to a computer or computer system in interstate or foreign commerce which damages such system, program, information, or code, or causes a withholding or denial of use of hardware or software, or transmits viruses which causes damage in excess of $1,000 or more during any one-year period, or modifies or impairs medical examination, diagnosis, treatment or care of individuals.

Subsec. (a)(5)(B)(ii)(II)(bb). Pub. L. 104–294, §604(b)(36)(A), which directed insertion of "or" at end of subsec., could not be executed because no subsec. (a)(5)(B)(ii)(II)(bb) existed subsequent to amendment by Pub. L. 104–294, §201(1)(E). See above.

Subsec. (a)(7). Pub. L. 104–294, §201(1)(F), added par. (7).

Subsec. (c)(1). Pub. L. 104–294, §201(2)(A), substituted "under this section" for "under such subsection" in subpars. (A) and (B).

Subsec. (c)(1)(B). Pub. L. 104–294, §604(b)(36)(B), struck out "and" after semicolon at end.

Subsec. (c)(2)(A). Pub. L. 104–294, §201(2)(B)(i), inserted ", (a)(5)(C)," after "(a)(3)" and substituted "under this section" for "under such subsection".

Subsec. (c)(2)(B). Pub. L. 104–294, §201(2)(B)(iii), added subpar. (B). Former subpar. (B) redesignated (C).

Subsec. (c)(2)(C). Pub. L. 104–294, §201(2)(B)(iv), substituted "under this section" for "under such subsection" and inserted "and" at end.

Pub. L. 104–294, §201(2)(B)(ii), redesignated subpar. (B) as (C).

Subsec. (c)(3)(A). Pub. L. 104–294, §201(2)(C)(i), substituted "(a)(4), (a)(5)(A), (a)(5)(B), or (a)(7)" for "(a)(4) or (a)(5)(A)" and "under this section" for "under such subsection".

Subsec. (c)(3)(B). Pub. L. 104–294, §201(2)(C)(ii), substituted "(a)(4), (a)(5)(A), (a)(5)(B), (a)(5)(C), or (a)(7)" for "(a)(4) or (a)(5)" and "under this section" for "under such subsection".

Subsec. (c)(4). Pub. L. 104–294, §201(2)(D), struck out par. (4) which read as follows: "a fine under this title or imprisonment for not more than 1 year, or both, in the case of an offense under subsection (a)(5)(B)."

Subsec. (d). Pub. L. 104–294, §201(3), inserted "subsections (a)(2)(A), (a)(2)(B), (a)(3), (a)(4), (a)(5), and (a)(6) of" before "this section" in first sentence.

Subsec. (e)(2). Pub. L. 104–294, §201(4)(A)(i), substituted "protected" for "Federal interest" in introductory provisions.

Subsec. (e)(2)(A). Pub. L. 104–294, §201(4)(A)(ii), substituted "that use by or for the financial institution or the Government" for "the use of the financial institution's operation or the Government's operation of such computer".

Subsec. (e)(2)(B). Pub. L. 104–294, §201(4)(A)(iii), added subpar. (B) and struck out former subpar. (B) which read as follows: "which is one of two or more computers used in committing the offense, not all of which are located in the same State;".

Subsec. (e)(8), (9). Pub. L. 104–294, §201(4)(B)–(D), added pars. (8) and (9).

Subsec. (g). Pub. L. 104–294, §604(b)(36)(C), substituted "violation of this section" for "violation of the section".

Pub. L. 104–294, §201(5), struck out ", other than a violation of subsection (a)(5)(B)," before "may maintain a civil action" and substituted "involving damage as defined in subsection (e)(8)(A)" for "of any subsection other than subsection (a)(5)(A)(ii)(II)(bb) or (a)(5)(B)(ii)(II)(bb)".

Subsec. (h). Pub. L. 104–294, §604(b)(36)(D), substituted "subsection (a)(5)" for "section 1030(a)(5) of title 18, United States Code" before period at end.

1994—Subsec. (a)(3). Pub. L. 103–322, §290001(f), inserted "adversely" before "affects the use of the Government's".

Subsec. (a)(5). Pub. L. 103–322, §290001(b), amended par. (5) generally. Prior to amendment, par. (5) read as follows: "intentionally accesses a Federal interest computer without authorization, and by means of one or more instances of such conduct alters, damages, or destroys information in any such Federal interest computer, or prevents authorized use of any such computer or information, and thereby—

"(A) causes loss to one or more others of a value aggregating $1,000 or more during any one year period; or

"(B) modifies or impairs, or potentially modifies or impairs, the medical examination, medical diagnosis, medical treatment, or medical care of one or more individuals; or".

Subsec. (c)(3)(A). Pub. L. 103–322, §290001(c)(2), inserted "(A)" after "(a)(5)".

Subsec. (c)(4). Pub. L. 103–322, §290001(c)(1), (3), (4), added par. (4).

Subsec. (g). Pub. L. 103–322, §290001(d), added subsec. (g).

Subsec. (h). Pub. L. 103–322, §290001(e), added subsec. (h).

1990—Subsec. (a)(1). Pub. L. 101–647, §3533, substituted "paragraph y" for "paragraph r".

Subsec. (e)(3). Pub. L. 101–647, §1205(e), inserted "commonwealth," before "possession or territory of the United States".

Subsec. (e)(4)(G). Pub. L. 101–647, §2597(j)(2), which directed substitution of a semicolon for a period at end of subpar. (G), could not be executed because it ended with a semicolon.

Subsec. (e)(4)(H), (I). Pub. L. 101–647, §2597(j), added subpars. (H) and (I).

1989—Subsec. (e)(4)(A). Pub. L. 101–73, §962(a)(5)(A), substituted "an institution," for "a bank".

Subsec. (e)(4)(C) to (H). Pub. L. 101–73, §962(a)(5)(B), (C), redesignated subpars. (D) to (H) as (C) to (G), respectively, and struck out former subpar. (C) which read as follows: "an institution with accounts insured by the Federal Savings and Loan Insurance Corporation;".

1988—Subsec. (a)(2). Pub. L. 100–690 inserted a comma after "financial institution" and struck out the comma that followed a comma after "title 15".

1986—Subsec. (a). Pub. L. 99–474, §2(b)(2), struck out last sentence which read as follows: "It is not an offense under paragraph (2) or (3) of this subsection in the case of a person having accessed a computer with authorization and using the opportunity such access provides for purposes to which such access does not extend, if the using of such opportunity consists only of the use of the computer."

Subsec. (a)(1). Pub. L. 99–474, §2(c), substituted "or exceeds authorized access" for ", or having accessed a computer with authorization, uses the opportunity such access provides for purposes to which such authorization does not extend".

Subsec. (a)(2). Pub. L. 99–474, §2(a), (c), substituted "intentionally" for "knowingly", substituted "or exceeds authorized access" for ", or having accessed a computer with authorization, uses the opportunity such access provides for purposes to which such authorization does not extend", struck out "as such terms are defined in the Right to Financial Privacy Act of 1978 (12 U.S.C. 3401 et seq.)," after "financial institution,", inserted "or of a card issuer as defined in section 1602(n) of title 15," and struck out "or" appearing at end.

Subsec. (a)(3). Pub. L. 99–474, §2(b)(1), amended par. (3) generally. Prior to amendment, par. (3) read as follows: "knowingly accesses a computer without authorization, or having accessed a computer with authorization, uses the opportunity such access provides for purposes to which such authorization does not extend, and by means of such conduct knowingly uses, modifies, destroys, or discloses information in, or prevents authorized use of, such computer, if such computer is operated for or on behalf of the Government of the United States and such conduct affects such operation;".

Subsec. (a)(4) to (6). Pub. L. 99–474, §2(d), added pars. (4) to (6).

Subsec. (b). Pub. L. 99–474, §2(e), struck out par. (1) designation and par. (2) which provided a penalty for persons conspiring to commit an offense under subsec. (a).

Subsec. (c). Pub. L. 99–474, §2(f)(9), substituted "(b)" for "(b)(1)" in introductory text.

Subsec. (c)(1)(A). Pub. L. 99–474, §2(f)(1), substituted "under this title" for "of not more than the greater of $10,000 or twice the value obtained by the offense".

Subsec. (c)(1)(B). Pub. L. 99–474, §2(f)(2), substituted "under this title" for "of not more than the greater of $100,000 or twice the value obtained by the offense".

Subsec. (c)(2)(A). Pub. L. 99–474, §2(f)(3), (4), substituted "under this title" for "of not more than the greater of $5,000 or twice the value obtained or loss created by the offense" and inserted reference to subsec. (a)(6).

Subsec. (c)(2)(B). Pub. L. 99–474, §2(f)(3), (5)–(7), substituted "under this title" for "of not more than the greater of $10,000 or twice the value obtained or loss created by the offense", "not more than" for "not than", inserted reference to subsec. (a)(6), and substituted "; and" for the period at end of subpar. (B).

Subsec. (c)(3). Pub. L. 99–474, §2(f)(8), added par. (3).

Subsec. (e). Pub. L. 99–474, §2(g), substituted a dash for the comma after "As used in this section", realigned remaining portion of subsection, inserted

"(1)" before "the term", substituted a semicolon for the period at the end, and added pars. (2) to (7).

Subsec. (f). Pub. L. 99–474, §2(h), added subsec. (f).

Effective Date of 2002 Amendment

Amendment by Pub. L. 107–296 effective 60 days after Nov. 25, 2002, see section 4 of Pub. L. 107–296, set out as an Effective Date note under section 101 of Title 6, Domestic Security.

Transfer of Functions

For transfer of the functions, personnel, assets, and obligations of the United States Secret Service, including the functions of the Secretary of the Treasury relating thereto, to the Secretary of Homeland Security, and for treatment of related references, see sections 381, 551(d), 552(d), and 557 of Title 6, Domestic Security, and the Department of Homeland Security Reorganization Plan of November 25, 2002, as modified, set out as a note under section 542 of Title 6.

Reports to Congress

Section 2103 of Pub. L. 98–473 directed Attorney General to report to Congress annually, during first three years following Oct. 12, 1984, concerning prosecutions under this section.

Appendix B

17 U.S.C. § 1201 Circumvention of Copyright Protection Systems[1]

(A) Violations Regarding Circumvention of Technological Measures.—(1)
(A) No person shall circumvent a technological measure that effectively controls access to a work protected under this title. The prohibition contained in the preceding sentence shall take effect at the end of the 2-year period beginning on the date of the enactment of this chapter.

(B)The prohibition contained in subparagraph (A) shall not apply to persons who are users of a copyrighted work which is in a particular class of works, if such persons are, or are likely to be in the succeeding 3-year period, adversely affected by virtue of such prohibition in their ability to make noninfringing uses of that particular class of works under this title, as determined under subparagraph (C).

(C)During the 2-year period described in subparagraph (A), and during each succeeding 3-year period, the Librarian of Congress, upon the recommendation of the Register of Copyrights, who shall consult with the Assistant Secretary for Communications and Information of the

[1] The WIPO Copyright and Performances and Phonograms Treaties Implementation Act of 1998 added chapter 12, titled "Copyright Protection and Management Systems," to title 17. Pub. L. No. 105-304, 112 Stat. 2860, 2863. The WIPO Copyright and Performances and Phonograms Treaties Implementation Act of 1998 is title I of the Digital Millennium Copyright Act. Pub. L. No. 105-304, 112 Stat. 2860. Retrieved from https://www.copyright.gov/title17/92chap12.html

DOI: 10.4324/9780429318726-10

Department of Commerce and report and comment on his or her views in making such recommendation, shall make the determination in a rulemaking proceeding for purposes of subparagraph (B) of whether persons who are users of a copyrighted work are, or are likely to be in the succeeding 3-year period, adversely affected by the prohibition under subparagraph (A) in their ability to make noninfringing uses under this title of a particular class of copyrighted works. In conducting such rulemaking, the Librarian shall examine—

(i) the availability for use of copyrighted works;

(ii) the availability for use of works for nonprofit archival, preservation, and educational purposes;

(iii) the impact that the prohibition on the circumvention of technological measures applied to copyrighted works has on criticism, comment, news reporting, teaching, scholarship, or research;

(iv) the effect of circumvention of technological measures on the market for or value of copyrighted works; and

(v) such other factors as the Librarian considers appropriate.

(D) The Librarian shall publish any class of copyrighted works for which the Librarian has determined, pursuant to the rulemaking conducted under subparagraph (C), that noninfringing uses by persons who are users of a copyrighted work are, or are likely to be, adversely affected, and the prohibition contained in subparagraph (A) shall not apply to such users with respect to such class of works for the ensuing 3-year period.

(E) Neither the exception under subparagraph (B) from the applicability of the prohibition contained in subparagraph (A), nor any determination made in a rulemaking conducted under subparagraph (C), may be used as a defense in any action to enforce any provision of this title other than this paragraph.

(2) No person shall manufacture, import, offer to the public, provide, or otherwise traffic in any technology, product, service, device, component, or part thereof, that—

(A) is primarily designed or produced for the purpose of circumventing a technological measure that effectively controls access to a work protected under this title;

(B) has only limited commercially significant purpose or use other than to circumvent a technological measure that effectively controls access to a work protected under this title; or

(C) is marketed by that person or another acting in concert with that person with that person's knowledge for use in circumventing a technological measure that effectively controls access to a work protected under this title.

(3) As used in this subsection—

(A) to "circumvent a technological measure" means to descramble a scrambled work, to decrypt an encrypted work, or otherwise to avoid, bypass, remove, deactivate, or impair a technological measure, without the authority of the copyright owner; and

(B) a technological measure "effectively controls access to a work" if the measure, in the ordinary course of its operation, requires the application of information, or a process or a treatment, with the authority of the copyright owner, to gain access to the work.

(b) Additional Violations.—(1) No person shall manufacture, import, offer to the public, provide, or otherwise traffic in any technology, product, service, device, component, or part thereof, that—

(A) is primarily designed or produced for the purpose of circumventing protection afforded by a technological measure that effectively protects a right of a copyright owner under this title in a work or a portion thereof;

(B) has only limited commercially significant purpose or use other than to circumvent protection afforded by a technological measure that effectively protects a right of a copyright owner under this title in a work or a portion thereof; or

(C) is marketed by that person or another acting in concert with that person with that person's knowledge for use in circumventing protection afforded by a technological measure that effectively protects a right of a copyright owner under this title in a work or a portion thereof.

(2) As used in this subsection—

(A) to "circumvent protection afforded by a technological measure" means avoiding, bypassing, removing, deactivating, or otherwise impairing a technological measure; and

(B) a technological measure "effectively protects a right of a copyright owner under this title" if the measure, in the ordinary course of its operation, prevents, restricts, or otherwise limits the exercise of a right of a copyright owner under this title.

(c) Other Rights, Etc., Not Affected.—(1) Nothing in this section shall affect rights, remedies, limitations, or defenses to copyright infringement, including fair use, under this title.

(2) Nothing in this section shall enlarge or diminish vicarious or contributory liability for copyright infringement in connection

with any technology, product, service, device, component, or part thereof.

(3) Nothing in this section shall require that the design of, or design and selection of parts and components for, a consumer electronics, telecommunications, or computing product provide for a response to any particular technological measure, so long as such part or component, or the product in which such part or component is integrated, does not otherwise fall within the prohibitions of subsection (a)(2) or (b)(1).

(4) Nothing in this section shall enlarge or diminish any rights of free speech or the press for activities using consumer electronics, telecommunications, or computing products.

(d) Exemption for Nonprofit Libraries, Archives, and Educational Institutions.—(1) A nonprofit library, archives, or educational institution which gains access to a commercially exploited copyrighted work solely in order to make a good faith determination of whether to acquire a copy of that work for the sole purpose of engaging in conduct permitted under this title shall not be in violation of subsection (a)(1)(A). A copy of a work to which access has been gained under this paragraph—

(A) may not be retained longer than necessary to make such good faith determination; and

(B) may not be used for any other purpose.

(2) The exemption made available under paragraph (1) shall only apply with respect to a work when an identical copy of that work is not reasonably available in another form.

(3) A nonprofit library, archives, or educational institution that willfully for the purpose of commercial advantage or financial gain violates paragraph (1)—

(A) shall, for the first offense, be subject to the civil remedies under section 1203; and

(B) shall, for repeated or subsequent offenses, in addition to the civil remedies under section 1203, forfeit the exemption provided under paragraph (1).

(4) This subsection may not be used as a defense to a claim under subsection (a)(2) or (b), nor may this subsection permit a nonprofit library, archives, or educational institution to manufacture, import, offer to the public, provide, or otherwise traffic in any technology, product, service, component, or part thereof, which circumvents a technological measure.

(5) In order for a library or archives to qualify for the exemption under this subsection, the collections of that library or archives shall be—

(A) open to the public; or

(B) available not only to researchers affiliated with the library or archives or with the institution of which it is a part, but also to other persons doing research in a specialized field.

(e) Law Enforcement, Intelligence, and Other Government Activities.—This section does not prohibit any lawfully authorized investigative, protective, information security, or intelligence activity of an officer, agent, or employee of the United States, a State, or a political subdivision of a State, or a person acting pursuant to a contract with the United States, a State, or a political subdivision of a State. For purposes of this subsection, the term “information security” means activities carried out in order to identify and address the vulnerabilities of a government computer, computer system, or computer network. (f) Reverse Engineering.—(1) Notwithstanding the provisions of subsection (a)(1)(A), a person who has lawfully obtained the right to use a copy of a computer program may circumvent a technological measure that effectively controls access to a particular portion of that program for the sole purpose of identifying and analyzing those elements of the program that are necessary to achieve interoperability of an independently created computer program with other programs, and that have not previously been readily available to the person engaging in the circumvention, to the extent any such acts of identification and analysis do not constitute infringement under this title.

(2) Notwithstanding the provisions of subsections (a)(2) and (b), a person may develop and employ technological means to circumvent a technological measure, or to circumvent protection afforded by a technological measure, in order to enable the identification and analysis under paragraph (1), or for the purpose of enabling interoperability of an independently created computer program with other programs, if such means are necessary to achieve such interoperability, to the extent that doing so does not constitute infringement under this title.

(3) The information acquired through the acts permitted under paragraph (1), and the means permitted under paragraph (2), may be made available to others if the person referred to in paragraph (1) or (2), as the case may be, provides such information or means solely for the purpose of enabling interoperability of an independently created computer program with other programs, and to the extent that

doing so does not constitute infringement under this title or violate applicable law other than this section.

(4) For purposes of this subsection, the term "interoperability" means the ability of computer programs to exchange information, and of such programs mutually to use the information which has been exchanged.

(g) Encryption Research.—

(1) Definitions.—For purposes of this subsection—

(A) the term "encryption research" means activities necessary to identify and analyze flaws and vulnerabilities of encryption technologies applied to copyrighted works, if these activities are conducted to advance the state of knowledge in the field of encryption technology or to assist in the development of encryption products; and

(B) the term "encryption technology" means the scrambling and descrambling of information using mathematical formulas or algorithms.

(2) Permissible acts of encryption research.—Notwithstanding the provisions of subsection (a)(1)(A), it is not a violation of that subsection for a person to circumvent a technological measure as applied to a copy, phonorecord, performance, or display of a published work in the course of an act of good faith encryption research if—

(A) the person lawfully obtained the encrypted copy, phonorecord, performance, or display of the published work;

(B) such act is necessary to conduct such encryption research;

(C) the person made a good faith effort to obtain authorization before the circumvention; and

(D) such act does not constitute infringement under this title or a violation of applicable law other than this section, including section 1030 of title 18 and those provisions of title 18 amended by the Computer Fraud and Abuse Act of 1986.

(3) Factors in determining exemption.—In determining whether a person qualifies for the exemption under paragraph (2), the factors to be considered shall include—

(A) whether the information derived from the encryption research was disseminated, and if so, whether it was disseminated in a manner reasonably calculated to advance the state of knowledge or development of encryption technology, versus whether it was disseminated in a manner that facilitates infringement under this title or a violation of applicable law other than this section, including a violation of privacy or breach of security;

(B) whether the person is engaged in a legitimate course of study, is employed, or is appropriately trained or experienced, in the field of encryption technology; and

(C) whether the person provides the copyright owner of the work to which the technological measure is applied with notice of the findings and documentation of the research, and the time when such notice is provided.

(4) Use of technological means for research activities.—Notwithstanding the provisions of subsection (a)(2), it is not a violation of that subsection for a person to—

(A) develop and employ technological means to circumvent a technological measure for the sole purpose of that person performing the acts of good faith encryption research described in paragraph (2); and

(B) provide the technological means to another person with whom he or she is working collaboratively for the purpose of conducting the acts of good faith encryption research described in paragraph (2) or for the purpose of having that other person verify his or her acts of good faith encryption research described in paragraph (2).

(5) Report to Congress.—Not later than 1 year after the date of the enactment of this chapter, the Register of Copyrights and the Assistant Secretary for Communications and Information of the Department of Commerce shall jointly report to the Congress on the effect this subsection has had on—

(A) encryption research and the development of encryption technology;

(B) the adequacy and effectiveness of technological measures designed to protect copyrighted works; and

(C) protection of copyright owners against the unauthorized access to their encrypted copyrighted works.

The report shall include legislative recommendations, if any.

(h) Exceptions Regarding Minors.—In applying subsection (a) to a component or part, the court may consider the necessity for its intended and actual incorporation in a technology, product, service, or device, which—

(4) does not itself violate the provisions of this title; and

(5) has the sole purpose to prevent the access of minors to material on the Internet.

(i) Protection of Personally Identifying Information.—

(1) Circumvention permitted.—Notwithstanding the provisions of subsection (a)(1)(A), it is not a violation of that subsection for a person to circumvent a technological measure that effectively controls access to a work protected under this title, if—

(A) the technological measure, or the work it protects, contains the capability of collecting or disseminating personally identifying information reflecting the online activities of a natural person who seeks to gain access to the work protected;

(B) in the normal course of its operation, the technological measure, or the work it protects, collects or disseminates personally identifying information about the person who seeks to gain access to the work protected, without providing conspicuous notice of such collection or dissemination to such person, and without providing such person with the capability to prevent or restrict such collection or dissemination;

(C) the act of circumvention has the sole effect of identifying and disabling the capability described in subparagraph (A), and has no other effect on the ability of any person to gain access to any work; and

(D) the act of circumvention is carried out solely for the purpose of preventing the collection or dissemination of personally identifying information about a natural person who seeks to gain access to the work protected, and is not in violation of any other law.

(2) Inapplicability to certain technological measures.—

This subsection does not apply to a technological measure, or a work it protects, that does not collect or disseminate personally identifying information and that is disclosed to a user as not having or using such capability.

(j) Security Testing.—

(6) Definition.—For purposes of this subsection, the term "security testing" means accessing a computer, computer system, or computer network, solely for the purpose of good faith testing, investigating, or correcting, a security flaw or vulnerability, with the authorization of the owner or operator of such computer, computer system, or computer network.

(7) Permissible acts of security testing.—Notwithstanding the provisions of subsection (a)(1)(A), it is not a violation of that subsection for a person to engage in an act of security testing, if such act does not constitute infringement under this title or a violation of applicable law other than this section, including section 1030 of title 18 and those provisions of title 18 amended by the Computer Fraud and Abuse Act of 1986.

(8) Factors in determining exemption.—In determining whether a person qualifies for the exemption under paragraph (2), the factors to be considered shall include—

(A) whether the information derived from the security testing was used solely to promote the security of the owner or operator of such computer, computer system or computer network, or shared directly with the developer of such computer, computer system, or computer network; and

(B) whether the information derived from the security testing was used or maintained in a manner that does not facilitate infringement under this title or a violation of applicable law other than this section, including a violation of privacy or breach of security.

(9) Use of technological means for security testing.—Notwithstanding the provisions of subsection (a)(2), it is not a violation of that subsection for a person to develop, produce, distribute or employ technological means for the sole purpose of performing the acts of security testing described in subsection (2), provided such technological means does not otherwise violate section (a)(2).

(k) Certain Analog Devices and Certain Technological Measures.—

(1) Certain analog devices.—

(A) Effective 18 months after the date of the enactment of this chapter, no person shall manufacture, import, offer to the public, provide or otherwise traffic in any—

(ii) VHS format analog video cassette recorder unless such recorder conforms to the automatic gain control copy control technology;

(iii) 8mm format analog video cassette camcorder unless such camcorder conforms to the automatic gain control technology;

(iv) Beta format analog video cassette recorder, unless such recorder conforms to the automatic gain control copy control technology, except that this requirement shall not apply until there are 1,000 Beta format analog video cassette recorders sold in the United States in any one calendar year after the date of the enactment of this chapter;

(v) 8mm format analog video cassette recorder that is not an analog video cassette camcorder, unless such recorder conforms to the automatic gain control copy control technology, except that this requirement shall not apply until there are 20,000 such recorders sold in the United States in any one calendar year after the date of the enactment of this chapter; or

(vi) analog video cassette recorder that records using an NTSC format video input and that is not otherwise covered under clauses (i) through (iv), unless such device conforms to the automatic gain control copy control technology.

(B) Effective on the date of the enactment of this chapter, no person shall manufacture, import, offer to the public, provide or otherwise traffic in—

(vii) any VHS format analog video cassette recorder or any 8mm format analog video cassette recorder if the design of the model of such recorder has been modified after such date of enactment so that a model of recorder that previously conformed to the automatic gain control copy control technology no longer conforms to such technology; or

(viii) any VHS format analog video cassette recorder, or any 8mm format analog video cassette recorder that is not an 8mm analog video cassette camcorder, if the design of the model of such recorder has been modified after such date of enactment so that a model of recorder that previously conformed to the four-line colorstripe copy control technology no longer conforms to such technology.

Manufacturers that have not previously manufactured or sold a VHS format analog video cassette recorder, or an 8mm format analog cassette recorder, shall be required to conform to the four-line colorstripe copy control technology in the initial model of any such recorder manufactured after the date of the enactment of this chapter, and thereafter to continue conforming to the four-line colorstripe copy control technology. For purposes of this subparagraph, an analog video cassette recorder "conforms to" the four-line colorstripe copy control technology if it records a signal that, when played back by the playback function of that recorder in the normal viewing mode, exhibits, on a reference display device, a display containing distracting visible lines through portions of the viewable picture.

(2) Certain encoding restrictions.—No person shall apply the automatic gain control copy control technology or colorstripe copy control technology to prevent or limit consumer copying except such copying—

(A) of a single transmission, or specified group of transmissions, of live events or of audiovisual works for which a member of the public has exercised choice in selecting the transmissions, including the content of the transmissions or the time of receipt of such transmissions, or both, and as to which such member is charged a separate fee for each such transmission or specified group of transmissions;

(B) from a copy of a transmission of a live event or an audiovisual work if such transmission is provided by a channel or service where payment is made by a member of the public for such channel or service in the form of a subscription fee that entitles the member of the public to receive all of the programming contained in such channel or service;

(C) from a physical medium containing one or more prerecorded audiovisual works; or

(D) from a copy of a transmission described in subparagraph (A) or from a copy made from a physical medium described in subparagraph (C).

In the event that a transmission meets both the conditions set forth in subparagraph (A) and those set forth in subparagraph (B), the transmission shall be treated as a transmission described in subparagraph (A).

(3) Inapplicability.—This subsection shall not—

(A) require any analog video cassette camcorder to conform to the automatic gain control copy control technology with respect to any video signal received through a camera lens;

(B) apply to the manufacture, importation, offer for sale, provision of, or other trafficking in, any professional analog video cassette recorder; or

(C) apply to the offer for sale or provision of, or other trafficking in, any previously owned analog video cassette recorder, if such recorder was legally manufactured and sold when new and not subsequently modified in violation of paragraph (1)(B).

(4) Definitions.—For purposes of this subsection:

(A) An "analog video cassette recorder" means a device that records, or a device that includes a function that records, on electromagnetic tape in an analog format the electronic impulses produced by the video and audio portions of a television program, motion picture, or other form of audiovisual work.

(B) An "analog video cassette camcorder" means an analog video cassette recorder that contains a recording function that operates through a camera lens and through a video input that may be connected with a television or other video playback device.

(C) An analog video cassette recorder "conforms" to the automatic gain control copy control technology if it—

(ix) detects one or more of the elements of such technology and does not record the motion picture or transmission protected by such technology; or

(x) records a signal that, when played back, exhibits a meaningfully distorted or degraded display.

(D) The term "professional analog video cassette recorder" means an analog video cassette recorder that is designed, manufactured, marketed, and intended for use by a person who regularly employs such a device for a lawful business or industrial use, including making, performing, displaying, distributing, or transmitting copies of motion pictures on a commercial scale.

(E) The terms "VHS format," "8mm format," "Beta format," "automatic gain control copy control technology," "colorstripe copy control technology," "four-line version of the colorstripe copy control technology," and "NTSC" have the meanings that are commonly understood in the consumer electronics and motion picture industries as of the date of the enactment of this chapter.

(5) Violations.—Any violation of paragraph (1) of this subsection shall be treated as a violation of subsection (b)(1) of this section. Any violation of paragraph (2) of this subsection shall be deemed an "act of circumvention" for the purposes of section 1203(c)(3)(A) of this chapter.

1202. Integrity of Copyright Management Information[3]

(b) False Copyright Management Information.—No person shall knowingly and with the intent to induce, enable, facilitate, or conceal infringement—

(1) provide copyright management information that is false, or

(2) distribute or import for distribution copyright management information that is false.

(c) Removal or Alteration of Copyright Management Information.—
No person shall, without the authority of the copyright owner or the law—

(1) intentionally remove or alter any copyright management information,

(2) distribute or import for distribution copyright management information knowing that the copyright management information has been removed or altered without authority of the copyright owner or the law, or

(3) distribute, import for distribution, or publicly perform works, copies of works, or phonorecords, knowing that copyright management information has been removed or altered without authority of the copyright owner or the law, knowing, or, with respect to civil remedies under section 1203, having reasonable grounds to know, that it will induce, enable, facilitate, or conceal an infringement of any right under this title.

(d) Definition.—As used in this section, the term "copyright management information" means any of the following information conveyed in connection with copies or phonorecords of a work or performances or displays of a work, including in digital form, except that such term does not include any personally identifying information about a user of a work or of a copy, phonorecord, performance, or display of a work:

(1) The title and other information identifying the work, including the information set forth on a notice of copyright.

(2) The name of, and other identifying information about, the author of a work.

(3) The name of, and other identifying information about, the copyright owner of the work, including the information set forth in a notice of copyright.

(4) With the exception of public performances of works by radio and television broadcast stations, the name of, and other identifying information about, a performer whose performance is fixed in a work other than an audiovisual work.

(5) With the exception of public performances of works by radio and television broadcast stations, in the case of an audiovisual work, the name of, and other identifying information about, a writer, performer, or director who is credited in the audiovisual work.

(6) Terms and conditions for use of the work.

(7) Identifying numbers or symbols referring to such information or links to such information.

(8) Such other information as the Register of Copyrights may prescribe by regulation, except that the Register of Copyrights may not require the provision of any information concerning the user of a copyrighted work.

(e) Law Enforcement, Intelligence, and Other Government Activities.— This section does not prohibit any lawfully authorized investigative, protective, information security, or intelligence activity of an officer, agent, or employee of the United States, a State, or a political subdivision of a State, or a person acting pursuant to a contract with the United States, a State, or a political subdivision of a State. For purposes of this subsection, the term "information security" means activities carried out in order to identify and address the vulnerabilities of a government computer, computer system, or computer network.

(f) Limitations on Liability.—

(1) Analog transmissions.—In the case of an analog transmission, a person who is making transmissions in its capacity as a broadcast station, or as a cable system, or someone who provides programming to such station or system, shall not be liable for a violation of subsection (b) if—

(A) avoiding the activity that constitutes such violation is not technically feasible or would create an undue financial hardship on such person; and

(B) such person did not intend, by engaging in such activity, to induce, enable, facilitate, or conceal infringement of a right under this title.

(2) Digital transmissions.—

(A) If a digital transmission standard for the placement of copyright management information for a category of works is set in a voluntary, consensus standard-setting process involving a representative cross-section of broadcast stations or cable systems and copyright owners of a category of works that are intended for public performance by such stations or systems, a person identified in paragraph (1) shall not be liable for a violation of subsection (b) with respect to the particular copyright management information addressed by such standard if—

(xi) the placement of such information by someone other than such person is not in accordance with such standard; and

(xii) the activity that constitutes such violation is not intended to induce, enable, facilitate, or conceal infringement of a right under this title.

(B) Until a digital transmission standard has been set pursuant to subparagraph (A) with respect to the placement of copyright management information for a category of works, a person identified in paragraph (1) shall not be liable for a violation of subsection (b) with respect to such copyright management information, if the activity that constitutes such violation is not intended to induce, enable, facilitate, or conceal infringement of a right under this title, and if—

(i) the transmission of such information by such person would result in a perceptible visual or aural degradation of the digital signal; or

(ii) the transmission of such information by such person would conflict with—

(I) an applicable government regulation relating to transmission of information in a digital signal;

(II) an applicable industry-wide standard relating to the transmission of information in a digital signal that was adopted by a voluntary consensus standards body prior to the effective date of this chapter; or

(III) an applicable industry-wide standard relating to the transmission of information in a digital signal that was adopted in a voluntary, consensus standards-setting process open to participation by a representative cross-section of broadcast stations or cable systems and copyright owners of a category of works that are intended for public performance by such stations or systems.

(3) Definitions.—As used in this subsection—

(A) the term "broadcast station" has the meaning given that term in section 3 of the Communications Act of 1934 (47 U .S .C . 153); and

(B) the term "cable system" has the meaning given that term in section 602 of the Communications Act of 1934 (47 U .S .C . 522).

1203. Civil Remedies[4]

(g) Civil Actions.—Any person injured by a violation of section 1201 or 1202 may bring a civil action in an appropriate United States district court for such violation.

(h) Powers of the Court.—In an action brought under subsection (a), the court—

(1) may grant temporary and permanent injunctions on such terms as it deems reasonable to prevent or restrain a violation, but in no event shall impose a prior restraint on free speech or the press protected under the 1st amendment to the Constitution;

(2) at any time while an action is pending, may order the impounding, on such terms as it deems reasonable, of any device or product that is in the custody or control of the alleged violator and that the court has reasonable cause to believe was involved in a violation;

(3) may award damages under subsection (c);

(4) in its discretion may allow the recovery of costs by or against any party other than the United States or an officer thereof;

(5) in its discretion may award reasonable attorney's fees to the prevailing party; and

(6) may, as part of a final judgment or decree finding a violation, order the remedial modification or the destruction of any device or product involved in the violation that is in the custody or control of the violator or has been impounded under paragraph (2).

(i) Award of Damages.—

(1) In general.—Except as otherwise provided in this title, a person committing a violation of section 1201 or 1202 is liable for either—

(A) the actual damages and any additional profits of the violator, as provided in paragraph (2), or

(B) statutory damages, as provided in paragraph (3).

(2) Actual damages.—The court shall award to the complaining party the actual damages suffered by the party as a result of the violation, and any profits of the violator that are attributable to the violation and are not taken into account in computing the actual damages, if the complaining party elects such damages at any time before final judgment is entered.

(3) Statutory damages.—(A) At any time before final judgment is entered, a complaining party may elect to recover an award of statutory damages for each violation of section 1201 in the sum of not less than $200 or more than $2,500 per act of circumvention, device, product, component, offer, or performance of service, as the court considers just.

(B) At any time before final judgment is entered, a complaining party may elect to recover an award of statutory damages for each violation of section 1202 in the sum of not less than $2,500 or more than $25,000.

(4) Repeated violations.—In any case in which the injured party sustains the burden of proving, and the court finds, that a person has violated section 1201 or 1202 within three years after a final judgment was entered against the person for another such violation, the court may increase the award of damages up to triple the amount that would otherwise be awarded, as the court considers just.

(5) Innocent violations.—

(A) In general.—The court in its discretion may reduce or remit the total award of damages in any case in which the violator sustains the burden of proving, and the court finds, that the violator was not aware and had no reason to believe that its acts constituted a violation.

(B) Nonprofit library, archives, educational institutions, or public broadcasting entities.—

(xiii) Definition.—In this subparagraph, the term "public broadcasting entity" has the meaning given such term under section 118(f).

(xiv) In general.—In the case of a nonprofit library, archives, educational institution, or public broadcasting entity, the court shall remit damages in any case in which the library, archives, educational institution, or public broadcasting entity sustains the burden of proving, and the court finds, that the library, archives, educational institution, or public broadcasting entity was not aware and had no reason to believe that its acts constituted a violation.

1204. Criminal Offenses and Penalties[5]

(j) In General.—Any person who violates section 1201 or 1202 willfully and for purposes of commercial advantage or private financial gain—

(1) shall be fined not more than $500,000 or imprisoned for not more than 5 years, or both, for the first offense; and

(2) shall be fined not more than $1,000,000 or imprisoned for not more than 10 years, or both, for any subsequent offense.

(k) Limitation for Nonprofit Library, Archives, Educational Institution, or Public Broadcasting Entity.—Subsection (a) shall not apply to a nonprofit library, archives, educational institution, or public broadcasting entity (as defined under section 118(f)).

(l) Statute of Limitations.—No criminal proceeding shall be brought under this section unless such proceeding is commenced within five years after the cause of action arose.

1205. Savings Clause

Nothing in this chapter abrogates, diminishes, or weakens the provisions of, nor provides any defense or element of mitigation in a criminal prosecution or civil action under, any Federal or State law that prevents the violation of the privacy of an individual in connection with the individual's use of the Internet.

Appendix C
HIPAA §164.308 Administrative Safeguards[1]

(a) A covered entity or business associate must, in accordance with §164.306:

(1) (i) Standard: Security management process. Implement policies and procedures to prevent, detect, contain, and correct security violations.

(ii) Implementation specifications:

(A) Risk analysis (Required). Conduct an accurate and thorough assessment of the potential risks and vulnerabilities to the confidentiality, integrity, and availability of electronic protected health information held by the covered entity or business associate.

(B) Risk management (Required). Implement security measures sufficient to reduce risks and vulnerabilities to a reasonable and appropriate level to comply with §164.306(a).

(C) Sanction policy (Required). Apply appropriate sanctions against workforce members who fail to comply with the security policies and procedures of the covered entity or business associate.

---

[1] 45 C.F.R. § 164.208

DOI: 10.4324/9780429318726-11

(D) Information system activity review (Required). Implement procedures to regularly review records of information system activity, such as audit logs, access reports, and security incident tracking reports.

(2) Standard: Assigned security responsibility. Identify the security official who is responsible for the development and implementation of the policies and procedures required by this subpart for the covered entity or business associate.

(3) (i) Standard: Workforce security. Implement policies and procedures to ensure that all members of its workforce have appropriate access to electronic protected health information, as provided under paragraph (a)(4) of this section, and to prevent those workforce members who do not have access under paragraph (a)(4) of this section from obtaining access to electronic protected health information.

(ii) Implementation specifications:

(A) Authorization and/or supervision (Addressable). Implement procedures for the authorization and/or supervision of workforce members who work with electronic protected health information or in locations where it might be accessed.

(B) Workforce clearance procedure (Addressable). Implement procedures to determine that the access of a workforce member to electronic protected health information is appropriate.

(C) Termination procedures (Addressable). Implement procedures for terminating access to electronic protected health information when the employment of, or other arrangement with, a workforce member ends or as required by determinations made as specified in paragraph (a)(3)(ii)(B) of this section.

(4) (i) Standard: Information access management. Implement policies and procedures for authorizing access to electronic protected health information that are consistent with the applicable requirements of subpart E of this part.

(ii) Implementation specifications:

(A) Isolating health care clearinghouse functions (Required). If a health care clearinghouse is part of a larger organization, the clearinghouse must implement policies and procedures that protect the electronic protected health information of the clearinghouse from unauthorized access by the larger organization.

(B) Access authorization (Addressable). Implement policies and procedures for granting access to electronic protected health information, for example, through access to a workstation, transaction, program, process, or other mechanism.

(C) Access establishment and modification (Addressable). Implement policies and procedures that, based upon the covered entity's or the business associate's access authorization policies, establish, document, review, and modify a user's right of access to a workstation, transaction, program, or process.

(5) (i) Standard: Security awareness and training. Implement a security awareness and training program for all members of its workforce (including management).

(ii) Implementation specifications. Implement:

(A) Security reminders (Addressable). Periodic security updates.

(B) Protection from malicious software (Addressable). Procedures for guarding against, detecting, and reporting malicious software.

(C) Log-in monitoring (Addressable). Procedures for monitoring log-in attempts and reporting discrepancies.

(D) Password management (Addressable). Procedures for creating, changing, and safeguarding passwords.

(6) (i) Standard: Security incident procedures. Implement policies and procedures to address security incidents.

(ii) Implementation specification: Response and reporting (Required). Identify and respond to suspected or known security incidents; mitigate, to the extent practicable, harmful effects of security incidents that are known to the covered entity or business associate; and document security incidents and their outcomes.

(7) (i) Standard: Contingency plan. Establish (and implement as needed) policies and procedures for responding to an emergency or other occurrence (for example, fire, vandalism, system failure, and natural disaster) that damages systems that contain electronic protected health information.

(ii) Implementation specifications:

(A) Data backup plan (Required). Establish and implement procedures to create and maintain retrievable exact copies of electronic protected health information.

(B) Disaster recovery plan (Required). Establish (and implement as needed) procedures to restore any loss of data.

(C) Emergency mode operation plan (Required). Establish (and implement as needed) procedures to enable continuation of critical business processes for protection of the security of electronic protected health information while operating in emergency mode.

(D) Testing and revision procedures (Addressable). Implement procedures for periodic testing and revision of contingency plans.

(E) Applications and data criticality analysis (Addressable). Assess the relative criticality of specific applications and data in support of other contingency plan components.

(8) Standard: Evaluation. Perform a periodic technical and nontechnical evaluation, based initially upon the standards implemented under this rule and, subsequently, in response to environmental or operational changes affecting the security of electronic protected health information, that establishes the extent to which a covered entity's or business associate's security policies and procedures meet the requirements of this subpart.

(b) (1) Business associate contracts and other arrangements. A covered entity may permit a business associate to create, receive, maintain, or transmit electronic protected health information on the covered entity's behalf only if the covered entity obtains satisfactory assurances, in accordance with §164.314(a), that the business associate will appropriately safeguard the information. A covered entity is not required to obtain such satisfactory assurances from a business associate that is a subcontractor.

(2) A business associate may permit a business associate that is a subcontractor to create, receive, maintain, or transmit electronic protected health information on its behalf only if the business associate obtains satisfactory assurances, in accordance with §164.314(a), that the subcontractor will appropriately safeguard the information.

(3) Implementation specifications: Written contract or other arrangement (Required). Document the satisfactory assurances required by paragraph (b)(1) or (b)(2) of this section through a written contract or other arrangement with the business associate that meets the applicable requirements of §164.314(a).

HIPAA §164.310 Physical Safeguards[2]

A covered entity or business associate must, in accordance with §164.306:

(a) (1) Standard: Facility access controls. Implement policies and procedures to limit physical access to its electronic information systems and

[2] 45 C.F.R. § 164.310

the facility or facilities in which they are housed, while ensuring that properly authorized access is allowed.

(2) Implementation specifications:

(i) Contingency operations (Addressable). Establish (and implement as needed) procedures that allow facility access in support of restoration of lost data under the disaster recovery plan and emergency mode operations plan in the event of an emergency.

(ii) Facility security plan (Addressable). Implement policies and procedures to safeguard the facility and the equipment therein from unauthorized physical access, tampering, and theft.

(iii) Access control and validation procedures (Addressable). Implement procedures to control and validate a person's access to facilities based on their role or function, including visitor control, and control of access to software programs for testing and revision.

(iv) Maintenance records (Addressable). Implement policies and procedures to document repairs and modifications to the physical components of a facility which are related to security (for example, hardware, walls, doors, and locks).

(b) Standard: Workstation use. Implement policies and procedures that specify the proper functions to be performed, the manner in which those functions are to be performed, and the physical attributes of the surroundings of a specific workstation or class of workstation that can access electronic protected health information.

(c) Standard: Workstation security. Implement physical safeguards for all workstations that access electronic protected health information, to restrict access to authorized users.

(d) (1) Standard: Device and media controls. Implement policies and procedures that govern the receipt and removal of hardware and electronic media that contain electronic protected health information into and out of a facility, and the movement of these items within the facility.

(2) Implementation specifications:

(i) Disposal (Required). Implement policies and procedures to address the final disposition of electronic protected health information, and/or the hardware or electronic media on which it is stored.

(ii) Media re-use (Required). Implement procedures for removal of electronic protected health information from electronic media before the media are made available for re-use.

(iii) Accountability (Addressable). Maintain a record of the movements of hardware and electronic media and any person responsible therefore.

(iv) Data backup and storage (Addressable). Create a retrievable, exact copy of electronic protected health information, when needed, before movement of equipment.

HIPAA §164.312 Technical Safeguards[3]

A covered entity or business associate must, in accordance with §164.306:

(a) (1) Standard: Access control. Implement technical policies and procedures for electronic information systems that maintain electronic protected health information to allow access only to those persons or software programs that have been granted access rights as specified in §164.308(a)(4).

(2) Implementation specifications:

(i) Unique user identification (Required). Assign a unique name and/or number for identifying and tracking user identity.

(ii) Emergency access procedure (Required). Establish (and implement as needed) procedures for obtaining necessary electronic protected health information during an emergency.

(iii) Automatic logoff (Addressable). Implement electronic procedures that terminate an electronic session after a predetermined time of inactivity.

(iv) Encryption and decryption (Addressable). Implement a mechanism to encrypt and decrypt electronic protected health information.

(b) Standard: Audit controls. Implement hardware, software, and/or procedural mechanisms that record and examine activity in information systems that contain or use electronic protected health information.

(c) (1) Standard: Integrity. Implement policies and procedures to protect electronic protected health information from improper alteration or destruction.

(2) Implementation specification: Mechanism to authenticate electronic protected health information (Addressable). Implement electronic mechanisms to corroborate that electronic protected health information has not been altered or destroyed in an unauthorized manner.

(d) Standard: Person or entity authentication. Implement procedures to verify that a person or entity seeking access to electronic protected health information is the one claimed.

---

[3] 45 C.F.R. § 164.312

(e) (1) Standard: Transmission security. Implement technical security measures to guard against unauthorized access to electronic protected health information that is being transmitted over an electronic communications network.

(2) Implementation specifications:

(i) Integrity controls (Addressable). Implement security measures to ensure that electronically transmitted electronic protected health information is not improperly modified without detection until disposed of.

(ii) Encryption (Addressable). Implement a mechanism to encrypt electronic protected health information whenever deemed appropriate.

HIPAA §164.314 Organizational Requirements[4]

(a)(1) Standard: Business associate contracts or other arrangements. The contract or other arrangement required by §164.308(b)(3) must meet the requirements of paragraph (a)(2)(i), (a)(2)(ii), or (a)(2)(iii) of this section, as applicable.

(2) Implementation specifications (Required).

(i) Business associate contracts. The contract must provide that the business associate will--

(A) Comply with the applicable requirements of this subpart;

(B) In accordance with §164.308(b)(2), ensure that any subcontractors that create, receive, maintain, or transmit electronic protected health information on behalf of the business associate agree to comply with the applicable requirements of this subpart by entering into a contract or other arrangement that complies with this section; and

(C) Report to the covered entity any security incident of which it becomes aware, including breaches of unsecured protected health information as required by § 164.410.

(ii) Other arrangements. The covered entity is in compliance with paragraph (a)(1) of this section if it has another arrangement in place that meets the requirements of §164.504(e)(3).

(iii) Business associate contracts with subcontractors. The requirements of paragraphs (a)(2)(i) and (a)(2)(ii) of this section apply to the contract or other arrangement between a business associate

[4] 45 C.F.R. §164.314

and a subcontractor required by §164.308(b)(4) in the same manner as such requirements apply to contracts or other arrangements between a covered entity and business associate.

(b) (1) Standard: Requirements for group health plans. Except when the only electronic protected health information disclosed to a plan sponsor is disclosed pursuant to §164.504(f)(1)(ii) or (iii), or as authorized under §164.508, a group health plan must ensure that its plan documents provide that the plan sponsor will reasonably and appropriately safeguard electronic protected health information created, received, maintained, or transmitted to or by the plan sponsor on behalf of the group health plan.

(2) Implementation specifications (Required). The plan documents of the group health plan must be amended to incorporate provisions to require the plan sponsor to—

(i) Implement administrative, physical, and technical safeguards that reasonably and appropriately protect the confidentiality, integrity, and availability of the electronic protected health information that it creates, receives, maintains, or transmits on behalf of the group health plan;

(ii) Ensure that the adequate separation required by §164.504(f)(2)(iii) is supported by reasonable and appropriate security measures;

(iii) Ensure that any agent to whom it provides this information agrees to implement reasonable and appropriate security measures to protect the information; and

(iv) Report to the group health plan any security incident of which it becomes aware.

Appendix D

Sec. 13410. Improved Enforcement[1]

(a) IN GENERAL.—

(1) NONCOMPLIANCE DUE TO WILLFUL NEGLECT.—Section 1176 of the Social Security Act (42 U.S.C. 1320d–5) is amended—

(A) in subsection (b)(1), by striking "the act constitutes an offense punishable under section 1177" and inserting "a penalty has been imposed under section 1177 with respect to such act"; and

(B) by adding at the end the following new subsection:

(C) "(c) NONCOMPLIANCE DUE TO WILLFUL NEGLECT.—

"(1) IN GENERAL.—A violation of a provision of this part due to willful neglect is a violation for which the Secretary is required to impose a penalty under subsection (a)(1).

"(2) REQUIRED INVESTIGATION.—For purposes of paragraph (1), the Secretary shall formally investigate any complaint of a violation of a provision of this part if a preliminary investigation of the facts of the complaint indicate such a possible violation due to willful neglect."

---

[1] The American Recovery and Reinvestment Act of 2009. TITLE XIII—The Health Information Technology for Economic and Clinical Health (HITECH) Act. SEC. 13410. Improved Enforcement. Retrieved from https://www.govinfo.gov/content/pkg/PLAW-111publ5/pdf/PLAW-111publ5.pdf

(2) ENFORCEMENT UNDER SOCIAL SECURITY ACT.—Any violation by a covered entity under thus subtitle is subject to enforcement and penalties under section 1176 and 1177 of the Social Security Act.

(b) EFFECTIVE DATE; REGULATIONS.—

(1) The amendments made by subsection (a) shall apply to penalties imposed on or after the date that is 24 months after the date of the enactment of this title.

(2) Not later than 18 months after the date of the enactment of this title, the Secretary of Health and Human Services shall promulgate regulations to implement such amendments.

(c) DISTRIBUTION OF CERTAIN CIVIL MONETARY PENALTIES COLLECTED.—

(1) IN GENERAL.— Subject to the regulation promulgated pursuant to paragraph (3), any civil monetary penalty or monetary settlement collected with respect to an offense punishable under this subtitle or section 1176 of the Social Security Act (42 U.S.C. 1320d–5) insofar as such section relates to privacy or security shall be transferred to the Office for Civil Rights of the Department of Health and Human Services to be used for purposes of enforcing the provisions of this subtitle and subparts C and E of part 164 of title 45, Code of Federal Regulations, as such provisions are in effect as of the date of enactment of this Act.

(2) GAO REPORT.— Not later than 18 months after the date of the enactment of this title, the Comptroller General shall submit to the Secretary a report including recommendations for a methodology under which an individual who is harmed by an act that constitutes an offense referred to in paragraph (1) may receive a percentage of any civil monetary penalty or monetary settlement collected with respect to such offense.

(3) ESTABLISHMENT OF METHODOLOGY TO DISTRIBUTE PERCENTAGE OF CMPS COLLECTED TO HARMED INDIVIDUALS.— Not later than 3 years after the date of the enactment of this title, the Secretary shall establish by regulation and based on the recommendations submitted under paragraph (2), a methodology under which an individual who is harmed by an act that constitutes an offense referred to in paragraph (1) may receive a percentage of any civil monetary penalty or monetary settlement collected with respect to such offense.

(4) APPLICATION OF METHODOLOGY.—The methodology under paragraph (3) shall be applied with respect to civil monetary penalties or monetary settlements imposed on or after the effective date of the regulation.

(d) TIERED INCREASE IN AMOUNT OF CIVIL MONETARY PENALTIES.—

(1) IN GENERAL.—Section 1176(a)(1) of the Social Security Act (42 U.S.C. 1320d–5(a)(1)) is amended by striking "who violates a provision of this part a penalty of not more than" and all that follows and inserting the following: "who violates a provision of this part—

"(A) in the case of a violation of such provision in which it is established that the person did not know (and by exercising reasonable diligence would not have known) that such person violated such provision, a penalty for each such violation of an amount that is at least the amount described in paragraph (3)(A) but not to exceed the amount described in paragraph (3)(D);

"(B) in the case of a violation of such provision in which it is established that the violation was due to reasonable cause and not to willful neglect, a penalty for each such violation of an amount that is at least the amount described in paragraph (3)(B) but not to exceed the amount described in paragraph (3)(D); and

"(C) in the case of a violation of such provision in which it is established that the violation was due to willful neglect—

"(i) if the violation is corrected as described in subsection (b)(3)(A), a penalty in an amount that is at least the amount described in paragraph (3)(C) but not to exceed the amount described in paragraph (3)(D); and

"(ii) if the violation is not corrected as described in such subsection, a penalty in an amount that is at least the amount described in paragraph (3)(D). In determining the amount of a penalty under this section for a violation, the Secretary shall base such determination on the nature and extent of the violation and the nature and extent of the harm resulting from such violation."

(2) TIERS OF PENALTIES DESCRIBED.—Section 1176(a) of such Act (42 U.S.C. 1320d–5(a)) is further amended by adding at the end the following new paragraph:

"(3) TIERS OF PENALTIES DESCRIBED.—For purposes of paragraph (1), with respect to a violation by a person of a provision of this part—

"(A) the amount described in this subparagraph is $100 for each such violation, except that the total amount imposed on the person for all such violations of an identical requirement or prohibition during a calendar year may not exceed $25,000;

"(B) the amount described in this subparagraph is $1,000 for each such violation, except that the total amount imposed on the person for all such violations of an identical requirement or prohibition during a calendar year may not exceed $100,000;

"(C) the amount described in this subparagraph is $10,000 for each such violation, except that the total amount imposed on the person for all such violations of an identical requirement or prohibition during a calendar year may not exceed $250,000; and

"(D) the amount described in this subparagraph is $50,000 for each such violation, except that the total amount imposed on the person for all such violations of an identical requirement or prohibition during a calendar year may not exceed $1,500,000."

(3) CONFORMING AMENDMENTS.—Section 1176(b) of such Act (42 U.S.C. 1320d–5(b)) is amended—(A) by striking paragraph (2) and redesignating paragraphs (3) and (4) as paragraphs (2) and (3), respectively; and (B) in paragraph (2), as so redesignated—(i) in subparagraph (A), by striking "in subparagraph (B), a penalty may not be imposed under subsection (a) if" and all that follows through "the failure to comply is corrected" and inserting "in subparagraph (B) or subsection (a)(1)(C), a penalty may not be imposed under subsection (a) if the failure to comply is corrected"; and (ii) in subparagraph (B), by striking "(A)(ii)" and inserting "(A)" each place it appears.

(4) EFFECTIVE DATE.—The amendments made by this subsection shall apply to violations occurring after the date of the enactment of this title.

(e) ENFORCEMENT THROUGH STATE ATTORNEYS GENERAL.—

(1) IN GENERAL.—Section 1176 of the Social Security Act (42 U.S.C. 1320d–5) is amended by adding at the end the following new subsection:

"(d) ENFORCEMENT BY STATE ATTORNEYS GENERAL.—

a. "(1) CIVIL ACTION.—Except as provided in subsection (b), in any case in which the attorney general of a State has reason to believe that an interest of one or more of the residents of that State has been or is threatened or adversely affected by any person who violates a provision of this part, the attorney general of the State, as parens patriae, may bring a civil action on behalf of such residents of the State in a district court of the United States of appropriate jurisdiction—

"(A) to enjoin further such violation by the defendant; or

"(B) to obtain damages on behalf of such residents of the State, in an amount equal to the amount determined under paragraph (2).

"(2) STATUTORY DAMAGES.—

a. "(A) IN GENERAL.—For purposes of paragraph (1)(B), the amount determined under this paragraph is the amount calculated by multiplying the number of violations by up to $100. For purposes of the preceding sentence, in the case of a continuing violation, the number of violations shall be determined consistent with the HIPAA privacy regulations (as defined in section 1180(b)(3)) for violations of subsection (a).

b. "(B) LIMITATION.—The total amount of damages imposed on the person for all violations of an identical requirement or prohibition during a calendar year may not exceed $25,000.

c. "(C) REDUCTION OF DAMAGES.—In assessing damages under subparagraph (A), the court may consider the factors the Secretary may consider in determining the amount of a civil money penalty under subsection (a) under the HIPAA privacy regulations.

d. "(3) ATTORNEY FEES.—In the case of any successful action under paragraph (1), the court, in its discretion, may award the costs of the action and reasonable attorney fees to the State.

e. "(4) NOTICE TO SECRETARY.—The State shall serve prior written notice of any action under paragraph (1) upon the Secretary and provide the Secretary with a copy of its complaint, except in any case in which such prior notice is not feasible, in which case the State shall serve such notice immediately upon instituting such action. The Secretary shall have the right—

"(A) to intervene in the action;

"(B) upon so intervening, to be heard on all matters arising therein; and

"(C) to file petitions for appeal.

"(5) CONSTRUCTION.—For purposes of bringing any civil action under paragraph (1), nothing in this section shall be construed to prevent an attorney general of a State from exercising the powers conferred on the attorney general by the laws of that State.

"(6) VENUE; SERVICE OF PROCESS.—

"(A) VENUE.—Any action brought under paragraph (1) may be brought in the district court of the United States that meets applicable requirements relating to venue under section 1391 of title 28, United States Code.

"(B) SERVICE OF PROCESS.—In an action brought under paragraph (1), process may be served in any district in which the defendant—

"(i) is an inhabitant; or"(ii) maintains a physical place of business.

"(7) LIMITATION ON STATE ACTION WHILE FEDERAL ACTION IS PENDING.—If the Secretary has instituted an action against a person under subsection (a) with respect to a specific violation of this part, no State attorney general may bring an action under this subsection against the person with respect to such violation during the pendency of that action.

"(8) APPLICATION OF CMP STATUTE OF LIMITATION.—A civil action may not be instituted with respect to a violation of this part unless an action to impose a civil money penalty may be instituted under subsection (a) with respect to such violation consistent with the second sentence of section 1128A(c)(1)."

(1) CONFORMING AMENDMENTS.—Subsection (b) of such section, as amended by subsection (d)(3), is amended—

(A) in paragraph (1), by striking "A penalty may not be imposed under subsection (a)" and inserting "No penalty may be imposed under subsection (a) and no damages obtained under subsection (d)";

(B) in paragraph (2)(A)—

(i) after "subsection (a)(1)(C),", by striking "a penalty may not be imposed under subsection (a)" and inserting "no penalty may be imposed under subsection (a) and no damages obtained under subsection (d)"; and

(ii) in clause (ii), by inserting "or damages" after "the penalty";

(C) in paragraph (2)(B)(i), by striking "The period" and inserting "With respect to the imposition of a penalty by the Secretary under subsection (a), the period"; and (D) in paragraph (3), by inserting "and any damages under subsection (d)" after "any penalty under subsection (a)."

(2) EFFECTIVE DATE.—The amendments made by this subsection shall apply to violations occurring after the date of the enactment of this Act.

(f) ALLOWING CONTINUED USE OF CORRECTIVE ACTION.—Such section is further amended by adding at the end the following new subsection: "(e) ALLOWING CONTINUED USE OF CORRECTIVE ACTION.—Nothing in this section shall be construed as preventing the Office for Civil Rights of the Department of Health and Human Services from continuing, in its discretion, to use corrective action without a penalty in cases where the person did not know (and by exercising reasonable diligence would not have known) of the violation involved."

Appendix E
15 U.S.C.

United States Code, 2011 Edition
Title 15 – COMMERCE AND TRADE
CHAPTER 2 – FEDERAL TRADE COMMISSION; PROMOTION OF EXPORT TRADE AND PREVENTION OF UNFAIR METHODS OF COMPETITION
SUBCHAPTER I – FEDERAL TRADE COMMISSION
Sec. 45 – Unfair methods of competition unlawful; prevention by Commission
From the U.S. Government Publishing Office, www.gpo.gov

§45. Unfair methods of competition unlawful; prevention by Commission[1]

(a) **Declaration of unlawfulness; power to prohibit unfair practices; inapplicability to foreign trade**

(1) Unfair methods of competition in or affecting commerce, and unfair or deceptive acts or practices in or affecting commerce, are hereby declared unlawful.

(2) The Commission is hereby empowered and directed to prevent persons, partnerships, or corporations, except banks, savings and loan institutions described in section 57a(f)(3) of this title, Federal credit

[1] 15 U.S.C. 45 – Unfair methods of competition unlawful; prevention by Commission. Retrieved from https ://www.govinfo.gov/app/details/USCODE-2011-title15/USCODE-2011-title15-chap2-subchapI-sec45

DOI: 10.4324/9780429318726-13

unions described in section 57a(f)(4) of this title, common carriers subject to the Acts to regulate commerce, air carriers and foreign air carriers subject to part A of subtitle VII of title 49, and persons, partnerships, or corporations insofar as they are subject to the Packers and Stockyards Act, 1921, as amended [7 U.S.C. 181 et seq.], except as provided in section 406(b) of said Act [7 U.S.C. 227(b)], from using unfair methods of competition in or affecting commerce and unfair or deceptive acts or practices in or affecting commerce.

(3) This subsection shall not apply to unfair methods of competition involving commerce with foreign nations (other than import commerce) unless—

(A) such methods of competition have a direct, substantial, and reasonably foreseeable effect—

(i) on commerce which is not commerce with foreign nations, or on import commerce with foreign nations; or

(ii) on export commerce with foreign nations, of a person engaged in such commerce in the United States; and

(B) such effect gives rise to a claim under the provisions of this subsection, other than this paragraph.

If this subsection applies to such methods of competition only because of the operation of subparagraph (A)(ii), this subsection shall apply to such conduct only for injury to export business in the United States.

(4)(A) For purposes of subsection (a), the term "unfair or deceptive acts or practices" includes such acts or practices involving foreign commerce that—

(i) cause or are likely to cause reasonably foreseeable injury within the United States; or

(ii) involve material conduct occurring within the United States.

(B) All remedies available to the Commission with respect to unfair and deceptive acts or practices shall be available for acts and practices described in this paragraph, including restitution to domestic or foreign victims.

(b) **Proceeding by Commission; modifying and setting aside orders**

Whenever the Commission shall have reason to believe that any such person, partnership, or corporation has been or is using any unfair method of competition or unfair or deceptive act or practice in or affecting commerce, and if it shall appear to the Commission that a proceeding by it in respect thereof would be to the interest of the public, it shall issue and serve upon such person, partnership, or corporation a complaint stating its charges in that respect and containing a notice of a hearing upon a day and at a place therein fixed at least thirty days after the service of said complaint. The person, partnership, or corporation so complained of shall have the right to appear at the place and time so fixed and show cause why an order should not be entered by the Commission requiring such person, partnership, or corporation to cease and desist from the violation of the law so charged in said complaint. Any person, partnership, or corporation may make application, and upon good cause shown may be allowed by the Commission to intervene and appear in said proceeding by counsel or in person. The testimony in any such proceeding shall be reduced to writing and filed in the office of the Commission. If upon such hearing the Commission shall be of the opinion that the method of competition or the act or practice in question is prohibited by this subchapter, it shall make a report in writing in which it shall state its findings as to the facts and shall issue and cause to be served on such person, partnership, or corporation an order requiring such person, partnership, or corporation to cease and desist from using such method of competition or such act or practice. Until the expiration of the time allowed for filing a petition for review, if no such petition has been duly filed within such time, or, if a petition for review has been filed within such time then until the record in the proceeding has been filed in a court of appeals of the United States, as hereinafter provided, the Commission may at any time, upon such notice and in such manner as it shall deem proper, modify or set aside, in whole or in part, any report or any order made or issued by it under this section. After the expiration of the time allowed for filing a petition for review, if no such petition has been duly filed within such time, the Commission may at any time, after notice and opportunity for hearing, reopen and alter, modify, or set aside, in whole or in part any report or order made or issued by it under this section, whenever in the opinion of the Commission conditions of fact or of law have so changed as to require such action or if the public interest shall so require, except that (1) the said person, partnership, or corporation may, within sixty days after service upon him or it of said report or order entered after such a reopening, obtain a review thereof in the appropriate court of appeals of the United States, in the manner provided in subsection (c) of this section; and (2) in the case of an order, the Commission shall reopen any such order to consider whether such order (including any affirmative relief provision contained in such order) should be altered, modified, or set aside, in whole or in part, if the person, partnership, or corporation involved files a request with the Commission which makes a satisfactory showing that changed conditions of law or fact require such order to be altered, modified, or set aside, in whole or in part. The Commission shall determine whether to alter, modify, or set aside any order of the Commission in response to a request made by a person, partnership, or corporation under paragraph [1] (2) not later than 120 days after the date of the filing of such request.

(c) **Review of order; rehearing**

Any person, partnership, or corporation required by an order of the Commission to cease and desist from using any method of competition or act or practice may obtain a review of such order in the court of appeals of the United States, within any circuit where the method of competition or the act or practice in question was used or where such person, partnership, or corporation resides or carries on business, by filing in the court, within sixty days from the date of the service of such order, a written petition praying that the order of the Commission be set aside. A copy of such petition shall be forthwith transmitted by the clerk of the court to the Commission, and thereupon the Commission shall file in the court the record in the proceeding, as provided in section 2112 of title 28. Upon such filing of the petition the court shall have jurisdiction of the proceeding and of the question determined therein concurrently with the Commission until the filing of the record and shall have power to make and enter a decree affirming, modifying, or setting aside the order of the Commission, and enforcing the same to the extent that such order is affirmed and to issue such writs as are ancillary to its jurisdiction or are necessary in its judgement to prevent injury to the public or to competitors pendente lite. The findings of the Commission as to the facts, if supported by evidence, shall be conclusive. To the extent that the order of the Commission is affirmed, the court shall thereupon issue its own order commanding obedience to the terms of such order of the Commission. If either party shall apply to the court for leave to adduce additional evidence, and shall show to the satisfaction of the court that such additional evidence is material and that there were reasonable grounds for the failure to adduce such evidence in the proceeding before the Commission, the court may order such additional evidence to be taken before the Commission and to be adduced upon the hearing in such manner and upon such terms and conditions as to the court may seem proper. The Commission may modify its findings as to the facts, or make new findings, by reason of the additional evidence so taken, and it shall file such modified or new findings, which, if supported by evidence, shall be conclusive, and its recommendation, if any, for the modification or setting aside of its original order, with the return of such additional evidence. The judgment and decree of the court shall be final, except that the same shall be subject to review by the Supreme Court upon certiorari, as provided in section 1254 of title 28.

(d) **Jurisdiction of court**

Upon the filing of the record with it the jurisdiction of the court of appeals of the United States to affirm, enforce, modify, or set aside orders of the Commission shall be exclusive.

(e) **Exemption from liability**

No order of the Commission or judgement of court to enforce the same shall in anywise relieve or absolve any person, partnership, or corporation from any liability under the Antitrust Acts.

(f) **Service of complaints, orders and other processes; return**

Complaints, orders, and other processes of the Commission under this section may be served by anyone duly authorized by the Commission, either (a) by delivering a copy thereof to the person to be served, or to a member of the partnership to be served, or the president, secretary, or other executive officer or a director of the corporation to be served; or (b) by leaving a copy thereof at the residence or the principal office or place of business of such person, partnership, or corporation; or (c) by mailing a copy thereof by registered mail or by certified mail addressed to such person, partnership, or corporation at his or its residence or principal office or place of business. The verified return by the person so serving said complaint, order, or other process setting forth the manner of said service shall be proof of the same, and the return post office receipt for said complaint, order, or other process mailed by registered mail or by certified mail as aforesaid shall be proof of the service of the same.

(g) **Finality of order**

An order of the Commission to cease and desist shall become final—

(1) Upon the expiration of the time allowed for filing a petition for review, if no such petition has been duly filed within such time; but the Commission may thereafter modify or set aside its order to the extent provided in the last sentence of subsection (b).

(2) Except as to any order provision subject to paragraph (4), upon the sixtieth day after such order is served, if a petition for review has been duly filed; except that any such order may be stayed, in whole or in part and subject to such conditions as may be appropriate, by—

(A) the Commission;

(B) an appropriate court of appeals of the United States, if (i) a petition for review of such order is pending in such court, and (ii) an application for such a stay was previously submitted to the Commission and the Commission, within the 30-day period beginning on the date the application was received by the Commission, either denied the application or did not grant or deny the application; or

(C) the Supreme Court, if an applicable petition for certiorari is pending.

(3) For purposes of subsection (m)(1)(B) of this section and of section 57b(a)(2) of this title, if a petition for review of the order of the Commission has been filed—

(A) upon the expiration of the time allowed for filing a petition for certiorari, if the order of the Commission has been affirmed or the petition for review has been dismissed by the court of appeals and no petition for certiorari has been duly filed;

(B) upon the denial of a petition for certiorari, if the order of the Commission has been affirmed or the petition for review has been dismissed by the court of appeals; or

(C) upon the expiration of 30 days from the date of issuance of a mandate of the Supreme Court directing that the order of the Commission be affirmed or the petition for review be dismissed.

(4) In the case of an order provision requiring a person, partnership, or corporation to divest itself of stock, other share capital, or assets, if a petition for review of such order of the Commission has been filed—

(A) upon the expiration of the time allowed for filing a petition for certiorari, if the order of the Commission has been affirmed or the petition for review has been dismissed by the court of appeals and no petition for certiorari has been duly filed;

(B) upon the denial of a petition for certiorari, if the order of the Commission has been affirmed or the petition for review has been dismissed by the court of appeals; or

(C) upon the expiration of 30 days from the date of issuance of a mandate of the Supreme Court directing that the order of the Commission be affirmed or the petition for review be dismissed.

(h) **Modification or setting aside of order by Supreme Court**

If the Supreme Court directs that the order of the Commission be modified or set aside, the order of the Commission rendered in accordance with the mandate of the Supreme Court shall become final upon the expiration of thirty days from the time it was rendered, unless within such thirty days either party has instituted proceedings to have such order corrected to accord with the mandate, in which event the order of the Commission shall become final when so corrected.

(i) **Modification or setting aside of order by Court of Appeals**

If the order of the Commission is modified or set aside by the court of appeals, and if (1) the time allowed for filing a petition for certiorari has expired and no such petition has been duly filed, or (2) the petition for certiorari has been denied, or (3) the decision of the court has been affirmed by the Supreme Court, then the order of the Commission rendered in accordance with the mandate of the court of appeals shall become final on the expiration of thirty days from the time such order of the Commission was rendered, unless within such thirty days either party has instituted proceedings to have such order corrected so that it will accord with the mandate, in which event the order of the Commission shall become final when so corrected.

(j) **Rehearing upon order or remand**

If the Supreme Court orders a rehearing; or if the case is remanded by the court of appeals to the Commission for a rehearing, and if (1) the time allowed for filing a petition for certiorari has expired, and no such petition has been duly filed, or (2) the petition for certiorari has been denied, or (3) the decision of the court has been affirmed by the Supreme Court, then the order of the Commission rendered upon such rehearing shall become final in the same manner as though no prior order of the Commission had been rendered.

(k) **"Mandate" defined**

As used in this section the term "mandate", in case a mandate has been recalled prior to the expiration of thirty days from the date of issuance thereof, means the final mandate.

(l) **Penalty for violation of order; injunctions and other appropriate equitable relief**

Any person, partnership, or corporation who violates an order of the Commission after it has become final, and while such order is in effect, shall forfeit and pay to the United States a civil penalty of not more than $10,000 for each violation, which shall accrue to the United States and may be recovered in a civil action brought by the Attorney General of the United States. Each separate violation of such an order shall be a separate offense, except that in a case of a violation through continuing failure to obey or neglect to obey a final order of the Commission, each day of continuance of such failure or neglect shall be deemed a separate offense. In such actions, the United States district courts are empowered to grant mandatory injunctions and such other and further equitable relief as they deem appropriate in the enforcement of such final orders of the Commission.

(m) **Civil actions for recovery of penalties for knowing violations of rules and cease and desist orders respecting unfair or deceptive acts or practices; jurisdiction; maximum amount of penalties; continuing violations; de novo determinations; compromise or settlement procedure**

(1)(A) The Commission may commence a civil action to recover a civil penalty in a district court of the United States against any person, partnership, or corporation which violates any rule under this subchapter respecting unfair or deceptive acts or practices (other than an interpretive rule or a rule violation of which the Commission has provided is not an unfair or deceptive act or practice in violation of subsection (a)(1) of this section) with actual knowledge or knowledge fairly implied on the basis of objective circumstances that such act is unfair or deceptive and is prohibited by such rule. In such action, such person, partnership, or corporation shall be liable for a civil penalty of not more than $10,000 for each violation.

(B) If the Commission determines in a proceeding under subsection (b) of this section that any act or practice is unfair or deceptive, and issues a final cease and desist order, other than a consent order, with respect to such act or practice, then the Commission may commence a civil action to obtain a civil penalty in a district court of the United States against any person, partnership, or corporation which engages in such act or practice—

(1) after such cease and desist order becomes final (whether or not such person, partnership, or corporation was subject to such cease and desist order), and

(2) with actual knowledge that such act or practice is unfair or deceptive and is unlawful under subsection (a)(1) of this section.

In such action, such person, partnership, or corporation shall be liable for a civil penalty of not more than $10,000 for each violation.

(C) In the case of a violation through continuing failure to comply with a rule or with subsection (a)(1) of this section, each day of continuance of such failure shall be treated as a separate violation, for purposes of subparagraphs (A) and (B). In determining the amount of such a civil penalty, the court shall take into account the degree of culpability, any history of prior such conduct, ability to pay, effect on ability to continue to do business, and such other matters as justice may require.

(2) If the cease and desist order establishing that the act or practice is unfair or deceptive was not issued against the defendant in a civil penalty action under paragraph (1)(B) the issues of fact in such action against such defendant shall be tried de novo. Upon request of any party to such an action against such defendant, the court shall also review the determination of law made by the Commission in the proceeding under subsection (b) of this section that the act or practice which was the subject of such proceeding constituted an unfair or deceptive act or practice in violation of subsection (a) of this section.

(3) The Commission may compromise or settle any action for a civil penalty if such compromise or settlement is accompanied by a public statement of its reasons and is approved by the court.

(n) **Standard of proof; public policy considerations**

The Commission shall have no authority under this section or section 57a of this title to declare unlawful an act or practice on the grounds that such act or practice is unfair unless the act or practice causes or is likely to cause substantial injury to consumers which is not reasonably avoidable by consumers themselves and not outweighed by countervailing benefits to consumers or to competition. In determining whether an act or practice is unfair, the Commission may consider established public policies as evidence to be considered with all other evidence. Such public policy considerations may not serve as a primary basis for such determination.

Appendix F

PART 681—IDENTITY THEFT RULES
Appendix A to Part 681—Interagency Guidelines on Identity Theft Detection, Prevention, and Mitigation[1]

Alerts, Notifications or Warnings from a Consumer Reporting Agency

1. A fraud or active duty alert is included with a consumer report.

2. A consumer reporting agency provides a notice of credit freeze in response to a request for a consumer report.

3. A consumer reporting agency provides a notice of address discrepancy, as defined in §641.1(b) of this part.

4. A consumer report indicates a pattern of activity that is inconsistent with the history and usual pattern of activity of an applicant or customer, such as:
   a. A recent and significant increase in the volume of inquiries;
   b. An unusual number of recently established credit relationships;
   c. A material change in the use of credit, especially with respect to recently established credit relationships; or

---

[1] 16 C.F.R. §681.1 PART 681—IDENTITY THEFT RULES, Electronic Code of Federal Regulations, e-CFR data is current as of December 31, 2019. Retrieve from https://www.ecfr.gov/cgi-bin/text-idx?SID=fddfe88d36b1e7881a1b76f4e8437d65&mc=true&node=pt16.1.681&rgn=div5#ap16.1.681_12.a

d. An account that was closed for cause or identified for abuse of account privileges by a financial institution or creditor.

Suspicious documents

5. Documents provided for identification appear to have been altered or forged.

6. The photograph or physical description on the identification is not consistent with the appearance of the applicant or customer presenting the identification.

7. Other information on the identification is not consistent with information provided by the person opening a new covered account or customer presenting the identification.

8. Other information on the identification is not consistent with readily accessible information that is on file with the financial institution or creditor, such as a signature card or a recent check.

9. An application appears to have been altered or forged, or gives the appearance of having been destroyed and reassembled.

Suspicious personal identifying information

10. Personal identifying information provided is inconsistent when compared against external information sources used by the financial institution or creditor. For example:

   a. The address does not match any address in the consumer report; or

   b. The Social Security Number (SSN) has not been issued, or is listed on the Social Security Administration's Death Master File.

11. Personal identifying information provided by the customer is not consistent with other personal identifying information provided by the customer. For example, there is a lack of correlation between the SSN range and date of birth.

12. Personal identifying information provided is associated with known fraudulent activity as indicated by internal or third-party sources used by the financial institution or creditor. For example:

   a. The address on an application is the same as the address provided on a fraudulent application; or

   b. The phone number on an application is the same as the number provided on a fraudulent application.

13. Personal identifying information provided is of a type commonly associated with fraudulent activity as indicated by internal or third-party sources used by the financial institution or creditor. For example:

   a. The address on an application is fictitious, a mail drop, or a prison; or

   b. The phone number is invalid, or is associated with a pager or answering service.

14. The SSN provided is the same as that submitted by other persons opening an account or other customers.

15. The address or telephone number provided is the same as or similar to the address or telephone number submitted by an unusually large number of other persons opening accounts or by other customers.

16. The person opening the covered account or the customer fails to provide all required personal identifying information on an application or in response to notification that the application is incomplete.

17. Personal identifying information provided is not consistent with personal identifying information that is on file with the financial institution or creditor.

18. For financial institutions and creditors that use challenge questions, the person opening the covered account or the customer cannot provide authenticating information beyond that which generally would be available from a wallet or consumer report.

Unusual use of, or suspicious activity related to, the covered account

19. Shortly following the notice of a change of address for a covered account, the institution or creditor receives a request for a new, additional, or replacement card or a cell phone, or for the addition of authorized users on the account.

20. A new revolving credit account is used in a manner commonly associated with known patterns of fraud. For example:

a. The majority of available credit is used for cash advances or merchandise that is easily convertible to cash (e.g., electronics equipment or jewelry); or

b. The customer fails to make the first payment or makes an initial payment but no subsequent payments.

21. A covered account is used in a manner that is not consistent with established patterns of activity on the account. There is, for example:

a. Nonpayment when there is no history of late or missed payments;

b. A material increase in the use of available credit;

c. A material change in purchasing or spending patterns;

d. A material change in electronic fund transfer patterns in connection with a deposit account; or

e. A material change in telephone call patterns in connection with a cellular phone account.

22. A covered account that has been inactive for a reasonably lengthy period of time is used (taking into consideration the type of account, the expected pattern of usage and other relevant factors).

23. Mail sent to the customer is returned repeatedly as undeliverable although transactions continue to be conducted in connection with the customer's covered account.

24. The financial institution or creditor is notified that the customer is not receiving paper account statements.

25. The financial institution or creditor is notified of unauthorized charges or transactions in connection with a customer's covered account.

Notice from Customers, Victims of Identity Theft, Law Enforcement Authorities, or Other Persons Regarding Possible Identity Theft in Connection With Covered Accounts Held by the Financial Institution or Creditor

26. The financial institution or creditor is notified by a customer, a victim of identity theft, a law enforcement authority, or any other person that it has opened a fraudulent account for a person engaged in identity theft.

Appendix G

6 U.S.C.
United States Code
Title 6 – DOMESTIC SECURITY
CHAPTER 6 – CYBERSECURITY
SUBCHAPTER I – CYBERSECURITY INFORMATION SHARING
Sec. 1501 – Definitions
From the U.S. Government Publishing Office, www.gpo.gov

§1501. Definitions[1]

In this subchapter:

(1) Agency

The term "agency" has the meaning given the term in section 3502 of title 44.

(2) Antitrust laws

The term "antitrust laws"—

(A) has the meaning given the term in section 12 of title 15;

[1] 6 U.S.C. 1501 – Definitions. Retrieved from https://www.govinfo.gov/app/details/USCODE-2018-title6/USCODE-2018-title6-chap6-subchapI-sec1501

(B) includes section 45 of title 15 to the extent that section 45 of title 15 applies to unfair methods of competition; and

(C) includes any State antitrust law, but only to the extent that such law is consistent with the law referred to in subparagraph (A) or the law referred to in subparagraph (B).

(3) Appropriate federal entities

The term "appropriate Federal entities" means the following:

(A) The Department of Commerce.

(B) The Department of Defense.

(C) The Department of Energy.

(D) The Department of Homeland Security.

(E) The Department of Justice.

(F) The Department of the Treasury.

(G) The Office of the Director of National Intelligence.

(4) Cybersecurity purpose

The term "cybersecurity purpose" means the purpose of protecting an information system or information that is stored on, processed by, or transiting an information system from a cybersecurity threat or security vulnerability.

(5) Cybersecurity threat

(A) **In general**
Except as provided in subparagraph (B), the term "cybersecurity threat" means an action, not protected by the First Amendment to the Constitution of the United States, on or through an information system that may result in an unauthorized effort to adversely impact the security, availability, confidentiality, or integrity of an information system or information that is stored on, processed by, or transiting an information system.

(B) **Exclusion**
The term "cybersecurity threat" does not include any action that solely involves a violation of a consumer term of service or a consumer licensing agreement.

(6) Cyber threat indicator

The term "cyber threat indicator" means information that is necessary to describe or identify—

(A) malicious reconnaissance, including anomalous patterns of communications that appear to be transmitted for the purpose of gathering technical information related to a cybersecurity threat or security vulnerability;

(B) a method of defeating a security control or exploitation of a security vulnerability;

(C) a security vulnerability, including anomalous activity that appears to indicate the existence of a security vulnerability;

(D) a method of causing a user with legitimate access to an information system or information that is stored on, processed by, or transiting an information system to unwittingly enable the defeat of a security control or exploitation of a security vulnerability;

(E) malicious cyber command and control;

(F) the actual or potential harm caused by an incident, including a description of the information exfiltrated as a result of a particular cybersecurity threat;

(G) any other attribute of a cybersecurity threat, if disclosure of such attribute is not otherwise prohibited by law; or

(H) any combination thereof.

(7) Defensive measure

(A) **In general**

Except as provided in subparagraph (B), the term "defensive measure" means an action, device, procedure, signature, technique, or other measure applied to an information system or information that is stored on, processed by, or transiting an information system that detects, prevents, or mitigates a known or suspected cybersecurity threat or security vulnerability.

(B) **Exclusion**

The term "defensive measure" does not include a measure that destroys, renders unusable, provides unauthorized access to, or substantially harms an information system or information stored on, processed by, or transiting such information system not owned by—

(i) the private entity operating the measure; or

(ii) another entity or Federal entity that is authorized to provide consent and has provided consent to that private entity for operation of such measure.

(8) Federal entity

The term "Federal entity" means a department or agency of the United States or any component of such department or agency.

(9) **Information system**

The term "information system"—

(A) has the meaning given the term in section 3502 of title 44; and

(B) includes industrial control systems, such as supervisory control and data acquisition systems, distributed control systems, and programmable logic controllers.

(10) Local government

The term "local government" means any borough, city, county, parish, town, township, village, or other political subdivision of a State.

(11) Malicious cyber command and control

The term "malicious cyber command and control" means a method for unauthorized remote identification of, access to, or use of, an information system or information that is stored on, processed by, or transiting an information system.

(12) Malicious reconnaissance

The term "malicious reconnaissance" means a method for actively probing or passively monitoring an information system for the purpose of discerning security vulnerabilities of the information system, if such method is associated with a known or suspected cybersecurity threat.

(13) Monitor

The term "monitor" means to acquire, identify, or scan, or to possess, information that is stored on, processed by, or transiting an information system.

(14) Non-Federal entity

(A) **In general**

Except as otherwise provided in this paragraph, the term "non-Federal entity" means any private entity, non-Federal government agency or department, or State, tribal, or local government (including a political subdivision, department, or component thereof).

(B) **Inclusions**

The term "non-Federal entity" includes a government agency or department of the District of Columbia, the Commonwealth of Puerto Rico, the United States Virgin Islands, Guam, American Samoa, the Northern Mariana Islands, and any other territory or possession of the United States.

(C) **Exclusion**

The term "non-Federal entity" does not include a foreign power as defined in section 1801 of title 50.

(15) Private entity

(A) **In general**

Except as otherwise provided in this paragraph, the term "private entity" means any person or private group, organization, proprietorship, partnership, trust, cooperative, corporation, or other commercial or nonprofit entity, including an officer, employee, or agent thereof.

(B) **Inclusion**

The term "private entity" includes a State, tribal, or local government performing utility services, such as electric, natural gas, or water services.

(C) **Exclusion**

The term "private entity" does not include a foreign power as defined in section 1801 of title 50.

(16) Security control

The term "security control" means the management, operational, and technical controls used to protect against an unauthorized effort to adversely affect the confidentiality, integrity, and availability of an information system or its information.

(17) Security vulnerability

The term "security vulnerability" means any attribute of hardware, software, process, or procedure that could enable or facilitate the defeat of a security control.

(18) Tribal

The term "tribal" has the meaning given the term "Indian tribe" in section 450b of title 25.

(Pub. L. 114–113, div. N, title I, §102, Dec. 18, 2015, 129 Stat. 2936.)

Short Title

Pub. L. 114–113, div. N, §1(a), Dec. 18, 2015, 129 Stat. 2935, provided that: "This division [enacting this chapter and sections 149 and 151 of this title, amending sections 131, 148, 149, and 150 of this title, section 1029 of Title 18, Crimes and Criminal Procedure, and sections 3553 and 3554 of Title 44, Public Printing and Documents, enacting provisions set out as notes under this section and sections 101, 131, and 151 of this title and section 301 of Title 5, Government Organization and Employees] may be cited as the 'Cybersecurity Act of 2015'."

Pub. L. 114–113, div. N, title I, §101, Dec. 18, 2015, 129 Stat. 2936, provided that: "This title [enacting this subchapter] may be cited as the 'Cybersecurity Information Sharing Act of 2015'."

Pub. L. 114–113, div. N, title II, §221, Dec. 18, 2015, 129 Stat. 2963, provided that: "This subtitle [subtitle B (§§221–229) of title II of div. N of Pub. L. 114–113, enacting subchapter II of this chapter and sections 149 and 151 of this title, amending sections 148, 149, and 150 of this title and sections 3553 and 3554 of Title 44, Public Printing and Documents, and enacting provisions set out as a note under section 151 of this title] may be cited as the 'Federal Cybersecurity Enhancement Act of 2015'."

Appendix H

18 U.S.C.
United States Code, 2011 Edition
Title 18 - CRIMES AND CRIMINAL PROCEDURE
PART I - CRIMES
CHAPTER 47 - FRAUD AND FALSE STATEMENTS
Sec. 1037 – Fraud and related activity in connection with electronic mail
From the U.S. Government Publishing Office, www.gpo.gov

§1037. Fraud and Related Activity in Connection with Electronic Mail

(a) In General.—Whoever, in or affecting interstate or foreign commerce, knowingly—

(1) accesses a protected computer without authorization, and intentionally initiates the transmission of multiple commercial electronic mail messages from or through such computer,

(2) uses a protected computer to relay or retransmit multiple commercial electronic mail messages, with the intent to deceive or mislead recipients, or any Internet access service, as to the origin of such messages,

(3) materially falsifies header information in multiple commercial electronic mail messages and intentionally initiates the transmission of such messages,

(4) registers, using information that materially falsifies the identity of the actual registrant, for five or more electronic mail accounts or online user accounts or two or more domain names, and intentionally initiates the transmission of multiple commercial electronic mail messages from any combination of such accounts or domain names, or

(5) falsely represents oneself to be the registrant or the legitimate successor in interest to the registrant of 5 or more Internet Protocol addresses, and intentionally initiates the transmission of multiple commercial electronic mail messages from such addresses, or conspires to do so, shall be punished as provided in subsection (b).

(b) Penalties.—The punishment for an offense under subsection (a) is—

(1) a fine under this title, imprisonment for not more than 5 years, or both, if—

(A) the offense is committed in furtherance of any felony under the laws of the United States or of any State; or

(B) the defendant has previously been convicted under this section or section 1030, or under the law of any State for conduct involving the transmission of multiple commercial electronic mail messages or unauthorized access to a computer system;

(2) a fine under this title, imprisonment for not more than 3 years, or both, if—

(A) the offense is an offense under subsection (a)(1);

(B) the offense is an offense under subsection (a)(4) and involved 20 or more falsified electronic mail or online user account registrations, or 10 or more falsified domain name registrations;

(C) the volume of electronic mail messages transmitted in furtherance of the offense exceeded 2,500 during any 24-hour period, 25,000 during any 30-day period, or 250,000 during any 1-year period;

(D) the offense caused loss to one or more persons aggregating $5,000 or more in value during any 1-year period;

(E) as a result of the offense any individual committing the offense obtained anything of value aggregating $5,000 or more during any 1-year period; or

(F) the offense was undertaken by the defendant in concert with three or more other persons with respect to whom the defendant occupied a position of organizer or leader; and

(3) a fine under this title or imprisonment for not more than 1 year, or both, in any other case.

(c) Forfeiture.—

(1) In general.—The court, in imposing sentence on a person who is convicted of an offense under this section, shall order that the defendant forfeit to the United States—

(A) any property, real or personal, constituting or traceable to gross proceeds obtained from such offense; and

(B) any equipment, software, or other technology used or intended to be used to commit or to facilitate the commission of such offense.

(2) Procedures.—The procedures set forth in section 413 of the Controlled Substances Act (21 U.S.C. 853), other than subsection (d) of that section, and in Rule 32.2 of the Federal Rules of Criminal Procedure, shall apply to all stages of a criminal forfeiture proceeding under this section.

(d) Definitions.—In this section:

(1) Loss.—The term "loss" has the meaning given that term in section 1030(e) of this title.

(2) Materially.—For purposes of paragraphs (3) and (4) of subsection (a), header information or registration information is materially falsified if it is altered or concealed in a manner that would impair the ability of a recipient of the message, an Internet access service processing the message on behalf of a recipient, a person alleging a violation of this section, or a law enforcement agency to identify, locate, or respond to a person who initiated the electronic mail message or to investigate the alleged violation.

(3) Multiple.—The term "multiple" means more than 100 electronic mail messages during a 24-hour period, more than 1,000 electronic mail messages during a 30-day period, or more than 10,000 electronic mail messages during a 1-year period.

(4) Other terms.—Any other term has the meaning given that term by section 3 of the CAN-SPAM Act of 2003.

(Added Pub. L. 108–187, §4(a)(1), Dec. 16, 2003, 117 Stat. 2703.)

References

The Federal Rules of Criminal Procedure, referred to in subsec. (c)(2), are set out in the Appendix to this title.

Section 3 of the CAN-SPAM Act of 2003, referred to in subsec. (d)(4), is classified to section 7702 of Title 15, Commerce and Trade.

Effective Date

Section effective Jan. 1, 2004, see section 16 of Pub. L. 108–187, set out as a note under section 7701 of Title 15, Commerce and Trade.

Appendix I
Valuable IT and Management Certifications

I. **Entry-Level IT Certifications**
- Cisco Certifications[1]
- Cisco Certified Technician (CCT)
- Cisco Certified Network Associate (CCNA)
- CompTIA Certifications[2]
- CompTIA IT Fundamentals (ITF+)
- Comp TIA A+
- CompTIA Network+
- CompTIA Security+
- Microsoft Certifications[3]
- Microsoft 365 Fundamentals
- Microsoft Technology Associate (MTA)
- Systems Security Certified Practitioner (SSCP)[4]

[1] https://www.cisco.com/c/en/us/training-events/training-certifications/certifications.html
[2] https://www.comptia.org/certifications
[3] https://docs.microsoft.com/en-us/learn/certifications/
[4] https://www.isc2.org/Certifications/SSCP

DOI: 10.4324/9780429318726-17

II. **Intermediate and Advance I T Certifications**

- Amazon Web Services (AWS) Certified Solutions Architect[5]
- Certified Ethical Hacker (CEH)[6]
- Certified Information Systems Security Professional (CISSP)[7]
- Cisco Certification
- Cisco Certified Network Professional (CCNP) [8]
- Cisco Expert-level Certifications (CCIE)[9]
- Cisco Certified Design Expert (CCDE)[10]
- Citrix Certifications[11]
- Citrix Certified Associate – Virtualization (CCA-V)
- CCA-N: Citrix Certified Associate – Networking
- Global Information Assurance Certifications (GIAC)[12]
- Google Certified Professional Cloud Architect[13]
- IBM Professional Certifications[14]
- Information Systems Audit and Control Association (ISACA) Certifications[15]
- Certified Information Systems Auditor (CISA)
- Certified Information Security Manager (CISM)
- Certified in Risk and Information Systems Control (CRISC)
- Certified in the Governance of Enterprise IT (CGEIT)
- Juniper Certifications[16]
- Linux Certifications[17]
- Microsoft Certifications[18]
- Microsoft certified solutions expert (MCSE)
- Microsoft certified solutions developer (MCSD)
- Microsoft Certifications
- Microsoft Certified: Azure Fundamentals[19]
- Microsoft Certified: Azure Administrator Associate[20]
- Microsoft SQL Server certifications
- Oracle Certified Professional[21]

---

5 https://aws.amazon.com/certification/certified-solutions-architect-associate/
6 https://cert.eccouncil.org/certified-ethical-hacker.html
7 https://www.isc2.org/Certifications/CISSP
8 https://www.cisco.com/c/en/us/training-events/training-certifications/certifications/professional.html
9 https://www.cisco.com/c/en/us/training-events/training-certifications/certifications/expert.html
10 https://www.cisco.com/c/en/us/training-events/training-certifications/certifications/expert/ccde.html
11 https://training.citrix.com/learning/landing-badges/digital-workspace
12 https://www.giac.org/
13 https://cloud.google.com/certification#certification_paths
14 https://www.ibm.com/certify
15 https://www.isaca.org/credentialing
16 https://www.juniper.net/us/en/training/certification/
17 https://www.lpi.org/our-certifications/summary-of-certifications
18 https://docs.microsoft.com/en-us/learn/certifications/browse/?resource_type=certification
19 https://docs.microsoft.com/en-us/learn/certifications/azure-fundamentals
20 https://docs.microsoft.com/en-us/learn/certifications/azure-administrator
21 https://education.oracle.com/certification

III. **Management Certifications**

- Project Management Professional (PMP)[22]
- Certified ScrumMaster (CSM)[23]
- Agile Certifications[24]

---

[22] https://www.pmi.org/certifications/project-management-pmp
[23] https://www.scrumalliance.org/get-certified/scrum-master-track/certified-scrummaster
[24] https://www.pmi.org/certifications/agile-certifications

INDEX

A

B

G

H

M

N

O

P

T

U

V

W

X

Y

Z

For Product Safety Concerns and Information please contact our EU
representative GPSR@taylorandfrancis.com
Taylor & Francis Verlag GmbH, Kaufingerstraße 24, 80331 München, Germany

www.ingramcontent.com/pod-product-compliance
Ingram Content Group UK Ltd.
Pitfield, Milton Keynes, MK11 3LW, UK
UKHW062047190926
475702UK00009B/1223
* 9 7 8 0 3 6 7 2 5 1 5 7 4 *